# Mac OS 9

## THE MISSING MANUAL

*The book that
should have been
in the box*

# Mac OS 9
## THE MISSING MANUAL

David Pogue

POGUE PRESS™
O'REILLY®

Beijing · Cambridge · Farnham · Köln · Paris · Sebastopol · Taipei · Tokyo

## *Mac OS 9: The Missing Manual*

by David Pogue

Copyright © 2000 Pogue Press, LLC. All rights reserved.
Printed in the United States of America.

Published by Pogue Press/O'Reilly & Associates, Inc., 101 Morris Street, Sebastopol, CA 95472.

| | |
|---|---|
| March 2000: | First Edition. |
| May 2000: | Second printing. |
| August 2000: | Third printing. |
| October 2000: | Fourth printing. |
| December 2000: | Fifth printing. |
| June 2001: | Sixth printing. |
| June 2002: | Seventh printing. |

This book is printed on acid-free paper with 85% recycled content, 15% post-consumer waste. O'Reilly & Associates is committed to using paper with the highest recycled content available consistent with high quality.

ISBN: 1-56592-857-1

# Table of Contents

# Part Three: The Components of Mac OS 9

# Part Four: Mac OS 9 Online

# Part Five: Plugging In to Mac OS 9

# The Missing Credits

## About the Author

David Pogue, award-winning *Macworld* magazine columnist, is the creator of the Missing Manual series. He has written or co-written 15 computer, humor, and music books, including the bestselling *PalmPilot: The Ultimate Guide; Macworld Mac Secrets;* and six books in the *...for Dummies* series (*Macs, iMacs, iBooks, Magic, Opera,* and *Classical Music*).

In his other life, David is a former Broadway show conductor, magician, and incorrigible pianist. He and his wife Jennifer Pogue, MD, live in Connecticut with their young son and daughter, as copiously documented at *www.davidpogue.com*.

He welcomes feedback about this book and others in the Missing Manual series by e-mail: *david@pogueman.com*. (If you're seeking technical help, however, please refer to the help sources listed in Appendix C.)

## About the Creative Team

**Nan Barber** (copy editor) works as a freelance writer and editor from her home near Boston. She graduated from Brown University in 1983 with a degree in Japanese Studies and traveled throughout Asia and Europe as a jewelry buyer before getting married in 1991. She's the managing editor of Salamander, a magazine for poetry, fiction, and memoirs, and executive editor of Bonjour Paris *(www.bparis.com)*.

**Dennis Cohen** (technical editor), a veteran of the Jet Propulsion Laboratory, Claris, and Aladdin Systems, has served as the technical reviewer for many bestselling Mac books, including several editions of *Macworld Mac Secrets*. He's the co-author of *AppleWorks 6 for Dummies*. He enjoys trapshooting, backgammon, bridge, and (especially) spending time with his Boston Terrier, Spenser. E-mail: *drcohen@mac.com*.

**David A. Freedman** created the cover design for the Missing Manual series (with assistance from illustrator Marc Rosenthal, who drew the Missing Manual dog). From his studio in Carlisle, Massachusetts *(df301@aol.com)*, David also designs logos and other graphics. Prior to establishing his design business, David worked for 20 years with Milton Glaser in New York City.

**Danny Marcus** (head proofreader), entered the book business as a freelance proofreader and copy editor in 1985 and lived the thrill of self-employment until he joined Pearson Education's Prentice Hall imprint in 1999. Danny has done work for several big New York trade houses, university presses, textbook publishers, and Lotus. He's also written eight pages so far of a new book on becoming an editorial freelancer: *I Get Paid to Stay Home, Read Books, and Point out Other People's Mistakes.*

**Phil Simpson**, the designer of this book's interior layout, works out of his office in Stamford, CT *(pmsimpson@earthlink.net)*, where he has had his graphic design business for 18 years. Experienced in many facets of graphic design, he is proud to be a long-time Macintosh user/supporter and honored to be part of the *Mac OS 9: The Missing Manual.*

## Other Acknowledgments

The Missing Manual series is a joint venture between Pogue Press—the team introduced on the previous pages—and O'Reilly & Associates, one of the most respected publishers on earth. It's only because Tim O'Reilly and his team had the vision to take a gamble on this concept that this book came into existence.

Creating this series was supposed to be my job; but the editorial and production teams at O'Reilly went *way* beyond the call of duty in guiding me, demonstrating at every step how deeply they care about creating outstanding, accurate, useful books. In particular, this book owes its existence to Tim O'Reilly, who gave life to the series; Cathy Record, the Missing Manuals' wonderful parent/product manager; Edie Freedman, whose visual genius shaped the MissingManual.com Web site and guided the book's design; and Allen Noren and his team, who took the Web site the rest of the way to reality. Sue Willing, Mark Brokering, Dana Furby, and Sara Winge were also delightful and integral parts of the books' birth.

My agent, David Rogelberg, first gave me the confidence to create this series and was its first believer. And my wife, Jennifer, provided the affection, humor, and enthusiasm I needed to create something from nothing—and love every minute of it.

Come to think of it, she *always* does that.

## The Missing Manual Series

Missing Manuals are designed to be authoritative, entertaining, superbly written guides to popular computer products that don't come with printed manuals (which is just about all of them). Watch for these other titles in 2000:

- AppleWorks 6: The Missing Manual *by Jim Elferdink and David Reynolds*

- iMovie: The Missing Manual *by David Pogue*

- Windows 2000: The Missing Manual *by Sharon Crawford*

- Windows ME: The Missing Manual *by Kathy Ivens*

- Mac OS X: The Missing Manual *by David Pogue*

- Quicken 2001: The Missing Manual *by Kathy Ivens and Thomas E. Barich*

# Introduction

For 25 million Macintosh computer users, Mac OS 9 is the last stop on a famous train. It's the last version of the operating system that changed the world, that put the Mac on the map and inspired such imitators as Microsoft Windows. After Mac OS 9, Apple Computer plans to introduce Mac OS X, a radically new operating system that looks and works nothing like the Mac we've come to know.

But Mac OS 9 doesn't feel like a has-been by any means. In fact, many Mac fans find that this Mac OS is better designed and more conducive to productivity than Mac OS X; after all, Mac OS 9 still offers such familiar and useful features as the Launcher, menu, Application menu, Control Strip, pop-up windows, collapsible windows, and so on. At the same time, Mac OS 9 incorporates under-the-hood improvements—the kind of technical tweaks that Apple doesn't bother advertising—that make it among the quickest, most stable versions of the Mac system software yet.

## What's New in Mac OS 9

According to Apple, Mac OS 9 offers over 50 new features. Most are subtle tweaks and improvements. About 18 of these features, however, are clearly big-ticket items:

- **Sherlock,** the Mac's built-in search program, is now called Sherlock 2. It features a new look, better organization, and the ability to restrict Internet searches to certain *kinds* of Web sites, such as shopping, news, or Mac information sites. (See Chapter 15.)

- The **Multiple Users control panel** protects a single Mac from accidental or deliberate damage by the hordes who share it (students, employees, lab members, or family members, for example). At the same time, each person who uses a particular machine sees only her own desktop picture, Web-browser bookmarks, documents, ★ menu configuration, and so on. (See Chapter 17.)

• You can now **speak your password** to gain access to your Mac, if it has a microphone. (Chapter 17 has the details.)

• You can **password-protect a file** with a single click. To open a file you've encrypted in this way, just double-click it and then enter the password. (Chapter 2 has the details.)

• Thanks to the **Keychain Access** control panel, you no longer have to memorize (or even type) the necessary passwords that let you into password-protected files, other networked Macs, FTP (Internet software) sites, and so on. (See Chapter 16.)

• You can now **share your Mac's files via the Internet.** (Chapter 16 offers step-by-step instructions.)

• **AppleScript** has been enhanced in many ways. Now, for example, it can control Macs anywhere on the Internet, respond to spoken commands, and much more. (Chapter 10 offers the details.)

• The **Software Update** control panel automatically consults a special database on the Internet whenever you go online. If it learns that Apple has released a new version of some component of the system software, it lets you know—and even offers to download and install that component automatically. (See Chapter 12 for specifics.)

• The **Network Browser** is more powerful than before. Now it can show you FTP sites and certain other Internet entities in addition to showing you other machines on your office network. (See Chapter 16.)

• **ColorSync** is better than ever at maintaining consistent colors throughout the scanning, image-processing, and color-printing process. (See Chapter 19.)

• Speaking of goodies of particular appeal to the printing industry, the new **FontSync** software lets you compare your installed set of fonts with those of your clients' Macs. Unpleasant font-substitution surprises are much less likely as a result. (See Chapter 13.)

• The 18 **WorldScript language kits** used to be sold separately. Now all the software you need to word process in several languages simultaneously—including non-Roman ones like Japanese and Cyrillic systems—or visit foreign-language Web sites are included with the system software. (Chapter 13 has the details.)

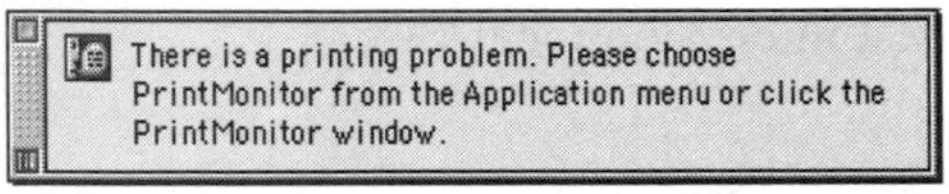

---

There is a printing problem. Please choose PrintMonitor from the Application menu or click the PrintMonitor window.

**Figure I-1:**
*In Mac OS 9, "notification-style" error messages don't commandeer your entire machine, as they used to. They're much subtler, and don't interrupt your work flow; you can keep working in other programs.*

- The PlainTalk **speech recognition software** still can't take dictation, but it's even better at executing commands (such as "Open AppleWorks" or "Make this bold"). (See Chapter 21.)

- **Less intrusive notification messages** no longer tie up your entire machine. Now, when the Mac needs your attention, it displays a quiet yellow box like the one shown in Figure I-1.

- The software known as Apple Remote Access lets you **dial into your Mac** from the road. For years, that's been an extremely useful feature for laptop travelers (who may have mistakenly left a particular document at home, for example)— but it's no longer an extra purchase. It's built right into Mac OS 9, as you can discover in Chapter 16.

- The **maximum file-size limit has grown**—from 2GB per file to two *terabytes* (a terabyte is 1,024 gigabytes). No, your AppleWorks files may not grow to that size; but if you create digital movies using programs like iMovie, Final Cut, or EditDV, this file-size improvement is a big deal. (Each *second* of digital video consumes 3.6 MB of disk space.)

- The **maximum number of open files on your Mac** has also grown—to more than 8,000. Here again, the benefit may not seem obvious; how many times do you have more than a few files open? Answer: almost always. Behind the scenes, the Mac OS itself opens many files you can't even see, such as the font-suitcase files in your System Folder. Because the open-file limit has grown, you can now have **512 font suitcases in your Fonts folder** (instead of 128, as in previous Mac OS versions). Chapter 19 has more on fonts.

- Mac OS 9 can run **Mac OS X programs,** thanks to the new CarbonLib extension.

## About this Book

Despite the many improvements in the Mac system software over the years, however, one feature has grown consistently worse since the original 1984 Macintosh: Apple's documentation. With Mac OS 9, in fact, you don't get a single page of printed instructions. To learn about the 2,000 pieces of software that make up this operating system, you're expected to use one of Apple's three mutually incompatible online help systems (Balloon Help, Apple Guide, and the Web-like Mac Help).

Unfortunately, as you'll quickly discover, these help systems are tersely written, offer very little technical depth, lack useful examples, and provide no tutorials whatsoever. You can't even mark your place, underline, or read it in the bathroom.

The purpose of this book, then, is to serve as the manual that should have accompanied Mac OS 9. In this book's pages, you'll find step-by-step instructions for using every Mac OS 9 feature, including those you may not even have quite understood, let alone mastered: desktop printing, ColorSync, Apple remote access, AppleScript, SimpleSound, QuickTime, and so on.

*Mac OS 9: The Missing Manual* is designed to accommodate readers at every technical level. The primary discussions are written for advanced-beginner or intermediate Mac users. But if you're a first-time Mac user, special sidebar articles called Up To Speed provide the introductory information you need to understand the topic at hand. If you're an advanced Mac user, on the other hand, keep your eye out for similar shaded boxes called Power Users' Clinic. They offer more technical tips, tricks, and shortcuts for the experienced Mac fan.

## About the Outline

*Mac OS 9: The Missing Manual* is divided into six parts, each containing several chapters:

- Part 1, **The Mac OS 9 Desktop,** covers everything you see on the screen when you turn on a Mac OS 9 computer: icons, windows, menus, scroll bars, the Trash, aliases, the  menu, contextual Control-key menus, and so on.

- Part 2, **Applications in Mac OS 9,** is dedicated to the proposition that an operating system is little more than a launch pad for *programs*—the actual applications you use in your everyday work, such as email programs, Web browsers, word processors, graphics suites, and so on. These chapters describe how to work with applications in Mac OS 9—how to launch them, switch among them, swap data between them, manage their memory, use them to create and open files, and control them using the AppleScript automation software.

- Part 3, **The Components of Mac OS 9,** is an item-by-item discussion of the individual software nuggets that make up this operating system. These chapters include a guided tour through the hundreds of icons in your System Folder and the Apple Extras folder on your hard drive.

- Part 4, **Mac OS 9 Online,** investigates Apple's claim that Mac OS 9 is "your Internet copilot." It covers all the special Internet-related features of Mac OS 9, including the Sherlock 2 Web-searching program, Web sharing, and Apple's online iTools services (which include free email accounts, secure file-backup features, Website hosting, and so on).

- Part 5, **Plugging Into Mac OS 9,** describes the operating system's relationship to equipment you can attach to your Mac: networks, disks, printers, microphones, and so on. Along the way, these chapters describe the QuickTime movie software, PlainTalk speech-recognition features, the Multiple Users feature, the ColorSync color-correction software, and setting up your own office network.

At the end of the book, three appendixes provide a menu-by-menu explanation of the Mac OS 9 Finder commands, guidance in installing this operating system, and a troubleshooting handbook.

## About→These→Arrows

Throughout this book, and throughout the Missing Manual series, you'll find sentences like this one: "Open the System Folder→Preferences→Remote Access folder."

That's shorthand for a much longer instruction that directs you to open three nested folders in sequence, like this: "On your hard drive, you'll find a folder called System Folder. Open that. Inside the System Folder window is a folder called Preferences; double-click it to open it. Inside *that* folder is yet another one called Remote Access. Double-click to open it, too."

Similarly, this kind of arrow shorthand helps to simplify the business of choosing commands in menus, as shown in Figure I-2.

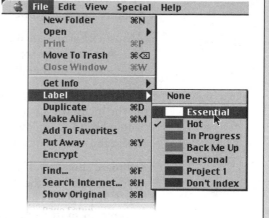

**Figure I-2:**
*In this book, arrow notations help to simplify folder and menu instructions. For example, "Choose File→Label→ Essential" is a more compact way of saying, "From the File menu, choose Label; from the submenu that than appears, choose Essential," as shown here.*

## About MissingManual.com

If you have an Internet account, visit the *MissingManual.com* Web site. Click the *Mac OS 9: The Missing Manual* link to reveal a neat, organized, chapter-by-chapter list of every piece of shareware and freeware mentioned in this book. (As noted on the inside back cover, having the software online instead of on a CD-ROM saved you 25 percent on the cost of the book.)

But the Web site also offers articles, tips, and updates to the book. In fact, you're invited and encouraged to submit such corrections and updates yourself. In an effort to keep the book as up-to-date and accurate as possible, each time we print more copies of this book, we'll make any confirmed corrections you've suggested. We'll also note such changes on the Web site, so that you can mark important corrections into your own copy of the book, if you like.

In the meantime, we'd love to hear your own suggestions for new books in the Missing Manual line. There's a place for that on the Web site, too, as well as a place to sign up for free email notification of new titles in the series.

## The Very Basics

To use this book, and indeed to use a Macintosh computer, you need to know a few basics. This book assumes that you're familiar with a few terms and concepts:

- **Clicking.** This book gives you three kinds of instructions that require you to use your mouse or trackpad. To *click* means to point the arrow cursor at something on the screen and then—without moving the cursor—to press and release the clicker button on the mouse (or laptop trackpad). To *double-click*, of course, means to click twice in rapid succession, again without moving the cursor at all. And to *drag* means to move the cursor while pressing the button continuously.

  When you're told to ⌘-*click* something, you click while pressing the ⌘ key (which is next to the Space bar). Such related procedures as *Shift-clicking, Option-clicking*, and *Control-clicking* work the same way—just click while pressing the corresponding key in the lower corner of your keyboard.

- **Menus.** The *menus* are the words at the top of your screen: File, Edit, and so on. (The  menu at the top left corner of your screen is a menu, too.) Click one to make a list of commands appear, as though they're written on a window shade.

  Some people click to open a menu and then release the mouse button; after reading the menu command choices, they click again on the one they want. Other people like to drag down the list to the desired command; only then do they release the mouse button. Either method works fine.

- **Keyboard shortcuts.** If you're typing along, it's sometimes disruptive to have to take your hand off the keyboard to use a menu. That's why many experienced Mac fans prefer to trigger menu commands by pressing key combinations. For example, in most word processors, you can press ⌘-B to produce a **boldface** word. When you read an instruction like "press ⌘-B," start by pressing the ⌘ key; while it's down, type the letter B, and then release both keys.

If you've mastered this much information, you have all the technical background you need to enjoy *Mac OS 9: The Missing Manual*.

---

**BREAKING NEWS**

## Mac OS 9.1 and Mac OS 9.2

In January 2001, Apple unveiled Mac OS 9.1, which offers one big-ticket new feature: a Window menu in the Finder. It lists every open desktop window, making it easy to summon a buried window by choosing its name.

If you press certain keys as you choose a window's name, you get all kinds of nifty extra features. For example, ⌘ closes a window, as though by remote control. ⌘-Shift closes a pop-up window—a great time saver. ⌘-Option brings a window to the front and closes all *other* windows. Control brings a window to the front and "windowshades" all other windows; and Control-Option brings a window to the front and *un*-windowshades all others.

Other changes are minor, but welcome: Mac OS 9.1's Applications folder is now called "Applications (Mac OS 9)," to help you find your programs when you move to Mac OS X. The General Controls, Sound, and Startup Disk control panels have been updated (see Chapter 12). The USB Printer Sharing control panel is all new: It lets you print on a USB printer that's connected elsewhere on your network.

Later in 2001, Apple released yet another touch-up: Mac OS 9.2, which offers bug fixes and much better speed as the "Classic" mode in Mac OS X. Both updaters—OS 9.1 and 9.2—are free downloads from the Apple Web site if you already have Mac OS 9-point-anything.

---

# Part One:
# The Mac OS 9 Desktop

1

# Window Opportunities

Xerox may have invented overlapping windows on a computer screen, and Microsoft may have gotten rich by tacking them onto DOS. But when the dust—and the lawyers—settled, it's the Mac OS that made windows famous. Even today, Mac windows are smarter and more flexible than their rivals on other computers.

But often enough, the downfall of the overlapping-windows concept is the overlapping part. As you create more files, stash them in more folders, and launch more programs, it's easy to wind up paralyzed before a screen awash with cluttered, overlapping rectangles. The Mac offers no Window menu that lets you bring a particular buried window to the front, nor a Tile command that neatly rearranges all open windows to give you an overview.

Fortunately, Mac OS 9 offers enough window tools to keep your windows reasonably tamed. (If you have Mac OS 9.1, see page 6 for even more window tips.)

## Window-Edge Gizmos

As in any window-based computer system, the edges of a Mac window are decorated by numerous clickable and draggable controls. Make using them second nature, and you'll find that you can summon and dismiss windows much more fluidly.

### Close Box

Especially for the novice, the most important window gadget is the Close box, the square in the upper-left corner (see Figure 1-1). Clicking it closes the window, which collapses back into the folder, file, or application icon from which it came.

The universal keyboard equivalent of the close box is ⌘-W (for *window*)—a keystroke well worth memorizing. If you get into the habit of dismissing windows with that deft flex of your left hand, you'll find it far easier to close several windows in a row, because you don't have to aim for successive Close boxes. Sometimes, as in Microsoft Word 98, extreme precision is required when using the Close box: Your cursor tip must click squarely in the square's center. But if you use the ⌘-W stroke instead of the mouse, you can't miss.

In many programs, something special happens if you're pressing the Option key when using the Close box, or even its ⌘-W equivalent: You close *all* open windows. This trick is especially useful in the Finder, where a quest for a particular document often leaves your screen plastered with open windows for which you have no further use. Option-clicking the Close box of any *one* window closes all of them—or just press Option-⌘-W. (If you've set up Mac OS 9 to make sound effects, as described in Chapter 3, you'll find the rapid-fire swishing sounds of these closing windows especially amusing.)

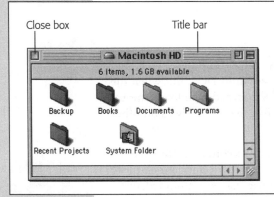

Close box          Title bar

**Figure 1-1:**
*If you learn nothing else about Macintosh windows, learn to make them go away: by clicking the Close box at the upper-left corner. (If you're used to Windows, this new location may take some getting used to.) The title bar's stripes aren't just for looks; they're supposed to be "grip strips," suggesting that you can move the entire window by dragging in the striped area.*

The Option-key trick doesn't close all windows on the Mac, by the way, only those in the current program. For example, Option-closing an AppleWorks document closes all *AppleWorks* windows—but your Finder windows remain open. Moreover, Option-closing works only in enlightened applications, such as AppleWorks, Quicken, and the Finder. (In this department, Microsoft is not yet enlightened.)

## Title Bar

The Mac OS 9 title bar (Figure 1-1) is grayer and more three-dimensional than title bars of Mac windows past, but otherwise the familiar horizontal pinstripes have been with us since the first Mac in 1984.

The title bar has several functions. First, when several windows are open, the presence of stripes tells you which window is *active* (in front). Second, the pinstripes act as a handle that lets you move the entire window around on the screen—a broader target than the thin edges on the remaining three sides of a window.

Most Mac users, however, overlook one of the title bar's most useful functions. In the Finder, after you've opened one folder that's inside another, the title bar's secret *folder hierarchy menu* is the simplest way to backtrack—to return to the enclosing window. Figure 1-2 reveals everything about the process except the key keystroke: to make this secret menu appear, press the ⌘ key as you click the name of the window. (You can release the ⌘ key immediately after clicking.)

**Figure 1-2:**
*Press ⌘ and click to summon the hidden folder-hierarchy menu. This Finder trick also works in AppleWorks, CodeWarrior, YA-NewsWatcher, GraphicConverter, FileMaker Pro, BBEdit, and StuffIt Deluxe!*

By choosing the name of a folder from this menu, you summon the corresponding window. When browsing the contents of the System Folder, for example, you can return to the main hard-drive window by ⌘-clicking the name System Folder and choosing Macintosh HD from the menu. (Keyboard lovers, take note: Instead of

---

**FREQUENTLY ASKED QUESTION**

## The Steve Jobs Window Look

*How do I windowshade a window that doesn't have a collapse box or title bar?*

Perhaps encouraged by the successes of its radical iMac and iBook hardware designs, today's Apple has undertaken a far riskier project: redesigning its *software.* Led by CEO Steve Jobs, the Apple interface design team has come up with a sleek new look for its applications, where each window re-

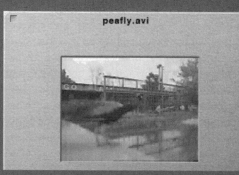

sembles a brushed, stainless-steel palmtop made by, say, Sony. You'll encounter this new Steve Jobs design in Mac OS 9's Sherlock 2 (see Chapter 15), QuickTime Player (Chapter 20), iMovie (the digital video-editing program included with iMac DV models), and Final Cut Pro (Apple's high-end video-editing program).

Unfortunately, "Steve Jobs" windows offer *fewer* features than the windows we came to know over the preceding 15 years. The stainless-steel windows don't have title bars at all, and therefore don't have the collapse or zoom boxes described in this chapter. Nor can you tell which window is active (in front), thanks to the loss of stripes in the title bar.

In most situations, you're out of luck; these familiar elements are simply not available in Steve Jobs windows. In the case of the Sherlock 2 searching program, however, a simple shareware fix can solve the problem. Window Fixer, available at *www.missingmanual. com*, brings to Sherlock 2 the familiar window control of OS versions gone by.

---

using this title-bar menu, you can also jump to the enclosing window by pressing ⌘-up arrow.)

But even that stunt pales in usefulness when you add the Option key to your ⌘-click. Doing so makes the current window close, even as you open the enclosing window. In effect, this keystroke lets you clean up after yourself as you back out of a nested window. Option-⌘-clicking a window's title bar is one of the most powerful weapons in your war against unnecessary window clutter. (Keyboard lovers, another note: You can do this, too, without the mouse—add Option to the ⌘-up arrow keystroke. You open the enclosing window and simultaneously close the inner one.)

---

*Tip:* When you click the title-bar area of an inactive window—one that's partly covered by a window in front—you bring the back window forward. But if you press ⌘ while dragging an inactive title bar, you can move a back window without bringing it to the front.

That technique is frequently useful when, for example, a back window is covering up some icons you're trying to manipulate. Better yet, the ⌘-dragging trick is built into Mac OS 9, not just the Finder. It works in every program—even Microsoft's.

---

The title bar does one other trick: by double-clicking the stripes, you can hide the body of a window, collapsing it into the title bar exactly as though you had clicked the Collapse box (described in an upcoming section). When you first install Mac OS 9, however, this feature is turned off. Apple was presumably thinking of easily alarmed novices who might assume, after making a window roll up accidentally, that they've just sent a window full of important files into the void. Turning on the title-bar double-click-to-collapse feature, therefore, requires a visit to the Appearance control panel. (Choose  →Control Panels→Appearance→Options, and turn on the "Double-click title bar to collapse windows" option.)

Once that's done, you can "windowshade" an active window by double-clicking its title-bar stripes. You can even roll up an *inactive* window by ⌘-double-clicking its dimmed title bar. (Here's another example where the ⌘ key lets you manipulate dimmed windows without bringing them to the foreground.)

## Zoom Box

A click on this square (see Figure 1-3) makes a desktop window just large enough to show you all of the icons inside it. If your monitor isn't big enough to show all the

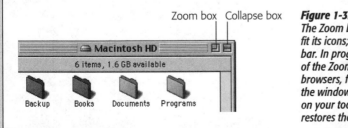

Zoom box  Collapse box

**Figure 1-3:**
*The Zoom box makes the window just big enough to fit its icons; the Collapse box hides all but the title bar. In programs other than the Finder, the behavior of the Zoom box varies. In word processors and Web browsers, for example, you can click the box to make the window as big as possible without encroaching on your toolbars. As always, however, a second click restores the window to its original size and shape.*

icons in a window, the zoom box resizes the window to show as many as possible. In either case, a second click on the Zoom box restores the window to its original size.

The equivalent control in a Windows PC window, by contrast, makes a window fill your screen, even if there's only a single icon inside the window. If you, a former Windows user, long for the days when the Zoom box made a window cover the entire desktop—including, perhaps, some work you were doing that the boss wouldn't approve of—no problem. Press Option as you click the Zoom box to make a Finder window fill the entire screen.

## Collapse Box

Click this doodad to "windowshade" any Mac window, so that the body of the window itself disappears. Only the title bar remains on the screen, floating like the Cheshire cat's smile.

"Rolling up" a window in this way is a popular window-management tool. In the Finder, doing so lets you see icons that are being covered by a window. In a word processor, this technique lets you type up a memo that requires frequent consultation of a spreadsheet behind it. When using the Appearance control panel (see Chapter 3), the collapse box lets you see the effects of a new photo you've chosen as your desktop backdrop, and so on.

---

**Tip:** If you enjoy the ability to roll up your windows in this way, consider giving your mouse a bigger target. Turn the entire striped title bar into a giant collapse box, as described in "Title Bar" earlier in this chapter.

---

The Collapse box harbors only one hidden feature, but it's very entertaining. If you Option-click it, *all* windows in the current program roll up simultaneously—great when you've got several Web browser windows open, for example, or word-processor documents. (Option-click the box again to un-windowshade all windows in that program.) If you turn on the Platinum sound effects in  →Control Panels→ Appearance→Sound, you'll find, in the rapid-fire *whish*ing of the windowshades, a rare moment of OS whimsy.

## Scroll Bars

Scroll bars appear automatically in any window that isn't big enough to show all of its contents. Without scroll bars in word processors, for example, you'd never be able to write a letter that's taller than your screen.

---

**Figure 1-4:**
*Three ways to control a scroll. The scroll-bar arrows (up and down) appear nestled together in Mac OS 9, as shown here; if you're an old-timer who prefers these arrows to appear on opposite ends of the scroll bar, visit your Appearance control panel, described in Chapter 3.*

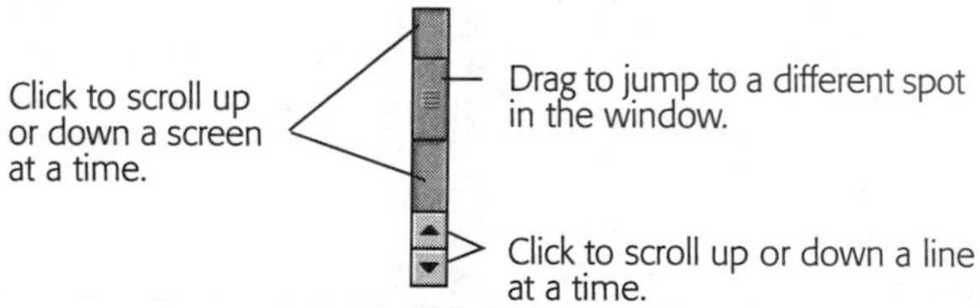

Click to scroll up or down a screen at a time.

Drag to jump to a different spot in the window.

Click to scroll up or down a line at a time.

---

You can manipulate a scroll bar in three ways, as shown in Figure 1-4.

It's worth noting, however, that the true speed expert eschews scroll bars altogether. Using your Page Up and Page Down keys lets you scroll up and down, one screen at a time, without having to take your hands off the keyboard to grab the mouse. The Home and End keys, meanwhile, are useful for jumping directly to the beginning or end of your document. (If you find some of these keys missing from your keyboard, install KeySwapper, available on this book's page at *www.missingmanual.com*.)

At first glance, you might assume that scroll bars are an extremely inefficient mechanism when you want to scroll a window *diagonally*—and you'd be right. Fortunately, the Mac OS includes an alternate scrolling system for such situations (see Figure 1-5).

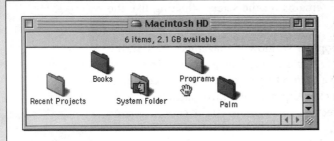

***Figure 1-5:***
*Position your mouse inside a Finder window (list views not included) or even an Internet Explorer window (5.0 and later); while pressing ⌘, you can drag—and scroll—in any direction. As you drag, the cursor changes shape, becoming a gloved white butler's hand. Where can you get that kind of service these days?*

## Window Edges

Dragging the faintly puffy border of a Mac OS 9 window doesn't reshape the window, as it does on a Windows PC. Instead, it *moves* the entire window in the direction you drag (see Figure 1-6).

*Tip:* In the early days of the Mac OS, you could move a Finder window only by dragging its title bar. The window edges make a much more flexible gripping region—but also make it possible, for the first time, to drag a window nearly entirely off the screen.

The next time you double-click a folder icon that refuses to open into a window, remember this quirk. It's possible that the window *is* open—off the screen. Scan the very edges of your monitor for a telltale puffy gray edge, which you can use to drag the wayward window back into view.

***Figure 1-6:***
*Drag the edge of a window to move it. As made clear earlier in this chapter, if the window is inactive (behind another window), you can move it without bringing it to the front by pressing ⌘ when dragging. The same tip applies to the window edges—dragging them with the ⌘ key pressed prevents an inactive window from popping to the front when you click.*

## Resize Box

The lower-right corner of every standard Mac window is ribbed, a design that's meant to imply that you can grip it by dragging. Doing so lets you resize and reshape the window (see Figure 1-7).

**Figure 1-7:**
*The resize box lets you change the size and shape of a window; it offers the only means of creating, for example, a tall, skinny window, or a short, wide one. You don't get much visual feedback as you're dragging—you see only the outline that the window will fill when you finally release the mouse.*

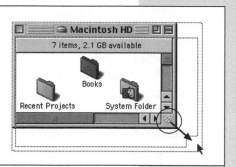

# Additional Finder-Window Controls

The window gadgets described so far in this chapter are available in every standard Mac window, regardless of the program you're using.

But windows in the Finder—the desktop—offer a few special gizmos of their own.

## Folder Proxy Icon

In the Finder, each window corresponds to either a folder or a disk. Each Finder-window title bar features a small icon, next to the window's name, representing the folder or disk from which this window was opened (see Figure 1-8). By clicking this tiny icon (until it darkens) and then dragging, you can move or copy the folder to a different folder or disk, without having to first close the window. (If this feature strikes you as unimpressive, you've never witnessed a hapless Mac novice making repeated attempts to drag an *open window* into the Trash in, say, System 7.5.)

**Figure 1-8:**
*The folder-proxy icon—in the title bar of every Finder window—can be useful when you've windowshaded (collapsed) a window so that only its title bar is visible. You can drag new icons into such a window—even though the window itself is hidden—by dropping them on the folder-proxy icon, as shown here.*

When dragging this proxy icon to a different place on the same disk, the usual folder-dragging rules apply: hold down the Option key if you want to *copy* the original folder. Without the Option key, you *move* the original folder. (You'll find details on moving and copying icons later in this chapter.)

## Information Strip

Just beneath a Finder window's title bar is the info strip (Figure 1-9). It tells you how many icons are in the window ("7 items," for example). The second number shown here is, oddly enough, the amount of free space remaining on the disk—a statistic that confuses many beginners, because it has absolutely nothing to do with *this window*.

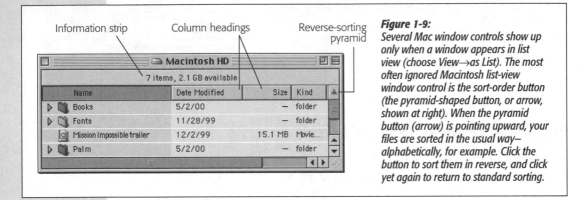

**Figure 1-9:**
*Several Mac window controls show up only when a window appears in list view (choose View→as List). The most often ignored Macintosh list-view window control is the sort-order button (the pyramid-shaped button, or arrow, shown at right). When the pyramid button (arrow) is pointing upward, your files are sorted in the usual way—alphabetically, for example. Click the button to sort them in reverse, and click yet again to return to standard sorting.*

**Tip:** The info strip shows you disk-space information for the entire disk, but not how much disk space this particular window's contents occupy. To find out *that* piece of information, make sure that no icon in the window is highlighted. Then choose File→Get Info→General Information (or press the keyboard equivalent, ⌘-I, or Control-click an empty area of the window and choose Get Info→General Information). The resulting Get Info window shows the size of the folder or disk whose window you're browsing, along with many other useful statistics.

## Column Headings

When a desktop window displays its icons in a list view, a convenient new strip of controls appears: the column headings (see Figure 1-9 again). (This band of column titles disappears when you choose View→as Icons.)

These column titles aren't just informational—they also serve as both buttons (for changing the way your files are sorted) and handles (for rearranging the column border). See "List View Notes" in the next section for details.

## The Reverse Sorting Button

At the upper-right of every list-view window is a tiny, striped, pyramid-shaped button, often overlooked. It determines the order of the file sorting in the current list view. When the pyramid is upright (or, put another way, when the arrow points upward), the newest files, or largest files, or files beginning with the letter A appear at the top of the list, depending on which sorting criterion you have selected. (Find it confusing that when the *smallest* portion of the pyramid is at the top, the *largest* files are listed first when viewed in size order? You wouldn't be the first.)

When you click the pyramid, however, the sort reverses: oldest files, smallest files, or files beginning with the letter Z appear at the top of the list. (The triangular pyramid icon turns upside down to indicate what's happening, as shown in Figure 1-9.)

Apple did the best it could at designing a "reverse sorting order" symbol to fit into a quarter-of-an-inch-square space. In fact, the designers of other software programs have followed suit—you'll find the identical symbol in email programs, in Sherlock (see Chapter 15), and anywhere else where reversing the sorting order of a list can be useful.

## Window Views: Icon, List, and Button

You can view the files and folders in a desktop window in any of three ways: as small or large icons, as a tidy list, or as kid-friendly launcher buttons. (Figure 1-10 shows the three different views.) Every window remembers its view settings independently.

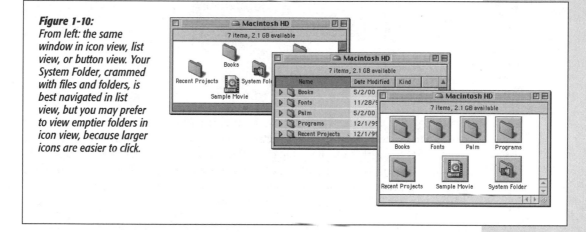

*Figure 1-10:*
*From left: the same window in icon view, list view, or button view. Your System Folder, crammed with files and folders, is best navigated in list view, but you may prefer to view emptier folders in icon view, because larger icons are easier to click.*

To switch a window from one view to another, most people choose View→as Icons (or View→as List, or View→as Buttons). If you have a large monitor, however, you may prefer this alternative method: while pressing the Control key, click anywhere inside the window. While the mouse button is pressed, a floating *contextual menu* appears at your cursor tip, from which you can easily choose View→as Icons, View→as List, or View→as Buttons. Using the contextual menu saves you a mouse trip to the top of the monitor.

## Icon-View Notes

In an icon view, each file, folder, and disk is represented by a small picture—an *icon*. This humble image, a visual representation of electronic bits and bytes, is the cornerstone of the entire Macintosh religion. (Maybe that's why it's called an icon.)

### Small-icon view

If you like the idea of icon views, but would prefer a more compact window listing, choose View→View Options. In the resulting window, choose the smaller icon size. As shown in Figure 1-11, you now have all the handy, freely draggable convenience of an icon view, along with the compact spacing of a list view.

### Keeping your icons neat and sorted

In general, you can drag icons anywhere within a window. Some people like to keep current project icons at the top of the window, for example, moving older stuff to the bottom.

**Figure 1-11:**
*Using the View Options command, you can specify either standard icons (left) or small ones. In small-icon view, the names of your files now appear beside, not under, the icons.*

If you'd prefer that Mac OS 9 impose a little discipline on you, however, it's easy enough to request a visit from an electronic housekeeper who tidies up your icons, aligning them neatly to an invisible grid. You can specify the size of this underlying grid by choosing Edit→Preferences, and choosing either Tight (which fits more icons per square inch, but very long file names may overlap) or Loose (in which icons are fairly far apart, so file names can't overlap).

Mac OS 9 offers an enormous number of variations on the "snap icons to the underlying grid" theme:

- **Aligning individual icons to the grid:** Press the ⌘ key while dragging an icon or several highlighted icons. When you release the mouse, you'll find that they all jump into neatly aligned position.

- **Aligning all icons to the grid:** Choose View→Clean Up. Now all icons in the window jump to the closest positions on the invisible underlying grid. This is a temporary status, however—as soon as you drag icons around, or add more icons to the window, the newly moved icons wind up just as sloppily positioned as before you used the command.

    If you'd rather have icons snap to the nearest underlying grid positions *whenever* they're moved, choose View→View Options. In the resulting dialog box, turn on the "Always snap to grid" option, and then click OK.

**Tip:** When the "Always snap to grid" option is turned on, any icons you drag jump into grid alignment when you release the mouse—unless you're pressing the ⌘ key at the moment when you let go.

In other words, the ⌘ key is the override key: when grid-snapping is turned on, ⌘ lets you drag an icon freely. When grid-snapping is turned off, ⌘ makes an icon snap into grid alignment.

Note, by the way, that neither of these grid-snapping commands—View→Clean Up and the "Always snap to grid" option—moves icons into the most compact possible arrangement. If one or two icons have wandered off from the herd to the lower-right corner of the window, they're merely nudged to the closest grid points to their present locations. They aren't moved all the way back to the crowd of icons elsewhere in the window. To make them jump back to the primary cluster, read on.

• **Sorting all icons for the moment:** If you choose View→Arrange→by Name, all icons in the window snap to the invisible grid *and* sort themselves alphabetically. Use this method to place the icons as close as possible to each other within the window, rounding up any strays. (The other subcommands in the View→Arrange menu, such as "by Size," "by Date Modified," and so on, work similarly, but sort the icons according to different criteria.)

As with the Clean Up command, View→Arrange serves only to reorganize the icons in the window at this moment. Moving or adding icons in the window means you'll wind up with icons out of order. If you'd rather have all icons remain sorted and clustered, try this:

• **Sorting all icons permanently:** This fascinating arrangement is the ideal solution for neat freaks who can't stand seeing icons out of place. It's a powerful feature that maintains sorting and alignment of all icons in the window, present and future—if you add more icons to the window, they jump into correct alphabetical position. If you remove icons, the remaining ones slide over to fill in the resulting gap.

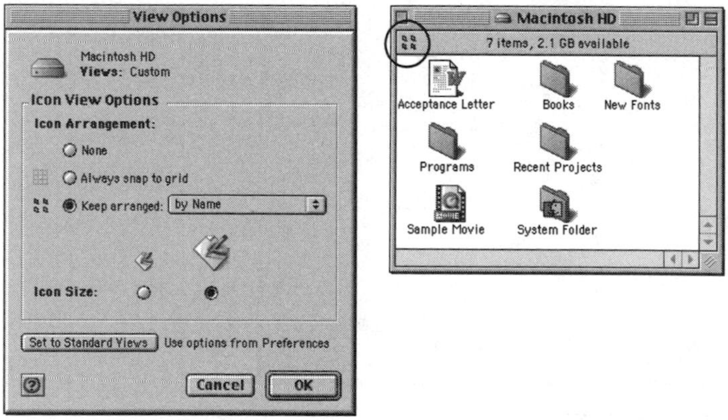

*Figure 1-12:*
*Use the View Options dialog box (left) to turn on permanent-cleanliness mode (right). The tiny four-square icon (circled) reminds you that you've turned on the Mac's spatial lockjaw feature, so that you don't get frustrated when you try to drag an icon into a new position and discover that it won't budge.*

To set this arrangement up, choose View→View Options. In the resulting dialog box, click the Keep Arranged button. From the pop-up menu, specify what order you want your icons to snap into, as shown at left in Figure 1-12. Click OK. As shown at right in Figure 1-12, your icons are now locked into sorted position, as compactly as possible.

---

***Tip:*** Although it doesn't occur to most Mac users, you can apply any of the commands described in this section—Clean Up, Arrange, Keep Arranged, and so on—to icons lying loose on your desktop. Even though they're not technically in any window at all, you can specify small or large icons, automatic alphabetical arrangement, and so on. Just use the commands in the View menu when no window at all is open, or use the contextual menu that appears when you Control-click the desktop.

---

## List-View Notes

In windows that contain a lot of items, the list view is a powerful weapon in the battle against chaos. The result is a tidy table whose informational columns reveal your files' names, dates, sizes, and so on.

The first column of a list view is always Name. You have complete control over any other columns: which of them should appear, in which order, and how wide they should be. Here's how to master these columns:

### Determining which columns appear

Choose View→View Options. In the dialog box that appears, you're offered on/off checkboxes for the different columns of information Mac OS 9 can show you, as shown in Figure 1-13.

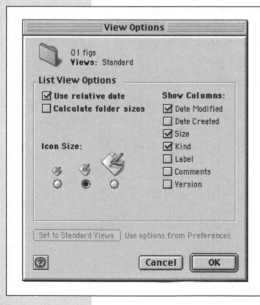

***Figure 1-13:***
*You can add up to seven columns of file information to a list view. The checkboxes you turn on here, in the View options dialog box, determine which columns of information appear in a list-view window. They also determine which commands are available in the View→Sort List submenu—after all, the Mac can't sort your list of files according to a criterion that you've made invisible.*

Most people live full and satisfying lives with only the three default columns—Date Modified, Kind, and Size—turned on. But the other columns can be helpful in special circumstances; the trick is knowing what information appears there.

- **Date Modified:** This date-and-time stamp indicates when a document was last saved. Its accuracy, of course, depends on the accuracy of your Mac's built-in clock (see page 190).

---

***Caution:*** Many an up-to-date file has been lost because a Mac user spotted a very old date on a folder and assumed that the files inside were equally old. But the modification date shown for a folder doesn't reflect the age of its contents! Instead, the date on a folder indicates only when items were last *moved* into or out of that folder. The actual files inside may be much more recent.

---

- **Date Created:** This date-and-time stamp shows you when a document was *first* saved. (Don't rely on the Mac's date and time stamps as proof that a student or employee met a deadline, however. Clever deadline-dodgers can change a file's creation date easily enough with the free editing program called ResEdit, included at *www.missingmanual.com.*)

- **Size:** With a glance, you can tell from this column how much disk space each of your files and folders is taking up. If the Size column is wide enough, you see the size written out in bytes; if the Size column is narrow, you see MB (megabytes; there are 1,048,576 bytes in a megabyte).

- **Kind:** In this column, you're shown what *kind* of icon each item represents. You may see, for example, "folder," "Photoshop document," "text clipping," "application," and so on.

- **Label:** Using the File→Label command, you can apply a colored (and written) *label* to icons of your choice. Doing so makes these icons easy to round up, or back up, later (see Chapter 2).

  If you've applied labels to your icons—most people don't bother—this column shows the written labels (such as "Essential" or "In Progress").

*Figure 1-14:*
*The Comments column is often worth making visible. If your monitor is big enough, you can make the Comments column a full 93 characters wide—enough to reveal the full life history of each icon. (Files you save from Netscape Communicator reveal the original Web-page address here, too.)*

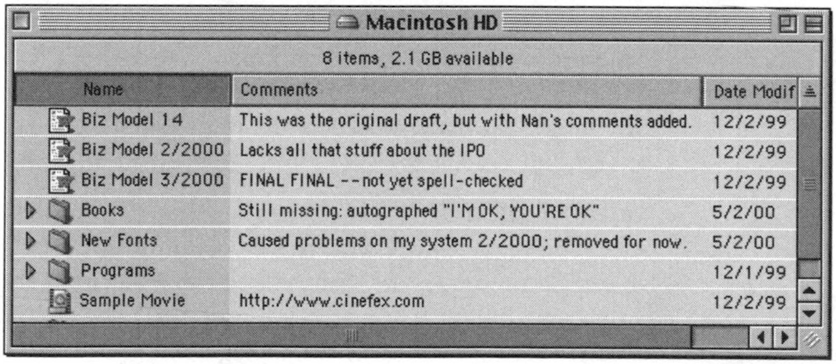

| Name | Comments | Date Modif |
|------|----------|-----------|
| Biz Model 1 4 | This was the original draft, but with Nan's comments added. | 12/2/99 |
| Biz Model 2/2000 | Lacks all that stuff about the IPO | 12/2/99 |
| Biz Model 3/2000 | FINAL FINAL -- not yet spell-checked | 12/2/99 |
| ▷ Books | Still missing: autographed "I'M OK, YOU'RE OK" | 5/2/00 |
| ▷ New Fonts | Caused problems on my system 2/2000; removed for now. | 5/2/00 |
| ▷ Programs | | 12/1/99 |
| Sample Movie | http://www.cinefex.com | 12/2/99 |

Macintosh HD — 8 items, 2.1 GB available

- **Comments:** This rarely seen column can actually be among the most useful. Suppose that you're a person who uses the Comments feature (highlight an icon, choose File→Get Info→General Information, type notes about that icon). The option to view the first line of comments about each icon can be very helpful, especially when tracking multiple versions of your documents, as shown in Figure 1-14.

- **Version:** In this column, you're shown the version numbers of your programs. For folders and documents, you see nothing but a dash. (Mac OS 9 offers no means of adding version numbers to your own files.)

### Rearranging the columns

You're stuck with the Name column at the far left of a window. But you can rearrange the other columns just by dragging their gray column headers horizontally, as shown in Figure 1-15.

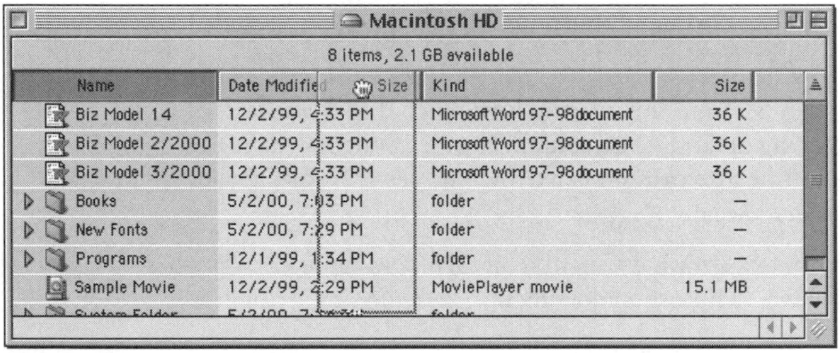

**Figure 1-15:**
As you rearrange columns, understanding where a column will wind up can be tricky: it will land to the left of the column it overlaps. Here, the Size column will wind up to the left of Date Modified–not to the right of it.

### Adjusting column widths

Place your cursor carefully on the dividing line between two column headings. When the cursor sprouts horizontal arrows from each side, you can drag horizontally. Doing so makes the column to the *left* of your cursor wider or narrower.

What's especially delightful about this activity is watching Mac OS 9 scramble to rewrite its information to fit the space you give it. For example, as the Size column gets narrower, a folder's size description changes from "16,429,056 bytes" to "15.6MB" and, finally, to "15…MB." The Date Modified (or Created) column is even more fun: As you make the column narrower, "Friday, June 2, 2000, 3:11 pm" shrinks first to "Fri, Jun 2, 2000, 3:11 pm," to "6/2/00, 3:11 pm," and finally to the terse "6/2/00."

### Resetting columns

After you've rearranged and resized columns until the list view is barely recognizable, it's simple to restore them to their original widths and sequence (Date Modified, Size, and Kind, in that order). Choose View→Reset Column Positions, and then click Reset in the confirmation dialog box.

### Specifying how the icons are sorted

Most of the world's list-view fans like their files listed alphabetically. It's occasionally useful, however, to view the oldest files first, largest first, and so on.

The column headings in a Mac OS 9 list view aren't just signposts; they're also buttons. Click one of them to sort the list of icons by that criterion. Click Name for alphabetical order, Date Modified to view newest first, Size to view largest files at the top, and so on. (You can perform the same function using the View→Sort List commands, or by Control-clicking inside a window and then choosing Sort List. But clicking a column title is usually much faster.)

### Taming the unruly list view

One of Mac OS 9's most attractive features is the tiny blue triangle that appears to the left of a folder's name in a list view. In its official occurrences, Apple calls these triangle buttons *disclosure triangles;* internally, the programmers call them *flippy triangles*. Either way, these triangles are fantastically useful: when you click one, you turn the list view into an outline, in which the contents of the folder are displayed in an indented list, as shown in Figure 1-16. Click the triangle again to collapse the folder listing. You're saved the trouble and clutter of having to open a new window just to view the folder's contents.

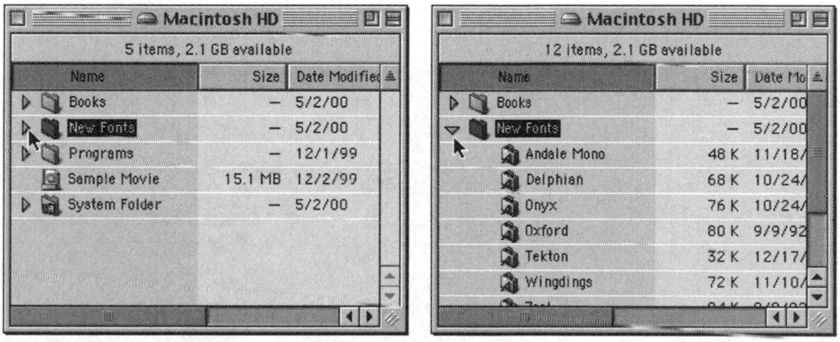

**Figure 1-16:**
*Click a "flippy triangle" (left) to see the listing of the folders and files inside that folder (right). Or press the equivalent keystrokes: ⌘-right arrow (to open) and ⌘-left arrow (to close).*

## Button-View Notes

The least popular window view, one that debuted in Mac OS 8.5, is Button view. Icons in this view open with a single click instead of the usual double-click, and each appears on a "pillow"—a fat border—that makes the icon an even easier target for clicking. All of this is designed for kids, the disabled, or efficiency addicts who find a second click superfluous.

Because Button-view icons are so big, most people dismiss them as impractical. But they can be useful when you're building a launching-bay window, for example, in which you store the icons of frequently accessed programs and documents. Moreover, you're not stuck with the jumbo icons; by choosing View→View Options, you can turn on the smaller icon option, which shrinks icon buttons to the size of normal icons.

In the final analysis, the biggest factor in the unpopularity of Button view maybe the unpleasant experience most people have with their initial encounter with button icons. That's when they discover—or so they believe—that buttons can't be moved. After all, a single click opens the corresponding icon, so dragging becomes impossible.

In fact, however, you can indeed move and copy button icons in the normal way. Just drag a button by its *name* instead of its icon.

## The View Options Command

As you've discovered if you read this far in chapter, many powerful window-customizing options lurk in the View→View Options command. The dialog box that appears (see Figure 1-13) varies slightly according to what kind of windows open at the time—a list, icon, or button view—but most of them remain constant, and several are very useful:

- **Use relative date (list views only):** In a list view, the Date Modified and Date Created columns generally display information in a format like this: "Sunday, November 11, 2000." (As noted earlier in this chapter, the Mac uses shorter date formats as the column gets narrower.) But when the "Use relative date" option is turned on, the Mac substitutes the word "Yesterday" or "Today" where appropriate, making recent files much easier to spot.

  (In fact, on some rainy Saturday when you have nothing better to do, use the Date & Time control panel to set your Mac's clock ahead one day. Launch any

---

**POWER USERS' CLINIC**

## Flippy Triangle Keystrokes

As you can tell from this chapter, Mac OS 9 offers an endless array of useful keystrokes that help you manipulate your folders and windows. The keystrokes that let you open and close flippy triangles in a list view, however, are worth committing to memory.

First, note that pressing the Option key when you click a flippy triangle lets you view a folder's contents *and* the contents of any folders inside it. The result, in other words, is a much longer list that may involve several levels of indentation.

If you prefer to use the keyboard exclusively, highlight the folder you want by typing the first letters of its name, or by pressing the up and down arrow keys. Then press ⌘-right arrow (to expand a flippy triangle) or ⌘-left arrow (to collapse the folder listing again). Here again, adding the Option key expands all levels of folder within the selected one.

Suppose, for example, that you find it useful to flag all files

in a newly installed System Folder with a certain label color— a problem-prevention technique described in Appendix B. You could perform the entire routine from the keyboard like this: Select the System Folder by typing the letters SY. Open it by pressing ⌘-O (the shortcut for File→Open). Highlight the entire contents by pressing ⌘-A (the shortcut for Edit→Select All).

Now that all folders are highlighted, press Option-⌘-right arrow. You'll have to wait a minute or more for the Mac to open every subfolder of every subfolder, but eventually, the massive list will appear, complete with many levels of indentation. Once again, press ⌘-A to highlight all visible files. From the File→Label command, choose the label color you want to apply to every element of your System Folder. Finally, press Option-⌘-left arrow to close every flippy triangle in the System Folder, and then ⌘-W to close the System Folder window and proceed with your life.

---

program and save a new document. When you reset your Date & Time control panel to the correct date, you'll see, as the creation date for your new document, the improbable label "Tomorrow"!)

- **Calculate folder sizes (list views only):** As described on page 20, the Mac generally shows only dashes in the Size column for folders. Turning on this checkbox forces the computer to add up the sizes of the files inside each visible list-view folder, finally displaying the grand total for each folder in the Size column. (This process takes time—sometimes several minutes—and applies only to the currently open window.)

- **Show columns (list views only):** Turn on the checkboxes corresponding to the columns you'd like to appear in the current window's list view, as shown in Figure 1-13.

  Appropriately enough, the choices you make here also affect which commands are listed in the View→Sort List command. The Sort List submenu lists such options as "by Name," "by Date Modified," and so on—which correspond to the checkboxes you turn on here.

- **Icon Size:** These three radio buttons offer you a choice of standard icon size for the current window. You're offered standard size, which is 32 *pixels* (screen dots) square; small size, 16 pixels square; and—in list view only—the tiny size, only 12 pixels square, so small that the individual illustration on the standard icon disappears entirely. (In addition to showing more icons per square inch, this tiny icon size offers a speed advantage. Because the Mac doesn't have to show you the actual Microsoft Word icon, AppleWorks icon, and so on, you can scroll through even enormous lists almost instantaneously.)

- **Icon Arrangement (icon and list views only):** These options govern whether, and how, your icons are kept neatly aligned with an invisible underlying grid, as described on page 18.

- **Set to Standard Views:** Click this button to make the current window adhere to a set of favorite window settings you've established in advance, as described in the next section.

## Setting Up Standard Views

As you've deduced from reading this chapter so far, Finder windows offer an almost infinite variety of file-listing styles. Every window of every disk can have a different assortment of information columns, display icons in different sizes, have different grid-alignment options, and so on. If, like most Mac fans, you prefer one particular arrangement, you may dread the prospect of having to perform the necessary setup steps for each of hundreds of different folders.

Fortunately, two built-in functions of Mac OS 9 make it easy to duplicate the favorite set of window settings: parent-window inheritance and the Standard Views command.

## Parent-Window Inheritance

Any new folder adopts the view settings of its parent window. If your hard drive displays your files as a grid-aligned, small-icon, date-sorted button view, so will any folders you create in the main hard drive window.

This information, of course, is most valuable when you've just bought your Macintosh, and haven't yet created dozens of new folders. Even if you've had your Mac for a while, however, it's not too late to set up the hard drive window the way you like it, content that its view settings will be passed on to future generations of folders.

## Standard Views

Mac OS 9 can memorize a complete set of favorite view settings for each of the three primary window types: list views, icon views, and button views. Once you've specified settings you like, applying them to other windows is a matter of two clicks.

To define the view settings you prefer, choose Edit→Preferences. In the Preferences dialog box that appears, click the Views tab. Use the pop-up menu to specify List, Icon, or Button, according to the kind of view you'd like to customize.

Now you can use the various checkboxes and buttons to define a standard look for the view you've indicated. These options are described in "Window Views: Icon,

---

**FREQUENTLY ASKED QUESTION**

### "Calculate Folder Sizes"

*When I sort my list view by size, I see only dashes for folder sizes. What am I doing wrong?*

Nothing at all; that's normal. When viewing a Finder window, you see a Size statistic for each *document.* For *folders,* however, you're shown only an uninformative dash.

Most Mac fans study this anomaly only momentarily, scratch their chins, and then get on with their lives. (Former Windows users don't even scratch their chins—on Windows PCs, folder-size information is *never* shown in a list view.)

The explanation: It can take a computer a long time to add up the sizes of all files inside a folder. Your System Folder, for example, contains over 1,000 files. So that you don't have to wait while the Mac does all of this addition, Mac OS 9 simply shows you a dash in the Size column for a folder.

On occasion, however, you really do want to see how big your folders are. In such cases, choose View→View Options, turn on "Calculate folder sizes," and click OK. You'll see the folder sizes slowly begin to pop onto the screen, from the top of the window downward, as the Mac crunches the numbers of the files within. (In older versions of the Mac OS, you could turn on the "Calculate folder sizes" option only globally, for all windows, resulting in a massive slowdown of the entire computer. In Mac OS 8 and later, you can use this option on a window-by-window basis. As a result, and because today's Macs are so fast, the "Calculate" option results in no measurable sluggishness for hard-drive folder windows.)

But now consider this anomaly: Suppose you've opted to sort a particular window by folder size (in other words, you've clicked the word Size at the top of the column). Turning on "Calculate folder sizes" bewilders the unprepared, as folders arbitrarily begin leaping out of order, forcing the list to rearrange itself once per second.

What's happening, of course, is that all folders *begin* at the bottom of the list, showing only dashes in the Size column. Then, as the Mac computes the size of your folders' contents, they jump into their correct sorted order at what may seem to be random intervals.

---

List, and Button" on page 17; you can set them up independently for list views, icon views, and button views. When you're finished, click OK.

The next time you open some window that doesn't match your favorite view settings, the solution is quick: choose View→View Options, and then click the Set to Standard Views button. When you click OK, the window will instantly whip itself into shape according to your previous specifications.

## Pop-Up Windows

After conducting many a focus group at its Cupertino, CA headquarters, Apple's software designers came to a grave conclusion: Mac fans were leaving far too many icons out on their desktops. Clutter is bad enough when it's your office desktop, but it's positively tacky on a computer screen.

That untidiness was the impetus behind the creation of *pop-up windows,* which Apple wants you to think of as drawers that pull out of the bottom of the screen for convenient icon stashing. After opening any folder or disk, you can create a pop-up window in either of two ways:

- Choose View→as Pop-up Window.

- Drag the window downward until your cursor is a half-inch from the bottom of the screen. The outline of your dragged window suddenly changes: now it's a tab, like the one on a file folder. Release the mouse. (This method has the advantage of letting you place the pop-up window wherever you wish at the bottom of the screen.)

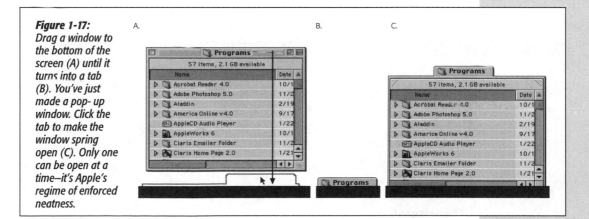

**Figure 1-17:**
*Drag a window to the bottom of the screen (A) until it turns into a tab (B). You've just made a pop- up window. Click the tab to make the window spring open (C). Only one can be open at a time—it's Apple's regime of enforced neatness.*

Either way, a new pop-up window is born (see Figure 1-17).

Pop-up windows behave oddly, and yet their idiosyncrasies can be useful. For example, pop-up windows are spring-loaded, refusing to remain open. They collapse back into tabs at the least provocation, including when you open any other window, double-click an icon within, switch into any other program, and so on.

This primal urge to collapse back into a tab at the bottom of the screen is the primary virtue of pop-up windows as a tidiness tool. It also makes them ideal for storing items for which you require quick access—programs and documents you might otherwise leave out on the desktop. Most Mac fans' first experiment with a pop-up window is to create a launching bay that houses the programs they use most often. (Technically speaking, they use the pop-up window to store *aliases* of such programs, as described in Chapter 2.)

It's easy to create multiple pop-up window tabs, stretching across the bottom of your screen; you'll quickly notice, however, that only one can be open at a time. Opening a second other pop-up window closes the first.

---

*Tip:* To move an item into a pop-up window, you can drag its icon onto the pop-up window's *tab.* The window dutifully springs open to receive its new document.

In other words, the fact that only one pop-up window can be open at a time doesn't prevent you from dragging icons *between* pop-up windows. Just open the first, and then drag an icon from inside it onto the tab of another pop-up window.

---

To turn a pop-up window back into a normal one, drag its tab upward until you can see the outline of its bottom edge, and then release. (Alternatively, click its tab and then choose View→as Window.)

As for closing pop-up windows from the keyboard, take your pick:

- ⌘-W makes an open pop-up window collapse back into its tab-like, bottom-feeding state.

---

**FREQUENTLY ASKED QUESTION**

## The Open Folder Pop-up Window Conundrum

*I opened my Programs folder and turned its window into a pop-up window. But now the folder is sitting on my hard drive with that darkened, hollow-looking icon that means it's open. How do I make it look like a normal, closed folder again?*

Unfortunately, every pop-up window leaves behind an open-folder icon, exactly as you describe. A pop-up window is, after all, still a window, and therefore the folder from whence it came

appears darkened and hollow as long as the pop-up window exists.

If this cosmetic problem is turning you into an insomniac, consider this cheat: Stash the open folder inside some *other* folder where you won't have to look at it. Then create an alias of the folder, as described in the next chapter. Put the alias into your main hard drive window, as a stand-in for the original folder. Alias icons, conveniently enough, *don't* turn dark and hollow when opened.

- Option-⌘-W makes an open pop-up window collapse *and* closes any open normal windows.

- Shift-Option-⌘-W—if you have that many fingers—closes and eliminates all pop-up windows at once, leaving the bottom of your screen tab-free.

# CHAPTER 2

# Icon Management

Before the Mac made *icons* famous, a computer's documents and programs were represented only by text listings. To open a letter you had written, you had to type out its name precisely.

Today, of course, every document, program, folder, and disk on your Mac is represented by an *icon:* an inch-tall picture that you can move, copy, or double-click to open. This chapter covers every aspect of managing, filing, naming, copying, deleting, and troubleshooting these cornerstones of the Mac OS.

## Icon Names

A Mac icon's name can have up to 31 letters and spaces. You can use letters, numbers, punctuation—in fact, any symbol you want except for the colon (:), which the Mac uses behind the scenes for its own folder-hierarchy designation purposes. (If you type a colon when renaming an icon, Mac OS 9 automatically substitutes a hyphen— a much more considerate behavior than showing you some rude error message.)

To rename an icon, you can use any of the following techniques:

- Click the file name itself, as shown in Figure 2-1.
- Click once on the icon, and then press Return or Enter to make the renaming rectangle appear. Type the new name, and then press Return or Enter.

---

*Tip:* If you simply want to add letters to the beginning or end of the file's existing name, press the right or left arrow key immediately after pressing Return or Enter. The insertion point jumps to the corresponding end of the file name.

---

*Tip:* The delay between your click on an icon's name and the appearance of its renaming rectangle is determined by, of all things, the Double-Click Speed setting in the Mouse control panel. The connection isn't as arbitrary as it might seem: the delay is designed to prevent accidental renamings by helping the Mac distinguish between a single click (to rename the file) and the first part of a double-click (to open it). Therefore, the wider you make the double-click speed window, the longer the renaming rectangle takes to appear.

- The most direct method of all: Click the file name and then flick the mouse, even a fraction of an inch, to make the renaming rectangle appear instantaneously. (The mouse movement tells Mac OS 9 that your click should be interpreted as an "I want to rename" click, not the first click in a double-click.)

**Figure 2-1:**
*Click an icon's name (top left). A rectangle appears around the name (top right). At this point, the existing name is highlighted; just begin typing to replace it (bottom left). When you're finished typing, press Return, Enter, or Tab to seal the deal and make the renaming rectangle disappear (bottom right).*

---

**POWER USERS' CLINIC**

## Designing Your Own Icons

You don't have to be content with the icons provided by Microsoft, Apple, and whoever else provided your software. Equipped with a graphics program like Photoshop, the painting module of AppleWorks, or a shareware program like GraphicConverter, you can easily draw your own icons to replace the originals.

To design an icon from scratch, create a document in your painting program that's 32 pixels square. As you design the new icon, be aware that Mac OS 9 has a tendency to "pour" the desktop background color into any white areas of the icon. (For example, if your new icon looks like somebody's head, even a single-pixel light-colored gap in the outline of the head—under the ear, say—is enough of an opening for the desktop color to fill the entire face.) To prevent that phenomenon, fully enclose the outline of your icon's shape with a dark outline.

When you're finished, choose Edit→Select All. In the Finder, highlight the icon that's going to receive the surgery. Choose File→Get Info. In the window that appears, click the existing icon, and then choose Edit→Paste. Close the Get Info window to see your icon with its new face. (To restore the original icon, repeat the procedure, but click the replacement icon and then choose Edit→Cut.)

It's also easy to modify the existing icon (instead of creating an all-new one). To do so, highlight the icon, choose File→Get Info, click the existing icon in the resulting window, and then choose Edit→Copy. Now you're ready to paste the image on your Clipboard into the graphics program for modification—or even onto another icon.

---

As you edit a file's name, remember that you can use the Cut, Copy, and Paste commands in the Edit menu to move selected bits of text around, exactly as though you were word processing. (In fact, editing file names is the *only* task those commands are good for in the Finder.) The Paste command can be useful when, for instance, you're renaming many icons in sequence (Quarterly Estimate 1, Quarterly Estimate 2, and so on).

Remember, too, that when the Finder sorts files, a space is considered alphabetically *before* the letter A. To force a particular folder to appear at the top of a list-view window, precede its name with a space.

## Selecting Icons

To highlight a single icon in preparation for printing, opening, duplicating, or deleting, click the icon once with the mouse. (In a list view, as described in Chapter 1, you can also click on any visible piece of information about that file—its size, kind, date modified, and so on.)

That much may seem obvious. But most first-time Mac users don't know how to manipulate *more* than one icon at a time—an essential survival skill.

To select multiple icons, press the Shift key as you click them in sequence—or drag a box around them, as shown in Figure 2-2. Each icon darkens to show that it has been selected. If you're highlighting a long string of icons and then include one more by mistake, you don't have to start over—instead, just Shift-click it again; the dark highlighting disappears. (If you do want to start over from the beginning, you can de-select all selected icons by clicking any empty part of the window.)

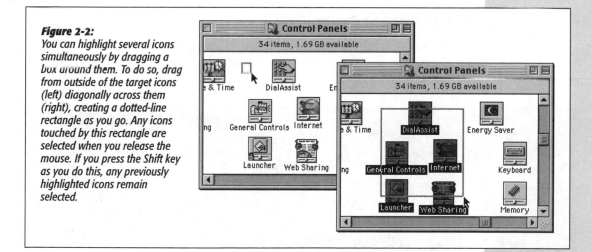

**Figure 2-2:**
*You can highlight several icons simultaneously by dragging a box around them. To do so, drag from outside of the target icons (left) diagonally across them (right), creating a dotted-line rectangle as you go. Any icons touched by this rectangle are selected when you release the mouse. If you press the Shift key as you do this, any previously highlighted icons remain selected.*

Once you've highlighted multiple icons, you can manipulate them all at once. For example, you can drag them en masse to another folder or disk by dragging any *one* of the highlighted icons: All other highlighted icons go along for the ride. This technique is especially useful when you want to back up a bunch of files by dragging them onto a different disk, or when you want to delete them all by dragging them to the Trash.

When multiple icons are selected, furthermore, the commands in the File menu—such as Print, Open, or Duplicate—apply to all of them simultaneously.

---

**POWER USERS' CLINIC**

### Selecting Icons from the Keyboard

For the speed fanatic, using the mouse to click an icon is a hopeless waste of time. Fortunately, you can also select an icon by typing the first couple letters of its name.

When looking at the main hard drive window, for example, you can type *AP* to highlight the Apple Extras folder. And if you actually intended to highlight the *Applications* folder instead, press the Tab key. Tab highlights the next icon in the window alphabetically. (Shift-Tab highlights the previous icon alphabetically.) You can use the arrow keys, too, to highlight a neighboring icon. All of these techniques work equally well in icon, list, or button views.

After having highlighted an icon in this way, you can manipulate it using the commands in the File menu—or their

keyboard equivalents: open (⌘-O), print (⌘-P), toss into the Trash (⌘-Delete), get information (⌘-I), duplicate (⌘-D), or make an alias, as described later in this chapter (⌘-M). If you have highlighted a disk icon, you can also press ⌘-E to eject it. You can't actually *move* a highlighted icon using only the keyboard (at least not without Easy Access, described in Chapter 13). For that, you must drag with the mouse.

If you're a first-time Mac user, you may find it excessively nerdy to memorize keystrokes for functions the mouse does perfectly well. If you make your living using the Mac, however, take the few minutes required to learn these tricks. The speed and efficiency of these keystrokes will reward you many times over.

---

## Moving and Copying Icons

Understanding when the Mac copies a dragged icon and when it just *moves* the icon bewilders many a beginner. However, the scheme is fairly simple; Figure 2-3 explains all.

---

**FREQUENTLY ASKED QUESTION**

### Moving, not Copying, to a Different Disk

*When I drag an icon to a different disk, the Mac always creates a duplicate. I wind up with the original file on my hard drive, and the copy on my backup disk. How can I move an icon to a different disk instead of copying it, so that the original doesn't remain on my hard drive?*

You can't.

Apple, in its empathy for the novice, has made it impossible to move an icon from one disk to another without making a copy of it. (Evidently the designers of the Mac OS worried that when you discovered the original file missing from your hard drive, you'd panic.) You have no choice but to manually delete the original from your hard drive after dragging it to the second disk.

---

## Copying as You Drag

There's one useful way to violate the golden rule of move-vs.-copy that's illustrated in Figure 2-3. If you press the Option key when you drag an icon to a different folder or window on the same disk, you create a duplicate. In other words, pressing Option as you drag makes Mac OS 9 behave exactly as though you had dragged the icon to a different disk.

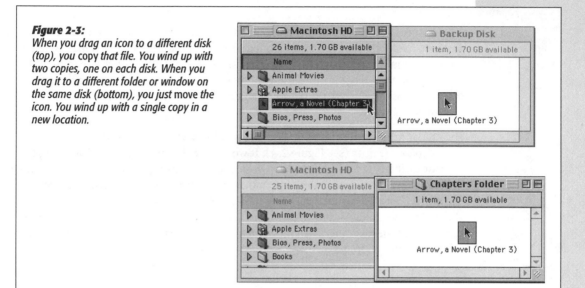

**Figure 2-3:**
*When you drag an icon to a different disk (top), you copy that file. You wind up with two copies, one on each disk. When you drag it to a different folder or window on the same disk (bottom), you just move the icon. You wind up with a single copy in a new location.*

---

**GEMS IN THE ROUGH**

## The Put Away Command

For years, Mac fans used the File→Put Away command exclusively for one purpose: ejecting a disk or CD. After all, the more logical-sounding Special→Eject Disk command had an annoying side effect: it left behind a residual ghost image of the disk's icon. (That behavior was left over from the 1984, pre-hard drive days.)

But in today's Mac OS, the Eject Disk command works properly. It's time for Mac users to rediscover the Put Away command. Its true function: to move icons on the desktop or in the Trash back to their previous folder locations on the hard drive.

For example, suppose you've double-clicked your Trash icon. You discover two icons waiting in the Trash window that shouldn't be deleted. Rather than trying to figure out what folder they originally came from, and shuffling windows around to receive them, just highlight the icons and then choose File→Put Away (or press ⌘-Y). Before your eyes, those icons disappear from the Trash window; Mac OS 9 has stored them safely in the folder from which they were dragged to the Trash, even if it was months ago.

Put Away also works on icons on the desktop, automatically flinging them back into the hard-drive folders from which they were once dragged. The command isn't always as successful here, however, because many desktop icons never *were* dragged out of a folder. Instead, they were downloaded, installed, or copied directly onto your desktop. In those situations, the Put Away command doesn't know where to put these icons, and has no choice but to show you an error message.

---

*Tip:* While the Mac is copying an icon, you can cancel the copying process in progress by pressing ⌘-period.

## Spring-Loaded Folders: Dragging Icons into Closed Folders

In its never-ending quest to create the operating system with the longest list of win-dow-management tools, Apple came up with a unique and powerful one called *spring-loaded folders.*

The feature is designed to solve a common problem: you want to drag an icon not just into a folder, but into a folder nested *inside* that folder. This awkward challenge would ordinarily require you to open the first folder, open the inner folder, drag the icon in, and then close both of the windows you had opened. As you can imagine, the process is even messier if you want to drag an icon into a sub-subfolder or even a *sub*-sub-subfolder.

Instead of fiddling around with all those windows, you can instead use the *spring-loaded folders* feature (see Figure 2-4). It works like this: with a single drag, drag the icon onto the first folder—but keep your mouse button pressed. After a few sec-onds, the folder window opens automatically, centered on your cursor. Still keeping the button down, drag onto the inner folder; its window, too, opens. Now drag onto the *inner* inner folder—and so on. When you finally release the mouse, all the win-dows except the last one close automatically. You've neatly placed the icon into the core of the nested folders.

**Figure 2-4:**
*Drag an icon onto a folder or disk icon (left), wait for the window to open (right), and continue dragging until you've reached your folder-within-a-folder destination. (If the inner folder you intend to open isn't visible in the window, you can scroll by dragging your cursor close to any edge of the window.)*

## Spring-Loaded Folders Without Dragging

Spring-loaded folders offer a corollary benefit that doesn't involve dragging an icon. Using almost the same technique, you can open a folder within a folder just to see what's inside.

To do so, learn the peculiar new skill known as a *click-and-a-half.* That's when you point to the outer folder, such as your System Folder, push the mouse button down-up-down—and freeze with the mouse button down. After a moment, the cursor changes to become a magnifying glass, and the System Folder window springs open, exactly as described in the previous section. Now you can proceed as described above, dragging your cursor onto an inner folder, then onto another inner folder, and so on. When you release the button, all windows close by themselves except the last one you opened.

### Making Spring-Loaded Folders Work

That spring-loaded folder technique sounds good in theory, but can be disconcerting in practice. For most people, the several-second wait before the first folder opens is almost enough wasted time to negate the value of the feature to begin with. Furthermore, when the first window finally does open, you're often caught by surprise. Suddenly your cursor—mouse button still down—is inside a window, sometimes directly on top of another folder you never intended to open. But before you can react, its window, too, has opened, and you find yourself off track and out of control.

Fortunately, you can regain control of spring-loaded folders using three tricks:

- Choose Edit→Preferences. Adjust the "Delay before opening" slider to a setting that drives you less crazy. For example, if you find yourself having to wait too long before the first folder opens, drag the slider toward the Short setting.

- Tap the Space bar to make the folder spring open at your command. That is, even with the Edit→Preferences slider set to the Long delay setting, you can force each folder to spring open when *you* are ready by tapping the Space bar as you hold down the mouse button.

  This powerful shortcut works both when you're dragging an icon into a folder-within-a-folder as well as when you're using the click-and-a-half method. True, you need two hands to master this one, but the control you regain is immeasurable.

- Whenever a folder springs open into a window, twitch your mouse cursor up to the title bar or information strip. Doing so ensures that your cursor won't wind up hovering on, and opening up, an inner folder by accident. Once parked on the info strip, you can take your time to survey the newly opened window's contents. Then you can plunge into an inner folder after gaining your bearings.

- If the spring-loaded nature of Mac OS 9 folders strikes you as more annoying than useful, you can turn the feature off entirely. Choose Edit→Preferences, and turn off the Spring-Loaded Folders checkbox.

## Aliases: Icons in Two Places at Once

By highlighting an icon and then choosing File→Make Alias, you generate an *alias,* a specially branded duplicate of the original icon (see Figure 2-5). It's not a duplicate of the file—just of the icon, requiring negligible storage space. When you double-click the alias, the original file opens. You can create as many aliases as you want of a single file. In other words, aliases let you, in effect, stash a file in many different folder locations simultaneously. Double-click any one of them, and you open the original icon, wherever it may be on your system.

***Tip:*** You can also create an alias of an icon by ⌘-Option-dragging it out of its window. (Aliases you create this way lack the word *alias* on the filename—a distinct delight to those who find the suffix redundant and annoying.) You can also create an alias by Control-clicking a normal icon and choosing Make Alias from the contextual menu that appears.

And if you use Sherlock (see Chapter 15), you can create an alias of any icon in the Items Found window by ⌘-Option-dragging it out of the window.

***Figure 2-5:***
*You can identify an alias by the tiny arrow badge on the lower-left corner—and by the italicized name.*

## What's Good About Aliases

An alias takes up almost no disk space, even if the original file is enormous. Aliases are smart, too: even if you rename the alias, rename the original icon, move the alias, and move the original file, double-clicking the alias still opens the original icon.

And that's just the beginning of alias intelligence: Suppose the original file is on a removable disk, such as a Zip disk. Suppose you make an alias of it, which you copy to your hard drive. When you double-click the alias, the Mac requests the Zip disk by name. Similarly, if the original file resides on a different machine on the network, your Mac attempts to connect to the appropriate machine, prompting you for a password (see Chapter 16)—even if the other machine is thousands of miles away and your Mac must dial the modem to connect.

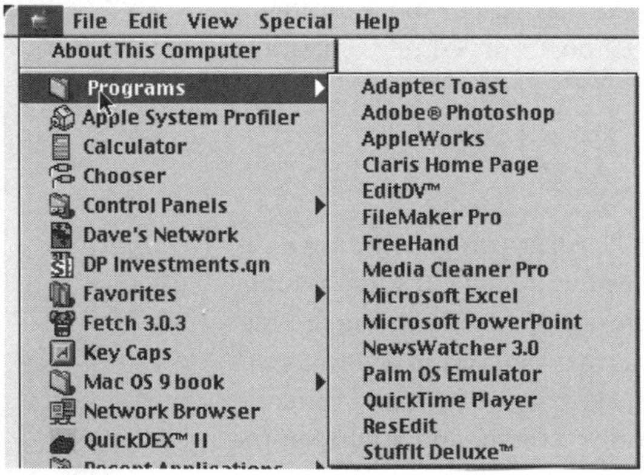

| File Edit View Special Help |
| --- |
| **About This Computer** |
| 📁 **Programs** ▶ |
| 🖥 Apple System Profiler |
| 🖩 Calculator |
| ⏱ Chooser |
| 🗂 Control Panels ▶ |
| 💻 Dave's Network |
| 📊 DP Investments.qn |
| 📚 Favorites ▶ |
| 🐾 Fetch 3.0.3 |
| 🔲 Key Caps |
| 📘 Mac OS 9 book ▶ |
| 💻 Network Browser |
| 🖱 QuickDEX™ II |
| 📁 Recent Applications ▶ |

Programs submenu:
Adaptec Toast
Adobe® Photoshop
AppleWorks
Claris Home Page
EditDV™
FileMaker Pro
FreeHand
Media Cleaner Pro
Microsoft Excel
Microsoft PowerPoint
NewsWatcher 3.0
Palm OS Emulator
QuickTime Player
ResEdit
StuffIt Deluxe™

***Figure 2-6:***
*The hierarchical Apple menu lets you create a convenient program-launching bay composed entirely of aliases to your favorite programs. (By preceding the folder's name with a space, you make it appear at the top of the menu for easier access.)*

There are as many different uses of aliases as there are Mac users. A few of the most common, however, run along these lines:

- Put the alias of a file, folder, program, or disk you use frequently into your  menu. (You'll find instructions on page 79.) Once the icon is listed there, you can open it from within any program, because your  menu is always available.

- Put the aliases of your favorite programs into a single folder to serve as a handy launching bay. Put that folder somewhere that's always convenient—in your  menu, for example, so that you can launch any of your programs with the kind of convenience illustrated in Figure 2-6.

    Alternatively, you might consider turning that launching-bay folder into a pop-up window that's always accessible at the bottom edge of your screen, as described in the previous chapter.

- Drop an alias of a document you're working on into your Macintosh HD→System Folder→Startup Items folder. When you turn on the computer each morning, that document opens automatically, so that it's waiting on the screen when you arrive at your machine. (If you use certain programs daily, such as your word processor, email program, or Web browser, you may as well save yourself the daily double-click by inserting aliases of these programs, too, into your Startup Items folder.)

- You can use the alias feature to save you slogging through the multiple dialog boxes required to access to another hard drive on the network. Details on this trick in Chapter 16.

- Suppose you're deep in your Preferences folder on a cleaning binge one afternoon. Consider making an alias of the Trash and placing it directly inside the Preferences window. This way, with each item you discard, you're saved the wrist-wearying cross-desk slide to the Trash icon. Anything you drop onto the alias is automatically placed in the real Trash.

- Many of Mac OS 9's most useful built-in file-management features rely, behind the scenes, on the *automatic* creation of aliases. These features include the Launcher (Chapter 3), the  menu, the Favorites command, and the Recent Items commands (all described in Chapter 5). If you're aware of these mechanisms, mastering the corresponding features becomes much easier.

**Figure 2-7:**
*If the alias can't find the original file, you're offered the chance to associate it with a different file—or to delete the orphaned alias icon.*

## Broken Aliases

It's important to understand that an alias doesn't contain any of the information you've typed or composed in the original. Don't copy an *alias* of your slide show to a Zip disk and then depart for the airport, hoping to give the presentation in your arrival city. When you double-click the alias, now separated from its original, you'll be shown the dialog box in Figure 2-7.

If you're on a plane 6,000 miles away from the hard drive on which the original file resides, click Delete Alias (to get rid of the orphaned alias you just double-clicked) or OK (to do nothing, leaving the alias where it is).

In certain circumstances, however, the third button—Fix Alias—is the most useful of all. Click it to summon a list of every icon on your computer; if you click one and then click Choose, you've just associated the orphaned alias with a different original icon.

Such techniques become handy when, for example, you click your AppleWorks icon on the Launcher (described later in this chapter), forgetting that you recently upgraded from AppleWorks 5 to AppleWorks 6. Instead of simply showing you an error message that says "AppleWorks 5 can't be found," the Mac shows you the box that contains the Fix Alias button. By clicking it, thus re-associating it with the new AppleWorks 6, you can save yourself the trouble of creating a new alias. From now on, double-clicking your AppleWorks alias launches the new version of AppleWorks.

## Using Labels

Here's a convenient Mac-only feature you can lord over your Windows-using friends: icon labels. This feature lets you tag selected icons with one of seven different labels, each of which has both a name and a color associated with it. To do so, highlight the icons and then choose File→Label; choose one of the seven provided labels from the submenu (such as Essential or In Progress). You can also apply a label by Control-clicking, as shown in Figure 2-8.

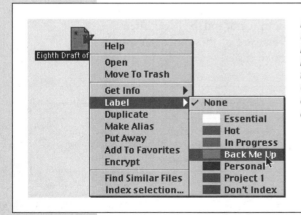

**Figure 2-8:**
*Use the File menu to apply a label tag to a highlighted icon. You can also apply a label by Control-clicking an icon and choosing a label from the contextual menu that appears. If you first highlight several icons, the Control-click trick still works—just Control-click any one of the highlighted icons. The label you choose will be applied to all highlighted icons.*

## What Labels Are Good For

After you've applied labels to icons, you can perform useful file-management tasks on all of them simultaneously, even if they're scattered across multiple hard drives. For example:

- Use Sherlock (see Chapter 15) to find all icons with a particular label. As shown in Figure 2-9, moving these icons en masse is a piece of cake.

Using labels in conjunction with Sherlock in this way is one of the most useful and inexpensive backup schemes ever devised. Whenever you finish working on a document that you'd like to back up, Control-click it and apply a label called, for example, Backup. At the end of each day, use Sherlock to round up all files with the Backup label—and then drag them as a group onto your backup disk.

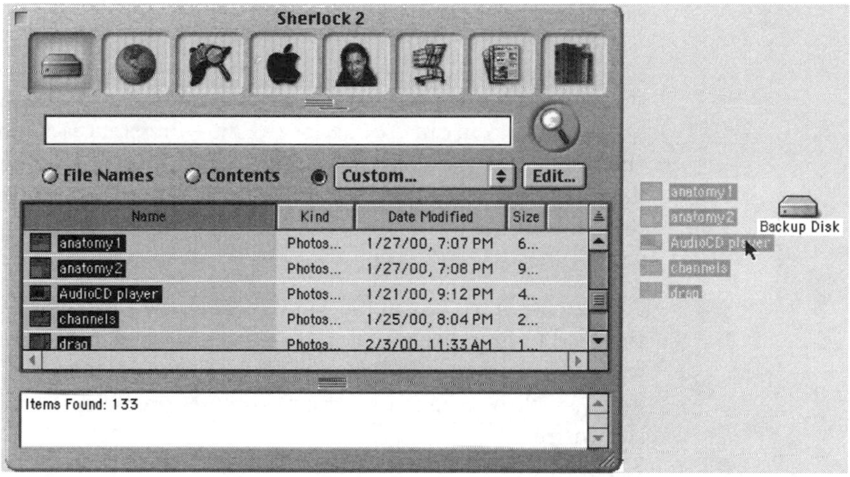

**Figure 2-9:**
*If you search your hard drive for icons with a particular label, backing them up as a group becomes very easy. Just choose Edit→Select All, and then drag any one of the highlighted icons out of the Sherlock window and into the target folder or disk.*

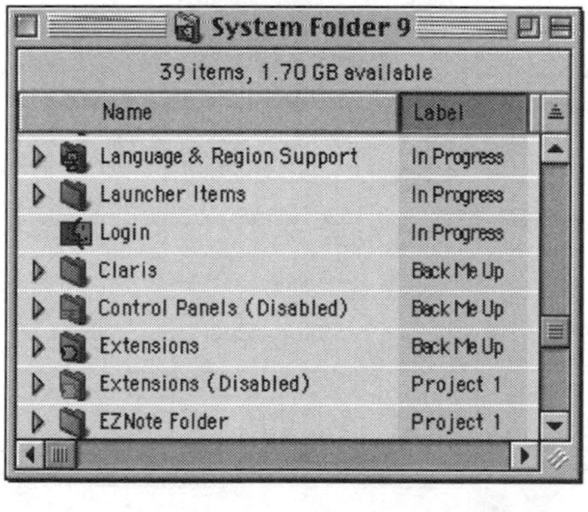

**Figure 2-10:**
*The ability to sort by label is only available if the label column is visible. Make it so by choosing View→View Options and turning on the Label checkbox.*

- Sort a list view by label. No other Mac sorting method lets you create an arbitrary order for the icons in a window. When you sort by label, the Mac creates alphabetical clusters *within* each label grouping, as shown in Figure 2-10.

This technique might be useful when, for example, your job is to process several different folders of documents; for each folder, you're supposed to convert graphics files, throw out old files, or whatever. As soon as you finish working your way through one folder, flag it with a label called Done. The folder jumps to the top (or bottom) of the window, safely marked for your reference pleasure, leaving the next unprocessed folder at your fingertips, ready to go.

- As described in Chapter 15, Mac OS 9's Sherlock program can search for words inside your files, no matter what the files are actually named. Before it can do so, however, you're required to *index* your hard drive (see page 267)—an extremely time-consuming feature.

You can use labels, however, to confine the indexing to folders that you actually might want to search. Create a label called, for example, Index This. Apply it to the folder icons for your e-mail, documents, and downloads. Then, when it comes time to index, you can use Sherlock's Edit→Preferences command to specify that you want *only* those folders indexed. Sherlock will now ignore all *other* folders—those containing no files worth searching, such as the System Folder, Applications folder, and so on. Both the indexing and the searching of your hard drive will be dramatically faster.

- You can use labels to flag the contents of a newly installed System Folder. When troubleshooting later, a glance will show you which icons have been added by the various applications and shareware downloads you've used—and therefore which items are likely to be causing your computer problems. See page 432 for step-by-step instructions.

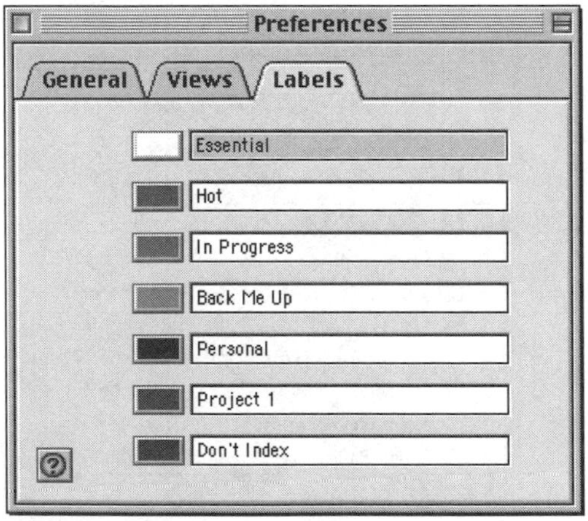

**Figure 2-11:**
In the Labels tab of the Preferences dialog box, you can change the predefined label text. Each label can be up to 31 characters and spaces long. You can also click the color square to summon the Color Picker dialog box, which you can use to specify a different label color. (The Color Picker offers several different color-selection methods, from the simple joy of the Crayons box to scientific mixtures of the primary colors by percentage.)

*Tip:* When you're finished using labels as described in the previous suggestions, you can *un*-label the icons you've marked. Just highlight them and then choose File→Label→None.

## Changing Labels and Label Colors

When you first install Mac OS 9, the seven labels in the File→Label menu are Essential, Hot, In Progress, Cool, and so on. Clearly, the label feature would be much more useful if you could rewrite these labels, tailoring them to your purposes.

Doing so is easy: choose Edit→Preferences. Click the Labels tab. Now you see the dialog box shown in Figure 2-11, where you can edit the text of each label.

*Tip:* If the notion of tinting your icons with colored labels disturbs your esthetic sense, change the label color to pure white. (The quickest way: in the Preferences dialog box, click the color swatch, click the Crayon Picker, and then click the upper-left crayon—the white one.) From now on, applying that label to an icon leaves it visually unchanged—but you still get the advantages of having placed the icon into that label category.

# The Launcher

The concept of the Launcher is simple: any icon you drag onto the Launcher window, shown in Figure 2-12, is installed there as a large, pillowed button. A single click, not a double-click, on this button opens the corresponding icon. In other words, the Launcher is an ideal parking lot for the icons of disks, folders, documents, and programs you frequently access.

Partly because of the large button size, and partly because of the halved clicking requirement, many Mac users don't respect the Launcher, considering it a tool for kids. But here and there, even among sophisticated Mac users, you can find the Launcher being used an essential software headquarters. As it turns out, you're not limited to the large button size; nor is your icon installation limited to the visible area of the Launcher.

## Setting Up Your Launcher

To bring the Launcher onto your screen, choose  →Control Panels→Launcher. (If you find it peculiar that the Launcher is listed as a control panel, when it's actually just a special window with no controls to change whatsoever, you're not alone.) The first time you open the Launcher, it contains only two icons, neither of which is especially useful: Script Editor and SimpleText. Feel free to remove these icons as described in the next section.

*Tip:* If you find the Launcher useful, you can set up the Mac to open the window each time you turn on the computer. To do so, choose  →Control Panels→General Controls. Turn on the checkbox called "Show Launcher at system startup."

Doing so ensures that the Launcher window will be waiting for you at each startup, even if you had closed it during the previous work session.

In many respects, this Launcher is a standard window. You can move it elsewhere on the screen by dragging its title bar or edges, change its size and shape by dragging the lower-right corner, "windowshade" (collapse) the window by clicking the upper-right tiny square, use scroll bars when they appear, and so on. But the Launcher window has two special talents:

### Installing a new icon

To add the icon of a favorite file, folder, or disk to your Launcher, just drag it into the Launcher window. After a moment, the fully formed Launcher button appears, bearing the icon and name of the file you dragged. Note that you haven't actually moved the original file—when you release the mouse, it remains exactly where it was. What you've actually done is to install an *alias* of that file onto your Launcher, as described below.

---

*Tip:* You can install many icons at once onto the Launcher—just drag them as a group, as described on page 33.

---

### Removing icons from the Launcher window

Because a single click on a Launcher button opens the corresponding icon, you can't remove a button from the Launcher just by dragging. Instead, press the Option key. While the Option key down, you can successfully drag Launcher buttons off the window and directly into the Trash. After a moment, the icon button disappears from the Launcher. (If it doesn't—an occasional occurrence—repeat the Option-drag. The second time is always successful.)

### Changing the button size

Depending on your screen size and sophistication level, you may prefer smaller or larger Launcher buttons. Switching is easy: while pressing the ⌘ key, click in a blank area of the Launcher window and keep the mouse button depressed. A small contextual menu appears at your cursor tip, listing a choice of three icon sizes: Small, Medium, and Large.

The small size accommodates a lot of icons within a limited-size Launcher window, but clips off long file names. The large size, on the other hand, can be seen from outer space, and the file names are actually enlarged automatically, on the premise that anyone who needs three-story buttons will probably appreciate larger text, too.

## Creating Launcher Pages

One of the Launcher's most useful (and most often overlooked) features is its multiple "pages" function. With just a minute of setup, you can create different Launcher screens, each offering a different set of icon buttons. You might create one set for you, another for your child, and so on—or different pages for different categories, such as applications, documents, and games.

Setting up such an arrangement offers another pleasant benefit: it teaches you exactly how the Launcher works.

1. **Open the Macintosh HD→System Folder→Launcher Items folder.**

   Here, in the Launcher Items window, are aliases of the items that show up on the Launcher as buttons. In other words, whenever you drag an icon onto the Launcher window to create a button, Mac OS 9 actually places an alias of it into the System Folder→Launcher Items folder.

   Another way to remove an alias from your Launcher window, in other words, is simply to drag its alias out of this Launcher Items folder. You can now see how easy it is to *rename* a Launcher button—just rename its alias in this window.

2. **Make a new folder by choosing File→New Folder.**

   The new, untitled folder appears.

3. **Give the new folder the name of the "topic button" you'll want it to have in your Launcher. Precede the name with a bullet.**

   To create a bullet symbol, hold down the Option key, and then type the number 8.

   Figure 2-12 illustrates the relationship you're building—any folder in the Launcher Items window whose name begins with a bullet turns into a new page full of buttons on the Launcher.

4. **Create up to six more topic buttons by creating bullet-named folders in this way.**

   The Launcher can show up to eight topic page buttons. Any icon in the Launcher Items window that *isn't* inside one of these bulleted folders appears on a special, default Launcher page called Applications. If you'd rather use that eighth slot for a topic button of your own, create eight bulleted folders—and remove all other icons from the Launcher Items window. (Place them all into the bulleted folders.)

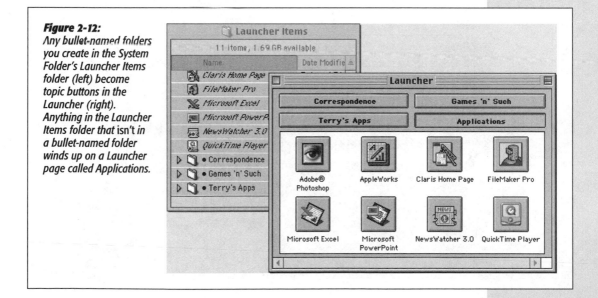

**Figure 2-12:**
*Any bullet-named folders you create in the System Folder's Launcher Items folder (left) become topic buttons in the Launcher (right). Anything in the Launcher Items folder that isn't in a bullet-named folder winds up on a Launcher page called Applications.*

5. **Close the Launcher Items window and the System Folder window. Install icons onto your various Launcher "pages" by dragging them onto the topic buttons.**

    Alternatively, of course, you can click a topic button to view its empty page, and then drag icons onto that page to install them.

---

*Tip:* You can move any Launcher button from one "page" to another by Option-dragging it onto the corresponding topic button at the top of the window.

---

As time goes by, you may want to rename or rearrange the icons on a particular Launcher page. To do so, you could double-click your way into Macintosh HD→System Folder→Launcher Items, as you did the first time. Fortunately, there's a faster way: Option-click one of the topic buttons. You jump instantly into the corresponding bulleted folder, deep within your System Folder→Launcher Items window.

## The Trash Icon

No single element of the Macintosh interface is as recognizable or famous as the Trash can in the lower-right corner of the screen. In many of the Mac's Hollywood movie appearances, for example, the producers have taken pains to disguise the  menu logo to make the on-screen computer seem less recognizable—but the Trash can is a dead giveaway every time.

You can discard almost any icon on your screen by dragging it onto the Trash icon. When the tip of your arrow cursor touches the center of the Trash icon, the little can turns black. When you release the mouse, you've succeeded in discarding whatever it was you dragged. (If you dragged files or folders—as opposed to a disk icon—the lid of the Trash-can icon pops off to the ground, displaced by the bulging refuse that peeks out of the top of the can.)

---

*Tip:* Learn the keyboard alternative to dragging something to the Trash: highlight the icon and then press ⌘-Delete. This technique is not only far faster than dragging, but requires far less precision, especially if you have a large screen. Mac OS 9 does all the Trash-targeting for you.

---

**FREQUENTLY ASKED QUESTION**

### The Case of the Vanishing Trash

*Help! My Trash can has disappeared. How can I get it back?*

Hate to disappoint you, but the Trash can *can't* disappear. You may have accidentally dragged it most of the way off the screen, but it's peeking out from the edge of the screen somewhere.

To find it, close all desktop windows and then press the Tab key, over and over again. Doing so highlights each desktop icon in alphabetical order–until you highlight whatever corner of the Trash can the Mac has left visible.

---

## Rescuing Files and Folders from the Trash

Icons that represent folders and files of any kind (such as programs and documents) sit in the Trash forever—or until you choose Special→Empty Trash, whichever comes first.

If you haven't yet emptied the Trash, you can double-click the Trash icon to review its contents—icons that you've placed on the waiting list for extinction. If you change your mind, you can rescue any of these items by dragging them out of the Trash window. (Or, more efficiently, highlight them and then press ⌘-Y—the keyboard shortcut of the File→Put Away command—which not only removes them from the Trash, but also puts them back into the folders from whence they came.)

## Emptying the Trash

If you're confident that the items in the Trash window are worth deleting, choose Special→Empty Trash. The Macintosh asks you to confirm your decision, reminding you in the process of how many items are in the Trash (see Figure 2-13). When you click OK, those files are deleted from your hard drive. (In cases of desperation, a program like Norton Utilities can resurrect deleted files, if used promptly after the deletion. In even more dire cases, companies like DriveSavers, *www.drivesavers.com,* can use sophisticated clean-room techniques to recover crucial information—for several hundred dollars.)

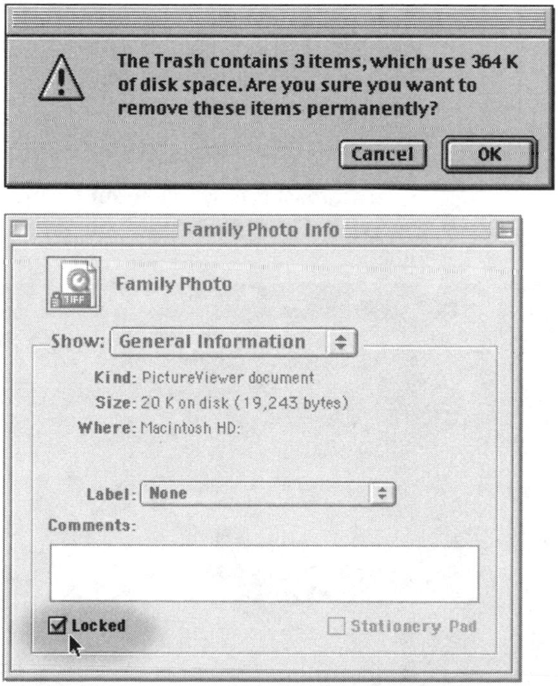

**Figure 2-13:**
*Top: Your last warning. Bottom: The Get Info window for a locked file. Locking a file in this way isn't military-level security by any stretch—any passing evildoer can unlock the file in the same way. But it does trigger a "Some items could not be deleted because they are locked" warning, bringing to your attention some important file you may have put into the Trash by accident.*

The Trash contains 3 items, which use 364 K of disk space. Are you sure you want to remove these items permanently?

Cancel    OK

Family Photo Info

Family Photo

Show: General Information

Kind: PictureViewer document
Size: 20 K on disk (19,243 bytes)
Where: Macintosh HD:

Label: None

Comments:

☑ Locked          ☐ Stationery Pad

## Locked Files and Folders

You may run into a complication when emptying the trash: You may be told that some of the items in the Trash are locked. This message merely means that someone, probably you, once highlighted one of the icons in the Trash, chose File→Get Info, and then turned on the Locked checkbox (see Figure 2-13, bottom).

### Turning Off the Trash Warning

The "Are you sure?" message that appears whenever you try to empty the Trash is, for the novice, a useful safety net. But after you've become a proficient Mac user, you may eventually develop a safety-net habit of your own: becoming sure about a file's trash-worthiness *before* placing it into the Trash. Thereafter, you'd probably just as soon have the Trash empty promptly at your command, without bothering you for confirmation.

By pressing Option as you choose Special→Empty Trash, you can suppress this confirmation box each time you empty

the trash. But even that trick is one step too many for the power user.

Fortunately, you can also instruct the Mac to suppress its confirmation box permanently. To do so, click the Trash icon, and then choose File→Get Info (or press ⌘-I). (Alternatively, Control-click the Trash icon and then choose Get Info→General Information from the contextual menu.) The resulting window offers a checkbox called "Warn before emptying." Turn off this checkbox, close the window, and savor the resulting time savings.

If you're told that a locked file is in the trash, you have two alternatives. First, you can open the Trash window to scan the contents for the presence of a tiny padlock stamped onto the lower-left corner of locked icons. By highlighting each locked icon, choosing File→Get Info, and then unchecking the Locked checkbox, you can unlock these files, rendering them trashable.

It's far faster, however, to simply press the Option key as you choose Special→Empty Trash. Doing so empties the trash, locked files and all, suppressing any warnings.

### Rescued Items

*Sometimes when I turn on my Mac, I find a folder in the Trash called Rescued Items From Macintosh HD. What is it? Can I delete it?*

Every self-respecting Macintosh program offers an Undo command that lets you undo the last step you took while working—or even the last several steps. Behind the scenes, this feature works because the program keeps multiple copies of your work in progress in an invisible folder on the hard drive called Temporary Items. When you quit the program, these invisible temporary files are deleted automatically.

But what happens if the Mac freezes, crashes, or "unexpectedly quits" before you've a chance to quit the program properly? The temporary files are stranded, orphaned, yet still in existence. When you turn the Mac on again, the operating system places them into the Trash in a new Rescued Items folder. Its thinking: Maybe you didn't have a chance to save your work before the freeze or crash—these temporary files might contain some of the typing you had done before the crash.

In practice, the rescued files are very rarely useful—but it's the thought that counts.

*Tip:* In Mac OS 9, for the first time, you can lock a *folder,* not just a file. To do so, highlight the folder. Choose File→Get Info→Sharing. In the resulting dialog box, you'll see the checkbox called "Can't move, rename, or delete this item (locked)"; check it to protect the folder.

On the other hand, you'll never be told that the Trash can't be emptied because it contains a locked *folder*–a locked folder can't even be *moved,* so nobody can move it into the Trash to begin with!

## "In Use" Messages

The other Trash-emptying complication arises when you're told that one of the items in the Trash is "in use." This message generally indicates that you're trying to delete an application or document that's still open, an extension (see Chapter 12), or a critical preference file. The solution is easy enough: close the offending application or document, if you can identify it—or just restart the computer with the Shift key pressed. Doing so turns off all extensions and closes all files, releasing all of Mac OS 9's claims on whatever is in the Trash.

# Password Protection

For the first time in Macintosh history, you can protect a file from prying eyes in ten seconds, without having to buy any add-on software. Mac OS 9 introduces password protection (encryption) of files, saving you the expense of buying commercial security software.

To secure a file in this way, follow these steps:

1. **Control-click the file icon. From the pop-up menu, choose Encrypt.**

   Alternatively, highlight the icon, and then choose File→Encrypt. Note that you can password-protect only *files,* not folders. (You *can* apply the Encrypt command to several highlighted icons at once—but you'll be asked to make up a password for each one individually.)

   The first time you try this experiment, a message appears, warning you that nobody, not even Apple, can open the protected file if you forget your password. That's true, by the way. If you ever hope to see your file again, *don't* forget your password! Click OK if you feel duly intimidated.

   Now the Apple File Security box appears, as shown in Figure 2-14.

2. **Type a password that's at least five characters long. Press Tab (or click in the second box), and type it again.**

   That ritual of typing the password twice is designed to protect you from making a typo that you'll never be able to reproduce.

   If you'd prefer not to have to remember and type out these passwords while *you* are seated at your Mac, leave the "Add to Keychain" box checked. (See details on the Keychain at the end of Chapter 16. For now, note that the Keychain is a Mac-wide, master password. You type it in *once*—as you sit down at your machine for a work session—and *all* of your password-protected files become openable. When you leave your Mac and "lock the Keychain," individual passwords become necessary once again for each protected file.)

### 3. Click Encrypt (or press Return).

Now a tiny key icon appears on the file icon you protected (as shown by the lower-left icon in Figure 2-14). When anyone double-clicks this file, one of three things may happen:

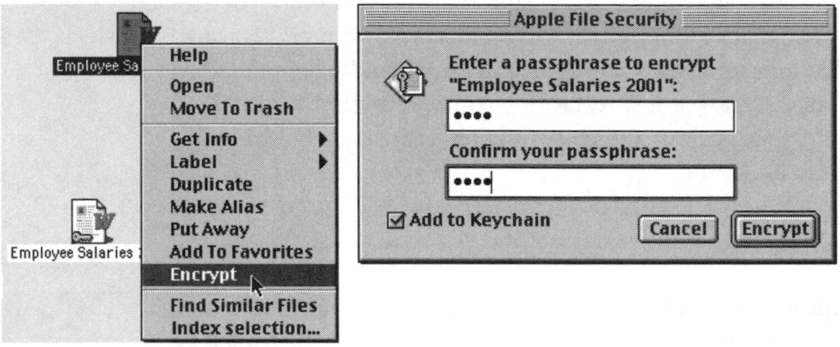

**Figure 2-14:**
*Password-protecting a file is as easy as Control-clicking it (left) and then making up a password for it (right). You don't actually see what you're typing: the Mac translates your typing into bullets (•••••), as a precaution against snoopers looking over your shoulder.*

- If you've "unlocked your Keychain" (see Chapter 16), the file opens promptly, as though it were never protected at all. (Only a one-second delay lets you know that anything's different.)

- If you've set up your Keychain, but haven't yet unlocked it by typing your master password, the Mac first asks you for the Keychain password. If you click Cancel (because you don't want to unlock the Keychain and make *everything* unprotected), the Apple File Security box asks you for this *file's* password.

- If you don't use the Keychain feature, or didn't use the "Add to Keychain" feature when encrypting this file, the Apple File Security box appears. If you correctly type the protected file's password and then click Decrypt, you're in; the file opens. If you type the wrong password, the Mac lets you try two more times before depositing you back in the Finder. You can double-click the icon to try again; but if you still can't produce the correct password, the contents of that juicy file will remain forever beyond your reach.

---

***Caution:*** When you successfully open a protected file, you've just *unprotected it.* After working with that document and closing it again, you must re-protect it if you still consider it confidential.

---

# The Desktop Database: Where Icons Live

One of the most important features of Mac icons is completely invisible. The vast majority of Mac users aren't even aware of its existence—but knowing about your invisible *Desktop database* can be extremely useful, especially in times of trouble-shooting.

As you may have noticed (and taken for granted), when you double-click the icon for a letter you've written, your word processor opens automatically. Moreover, every document you create bears the same matching document icon, visually related to the program that created it.

Both of these relationships are maintained by a database on your hard drive, composed of two invisible files called the Desktop files. (If you become handy with Sherlock, as described in Chapter 15, you can actually see these invisible files—they're called Desktop DB and Desktop DF.) These files store the relationships between your applications, aliases, documents, and their icons, along with the information that appears when you highlight an icon and choose File→Get Info.

Knowing about the Desktop database is primarily useful when you're trying to troubleshoot these two problems:

- *Your Mac has been getting slower over time.* As it turns out, the Desktop database must store the color graphic for every icon that crosses your hard drive's path. Every program you install, every shareware game you download, inserts into your Desktop database a set of color icons. Even if you subsequently delete those programs, their icons remain in your Desktop database.

---

**UP TO SPEED**

## Drag-and-Drop

One of the most respected characteristics of the Mac OS is its ability to launch the appropriate application when you double-click a *document.* For example, when you double-click a Microsoft Word document, Microsoft Word itself launches automatically.

In the Internet age, however, many of the documents that find their way onto your hard drive were created by other people, using software you don't own. Graphics files and text files, in particular, may land on your Mac, separated by miles of wiring from the GraphixMaster III or WordProPlus 3.4 programs that created them.

When you double-click such documents, the Mac makes an effort to find a program on your hard drive that *can* open them (see page 109 for details). It's often less trouble, though, to drag the mystery download files onto the *icon* of a program you'd like to use. Dragging a downloaded graphics file onto your copy of PictureViewer or Photoshop is a quick and easy way to open it; dragging a downloaded text document onto your word processor icon works well, too.

Nor do you have to drag such document icons onto the actual program icons. You can also drag them onto *aliases* of the program icons, Launcher buttons, the Application switcher (see page 105), and so on.

---

If you've worked in graphics, you know that color images can take up a lot of disk space. Over time, therefore, all of these icons, many of which are no longer needed, inflate the size of your Desktop database. Windows and programs may open more slowly as a result, and the computer may take longer to start up.

- *Icons appear on the screen with a blank, or "generic," look.* These plain white icons indicate that the Desktop database has become confused; it's unable to supply the correct images for the icons based on its knowledge of the program that created them. (A confused Desktop database is only one cause of the blank-white-icon syndrome, however. Blank icons may also appear if the Desktop database never *did* know what program created the files. Downloaded graphic files from the Internet, for example, almost always appear blank. Your Mac has no idea of what graphics program was used to create them.)

In both cases, the solution is simple: force the Mac to rebuild the Desktop database, flushing out orphaned and unused icon images, and updating the program/document relationships based on what's on your hard drive at this moment.

To rebuild the Desktop files, restart the computer. Near the end of the extension-loading process (the appearance of icons at the bottom of your screen), press and hold the ⌘ and Option keys until you see the words "Rebuild the Desktop file on Macintosh HD?" (You'll be asked about each of your disks, if you have more than one, separately.) If you answer in the affirmative, Mac OS 9 takes a moment to survey the icons on your hard drive, and builds a clean, fresh Desktop database as a result.

---

*Tip:* If you're using the Multiple Users feature described in Chapter 17, you don't have to restart the Mac to rebuild the desktop. Instead, just log out. Press the ⌘ and Option keys just after you enter your password and click OK. (Only people with Owner and Normal accounts can perform this stunt, however.)

---

# CHAPTER 3

# Interior Decoration

From the day it was born, the Macintosh was the computer for the individualist. To this day, corporations purchase thousands of Windows PCs—but when they go home at night, the executives often keep Macs for their personal use.

In other words, when you bought a Macintosh, you already made a dramatic act of self-expression. But that's only the beginning: now it's time to bend the computer screen itself to your personal sense of design and fashion.

## Designing Your Desktop

Cosmetically speaking, the greatest contribution of Mac OS 9 is its collection of full-screen desktop pictures. These swirling 3-D images manage to be visually interesting; yet they're neither as distracting as the nature photos, nor as commercial as the Mac OS logos, provided as desktop pictures in previous Mac OS versions.

### Desktop Patterns and Pictures

The command center for dressing up your Desktop—the backdrop of your screen—is the Appearance control panel (see Figure 3-1).

Although the design of this window may not make it clear, you can actually perform two different functions here: You can paste a full-screen photo over your entire desktop backdrop, or you can choose to have a smaller image *tiled* (repeated) until it fills the entire screen.

#### Applying a photo to your desktop

If a full-screen picture already appears on your desktop—as it does when you first install Mac OS 9—you must first click the Remove Picture button before you can select a different picture. (Doing so doesn't actually remove the picture file from your hard drive; it simply stops using that file as your desktop picture.)

At this point, the button in the lower-right corner of the Appearance window says Place Picture. Now you're ready to choose a new graphics file—in JPEG, GIF, Photoshop, or PICT format—to hang on the wall of your computer screen. You can do so in either of these two ways:

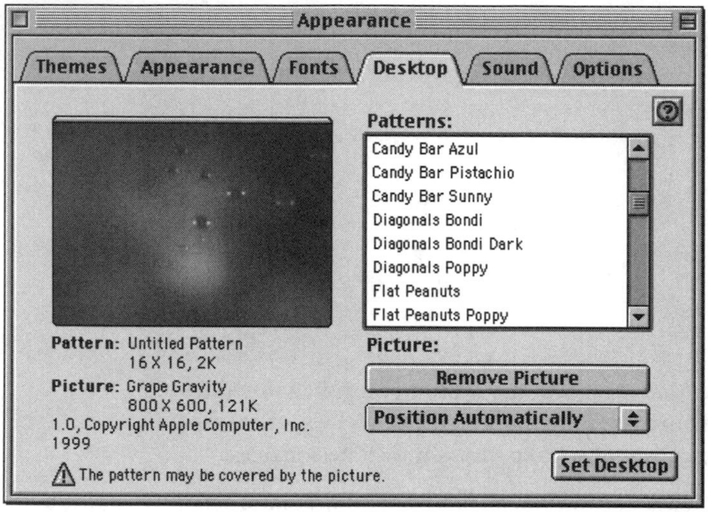

*Figure 3-1:*
*The Desktop tab of the Appearance control panel controls the pattern or picture that fills the background of your Mac screen. Open it by choosing ⌘→Control Panels→ Appearance. When the Appearance program opens, click the Desktop tab, as shown here.*

- Click Place Picture. The standard Open File dialog box appears, as described in Chapter 8; you're shown the contents of the Macintosh HD→System Folder→Appearance→Desktop Pictures folder. Here you'll find several folders filled with ready-made full-screen pictures. These Mac OS 9-provided folders are named as follows: 3-D Graphics (various computer-generated images of alien vehicles on the march); Convergency (several blurry, colorful graphics that look like someone's camera went off by accident); Ensemble Pictures (computer-generated illustrations, in iMac color schemes, that look like electron microscope photos); and Photos (of bottles, flowers, and window shutters).

By all means, click Show Preview; single-click each of these graphics in turn; and consider how each would affect your personality if you had to look at it all day, every day. You may find one that you like—or you may decide that a photo of your own would be a superior choice.

If so, click the Desktop Pictures pop-up menu *above* the list; choose Desktop; and then double-click your way into whatever folder contains your desired graphics file. Double-click the one you want.

- You can also drag any graphics file directly onto the miniature desktop of the Appearance control panel, as shown in Figure 3-2.

In either case, the Appearance control panel now shows you a miniature version of what your desktop will look like when you click the Set Desktop button, also shown in Figure 3-2.

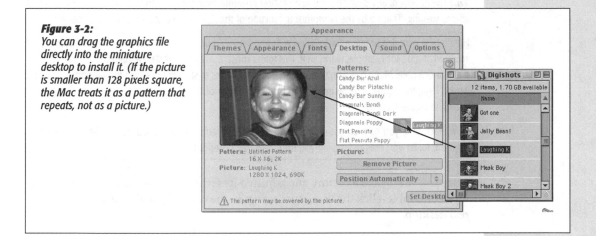

**Figure 3-2:**
*You can drag the graphics file directly into the miniature desktop to install it. (If the picture is smaller than 128 pixels square, the Mac treats it as a pattern that repeats, not as a picture.)*

Unless you're a graphics expert or a very lucky person, the photo file you chose in the previous steps probably isn't exactly the same size as your screen. Fortunately, the Mac offers a number of solutions to this problem. Using the pop-up menu just above the Set Desktop button (see Figure 3-2), you can choose any of these options:

- **Tile on Screen:** If your graphic is smaller than the screen, this option makes it repeat over and over until the multiple images fill the entire monitor. (If your picture is *larger* than the screen, no such tiling takes place—you see only the upper-left corner of the graphic.)

- **Center on Screen:** This command centers the photo neatly on the screen. If the picture is smaller than the screen, it doesn't fill the entire background; whatever desktop pattern you've chosen, as described "A picture and a pattern," below, provides a frame for the picture. If the picture is larger than the screen, you see only the middle—the edges of the picture are chopped off as they extend beyond your screen.

- **Scale to Screen:** This choice, among the most useful, makes your picture fit the screen as closely as possible without distortion. In other words, a small picture gets enlarged, and a large picture gets reduced, so that its largest dimension stretches from edge to edge of your screen. Of course, most graphics aren't exactly the same *shape* as your screen, so you'll probably see gaps on both sides of—or above and below—the picture. These gaps are filled in by the desktop pattern, as described in "A picture and a pattern," on the next page.

- **Fill Screen:** Use this one at your peril. It makes your graphic file fill every inch of the desktop, even if it must reduce, enlarge, and distort the graphic to do so.

- **Position Automatically:** This option behaves the same as Scale to Screen, described on the previous page.

---

*Tip:* The novelty of any desktop picture, no matter how interesting, is likely to fade after several months of all-day viewing. That's why the randomizing function of the Appearance control panel is so delightful.

Here's how it works: Create a folder filled with images you'd like to use as desktop pictures. (A group of scanned photos, for example, works well. This folder must reside on your startup hard drive—if it's on a Zip disk, for example, Mac OS 9 won't be able to find the images at startup time, and the randomizing won't work.) Drag this folder directly into the miniature desktop of the Appearance control panel, exactly as shown in Figure 3-2.

Now, each time you turn on your Mac, its desktop will be automatically filled with a different selection from the folder you dragged, saving you from death by boredom.

---

After you've selected a picture and adjusted its settings to your taste, click Set Desktop—or double-click the miniature screen in the control panel—to apply it to your real desktop.

### Applying a pattern to your desktop

There's nothing like personalizing your Mac by filling the screen with a single photo of your favorite person, place, or thing. But detailed full-screen photos can make it harder to spot icons you've left out on the desktop. It's sometimes more useful to cover your screen with a tiled, repeating rectangle—of a solid color, for example.

Selecting a pattern to cover your screen is easy: just click one of the named patterns in the list at the right side of the Appearance control panel. The miniature desktop to their left instantly illustrates the effect. If you approve, click Set Desktop (or double-click the miniature desktop) to apply the pattern to your actual desktop.

### A picture and a pattern

You can have both a pattern *and* a picture, by the way; the pattern lies behind the picture, filling in any gaps between your selected picture and the edges of the screen. (On the other hand, if you've selected the Fill Screen option for the picture, it *covers up* any pattern you've selected—a phenomenon that confuses many a Mac fan, who wonders why the pattern controls don't seem to work.)

### Adding to the list of patterns

Although you can't delete any of the built-in patterns, you can add, delete, and rename patterns of your own.

To add a new pattern, copy a picture out of a graphics program or from a Web page. Open the Appearance control panel, click the Desktop tab, click the Patterns list, and then choose Edit→Paste. (The pattern can be as large as you like, but when you apply it to your desktop, it will shrink to 128 *pixels* [screen dots] square, or less.) Your newly pasted pattern shows up with the name Untitled Pattern; while it's still highlighted, you can Edit→Pattern Name to give it a more descriptive name. You can also delete it from the list by choosing Edit→Clear.

## Fonts, Sounds, and Colors

Although the desktop is certainly the most prominent visual element of your screen, it's not the only way you can interior-decorate your Mac. Using the Appearance control panel, you can also specify the typefaces, colors, and even sound effects you want to make part of your Mac experience.

### Changing the system fonts

Using the Fonts tab of the Appearance control panel (&#63743;→Control Panels→Appearance), you can specify the typefaces you prefer for use in the menus, windows, and icons of Mac OS 9.

- **Large System Font:** This first pop-up menu offers a choice of seven superbly designed fonts for use in your menus and window titles. Most people use Charcoal, the factory-installed typeface, and the one most often associated with the Mac—but you may find that Gadget gives the Mac a fresher look, or that Textile or Capitals makes menus easier to read from a distance.

**FREQUENTLY ASKED QUESTION**

## Freedom of Menu Fonts

*Why do I see only seven fonts listed in the Large System Font pop-up menu? Where are the rest of my fonts?*

The seven typefaces listed in the Large System Font pop-up menu have something special in common: they all share precisely the same spacing and height. That's important, because your various software programs are designed to place each successive letter in, for example, the name of the menu a certain distance from the previous one.

If Apple gave you a free choice of typefaces for use in the menus, you might choose one whose spacing is larger or smaller than the basic seven. The result would be unreadable—one menu title might even collide with the next. Therefore, Apple offers you only fonts whose measurements are sure to work in every program's menus.

If this limitation bothers you, however, install AppearanceHopper, a shareware program available at *www.missingmanual.com*. It lets you experiment with using different fonts and sizes in your menus.

- **Small System Font:** This pop-up menu controls which typeface is used inside dialog boxes for explanatory text—such as, ironically, the words "for explanatory text and labels" underneath the pop-up menu itself. You can choose any typeface you'd like, as long as it's Geneva.

- **Views Font and Size:** Using the much more generous selection of fonts in this pop-up menu (see Figure 3-3), you can specify what typeface you want used for your icons in Finder windows (see Chapter 1). Better yet, using the Size pop-up menu, you can also specify a different type *size*—a terrific feature if your eyesight is going, or if you're giving a Mac lesson to several people clustered around your screen.

The checkbox at the bottom of the Fonts tab may be the most powerful click you can make here: it turns on *anti-aliasing*, or edge-smoothing, for all text, anywhere it appears on your Mac: in word processing documents, email messages, Web pages, and so on (see Figure 3-4).

**Figure 3-3:**
*Using the Fonts tab (left), you can specify a typeface for your menus and icons (right). (Note to producers of alien-invasion movies: You can make Mac OS 9 look like the OS from a distant galaxy by changing the Views Font to a non-alphabetic font like Symbol or Wingdings, as shown here.)*

**Figure 3-4:**
*Large type on the screen looks less jagged when font smoothing is turned on (bottom). The result is smoother, more commercial-looking type, especially at larger type sizes and at irregular type sizes, such as 21 points (top).*

At smaller type sizes, such as 12-point and smaller, you might find that text is actually *less* readable with font smoothing turned on. For that reason, the Size pop-up menu lets you choose a minimum point size for anti-aliasing. If you choose 14 from this pop-up menu, for example, then 12-point (and smaller) type, like that in most word-processing and email text, still appears crisp and sharp; only larger type, such as headlines, displays the graceful edge smoothing.

### Sound effects

If you click the Sound tab of the Appearance control panel, you can unlock the single most polarizing feature of the entire Mac OS, one that either thrills or disgusts everyone who encounters it: sound effects. When you choose Sound track→Platinum Sounds, Mac OS 9 produces tiny, subtle sounds to accompany every mouse movement, including pulling down menus, clicking, scrolling, dragging icons and windows, emptying the Trash, and so on. (The checkboxes below the pop-up menu give you control over exactly which categories of sounds play.)

Some people enjoy the effects, savoring the psycho-acoustic sense of precision that the little chirps and squeaks lend to everyday computing activities. Other people—particularly those who work in libraries, operating rooms, and churches—find the sounds annoying, and keep them turned off.

(Both groups may well wonder why the Sound track pop-up menu lists only a single option, called Platinum Sounds. During early testing of Mac OS 8.5, in which this feature made its debut, this pop-up menu listed several different "soundtracks," each offering a different collection of sound effects. At the eleventh hour, however, Apple decided that the wackier soundtracks risked damaging the Mac's reputation for elegance and class—and that one soundtrack was enough.)

### Changing the highlighting color

When you drag your cursor across it, text changes color to indicate that you've selected it. Likewise, when your mouse slides down a menu, each command changes color as the tip of the cursor touches it.

Exactly *which* color the text and menus become is up to you. Open the Appearance control panel ( →Control Panels→Appearance) and then click the Appearance tab. There you'll find these three pop-up menus:

• **Appearance:** This, the most pointless pop-up menu in the history of computerdom, is a remnant of a never-released version of the Appearance control panel, in which you could choose dramatically different looks for the entire Mac interface. Ultimately, Apple chose not to release any of these alternate Appearance schemes, afraid that it might do too much damage to the Mac's recognizable look (and crash too many programs)—and so left in this control panel a pop-up menu containing only a single choice. (The shareware hit Kaleidoscope, described at the end of this chapter, picks up where the abandoned Appearance feature left off.)

• **Highlight Color** and **Variation:** The Highlight Color pop-up menu governs the highlighting color for text; the Variation pop-up menu determines the color of menu selections, progress bars, the scroll-bar box, and other Mac OS accents. (If none of the text-highlight choices appeals you, choose Other; the Color Picker dialog box appears, from which you can choose any color in the rainbow.)

### The Options tab

The rightmost tab would have been better named "A coupla settings we had nowhere else to stick." It offers these two choices:

• **Smart Scrolling.** Turn this option on if you'd like both scroll arrows at the same end of your scroll bars, as shown at right in Figure 3-5, instead of at opposite ends.

• **Double-click title bar to collapse windows.** You can already collapse a Mac window, windowshade-like, into just a title bar: just click the collapse box in the upper-right corner, as described on page 13. But if you'd like a broader target, turn on this option; now you can click anywhere in the entire title bar to "windowshade" the window.

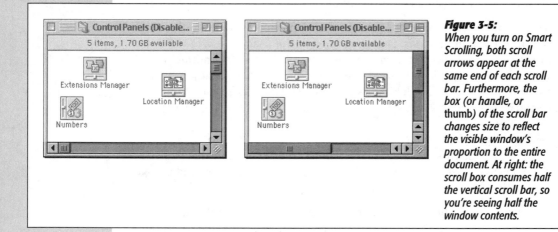

**Figure 3-5:**
*When you turn on Smart Scrolling, both scroll arrows appear at the same end of each scroll bar. Furthermore, the box (or handle, or thumb) of the scroll bar changes size to reflect the visible window's proportion to the entire document. At right: the scroll box consumes half the vertical scroll bar, so you're seeing half the window contents.*

## Saving your Schemes as Themes

After spending several hours adjusting your desktop picture, fonts, sounds, and colors into a glorious, unified, harmonious whole, the artistically inclined Mac user may want to save all these parameters under a single name so that you can recall the entire suite of settings later with a single click. That's the purpose of the first tab in the Appearance control panel, the one called Themes.

When you click it, you'll see that you can scroll through about a dozen ready-made themes, each with a different combination of background pattern, font choices, highlighting colors, and sounds. You can apply one of these themes to your desktop just by double-clicking it.

To create your own theme that will subsequently appear in this scrolling list, begin by setting up the other tabs of this control panel—Appearance, Fonts, Desktop, and so on—to create a look and feel (and sound) you like. Then, on the Theme tab, you'll see a new option, reflecting your choices, called Custom Theme.

**Figure 3-6:**
*Click Save Theme to name a collection of settings you've created. You can remove any of your homemade themes by clicking its representation here and then choosing Edit→Clear. (You can't remove any of the themes that come pre-installed in Mac OS 9.)*

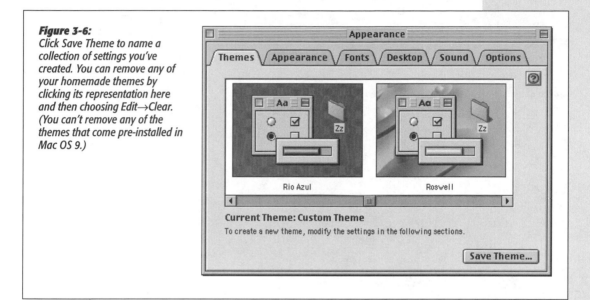

To save this masterpiece, click Save Theme (see Figure 3-6). Now you're asked to name the theme; do so, and then click OK. From now on, you can summon this overall Mac design scheme by double-clicking your newly named theme on the Themes tab.

**POWER USERS' CLINIC**

## Beyond Appearance

The built-in desktop-decoration features of the Appearance control panel offer plenty of design tools for the average Mac fan. But if you feel limited, two shareware programs, both available at *www.missingmanual.com*, let you take the Mac OS far beyond its recognizable condition.

AppearanceHopper, for example, eliminates the Appearance control panel's limitations on font choices (and font sizes) for your menus and window names.

It also lets you change where the scroll arrows appear on scroll bars, and how alias icons appear on your screen.

Kaleidoscope, a wildly popular control panel, tweaks far more than just the desktop and menu font of Mac OS 9—it can make windows, buttons, and menus wavy, striped, or even more abstract, as shown here. Because you can download new Kaleidoscope modules from the Internet, the variety never needs to end.

# CHAPTER 4

# Controlling Your Desktop

A s in any modern operating system, you control your Macintosh using *menus*—lists of commands that pertain to the task at hand. In Mac OS 9, however, menus lurk in some unexpected places. The menu bar at the top of the screen is only half the story: Contextual (Control-key) menus and the pop-up menus of the Control Strip are sometimes even more useful.

## The Menu Bar

In the early days of Macintosh, you could open Mac menus—the words File, Edit, View, and Special above the desktop—only by keeping the mouse button pressed continuously as you dragged down the list of commands.

Today, you can still drag continuously down Mac menus. But you may find it more efficient, and less conducive to muscle strain, simply to *click* the name of a menu (File, for example). The menu drops down by itself and remains open for 15 seconds. During that interval, you have two choices: either make a menu selection by clicking one of the commands, or dismiss the menu by pressing a key or clicking anywhere else on the screen.

## Submenu Tactics

Many of today's Mac menu commands offer *submenus*, as shown in Figure 4-1. Lists of submenu commands appear automatically when you drag onto them—you don't have to click to make the sub-commands appear. You do, however, have to click one of these sub-commands to activate it.

## Keyboard Shortcut Symbols

As experienced Mac fans know, the symbols that appear down the right side of a typical menu indicate keyboard alternatives to using the menu commands. Suppose you notice that the New Folder command, in the File menu, bears the legend ⌘-N. That notation tells you that instead of using the mouse to click File→New Folder, you can instead type the letter N while pressing the ⌘ key (which is next to the Space bar). In theory, the keyboard equivalents for menu commands make work go faster by eliminating the need to use the mouse.

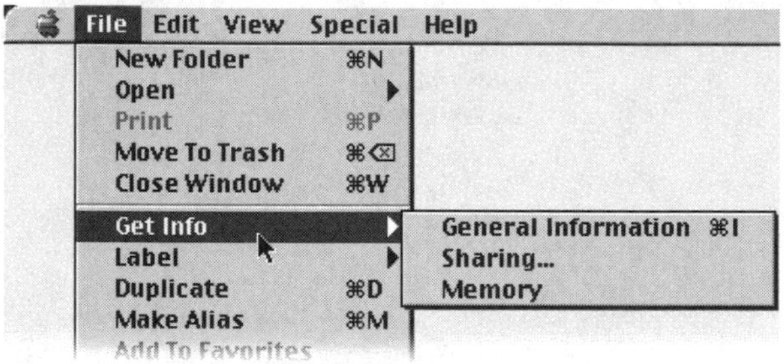

**Figure 4-1:**
*Two specialized Mac submenus offer a special, undocumented feature: they let you choose either the primary menu command or one of its submenu commands. Both the  menu and the Get Info command offer this feature.*

In practice, however, most Mac fans' good intentions to start mastering keyboard shortcuts hit a wall when they encounter less recognizable menu symbols. What keys, for example, should you press when you see ⌘-⌥-⇧-T? Other than the ⌘ logo, none of these symbols actually appears on your keyboard, and no translation key is readily available.

You can interpret such menu symbols according to this cheat sheet:

- ⌃: The Control key, usually found in the lower-left corner of your keyboard.

- ⇧: The Shift key.

- ⌥: The Option key, which is on the bottom row of keys, on the left side.

- ⌅: The Enter key, which you'll find on the far right side of your keyboard, usually on the numeric keypad. (On laptops, it's just to the right of the Space bar instead.)

The Delete-key symbol is shown next to Move To Trash in the figure above.

## Contextual (Control-key) Menus

As useful as the menu-bar menus are, Mac OS 9's vast set of *invisible* menus can be even more powerful. You summon these hidden menus one at a time—by Control-clicking various places on the screen. In slow motion, the process works like this:

1. **Press and hold the Control key at the lower-left corner of your keyboard.**

   The cursor changes shape, as shown in Figure 4-2.

2. **While the Control key is down, use the mouse to click an object on your screen; keep the button pressed.**

At this point, a list of commands springs out of your cursor tip, and remains available as long as you keep the button pressed (Figure 4-2, right). This miniature menu is known as a *contextual* menu, because the commands in it change depending on the context. If you click an icon, you're offered commands like Move To Trash and Duplicate. If you click an empty space in a window, the contextual menu offers Sort List and View Options. And if you click the desktop itself, you get commands like New Folder and Change Desktop Background.

**Figure 4-2:**
*With the Control key pressed, a tiny menu icon sprouts on your cursor, indicating that a contextual menu will appear when you click. (The cursor may not change shape in all programs, however.) At right: the commands that appear depend on what you're clicking.*

Other useful contextual menus appear when you click the Trash, window title bars, disk icons, and folder icons. The beauty of contextual menus is that, unlike menu-bar menus, they never, ever display *dimmed* (unavailable) commands. After all, by definition, a contextual menu shows only commands that make sense in this *context* — at this time and when clicking this object.

## Exclusive Contextual-Menu Commands

Most of the commands in a contextual menu are also in the traditional menu bar. When you Control-click a document icon, for example, you get commands like Open, Get Info, Label, Make Alias, and Add To Favorites—all of which are also listed in the File menu. The primary benefits of contextual menus, in other words, are a savings in mouse travel and a savings in menu-bar hunting. (Because contextual commands are collected into one pop-up menu, you don't have to read several menus to find the command you want.)

A few commands, however, appear *only* in contextual menus—functions unavailable to the masses who haven't yet discovered contextual menus. The primary examples include:

• **Find Similar Files:** This command appears only when you Control-click a document icon. It launches Sherlock (see Chapter 15), which proceeds to scour your hard drive for a list of documents that do indeed resemble the one you Control-clicked. If you Control-click, say, a contract written in Microsoft Word, Sherlock shows you a list of other Microsoft Word contracts on your hard drive.

This impressive feature works only if you have first *indexed* your hard drive using Sherlock, as described in Chapter 15. It also works best if your expectations aren't sky-high: If you Control-click a graphics file that shows Wayne Newton, don't expect Sherlock to locate other photos of Vegas lounge acts. Sherlock can identify documents only by the words inside them.

- **Index Selection:** Use this contextual command to force Sherlock to index the folder or disk you're clicking.

This contextual command can be very powerful. Most people aren't, in fact, in the habit of letting Sherlock index their entire hard drives. But almost everyone occasionally needs to search for a document whose name and location they can't remember. Using this feature, you can force Sherlock to index only a single folder, so that you can then search for the words inside the files it contains.

- **Attach a Folder Action:** A *folder action* is a software robot that processes a document automatically when it's dropped into a particular folder, courtesy of the built-in Mac OS automation program called AppleScript. You'll find details of folder actions in Chapter 10; for now, notice that this folder-only contextual menu is the mechanism you use to attach an AppleScript to a certain folder.

- **Change Desktop Background:** You get this command when you Control-click the desktop itself—the colored backdrop of your screen. It takes you directly to the Desktop tab of the Appearance control panel, described in the previous chapter, where you can change the color, photograph, or pattern that fills the background of your screen.

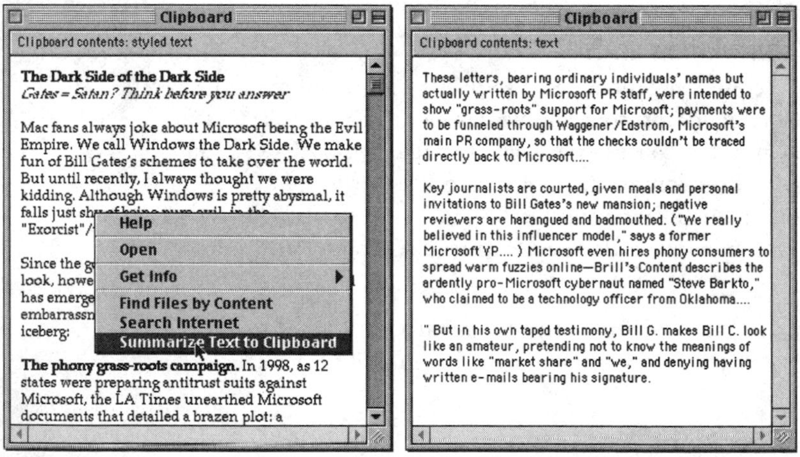

**Figure 4-3:**
*Use the Summarize Text to Clipboard command to create a summary (right) of a longer document (left). For even more fun, you can even summarize the summary—just Control-click the Clipboard window (right) and choose the same command again, ad infinitum.*

This command, too, is worth using; it's much more direct than opening the  menu, sliding down to the Control Panels command, opening Appearance, and so on.

- **Summarize Text to Clipboard.** Few secret commands are as secret, or as intriguing, as this one. It appears only under certain circumstances—namely, when you've highlighted some text in text-processing programs like Claris Emailer, America Online, and the Clipboard window itself (choose Edit→Show Clipboard).

  When you choose Summarize Text to Clipboard, the Mac analyzes the sentences you've highlighted, and instantly produces a much shorter summary. (It doesn't actually do any creative rewriting; instead, it chooses the most statistically significant sentences to include in the summary.) This summary appears in the Clipboard window, which opens automatically (see Figure 4-3).

## Adding to Contextual Menus

As useful as contextual menus are, the built-in Mac OS 9 set is only the beginning. It's very easy to add new commands to these menus (and, if you're a programmer, to write new modules for them).

You can get these additional contextual-menu commands at *www.control-click* or *www.missingmanual.com,* among other places; Figure 4-4 shows a few of them in action.

Some of the add-ons come with their own installers; others require you to place the new contextual-menu module yourself. To do so, open Macintosh HD→System Folder, and then drag the downloaded module into the Contextual Menu Items folder. When you restart the computer, you'll find new commands listed in the appropriate contextual menus. (Removing commands from your contextual menus is just as easy: Drag the corresponding modules out of your Contextual Menu Items folder, and then restart the computer.)

**Figure 4-4:**
*FinderPop is a shareware contextual-menu add-on that lets you see what's inside the folder without having to open it–just by clicking. It also lets you manage programs–switching to another program, hiding or showing all programs, listing all Finder windows, and so on. StuffIt Deluxe and Documents to Go are examples of commercial programs that also add commands to the contextual menu.*

# The Control Strip

The Control Strip (see Figure 4-5) is a clever enhancement, built into Mac OS 9, that lets you change Macintosh settings directly, without going to the trouble of opening the corresponding control panels. With a couple of deft clicks, you can change your speaker volume, choose a different track to play on a music CD, disconnect from the Internet, and so on. In general, each Control Strip tile duplicates the functions of the control-panel programs found in your &#63743;→Control Panels folder, offering a quick way to adjust key settings without having to open those corresponding programs.

**Figure 4-5:**
*The Control Strip spends most of its time as a subtle gray tab hugging the left edge of your screen (top). It expands to full width (bottom) when you click the tab, and collapses again when you click the tab a second time.*

## How the Control Strip Works

To open the Control Strip, which normally hugs the edge of your screen in its timid way, click the gray tab as shown in Figure 4-5. Once it's open, you can see that it's composed of individual tiles, each of which is a pop-up menu that controls a specific aspect of your Mac.

---

**Tip:** The beauty of the Control Strip is that it's always available, no matter what you're doing on the Macintosh. When open, it lies in front of any other programs. The downside, however, is that its very collapsibility makes many Mac fans avoid it. After all, you have to find, and then click, the tab to open it before accessing any of its goodies—and then click the tab again when you're finished.

You don't have to use the tab to summon and dismiss the Control Strip, however. Using the ⌘-Control-S keystroke, you can make the fully open Control Strip appear and disappear at your command. (You can choose a different key combination in &#63743;→Control Panels→Control Strip. When the control panel opens, click "Hot key to show/hide," and then click "Define hot key.")

---

### Adjusting and moving the Control Strip

Most Mac fans suffer in silence, convinced that the Control Strip is locked forever in the lower-left corner of the screen. Fortunately, it's easy enough to move the Control Strip up or down on the screen—just Option-drag the tab. In fact, you can even drag the Control Strip all the way to the *right* side of the screen, provided you're holding down the Option key as you drag.

Similarly, you can rearrange the order of the individual tiles on the Control Strip. The trick, once again, is to hold down the Option key as you drag. The cursor turns into a tiny cartoon hand to signal that it's ready for the hard labor of moving tiles.

### Adding and removing Control Strip tiles

Behind the scenes, each tile on the Control Strip is represented by an icon in the System Folder→Control Strip Modules folder. You can add Control Strip items that you've downloaded from the Internet simply by dropping them into this Control Strip Modules folder—or, easier still, by dropping them onto the System Folder icon itself. (The Mac offers to file them into the proper inner folder automatically.)

Likewise, you can remove tiles from your Control Strip by dragging them *out* of this folder. (If you're familiar with other Mac OS 9 quick-access mechanisms, including the Launcher, <apple> menu, Favorites, and contextual menus, you may be recognizing a pattern. The choices offered by these features, too, are represented by icons in corresponding folders inside the System Folder.)

Fortunately, you don't have to burrow into your System Folder every time you want to add or remove Control Strip tiles. You can drag new Control Strip modules directly from the desktop *onto* the open Control Strip, where the new tile immediately appears. (Behind the scenes, a copy has actually been placed into the System Folder→Control Strip Modules folder.)

Similarly, you can remove tiles just by dragging them from the Control Strip directly into the Trash—provided you remember to hold down the Option key as you drag.

---

*Tip:* Just installing a Control Strip module into your System Folder→Control Strip Modules folder doesn't necessarily mean that it will show up on your Control Strip. The Mac is smart enough to hide modules that wouldn't work on your Mac model anyway. For example, a standard Mac OS 9 installation dumps modules for TV Mirroring into your Control Strip Modules folder—but no such tile appears on your Control Strip unless your model has TV output jacks on the back panel.

---

## The Standard Mac OS 9 Control Strip Tiles

When you first install Mac OS 9, your Control Strip has about 14 tiles, depending on whether your Mac is a laptop or desktop model. Not all of them are equally useful, however; it's well worth removing the ones you don't use. After all, the fewer tiles, the quicker you can find the one you're actually looking for.

In this discussion, the *modules* are listed alphabetically, as they appear in your System Folder→Control Strip Modules folder. The *commands* in each module are described here from *bottom to top* of each tile's pop-up menu. That's because the Control Strip's pop-up menus are cleverly designed with the most important commands closest to your initial mouse click—that is, at the bottom of the pop-up menu. (If you move your Control Strip to the *top* of your screen by Option-dragging its tab, the software is smart enough to flip these pop-up menus *upside-down,* once again placing the important commands closest to your cursor—which is now at the *top* of the flipped Control Strip menus.)

The following descriptions omit the self-explanatory commands like "Open File Sharing Control Panel." Each such command opens the Control Strip tile's corresponding program in the  →Control Panels folder.

---

*Tip:* To identify the tiles on your Control Strip, turn on Balloon Help. (To do so, choose Help→Show Balloons.) Now, as your cursor passes over each Control Strip tile, a pop-up balloon identifies the tile by name and hints at how to use it.

---

### AirPort Control Strip

If you have this Control Strip item, you'd remember having paid $100 for an AirPort card, which lets any modern Mac model communicate, like a cordless phone, with an AirPort base station up to 150 feet away. Doing so lets you surf the Web from your laptop in the TV room, for example, or to share files with someone across the dormitory from you.

This meter shows your signal strength (which decreases the farther you move from the base station). Its popup commands include:

• **Turn AirPort Off.** You'd do this to save laptop battery power, for example.

• **[Base Station Names.]** Choose one of the names here to specify which base station you want to use for connecting to the Internet or local network. (It's intended for school or office situations, where you may have several base stations to choose from.)

• **Computer to Computer.** If you'd rather hook into another AirPort-equipped Mac than to the Internet, choose this command. Now you can use the Network Browser or Chooser to access other Macs' hard drives, exactly as described in Chapter 15—except this time, you're not wired to anything.

• **Open AirPort.** This command opens the AirPort application (which also appears in your  menu), for more detailed administration of your AirPort setup.

### AppleTalk Switch

AppleTalk is the Mac's networking software. If your Mac is connected to another Mac or to a laser printer, AppleTalk must be *active* (turned on). (AppleTalk doesn't affect your ability to connect to the Internet.)

If you're not on an office network, however, you can save memory, startup time, and (on a laptop) battery power by turning AppleTalk off. This tile, when clicked, offers a choice of two commands: AppleTalk Active and AppleTalk Inactive. There are two other ways to turn AppleTalk on and off—in the  →Chooser, and in the  →Control Panels→AppleTalk control panel—but the Control Strip tile is by far the most direct route.

*Tip:* When considering whether or not to remove the AppleTalk Switch Control Strip module, the primary consideration isn't whether or not you want AppleTalk to be on. It's whether or not you frequently need to *switch* it on and off. Anyone whose Mac is a member of a network probably never turns AppleTalk off, and so should consider removing this Control Strip module altogether. Likewise, if your Mac isn't connected to any other Macs, you probably never turn AppleTalk *on,* and so can safely remove the AppleTalk Switch module.

### Battery Monitor

You'll see this tile only when using a laptop, such as a PowerBook or iBook; it's your battery gauge. It offers three commands: Hide/Show Time Remaining, Hide/Show Battery Consumption, and Hide/Show Battery Level. Figure 4-6 details how these controls govern the appearance of the Control Strip tile itself.

**Figure 4-6:**
*Use the Battery Level command to hide or show a battery-charge bar graph. The Battery Consumption command controls the presence of an alternate graph—a little fuel gauge. The Time Remaining command hides or shows the hours and minutes left in the current charge.*

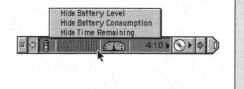

### CDStrip

In addition to computer CDs, your Mac's CD-ROM player can also play music CDs, so that you can listen to music as you work. The primary "front panel" for your virtual CD player is the AppleCD Audio Player program, as described in the next chapter.

When you'd rather not launch an entire application just to control your music CDs, however, this Control Strip tile suffices. Its commands include:

- **Track 1, Track 2...:** At the bottom of the menu is a list of the tracks on the CD that's currently inserted, if any. Choose a track name to start playing that song.

  Obviously, the names of these tracks aren't very helpful; at very few parties do people say, "Hey, have you heard track 11 of the new Elton John CD?" Fortunately, you can replace these designations with the actual song names by using AppleCD Audio Player.

- **Stop, Eject:** Use these commands exactly as you might expect. The Stop command halts playback—but unlike the Pause command, it doesn't remember where you stopped. When you play again, the music begins at the beginning of the CD. And the Eject command, of course, spits the CD out of your Mac.

- **Skip Track, Back Track:** These two commands jump to the next or previous song on the CD, respectively.

- **Pause/Play:** The wording of this command changes from moment to moment. Before the music has begun to play, or after you've used the Stop command, this command says Play; when playback resumes, you'll hear the track indicated by a dot. If a music CD is playing, the command says **Pause [Playing]**, which makes playback freeze in its tracks. After you've used this Pause command, it changes to say **Play [Paused]**, which makes playback resume at the same spot in the music.

- **Normal/Shuffle:** To the frustration of many unsuspecting Mac fans, this command is *never* available; it appears dimmed in the pop-up menu. It's an indicator, not a command. Its purpose is to show you the current playback mode for the CD that's playing—Normal mode, where the tracks play in sequence, or Shuffle, in which the tracks play in a random order. You can't switch between modes using the Control Strip; you must use the AppleCD Audio Player program, described in the next chapter.

- **3D Stereo:** This command appears only if your Mac model offers 3D stereo simulation, such as an iMac or an iBook with connected headphones. When the dot appears beside this command's name, the 3D effect is turned on, making it sound as though there are speakers not only to your left and right, but also behind you.

- **Repeat:** This option is available only when a music CD is actually inserted. When Repeat is selected (so that a dot appears), the CD plays again from the beginning after reaching the end; otherwise, the music simply stops when the CD reaches its conclusion.

- **Auto Play:** When this option is turned on, as indicated by a dot next to its name, any music CD you insert begins playing automatically, saving you the effort of having to use the Play command. (To turn this option off, choose its name so that the dot disappears.)

- **ATAPI CD-ROM [Name of your CD-ROM drive]:** At the top of this tile's pop-up menu, above the first light gray line, is a list of all your CD-ROM drives. Of course, you probably have only one, and its name is probably ATAPI CD-ROM.

If you were a particularly wealthy individual, however, with multiple CD-ROM drives attached to your Mac, you'd see each of them listed here. By choosing a drive's name, you could indicate which drive the other Control Strip commands should control. (The currently selected CD-ROM drive displays a dot beside its name.)

### Energy Settings

You can think of this tile as the representative of the Energy Saver control panel, described in Chapter 12. It is primarily useful for controlling the trade-off between speed and battery savings on Apple laptops, although the same tile is inexplicably available on iMacs, as well.

The **Sleep Now** command puts your laptop or desktop computer promptly to sleep, darkening the screen and putting the computer into a low-power, dormant state. (You might think of this function as the Mac's built-in screen saver.) Press a key, or click the mouse, to wake it up again.

The next command in this pop-up menu, **Spin Down Hard Disk,** immobilizes what may be the biggest battery guzzler on a laptop: the hard drive. (The disadvantage of halting the hard drive's spinning is that you'll experience a 10-second delay the next time you use the mouse or keyboard to do almost anything—the time it takes for the hard drive to begin spinning again.)

Behind the scenes, the next commands, **Better Conservation** and **Better Performance,** move the sliders in the Energy Saver control panel that govern how quickly your screen, hard drive, and processor "go to sleep" to save energy.

---

**Tip:** When you're running on battery power, Better Conservation is the factory-selected choice—a terrible handicap when you're trying to play QuickTime movies, give a presentation, or crunch numbers on a deadline. When speed counts, Better Performance is by far the better choice.

---

### File Sharing Strip

If your Mac is connected to other computers in the office, you can use the File Sharing feature to make certain folders on your hard drive available to other people on the network. (See Chapter 16 for details on Mac networking.) If your Mac isn't connected to other Macs, by all means remove this tile from your Control Strip.

It offers three sets of commands. **Turn File Sharing On/Off** is a shortcut for opening the Control Panels→File Sharing control panel and then clicking the Start button (which is the master switch for sharing folders on your hard drive).

At the top of the pop-up menu, you see a list of other people on the network who are at this moment connected to your Mac and looking through your folders. (If anyone is, in fact, connected, the File Sharing Strip tile itself changes its look; a tiny pair of stylized heads on the tile let you know that your Mac is being visited.) The names of connected Mac users in this list can be confusing, because they're not actually commands; they're listed purely for your information. In other words, choosing a name from this list does absolutely nothing.

---

**Tip:** As many frustrated Mac fans have discovered, you can't eject or rename a disk while File Sharing is turned on. One of the most frequent uses of this Control Strip tile, therefore, is to turn off File Sharing long enough for you to rename a Zip disk, for example, or eject a CD.

---

### Keychain Strip

New to Mac OS 9, this module will grow in usefulness as more Internet programs recognize the Mac OS 9 Keychain feature, which is described in Chapter 16. (In brief: the Keychain is a master password that automatically enters all *other* passwords required for network Macs, Internet FTP sites, and—someday—Web sites, saving you an immense amount of typing and memorization. The idea is that you "unlock your keychain" when you sit down at the Mac, thus proving that you are you. When you leave the Mac, you can lock the keychain again, so that individual passwords are once again required by all of those various network elements.)

By far the most useful command here is **Unlock Keychain**, which summons the master password dialog box. (Once you've entered your password, the icon of this Control Strip tile changes from a padlock to a key, making it easy to spot the fact that your Mac is now in password-free, unlocked condition. At this point, a new **Lock** command appears at the bottom of the pop-up menu.)

The **Show Available Keychains** command opens the System Folder→Preferences→ Keychains folder, so that you can see and manipulate the icons representing each of your keychains. Finally, the **Open Keychain Access** command opens the Keychain Access control panel, which is described in Chapter 12.

### Location Manager Controls

You can read about the Location Manager in detail in Chapter 12. It's a powerful but very complex control panel that can change many location-related Mac settings with a single click. It was originally designed to accommodate laptop owners who use their machines at two or more different locations, each with a different network setup and local Internet phone number. Using the Location Manager—and, in particular, this Control Strip module—you can choose the name of a particular location, such as Downtown Office, to switch many such settings at once.

At the bottom of the pop-up menu are the names of any Locations you've set up using the Location Manager control panel. The **None (Off)** command returns your Mac to whatever control panel settings were in force before you switched to any of your defined Locations. Finally, the **Open Location Manager** command opens the Location Manager control panel itself, where you can set up new Locations and perform other administrative duties.

### Media Bay

PowerBook owners are the target audience for this indicator, which shows, at a glance, what equipment is currently inserted into each of the laptop's two side compartments. (Zip drives, CD-ROM drives, floppy drives, and extra batteries are some of the gadgets PowerBook owners can insert into these two matching bays.)

### Monitor BitDepth

Today's Mac monitors offer different *bit depth* settings, each of which permits the screen to display a different number of colors simultaneously. This tile duplicates the functions of the Monitors control panel (see Chapter 12), offering such settings as 256, Thousands, Millions, and so on. On a few machines, such as the iBook, you're even offered a 256 Grays option, which produces a grayscale image that resembles an old black-and-white TV show.

In the early days of Macintosh, higher color settings required a sacrifice in speed; the Mac took time to compute the color for each of thousands of individual dots that make up the screen image. Today, however, there's very little downside to leaving your screen at its maximum bit depth setting ("Millions of Colors"). Photos, in particular, look best when your monitor is set to higher bit depth settings. The "256 Colors" option, on the other hand, makes photos look blotchy; it's useful only for certain computer games that, having been designed to run on ancient Macs, require the lower color setting.

### Monitor Resolution

All desktop screens today, and even some Mac laptop screens, can make the screen picture larger or smaller, thus accommodating different kinds of work. You do this magnification or reduction by switching among different *resolutions* (the number of dots that compose the screen). This pop-up menu lists the various possible resolution settings for your screen: 640 x 480, 800 x 600, and so on. (You can use the Monitors control panel, described in Chapter 12, to access the same choices—but the Control Strip is quicker.)

When you use a low resolution setting, such as 640 x 480, the dots that make up your screen image get larger, thus enlarging (zooming in on) the picture—but showing a smaller slice of the page. Use this setting when, for example, playing a small QuickTime movie, so that it fills more of the screen. At higher resolutions (such as 800 x 600), the screen dots get smaller, making your windows and icons smaller, but showing more overall area. Use this kind of setting when you want to see as much screen area as possible: when working on two-page spreads in a page-layout program, for example.

### Printer Selector

Using this Control Strip tile, you can specify which office laser printer you want to use for your next printout.

If you don't have multiple laser printers at your disposal, throw away this tile; it does you no good. (It doesn't, for example, list or let you switch among inkjet printers, such as the popular and inexpensive printers from Epson, Canon, and Hewlett-Packard.)

### Remote Access Control Strip

Remote Access is the program that controls your modem connection to the Internet. It's where you record the phone number your Mac dials, your name and password, and other Internet settings. (If you connect by cable modem, DSL line, T-1 line, or any other method, you don't need the Remote Access control panel—or this tile.)

- **Connect [Disconnect]:** As described in Chapter 14, the Mac does two things when you launch, say, your Web browser. First, it dials into the Internet, opening a phone-line connection; second, it actually launches your Web browser and allows it to communicate with the Internet over the open phone connection.

  But when you then *quit* your Web browser, the phone connection doesn't stop. The Mac remains online, assuming that you may now want to run a different Internet program (your email program, for example). The computer doesn't actually hang up its phone call until 10 minutes after your last online activity.

  The Control Strip's Disconnect command lets you hang up the phone on command, without having to wait. The Connect command, on the other hand, places that call to the Internet, opening up a connection so that you can use your Internet software.

- **Default, [other Internet setups]:** Between the light gray lines in the Remote Access tile is a list of Internet settings you've created in the Remote Access control panel. Most people have only one Internet account (usually called Default), and have no need for this flexibility. Some people, however, switch regularly between, say, America Online and an Internet (ISP) account. Laptop owners may travel between two hub cities, each requiring a different local Internet phone number. Using these commands, you can switch to an appropriate account or phone number without having to open the Remote Access control panel.

- **Status Display:** When you choose this command, a dialog box appears, offering three kinds of information you can opt to have displayed on the Control Strip tile's icon itself. **Icon Only** means that only the telephone-pole icon appears. **Time connected** shows how long you've been online—a relic of an era before unlimited Internet account plans (but a useful indicator if you're a surfaholic). And **Time remaining** shows how many minutes remain until you're automatically disconnected (an obsolete setting, as modern Internet access companies don't limit the length of each Internet session).

- **Remote Access Status: Idle [Connected]:** This final pop-up menu item isn't a command; it's a status indicator that lets you know, at a glance, whether or not your modem is still connected to the Internet.

### Sound Volume

Use this slider to control your Mac's speaker volume. The changes you make here correspond to those in the ⌘→Control Panels→Sound control panel.

### SoundSource Strip

When you use one of the Mac's sound-recording programs, such as SimpleSound (see Chapter 20), you have a choice of *what* to record. You may decide to record a sound from a music CD you're playing, the built-in microphone of an iMac or PowerBook, an external mike you've plugged into your iBook or Power Mac, and so on. This pop-up menu lists all available sound sources, and lets you specify which one you want to record. (The current selection is indicated in italics at the top of the pop-up menu.)

### Speakable Items

This tile appears only if you've installed the Mac's speech-recognition software (called PlainTalk, and described in Chapter 21). Its sole function: To turn the Speakable Items function on or off—in other words, to make your Mac start and stop listening to your voice commands.

### TV Mirroring

Throughout Mac history, occasional models have offered a unique feature: the ability to view the Mac's image on a TV connected to the Mac's back panel. (Power Mac towers with the A/V card option and bronze-keyboard PowerBook G3 models, among others, have included this feature.) You use this module to control various aspects of this setup.

The commands in this module differ by Mac module, but the essence is the same. Using the **TV Mirroring On** command, you can make the same screen picture appear on both the Mac's monitor and the attached TV. Such an arrangement can be useful when, for example, you're presenting a slide show for an audience. (As shown in Figure 4-7, the TV Mirroring icon smiles to indicate that a TV is connected.)

The **Use NTSC Standard** and **Use PAL Standard** commands let you specify whether you're using American or European TV equipment, respectively; **Overscan** enlarges the output image to fill the TV screen, sometimes clipping the edges of the picture (including the menu bar) in the process; **Best for Graphics/Best for Video** may improve the TV picture when you're showing, say, a PowerPoint slide show ("Graphics") or a QuickTime movie ("Video"); and **Leave Monitor On** means that the Mac's screen works, too. (A few, especially cruddy monitors show distortion or snow when you're using TV Mirroring. That's when you'd want to turn *off* the Leave Monitor On option.)

### Video Mirroring

A few, specially blessed Macs (including the bronze-keyboard PowerBook G3) let you attach an external monitor or TV—but not just to display a duplicate image of the Mac's own screen, but instead to *extend* it, as though you've tacked a two-foot addition onto the right of your built-in Mac screen. Such an arrangement is fantastically useful when (a) working in palette-crazed programs like Photoshop and Premiere, or (b) trying to make your Windows-using friends feel inferior.

As shown in Figure 4-7, this Control Strip module lets you turn Mirroring on (Mac and external screen show the same thing) or off (external screen acts as additional real estate).

**Figure 4-7:**
*When Video Mirroring is turned off (top), the external screen acts as an extension of the built-in screen. When Mirroring is on (bottom), the Mac and external screen show the same image, and the icon shows a double face (bottom).*

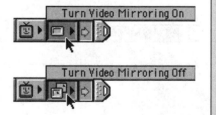

### Web Sharing CS

Web Sharing is the curious little feature that lets you designate a Web-page folder that you want to make available to other Macs on your network. (Chapter 14 offers detailed instructions.) If your Mac doesn't have a full-time Internet connection or network, you have no use for Web Sharing (or this tile).

Like the File Sharing feature, Web Sharing comes with a Control Strip tile—this one—that lets you turn the sharing on and off. This tile also shows your Mac's current *IP address,* which, as far as your potential dial-in guests are concerned, is your Mac's Internet address.

## Other Control Strip Tiles Worth Installing

Some programs, such as EditDV (from Digital Origin) and Conflict Catcher (from Casady & Greene), install their own tiles onto your Control Strip as part of their regular installation process. Others are the free or shareware programs that make Mac life more enjoyable. A few (available from *www.missingmanual.com*) are these:

- **BunchOApps:** Despite having been written in 1994, this application-manager Control Strip tile works like a champ. It lists and launches recently opened programs plus any other favorites that you designate.

- **Quit CSM:** Shows a graph of your Mac's free memory, right there in the Control Strip. (CSM stands for Control Strip Module.) When you click the tile, you're offered Quit commands for each running program, a Quit All command, various Hide and Show commands, and other useful functions.

- **EasyFontPreview:** Shows a list of the fonts on your Mac—and lets you see the alphabet in that typeface.

- **StripBandit:** A smile-inducing representative of a specialized class of Control Strip modules—those designed for pure entertainment. This one is for vacationers just back from Vegas: click the tile to roll the "slot machine" dials (see Figure 4-8).

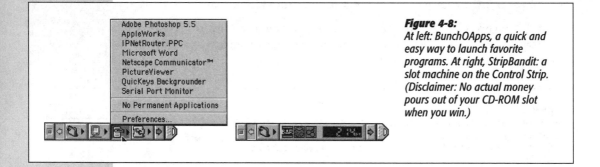

**Figure 4-8:**
At left: BunchOApps, a quick and easy way to launch favorite programs. At right, StripBandit: a slot machine on the Control Strip. (Disclaimer: No actual money pours out of your CD-ROM slot when you win.)

# Mastering the Apple Menu

Enjoy the fact that your  menu icon displays the six colored stripes of the original Apple logo—it's the last surviving memory of the logo's glory days, before Steve Jobs retook control of Apple and redid the logo in pure white. It's also a holdover from the very first color Macintosh, almost unchanged in look and function.

That function, of course, is to serve as the North Star of menus. Below the "About this Program" command and the light gray line, the  menu commands make up a reliable and permanent listing that never varies, no matter what program you're using. Unlike your other menus, this one's contents never changes, making the  menu an excellent place for listings of programs and documents that you frequently launch.

When you first install Mac OS 9, the  menu comes equipped with several useful utility programs, such as the Calculator; you'll find these programs documented in this chapter. It's much more important, however, for you to recognize that you can easily *change* the contents of the  menu, adding items you often open and deleting things you never use.

## How to Modify the  Menu

Every item in the  menu is represented by a corresponding icon in the System Folder→Apple Menu Items folder. Figure 5-1 should make this relationship clear.

By placing it into the System Folder→Apple Menu Items folder, you can install virtually any kind of icon (or alias thereof) into the  menu. Each kind of icon offers its own payoff:

• **A document:** Suppose there's some spreadsheet of part numbers that you frequently need to consult. By installing it into your ▆ menu, you never again have to rummage through your hard drive looking for it. The same trick works for frequently used applications, of course—if you haven't installed aliases of your word processing program, email program, and Web browser into your ▆ menu, you're wasting time every time you need them.

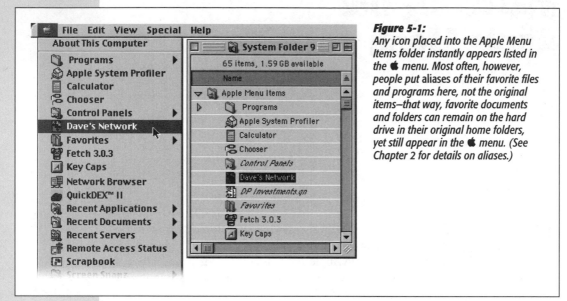

**Figure 5-1:**
*Any icon placed into the Apple Menu Items folder instantly appears listed in the ▆ menu. Most often, however, people put aliases of their favorite files and programs here, not the original items—that way, favorite documents and folders can remain on the hard drive in their original home folders, yet still appear in the ▆ menu. (See Chapter 2 for details on aliases.)*

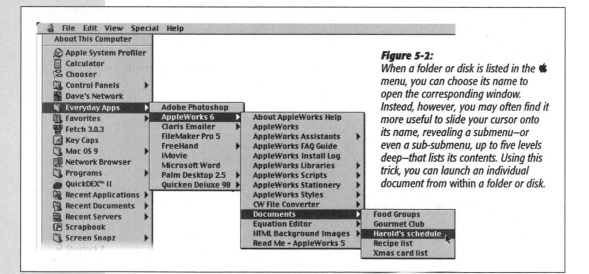

**Figure 5-2:**
*When a folder or disk is listed in the ▆ menu, you can choose its name to open the corresponding window. Instead, however, you may often find it more useful to slide your cursor onto its name, revealing a submenu—or even a sub-submenu, up to five levels deep—that lists its contents. Using this trick, you can launch an individual document from within a folder or disk.*

**Tip:** Items in the  menu appear alphabetically. If you'd like some item listed at the *top* of the menu, therefore, precede its name (in the System Folder→Apple Menu Items folder) with a space. Additional spaces make the item appear even higher on the list.

- **A folder:** In its effort to be your time-saving slave, the  menu not only lists folders, but turns them into submenus that let you access their contents, as shown in Figure 5-2.

**Tip:** If your  menu doesn't offer folder submenus like the ones in Figure 5-2, somebody must have turned this feature off. The on/off switch is in the Apple Menu Options control panel (choose →Control Panels to see this control panel).

- **Your hard drive:** Following the trick proposed in Figure 5-2 to its logical conclusion, many Mac fans place an alias of the *hard drive icon itself* into the  menu. Thereafter, they have complete access to every single item on the hard drive— simply by choosing it from this menu. You may have to burrow through several submenus (representing folders within folders on your hard drive) to find a particular document, but at least you won't have to open and then close numerous windows.

- **The Trash:** A few people even put an alias of the Trash can into the  menu. Doing so provides a quick way to open the Trash window to survey its contents before emptying the Trash, even if you're not working in the Finder.

- **Automated Tasks:** In the Macintosh HD→Apple Extras→AppleScripts folder is the often-overlooked folder called Automated Tasks. Inside this folder are five *AppleScripts*—tiny programs that perform a single, very specific task when double-clicked (see Chapter 10). (Three more such AppleScripts lurk in the Apple Extras→AppleScripts→More Automated Tasks folder.)

Among these marginally useful scripts is one fantastically useful one, called Add Alias to Apple Menu. Place this icon into your Apple Menu Items folder, so that it now appears in  menu, as shown in Figure 5-3. From now on, adding a new

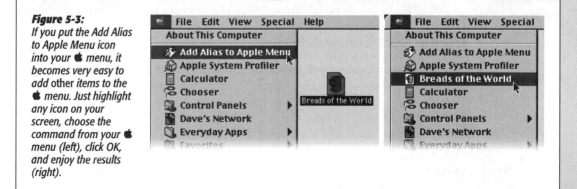

**Figure 5-3:**
*If you put the Add Alias to Apple Menu icon into your  menu, it becomes very easy to add other items to the  menu. Just highlight any icon on your screen, choose the command from your  menu (left), click OK, and enjoy the results (right).*

icon to your  menu doesn't require the usual hassle of opening your System Folder, then opening the Apple Menu Items folder, and so on. Instead, adding something to the  menu is a matter of a single step; Figure 5-3 offers the details. Moving this particular AppleScript into your  menu is an excellent idea.

- **The Apple Menu Items folder:** In a strange twist of recursive logic, many Mac fans open the System Folder, make an alias of the Apple Menu Items folder, and insert that alias *into* the Apple Menu Items folder from which it came! The result: the Apple Menu Items folder is now listed *in* your  menu.

This arrangement makes it much more convenient to make changes to your  menu; whenever you want to add or remove something from the menu, choose the name of the Apple Menu Items folder. The Apple Menu Items window opens, giving easy access to the icons inside, which you can now trash, rename, or otherwise manipulate.

---

**TROUBLESHOOTING MOMENT**

## The Broken Desk Accessory Drag-and-Drop

*I dragged the Stickies program onto my System Folder to install it into my  menu, as I've done with desk accessories for 15 years. But instead of automatically being placed into the Apple Menu Items folder, like the Mac always used to do, Stickies just clunked into the System Folder itself, doing me no good at all. What's going on?*

You're correct that, for the first 15 years of its existence, the Mac auto-routed desk accessory programs into the Apple Menu Items folder when you dropped them onto the System Folder. You're also correct that the Mac no longer auto-files several of the standard "desk accessories" in this way. The Note Pad, Remote Access Status program, Stickies, Network Browser, and even Sherlock 2 fall into this category. (Only a few programs still auto-route themselves, including the Chooser and Key Caps.)

The explanation: Mac OS 9 is the stepping stone between the traditional Mac OS and the advanced, next-generation, Unix-based Mac OS X, projected to become available in 2000. In Mac OS X, desk accessories, the mini-programs for which the  menu has traditionally been home, are a thing of the past. Only full-blown applications populate the  menu (and the Mac itself, for that matter).

Over time, therefore, Apple has been stealthily replacing standard desk accessories with identical-looking full-blown *applications*. Because these items still appear in the  menu and work as they always have, you might not have noticed this transition—except when you dropped them onto the System Folder for auto-filing, and discovered that the Mac no longer recognizes them as  menu items.

---

## About This Computer

The first command in the  menu is the only one that's not represented on your hard drive by its own icon. It's About This Computer, which produces the dialog box shown in Figure 5-4, a display teeming with information about your system software and memory usage.

---

***Tip:*** Ironically, the About This Computer window doesn't reveal a shred of information that's actually about this *computer*, such as its model name or processor specs. For that information, choose the *next* command in the  menu, Apple System Profiler.

---

Among the most useful bits of information provided here: Built-in Memory (how much RAM your Mac has), Largest Unused Block (how much free memory remains), and the list of currently open programs. To find out how to interpret and capitalize on these statistics, see Chapter 7.

**Figure 5-4:**
*The highlights of the About This Computer window include memory statistics, the version of the Mac OS you're running (in the upper-right), and a list of all running programs. The memory bars indicate how much memory each program has set aside for itself; the colored portion indicates how much of that memory it's actually using.*

About This Computer

MacOS 9

Version: Mac OS 9.0          PowerPC Enabler 9.0
Built-in Memory: 128 MB
Virtual Memory: 129 MB used on Macintosh HD
Largest Unused Block: 47.2 MB          ™ & © Apple Computer, Inc. 1983–1999

| | | |
|---|---|---|
| Adobe® Photoshop | 17.1 MB | |
| Claris Emailer | 4.9 MB | |
| Mac OS | 32.9 MB | |
| Microsoft Word | 10.9 MB | |
| Netscape Communicator™ | 12.7 MB | |

---

**GEM IN THE ROUGH**

## The Last Easter Eggs

In the Golden Age of Macintosh, programmers delighted in planting secret displays, sounds, or even animations inside their software. These so-called *Easter eggs* were usually tributes to themselves—hidden credits—that only appeared on the screen when you performed some very unlikely sequence of steps, such as clicking repeatedly in the same spot 56 times while holding down the M key.

Software companies don't like Easter eggs, however. Because they're secret and never actually encountered by the hundreds of beta testers who look for bugs in fresh software, Easter eggs can introduce bugs or glitches. Worse, in today's ultra-competitive Silicon Valley job market, Easter eggs constitute a virtual shopping list for predators like Microsoft, who regularly sends job offers to Apple's talented programmers.

That second reason is Steve Jobs's justification for banning Easter eggs in the Mac OS. Two remain in Mac OS 9, however, evidently slipped in before Jobs's decree. Both are related to the  menu→About This Computer command.

To see a color picture of Apple's Cupertino headquarters (and a scrolling list of everyone who's ever worked on the Mac OS), choose the command while pressing Option.

To see the names of the people who wrote Mac OS 9, choose the command while pressing Control, Option, and ⌘. (Both tricks change the actual wording of the command, too.)

Either way, enjoy the resulting displays; they may be Apple's very last Easter eggs.

# The Standard ď Menu Items

Although you get the most mileage out of the ď menu when you tailor it to your tastes, several useful programs come pre-installed there. Here's a rundown.

## Apple System Profiler

Since this program debuted in January 1997, Apple System Profiler has arrived into the homes and offices of 15 million people. Yet only a tiny handful of Mac users have ever actually opened Apple System Profiler, let alone understood it.

That's as it should be: the program's primary function is to serve as a spy, a mole placed inside your Macintosh by Apple's tech-support staff. When you call the Apple help line, the technicians on the other end no longer need to pull out their hair by the clump, unable to determine your Mac configuration. Instead, they can calmly ask you to choose ď→Apple System Profiler and read the statistics it reveals about your system. Apple System Profiler puts every conceivable shred of information about your Mac, disks, control panels and extensions, applications, and other details into a single centralized location, suitable for rattling off over the phone to somebody who's trying to help you. (Using the File→New Report command, you can also save the same information into a text file or compact Apple System Profiler document, which you can then send by email.)

The program's display screen is broken down into tabs. They are:

- **System Profile:** This screen indicates your Mac OS version, memory and virtual memory statistics, and other hardware details. Hunt long enough, and you'll find out whether your Mac has a built-in modem, the name of your Mac model, what chip is inside (and its speed), and so on.

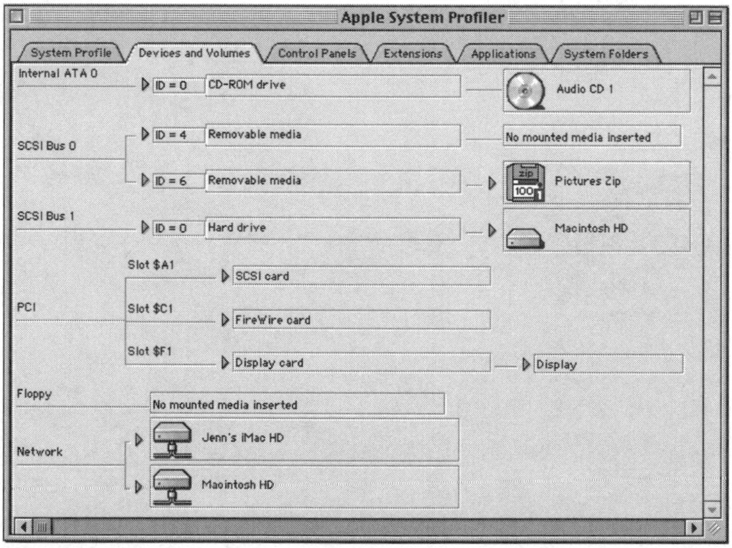

**Figure 5-5:**
Click the tiny triangles to expose the details about the corresponding aspects of your machine. Most of these morsels are extremely technical, of value primarily to technicians trying to help you troubleshoot. You can switch from one screen of information to another either by clicking the tabs, choosing from the Commands menu, or pressing ⌘-1 through ⌘-6.

- **Devices and Volumes:** Think of this screen as Disk Central (see Figure 5-5). It specifies exactly what disks are attached to your Mac, both inside and outside, including hard drives, Zip drives, CD-ROM drives, and so on. The primary horizontal branches of the "tree" (such as "Internal ATA 2" and "USB 0") represent your Mac's *buses*—chains of sequential circuitry through which information flows inside your Mac.

- **Control Panels** and **Extensions:** These two screens list and identify every control panel and extension in your System Folder. The vast majority of Mac problems are, in fact, software problems, and most are introduced by old, buggy, or non-Apple control panels and extensions. That's why this listing of such files can be so useful to a troubleshooter. (Click an item in the list to read a short description of its purpose.)

- **Applications:** Here you can read an alphabetical list of every program on your Mac. This listing makes it easy to spot duplicates and outdated versions. (How many copies of SimpleText do *you* have? Extra credit if you have fewer than seven.)

## Calculator

This humble, black-and-white, four-function calculator is the oldest surviving piece of the Mac OS, lingering in the  menu almost unchanged since 1984. It works exactly like a pocket calculator, except that it has far fewer functions and no CE button. Three of its idiosyncrasies:

- You don't have to click the tiny buttons with your mouse. Instead, you can control the Calculator by pressing the keys on the number pad of your keyboard, whose layout matches that of the Calculator. You can press the Enter key as a substitute for the = key.

- As on most computers, you use the / and * buttons (or keys on the keyboard) to represent division and multiplication, respectively.

- The Calculator doesn't have a memory function; if you make a typo while entering a long string of numbers, your only recourse is to click the C button (or press the letter C on your keyboard) to erase everything you've entered and start over.

  Fortunately, you can also type out the long string of calculations in a word processor, or even a program like Stickies. Highlight the calculation you've typed, choose Edit→Copy, switch to the Calculator, and then choose Edit→Paste. The previously typed numbers fly into the Calculator in sequence, finally producing the grand total on its little screen. (You can then use the Edit→Copy command to copy the result back out of the Calculator, ready for pasting into another program.)

---

*Caution:* When solving a long calculation, the Calculator doesn't observe parentheses. In other words, it doesn't resolve multiplication and division before addition and subtraction, as is standard in mathematics. It simply crunches the numbers from left to right, regardless of the operators.

## Chooser

Once considered the most useful  menu item, the Chooser is rapidly fading in importance. This little program was originally designed to be the Grand Central Station for administering gadgets that plugged into the Mac's serial ports (the modem and printer port)—such as printers, modems, and network cables.

Today's modern Mac, however, doesn't even *have* modem and printer ports. USB, FireWire, and Ethernet ports have replaced them. Moreover, the Network Browser program described later in this chapter supplants the network-navigation features of the Chooser. Still, for many veteran Mac users, the Chooser is a reassuringly familiar piece of software, still admirably performing these functions:

• **Choosing a printer.** If your Mac has more than one printer attached—this means you, people who work in large offices—the Chooser window lets you specify which one you want to use for the next printout (see Figure 5-6). (If you work on a network whose printers are primarily laser printers, you may prefer the Desktop Printing feature, described in Chapter 19—a much more convenient method of switching printers.)

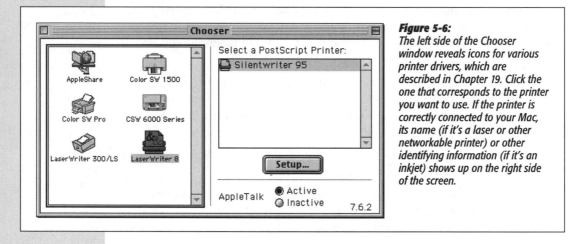

**Figure 5-6:**
The left side of the Chooser window reveals icons for various printer drivers, which are described in Chapter 19. Click the one that corresponds to the printer you want to use. If the printer is correctly connected to your Mac, its name (if it's a laser or other networkable printer) or other identifying information (if it's an inkjet) shows up on the right side of the screen.

• **Turning AppleTalk on and off.** AppleTalk is the Mac's networking circuitry; when it's off, your Mac can't communicate with any other machines on a network. (You can read more about AppleTalk in Chapter 16.) The Chooser offers buttons called AppleTalk Active and AppleTalk Inactive; unfortunately, in some circumstances, they don't actually work, thanks to a strange incompatibility with the underlying and much more modern Open Transport networking software. A much more reliable method of turning AppleTalk on and off is the AppleTalk control panel (see Chapter 12) or the AppleTalk Control Strip tile (see Chapter 4).

• **Connecting to another Mac on the network.** If your Mac is part of a network, you can access the contents of another Mac's hard drive by clicking the AppleShare icon in the Chooser. The names of other networked Macs show up on the right side of the window; you can double-click one of their names as the first step in connecting to it. (See Chapter 16 for details on networking.)

If you're an old-timer on the Mac, used to connecting to networked Macs this way, feel free to continue using this method. (In fact, here's a tip: you can control the entire process from the keyboard. After opening the Chooser, type A to highlight the AppleShare icon, press Tab to highlight your network zones list—if any—or the right side of the window, press Return or Enter to open the highlighted Mac in the list, and so on.)

But today, using the Chooser to connect to your network requires an unnecessary number of steps, and the interface needs streamlining. Using the Network Browser program described later in this chapter is far more satisfying.

- **Switching to your fax modem.** If your Mac has a fax modem attached, an icon in the Chooser window represents it. By clicking that icon, you ensure that the next time you use the File→Print command in one of your programs, you send the document as a fax instead of printing it.

Virtually every fax software package today, however, offers a far more direct route to sending a document via fax. For example, in Global Village and FaxSTF fax programs, you generate a fax just by holding down specified keys, such as ⌘ and Shift, as you choose File→Print, bypassing the Chooser business altogether.

Thanks to such shortcuts, modern replacements like the Network Browser, and the well-known contempt for the Chooser harbored by Apple's Steve Jobs, it's a safe bet that this humble desk accessory will disappear completely in Mac OS X.

## Control Panels

This item is nothing more than an alias in your  menu, placed there for your convenience by Apple. It gives you direct access to the contents of the System Folder→Control Panels folder, so that you can open one of the control panels with a single menu selection.

## Favorites

After years of watching Microsoft pilfer great ideas from the Mac OS, Apple decided that two could play that game—and it stole a feature right back. The Add to Favorites command (in the Mac OS 9 File menu) places the names of icons you've highlighted into the  menu→Favorites command, as shown in Figure 5-7. In other words, this Favorites scheme is yet another mechanism that lists your favorite files for quick access—much like the Launcher, pop-up windows, and the  menu itself.

Also like those other mechanisms, this one relies on a special folder inside your System Folder; it's called, reasonably enough, Favorites. Every time you use the Add to Favorites command as illustrated in Figure 5-7, the Mac puts an alias of the highlighted icon into this Favorites folder.

This behind-the-scenes transaction is worth knowing about, if only because it offers the sole method of *removing or renaming* something from the →Favorites listing. That is, choose ♦→Favorites to open the Favorites window; throw away or rename any of the aliases in it; and then close the window. The ♦→Favorites submenu updates itself instantly.

---

**Tip:** Instead of using the Add to Favorites command in the File menu, you can also add an icon to the Favorites submenu by Control-clicking it. Choose Add to Favorites from the contextual menu that appears.

---

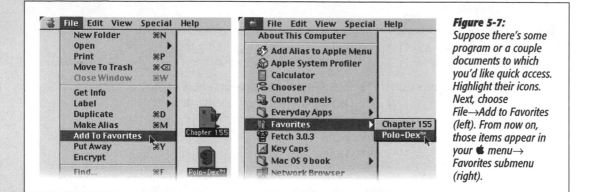

**Figure 5-7:**
*Suppose there's some program or a couple documents to which you'd like quick access. Highlight their icons. Next, choose File→Add to Favorites (left). From now on, those items appear in your ♦ menu→ Favorites submenu (right).*

## Key Caps

The Mac is capable of creating hundreds of different typographical symbols—the currency symbols for the Yen and British pound, diacritical markings for French and Spanish, various scientific symbols, trademark and copyright signs, and so on. Obviously, these symbols don't appear on your keyboard; to provide enough keys for all of the symbols, your keyboard would have to be the width of Wyoming. Fortunately, you can indeed type the symbols—but they're hidden behind the keys you do see.

The treasure map that reveals their locations is Key Caps. When you first open this program, you see a diagram of your keyboard. Use the Key Caps menu to specify the font you want to use (because every font contains a different set of symbols). As you press the various modifier keys at the bottom of your keyboard—Option, ⌘, and Control, for example—the Mac shows you what symbols will be produced by pressing the corresponding letter keys. Figure 5-8 should make the process clear.

After having found the symbol on the Key Caps map, you can proceed in one of two ways. First, you can note which keys you're supposed to hold down to produce a certain symbol, as described in Figure 5-8, and then type it into whatever document you're working on.

Second, you can simply click the symbol on the Key Caps map, thus typing the symbol into the box at the top of the window. You can then highlight the typed symbol with your mouse, choose Edit→Copy, switch to your word processor, and then choose Edit→Paste. The symbol you copied now appears in whatever you've been typing, and you've been saved from having to memorize the key combination that produces it.

*Tip:* As many unhappy Mac fans have discovered, the key squares in Key Caps are too small to show much detail in some elaborate fonts. But if you click the Zoom box in the upper-right corner of the window, Key Caps becomes Super Key Caps, jumping to double size—and providing more than enough headroom for the juiciest typefaces.

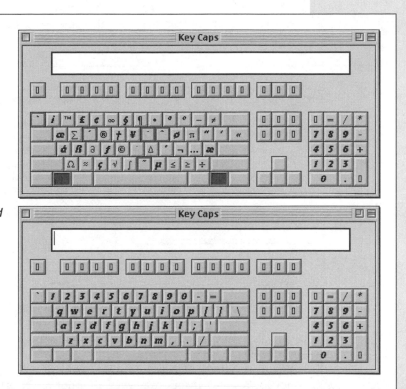

*Figure 5-8:*
*Suppose you're trying to find out what key combination produces the yen symbol. Experiment by holding down various combinations of the Shift, Option, ⌘, and Control keys until you see the ¥ symbol. In this example, the blackened key on the bottom row corresponds to the Option key that's being held down at this moment (top). When you release the key, you can see that the Yen symbol is assigned to the Y key (bottom). You can now return to your document and press Option-Y to produce the symbol.*

---

**UP TO SPEED**

## Dead Keys

As you can see in Figure 5-8, a few keys, such as the e, u, n, and I, show a dark gray border in Key Caps whenever you press the Option key. That border is the Mac's way of illustrating the *dead keys*—keys that do nothing when you first press them. Try pressing Option-e in your word processor; you'll see that nothing happens. Yet.

Dead keys are very useful, however, because they affect the *next* key you type. When you type a normal key after pressing a dead keystroke, you get an accent mark over it. For example, press Option-e, then regular e, to get é. Press Option-i, then regular i, to get î, and so on. You make the Spanish ñ and the German ü using a similar technique.

The top image in Figure 5-8 shows where these dead keys hide, and which accent marks they produce.

---

## Network Browser

After receiving one too many emails from corporate customers irritated with having to connect to networked Macs using the Chooser, Apple's designers got serious. In Mac OS 8.5, they created the Network Browser, an ingeniously simple program that displays an icon for every disk on every computer in every zone of the network. Then, in Mac OS 9, they enhanced the Network Browser with the ability to display the icons of certain Web sites and other Internet entities. (The tutorials in Chapter 16 cover this program in more depth.)

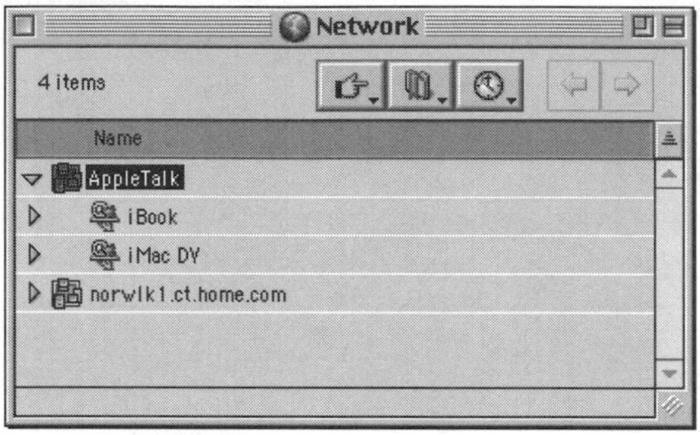

**Figure 5-9:**
*The Network Browser is a map of the network to which your Mac is connected. The leftmost icons are called "neighborhoods"—your office network is one of them. Within a neighborhood is a list of the computers in that network—if you have a large office that uses network routers, each zone has its own icon. By double-clicking, you can burrow down all the way to an individual hard drive whose files you want to access.*

Configuring the Network Browser to display the network nodes and Internet sites to which you want access is a task for the professional network administrator; fortunately, using the Network Browser once the network is operational is extremely easy.

### Using the Network Browser

When you launch Network Browser, the icons that appear depend on whether or not you're on a network, and whether or not you're connected to the Internet.

---

**TROUBLESHOOTING MOMENT**

## The Auto-Dialing Network Browser

*Whenever I so much as open the Network Browser program, it dials the Internet. Drives me crazy. What's going on?*

You're witnessing a side effect of the program's ability to show you Web sites and FTP servers alongside your own network in the same window. Whenever you launch the program, it attempts to connect to the Internet, in preparation for showing you the contents of Web and FTP servers there.

Unfortunately, there's no convenient way to stop it. If your

purpose in using the Network Browser was to connect to another Mac on your local network, you can use the AppleShare icon in the Chooser instead (see "Chooser" earlier in this chapter). Alternatively, you can open the  →Control Panels→Remote Access control panel, click Options, click Protocol, and turn off "Connect automatically when starting TCP/IP applications." Now Network Browser won't dial automatically when launched—but neither will your Web browser or email programs.

No matter what icons you see, however, the process of accessing the contents of the computers that show up is always the same: just double-click icon after icon, burrowing ever closer, until the folder or hard drive you seek appears on your desktop.

For example, suppose you're on a small network—a handful of Macs, all connected by Ethernet (see Chapter 16). The Network Browser first shows you an icon called AppleTalk. (AppleTalk is one of what Apple calls "neighborhoods"—the highest level of icons that shows up in the Network Browser.) Double-click the AppleTalk icon (or click its flippy triangle button) to view the names of other Macs on your network. Double-click one of them (or click their flippy triangles), to access their contents.

Along the way, you may be asked for your name and password, thus proving that you're authorized to meddle with the contents of the computer you're breaking into. If you're smart, you'll take this opportunity to check the Add to Keychain checkbox (see page 301), so that you won't have to enter them again the next time you connect. Finally, an icon for the actual shared hard drive or folder appears, which you can double-click to open. (For more detail on networking and sharing files, see Chapter 16.)

If you've been burrowing toward your goal by double-clicking icons in the Network Browser (instead of using the triangle buttons), you can use the arrow buttons at the top of the window to re-trace your steps, exactly as in a Web browser. Click the Back arrow enough times, and you finally arrive at the original overview of your network.

### What to do when you get there

As you navigate the Network Browser, it's useful to remember that all of the Finder list-view keystrokes and shortcuts described in Chapter 1 work in this window, too. You can type the first letter of an icon to highlight it, move up and down the list by pressing the arrow keys, reverse the sorting order by clicking the tiny pyramid button above the right scroll bar, and rotate a flippy-triangle button by pressing ⌘-right arrow, and so on.

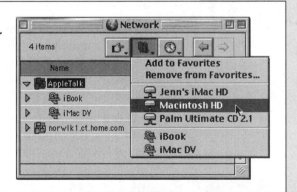

**Figure 5-10:**
*The three cryptic icons at the top of the Network Browser window are actually pop-up menus. The first, called Shortcuts, lists your Neighborhoods (network zones or Internet domains); the middle one is your list of Favorites, separated into clusters of Neighborhoods, zones, and servers; on the right is the list of Recent items—servers you've most recently accessed.*

You'll also recognize the Favorites mechanism, represented here by the middle icon (see Figure 5-10). When a hard drive, computer, zone, or network icon is highlighted in the list, you can click that icon and, from the pop-up menu, choose Add To Favorites, making it more conveniently accessible the next time you want to connect. (Anything you add to this Favorites pop-up menu is simultaneously added to the →Favorites submenu, by the way.)

---

*Tip:* Instead of using the Add To Favorites command, you may find it more direct to drag an icon from the Network Browser window directly onto the Favorites icon (which looks like a folder with a ribbon on it). The result is the same—the icon you dragged now appears in the Favorites icon's pop-up menu.

---

If you know you'll want access to some server again, but would rather not fuss with the Favorites command, you can also drag an icon out of the Network Browser window to your desktop. There it becomes an alias that, henceforth, you can double-click to open the corresponding hard drive or server—without involving the Network Browser at all.

### Recent Applications, Recent Documents

As you open and close your various programs and files, Mac OS 9 tracks them. It maintains a list of the most recent programs you've used in the →Recent Applications submenu, and a list of the most recent documents you've had open in the →Recent Documents submenu. By choosing its name, you can conveniently launch one of these files, without having to hunt down the actual icon on your hard drive.

---

*Tip:* Behind the scenes, Mac OS 9 creates aliases of the programs and documents you use, and stores them in special System Folder folders. Recent programs are maintained in the System Folder→Apple Menu Items→Recent Applications folder; recent documents, meanwhile, are tracked in the System Folder→Apple Menu Items→Recent Documents folder. You're free to throw away these alias icons whenever you like, thus eliminating the Recent Applications and Recent Documents submenus temporarily. Doing so can be useful when, for example, you go out for lunch, leaving your Mac available for inspection by your boss, and would rather not leave behind tracks that show what you've been doing all day.

---

You control how many programs Mac OS 9 tracks using, of all things, the Apple Menu Options control panel (see page 188). There's no downside to increasing this number—many power users let the Recent Applications command track the most recently used 30 or 40 programs, eventually turning the command into the virtual launching bay for every application on the hard drive.

On the other hand, if you type a zero into the Applications or Documents box, you turn off the recent-file-tracking feature. In fact, doing so eliminates the Recent Applications or Recent Documents command from the  menu altogether.

## Recent Servers

This command is useful exclusively for people whose Macs are on an office network. It lists the Macs to which you have most recently connected.

For a detailed explanation of how this mechanism works (by placing aliases into the

---

System Folder→Apple Menu Items→Recent Servers folder), consult the previous paragraphs. The same process for eliminating this command from your  menu applies—open →Control Panels→Apple Menu Options program, and then type a zero into the Servers box.

---

**FREQUENTLY ASKED QUESTION**

## Where's the Note Pad?

*Yeah! What happened to the Note Pad?*

For the first time since the invention of the Macintosh, the handy little note-taking program called Note Pad is missing from the Mac OS 9  menu. No end of wailing and hand-wringing ensued among the online community of Mac fans, who felt that Apple had robbed them of an under-appreciated gem.

Actually, the Note Pad isn't missing from Mac OS 9—just from the  menu. You'll find it, healthy and unharmed, in the Apple Extras folder on your hard drive. If you feel that the  menu is the proper place for this little program, by

all means drag it into the System Folder→Apple Menu Items folder. All will be well with the world once again.

If you're a math teacher, you may soon discover another traditional -menu item that's moved to a new address: the Graphing Calculator. It's now in the Applications folder on your hard drive. So is SimpleSound, the former  menu occupant that you can use to make sound recordings.

Finally, there's the Jigsaw Puzzle, the frivolous little time-waster that's taken up an -menu slot for nearly a decade. Don't bother hunting through your Applications folder for that little item—beginning with Mac OS 9, Apple has retired it for good.

---

## Remote Access Status

If you have an Internet account (as opposed to an America Online account), by now you're probably aware that when you open your Web browser or e-mail program, your Mac dials. But when you quit that program, the Mac doesn't hang up—it holds the line, on the premise that you might want to use another Internet program while the connection is still open.

Mac OS 9 is crawling with features that let you hang up that phone connection on demand. You can use the Disconnect button in the Remote Access control panel. You can use the same control panel's Options button to specify an auto-disconnect time interval (15 minutes, for example). You can also use the Disconnect command in the Remote Access Control Strip tile (described in the previous chapter). (More on this topic in Chapter 14.)

This little program, Remote Access Status, is yet another method. Its streamlined, compact window offers a single feature—a big, fat Disconnect button. (When you're not online, the button says Connect.) You might prefer this method if you connect and disconnect from the Internet several times a day; in that situation, you can park the Remote Access Status window in a corner of your screen, where it's more accessible than any of the other hangup methods. And while you're online, the little display window indicates your connection speed; little phony "status lights" show when you're sending or receiving data.

---

*Tip:* You can set up Remote Access Status to open by itself whenever your modem dials the Internet. To do so, choose ●→Control Panels→Remote Access. Click Options, then Connection. Turn on "Launch Status application when connecting." Click OK.

The next time the Mac dials, it opens the Remote Access Status window automatically.

## Scrapbook

When you use the Edit→Copy command in any program, you place a copy of the highlighted text, graphics, music, or sound onto the invisible Macintosh Clipboard. You're now free to paste that material (using Edit→Paste) as many times as you like, into the same program or into different programs. The problem with the Clipboard, however, is that it only holds a single copied blob of material, which is erased forever when you turn off the computer.

The Scrapbook program solves both problems. It can permanently store graphics, text, sounds, movies, spreadsheet data, and almost anything else that can be copied. To transfer material into the Scrapbook, first copy it out of another program (using the Edit→Copy command), then open the Scrapbook and paste it (using Edit→Paste). (A more direct method: in many Mac programs—Word 98, AppleWorks, the desktop itself, and so on – you can drag highlighted material directly into the Scrapbook window.)

The Scrapbook automatically creates a new "page" to hold material you've pasted or dragged. Using the scroll bar (or by pressing your keyboard's arrow keys), you can view the various pages of the Scrapbook. Use the Edit→Copy command to retrieve something from the Scrapbook at a later date—you might, for example, keep your logo in the Scrapbook, so that you can grab it for pasting into your word processor at will.

To remove a page from the Scrapbook, use the Edit→Clear command.

*Caution:* The Scrapbook understands many kinds of data, but not all. For example, if you paste Word 98 text into the Scrapbook, you lose style-sheet information (but not text-formatting information). The Scrapbook doesn't take kindly to EPS graphics, either.

## Sherlock 2

Sherlock 2, by far the most useful new feature in Mac OS 9, is a glorified Find command. It helps you locate files on your hard drive, words in your files, or Web sites on the Internet. The program is so flexible and powerful, in fact, that it gets a chapter of its own—Chapter 15.

# Stickies

When choosing a computer, many people agonize over which kind to get: Macintosh or Windows. But after spending weeks weighing the pros and cons, considering price and simplicity, software and hardware, service and support, many a soul winds up choosing Macintosh because of this delightful, yet almost microscopic, piece of software: Stickies.

Stickies puts electronic sticky notes onto your screen, in your choice of pastel colors, each with your choice of typeface (see Figure 5-11). To create a new note, choose File→New Note, and then just type the note—a to-do list, brainstorm, Web address you want to visit later, or what have you.

**Figure 5-11:**
*When you click the close box of a sticky note (shown by the cursor at left), the Mac reminds you that you're about to eliminate it forever, and offers you the opportunity to save it as a text file on your desktop. Double-click a title bar to collapse a note into just its top line (right).*

You can make the most of Stickies by getting used to its hidden features:

- Instead of typing into a note, you can also paste text into it. You can also drag text into it, either from a drag-and-drop word processor like SimpleText, AppleWorks, or Word 98, or by dropping the icon of a text-clipping file (see page 138) into a note window.

- To change the typeface of a note, use the Note→Text Style command. (You can't change the font *within* a note, but each note can have its own typeface.) After setting up a color (by using the Color menu), position (by dragging the title bar), and typeface that you like, you can make Stickies memorize the look of this customized note by choosing Edit→Use As Default. Subsequent new notes will match the one you've set up.

---

***Tip:*** Setting a default note size and style is all well and good. But man does not live on yellow Helvetica alone. Wouldn't it be useful to be able to set up, say, five or six different Stickies note styles—one each for Internet information, shopping lists, journal-keeping, and so on?

You can. After adjusting a note's color, font, size, and even starter text (such as "URL To Check Out"), choose File→Close; click Save; turn on "Save as Stationery"; type the name for this Sticky style; click Desktop; and then click Save. You wind up with a special icon on your desktop (which you can move to your  menu). Every time you double-click this icon, you get a new blank note that looks exactly like the one you saved.

---

- A sticky has no scroll bars. To navigate, press the arrow keys to move up and down, or the Home or End keys (or ⌘-up arrow and ⌘-down arrow) to jump to the top and bottom of the note.

- When you choose File→Quit, Stickies asks if you want it to launch automatically every time you turn on the computer. If you say yes, Mac OS 9 places an alias of the Stickies program in your system folder→Startup Items folder, so that your Stickies are waiting and ready on the screen every time the Mac turns on.

- The Zoom box (at the upper-right of the current note) makes the note snap back to its previous size and shape—or, when Option-clicked, makes it collapse into a thin horizontal bar. The resize box (lower right of each note) lets you change the shape and size of the window.

- You can collapse a note so that only its first line is visible in a narrow, floating strip. To do so, Option-click its zoom box, as shown on the right in Figure 5-11. Actually, doing so is even easier if you open the  →Control Panels→Appearance →Options tab and turn on "Double-click title bar to collapse windows." From now on, you can collapse a sticky note just by double-clicking its tiny title bar.

---

**Tip:** If you have a Mac model with programmable function keys, such as the iMac DV, PowerBook, or another USB-equipped model (see page 105), consider assigning Stickies to one of these keys. Because it launches quickly, Stickies then becomes an extremely useful note-taking element in your life; whenever inspiration strikes, you can just slap, say, the F10 key. Your Stickies appear, ready for typing, in less than a second.

---

# Part Two:
# Applications in Mac OS 9

2

# Using Programs in Mac OS 9

W hat *is* an operating system, anyway? When you get right down to it, an OS is nothing more than a home base from which to launch *applications* (software programs). The world is filled with modern, beautifully written operating systems that almost nobody uses because few programs run on them—the Be OS, for example.

Not only do tens of thousands of programs run on the Mac OS, but in these days of 64 or 128-megabyte RAM installations, it's the rare Mac user who doesn't regularly run several programs simultaneously. Just turning on the computer, in fact, launches several programs automatically, including the Finder.

When you run applications simultaneously, however, the road gets bumpy. Now you must become aware of memory management—after all, each program you launch chips away at the finite memory pool available in your machine. You have a screen-management problem, too, because each program occupies its own windows, covering up your desktop and sometimes making it difficult to understand what program you're actually in. Finally, you sometimes have a stability problem. Operating systems like the Mac and Windows 98 maintain a single bubble of memory for all open programs—if one of them crashes or freezes, it can wipe out the entire bubble, usually forcing you to restart the machine.

In the upcoming Mac OS X, every program will open into its own memory bubble, eliminating the stability hassle of multitasking. This chapter provides help with the remaining problems.

# Launching Mac Programs

You can launch (open) a Macintosh program in any of several ways:

• Double-click an application's icon in the Finder.

• Highlight an application icon and then press ⌘-O (the equivalent of the File→ Open command) or ⌘-down arrow.

• Choose a program's name from the  menu, if you've installed it there (see the previous chapter). Or use the submenus of the  menu's Recent Applications or Favorites commands.

• On Mac models with programmable Fkeys (current iMacs, PowerBooks, and iBooks, for example), press the corresponding key. (Chapter 12 has details on assigning applications to your Fkeys.)

---

**Tip:** If you press Option as you open an application icon in the Finder, you automatically close the window that contains the icon. Later, when you quit the program and return to the Finder, you'll find a neat, clean desktop, free of loitering windows.

---

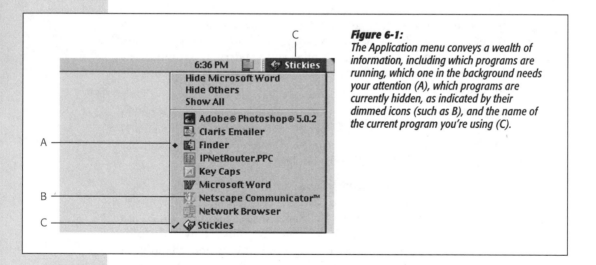

**Figure 6-1:**
The Application menu conveys a wealth of information, including which programs are running, which one in the background needs your attention (A), which programs are currently hidden, as indicated by their dimmed icons (such as B), and the name of the current program you're using (C).

When you launch a program, the Mac reads its computer code, which lies on your hard drive surface, and feeds it quickly into RAM (memory). During this brief interval, any menu-bar menus (File, Edit, and so on) disappear, replaced by a blank white bar that names the program you're opening.

You're free to change your mind about opening the program, by the way, if you do so within about one second of launching it: Just press the keystroke ⌘-period, several times in succession.

If you don't interrupt the launch in this way, however, the program completes its startup sequence. What happens next depends on the program you're using. Most present you with a new, blank, untitled document. Some, such as FileMaker and PowerPoint, welcome you instead with a question: Do you want to open an existing document or create a new one? In AppleWorks, the welcome screen may ask you to specify what *kind* of new document you want to create. And a few oddball programs, such as Photoshop, don't open any window at all when first launched. The appearance of tool palettes is your only evidence that you've opened a program at all.

## Switching Programs: the Application Menu

Mac OS 9 includes an elegant solution to tracking the programs you've opened: the Application menu.

Beginners who read Mac books and articles may be confused by references to the Application menu, since the word Application doesn't actually appear anywhere on the screen. Instead, the Application menu is represented by an icon, as shown in Figure 6-1.

### Switching Programs

The primary purpose of the Application menu is simple: it lists all open programs. Only one—the one with a checkmark beside its name—can be in front, or *active*, at a time.

You can also identify the current program simply by reading its name in the upper-right corner of the screen. (If this strikes you as an unremarkable feature, you probably don't remember the days when the current program's name *didn't* appear on the screen. Many a novice called for help in a panic, unable to find, for example, the Finder's Shut Down or Empty Trash commands—because they had no way of knowing that they were still in, for example, ClarisWorks. Now a glance at the upper-right corner of the screen identifies the currently active program.)

---

*Tip:* If the upper-right corner of your screen shows only the icon, but not the name, of the current program, then one of two things has happened. If you're using a program with lots of menus, such as Microsoft Word, then Mac OS 9 may have run out of menu-bar space to show the actual words *Microsoft Word*. It hides the application name to make more room for Word's own menus.

Second, it's possible that *you* hid the name. The tiny ribbed bar just to the left of the Application menu icon (see Figure 6-1) is a button. Clicking it hides the program's name; clicking again shows the name.

And if you seek some happy medium, you can *drag* this ribbed bar horizontally, revealing only as much of the application name as you want.

---

To make a different program active, you can repeat whatever technique you used to launch the program to begin with: choose its name from the  menu, double-click its icon, press its Fkey, and so on.

Most people, however, switch to a different program by choosing its name from the Application menu. Doing so makes the program, along with any of its open windows and toolbars, pop to the front.

---

*Tip:* You can also bring a different program to the front without using the mouse. Press ⌘-Tab repeatedly to cycle through all open programs, in alphabetical order, until you arrive at the one you want. (Watch the current application's name change at the upper-right corner of your screen as you press ⌘-Tab.)

To move *backward* through the open programs, press *Shift-*⌘-Tab.

---

### Changing the Application-Switching Keystroke

It didn't take long for Apple to hear from power users when the ⌘-Tab keystroke debuted. That same keystroke is already assigned to useful functions in many programs, including Microsoft Word, FileMaker 4, and QuarkXPress. Imagine the dismay of these Mac users who pressed ⌘-Tab to activate some QuarkXPress feature, and instead found themselves jettisoned out of the program entirely!

As it turns out, though, you can substitute a different key combo for the program-switching keystroke. You'll find the mechanism to do so in an unlikely place: the Help menu.

Choose Help→Mac Help. In the search blank at the top of the window, type *switching,* and then click Search. In the list of resulting Help topics, click "Switching between open programs." Scroll to the bottom of the help screen; click the blue underlined words "Help me modify the keyboard shortcuts." Answer Yes to each of the next two questions you're asked; specify the key you want to hold down from the choices you're shown, and then type the letter key you want (or /t for the Tab key). Using this mechanism, for example, you might choose *Control*-Tab, or *Option*-Tab, or ⌘-` (the upper-left key on the keyboard) as your keyboard-switching stroke.

---

## Hiding Programs

Suppose that when you try to save an enormous Photoshop file, an error message tells you that your hard disk is full. Using the Application menu, you could switch to the Finder to make room by discarding files. But you'd quickly discover the difficulty of the task: the Photoshop picture would still be filling your screen, blocking your access to the files you're trying to discard—and covering up the Trash icon itself.

If the open programs on your Mac are like overlapping sheets of paper on a messy desk, then *hiding* a program makes its sheet of paper transparent. In the Photoshop example, you could switch to the Finder and then use the Application menu's Hide Others command (see Figure 6-1), thus making the windows of all *other* programs disappear. When a program is hidden, its icon appears dimmed in the Application menu (see Figure 6-1 again), and all of its windows, tool palettes, and button bars disappear. You can bring them back only by bringing the program to the front again (by choosing its name from the Application menu, or by doing anything you'd do to launch the program, such as double-clicking its icon).

The Application menu also offers a Hide command that applies only to the currently active program ("Hide AppleWorks," for example). But if your aim is to hide only the program you're using at this moment, the Option key provides an easier, faster method. For example:

• Option-click any visible portion of the desktop. The program you were in vanishes.

---

- With the Option key pressed, choose any other program's name from the Application menu. You switch to that program *and* hide the one you were using.

- Option-click another program's tile on the *Application palette,* described in the next section. Once again, you switch programs, hiding the one you were using at the time.

---

**POWER USERS' CLINIC**

## The Best Macro You Can Write

Suppose you're word processing—and now you want to throw away some files, open a program, make a backup, eject a CD, or perform some other housekeeping function. For any of these tasks, you need to get back to the desktop—and hide *all* other programs. Unfortunately, doing so is a cumbersome two-step process on the Mac—switch to Finder, then use the Hide Others command in the Application menu—and no keyboard shortcuts are available. What the Mac OS really needs is a single keystroke that lets you jump to the Finder *and* hide all other programs.

It's easy enough to create an AppleScript to perform this function (see Chapter 10 for AppleScript basics). You can

then assign your AppleScript to a keystroke using a program like QuickPop (available at *www.missingmanual.com*) or, more conveniently, using the programmable Fkey feature of recent iBook, iMac, or PowerBook models, as described at the end of this chapter.

If you use a macro program like QuicKeys (CE Software) or OneClick (Westcode), on the other hand, creating a switch-and-hide macro (and assigning it to a keyboard combination) is easier still.

All of this sounds like a lot of work, but it's well worth the trouble. You'll find yourself using your jump-to-desktop keystroke more often than you can imagine.

---

## The Application Palette

When you're doing a lot of switching between two programs—when writing a report in Word that requires you to refer, once per paragraph, to a graph in Excel, for example—you'll soon discover the dark side of the Application menu. Using the mouse to switch between two programs listed in the Application menu over and over again can drive you quietly mad.

Nor is the ⌘-Tab keystroke practical for this situation. If you're running several other programs, you have to press the keystroke many times in succession to cycle all the way from Excel to Word.

It's for just such cases that Apple created the Application *palette.* To make it appear on your screen, see Figure 6-2.

Once the palette appears, you can jump directly to any of the listed programs with a single click. The tile you click darkens to indicate the newly crowned active program. (As noted earlier, you can *Option*-click to hide the windows of the previous program in the process.)

Because everyone's monitor and eyesight are different, Apple designed this palette to be the single most customizable interface element of Mac OS 9. You can twist, drag, and tweak this palette beyond recognition. For example, you can change its:

• *Position:* Move the palette by dragging either its thin edges or its narrow title bar (which, if the palette is wide enough, says *Applications*). Or just drag anywhere inside the palette while pressing the ⌘ key.

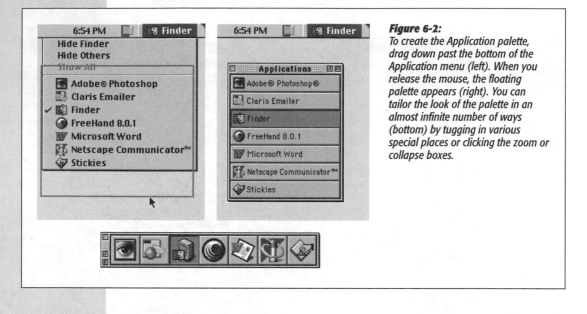

**Figure 6-2:**
*To create the Application palette, drag down past the bottom of the Application menu (left). When you release the mouse, the floating palette appears (right). You can tailor the look of the palette in an almost infinite number of ways (bottom) by tugging in various special places or clicking the zoom or collapse boxes.*

• *Width:* Carefully position your cursor just inside the right border of the palette. When it changes to a double-headed arrow, drag horizontally to make the palette wider or narrower.

• *Identifying labels:* If you'd prefer to see only the icons of your running programs, but not the names, click the zoom box (the second of the three tiny squares in the title bar). The result is a tall, skinny Applications palette that you can drag to the very edge of your monitor, where it's less likely to get in the way of your document windows.

• *Icon size:* Option-click the zoom box to enlarge the icons (and the tiles of the palette itself). Option-click again to restore the original small icons.

• *Orientation:* If you'd prefer a horizontal layout of the palette tiles, Shift-Option-click the zoom box. You can then drag the resulting wide, short bar to the very bottom of the screen, where it resembles the Taskbar in Windows.

• *Anything else:* Using a free program like AppSwitcher Control (available at *www.missingmanual.com*), you can go to preposterous extremes in changing additional characteristics of the palette. Instead of alphabetical order, you can make your icons appear in the order in which they were launched—or reverse order. You can hide the window edges and title bar, making the strip even more compact; specify a default position for the palette; and change the default width for the program names.

## Using the Application Palette for Drag-and-drop

As described on page 107, the Mac is savvy when it comes to the relationship between documents and applications. If you double-click an AppleWorks document icon, for example, the AppleWorks program launches automatically and shows you the document.

But these days, it's occasionally useful to open a document using a program 'other than the one that created it. Perhaps, as is often the case with downloaded Internet graphics, you don't *have* the program that created it, or you don't know which one was used. This technique is also useful when you want to open a Read Me file into your word processor, such as Word, instead of the usual SimpleText program.

In such cases, the application palette is handy: just drag the mystery document onto one of the palette's tiles, as shown in Figure 6-3. Doing so forces the program to open the document (if it can).

**Figure 6-3:**
*To open a document using a program that didn't create it, drag the document icon from the desktop onto the corresponding tile of the Application palette.*

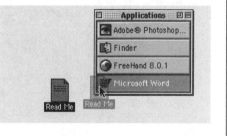

# Launching Applications from the Keyboard

Every Macintosh is born with a row of keys across the top row of the keyboard labeled F1, F2, and so on. In most programs, these *Fkeys,* or *function keys,* do absolutely nothing. The vast majority of Mac users never even touch these keys, having been trained to consider them useless.

But these keys can be fantastically useful. It's true that they generally have no predetermined functions—but that's by design. The keys are provided so that you can define your *own* functions for them, and chief among these uses is launching your favorite programs. You can map F1 to your email program, F2 to Netscape Navigator, F3 to Sherlock, and so on.

Assigning these keys to launch your favorite programs once required a macro program, such as the commercial QuicKeys or OneClick, or the shareware QuickPop. Fortunately, the designers at Apple were recently inspired to build this feature right into the Mac OS. If you have a Macintosh that came with a USB (translucent) keyboard, you can use the Keyboard control panel to assign each Fkey to a different favorite application.

## Opening the Keyboard Control Panel

When you press an Fkey whose function you haven't yet assigned, you get the message that says, in effect, "That key hasn't been assigned; want to set it up?" Click Open. Alternatively, you can choose  →Control Panels→Keyboard; when the Keyboard control panel opens, click Function Keys. Either way, you wind up in the Function Keys dialog box. See Figure 6-4 for instructions in using this dialog box to assign Fkeys to your favorite programs.

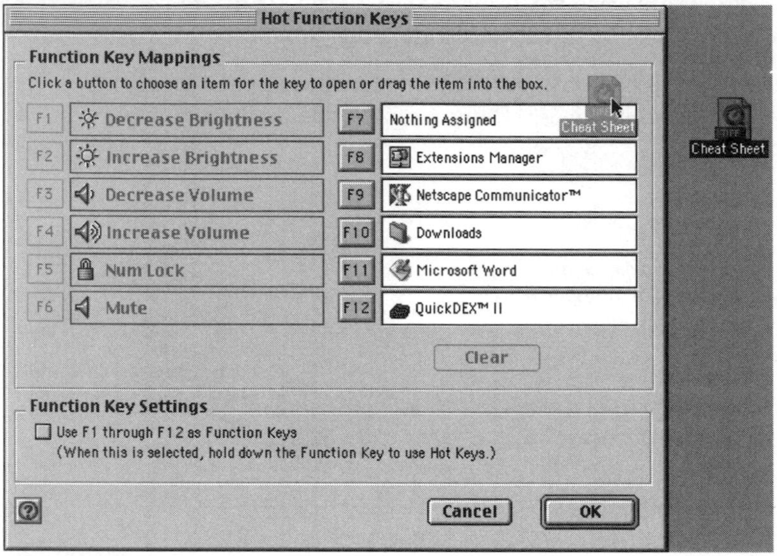

**Figure 6-4:**
*Deep within the Keyboard control panel lies this Fkey-assignment screen. Here, you can map your favorite programs to any of your otherwise unused Fkeys at the top of your keyboard. Do so by dragging the icon of a program directly onto the corresponding Fkey slot, as shown here, or by clicking the button to the left of a slot and then choosing a program from the list of your hard drive contents. (To unassign an Fkey, click its slot and then click Clear, or simply assign a different program to it.)*

You're not limited to assigning programs to your Fkeys, however, you can also assign documents, control panels, servers on the network (by assigning an Fkey to open its alias), and even folders and disks. For most people, however, applications are the most useful targets.

---

***Tip:*** Launching a program isn't the only useful task for which you can use an Fkey. After the program is already running, you can bring it to the front by pressing the same Fkey again.

---

Once you've set up your Fkeys to launch favorite files and programs, your only remaining task is to remember which Fkey launches which program. If you bought an iBook, your iBook accessories included a set of small white stickers expressly for this purpose. (They go above the Fkeys, on the surface of the iBook, not on the keys themselves.) If you have any other Mac model, labeling the Fkeys is left to you; Scotch tape and a felt-tip marker constitute a frequently used arrangement.

# Type and Creator Codes

Every operating system, including Mac OS and Windows, needs a mechanism to associate documents with the applications that created them. When you double-click a Microsoft Word document icon, for example, you want Microsoft Word to launch and open the document. (The ancient operating system known as DOS didn't have such a system. To open a document, you had to *type out* the name of the program you wanted to open!)

In Windows, every document bears a file-name suffix, usually three letters long—if you double-click something called *memo.doc,* it opens in Microsoft Word; if you double-click *memo.wri,* it opens in Microsoft Write; and so on.

The Mac uses a similar system, except that you never see the identifying codes. Mac *creator codes,* as they're known, are invisible. Apple carefully monitors and tracks these four-letter codes in conjunction with the various Mac software companies so that no two codes are alike.

It's possible to live a long and happy life without knowing anything about these codes; indeed, the vast majority of Mac fans have never heard of them. But understanding how to see and change creator codes—and their siblings, *type codes*—can be useful in troubleshooting, keeping your files private, and appreciating how Mac OS 9 works.

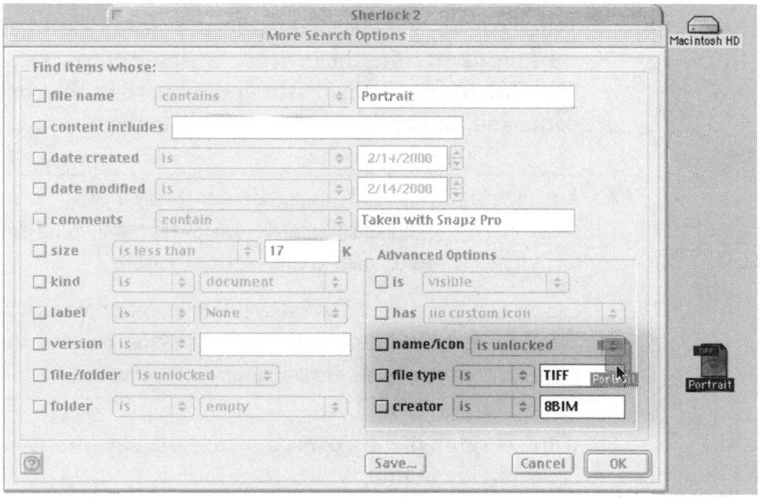

**Figure 6-5:**
*Drag any icon from the desktop directly into the Sherlock More Search Options screen to view the icon's creator code. As a little experimentation will soon show you, the creator code for a program and the documents it creates are identical–MSWD for Microsoft Word, FMP3 for FileMaker Pro, and so on. That's the entire point–the creator code tells Mac OS 9 which program to open when you double-click a document. (Capitalization and spaces count–if you see a creator code that appears to have only three letters, then a space is also part of the code.)*

## Discovering a Program's Creator Code

To see the creator code for a particular file, choose  →Sherlock; click Edit (the button just below the search blank); and then drag the icon in question anywhere onto the Sherlock screen, as shown in Figure 6-5. Sherlock instantly shows you the creator code, among many other statistics.

## The Type Code

When you use the drag-and-drop procedure shown in Figure 6-5, Sherlock also reveals the second four-letter code in the DNA of every Macintosh icon—the *type code*. This code doesn't identify what program created the file; instead, it specifies the document's file format. Photoshop, for example, can create graphics in any of dozens of different formats: GIF, JPEG, TIFF, and so on. If you inspect your Photoshop documents, you'll discover that they all share the same creator code (8BIM)—but have a wide variety of type codes. Same thing with Microsoft Word or AppleWorks: each can create many different kinds of documents, such as plain text files, Rich Text Format files, and so on—but they always bear the creator code of Microsoft Word or AppleWorks.

---

*Tip:* If the type code is supposed to identify the file format of a *document,* does an *application* have a type code?

It does: APPL.

---

## How Type and Creator Codes Work

When you double-click a document, Mac OS 9 studies its creator code. It then consults the *desktop file,* the invisible database of icons and codes described on page 51. This desktop file is the master index that lists the correspondence between creator codes and the applications that generate them.

---

*Tip:* Together, the type and creator codes also specify what *picture* appears on a particular icon. When you see an icon that looks like a plain white piece of paper with a dog-eared corner, the Mac can't find an entry for its type and creator codes in your desktop database.

Usually a blank document icon indicates that the parent program isn't on your Mac. Occasionally, however, it means that your desktop database has become corrupted or confused. Appendix C shows you how to *rebuild* your desktop file, eliminating any such corruption.

---

If the desktop file discovers a match—if, say, you double-clicked a document with creator code BOBO, which corresponds to the AppleWorks entry in your desktop database—then the corresponding program opens the document, which now appears on your screen.

If the desktop file discovers no match, however, the situation is much more interesting. The Mac believes that the program needed to open your document isn't on the hard drive. (This situation happens more often than you might think—graphics or word processing files you download from the Internet, for example, were created on somebody else's computer, perhaps using programs you don't own.)

---

For many years, double-clicking such an orphaned document produced nothing more than an error box—the dreaded "Application not found" message. But in more modern Mac versions, including Mac OS 9, a clever piece of software called File Exchange intervenes. As shown in Figure 6-6, this control panel's purpose is to say: "I couldn't find the program that created this document, but that doesn't mean you can't look at it. Here are the programs on your hard drive that *can* open it. Choose the one you want to use."

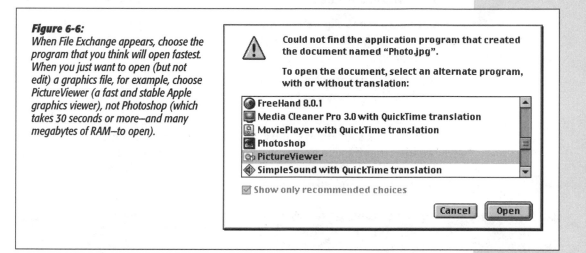

**Figure 6-6:**
*When File Exchange appears, choose the program that you think will open fastest. When you just want to open (but not edit) a graphics file, for example, choose PictureViewer (a fast and stable Apple graphics viewer), not Photoshop (which takes 30 seconds or more—and many megabytes of RAM—to open).*

How does File Exchange work its magic? By studying the *type* code of the icon you double-clicked. File Exchange then compares that type code with the desktop database file, searching for programs that claim to be able to open files of that type.

Here's a common real-world example of the entire process:

1. **You download a picture from the Web.**

   For example, suppose you're in Microsoft Internet Explorer. You hold the mouse button down while pointing to a picture of a body builder, and choose Save Image to Disk from the pop-up menu. You save the graphic file onto your desktop, where it appears as a plain blank icon.

   The plain blank icon tells you immediately that your Mac doesn't recognize the downloaded graphics file's creator code. Translation: You don't have the program that was used to generate it.

2. **You double-click the blank icon on your desktop.**

   You hear the hard drive rustling as File Exchange searches your desktop database for programs that can open the graphics file. (If you've turned off File Exchange, using the Extensions Manager program described in Chapter 12, you get an "application not found" message instead, and the story ends.)

In this example, suppose that the graphics file you saved off the Web is a GIF (graphics interchange format) file, one of the most popular graphics formats used on Web pages. The type code for every GIF file is GIFf.

3. **The File Exchange window opens, showing a list of every program on your hard drive that can open files with type code GIFf.**

Every program on your hard drive, when installed, informed your desktop database what kinds of document it can open. File Exchange consults this listing now.

As you can see in Figure 6-6, you're asked to make a selection from the list of programs. (Tip: To scroll this list, you can type the first letter of the program you want.)

4. **Double-click the program you want to open. The graphics file opens at last, using the program you selected.**

That's *usually* what happens, anyway. In practice, certain characteristics of the file you double-click sometimes confuse either File Exchange or the desktop database. The result is that the File Exchange list sometimes contains programs that cannot, in fact, open the document you double-clicked. (AppleWorks, for example, thinks that it can open almost anything—it sometimes can't.)

---

**POWER USERS' CLINIC**

## Changing Type and Creator Codes

Most Mac fans aren't even aware of type and creator codes. Even fewer know how to *change* them.

Yet changing the type or creator code of a file can occasionally be useful. For example, you can change the codes of a confidential document so that when some unauthorized snooper double-clicks it, only an error message results. You might also decide to change the creator code of some downloaded file (such as a JPEG graphic) so that it opens automatically into a different program (such as Photoshop).

Changing these codes requires a piece of shareware like FileTyper, available at *www.missingmanual.com.* Just drag the

icon in question onto the FileTyper icon. A dialog box like the one shown here appears, into which you can type new type and creator codes.

If you're changing these codes for the sake of security, consider swapping the *case* of the letters of the code—make capital letters lowercase, and vice versa—as a means of confusing your Mac but reminding yourself of the original codes, so that you can restore the file later. (Just be careful not to assign a live, *real* code to your document. When some snooper tries to double-click it, the parent program may try to open it, with crashy results.)

# CHAPTER 7

# Managing Your
# Mac's Memory

I n an ideal world, you would never have to think about how your Mac uses memory (RAM). Apple wouldn't sell computers that run out of memory, and the operating system would be smart enough to assign just the right amount of memory to each program you use.

Unfortunately, Macs in the real world are more complicated. Some Mac models, such as first-generation iMacs and iBooks, came with only 32 MB (megabytes) of memory installed—barely enough to turn on and run a single program. Worse, even on machines with enormous amounts of installed RAM, the occasional "out of memory" message still makes its unwelcome appearance.

When everything is working smoothly, you never need to think about memory. Put another way, this chapter is a glorified troubleshooting course. Fortunately, as you'll soon find out, there's no voodoo involved in understanding memory. A few simple rules govern Mac OS 9's memory usage.

## Where Your Memory Goes

When you turn on the computer, Mac OS 9 itself uses 20 to 30 MB of memory, depending on the Mac model. In other words, before you've launched a single program, over half of the standard original iBook's or iMac's 32 MB of memory is already used up. (That memory is dedicated to all the standard Mac functions, including the Finder program, turning on all the Internet and networking functions, preparing your CD-ROM drive for use, and so on.)

Now you begin to open the programs you'll be using, keeping in mind that each comes pre-assigned with a certain memory appetite: Microsoft Word (9 MB),

Quicken Deluxe (5 MB), a Web browser (4 MB or more), AppleWorks or Palm Desktop (2 MB each), and so on. The total appetites can't exceed the free memory you have left. Clearly, on a 32-MB Mac, Mac OS 9 doesn't leave you much room for opening more than a couple of useful programs.

---

### Memory Facts to Remember

If you're new to computers, you may well be confused by all this discussion of memory, megabytes, and RAM. And no wonder: You probably didn't grow up knowing about RAM, and there's no real-world equivalent.

When your computer is turned off, all of your information is safely stored on the hard drive, the same way the movies on videotapes are preserved even when the TV is off. When you double-click an icon, however, the Mac copies the information contained in that document from the hard drive into its electronic memory—its RAM.

RAM is nothing but circuitry. (It looks like a circuit board about the size of a stick of Juicy Fruit.) When something is in memory (RAM), it's delivered extremely quickly to your Mac's processor (its brain); when you type, for example, the letters appear instantly on the screen. A computer uses RAM (and not the hard drive) to store the contents of what

you're working on for the sake of speed—the hard drive is hundreds of times slower than RAM, much too slow at delivering information to the Mac's processor chip.

But RAM has two drawbacks: it's expensive, and it can hold information only while the computer is turned on. That's why the Mac has both a hard drive (inexpensive and permanent) and RAM (costly and fragile). The hard drive is big enough to hold hundreds of different programs, but most Macs can only run a handful of programs simultaneously before running out of RAM. Most of the time, that's fine—*you* can probably only work on a few things simultaneously, too.

It's important not to confuse RAM with disk space. When you get an "out of memory" message, don't try to solve the problem by putting icons into the Trash. Doing so makes more free *disk space*, but doesn't affect your computer's *memory* at all.

---

Of course, you can always quit one program before using the next, so that your 12 free megabytes are used by only one program at a time. That is, you could launch Microsoft Word, work for a while, and then choose File→Quit before opening your email program. But that quitting business wastes time—each time you launch or quit a program, you must wait for 15 seconds or so. Furthermore, having to quit one program before launching the next makes it much more difficult to copy information between the two programs, or to refer to the information in one program while writing about it in another. Clearly, a Mac runs faster and much more comfortably when this quitting-and-relaunching routine isn't necessary.

Installing more RAM is always an attractive option, especially on Macs with only 32 MB of RAM preinstalled. Today's Mac models are extremely easy to open—you can install one of the little RAM expansion boards just by lifting the keyboard (on iBooks), folding down the side (Power Macs), or pulling out a little drawer (modern iMac models). A typical 64-MB RAM upgrade costs, at this writing, about $100. Before making that extra expenditure, make sure you're maximizing the use of the RAM you already have.

---

## Getting More Mileage from Your Memory

It's easy to see where all your memory is going. In the Finder, choose ⌘→About This Computer. As shown in Figure 7-1, you're shown a graph that reveals a wealth of information about the memory on your machine.

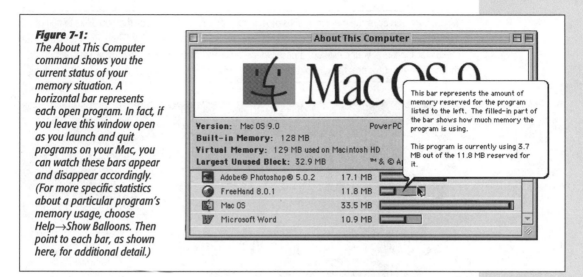

**Figure 7-1:**
*The About This Computer command shows you the current status of your memory situation. A horizontal bar represents each open program. In fact, if you leave this window open as you launch and quit programs on your Mac, you can watch these bars appear and disappear accordingly. (For more specific statistics about a particular program's memory usage, choose Help→Show Balloons. Then point to each bar, as shown here, for additional detail.)*

This Grand Central station for memory statistics includes this information:

- **Version:** This line indicates what version of the Mac operating system you're running—Mac OS 9, Mac OS 9.0.2, or whatever.

- **Built-in Memory:** This critical statistic indicates how much actual RAM is installed in your Mac.

- **Virtual Memory:** As described later in this chapter, *virtual memory* is a special computer trick that fools your Mac into believing that it has more RAM than it does. This line tells you whether or not this feature is turned on, and how much fake memory it's buying you.

- **Largest Unused Block:** You might expect this number to show the total amount of free memory remaining on your Mac. Instead, however, it shows you only a part of that amount—the *largest* unused block. Other, smaller blocks may also be available, which you can use to run programs with smaller memory appetites. (For details, see the sidebar "When To Care about Memory Fragmentation.")

- **Bar Graphs:** These colored memory bars show you, at a glance, which of your open programs are memory hogs. The longer the bar, the more RAM a program is consuming.

Of special interest: the relative size of the blue and gray areas of each bar. The blue portion shows what portion of a program's RAM appetite it's actually using. (It's possible for a program, when launched, to claim more RAM than it needs.)

If you see just a bit of gray at the right end of the memory bar, you're in good shape. If more than half of the bar is gray, however, it's likely that one of your programs has reserved more RAM for itself than necessary. See "Adjusting a Program's Memory Allotment" in the following section.

---

*Tip:* If, upon surveying the memory graphs of your open programs, you decide that you'd like to quit one of them in order to make more memory available, just Control-click its graph bar. Then, from the contextual menu that appears at your cursor tip, choose Open. You've just switched into the program in question. Now choose File→Quit (or press ⌘-Q) to close down the program, thus freeing up the memory it was using.

---

**POWER USERS' CLINIC**

## When To Care about Memory Fragmentation

You can launch a Mac program only if there's enough free memory in one continuous chunk. If you've got 6 MB free, but it's chopped up into several smaller pieces, you may get an "out of memory" message when you try to launch a program that requires less than 6 MB of RAM. (That's why the statistic in Figure 7-1 says "Largest unused block," not "Total Memory Available.")

When your memory is chopped up like this, it's said to be *fragmented.* To defragment your memory, you can either quit all the programs or restart the computer.

So how does memory get fragmented? As you launch programs, they consume successive chunks of memory, like cars parking in sequence along a city curb. Suppose you launch three programs, and then quit the second one. You've just created a little chunk of memory, a hole, in between the two programs that are still running. You've effectively split your free RAM into two different smaller chunks.

Not one person in 100 actually worries about memory fragmentation. Most people never know that it even goes on, because their Macs have so much memory that a little fragmentation is never an issue.

But if, as your day goes on, "Not enough memory to open this program" messages seem to appear more frequently when you try to launch programs, memory fragmentation could be at fault. One possible strategy is to launch programs you plan to use all day—your email and word processor programs, for example—*first,* just after the computer turns on. Launch last the programs that you think you may be quitting and launching again.

## Decreasing Mac OS 9's Memory Appetite

If 18 or 20 MB strikes you as an excessive amount of memory to give up just in the act of turning the computer on, you're not alone. Fortunately, depending on how many Mac OS 9 features you're willing to give up, you can shave about 5 MB from that tab. Although the following exercise might be a lot of work for 5 MB RAM refund, it can be useful in certain occasional situations when you need every shred of memory you can get—and it constitutes an excellent lesson in how the Mac OS works.

As it turns out, almost every memory-eating feature of the Mac OS—the ability to send faxes, play CD-ROMs, use the Internet, and so on—is represented by an icon on your hard drive. You'll find them in your System Folder, in subfolders called Extensions and Control Panels. (Chapter 12 describes each of these items.) Because Apple equips every Macintosh to be ready for every possible feature, your Mac is probably running far more of these extensions and control panels than necessary for your individual purposes.

Fortunately, you can selectively turn them on and off. If you're not connected to an office network, for example, you can turn off almost a dozen of these miniature programs; if you don't do any color printing, you can turn off another six; and so on.

The master switch for the control panels and extensions is Extensions Manager. You open this program by choosing  →Control Panels→Extensions Manager. (You can also open Extensions Manager by pressing the space bar while the computer is starting up.) For details on using Extensions Manager, plus a guide to the various control panels and extensions you can turn off, see Chapter 12.

There are two other ways you can control the amount of memory Mac OS 9 itself consumes: by adjusting the *disk cache,* and by using *virtual memory.* You can read about both of these advanced features later in this chapter.

## Changing a Program's Memory Allotment

Every application comes from the software company with a predetermined memory appetite—an amount of RAM that the program claims for itself when you double-click its icon. In a number of situations, however, you can make your Mac and yourself happier by adjusting this number. For example:

- When you use a program, you get out-of-memory messages. This situation is by far the most frequently encountered Mac-related memory problem. You need to allow the program to use more memory.

- A program behaves slowly or strangely. You might see strange visual anomalies— half of a toolbar floating where it shouldn't be, for example—or maybe you can't get some dialog box to appear. These are classic indications that your program is gasping for RAM.

- When you look at your About This Computer display (see Figure 7-1), you see that a large percentage of the bar is gray instead of blue. In this instance, you might consider giving the program a *smaller* memory appetite, in order to make more memory available to your other programs. (On the other hand, remember that some programs—such as Photoshop—don't use memory at all when no document is open. Check the memory bars, in other words, when you've got a typical document open.)

As you read the following instructions for changing a program's memory allotment, don't feel that you're doing something unauthorized or dangerous. When you allow a program more memory, you may actually be making things right—the marketing departments of modern software companies often pressure their programmers to set a low memory requirement. After all, memory is expensive, and RAM-greedy software decreases sales. By increasing the memory requirement, you may, in fact, be restoring your software to the memory setting it was born to have.

## Step 1: Highlight the Application Icon

To adjust the memory size for a program, highlight its icon. This step frequently throws beginners, because the icon you highlight must meet the following three requirements:

- **You can't adjust the memory appetite for a program that's currently** *running.* Check your Application menu (see page 101). Do you see the name of the program you're adjusting? If so, choose its name, and then choose File→Quit.

- **You can't adjust the memory appetite for a folder.** Most programs sit on your hard drive inside a folder of the same name. For example, your copy of America Online is inside a *folder* called America Online. Be sure you've opened that folder and highlighted the application icon inside it. (The actual America Online icon is triangular.)

- **You can't adjust the memory appetite for an alias.** You can read about aliases on page 37. For now, it's enough to note the typography of an icon's name. Is it italicized? If so, you're looking at the alias of the application, not the application itself. Fortunately, it's easy enough to track down the actual application icon: after highlighting the alias, choose File→Show Original. The Mac instantly opens whatever window contains the original application icon, which shows up highlighted. Now you can proceed with step two.

- **You can't adjust memory in Simple Finder mode.** You can read about this peculiar, stark desktop mode at the end of Chapter 17; but if the File menu doesn't contain a Get Info command *at all,* switch out of Simple Finder mode using the Edit→Preferences command.

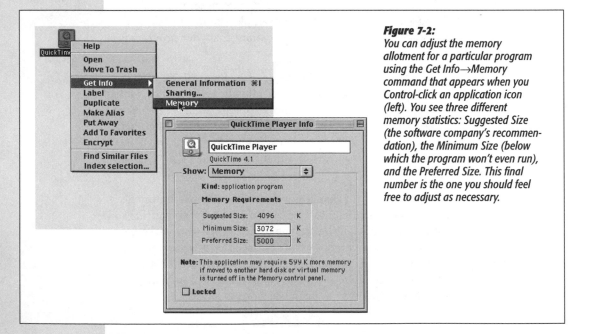

**Figure 7-2:**
*You can adjust the memory allotment for a particular program using the Get Info→Memory command that appears when you Control-click an application icon (left). You see three different memory statistics: Suggested Size (the software company's recommendation), the Minimum Size (below which the program won't even run), and the Preferred Size. This final number is the one you should feel free to adjust as necessary.*

## Step 2: Open the Get Info Memory Panel

Next, open the Get Info/Memory window for the highlighted icon. You can do so by choosing File→Get Info→Memory, or by using the application's contextual menu, as shown in Figure 7-2. (You can also press the keystroke ⌘-I, and then choose Memory from the pop-up menu in the middle of the resulting dialog box.)

Edit the number in the bottom box—the Preferred Size. If you've been having trouble with the program or getting memory error messages, increase this number by 10 percent. (If the problems persist, increase it another 10 percent.) If you'd like to decrease this number, you can do that, too, taking care not to set it below the number shown in the Minimum Size box. In fact, you'd rarely want to set this number below the Suggested Size statistic (see Figure 7-2), unless you're convinced that the program is setting aside much more RAM for itself than necessary for the projects you're doing.

After changing the Preferred Size number, close the Get Info window. The job is done.

---

**Tip:** You're most likely to encounter out-of-memory messages when using graphics-intensive programs like Photoshop, PowerPoint, the AppleWorks graphics modules, and–especially–Web browsers. (Web browsers also run out of RAM because they attempt to run such auxiliary software as Java applications and *plug-ins* that let your Web browser play video, audio, and animations.) When such programs give you trouble, increasing their memory allotments should be your first resort.

---

# Virtual Memory: Trading Speed for RAM

As the beginning of this chapter makes clear, your Mac has two different areas that can hold information: the *hard drive* and the *memory*. But because it's so slow, the hard drive is unsuitable for holding documents and programs while you're working on them.

In the early days of personal computing, however, RAM was astronomically expensive. People whose Macs had limited RAM—which is to say, *all* Mac owners—were willing to sacrifice some speed in order to be able to run more than one program simultaneously. Accordingly, Apple engineers came up with a technical scheme called *virtual memory,* which tricks the Mac OS into treating an area of the hard drive as extra RAM. If your Mac had four megabytes of RAM, but you wanted to launch two 3 MB programs simultaneously, virtual memory was your savior.

## Using Virtual Memory as Extra RAM

To this day, some people use virtual memory for its original intended purpose. If you're running Mac OS 9 on a Mac with only 32 MB of RAM, you can simulate having, say, 40 MB by choosing ⌘→Control Panels→Memory, setting virtual memory to 40, and then restarting the computer (Figure 7-3). The Mac always dedicates all of its available RAM to whichever program is in front, so you probably won't notice any slowdown while working in any one program. When you *switch*

---

from one program to another, however, the Mac must shuffle information from the hard drive into RAM, which makes the switch take longer. It's this sluggishness while switching that gives virtual memory its reputation for slowing down the Mac.

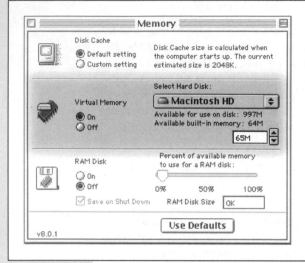

**Figure 7-3:**
*On a 64 MB Mac, virtual memory comes set to 65 MB—in other words, you're only gaining one megabyte of simulated RAM. That's because these days, virtual memory isn't often required for keeping multiple programs open; it's used for its side effect benefits of speed and RAM savings.*

### Using Virtual Memory to Save RAM and Launch Time

Every Mac model sold today comes with at least 64 MB of memory. Few people, in other words, still need to use virtual memory just to keep a couple of programs open at the same time. Yet strangely enough, Apple recommends keeping virtual memory turned on—and turns it on at the factory—no matter how much RAM you have. (See Figure 7-3 for a typical example.)

The reason is extremely technical, but it boils down to this: when virtual memory is turned on, you gain two benefits. First, most programs use up less RAM than when virtual memory is off; the fine print at the bottom of the Get Info screen, as shown in Figure 7-2, tallies the savings for you. Microsoft Word, for example, requires 9 MB of RAM when virtual memory is on, but 13.5 MB when it's off. Second, programs launch faster when virtual memory is on, because not all of their computer code must be copied into RAM from the hard drive.

To gain these benefits, virtual memory must be turned on—but only slightly. As shown in Figure 7-3, if your Mac has plenty of RAM, the best setting for virtual memory is *one megabyte more* than the amount of actual RAM your Mac has.

### The Disk Cache: Trading RAM for Speed

When perusing the Memory control panel (see Figure 7-3), you may have wondered about the first set of controls in that window, called Disk Cache. This is another memory-related feature that Apple sets at the factory, and that you'll rarely need to adjust.

The *disk cache* (pronounced *cash*) is a speed trick. Mac OS 9 sets aside a small amount of your Mac's RAM as a temporary high-speed storage shelf for information your Mac has just used, and is likely to use again shortly. Suppose, for example, that you highlight some text in your word processor and apply the Times font. To find out what this typeface looks like, the Mac must read some information from your hard drive, which takes a full second. Moments later, you highlight another passage of text, and again apply the Times font. This time, the typeface changes instantly, because the letter shapes in the Times font are already in the disk cache. The Mac doesn't have to consult the hard drive a second time.

---

**FREQUENTLY ASKED QUESTION**

## Why is Virtual Memory Set So High?

*Apple recommends that I keep virtual memory turned on—for best speed, though, they say I should only use one megabyte's worth of virtual, hard-disk memory. But in the Memory control panel, I can't set virtual memory to anything close to 1 MB. In fact, 65 is the lowest it will go!*

To keep its virtual memory scheme as fast as possible, Mac OS 9 doesn't reserve only one extra megabyte of space on the hard drive. Instead, it takes up as much space as you have actual RAM, *plus* the amount of additional virtual memory you'd like. Your Mac evidently has 64 megs of RAM, so the least hard drive space you can sacrifice is 65. If your Mac had 128 megs, you'll lose a minimum of 129 megs of hard drive space, and so on.

That's because virtual memory works by transferring information rapidly between actual RAM and the hard drive. It's far faster for the Mac to put down the contents of RAM into precisely corresponding locations on the hard drive than to cram fresh data into a single extra megabyte of disk space. The transfer is faster when the slots for information in RAM and on the hard drive correspond, the same way it's faster for a handbell player to put every handbell exactly back into its original location—in its rack of eight handbells in front of her—after each brief use.

The virtual memory scheme explains another frequently asked question, too: why the sizes of the folders and files on your hard drive never add up to the total amount of disk space your Mac reports as being used. A huge chunk of your hard drive is being used by the invisible virtual memory *swap file*—the space the Mac uses to "set down" its RAM contents when juggling information.

---

*Tip:* The best way to see the disk cache in action is on your desktop. Just after turning on the computer, open a large list-view folder that contains lots of icons—your System Folder, for example. Even on the fastest Mac, it takes a moment or two for all the icons to appear.

Now close the window and open it again. This time, the icons inside appear instantly—because the picture of that open window had already been stored in the disk cache. The disk cache works by speeding up almost anything you do the *second time* you do it (and thereafter—or until more recent information displaces it in the disk cache).

---

Unless you fiddle with the Memory control panel, the Mac reserves about three percent of its RAM for use by the disk cache—one megabyte for every 32 installed in your machine. That's the "Default setting," as identified in the Memory control panel. Part of the 20 MB of memory consumed by Mac OS 9 when you turn on the computer is the RAM dedicated to the disk cache.

If, in desperate times, you need a little more free RAM for running programs, you can click "Custom setting," click Custom in the warning dialog box, and reset the "Size after restart" to a lower number (by clicking the down arrow button). When you restart the computer, the memory that had been reserved for the disk cache is returned to the pot available to your programs—but you may discover that the Mac doesn't run quite as quickly as before.

On the other hand, if your Mac has several thousand gallons of RAM to spare, you might be tempted to increase the disk cache in hopes of speeding up your machine. In fact, you probably won't notice any speedup; there isn't much more the disk cache can store for subsequent use during a given work session. Meanwhile, you're taking away RAM that might have been used by the programs themselves.

## RAM Disk: The Ultimate Speed Trick

For the last several pages, you've been reading about methods of trading RAM for speed. The most radical and often overlooked trick of this kind is the RAM disk—a Mac OS feature that creates the icon of a virtual hard drive on your screen. But this hard drive is made of RAM—and therefore, anything you put on it runs 100 times faster than it would from your hard drive. Here are some of the ways a RAM disk can speed up your life:

- When you surf the Web, you can direct the *cache files* to be stored on the RAM disk. (Cache files are the tiny snippets of graphics and text that compose each Web page you visit, which are normally stored on your hard drive as you surf.) Now each Web page loads more quickly, because the Mac requires less time to store the cache files. And recalling a Web page to the screen (when you click the Back button in your browser, for example) is instantaneous, because those cache files are dished up to your screen 100 times faster. (RAM required: about 5 MB.)

- If you use a particular gigantic program every day, one that normally requires 30 seconds or so to launch, copy it onto the RAM disk. The RAM-based copy opens in a fraction of the time. (RAM required: the size of the program.)

- On some older PowerBooks, you can easily double the amount of working time provided by each battery charge. Doing so entails turning the RAM disk into a startup disk. (Create the smallest System Folder possible, copy it onto the RAM disk, and then use the Startup Disk control panel to designate the RAM disk as the startup disk.) Not only does the computer start up astonishingly fast in such a configuration, but because the hard drive is one of the largest consumers of laptop power, your battery seems to last forever. As a bonus, the computer is utterly silent. (RAM required: 50 MB or more, depending on how much you strip down your System Folder. This trick doesn't work, alas, on current Apple laptop models.)

Before salivating over the potential acceleration a RAM disk can provide, be warned: any space you allot to your RAM disk is subtracted directly from your available memory. If you create a 10-megabyte RAM disk, a 64 MB Mac has only 54 megs left to use for the Mac OS and your programs. The RAM disk is a luxury exclusively for Macs with plenty of RAM.

## Creating a RAM Disk

From the ⌘ menu, choose Control Panels→Memory. Create the RAM disk as shown in Figure 7-4, and then restart the computer.

**Figure 7-4:**
*To create a RAM disk, click the On button (A). Next, drag the slider (B) to the right until the RAM Disk Size (C) is as large as you want your virtual disk to be. On some Mac models, you're also offered the Save on Shut Down checkbox (D). When this option is selected, the Mac backs up the contents of your RAM disk onto the hard drive when you turn off the Mac. When you turn it on again, you'll find your RAM disk magically intact, complete with those files.*

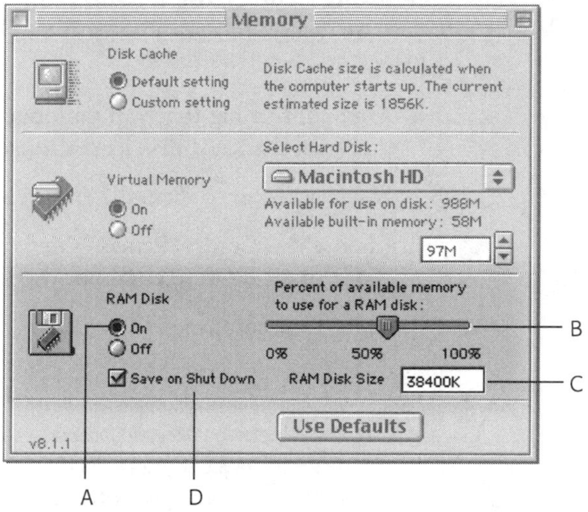

When the machine comes to, you'll find, at the right side of your screen, the icon for what appears to be a brand-new hard drive called RAM Disk. Try dragging an application onto it; you'll be astounded at the copying speed. Then try double-clicking the program you copied onto it. The program launches with freakish speed.

## How Fragile is the RAM Disk?

The RAM disk itself is almost indestructible. You have to go to considerable effort, as described in the next section, to get its icon off your screen.

The *contents* of the RAM disk, however—the files on it—are another story. You can safely restart the computer without losing them. Even if the computer freezes or crashes, the contents of the RAM disk survive as long as you *restart* the computer (by pressing ⌘-Control-power button).

When you *shut down* the computer, however, all the files on the RAM disk are obliterated. (When you use the Shut Down command, the Mac shows you a warning to this effect.)

On the other hand, if you turn on the Save on Shut Down option in the Memory control panel, using the Shut Down command is perfectly safe; the Mac copies your files onto the hard drive before shutting down, and then restores them to the RAM disk the next time you turn the machine on. If you're using a laptop, and your battery runs out of power, you're still okay, because a battery too weak to keep your laptop running still has the juice to preserve the contents of RAM for several weeks.

The greatest threat to the files on your RAM disk, therefore, is the sudden and complete loss of power, as when a blackout cuts electricity to your outlets, or when you deprive your laptop of both its battery and its power cord.

## Deleting or Resizing a RAM Disk

You can resize or delete a RAM disk only when it's completely empty. The steps go like this:

1. **After confirming that you no longer need any of the files on your RAM disk, highlight the RAM disk icon. Choose Special→Erase Disk.**

   You're asked to confirm the erasure. Click Erase, if that's your intention.

2. **Choose  →Control Panels→Memory. Drag the slider to change the RAM disk's slider, or click Off to eliminate the RAM disk.**

3. **Restart the computer.**

---

**Tip:** As with almost any built-in feature of the Mac OS, the shareware world offers a better alternative. AppDisk, available at *www.missingmanual.com*, creates a RAM disk, exactly like the Memory control panel. But you create the RAM disk just by double-clicking the AppDisk icon; you resize the RAM disk just by changing the memory size in AppDisk's Get Info box; and you quit the RAM disk just by choosing File→Quit from the AppDisk menu. No restarting is necessary for any of these tasks. The shareware programs ShrinkWrap (*www.aladdinsys.com*) and Apple's free DiskCopy (*www.apple.com*) aren't quite so straightforward, but also let you create, resize, and quit RAM disks without having to restart the computer.

---

## Using a RAM Disk for Web-Browsing Acceleration

One way to use your RAM disk is simply to copy applications and documents onto it that you'd like to open and save especially quickly. The more popular use, however, is using it to store the cache files that your Web browser generates as you surf the Internet, which speeds up both the appearance of Web pages and their reappearance when you click the Back button in your browser.

For this technique, create a RAM disk of about 5 or 10 MB, depending on the length of your browsing sessions. Once you see the RAM disk icon alive and well at the right side of your screen, proceed like this:

1. **In your Web browser, choose Edit→Preferences. Click the Advanced icon.**

   The next step depends on which Web browser you're using.

2. **In Microsoft Internet Explorer, click Change Location. In Netscape Communicator, click Cache, then Choose.**

   The standard Open File box appears (see Chapter 8).

---

3. **Click the Desktop button. Click your RAM disk icon, and then click the Select button below the list.**

Close the Preferences window. Next time you launch your Web browser, your cache files will collect on the RAM disk, not the hard disk, and you'll feel a noticeable surge in speed—especially on slower Macs using a modem connection.

# The Save and Open Dialog Boxes

The least satisfying moment in using a computer may be the first time you save a newly typed document. You open the File menu, and then you choose Save or Save As. The computer responds by showing you a dialog box, in which you're supposed to type a name for, and specify the file format for, the file you're saving.

To the beginner, these specifications are confusing and unnatural. They bear no resemblance to any real-world process—nobody asks you to name cookies you've just baked, or what file format you'd like them to assume as they come out of the oven.

But it gets worse. In the Save dialog box, you're also asked where on your hard drive you want the new document stored. Filing a document away in a folder *does* have a real-world equivalent; that's why it's so easy to understand the folder icons on the Mac desktop. Unfortunately, compared with the Finder's self-explanatory folder display, the Save dialog box's presentation of your hard drive's contents is about as friendly as a tax form, as Figure 8-1 illustrates.

**Figure 8-1:**
*The Save dialog box, an inevitable part of Mac computing, displays a map of the folders on your hard drive (left). Because it shows you only the contents of one folder at a time, however, it's not nearly as easy to figure out as the desktop itself (right).*

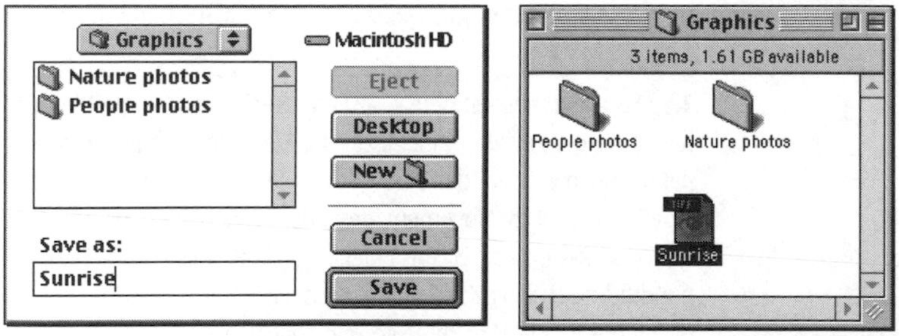

All of these factors conspire to make the Save dialog box—and its sibling, the Open file dialog box—among the most challenging parts of the Mac operating system.

With the dawn of Mac OS 8.5, Apple made a noble attempt to address the deficiencies of these troublesome dialog boxes. It created replacement dialog boxes that behave much more like Finder list-view windows (see Figure 8-4). At first, you didn't see much of these new Open and Save dialog boxes (which Apple calls Navigation Services); Mac programs must be specifically rewritten to take advantage of them. Still, over time, more Mac programs will incorporate these friendlier dialog boxes; this chapter covers both the older and, starting on page 131, the newer Open and Save versions.

# The Save File Dialog Box

To view the Save File dialog box, launch almost any program that has a Save or Export command in the File menu: your word processor, email program, or SimpleText, for example. Type a couple of words, if necessary, and then choose File→Save. The Save dialog box appears.

In essence, this dialog box provides a list of folders on your hard drive. By navigating this list, you can specify exactly where you want to file your newly created document. (For your reference, the names of your *documents* also appear in this list. But since you can't save a document into another document, their names appear dimmed. Only folder names appear black and thus available.)

## Saving Onto the Desktop

If you prefer simplicity to complexity, you can easily avoid confronting the teeming swarms of features presented by this box. Just type a name for the file, click the Desktop button, and then click Save.

Using the Desktop button ensures that your file won't fall accidentally into some deeply nested folder where you'll never see it again (a common occurrence among first-time computer users). Instead, the newly minted document will be waiting for you on the desktop itself—not in any folder at all—when you quit your program or close its window. From there, you can drag it manually into any folder you like.

Novices aren't the only Mac fans who have embraced this foolproof technique. Power users appreciate the fact that a newly created document is one that they're likely to want to open again soon. The desktop, which doesn't require opening any windows at all, is the most exposed and convenient place for such documents.

---

*Tip:* For even more efficiency, you can use the saving-onto-the-desktop method without ever taking your hands off the keyboard, thanks to the Mac's copious keyboard shortcuts. Suppose you've just typed a paragraph in your word processor. Press ⌘-S (the equivalent of File→Save) to open the Save dialog box; type a name for the document; press ⌘-D (the equivalent for the Desktop button); and then press either ⌘-S, the Return key, or the Enter key (all of which are equivalents for the Save button). After several hundred repetitions, this keyboard sequence becomes second nature, reducing the intrusion of the Save dialog box to a fleeting three-second appearance.

---

## Navigating in the Save File Dialog Box

If the saving-onto-the-desktop method doesn't strike your fancy, you can use the Save dialog box's various controls to navigate your way into any folder on your Mac. The difficulty is that the Save dialog box shows the contents of only one folder at a time.

Suppose you've just used the File→Save command. The Save dialog box appears, but you don't recognize the list of folders and files in the list. (It's generally the folder that contains the program or document itself, or the folder in which you last saved a document.) If you click Save now, you'll file your document away inside that random folder, where you may have difficulty locating it again later. In times like these, knowing how to navigate the folders on your hard drive from within this narrow list becomes a crucial skill.

As noted above, clicking the Desktop button (or pressing ⌘-D) is often a wise first step. It takes you immediately to a recognizable landscape: the desktop, where your hard drive, other disks, and Trash appear. From here, you can double-click your hard drive icon to see its contents; then the Applications folder to see *its* contents; and so on. In this way, you can double-click your way into any folder on any disk (see Figure 8-2).

*Figure 8-2:*
*The cursor originally appeared in the "Save this document as:" box at the bottom of the Save File dialog box. But by pressing the Tab key, you highlight the upper list (indicated by the fat black border). At this point, you can navigate the list or highlight an icon by typing the keys on your keyboard. At bottom: the pop-up menu above the list shows where you are in the hierarchy of folders on your hard drive.*

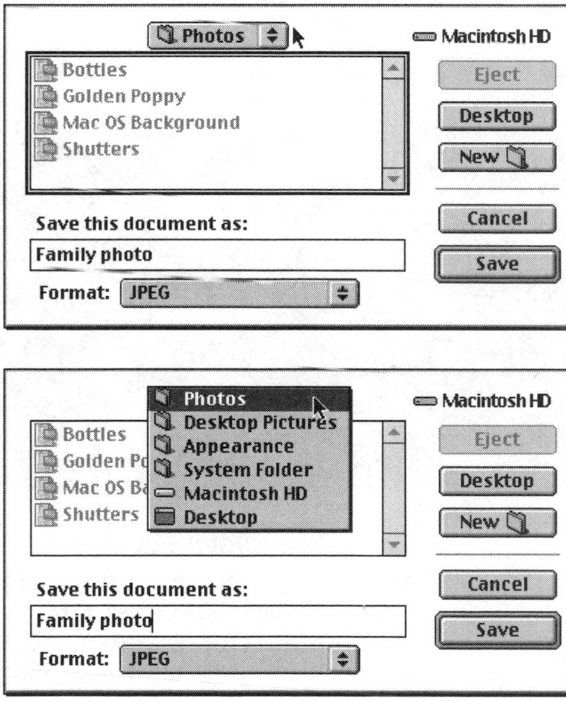

But backing out is more difficult. Once you're viewing the contents of the Applications folder, how do you backtrack so that you're once again viewing the contents of the hard drive? A map is available: it's the pop-up menu at the top of the list (see Figure 8-2, bottom). This pop-up menu strikes many people as confusing, because it shows the path you've taken *upside-down*. The desktop, for example, is always listed at the bottom. The hard drive name appears just above it. As you read *up* the list, you see the names of the various folders you've opened. Choose any disk or folder name in this list to view its contents.

---

**WORKAROUND WORKSHOP**

## Never Lose Another File: the Documents Folder

As this chapter makes clear, one way to avoid accidentally saving new documents into the wrong folders is to click the Desktop button first. That way, all freshly minted documents' icons are born on your desktop, where they're impossible to miss.

But as a more effortless alternative, Apple offers a mechanism called the Documents folder. To turn it on, choose  →Control Panels→General Controls. In the lower-right corner of the resulting dialog box (see page 200), click "Documents folder."

The next time you use the File→Save command, the Save File dialog box will appear as usual—but it shows you the contents of a new folder on your hard drive called Documents. In fact, every time you use the File→Save command—in any program—Mac OS 9 will propose this folder as the new home of whatever document you've just created. You're free, as always, to navigate to some other folder location, but the Documents folder will suggest itself as the new-document receptacle the next time, and every time after that.

What's the benefit? First, you never need to wonder where a particular document got saved—just open your hard drive window and then the Documents folder to find it. Second, it's now very easy to make a backup copy of your important documents, because they're all in a single folder.

Finally, whenever you use the File→Open command from within any program, the Mac once again shows you the contents of the Documents folder. All of your documents are now staring you in the face; you don't have to navigate through hard drive folders to locate the one you want. In other words, not only does the Documents folder save you time when creating a new file, but also when retrieving it.

(If the contents of the Documents folder becomes cluttered, feel free to make sub-folders inside it to hold your various projects.)

---

## Navigating Without the Mouse

When the Save dialog box first appears, the "Save file as:" box is generally highlighted, so that you can type a name for the newly created document. At first glance, then, you might suppose that the Save dialog box isn't set up to be controlled without the mouse—after all, if typing types the name of the new file, how can it control the list of folders?

But in fact, this dialog box is elaborately rigged for keyboard control. The trick is to press the Tab key, which highlights the *list*. (Press it again to highlight the "Save file as:" blank again.) A fat black border outlines the list to indicate that you've now entered keyboard-navigation mode (see Figure 8-2).

Once the list is highlighted, you can type the following keys to navigate:

- Press letter keys to highlight the corresponding folder icons. To highlight the System Folder, for example, you could type SY. (If you type too slowly, your key presses will be interpreted as separate initiatives—highlighting first the Stuff folder and then the Youth folder, for example.)

- Press the Page Up or Page Down keys to scroll the list up or down. Press Home or End to scroll to the top or bottom of the list. (Press the letter A or Z to *highlight* the top or bottom folder in the list.)

- Press the arrow keys (up or down) to highlight successive folders in the list.

- When a folder is highlighted, you can open it by pressing the Return or Enter key (the equivalent of clicking the Open button). You can also press ⌘-O or ⌘-down arrow to open it.

---

*Caution:* Press Return or Enter to open a folder *only* when the list bears the fat black "keyboard navigation" border. If you press Return or Enter when the cursor is in the "Save file as:" blank, you trigger the Save button instead, which could save your half-named or untitled document into some random folder where you'll have trouble finding it again.

---

- Here's the most useful, but hardest to remember tactic: After opening a folder, you can back out of it by pressing ⌘-up arrow. Doing so takes you one step closer to the desktop level. For example, if you're viewing the contents of your System Folder, ⌘-up arrow shows you the list of folders (including the System Folder icon) in the hard drive window. (Clicking the name of your hard drive— at the upper-right corner of the dialog box—performs the same function.)

- Suppose you have several disks attached to your Mac: your hard drive, a Zip drive, a CD-ROM, and so on. You can press ⌘-right arrow or ⌘-left arrow to cycle from disk to disk; the Save File dialog box list changes to reflect the contents of each one.

- You can "click" the Desktop, Eject, New Folder, and Save buttons by pressing ⌘-D, -E, -N, or -S, respectively. To "click" the Cancel button, press the Esc key or ⌘-period.

### The File Format Pop-up Menu

Although it's by no means universal, the Save dialog box in many programs offers a pop-up menu of file formats below the "Save file as:" blank. Use this pop-up menu when you want to prepare a document for use by somebody else—somebody whose computer doesn't have the same software. For example, if you've typed something in AppleWorks, you can generate a document that can be opened by Microsoft Word by choosing the corresponding command from this pop-up menu. If you've used Photoshop to prepare a photograph for use on the Web, this pop-up menu is where you specify JPEG format (the standard Web format for photos), and so on.

## The Open File Dialog Box

The dialog box that appears when you choose File→Open is almost identical to the Save File dialog box—but simpler (see Figure 8-3). Because you encounter it only when you're opening an existing file, this dialog box doesn't have a New Folder button, Save button, "Save file as:" field, and so on. Nor do you have to worry about distinguishing between two areas where you can type. Because there is no "Save file as:" field, any keys you press are for navigation.

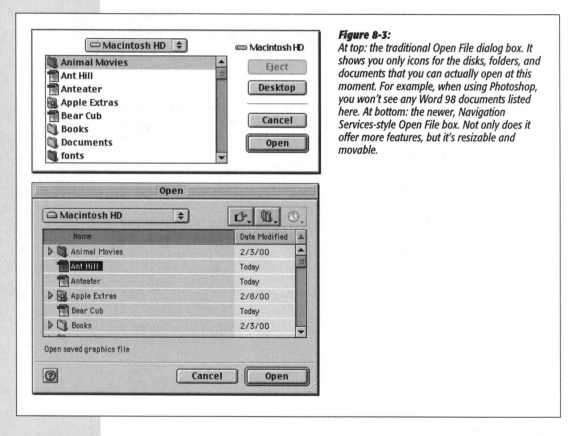

**Figure 8-3:**
At top: the traditional Open File dialog box. It shows you only icons for the disks, folders, and documents that you can actually open at this moment. For example, when using Photoshop, you won't see any Word 98 documents listed here. At bottom: the newer, Navigation Services-style Open File box. Not only does it offer more features, but it's resizable and movable.

Most of the other Save File dialog box controls, however, are equally useful here. Once again, you may find that beginning your navigation with a click on the Desktop button (or by pressing ⌘-D) gives you a useful overview of your Mac when you're beginning to search for a particular file. Once again, you can open a folder or disk by double-clicking its name in the list, or navigate the list by pressing the keystrokes described in the previous section. And once again, you can use the pop-up menu above the list (or the ⌘-up arrow keystroke) to back *out* of a folder that you've opened.

When you've finally located the file you want to open, do so by double-clicking it or by highlighting it (which you can do from the keyboard) and then pressing Return, Enter, or ⌘-O.

In general, most people don't encounter the Open File dialog box nearly as often as they do the Save File dialog box. That's because the Mac offers many more convenient ways to *open* a file—double-clicking its icon in the Finder, choosing its name from the  →Recent Documents command, and so on—but only a single way to *save* a new file.

# Navigation Services

After listening to their customers complain about the Save and Open dialog boxes for over a decade, Apple's designers finally gave these critical Mac OS elements an overhaul. The good news: the new look offers useful new features and feels a good deal more modern.

## Where to find Navigation Services

The bad news: you'll encounter these new boxes only occasionally; the majority of Mac programs still offer the older Open and Save dialog boxes. Only a few software companies have begun rewriting their programs to take advantage of the new versions.

Even in Mac OS 9, only a few programs take advantage of the new look—such as Sherlock 2, Apple System Profiler, and the Appearance, Internet, and File Exchange control panels. All *recent* Apple software, such as AppleWorks 6 and iMovie, capitalize on the new features; but many older programs in Mac OS 9, including Extensions Manager, Stickies, and Palm Desktop, have not yet been updated. Nor have most popular commercial programs—Microsoft Office 98, Adobe Photoshop 5, and the like.

In other words, in redesigning these dialog boxes, Apple intended to make life simpler for its fans, but wound up making it doubly complicated. For the next few years at least, Mac fans must know how to operate *both* kinds of dialog boxes.

## What's New in Navigation Services

It's easy to see the potential in the new dialog boxes, however. By far the most dramatic improvement is that—in the Open box (Figure 8-3)—you see a flippy triangle (also known as *a disclosure triangle*) next to each folder, exactly as in a list view in the Finder. Now, when you want to open a folder within a folder, you don't have to double-click—you can just click this little triangle, as shown in Figures 8-3 and 8-4. The significance is that, for the first time, you can keep your folder-within-folder path in sight at all times when navigating these dialog boxes.

That aid to keeping your place is only the beginning of the new features, however. Also like Finder list-view windows, these dialog boxes let you change the way your files and folders are sorted (see Figure 8-4). You can also move one of these windows (by dragging its title bar), resize it (by dragging the lower-right corner), or even send it to the background (by clicking outside its boundaries or by using the Application menu).

---

**Tip:** When the new Open or Save dialog box is on the screen, you can drag the icon of any folder or disk from your desktop directly into the dialog box list. Mac OS 9 instantly shows you what's in that folder or disk. This shortcut can save you time when you want to save a file into, or open a file from, a deeply nested folder that's already visible in the Finder.

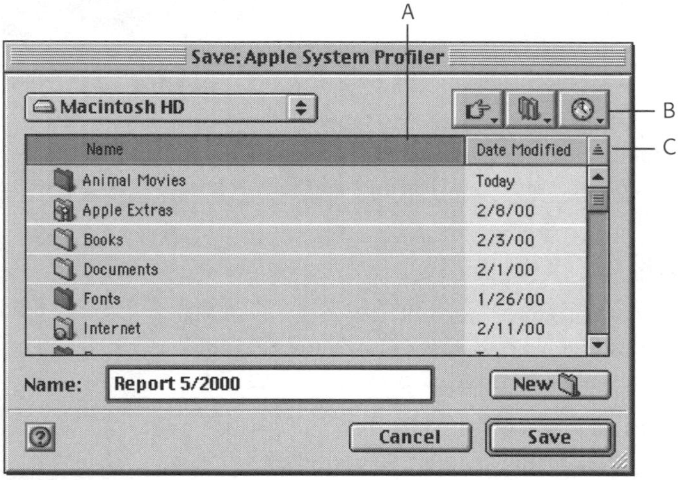

---

*Figure 8-4:*
*A tour of the vastly improved Save File dialog box, circa 2000. (A) Click either Name or Date Modified to sort the list alphabetically or by date. (B) The Shortcuts, Favorites, and Recent Items pop-up menu/ icons. (C) Click this pyramid button to reverse the sorting order (Z to A or oldest first, for example).*

Most of the same keyboard commands described on page 129 also work in these new dialog boxes (including Tab, ⌘-D, ⌘-up and down arrow keys, and so on). The ⌘-right and left arrow keys, however, no longer show you the contents of one disk after another. Instead, in the Open File dialog box, these keystrokes open and close the flippy triangle of a highlighted folder. (In the Save File dialog box, they do nothing.)

The three icons at the upper-right corner of each dialog box are actually pop-up menus (see Figure 8-4). Apple omitted text labels for these menus, leaving you to guess their functions. Here's the cheat sheet:

• The first icon/pop-up menu is called Shortcuts. It lists every disk that's in or connected to your Mac, so that you can immediately see what's on one disk or another. This menu also contains a Desktop command (the equivalent of the Desktop button in the older boxes), a Connect to Server command (for use when you know the exact IP address of a particular Mac on the network), and a Network command, which reveals the icons for any computers connected to yours on the office network (exactly like the Network Browser, described in Chapter 5).

• The second icon/pop-up menu is called Favorites. Its purpose is to list the disks, servers, folders, and other items you use frequently, so that you don't have to go burrowing through your folders every time you want access. (Whatever is listed here also shows up in the Favorites command in your  menu, which is described in Chapter 5; here, however, you see *only* the Favorites that make sense— that is, only documents your program can actually open, for example.)

---

***Tip:*** You can install a new item into this Favorites menu simply by dragging it from the list in this dialog box directly onto the Favorites menu/icon. (You can also do so the obvious way: by highlighting an icon in the list and then choosing Add to Favorites from the Favorites icon/pop-up menu.)

---

• The third pop-up menu, which bears a clock icon, lists the folders, disks, network zones, and network servers you've opened most recently. (You can change the number of items listed by changing the Servers setting in the →Control Panels→Apple Menu Options control panel.) If you haven't, in fact, ever opened a document from within the program you're now using, this icon appears dimmed when using the Open command.

---

**POWER USERS' CLINIC**

## Electronic Stationery

In the lower-right corner of the Save File dialog box—or in the File Format pop-up menu—you may encounter an option called Stationery. When you save a file using this option, you create a uniquely gifted document icon: Whenever you double-click it, Mac OS 9 instantly peels off a perfect, new, untitled *duplicate* of the original file.

By far the most popular use of this feature is to store your letterhead in one of your word-processing documents. Suppose, for example, that you've scanned in your logo and pasted it into the header of an AppleWorks or Word 98 document. You've neatly typed in, and formatted, your return address beneath the logo. And you dearly hope that you won't have to repeat all this work the next time you need to print out a letter on your new "letterhead" paper.

You won't. Choose File→Save, click Desktop, name your document, choose the Stationery file format, and click Save. When you exit your word processor, you'll see the resulting icon on your desktop.

When you double-click it, you *won't* open the original letterhead file, which is now protected. Instead, you'll open a perfect copy of it—but your word processor will treat it as a new, untitled document.

At any time, you can turn your stationery document back into a normal, editable one. Highlight the icon, choose File→Get Info, and turn off the Stationery Pad checkbox. (Using the same method, you can convert an existing document *into* a Stationery document.)

---

# Moving Data

T he original 1984 Mac didn't make jaws drop because of its speed, price, or sleek looks. What amazed people most was the simplicity and elegance of the user interface. At some point in every Apple demo, the presenter copied a graphic drawn in a painting program (MacPaint) and pasted it directly into a word processor (MacWrite), where it appeared nestled between typed paragraphs of text.

We take this example of data exchange for granted today; but in that pre-Windows, pre-Macintosh era, that simple act struck people like a thunderbolt. After all, if this little computer let you copy and paste between different programs, it could probably do anything.

Today, the Mac is even better at helping you move and share your hard won data. Mac OS 9 offers several different ways to move information within a single document, between documents, between different programs, and even between the Mac and Windows computers. This chapter leads you through this broad range of data-exchange mechanisms.

## Moving Data Between Documents

You can't paste a picture into your Web browser, and you can't paste MIDI music information into your word processor. But you can put graphics into your word processor, paste movies into your database, insert text into Photoshop, and combine a surprising variety of seemingly dissimilar kinds of data.

# Cut, Copy, and Paste

The original copy-and-paste procedure of 1984—putting a graphic into a word processor—has come a long way. Most experienced Mac users have learned to trigger the Cut, Copy, and Paste commands from the keyboard, quickly and without even thinking. Here's how the process works in slow motion:

1. **Highlight some material in the document before you.**

   In most cases, this means highlighting some text (by dragging through it) in a word processor, layout program, Web-design program, or even a Web page in your browser. You can also highlight graphics, music, movie, database, and spreadsheet information, depending on the program you're using.

2. **Use the Cut or Copy command.**

   You can trigger these commands in one of three ways. First, you can choose the Cut and Copy commands found in the Edit menu of almost every Mac program. Second, you can press the keyboard shortcuts ⌘-X (for Cut—think of the X as representing a pair of scissors) or ⌘-C (for Copy). Finally, you can press the F2 or F3 keys, respectively (at the top row of your keyboard).

---

***Tip:*** Few people are aware that the first four Mac function keys, F1 through F4, trigger the Undo, Cut, Copy, and Paste commands in the standard program's Edit menu. The order corresponds to the Z, X, C, and V keys on the *bottom* row of your keyboard, which (when combined with the ⌘ key) perform the same four functions.

But on the iBook and recent PowerBook models, the F1 through F4 keys govern screen brightness and speaker volume. The function keys perform their Undo, Cut, Copy, and Paste functions only if you simultaneously press the Fn key at the lower-left corner of the keyboard.

---

   When you do so, the Macintosh memorizes the highlighted material, socking it away on an invisible storage pad called the Clipboard. (If you chose Copy, nothing visible happens. If you chose Cut, the highlighted material disappears from the original document.)

   At this point, most Mac fans take it on faith that the Cut or Copy command actually worked—but if you're in doubt, switch to the Finder, using the Application menu, and then choose Edit→Show Clipboard. The Clipboard window appears, showing whatever you've copied.

3. **Click the cursor to indicate where you want to material to reappear.**

   This may entail switching to a different program, a different document in the same program, or simply a different place in the same document. (Using the Cut and Paste commands within a single document may be these commands' most popular function; it lets you rearrange sentences or paragraphs in your word processor.)

4. **Choose the Paste command.**

Here again, you can do so either from a menu (choose Edit→Paste) or from the keyboard (press ⌘-V, or the F4 key on the top row of your keyboard). The copy of the material you had originally highlighted now appears at your cursor—that is, if you're pasting into a program that can accept that kind of information. (You won't have much luck pasting, say, a paragraph of text into Quicken.)

The most recently cut or copied material remains on your Clipboard even after you paste, making it possible to paste the same blob repeatedly. Such a trick can be useful when, for example, you've designed a business card in your drawing program and want to duplicate it enough times to fill a letter-sized printout. On the other hand, whenever you next copy or cut something, whatever was already on the Clipboard is lost forever.

---

**Tip:** Most people manage to survive the Clipboard's one-item-at-a-time rule. But if you'd prefer a Clipboard that can store an unlimited amount of copied material, consider a shareware alternative like EZNote, available at *www.missingmanual.com.*

---

## Drag-and-Drop

As useful and popular as it is, the Copy/Paste routine doesn't win any awards for speed; after all, it requires four steps. In many cases, you can replace that routine with the far more direct (and enjoyable) drag-and-drop method. Figure 9-1 shows how it works.

**GEM IN THE ROUGH**

### Styled Text

When you copy text from, for example, Word 98, and then paste it into another program, such as the Scrapbook (in your  menu), you may be pleasantly surprised to note that the formatting of that text—bold, italic, your choice of font, size, and color, and so on—appears intact in the Scrapbook. You're witnessing one of the Mac's most useful but under-publicized features: its support for *styled text* on the Clipboard.

Not every program transfers the formatting along with the copied text. (Netscape Communicator, for example, lets you copy only plain, unformatted text.) But most do: Word (and other word processors), Excel, PowerPoint, FileMaker, AppleWorks, SimpleText, Internet Explorer, America Online, FreeHand, Illustrator, and so on.

Every time you paste text copied from one of these programs, the pasted material appears with the same typographical characteristics it had in the original program. Over time, this tiny time-saver spares us years' worth of cumulative re-formatting effort—yet another tiny favor the noble Macintosh does mankind.

Almost every component of Mac OS 9 itself works with the drag-and-drop technique, including the Note Pad, Stickies, Network Browser, Sherlock 2, the Appearance control panel, and the Scrapbook, along with such utilities as SimpleText, QuickTime Player, and Apple System Profiler. Most popular commercial programs offer the drag-and-drop feature, too, including email programs and word processors, Microsoft applications, America Online, and so on.

### When to use drag-and-drop

As shown in Figure 9-1, drag-and-drop is ideal for transferring material between windows or between programs. It's especially useful when you've already copied something valuable to your Clipboard, because drag-and-drop doesn't involve (and doesn't erase) the Clipboard.

ELEMENTS OF LIBRARY TALK

Brief history of electrons
Transition into quantum theory
Surprise Ralph Nader appearance
Pros/cons of quark research
Lunch break
Group discussion

FINAL SEQUENCE

Surprise Ralph Nader appearance
Brief history of electrons
Transition into quantum theory

Group discussion
Pros/cons of quark research

**Figure 9-1:**
*Highlight some material (left). Click in the middle of the highlighted area; drag to another place in the document, into a different window, or into a different application. As your cursor enters the target window, a shaded outline appears inside the window's boundaries—the Mac's way of letting you know that it understands your intention. When you release the mouse, the highlighted material appears in its new location.*

Its most popular use, however, is rearranging the text in a single document. In, say, Word 98 or AppleWorks, you can rearrange entire sections, paragraphs, sentences, or even individual letters, just by dragging them—a terrific editing technique.

---

**Tip:** When you use drag-and-drop to move text within a document, the Mac *moves* the highlighted text, deleting the highlighted material from its original location. If you press Option as you drag, however, you make a *copy* of the highlighted text.

---

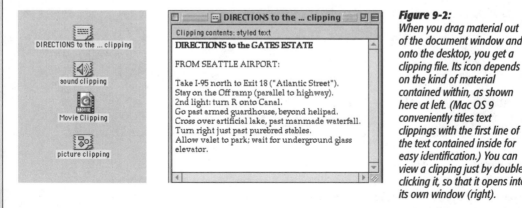

DIRECTIONS to the ... clipping

sound clipping

Movie Clipping

picture clipping

DIRECTIONS to the ... clipping

Clipping contents: styled text

**DIRECTIONS to the GATES ESTATE**

FROM SEATTLE AIRPORT:

Take I-95 north to Exit 18 ("Atlantic Street").
Stay on the Off ramp (parallel to highway).
2nd light: turn R onto Canal.
Go past armed guardhouse, beyond helipad.
Cross over artificial lake, past manmade waterfall.
Turn right just past purebred stables.
Allow valet to park; wait for underground glass
elevator.

**Figure 9-2:**
*When you drag material out of the document window and onto the desktop, you get a clipping file. Its icon depends on the kind of material contained within, as shown here at left. (Mac OS 9 conveniently titles text clippings with the first line of the text contained inside for easy identification.) You can view a clipping just by double-clicking it, so that it opens into its own window (right).*

### *Using drag-and-drop to the desktop*

You can also use drag-and-drop in the one program you use every single day: the Finder itself. As shown in Figure 9-2, you can drag text, graphics, sounds, and even movie clips out of your document windows and directly onto the desktop. There your dragged material becomes an icon—a *clipping file.*

When you drag a clipping from your desktop *back* into an application window, the material in that clipping reappears. Drag-and-drop, in other words, is a convenient and powerful feature; it lets you treat your desktop itself as a giant, computer-wide pasteboard—an area where you can temporarily stash pieces of text or graphics as you work.

---

***Tip:*** When the material you drag to the desktop contains nothing but an Internet address, such as an email address or Web page URL, Mac OS 9 gives it a special icon and a special function: you've created an *Internet location document.* When you double-click one of these, it doesn't show you the text inside, like a normal text clipping; instead, it actually launches your email program, FTP program, or Web browser and fills in the Internet address automatically. You can read more about Internet location files in Chapter 14.

---

## Publish and Subscribe

Here's yet another relative of the Copy and Paste duo: the Publish and Subscribe commands. In this scenario, your pasted material is "live": When you edit the original source material, any copies of it—even if they're in other documents—update themselves to reflect the changes. You might publish-and-subscribe your masthead, for example, so that when you update it, all of your subscribed documents change automatically.

Unfortunately, setting up a Publish/Subscribe relationship requires even more steps than Copy/Paste. Furthermore, not every program offers this feature. As a result, Publish and Subscribe is the Forgotten Feature, used by only a tiny number of Mac fans in very specialized circumstances. With each successive release of new Mac software—including Apple's own AppleWorks 6—these commands continue to disappear from the Edit menus of the world.

If the idea of self-updating pasted material intrigues you, however, here's the procedure:

1. **Create a document in a program that offers Publish and Subscribe features.**

   Some programs that do: Excel, Word, AppleWorks 5, WordPerfect, Photoshop, PageMaker, and FreeHand.

2. **Highlight some text or graphics. Choose Edit→Create Publisher.**

   The wording and placement of this command may vary. In Word 98, for example, it's in the Edit→Publishing submenu; in FreeHand 8, it's in the Edit→Editions submenu.

   Now the Save File dialog box appears, in which you're supposed to type a name for the *Edition file* you're about to create. In other words, the Publish and Subscribe mechanism requires that you generate a document on your hard drive that serves as a temporary holding tank for the stuff you'll be re-using.

3. **Name and save the Edition file. Click Publish (or Save, or OK).**

In most programs, a gray border now appears around the material you've just published, reminding you that other documents will soon be referring to it.

4. **Save the document that contains the published material.**

If you don't, the intermediary Edition file will be orphaned and useless.

5. **Open the destination document. Click to indicate where you want the published material to appear.**

You can open a different program altogether, a different document in the same program, or just a different spot in the original document.

6. **Choose Edit→Subscribe To.**

The exact wording and location of this command, too, may vary by program. Now an Open File dialog box appears; the Edition file you've most recently published is automatically highlighted.

7. **Open the Edition file you want.**

The material in it appears in your document, once again surrounded by a gray, nonprinting outline. Because this text or graphic comes from another document, you can't do much with it—you can't correct a typo, for example. Depending on the program, however, you may be able to change its font or other formatting.

---

***Tip:*** You can subscribe to the same Edition file over and over again in different documents (or even the same document). When original source material changes, all of the "subscriber" documents update automatically.

---

Now the fun begins: you can make changes in the source material and watch the revision appear automatically in any subscribed documents.

8. **Open the original document from Step 1. Edit the published material and then choose File→Save.**

Now return to the destination document. If you had used the automatic-update option (instead of the manual-update option offered in most programs), you'll see that the subscribed material has indeed been magically updated to reflect your edits.

## Export/Import

When it comes to transferring large chunks of information—especially address books, spreadsheet cells, and database records—from one program to another, none of the data-transfer methods described so far in this chapter do the trick. For these purposes, use the Export and Import commands found in the File menu of almost every database, spreadsheet, email, and address-book program.

These Export/Import commands aren't part of Mac OS 9, so the manuals (if any) of the applications in question should be your source for instructions. For now, however, the power and convenience of this feature are worth noting—it means that your four years' worth of collected names and addresses in, say, an old program like Dynodex can find its way into a newer program, such as Palm Desktop, in a matter of minutes.

# Exchanging Data with Windows PCs

It's no surprise that the Mac is great at transferring information among Mac programs. The greater challenge is crossing platforms: transferring files between Macs and Windows computers.

Fortunately, Apple has done a lot of work to make such transfers easy. Documents these days usually take one of three roads between your Mac and a Windows machine: you transfer it on a disk (such as a floppy or Zip disk), over an Ethernet cable (if you're on an office network), or as an attachment to an email message.

## Preparing the Document for Transfer

Without special adapters, you can't plug an American appliance into a European power outlet, play a CD on a cassette deck, or open a Macintosh file in Windows. Before sending a document to a colleague who uses Windows, you must be able to answer "yes" to both of these questions:

- **Is the document in a file format Windows understands?** Most popular programs are sold in both Mac and Windows flavors, and the documents they create are freely interchangeable. For example, documents created by AppleWorks, Word 98, Excel 98, PowerPoint 98, FileMaker, Photoshop, FreeHand, Illustrator, Finale, and many other Mac programs don't need any conversion; the corresponding Windows versions of those programs open such documents with nary a hiccup.

   Files in one of the standard exchange formats don't need conversion, either. These formats include JPEG (the photo format used on Web pages), GIF (the cartoon/logo format used on Web pages), HTML (raw Web page documents before they're posted on the Internet), Rich Text Format (a word processor exchange format that maintains bold, italic, and other formatting), plain text (no formatting at all), QIF (Quicken Interchange Format), MIDI files (for music), and so on.

   But what about documents made by Mac programs that have no Windows equivalents? If you send such documents to your Windows comrades, you'll get nothing in reply except a frustrated mutter. Do your recipients the favor of first saving such documents into one of the formats listed in the previous paragraphs.

   AppleWorks 5 is a good example. (It's available for Windows, but few Windows users outside of the world of education have it.) To prepare an AppleWorks word processor document for transmission to a Windows computer, choose File→Save As; from the File Type pop-up menu, choose WinWord; name this special version of the document; and then click Save. (AppleWorks 6 lacks this option.)

- **Have you added the correct three-letter file name suffix?** As you can read in Chapter 6, every document on your hard drive has a pair of invisible four-letter codes. These codes associate each document with the program that created it.

The corresponding codes in Windows are not invisible, and they're not four letters long; instead, they're generally three-letter suffixes tacked on to the end of your files' names. If you plan to send a document to a Windows user, you must manually add this suffix. Here are some of the most common such codes:

| Kind of document | Suffix | Example |
|---|---|---|
| Microsoft Word | .doc | Letter to Mom.doc |
| Excel | .xls | Profit Projection.xls |
| PowerPoint | .ppt | Slide Show.ppt |
| FileMaker Pro 3, 4 | .fp3 | Recipe file.fp3 |
| JPEG photo | .jpg | Baby Portrait.jpg |
| GIF graphic | .gif | Logo.gif |
| Web page | .htm | Index.htm |

**POWER USERS' CLINIC**

### Bringing Windows Documents to the Mac

When a Windows document arrives on the Mac, it's technically an orphan. Because it was created on Windows, it doesn't have the invisible four-letter type and creator codes (see page 107) that let the Mac know which Mac program should open it. Yes, a Windows document does have a three-letter code at the end of its name. But that code identifies the document only to a Windows PC, not to the Mac OS.

That's where File Exchange comes in. This control panel (⌘→Control Panels→File Exchange) is the go-between that associates each three-letter Windows code with a Mac type and creator code. Thanks to this little control panel, when you double-click the icon of a Windows document, a Mac program launches and opens it. (For details on File Exchange, see Chapter 12.)

### By Disk

Once you've created a document destined for a Windows machine, your next challenge is to get it *onto* that machine. One of the most convenient methods is to put the file on a disk—a floppy disk or Zip disk, for example—which you then hand to the Windows user. (Modern Macs don't have built-in floppy drives, of course, but millions of older Macs do, and any Mac can be equipped with an external, add-on drive.)

In theory, this kind of exchange shouldn't be possible, because Macs and PCs format disks differently. When you insert a Mac floppy disk into a PC, for example, an error message declares it to be unreadable—and Windows offers to "correct" the problem by erasing the disk.

### How the Mac reads Windows disks

Fortunately, although Windows can't read Mac disks, the Mac can read Windows disks. The control panel called File Exchange does the translation automatically; when you insert a Windows-formatted floppy, Zip, Jaz, SuperDisk, or CD into your Mac, its icon shows up on the screen just like a Mac disk (see Figure 9-3). You can drag files to and from this disk (or its window), rename files, delete files, and so on, exactly as though you're working with a Mac disk. (It doesn't operate nearly as quickly as a Mac disk, however.)

*Figure 9-3:*
*The special icon helps you understand why the PC disk seems so slow when inserted into your Mac.*

PC Documents

### Creating a Windows disk on the Mac

You can even *create* a Windows disk on your Macintosh, as long as you're willing to erase it in the process. Click a floppy disk icon, and then choose Special→Erase Disk. In the resulting dialog box, use the pop-up menu to specify "DOS 1.4 MB" format—and then click Erase. After the erasing process is over, you can insert the floppy into both Macs and PCs with equal success.

---

*Tip:* The Special→Erase command can format floppy disks for use in Windows, but not Zip or Jaz disks. To prepare those disks for use on a PC, launch the Iomega Tools program that came with your drive (or better yet, the updated version that may await at *www.iomega.com*). Click the Erase icon and then, in the resulting dialog box, choose DOS from the pop-up menu.

---

## By Network

If you're willing to spend about $125 and a couple of hours in Software Configuration Land, programs like DAVE and PC MacLan let Macs and PCs join the same Ethernet network. From there, it's a simple matter to drag files from one machine's icon to another, exactly as described in Chapter 16.

## By Email Attachment

Among the most popular means of transferring files between Mac and Windows is plain old email. When using Microsoft Outlook Express, for example, you can drag any icon from your desktop directly into the email message window—and the deed is done. The file you dragged will arrive within seconds in the email box of your lucky recipient.

For many people, however, the email-attachment route is fraught with frustration. At times, it seems as though half of all attachment files arrive at the other end in unopenable condition.

In many cases, the problem boils down to the issues described on page 141-142—either you're sending a document that Windows can't open, or you failed to add the three-letter suffix to the file's name. In many other cases, however, the problem is the shrinking and encoding performed by every email program.

---

**FREQUENTLY ASKED QUESTION**

## What Are These Bizarre Files?

Suppose you insert a PC disk into your Mac. When you then insert the disk into a Windows PC, you may be alarmed to discover a handful of files and folders that weren't there when the disk was in the Mac. They have mysterious names like Finder.dat, TheFindByContentFolder, TheVolume-SettingsFolder, Desktop, and OpenFolderListDF. You can throw these files away, if you like, but they reappear every time the disk visits another Macintosh.

Believe it or not, these files populate every *Macintosh* disk, too—but on the Mac, they're invisible. They store information about the size, position, and look of the disk window and its files. The Desktop file, for example, is part of the desktop database described on page 51. In most cases, you can just ignore these files when using the disk on a PC. If you don't plan to reinsert the disk into your Mac, you can throw the files away.

After discarding the mysterious files, there's only one way to prevent them from reappearing upon the disk's next Mac insertion: lock the disk first. (While the disk is in the PC, right-click its icon; click Properties; click Read-Only.) Of course, that means you won't be able to change the contents of the disk when it's in the Mac—but at least you'll deprive the Mac of the chance to spew those invisible files.

---

### File compression and encoding

The technology behind email attachments is somewhat technical, but extremely useful in understanding why some attachments don't make it through the Internet alive.

When you send an email attachment, your email program does two things. First, it may *compress* the attached file so that it takes less time to send and receive.

The second process is more technical. Surprising as it may seem, the Internet cannot, in fact, transmit files—only pure text. Your email program, therefore, takes an additional moment to *encode* your file attachment, converting it into a stream of text gibberish that will be reconstructed by your recipient's email program.

Each of these processes can foul up file attachments.

- **File compression problems:** Most Mac email programs compress outgoing files using the StuffIt method—but Windows recipients can't open StuffIt files. When sending files to Windows computers, therefore, you can turn off the StuffIt compression option in your email program. (Alternatively, you can bid your recipient to download StuffIt Expander for Windows, available at *www.aladdinsys.com,* which can indeed open StuffIt attachments. But unless your correspondent is related to you by blood, don't expect a warm reception to this suggestion.)

America Online is a particular problem. When you attach multiple files to a single email message, AOL uses StuffIt compression automatically—and you can't override this behavior. When sending files to Windows friends from AOL, therefore, attach only a single file per email message.

- **File encoding problems:** Most email programs offer a choice of encoding schemes, which bear such unfriendly names as Base64, uuencode, and AppleDouble. (Consult the Help command of your email program to find out how to set these preferences.) If you have a choice in your particular email program, use AppleDouble. File attachments encoded using this method arrive intact on both Mac and Windows machines.

### Problems receiving Windows files

When your Mac receives Windows files by email, the problems aren't so severe. Most of the time, your email program decompresses and decodes file attachments automatically. When it doesn't, you can drag the downloaded file onto the icon of the free utility program StuffIt Expander (which is on the hard drive of every recent Mac, in a folder called Internet). StuffIt Expander can convert almost any Internet file in existence back into human form.

It's worth noting once again, however, that not every file that came from Windows *can* be opened on a Macintosh, and vice versa. A file whose name ends in *.exe,* for example, is a double-clickable Windows application, which doesn't run on the Mac (at least, not unless you've gone to the expense and trouble of installing a Windows emulator program like VirtualPC or SoftWindows). See the list on page 142 for some examples of files that transfer well from Windows to Mac and don't need converters or adapters of any kind.

# An Introduction to AppleScript

Ask a crowd of Mac users how many use AppleScript, and only a few hands are likely to go up. After all, AppleScript is a *programming language;* everyone knows that it takes years to learn how to write computer code.

But even if you're not aware of it, you use AppleScript all the time—or, more specifically, you use the software-to-software messages that AppleScript generates, which are called *Apple events.* Behind the scenes, numerous components of your Mac communicate with one another by sending Apple-event messages. When you click the Show Original button for an alias, or use the Get Info command in Sherlock, or click any icon on your Launcher, it's an Apple event that tells the Finder how to respond. Using AppleScript, you can send your own Apple events to your software.

That hypothetical survey of random Mac users is still revealing, however; it's true that very few Mac users write their *own* AppleScript programs. That's too bad, because as programming languages go, AppleScript is easy to understand. For example, here's a fragment of actual AppleScript "code":

```
open the file "Energy Saver" of the folder "Control Panels" of
the folder "System Folder" of the startup disk
```

You probably don't need a manual to tell you what this miniature program does. It opens the Energy Saver control panel (which is in your Control Panels folder, in the System Folder of your hard drive).

You can think of the AppleScript programs you write (which are often called *scripts)* as automated software robots. A simple AppleScript might perform some simple daily task for you: backing up your Documents folder before shutting down the Mac, for example.

A more complex script can be pages long; in professional printing and publishing, where AppleScript enjoys its greatest popularity, a script might connect to a photographer's hard drive elsewhere on the Internet, download a photo from a pre-determined folder, color-correct it in Photoshop, import it into a specified page-layout document, print a proof copy, and send a notification email to the editor—automatically. A real-world example is similar: At TV Guide, AppleScripts auto-matically download, print, and convert (to TV Guide's preferred graphics format) 600 advertiser-submitted ad graphics a day, unattended. Clearly, in a business where hundreds of documents must be processed in tediously repetitive ways, a software slave like AppleScript is well worth the time it takes to master.

In Mac OS 9, AppleScript has been enhanced and expanded. The new features include the ability of a script to communicate with another Mac on the Internet. Other new features include:

- **Scriptable speech recognition.** A new program called Speech Listener lets you create scripts that listen for specific phrases, and even respond.

- **Sherlock control.** New commands in the AppleScript language let you manipu-late the Sherlock search program—to specify a particular "channel" of Internet sites you want to search, for example—by script.

- **A more scriptable Apple System Profiler.** As you can read in Chapter 5, Apple System Profiler is the program that lets troubleshooters and help-desk staffers figure out your Mac's configuration. Now such people can find out the specs of your Mac over a network, using AppleScript.

- **A scriptable Memory control panel.** An AppleScript can turn virtual memory on or off, set up a RAM disk, or perform other manipulations of the Memory con-trol panel.

## Recording in "Watch-Me" Mode

If you have no interest in learning to program, you're forgiven; you're not alone. But almost every Mac user can benefit by understanding what AppleScript can do, why it's important in certain industries, and how it may be useful in special situations. Even skimming this chapter will give you an appreciation of AppleScript's power—and yet another reason to relish being a Mac user: Windows has no equivalent of AppleScript.

You can, if you wish, create a script by typing out the computer commands one at a time, just as computer programmers do the world over. Details on this process later in the chapter.

But if the task you want it to handle isn't especially complex, and involves only the Finder, you can create a script just by doing the job manually—using menu com-mands, dragging icons, opening windows, and so on—as AppleScript watches. As you do so, AppleScript can type out its *own* instructions, building the script as you work.

## A Simple Auto-Recorded Script

Try this experiment, for example. It's a script that creates a brightly colored, can't-miss-it folder into which you can stuff your newly created documents each day for backup:

1. **Open Script Editor.**

   Script Editor, the heart of the AppleScript suite, is in your Apple Extras→AppleScript folder. It looks like Figure 10-1 (except that the window appears empty when it first opens). If you don't see an open window like the one illustrated, choose File→New Script.

***Figure 10-1:***
*The Script Editor in action. Type a short description into the top window, if you like—or eliminate the top window by collapsing the "flippy triangle" button beside it. This script appears already formatted with boldface and indents because it was created using "watch-me" mode.*

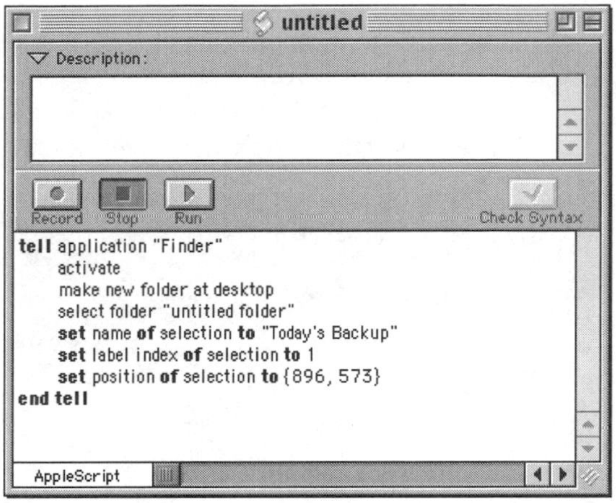
untitled
Description:
Record
Stop
Run
Check Syntax
tell application "Finder"
activate
make new folder at desktop
select folder "untitled folder"
set name of selection to "Today's Backup"
set label index of selection to 1
set position of selection to {896, 573}
end tell
AppleScript

2. **Click Record.**

   Script Editor is about to write out the AppleScript translation of each mouse movement, click, and menu command you perform from now on. In this experiment, you'll create a new folder, name it, label it, and then move it to a convenient position on the desktop.

3. **Click your desktop. Choose File→New Folder. Type *Today's Backup* and then press Return.**

   You've just made a new folder on your desktop. If you sneak a peek at your Script Editor window, you'll see that it has begun to notate the computer commands that represent what you've done so far. In the next section, you'll find out how to interpret these commands.

   So that you can't miss it when it's time to back up your work for the day, apply a label to your new folder:

4. **Choose File→Label→Essential (or whichever label you prefer).**

   Finally, you should move this backup folder away from your hard drive, where it's too easy to get lost:

5. **Drag the Today's Backup folder to a new position on the screen—just above the Trash, for example.**

   That's all this modest AppleScript will do: Create a new folder, name and label it, and then drag it to a new spot.

6. **Click in the Script Editor window, and then click Stop.**

   Your newly created script is complete, as shown in Figure 10-1.

To try out this masterful automation sequence, click your desktop and then throw away the Today's Backup folder, so that you can start fresh. Once again, return to Script Editor—but this time, click Run.

In rapid, ghost-driven sequence, you'll see AppleScript create *another* Today's Backup folder, label it with a color, and drag it to precisely the spot on the screen where you dragged the first one by hand—all in a fraction of a second. The script you've created isn't the world's most useful, but it illustrates how powerful and fast AppleScript can be.

---

**FREQUENTLY ASKED QUESTION**

## Boldface Words in Scripts

*Why does Script Editor put random words in bold type?*

They're not actually random.

Consider this: In spoken English, some words always arrive together in the same sentence. For example, you can't use the word *put* in a sentence without also specifying *where;* and when you say the word *if,* you'll also need to say (or imply) the word *then.*

The same phenomenon occurs in AppleScript. Some AppleScript commands require pairs or trios of related words to appear together. The boldface simply helps you match them up; it serves as a visual aid in making sure you've included all pieces of a particular command.

For example, every AppleScript begins with the *tell* command,

which gets the attention of the program you're about to control—and ends with the *end tell* command, which tells that program that it can stop paying attention. These commands always appear in bold type, because they belong to each other. (If you see one or the other when it's *not* in bold, then you've forgotten to insert the matching component. The boldface only appears when everything's *correctly* matched.)

Similarly, the *set* command in the sample script you recorded in this section must be accompanied by an *of* term (which tells the script *what* to manipulate) and a *to* term (which tells the script *how* to manipulate it). All three terms are bolded, as in "set name of selection to 'Today's Backup.'"

Commands that don't require multiple pieces, on the other hand, such as *select,* don't appear in bold.

---

## Understanding AppleScript Commands

Eventually, you'll discover that scripts you create in "watch-me" mode are fairly limited. Very few programs other than the Finder are "recordable" (let you create scripts by performing tasks manually), and the scripts you create this way aren't very intelligent. If your AppleScript ambition extends beyond creating folders and dragging them around, you'll eventually have to learn to type out AppleScript codes of your own.

As a first step in understanding the AppleScript language, study the codes written by Script Editor in the previous example. As it turns out, much of this script consists of standard AppleScript jargon that appears in *every* script. The little folder-creating script you just made includes these commands:

```
tell application "Finder"
   activate
   make new folder at desktop
   select folder "untitled folder"
   set name of selection to "Today's Backup"
   set label index of selection to 1
   set position of selection to {896, 573}
end tell
```

Here's a line-by-line analysis of what they do:

### tell application "Finder"

Every script begins with a line like this. It specifies which Mac program is about to be controlled by your script. It brings that program to attention.

Complex scripts can span *several* programs—grabbing information from FileMaker and pasting it into PageMaker, for example. In those longer scripts, you'd see "tell application 'FileMaker Pro'" at the beginning of the steps that involve the first program, and then "tell application 'PageMaker'" later in the script, where the steps pertain to PageMaker.

### activate

This command means, "Bring the abovementioned program to the front." Technically, you don't have to make the Finder the active program to perform the simple folder-creation steps in this script—AppleScript could create, name, label, and move your Today's Backup folder even while the Finder is in the background. But Script Editor inserted this step automatically because, when it recorded your actions, *you* made the Finder the active program (by clicking the desktop). You're welcome to delete this step from your Script Editor window.

(This is only the first of many examples you'll find in which Script Editor records wordier scripts than necessary. Hand-typed scripts, like those described later in this chapter, are often more compact and faster in execution.)

### make new folder at desktop

The beauty of AppleScript is that it's a lot like English. This command, of course, tells the Finder to create a new folder at the desktop level. If you had made the new folder in your hard drive window, this command would say, "make new folder at startup disk," and so on.

### select folder "untitled folder"
### set name of selection to "Today's Backup"

These steps highlight the new folder, making it the selected item ("the selection")— and then change its name. Note that Script Editor leaves out words like "the," but if

---

inserting such articles would make AppleScript easier for you to understand, you're welcome to use them. You could have written, for example, "Select *the* folder 'untitled folder'; set *the* name of *the* selection to 'Today's Backup.'" The script would work equally well.

### set label index of selection to 1

The *label index* just means the *label*, as it appears in your File→Label menu. The Mac doesn't refer to these labels as Essential, Hot, In Progress, and so on, because you might change these labels at a later time. Instead, it refers to them by number, 1 through 7, as they're listed in the File→Label menu.

If you wanted your script to apply the second label ("Hot," for example) to your icon instead, you could change the 1 in your script to a 2 (or some other number under 8).

### set position of selection to {896, 573}

This is the script step that actually moves your icon to the specified position. The numbers represent coordinates as measured in pixels (screen dots) from the upper-left corner of your screen (vertically and horizontally, respectively). If the coordinates were {0, 0}, your icon would jump into the upper-left corner of the screen; if they were {0, 800}, it would jump to the upper-right corner, and so on. (Don't move an icon beyond your monitor's edges, as indicated by the resolution number in your Monitors control panel—you'll make it jump clear off the desktop into oblivion!) The icon's position is measured from its own upper-left corner.

---

***Tip:*** On some lazy Sunday afternoon, try this: In Script Editor, click Record. Now return to your desktop and drag the hard drive around the screen—over and over again, to a new position each time, perhaps 12 or 15 moves. Return to Script Editor, click Stop, and then Run. You'll see AppleScript duplicate your moves, so that the hard drive icon appears to jump all over the monitor, rabbit-like—much to the bewilderment of any onlookers.

---

### end tell

This command tells the Finder that it can stop paying attention to AppleScript, which is finished having its way. "End tell" always accompanies the "tell" command that begins a script; they form the bookends that delineate the instructions to the program in question. (AppleScripters call the entire chunk, beginning with "tell" and ending with "end tell," a *tell block.*)

---

***Tip:*** You can change the fonts and formatting Script Editor uses to write out your scripts. Choose Edit→AppleScript Formatting, click a category of formatting, and then use Script Editor's Font and Style menus to choose new type specs.

---

## Another "Watch-Me" Example: Labeling a Clean System Folder

The "Today's Backup" script is high on instructional value, but low on utility. If you want to save it for future use, by all means choose File→Save (and see "Saving a Script" in the next section). Otherwise, just close its window without saving.

---

Here's a slightly more practical example. As Appendix B makes clear, one of the smartest steps you can take after installing a new, fresh System Folder is *labeling* all of its icons. That way, when you're having to troubleshoot a month later, a quick glance will help you identify the suspect components—they'll be the only extensions, control panels, and other elements that *aren't* orange (or whatever label color you used).

This script performs the labeling automatically.

1. **In Script Editor, choose File→New Script, and then click Record.**

   As before, you're about to perform the steps manually as Script Editor writes the script for you.

2. **Click your desktop. Open your hard drive, and then open your System Folder. Open the Control Panels folder.**

   The files that can cause instability and crashes on your Mac are housed in the Control Panels, Extensions, Preferences, and Fonts folders. These are the folders whose contents you're about to flag with a colored label.

3. **Choose Edit→Select All, and then choose File→Label→Essential. Close the window.**

   You've just applied a colored label to all of the icons in the Control Panels folder.

   Of course, you can use any of the provided labels instead of "Essential," or you can (later) use the Edit→Preferences command to rename "Essential" to, for example, "Clean Install Labels."

4. **Open the Extensions folder, and then repeat step 3. Open the Fonts folder; repeat step 3. Open Preferences; repeat step 3.**

   All of the Apple-authorized, factory-installed icons in the Control Panels, Extensions, Fonts, and Preferences folders are now colored with that label.

5. **Close all windows. Click the Script Editor window, and click Stop.**

   Your script is finished. If you click Run, you'll see your script fly into action; of course, you'll see it apply the same color to the already-colored icons, so the effect isn't terrifically spectacular. (To make it more impressive, edit the script. Change every occurrence of "label index 1" to "label index 2," for example, so that the script applies a *different* label color in each of the affected folders.)

To preserve this script for future use, read on.

## Saving a Script

Before you save a script, let Script Editor check its *syntax*—in other words, check for programming errors. Do that by clicking the Check Syntax button at the right side of the window.

*Note:* The Check Syntax button won't find any errors if you created a script using the "watch-me" system; after all, Script Editor itself wrote the script, so of *course* it's perfect. But when you begin to write scripts by hand, as described later in this chapter, the Check Syntax button will become a useful tool.

If Script Editor finds your script to be correctly written, you'll get no reaction from Script Editor except to see your script formatted, as shown in Figure 10-2.

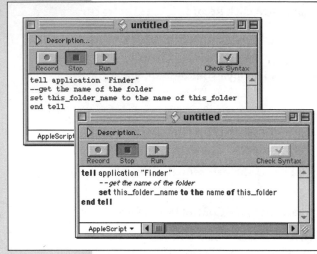

**Figure 10-2:**
*If you type an AppleScript manually, it appears just as it would in a word processor (top left), with no special formatting. After you've clicked the Check Syntax button, however, and have been given Script Editor's seal of approval, the tell block is indented, and certain commands are set in bold or italic type (lower right).*

At this point, you're ready to save your script. You start as you would in any Mac program, by choosing File→Save. The Save Script As dialog box appears (using the look and features of Navigation Services, described on page 131). Name your script and choose a location for it, by all means—but the important step to take here is to choose a *format* for your completed script (see Figure 10-3). Your choices are:

- **Text.** This option is useful only for studying purposes. It can't actually run like a normal script.

- **Compiled script.** This option is useful primarily if you plan to let another *program* run your finished script. Outlook Express, Claris Emailer, and Palm Desktop, among other programs, are known as *attachable* programs: they have an AppleScript menu, which you can populate with scripts of your own. A compiled script is not double-clickable, like a Classic applet (described next).

- **Classic applet.** Choose this option if you want to create a stand-alone, double-clickable, application-like script. This kind of self-running script is, for most people, by far the most attractive option. You can put the resulting script into your  menu, for example, so that you can trigger it whenever you like, just by choosing its name. Or you can put the finished script into, say, your Startup Items folder to run automatically at startup (to play a welcome movie, for cxample). Many people create a script that backs up their Documents folders—and they store this script in the System Folder→Shutdown Items folder, so that it runs automatically when they shut down the machine.

When you choose this option, you're offered two additional checkboxes. If you choose Stay Open, the "applet" you've created remains running after it's launched. You'd use this setting when creating very complex scripts that remain open in order to process commands from *other* scripts.

The other checkbox here is Never Show Startup Screen. In general, you'll want this option turned on; see Figure 10-3 to see what happens if you turn it off.

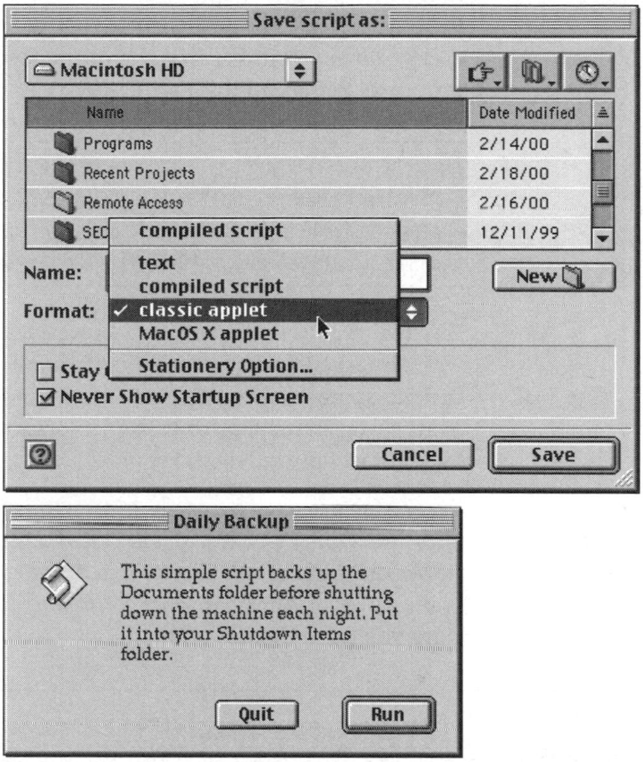

*Figure 10-3:*
*When you save a script, use the Format pop-up menu (top) to specify its format, which will have a lot to do with determining how useful your script is. (Use one of the Applet choices to create a double-clickable application.) If you turn off Never Show Startup Screen, then whatever description you provided for your script appears whenever the script runs (bottom). You, or whoever is using your script, must click either Run or Quit after reading the welcome message.*

- **Mac OS X applet.** Creates a double-clickable, self-running script that can run on Macs that have Mac OS X *or* Mac OS 9 with the extension called Carbon Lib installed. (You're offered the same two checkboxes described in the previous paragraphs.)

- **Stationery Options.** If you plan to create several scripts, all variations of a single script, choose this command and click Stationery. Thereafter, opening your script will create a new, untitled duplicate of the one you're saving now. (For more on Stationery, see page 133.)

# Writing Commands by Hand

Using the "watch-me" mode described so far in this chapter, you can create only very simple scripts. You can unleash the real power and utility of AppleScript only by typing out the script steps one by one, testing your work, debugging it, reworking it, and so on.

## Scriptable Programs

Most of the introductory articles you'll read about AppleScript, and the examples provided so far in this chapter, discuss scripts that perform useful tasks *in the Finder*—that is, scripts that manipulate your files, folders, disks, and so on. That's because the Finder is an extraordinarily *scriptable* program: AppleScript can control almost every element of it. It's also one of the few *recordable* programs—that is, applications that let Script Editor write scripts automatically in "watch-me" mode.

---

*Tip:* Other Mac OS 9 programs and control panels that you can control with AppleScript scripts are Sherlock, File Sharing, Remote Access, Web Sharing, the application switcher, the Help Viewer, Location Manager, Appearance, Apple Menu Options, File Exchange, the Keyboard control panel, Apple System Profiler, ColorSync, Mouse, Memory, and the Desktop Printing software (including the LaserWriter 8 printer driver).

---

The real beauty of AppleScript, however, is that it can control and communicate with almost every popular Mac program: FileMaker, AppleWorks, Microsoft applications, some Adobe programs, and so on. Because of this convenient AppleScript feature, you can create, for example, a script that transfers selected messages in Outlook Express into a FileMaker database for permanent archiving.

Every Mac program on earth understands four AppleScript commands: Open Application, Quit, Print, and Open Document. (These four commands constitute what AppleScript gurus call the Required Suite of commands.) Every *decent* Mac program, however, offers far more commands, thus tailoring AppleScript to the kind of work you do in that program.

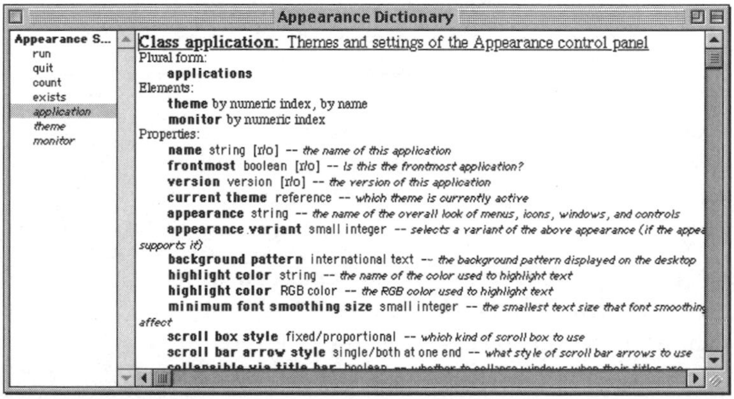

*Figure 10-4:*
*The Dictionary for a program lists the Apple events it understands. If you click one of the commands on the left side of the window, you see an explanation of how to use it on the right side of the window. Unfortunately, you don't get any examples; it's up to you to try each of the commands to see what it does and how it works.*

But before you can write a script that manipulates, say, Palm Desktop, you need to learn which commands Palm Desktop can understand. To do that, open Script Editor. Choose File→Open Dictionary. (The list of AppleScript commands a program understands is called its *dictionary.*) Navigate to, and then double-click, the Palm Desktop application icon. You'll be shown an impressive split window that lists every AppleScript command (every Apple event) Palm Desktop can respond to (see Figure 10-4).

---

***Tip:*** You can also open a dictionary by dragging a program's icon onto the Script Editor icon.

---

That's not to say, of course, that these commands make much sense to someone who's never written a computer program before; these commands, and scripts that incorporate them, still require study and experimentation. But a glance at a program's AppleScript Dictionary is a good way to assess its scriptability—and therefore how much the software company has embraced the Macintosh way.

## Four Sample Scripts

In the following simple, hand-typed examples, you'll encounter new kinds of *tell blocks,* scripts that control more than one program at a time, and scripts that do things you can't even do manually. If you look over these examples carefully—and type them up for yourself in Script Editor—you'll begin to see how English-like AppleScript can be. (You may also wind up with some useful scripts that can make your Macintosh life easier.)

### Changing your Mac's scroll bar style

By opening the dictionary of the Appearance control panel, you'll discover that you can actually script almost every aspect of your Mac's look. In fact, the Appearance Dictionary (see Figure 10-4) reveals commands available to AppleScript that aren't even available in the Appearance program itself!

Open Script Editor, choose File→New Script, and type out this script, for example:

```
tell application "Appearance"
   set scroll bar arrow style to both at one end
end tell
```

When you click Run, you'll see that both of the scroll-bar arrow buttons appear at the bottom of your vertical scroll bars (and the right end of horizontal scroll bars). By changing the phrase "both at one end" to "single" in the script above, your script can restore them to opposite ends of the scroll bar.

What's the big deal? Doesn't the Smart Scrolling option in the Appearance control panel do exactly the same thing? Yes, but Smart Scrolling *also* changes the style of the scroll *box* (the ribbed handle that you drag inside the scroll bar). Only by using AppleScript can you control each aspect of the scroll bars independently.

For example, if you replace the middle line in the script on page 157 with this—

```
set scroll box style to proportional
```

—then you've just changed the scroll *box* style without changing the scroll *arrow* style.

### Auto-backup before shutting down

Suppose you'd like the Mac, just before it shuts down each night, to back up your Documents folder to a Zip disk. AppleScript can do the job automatically. In Script Editor, choose File→New Script, and then type this:

```
tell application "Finder"
   move folder "Documents" to disk "Backup Zip" with replacing
end tell
```

In this example, your Zip disk is called Backup Zip; if it has a different name, change the script above accordingly. This script also assumes that your Documents folder is sitting on your desktop. If it's on your hard drive instead, the second line would look like this:

```
move folder "Documents" of startup disk to disk "Backup Zip"
with replacing
```

You may wonder, by the way, why the primary command here is *move folder* and not *copy folder*. As it turns out, the Copy command in AppleScript isn't smart enough to *replace* an existing folder of the same name. Because you probably plan to run this auto-backup script every day, you'll want it to wipe out *yesterday's* Documents backup each time you run it. That's why the "move" command—in conjunction with its optional modifier phrase "with replacing"—is the one you want. It makes the Mac copy the Documents folder to the Zip, *replacing* the Documents folder that's already there, without asking for confirmation or showing an error message. (If the Backup Zip isn't in your Zip drive at the time you run the script, though, you *will* get an error message.)

Once you've created this little script, save it as a Classic Applet or Mac OS X Applet and put it into your System Folder→Shutdown Items folder, so that it runs automatically whenever you turn off the Mac.

### Instant RAM disk

Among the Mac elite, one particular Web-browsing speed trick is passed from generation to generation: If you store your Web browser's *cache files* on a RAM disk (see page 120), Web surfing goes much faster.

Chapter 7 makes it clear that you can create a RAM disk very easily using an add-on program like AppDisk or ShrinkWrap. But if you'd rather use the built-in Apple RAM disk feature described in that chapter, and you create such a RAM disk regularly, you may prefer this AppleScript. It turns on the RAM disk and then restarts your Mac (which is required whenever you create or destroy a RAM disk).

You may find this script especially interesting because it controls two different programs in the same script: first the Memory control panel, and then the Finder. Technically, you'd say that this script has two *tell blocks:*

```
tell application "Memory"
    set the state of RAM disk to active after restart
    set the size of RAM disk to 5242880
end tell
tell application "Finder"
    restart
end tell
```

The first steps turn on the RAM disk option in the Memory control panel, and then set the RAM Disk Size slider to 5120K. (The third command in the script says "5242880" because AppleScript measures memory in bytes, of which there are 1,024 per kilobyte. You're welcome to change this number in your script.) The second set of steps restarts the Mac (after closing all your programs and asking if you'd like to save unsaved documents).

If you save this script as a Classic Applet or Mac OS X Applet, you'll be able to create a 5MB RAM disk just by double-clicking it. Creating a second script that *eliminates* the RAM disk should be easy: Duplicate the script above, changing the second line so that it ends *inactive after restart* and eliminating the third line.

### Triple shutdown

Every now and then, you might find it useful to quit all running programs (except the Finder). You might want to do so in order to defragment your RAM (see page 114), for example, or to make RAM room for a very large program you're about to launch. Unfortunately, there's no one-step command that quits all of your open programs—but you can create one yourself.

Every Mac program on earth understands the Quit command when sent by AppleScript. All you have to do, then, is to send that command to each of the programs you're likely to have open. If you spend most of your time in AppleWorks, Outlook Express, and Internet Explorer, for example, your script might look like this:

```
tell application "AppleWorks"
    quit
end tell
tell application "Outlook Express"
    quit
end tell
tell application "Internet Explorer"
    quit
end tell
```

If some of these programs aren't actually running at the time you run this script, your Mac will just pause, puzzled, for about two seconds, as it tries to send the Quit command to nonexistent applications; no harm done.

## Advanced AppleScript

No single chapter—in fact, no entire book—can make you a master AppleScript programmer. Gaining that kind of skill requires weeks of experimentation and study, during which you'll gain a lot of appreciation for what full-time software programmers endure every day. AppleScript, despite its friendly, English-like appearance, uses many of the same structures and conventions as "real" programming languages.

By far the best way to learn AppleScript is to study existing scripts, like the ones in your Apple Extras→AppleScript folder, and to take the free online training courses listed at the end of this chapter. Trying to figure out these scripts, running them after making small changes here and there, and emailing the authors when you get stuck are some of the best ways to understand AppleScript.

Figure 10-5, for example, is a script called Add Alias to Apple Menu. It's one of the professionally written sample scripts that come with Mac OS 9. To open it, open Script Editor; choose File→Open; navigate to your Apple Extras→AppleScript→ Automated Tasks folder; and double-click Add Alias to Apple Menu. A quick glance tells you a lot about the tricks of professional scripters:

- **Description.** Careful script writers *document* their work; they add lots of notes and explanatory comments for the benefit of whoever might want to study or amend the script later (which is often themselves). Adding a description of the script's function in the Description box (at the top of the Script Editor window) is a good first step.

- **Variables.** Ever seen a legal contract? It often begins, "This contract is between John F. Grisham, Esquire, of 2234 Mission Bell Lane, New Orleans, LA ('AUTHOR'), and Time Warner Publishing, Inc., 23 Avenue of the Americas, New York, NY ('PUBLISHER')." The names John Grisham and Time Warner never appear again in the contract—instead, the lawyers refer only to AUTHOR and PUBLISHER.

  Those lawyers are using *variables*—made-up terms that serve as stand-ins for more complicated ideas, which help to simplify the script, clarify its purpose, and save typing. In AppleScript, as in real programming, you can define your own variables. In the third line of the Add Alias to Apple Menu script, for example, you can see the command "set theList to selection." That command tells AppleScript that you're defining your own variable called *theList,* which will henceforth mean "whatever icons are currently selected." (For some reason, AppleScripters tend to use variable names where the first letter is lowercase, but subsequent words appear with no spaces and capital letters, *somethingLikeThis.)*

  Note that the rest of the script contains many references to "theList." Using "theList" as shorthand for "the selection" saves the programmer some typing and makes the meaning of the script clearer.

- **Subroutines.** The twelfth line of the script says, "MakeAppleAliases(theList)." That step tells the script *not* to proceed down the list of commands in sequence, like the scripts described so far in this chapter, but instead to jump to a *subroutine*—

a separate set of commands that's been separated from the first batch for clarity. In this case, the subroutine begins several lines later ("**on** MakeAppleAliases (theList)").

• **Nested "if" statements.** You might tell an underling, "If you have time this afternoon, would you please run to the store? If the steaks are still on sale, buy three pounds; otherwise, buy just one pound." That, believe it or not, is a *nested "if" statement.* In other words, the steak-buying will take place only if the underling has time this afternoon.

The Add Alias to Apple Menu script is filled with nested "if" statements. For example, the third line says, in essence, "If there's only one highlighted icon"; the next line says, "…and if it's an application icon." The script proceeds only if both of those criteria are true.

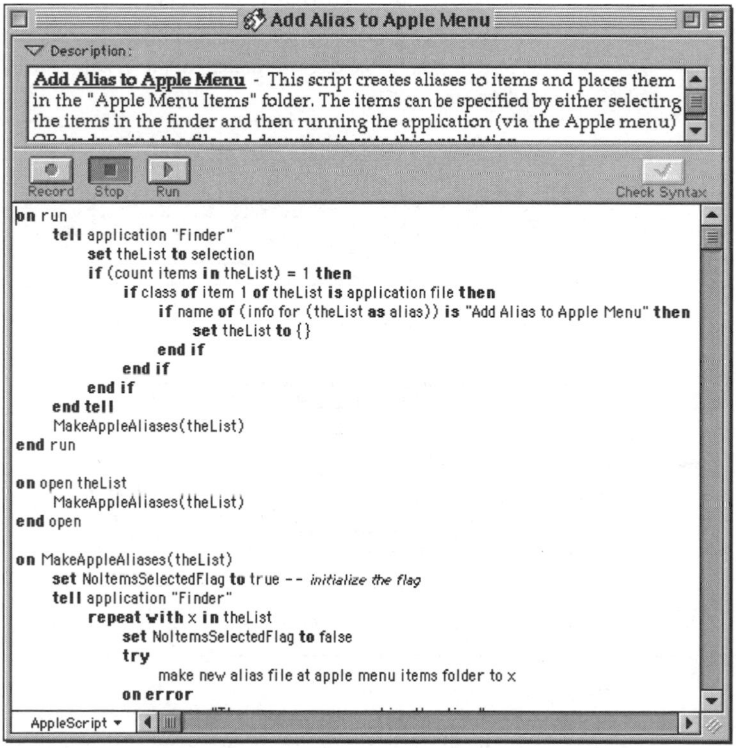

**Figure 10-5:**
The Add Alias to Apple Menu script is a classic AppleScript example. It contains variables, subroutines, nested "if" statements, and many other common elements of professionally written scripts. (After typing a description into the box at the top of the window, you can click the flippy triangle to the left of the Description box to hide the entire thing, thus maximizing your script-writing space.)

• **Comments.** Do you see the italicized comment, "--*Initialize the flag*"? That's the programmer's note to herself, or to anyone else who studies the script. It's a *comment;* when AppleScript runs the program, it ignores comments. You create one by typing two hyphens (--); when you click the Check Syntax button, Script Editor automatically sets what follows in italics.

*Tip:* If you want to type a out a longer comment—a whole paragraph between commands in your script—just precede and follow it with a parenthesis and asterisk (*like this*).

- **Looping.** The paired commands "repeat" and "end repeat" create a loop—a set of commands that AppleScript repeats over and over again until something (which you've specified) interrupts it. In the case of the Add Alias to Apple Menu script, the script loops until it's added *all* of the highlighted icons to the  menu—at which point it displays either an error message or a success message.

- **Dialog boxes and buttons.** If you ever want to play programmer for a day, open Script Editor and try creating dialog boxes and buttons of your own. The script command "display dialog" (followed, in quotes, by whatever message you want to appear on the screen) is all you need, as shown in Figure 10-6.

*Tip:* Instead of a dialog box, you can also interact with the person using the computer by making the Mac *speak.* (See Chapter 21 for more on speech.) Just use the "Say" command. If your AppleScript contains the line, *say "Hey! Pay some attention to me!" using "Zarvox,"* then the Mac speaks that line using the voice called Zarvox.

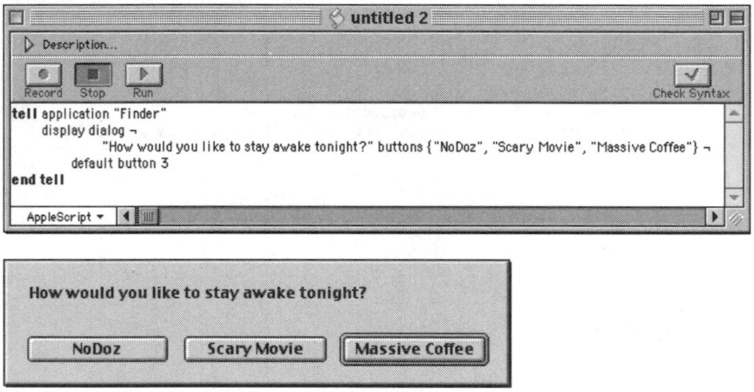

**Figure 10-6:**
*The script shown at top produces the dialog box shown at bottom. The "buttons" command lets you create your own buttons (up to three of them, punctuated exactly as shown here); the "default button" command tells the script which of your buttons should have the fat black border (which indicates the default button, the one you can "click" just by pressing the Return key). "Default button 3" means that the third button is the default button.*

- **Line breaks.** When a line of AppleScript code gets too long, it's hard to read—especially if it's wider than the Script Editor window itself. AppleScript pros therefore insert a special *continuation symbol* that makes the text wrap to the next line, which lets AppleScript continue to treat the entire phrase as a single command. You create this symbol by pressing Option-Return. (Several of these line-break characters appear in the scripts shown in Figures 10-5 and 10-6.)

*Caution:* Don't use a line-break character in the middle of a phrase that appears inside quotation marks; such AppleScript commands must remain together on a single line.

- **Try…On error…End try.** This suite of three commands appears frequently in polished AppleScript scripts—including the one shown in Figure 10-5. In essence, it tells the Macintosh: "Try to do this. If it doesn't work out, show this error message." Here's an example:

```
tell application "Finder"
   try
      make new folder at startup disk with properties {name:
"Backup Folder"}
   on error
      display dialog "A folder already has that name."
   end try
end tell
```

This script tries to make a new folder on the startup disk named Backup Folder. But if there's already a folder there by that name, the AppleScript gets an error—and shows the error message you specify.

### What Else AppleScript Can Do

In general, the online help provided with Mac OS 9 can be skimpy and scattershot; you're lucky if you can find good, hard, specific information that goes beyond the basics about a particular feature.

The online help provided with AppleScript, however, is a different story. It's still terse and unfriendly, but it's seething with useful examples—and it's copious enough to serve as a detailed overview of AppleScript's powers. There you'll find out, for example, that simple scripts can:

- Manipulate specific files and folders (copy, delete, rename, or label them, for example)

- Read, copy, or insert text into the Comments field of a certain icon's Get Info window

- Use artificial intelligence to create a summarized version of a longer text document

- Use the Speech Listener program to create scripts that respond to spoken commands.

## Folder, Network, and Internet Scripts

As noted earlier in this chapter, most people trigger scripts by saving them as Classic Applets or Mac OS X Applets—and then double-clicking the resulting script icons. But AppleScript has become much more flexible in recent years; now a script can control a program elsewhere on your network, even elsewhere on the *Internet;* you can also set up a script to run whenever somebody fiddles with a particular folder. Here's how to work these specialized AppleScript features:

## Folder Actions

A *folder action* is a script that the Mac triggers automatically whenever something happens to a particular folder—such as when you open, close, move, resize, or change the contents of a folder while its window is open.

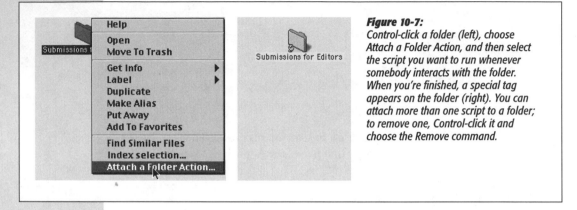

**Figure 10-7:**
*Control-click a folder (left), choose Attach a Folder Action, and then select the script you want to run whenever somebody interacts with the folder. When you're finished, a special tag appears on the folder (right). You can attach more than one script to a folder; to remove one, Control-click it and choose the Remove command.*

To attach a script to a folder, follow the steps shown in Figure 10-7. For example, here's one that notifies you whenever somebody has put new files into a particular folder:

```
on opening folder this_folder
    tell application "Finder"
        set the folder_name to the name of this_folder
        display dialog "Someone has put new files into the folder
called " & ¬
            the folder_name giving up after 30
    end tell
end opening folder
```

This script incorporates several useful AppleScript techniques you haven't yet seen in this chapter. For example:

- **on opening.** This phrase tells the Mac that the script should run when the folder is opened. It's related to the "on run" command, which always appears at the beginning of a *drag-and-drop* script—that is, a script that runs when another icon is dropped onto it in the Finder. (The Add Alias to Apple Menu script described earlier in this chapter also begins with the "on run" command.)

- **this_folder.** All folder-action scripts refer to the folder in question as "this_folder." It's no secret to the Mac which folder "this folder" refers to, because you *told* it which folder when you Control-clicked (see Figure 10-7).

- **folder_name.** This term, on the other hand, *isn't* a standard AppleScript term; it's a *variable,* as described earlier in this chapter. In order not to have to type *the name of this_folder* over and over again, the programmer uses the word "folder_name" to represent that longer phrase.

- **&.** When you're composing the message that you want to appear in a dialog box (as indicated by the "display dialog" command above), you can attach facts and figures to the text you typed. In this example, the fourth line of the script creates a dialog box that says, "New items have been placed in folder Fish Heads" (if that's what the folder is called).

- **Giving up after 30.** This optional modifier phrase affects the "display dialog" command. It means, "If nobody clicks this dialog box's OK button after 30 seconds, then nobody's at the Mac. Just make the dialog box go away by itself."

After you've attached this script to a folder, nothing happens when you drop a new file into the folder. But the next time you *open* the folder, a message appears, saying, "Someone has put new files into the folder called 'Submissions,'" so that you can keep tabs on (for example) what your network buddies have been submitting while you were working on other things.

---

**POWER USERS' CLINIC**

## Scripting Additions

Much of Apple's power comes in the form of add-on files called *scripting additions.* You can think of them as plug-ins, each of which adds a particular new feature to AppleScript's repertoire. They sit in your System Folder→ Scripting Additions folder. In Mac OS 9, you can find scripting additions that let your scripts manipulate your Keychain, Keyboard control panel, Desktop Printing software (see Chapter 19), and so on.

Like a standard application, each of these additions has its own *dictionary*—its own specialized AppleScript commands that you can use in your scripts. You view these new com-mands just as you would when studying the vocabulary of a program: by opening Script Editor, choosing File→Open Dictionary, and then navigating to, and opening, the scripting addition you want.

The AppleScript commands that folder actions can understand are among those in the Standard Additions scripting addition. There you'll discover five folder-action commands, called *opening folder, closing folder window for, moving folder window for, adding folder items to,* and *removing folder items from.* One of these commands must begin any script that you attach to a folder.

---

**Tip:** If you'd like to be notified *immediately* when someone adds files to a folder, use the "add - new item alert" script instead of the one listed above. You can find this useful script, along with a powerful assortment of other ready-made folder-action scripts, in your System Folder→Scripts→Folder Action Scripts folder.

The "add - new item alert" script, however, requires that the folder be *open* when new icons are put into it; no folder action can alert you immediately when someone puts new files into a *closed* folder.

---

For much more detail on folder actions, including many examples worth studying, open Script Editor, choose Help→AppleScript Help, and search for *folders.*

## Controlling Programs Over the Network or Internet

Thanks to a feature called *program linking,* a script can send AppleScript commands to applications that aren't even on your Mac, but on machines elsewhere on the network—or elsewhere on the planet, thanks to the Internet. In high-horsepower

AppleScript operations, this feature can come in handy in several circumstances: when you want to install software onto, or back up, all the Macs on your network (without having to run around to each machine), for example, or splitting up intensive computational duties among several Macs.

### Setting up the Mac you'll be controlling
The setup goes like this:

1. **Visit (or contact the owner of) the Mac whose software you intend to control. Make sure you've been assigned a name and password.**

   This setup works exactly like the one described on page 286. You set up the remote Mac as though you're going to connect to it over the standard office network; you use the same name and password.

2. **On that same Mac, choose  →Control Panels→File Sharing.**

   The File Sharing control panel opens. (If you're setting up a Mac that's running some version of System 7.6, open the Sharing Setup control panel instead.)

3. **If the bottom button says Start, click it.**

   You've just turned on the master switch for program linking (which means "remote control by AppleScript").

   If you'll be connecting to this machine via Internet, also turn on the "Enable Program Linking clients to connect over TCP/IP" checkbox.

   Now you have to specify *who*, on the network, has the power to control this Mac's programs remotely.

4. **While the File Sharing control panel is still open, click Users & Groups. Double-click the icon for each person to whom you're granting remote-control powers, choose Show→Sharing, and turn on "Allow guests to link to programs on this computer."**

   For details on the Users & Groups system of setting up names and passwords for your co-workers, see Chapter 16.

---

***Tip:*** At this point, your network buddies can theoretically control any application on this Mac. If you'd like to declare one of these programs off-limits to remote-control manipulation, quit the program (if it's running), highlight its icon, choose File→Get Info→Sharing, and turn off "Allow remote program linking" in the Get Info window that appears.

---

5. **Close the control panel, saving changes if you're asked to do so.**

Your setup of the Mac to be controlled is complete. Repeat the steps for any other Macs on the network you'll want your AppleScripts to control.

### Writing the remote-control script

The key to making a remote-control AppleScript work is telling Script Editor which application on which Mac you want to control. To do so, just write, in a new Script Editor window, this humble, temporary script:

```
choose application
```

Then click the Run button. The all-important dialog box shown in Figure 10-8 appears. This is your chance to specify which Mac, and which *program* on that Mac, you want to control—even if you intend to send your script via the Internet.

After you follow the steps shown in Figure 10-8 and click OK, a new window appears in Script Editor: the Result window. It contains the precise text you'll need to use, when writing your script, to specify the particular program on the particular Mac you intend to control.

Then, instead of beginning your script with the usual "tell application 'Finder'" (or whatever the application is), substitute the longer phrase shown in the Result window. You'll wind up with a step like this, in other words:

```
tell application "Finder" of machine "iMac DV"
```

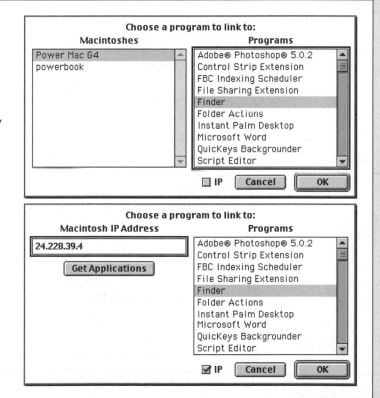

**Figure 10-8:**
*Click the name of the machine you want to control from the list on the left; click the name of the zone (if any) and then the name of the application from the list at right (top). If you'll be sending this script message over the Internet, click the IP checkbox. In the resulting window (bottom), type the IP address of the Mac you want to control (which you can find out by opening its File Sharing control panel), clicking Get Applications, and then selecting the program you want from the resulting list.*

Then write your script as usual. When you run the finished product, you'll be instructing programs on that other Mac on the network—or that other Mac on the Internet—from the comfort of your own screen.

---

## AppleScript Over the Internet

To control a Mac elsewhere on the Internet via AppleScript, follow the steps described in this section. There's only one difference: Instead of naming the machine on your network (in the opening line "tell application 'Finder' of machine 'iMac DV,'" for example), substitute the code *eppc://* plus the *IP address* of the machine you're controlling. Your opening line might, therefore, be: "tell application 'Finder' of machine 'eppc://24.229.28.3.'"

As you can read in Chapter 16, every Mac connected to the Internet has an *IP address* (a numerical Internet address). You can find out a Mac's IP address by opening the File

Sharing control panel; the number appears on the main Start/Stop screen.

The trouble arises when you're setting up a Mac that can connect to the Internet only by modem. In that case, its IP address changes *every time* it connects to the Internet. Furthermore, odds are good that that Mac won't be online when you try to send your AppleScript command to it.

In other words, you can send AppleScript commands *only* to Macs that have a full-time Internet connection, such as a cable modem, DSL, or corporate network.

---

### A great example

Even if you don't manage a huge network of load-sharing Macs in a printing plant, you can still get mileage out of the AppleScript network-control feature. Suppose, for example, that your small office has three Macs; at the end of each day, you've been wearily trudging over to each one to shut it down, in an effort to save power.

Now that you know the secret, a simple AppleScript can do the dirty work for you. This is all it takes:

```
tell application "Finder" of machine "iMac DV"
   beep
   say "This machine will shut down for the night in 30 sec-
onds."
   delay 30
   shut down
end tell
```

Copy and paste this block over and over again, each time substituting the name of another Mac on your network that you'll want to shut down with this single script.

The first line specifies which machine you want to control. The second beeps to get the attention of any late worker who's still seated in front of it. The "say" command uses the Macintalk speech voices (see Chapter 21) to utter a verbal warning; the "delay" command makes the AppleScript pause for a number of seconds you specify—in this case, to give that straggler a chance to wrap it up. And finally, the "shut down" command turns off that Mac, wherever it may be in the world.

---

*Tip:* When you run this script, you'll be prompted for your name and password. Storing that information in the Keychain (see Chapter 16) neatly eliminates that inconvenient step.

## Where to Learn More

As noted earlier, AppleScript isn't something you can master in a day or two. Fortunately, few Mac technologies have more ardent fans than AppleScript, and free beginners' (and experts') tutorials are available all over the Web.

Begin your quest at Apple's AppleScript Web site, *www.apple.com/AppleScript*. Unless it's changed since this writing, you'll find an excellent, step-by-step tutorial in hand-coding scripts, as well as links to these outstanding online AppleScript guides:

- **Bill Briggs' AppleScript Primers**—Dozens of articulate, thoughtful tutorials for the beginning scripter.

- **AppleScript Guidebooks.** Download and install these additions to your Help→Help Center menu. Each adds, to your built-in Mac help system, detailed instructions on various specialized AppleScript topics: Open Transport, subroutines, speech, program linking, and so on. Each includes several dozen sample scripts for you to dissect.

- **AppleScript mailing lists.** Sign up for one of these free, email-based discussion lists whose members are all AppleScript fans. Apple runs one; the MacScript list is independent.

Other links take you to commercial AppleScript training course offerings, technical encyclopedias that describe every single AppleScript command in detail, AppleScript news sites, and so on.

# Part Three:
# The Components of
# Mac OS 9

3

# What's in the System Folder

When people talk about Mac OS 9, they're generally talking about the contents of *one folder* on your hard drive: the System Folder. If you've ever had a hankering to *see* Mac OS 9, to survey its components arrayed before you like the pieces of a car engine, just double-click your System Folder icon.

Without the System Folder, a Macintosh can't even turn on. When you upgrade from, say, Mac OS 9 to Mac OS 9.0.4, it's the System Folder that gets changed. And when mysterious glitches begin to affect your Mac, some component in the System Folder is usually at fault.

## What's in the Mac OS 9 System Folder

Every Mac OS 9 System Folder contains roughly the same standard chunks of software, organized in the same set of System Folder sub-folders (see Figure 11-1). Some are more important than others, but all are worth knowing about.

### Appearance

This subfolder contains three folders, each of which pertains in some way to the Appearance control panel (see Chapter 3): Desktop Pictures, Sound Sets, and Theme Files.

- **Desktop Pictures** contains several folders full of picture (JPEG) files, each suitable for use as a full-screen desktop "wallpaper" image. When you click the Place Picture button in the Appearance control panel (see page 53), this folder's contents appear.

*Tip:* Whenever you drop certain kinds of graphics files (such as JPEG, GIF, or Photoshop images) onto the System Folder icon, the Mac offers to file them away in the System Folder→Appearance→Desktop Pictures folder.

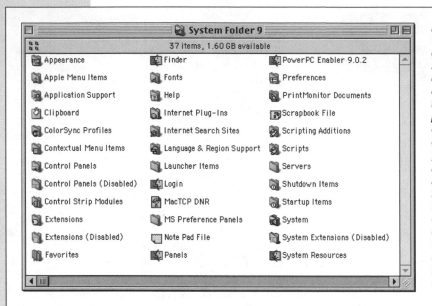

**Figure 11-1:**
*When named properly, each folder in the System Folder automatically displays a special folder icon that hints at its purpose. Except when organizing your fonts or your* ⌘ *menu, you'll have little reason to open or meddle with these folders in everyday work. But being aware of their functions and contents can be useful when you want to customize or troubleshoot your computer.*

- The **Sound Sets** folder contains a single item: Platinum Sounds. When designing Mac OS 8.5, Apple planned to offer a variety of "soundtracks" to accompany your mouse movements in the final version, Apple ripped out the option to change soundtracks. Unfortunately, this last-minute change left several orphaned features in the Mac OS, such as the Sound Track pop-up menu (page 59) and this folder, which—unless you make new soundtracks yourself—will never contain more than this single sound set.

*Tip:* Although Apple doesn't provide more than one "soundtrack" file, it's easy to make your own–if you're handy with the free ResEdit program (available from *www.missingmanual.com,* for example). Duplicate and rename the Platinum Sounds icon in your Sound Sets folder. Then open the new file with ResEdit. By copying and pasting, you can replace the standard Mac OS 9 sounds with ones that you've recorded. You can make your various mouse activities sound more comical, more musical, or more violent, depending on your mood.

After you've created additional sound-sets files, you can use the Appearance control panel's Sound tab to switch among your newly created "soundtracks." You can also install the soundtrack files onto another Mac by drag-and-dropping them onto its System Folder.

• A *theme file,* such as those in the **Theme Files** folder, stores a set of *themes*—collections of saved preferences from the Appearance control panel. (See page 60 for more on themes.) If you've never created a theme of your own, the Theme Files folder contains two icons: one containing the standard Apple Platinum theme (which defines your gray-tinted menu bar, gray puffy window edges, and other visual accents) and one containing Ensemble Themes (the various factory-installed themes shown in the Appearance control panel's Themes tab).

**UP TO SPEED**

## System Folder Drag-and-Drop

The Mac OS 9 System Folder contains a staggering 2,000 individual icons. Each plays a part in making your Mac run.

But a System Folder crammed with 2,000 unfiled icons would be an unholy mess: you'd have a hard time finding a file you need, troubleshooting your system, and understanding how your Mac works.

That's why, over the years, Apple has been subdividing the System Folder by creating specially named folders *inside* it, each with a special icon to identify it as an official Mac OS 9 entity. These special folders each contain one special category of system software: they're called Apple Menu Items, Fonts, Control Panels, Preferences, and so on (see Figure 11-1).

But in its efforts to make the System Folder contents better organized, Apple also makes them harder to access. In the days before these subfolders existed, you could remove (for example) a control panel just by opening the System Folder and dragging the appropriate icon directly out; today, you must open the System Folder, *then* open the Control Panels folder, and so on.

Fortunately, putting such elements *into* your System Folder becomes ever easier. With each new OS version, Apple adds more drag-and-drop auto-routing smarts to its System Folder icon. That is, when you drag some new System Folder com-

ponent directly onto the System Folder a font, a control panel, an extension—the Mac offers to place it into the correct inner folder automatically, as shown here.

If you click OK, Mac OS 9 places the drag-and-dropped icon into the proper subfolder automatically. You can even drop several System Folder-related icons, or a whole folder full of them, onto the System Folder icon. (If the message says, *"Some* of the items need to be put into special folders," beware: The Mac doesn't recognize

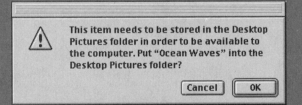

some of them. Not all of the icons you're dragging will be filed into subfolders.)

You may be surprised by how many different kinds of files have homes in the System Folder. You can read about each of the following self-filing icon types in this chapter: Chooser printer icons, desktop pictures, sound sets, theme files, desk accessories, -menu applications, ColorSync profiles, contextual menu modules, Control Strip modules, control panels, shared libraries, Location Manager modules, modem scripts, scripts and scripting additions, extensions, fonts, help files, Internet search sites, AppleScript scripts, sound files, and so on. Throw any of these items onto your System Folder icon, and the Mac puts them into their proper locations.

It's just a shame that our kitchens and offices don't work the same way.

If you decide to create a Theme of your own, as described on page 60, it gets saved into a third theme file called Custom Themes. (This icon magically appears in the Theme Files folder when you save a theme in the Appearance control panel.) All subsequent themes you name and save, in fact, are then incorporated into this Custom Themes file.

---

*Tip:* Very few Mac fans make much of the Themes feature. But if you get a kick out of creating, naming, and saving custom visual design schemes, note that you can transfer the Custom Themes file from Mac to Mac, thus duplicating your saved settings on other machines. (You don't have to place the Custom Themes file manually into the System Folder→Appearance→Theme Files folder; just drag it onto the System Folder. The Mac offers to file it for you automatically.)

---

## Apple Menu Items

Each icon in this folder also appears in the  menu. You'll find a complete discussion of this relationship, and of the standard items that come pre-installed here, in Chapter 5.

### The Death of Desk Accessories

In early versions of the Mac OS, the  menu was exclusively the domain of tiny programs called *desk accessories,* such as the Calculator and Note Pad. In the days when you could run only a single Mac program at a time, desk accessories were a big deal: you could open one even if a "real" program was already running.

Now that every Mac multitasks as easily as you can blink while breathing, Apple doesn't see much point to that old software format. Why not, Apple reasons, just list *regular* applications in the  menu? Over the years, bodysnatcher-like, Apple has been quietly killing off the standard desk accessories and replacing them with identical-looking *applications* with the same names. In Mac OS 9, only two true desk accessories survive: the Chooser and the humble Calculator.

If you're a genuine power user, you might be challenging the notion that today's  menu applications behave *exactly* like desk accessories once did. "Desk accessory icons," you might be frowning, "when dropped onto the System Folder icon, got placed into the Apple Menu Items folder automatically. Application icons don't."

True enough, genuine applications like Word and AppleWorks don't fall into the Apple Menu Items folder when you drop them onto the System Folder icon. That's because the auto-filing feature of the System Folder is determined by the drag-and-dropped icon's *type and creator codes* (see page 107). For a desk accessory, the type code is always *dfil;* for an application, it's APPL, which the System Folder doesn't recognize for auto-filing.

But Apple was sneaky on this one: It defined a special variant of application type code, APPD, which means, "This is an application that should be filed in the Apple Menu Items folder, like a desk accessory." When you drag the icons of the Apple System Profiler or Key Caps onto the System Folder icon, for example, the Mac offers to put them into the Apple Menu Items folder.

Only one mystery then remains: Why don't such desk accessory–like Apple Menu Items as the Note Pad, Scrapbook, and Stickies also have the APPD type code? When you drop *them* onto the System Folder, they just land with a clunk in the System Folder itself. Maybe Apple's been too busy to get around to changing them.

## Application Support

When you install a new program, it may require certain software components to be in your System Folder for its own use. To prevent your System Folder from becoming randomly littered with such components, Apple created this special subfolder. Yours may contain support files for programs from Adobe, the RealAudio plug-in, and DataViz translation programs, for example.

The most important thing to know about Application Support is that its contents are for the exclusive use of your *programs.* Don't waste time double-clicking a file in Application Support; you'll get only an error message.

## Claris

The Claris folder isn't actually part of Mac OS 9. But because it contains support files for AppleWorks 4 and 5, however, which came with many iMacs and iBooks, this folder is present on many Macs. (Why doesn't AppleWorks—Apple's own software—use the Application Support folder, which would be a more appropriate storage bin for these files? Because the AppleWorks program, once called ClarisWorks and owned by Claris Corporation, predates the introduction of the Application Support folder. Meanwhile, AppleWorks 6 doesn't create a Claris folder; it keeps its junk in its own folder.)

## Clipboard

You can read more about the Clipboard on page 136. (Chapter 9) There you'll read that when you use the Cut or Copy command, highlighted material is placed onto an invisible Mac storage plate called the Clipboard. Behind the scenes, however, the Clipboard isn't actually invisible—this file in your System Folder holds whatever you've most recently cut or copied. By double-clicking this icon, you open a window that shows the most recently cut or copied material.

## ColorSync Profiles

ColorSync is a sophisticated but easy-to-use technology that maintains color fidelity when an image is scanned, viewed on your monitor, and printed—which is a surprisingly difficult task for a computer. For instructions on using ColorSync, see page 366.

This folder contains the *profiles* (color-display information) for dozens of printers and monitors. (CSW stands for Color StyleWriter.) These are the choices that appear when you click the Color button in your Monitors control panel.

---

*Tip:* You can save considerable disk space, and simplify your life, by throwing away all of the profiles that *don't* match equipment you actually use.

If you ever actually do need one of the profiles, you can always use the Custom option of your Mac OS 9 Installer (see Appendix B) to reinstall it.

---

## Contextual Menu Items

The software nuggets in this folder add features to your *contextual menus*—the cursor-tip pop-up menus that appear when you Control-click an object on your screen. As described on page 67, you can add new commands to these contextual menus by adding appropriate modules to your System Folder.

But knowing about this folder is much more useful when you want to *remove* one of the add-ons you've installed. Just open this folder and drag the corresponding icon out of the window (or to the Trash). The next time you turn on the Mac, the corresponding commands will be gone from your Control-key menus.

## Control Panels

Here lurk dozens of control panels and control-panel-like applications that define how your Mac works: whether its speakers are loud or soft, what color its screen background should be, what Internet number you tell the Mac to dial, and so on. These programs are so important that they merit their own chapter, Chapter 12.

## Control Panels (Disabled)

See page 195 for a discussion of Extensions Manager, which lets you turn various control panels on and off. When you turn one off, the Mac simply re-files the control panel into the Control Panels (Disabled) folder, where Mac OS 9 ignores it.

You can turn that control panel back on by using the Extensions Manager program again—or by dragging it manually from the Control Panels (Disabled) folder into the Control Panels folder.

## Control Strip Modules

Chapter 4 describes the useful pop-out command center known as the Control Strip. Each tile on the Strip controls a different Macintosh function: your speaker level, network settings, and so on.

Each tile on the Strip is also represented by an icon in this Control Strip Modules folder. As Chapter 4 points out, you can add tiles to, and remove them from, the Control Strip just by dragging them on and off the strip; but you can also do so by dragging Control Strip modules into, or out of, this folder.

## Extensions

An *extension* is a small software blob, housed in this folder, that adds one single feature to your Mac. One extension lets you get onto the Internet; another lets you print; another lets your Mac read CD-ROM discs; and so on. Chapter 12 contains a description of these items.

This folder is also the final resting place for the *drivers* your Mac needs—individual software modules that communicate with the various hardware gadgets plugged into your Mac, such as scanners, printers, and USB devices. (Each printer icon that shows up in your Chooser, for example, corresponds to an icon in the Extensions folder.) This folder also houses *shared libraries,* which are chunks of software that may be used by more than one of your applications, and which have therefore been incarnated as detachable modules in your Extensions folder.

## Extensions (Disabled)

Using the Extensions Manager program described in Chapter 12, you can *turn off* extensions—a common technique when you're troubleshooting or trying to save memory. When you turn one off, it isn't actually deleted from your Mac—instead, it's just moved into this folder, where the Mac ignores it. To restore it, you can either drag an extension back into the regular Extensions folder—or just use Extensions Manager to turn it back on.

## Favorites

This folder contains the aliases of files, folders, disks, or networked disks that you've designated as your Favorites—a mechanism described in Chapter 5.

---

*Tip:* To remove something from your  menu→Favorites command, you're supposed to remove it from this Favorites folder. To do so, start by choosing →Favorites to open the Favorites window quickly and efficiently, ready for editing.

---

## Finder

The Finder—the world of folders and icons that appears when you first turn on your Mac—may not seem like an application, along the lines of AppleWorks or Outlook Express. In fact, however, it is an application, and this is its icon. (Because the Finder is *always* running, you don't, and can't, double-click its icon.) Without this icon in the System Folder, your Mac doesn't operate.

## Fonts

Your Mac's collection of typefaces, or fonts, is represented not only in the Font menu of your word processor, but also by icons inside this folder. Each suitcase-shaped file in this folder may contain a handful—or dozens—of individual typefaces at different sizes. Chapter 19 covers the basics of font-file manipulation; for now, it's enough to note that you install a new font by dropping it onto your System Folder icon, and remove a font by dragging its icon out of this Fonts folder. In both cases, you must quit any running programs before making changes to the Fonts folder.

## Help

This folder contains the text and graphics that appear when you choose Help→Mac Help—the only instruction manual Apple provides with Mac OS 9.

*Tip:* Ordinarily, you view the contents of the Help folder using Mac OS 9's built-in Help command. As it turns out, however, the Mac's Help program is actually a tiny Web browser, and the files in your Help folder are Web-page documents and GIF graphics.

You can prove this to yourself by launching your Web browser, such as Navigator or Internet Explorer, and then choosing File→Open. Navigate your way into the System Folder→Help folder, and open the Help Center document. Now you're actually using the Mac Help system from within your Web browser, which gives you several important features that are missing from the Mac's Help program—including copying text, opening multiple help topics at once, and creating bookmarks.

## Internet Search Sites

In Chapter 15, you can read about the Sherlock program's ability to search the Web right from your desktop. To pull off that trick, Sherlock relies on the special files in this folder, each of which teaches Sherlock how to search one specific Web site (Amazon, Apple, Infoseek, and so on).

If you become a real Sherlock maven, you may decide to enhance Sherlock with additional search modules, which you can download from the Internet. To install one, drag it onto the System Folder icon; the Mac automatically offers to place it into this Internet Search Sites folder.

## Language & Region Support

Although you may not realize it, Apple gave you several hundred dollars' worth of free add-on software with Mac OS 9: its complete collection of *language kits,* each of which cost $79 each before Mac OS 9. Each kit lets your Mac word process in a different language, even if that language word processes from right to left across the screen, proceeds from top to bottom, requires special fonts, and so on. Chapter 13 contains a full description of this feature; for now, it's enough to know that this folder stores the various modules that teach your Mac how to word process in these Roman and non-Roman languages. (Feel free to throw away the language modules you don't use.)

## Launcher Items

You can read about the Launcher in Chapter 2. There you'll discover that this folder contains aliases for each item that appears on your Launcher—and folders for each "page" of the Launcher.

*Tip:* You don't actually have to access this folder to add icons to, or remove icons from, the Launcher; Chapter 2 reveals how you can simply drag items on or off the Launcher. Knowing about this folder is still very useful, however: opening it and editing the names of the icons inside is still the only way to *rename* a Launcher icon.

## Login

This miniature program is responsible for bypassing the Finder whenever you use the Multiple Users feature described in Chapter 17. In other words, whenever you first turn on the Mac or use the Special→Log Off command, the Login application shows you a list of every person who's been given an account on that machine.

## Mac OS ROM

In the early days of Macintosh, the *ROM chip* was a piece of silicon—part of the Mac circuitry—etched with the permanent instructions that make a Mac a Mac: the instructions for drawing windows, making menus, displaying the Trash can, and so on. Eventually, Apple discovered that replacing this physical chip with a *file* in your System Folder offered several advantages—for example, the software-based ROM is much easier to update when bugs are discovered, and it also allows the Mac to start up faster. Current Mac models, including the iMac and iBook, use this more modern scheme. Put another way, the Mac OS ROM file in your System Folder is astoundingly important—without it, the Mac can't start up at all.

## MacTCP DNR

This file contains crucial behind-the-scenes software your Mac needs to connect to the Internet.

## Note Pad File

If you've experimented with the Note Pad, described in Chapter 13, you may have discovered that this stripped-down word processor has no Save command. Instead, anything you type there is auto-saved in this file (which doesn't exist unless you've actually opened the Note Pad). In fact, you can double-click this file to open the Note Pad to view its contents—one of the few System Folder elements that, when double-clicked, gets you anything more than an error message.

---

***Tip:*** You can duplicate this file, thus winding up with multiple Note Pad Files. You might store, for example, a different kind of information in each one. Double-click the one you want to open; the Note Pad program opens automatically.

---

## Panels

This file contains the software that creates the kid-friendly Panels screen described in Chapter 17.

## Preferences

Welcome to one of the busiest folders on the Mac. Every control panel, every application, every Web page you visit creates a tiny file in this folder. Each preference file saves the settings you've made in that control panel, application, or Web page: the font you prefer, the phone number your Mac dials for Internet access, your Web browser's bookmarks list, and so on. In general, it's easy to figure out which preference file corresponds to which program—the preference files have names like Adobe Photoshop Prefs, Control Strip Preferences, and FileMaker Prefs.

In general, you can ignore the contents of the Preferences folder. They should enter your consciousness only in two circumstances: first, when you're troubleshooting a particular program (see Appendix C), and second, when you've performed a "clean install" of your System Folder (see Appendix B).

## PrintMonitor Documents

Thanks to a feature called background printing (see Chapter 19), while the computer is printing, you can continue using other programs. In the meantime, the Mac processes the printouts in the background. This folder contains the printouts it's working on—the ones it has yet to finish printing. That's why, most of the time, this folder is empty.

## Scrapbook File

Chapter 5 contains a description of the Scrapbook program; this file stores the various pictures, sounds, movies, and blocks of text that you paste into the Scrapbook. You can double-click this file to open the Scrapbook.

---

*Tip:* By duplicating the Scrapbook file (choose File→Duplicate), you can actually create multiple Scrapbook files, each containing a different collection of pictures, sounds, and so on. Just double-click the one you want to open. (For easier access, consider putting aliases of these Scrapbook files into your  menu, as described in Chapter 5.)

---

## Scripting Additions, Scripts

These folders contain support files for AppleScript, the Mac-automation feature described in Chapter 10.

## Servers

As described in Chapter 16, it's relatively easy to bring the hard drive of another Mac in your office onto your desktop, thanks to the Mac's built-in networking software. If you do so using the Chooser—a technique also described in Chapter 16—you're offered a checkbox that offers to bring that hard drive onto your screen every time you turn on your computer.

Turning on that checkbox creates an alias in this Servers folder; that's how the Mac remembers which hard drives you want to see again. (If you find aliases in this folder for hard drives you no longer need every day, throw them away. Your Mac's quest for these hard drives every morning makes your Mac take longer to start up.)

## Shutdown Items, Shutdown Items (Disabled)

Not many Mac fans use this folder, but it's a useful feature in certain circumstances. Any icon you put into this folder gets magically double-clicked every time you turn off the computer. Some people put sound files into the Shutdown Items folder, so that the Mac says, for example, "I'm... so... c-c-c-cold—it's getting dark!..." before popping off. Others use this folder to store the alias of an automatic backup program, or an AppleScript (see Chapter 10) that performs some other end-of-day cleanup procedure.

Using Extensions Manager (see Chapter 12), you can control which of these Shutdown Items are triggered. Whenever you turn one off in Extensions Manager, the Mac actually moves the shutdown item into the Shutdown Items (Disabled) folder, where it gets ignored. When you turn that shutdown item on again in Extensions Manager, the Mac moves it back into the regular Shutdown Items folder.

## Startup Items, Startup Items (Disabled)

This folder is the flip side of the Shutdown Items feature: any icon or alias that you put into *this* folder gets automatically double-clicked when you turn *on* the computer. This more popular feature is useful for auto-launching the programs you use every day, saving you a couple of clicks and some waiting. For example, if you check your email every morning and then start word processing, put the aliases of Outlook Express and AppleWorks into the System Folder→Startup Items folder. Now those two programs will launch themselves when you turn the computer on. Putting *documents* into this folder can be useful, too—store an alias of the chapter, spreadsheet, or drawing you've been working on, for example, so that it's open and waiting just after you turn on the computer.

Mastering the Startup Items entails learning three useful tricks:

- The items in the Startup Items folder open alphabetically. For example, if you want the AppleWorks window waiting for you after all other startup items have opened, make it launch last by adding the letter Z to the beginning of its name.

- Suppose that you know you'll want to *use* AppleWorks and Internet Explorer each day, and would like them already running when you sit down at your Mac. But suppose that you want your desktop windows—not AppleWorks or Internet Explorer windows—to greet you when you arrive at the machine.

  The secret: Put an alias of your *hard drive* into the Startup Items folder, too—and name it to load last of all.

- If you're anxious to get to work just after your Mac has started up, you can prevent your startup items from launching at all. To do so, press and hold the Shift key *just* as your extension icons are finished loading—during the interval when the screen is blank, just before the Trash appears.

The (Disabled) folder contains the icons for any startup items you've turned off using Extensions Manager (see Chapter 12).

## System, System Resources

These crucial files, together with the Finder and Mac OS ROM files described earlier, *are* the Mac OS. These chunks of software control the Mac, allowing it to turn on and function. If you move the System file out of the System Folder, for example, all of the special folders described in this chapter—Apple Menu Items, Launcher Items, and so on—lose their specially designed folder icons, which is your signal that you've just incapacitated the computer.

This is not to say, however, that you should never touch the System file. While it's foolish to *move* this file, *double-clicking* it is harmless and sometimes useful, as shown in Figure 11-2.

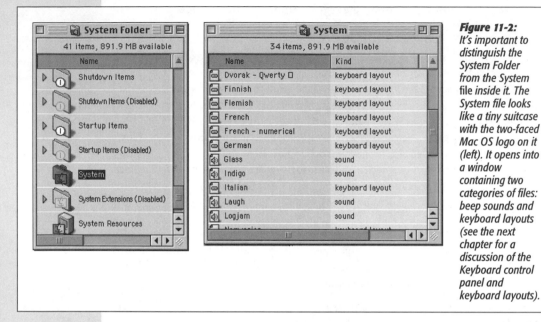

**Figure 11-2:**
*It's important to distinguish the System Folder from the System file* inside it. The System file looks like a tiny suitcase with the two-faced Mac OS logo on it (left). It opens into a window containing two categories of files: beep sounds and keyboard layouts (see the next chapter for a discussion of the Keyboard control panel and keyboard layouts).

---

## Blessed Be Thy System Folder

If you look at your System Folder window in icon view (choose View→as Icons), you'll discover that every folder described in this chapter has its own unique, attractively designed icon. The Extensions folder displays a tiny jigsaw-puzzle piece, the Apple Menu Items folder displays a tiny Apple logo, and so on.

Mysteriously enough, if you drag one of these folders out of the System Folder, that handsome folder icon becomes an ordinary blue folder icon, like Cinderella's carriage turning back into a pumpkin.

The custom icons appear only on folders with the exact names Mac OS 9 requires, and only within the current System Folder. It's perfectly possible to have more than one System Folder on your hard drive—but only one displays the two-faced Mac OS logo. That working System Folder is

called, by the programmers, the *blessed* System Folder. Only this one displays the Mac OS logo, offers the kind of auto-filing drag-and-drop smarts described in the beginning of this chapter, and puts special icons on its interior folders.

This knowledge can be useful in times of troubleshooting. If the Mac won't let you throw away some font, for example, move the entire Fonts folder on to the desktop. Now that it's no longer part of the blessed System Folder, you can open it, throw away a corrupted font suitcase, and so on. (And if you're having trouble with the folder itself—can't throw it away, for example—you can create a new folder of the same name inside the System Folder window. Then you can move the contents of the corrupted folder on your desktop into its replacement—after making sure you're not simply re-copying the corrupted file within it.)

---

## Text Encodings

This folder contains another set of files for Mac OS 9's multiple-language feature, which lets you, for example, view both English and Japanese in the same word processing document (see Chapter 13). You're welcome to discard the icons for any languages you don't regularly use on your Mac.

# Control Panels and Extensions

Your Mac can run without any of the control panels and extensions in your System Folder, but it wouldn't be much fun. These small software chunks add dozens of useful features to the basic machine. They permit you to print, go online, use CD-ROMs, connect over a network, change the look of your screen, and much more. Without these add-ons, in fact, you wouldn't be able to do much with your Mac beyond mindlessly dragging icons in and out of folders.

Control panels and extensions sit in their own, similarly named folders within the System Folder. Many of them—especially extensions—do their magic when you first turn the computer on. The Mac loads them into its memory during the startup process, after which they hover like ghosts in your Mac's memory, waiting for their cue to perform. Virus checkers, screen savers, and Internet dialing software all fall into this category.

It's worth knowing what these things are, if only for the purposes of troubleshooting; the fewer extensions and control panels you have running, the more stable your computer will be, and the faster it starts up. As you'll see in the following discussion, a few of these software nuggets are so important that they merit chapters of their own; all the others are described in the following pages.

## The Mac OS 9 Control Panels

Each Mac control panel changes the settings for a different aspect of your computer's behavior. Because the Mac is marketed to the broadest possible audience, it includes hundreds more options than any one person would ever need. Let this chapter be your guide to adjusting the control panels that need adjusting, and—using Extensions Manager, described later in this section—turning off the ones you can't imagine ever needing.

---

***Tip:*** Speaking of useless items, you can have a long and happy life without adjusting—or even reading about—every single control panel described here. Only a few offer must-see features for every Mac user: the control panels called Energy Saver, Date & Time, General Controls, Internet, and Extensions Manager.

---

### What's Really In Those Folders

Most items in your Extensions folder are standard system extensions—tiny programs that load into memory when you turn on the computer, and remain in the background.

In the Control Panels folder, on the other hand, many of the items—including Appearance, Keyboard, Monitors, and Energy Saver—are actually applications. Unlike true control panels (of type code CDEV, popular ten years ago), these new "control panels" work correctly even when they're not in your System Folder. And unlike true control panels, these programs' names show up in your Application menu (see page 101) when they're open. Still, most people think of them as control panels because they come in the Control Panels folder. And thanks to a special type code (APPC), these programs fall

automatically into the Control Panels folder when you drop them onto your System Folder icon, which makes them seem even more like standard control panels.

The Extensions folder contains many self-loading startup tidbits as described earlier. But it also houses Chooser icons (the software that communicates with various printers) and *shared libraries* (detachable chunks of code that several different programs may share—notably Microsoft Office programs). None of this should concern you—if anything, it should make you relieved that not every item in your Extensions folder is using up memory and increasing the risk of conflicts, as true extensions do. (Appendix C has more on Mac extension troubleshooting.)

## Appearance

Chapter 3 is a grand tour of this program, which is the command center for tailoring the look (and sound) of your desktop.

## Apple Menu Options

This control panel has two functions. First, it contains the on/off switch for *submenus* in your  menu (see Figure 12-1). Second, it lets you specify how many recent documents, programs, and networked disks you want listed in the  menu.

---

***Tip:*** There's no reason not to list a very high number in the Documents and Applications blanks of the Apple Menu Options control panel. It's very useful to have instant access to the most recent, say, 50 programs you've used.

On the other hand, if your Mac isn't connected to a network, you may as well put 0 into the Servers blank. Doing so makes the Servers command disappear entirely from the  menu, removing one more bit of unnecessary clutter from your life.

---

## AppleTalk

Using this control panel, you answer one simple question: how is your Mac connected to the office network? If your Mac is connected by an Ethernet cable (see Chapter 16), choose Ethernet or Ethernet Built-in from the pop-up menu; if you have an AirPort card for wireless networking, choose AirPort; if you have an older Mac, one that has a printer port, and you're connected using the inexpensive but slow LocalTalk cables, choose Printer Port. (The Remote Only option is useful only if you plan to dial into your Mac from the road, a trick described in Chapter 16.)

If you're *not* connected to an office network (or laser printer), the setting here is irrelevant. In fact, you can turn this control panel off using Extensions Manager, described later in this section.

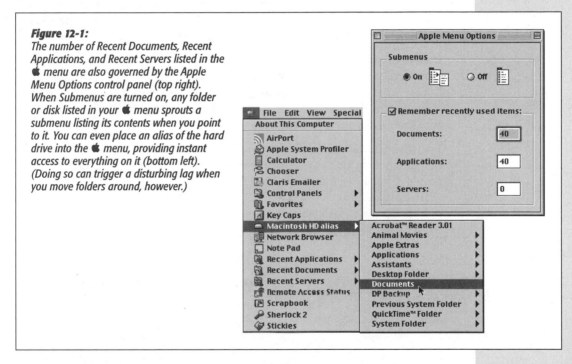

**Figure 12-1:**
*The number of Recent Documents, Recent Applications, and Recent Servers listed in the  menu are also governed by the Apple Menu Options control panel (top right). When Submenus are turned on, any folder or disk listed in your  menu sprouts a submenu listing its contents when you point to it. You can even place an alias of the hard drive into the  menu, providing instant access to everything on it (bottom left). (Doing so can trigger a disturbing lag when you move folders around, however.)*

## ColorSync

This control panel is part of the software suite that attempts to maintain color fidelity throughout the life of a scanned image: from scanner to monitor and finally to color printout. For details, see Chapter 19.

## Control Strip

The Control Strip is a convenient shortcut to many of the control panels described in this chapter. For complete details, see page 68.

## Date & Time

Your Mac's conception of what time it is can be very important. Every file you create or save is stamped with this time; every email you send or receive is marked with this time; and when you drag a document into a folder that contains a different draft of the same thing, the Mac warns you that you're about to replace an older or newer version—but only if your clock is set correctly.

The Date & Time control panel (see Figure 12-2) offers these settings:

- **Current Date, Current Time.** To specify the current date or time, click one of the numbers in these boxes. Then adjust the corresponding number either by typing the numbers, pressing your up or down arrow keys, or by clicking the tiny up or down arrow *buttons.* To jump to the next number for setting, press either the Tab key or the right arrow key on your keyboard. (Of course, if you use the Use the Network Time Server option described below, your Mac can set its *own* clock.)

- **Date Formats, Time Formats.** If you think that 7/4 means July 4, skip this section. But if, as a European or Australian, you interpret it as April 7, you can click Date Format to summon the dialog box shown in Figure 12-2, where you can rearrange the sequence of date elements. All of the options in this dialog box affect how dates are displayed in list-view Finder windows.

The Time Formats button works similarly—it summons a dialog box where you can specify how you want the time displayed on the Mac. For example, some people prefer a 12-hour clock ("3:05 PM"), and others prefer a military or European-style, 24-hour clock ("1505"). A Region pop-up menu lists 18 ready-made settings for countries where the Mac is popular. If none of those suit your fancy, use the Long Date pop-up menus to specify some radical new order for the elements of your dates.

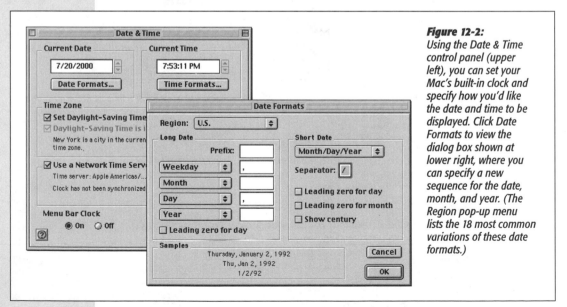

**Figure 12-2:**
Using the Date & Time control panel (upper left), you can set your Mac's built-in clock and specify how you'd like the date and time to be displayed. Click Date Formats to view the dialog box shown at lower right, where you can specify a new sequence for the date, month, and year. (The Region pop-up menu lists the 18 most common variations of these date formats.)

- **Set Daylight-Saving Time Automatically; Set Time Zone.** You'd be surprised how important it is to click Set Time Zone and then select, from the scrolling list, a city in your current time zone. If you don't do so, the email and documents you send out—and the Mac's conception of what documents are "older" and "newer"—could be hopelessly skewed.

  Once you've set your time zone, you can specify whether or not you want the Mac to adjust its clock for daylight-saving time automatically—a terrific feature.

  If you turn off the Set Daylight-Saving Time checkbox, then you must remember to change your Mac's clock manually whenever daylight-saving time begins or ends—which, fortunately, is as easy as checking the "Daylight-Saving Time is in effect" checkbox. (This checkbox is unavailable if you've opted to have your Mac adjust the clock automatically.)

- **Use a Network Time Server.** This option means, "Set the clock automatically by consulting a scientific clock on the Internet." When turned on, the Mac will set its own clock at regular intervals, adjusting it to within fractions of a second by connecting to sophisticated atomic-clock Internet sites. You schedule this automatic updating by clicking the Server Options button.

- **Menu Bar Clock.** Use these On/Off buttons to specify whether or not you want the current time and/or date to appear, at all times, at the top of your screen. By clicking Clock Options, you summon an immense array of options that govern this digital clock display: whether or not you want to include designations for AM and PM, the day of the week, a blinking colon, a different color or typeface for the digits, and so on. If you have a laptop, you can even choose to eliminate the battery-charge gauge that appears next to the clock on your menu bar.

  You can also specify that you want your Mac to chime (actually, beep) on the hour, half-hour, and/or quarter hour, like some kind of high-tech grandfather clock. (The Select Chimes pop-up menus let you specify which of your Mac's built-in sounds you want to use for each of these chime sounds. The sounds called Temple, Purr, Glass, and Submarine make not-too-annoying choices.)

---

*Tip:* Your menu-bar clock generally shows the current time. When you need to know today's date, just click the clock. Click again, or just wait a few seconds, to view the time once again.

---

## DialAssist

In Chapter 16, you can read about dialing into your home-base Mac while traveling on the road. That's the only time this control panel is useful; it lets you specify complicated numbers to dial—credit-card numbers, long-distance prefixes, the 9 or 8 you may need to dial for an outside line, and so on—using simple pop-up menus.

## Energy Saver

The Energy Saver program is good for you and your Mac in a number of different ways. By blacking out the screen after a period of inactivity, like a screen saver, it prolongs the life of your monitor. By putting the Mac to sleep (or shutting it down) a half an hour after you've stopped using it, Energy Saver cuts down electricity costs and pollution. By turning the computer *on* ten minutes before you arrive at your desk each morning, it saves you time. And if your Mac is a laptop, Energy Saver extends the length of the battery charge by controlling the activity of the hard drive, screen, and processor.

### Automatic sleep settings

When you first open Energy Saver, you're shown a slider that controls when the Mac will automatically go to sleep: 30, 40, or 60 minutes after your last activity, for example. ("Activity" is mouse movement, keyboard action, or Internet data transfer; Energy Saver will never put the Mac to sleep in the middle of a download, although it may darken the screen.)

At that time, the screen goes dark, the hard drive stops spinning, and your processor chip slows to a crawl. Your Mac is now in *sleep* mode, using only a fraction of its usual electricity consumption. To wake it up when you return to your desk, press any key; everything you were working on, including open programs and documents, is still on the screen, exactly as it was. (To turn off this automatic sleep feature entirely, drag the slider to Never.)

---

***Tip:*** The "Shut down instead of sleeping" checkbox makes the Mac shut itself down (instead of sleeping) after the specified period of inactivity. If you're the kind of person who, when called away from the desk, generally doesn't return for the rest of the day—because you're a paramedic, computer consultant, or work-at-home parent, for example—you might prefer this option.

---

For more control over the sleeping process, click Show Details. Now you're offered *three* sliders: one each for the computer itself, the monitor, and the hard drive. If you turn on the "Separate timing" checkboxes, you can specify independent sleep settings for the screen and the hard drive.

---

***Tip:*** If you find yourself impatient with the ten seconds it takes the Mac to wake up when you press a key, consider putting your Mac into *light sleep.* To do so, turn on "Separate timing for display sleep," and drag the slider so that the monitor (the middle slider) goes to sleep sooner than the Mac itself (the top slider). Now the screen goes dark after its specified period, but awakens *instantly* when you touch a key or click the mouse. This setup doesn't save as much electricity as regular sleep, but protects the screen equally well, and spares you those ten-second wakeup periods.

---

### Scheduled startup and shutdown

By clicking the second icon at the top of the Energy Saver window, you can set up the Mac to shut itself down and turn itself back on automatically. If you work 9 to 5, for example, set the Mac to turn itself on at 8:45 AM, and shut itself down at 5:30 PM—an arrangement that conserves electricity, saves money, and reduces pollution, but doesn't inconvenience you in the least. In fact, you may come to forget that you've set up the Mac this way—you'll never actually see it turned off.

**Note:** The Mac doesn't shut down automatically if you've left unsaved documents open on the screen. Remember, too, that if you schedule the Mac to shut off at night, automatic middle-of-the-night tasks like Sherlock's hard drive indexing (see Chapter 15) won't take place at all.

### Laptop options

If you have a PowerBook or iBook, the Energy Saver has a few additional controls and another function: to extend the life of each battery charge when you're traveling. First, above the sliders, it displays a new pop-up menu that offers two choices: Power Adapter and Battery. In other words, you can create two separate slider settings—one for use when the laptop is plugged in, and another when you're running off battery power. The theory is that when running from the battery, you'll want the various laptop components to go to sleep after relatively short periods of inactivity, thus conserving juice—but when you're plugged into a wall socket, you'd rather not have those annoying lapses of service.

**Tip:** There's no downside to setting the laptop *never* to sleep when it's plugged in. Chances are, when you're not using it, you'll close the lid anyway (which, of course, puts it to sleep). And by clicking Show Details and dragging the top slider all the way to Never, you rule out the possibility that the laptop will blink to sleep while you're in the middle of a presentation or reading a speech from its screen.

At the top of the Energy Saver window, laptop owners find a third icon button called Advanced Settings. Clicking it summons a screen full of new checkboxes that offer additional wake/sleep options for your laptop. Depending on your laptop model, they may include:

- **Preserve memory contents on sleep.** Whenever the laptop goes to sleep, this option makes it take 20 additional seconds to store, in a giant invisible file on your hard drive, a copy of everything that's in memory, including unsaved open documents. Doing so is a safety net for a fairly unusual situation: you put the laptop in the closet for three weeks or more, so long that the battery eventually dies. In that circumstance, the "Preserve memory contents" option could save your bacon—when power is restored and you turn the computer on again, you'll find all your documents open on the screen, exactly as you had left them before the lights went out. Otherwise, unsaved changes would have been lost forever.

  Still, most people leave this option off—the 20-second delay before sleep is too high a price to pay for that very hypothetical safety net.

- **Wake for network administrative access.** This option and the next, **Wake for other network activity,** are unavailable on most laptops. They exist exclusively for the purchasers of the software suite called Apple Network Administrator, which lets the network guru in an office control (and, with this checkbox, even wake up) laptops that are sleeping on the network.

- **Wake when the modem detects a ring.** This checkbox can be useful in two circumstances: first, if you use your laptop as a fax machine that accepts incoming faxes (a function of the FaxSTF software that's included with most Apple laptops), and second, if you dial into your Mac from the road (see Chapter 16). In either case, when a phone call reaches the laptop's modem, the computer wakes up and accepts the call—if this option is turned on.

- **Wake when the computer is opened.** Why did it take the laptop makers so long to think of this? If you open a laptop's lid, of *course* you intend to use it, so why shouldn't it wake up from sleep automatically?

- **Reconnect to servers on wakeup/Remember my passwords.** If, at the moment your laptop goes to sleep, you had brought the hard drives of other Macs on the network onto your screen (see Chapter 16), this option brings them *back* onto the screen when the computer wakes up.

- **Allow processor cycling.** This important option perhaps shouldn't be buried so deeply in the Energy Saver control panel. When turned on, it lets your main processor chip take infinitesimal catnaps between operations. The result is that your battery charge lasts much longer—about another 25 minutes per charge—but the computer is slower. Processor cycling is fine when you're reading email or word processing, but it can dramatically slow down QuickTime movies, Photoshop calculations, and other intensive operations.

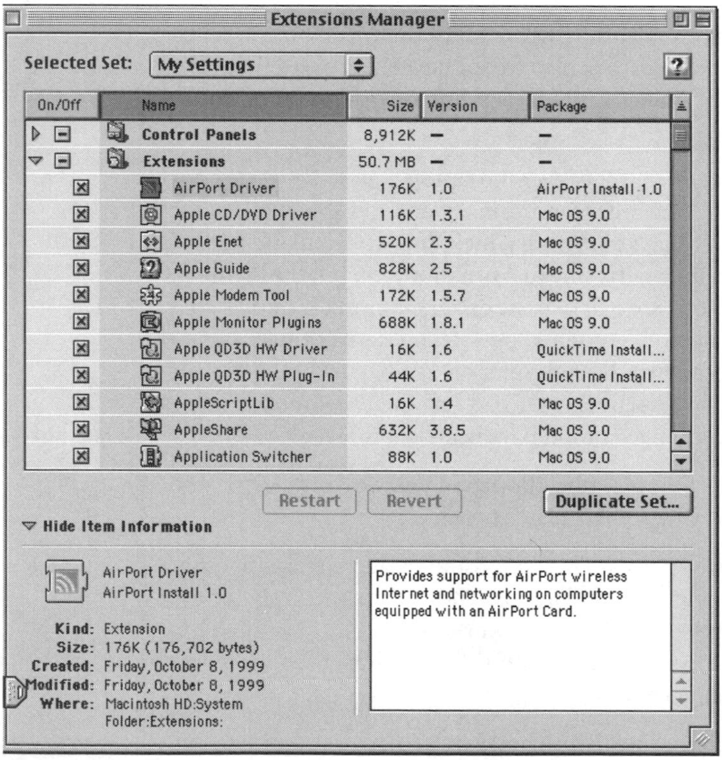

**Figure 12-3:**
*The Extensions Manager window is, in many respects, like a standard Finder window. You can sort the list by clicking the column titles (such as Size and Version), adjust the column widths by dragging the vertical dividers (which works, for some reason, only for the Name and Package columns), sort the list in reverse by clicking the pyramid button above the scroll bar, collapse one of the folders by clicking the "flippy triangle" to its left, and so on. The "Package" column can be especially useful—it often lets you know what program dumped these particular items into your System folder.*

# Extensions Manager

Each of the control panels and extensions described in this chapter adds a particular enhancement to Mac OS 9. Unfortunately, each also makes your Mac take longer to start up, uses up more memory, and decreases your Mac's stability. That's why Apple has blessed us with Extensions Manager, a control panel that lets you turn *other* control panels and extensions, as well as items in your Startup Items and Shutdown Items folders, on or off.

You can open Extensions Manager as you would any control panel—by choosing its name from the Apple menu→Control Panels command. More often, however, you'll want to open it during the startup process, so that you can turn some features on or off in preparation for the computing session that's about to begin. To do so, press the Space bar just after you turn the Mac on. Eventually, the Extensions Manager window appears (see Figure 12-3).

Your principal activities in Extensions Manager will be (a) clicking the checkboxes at the left side to turn items on or off, and (b) finding out what these items are for.

---

*Tip:* You can jump to any item in the Extensions Manager list by typing the first letter or two of its name.

---

### Turning extensions or control panels on and off

To turn something on or off, click the checkbox to the left of its name: The X means on. If you summoned Extensions Manager by holding down the Space bar while the computer was starting up, click Continue to finish starting up your computer. If you opened Extensions Manager instead by choosing its name from the  →Control Panels command, click Restart; the computer turns off, then on, with your newly chosen set of control panels and extensions in effect.

And how are you supposed to know which ones to turn off? The basic rule is: for best stability, greatest memory savings, and quickest startup time, turn off as many as possible. Use this chapter as your guide; if you don't do scanning or color print ing, for example, turn off all the ColorSync items. If you're not on an office network, turn off File Sharing (control panel and extension), and so on. The Show Item Information command, described next, supplies more guidance.

---

*Tip:* When you open Extensions Manager by choosing  →Control Panels→Extensions Manager (instead of by holding down the Space bar during startup), you get a bonus feature: a menu bar. It's loaded with additional features that make Extensions Manager more useful.

For example, the File menu contains commands that let you duplicate, rename, delete, or create a text report about one of your sets. When you've highlighted something in the list, the Edit menu offers the Find Item command, which jumps to the actual icon in your System Folder, ready for deleting, opening, or renaming. And the View menu lets you rearrange the list of control panels or extensions, making clusters of them alphabetically, by the System Folder folder in which they sit, or by the *package* (software installer) that gave them to you in the first place.

---

## Getting information

Extensions Manager makes a decent effort to explain the purpose of each control panel and extension—an effort limited only by the abilities of programmers to describe their creations in plain English.

To view the description of any item, click it once, and then click the Show Item Information triangle below the list. A new panel of the Extensions Manager screen appears, revealing, in most cases, a description of the item you clicked. Sometimes you get lucky: "Mouse: Use this control panel to set the tracking and double-click speed of your mouse." Sometimes you don't: "ATI Resource Manager manages video memory for ATI Components." Still, some verbiage is better than none.

---

***Tip:*** If the Extensions Manager descriptions leave you wanting, download the program called Extensions Overload, a shareware program available at *www.missingmanual.com*. Although it's not written by an English major either, it exhibits the fruits of far more research and effort than the built-in Extensions Manager descriptions.

---

**FREQUENTLY ASKED QUESTION**

## What is Extensions Manager Trying to Tell Me?

*Sometimes when I open Extensions Manager, I get an incomprehensible error message. It wants me to click buttons called Revert, Update, or Cancel, or something, none of which I understand. What should I do?*

Extensions Manager is complaining that you've been messing around inside the System Folder. Apparently you, someone you love, or a software installer you've used recently has moved some extensions or control panels into, or out of, the Extensions or Control Panels folders. Extensions Manager is saying, in effect: "How am I supposed to activate the list of extensions you specified when some of them aren't even here?"

Sometimes the message says: "The selected set does not match the contents of your System Folder." In this case, someone has dragged icons between the Extensions and Extensions (Disabled) folders in your System Folder—or the Control Panels and Control Panels (Disabled) folders—which is normally Extensions Manager's job.

You're offered three buttons. The Update button opens Extensions Manager as planned—but Mac OS 9 changes the on/off checkboxes in the list to reflect the current state of affairs in your System Folder. For example, if you had dragged the Mouse control panel into the Control Panels (Disabled) folder, its checkbox appears off. In most cases, this is what you want.

The Revert button opens Extensions Manager, but the list now looks exactly as it did before you moved things around in your System Folder. To make this list reflect reality, Mac OS 9 moves extensions and control panels in your System Folder *back* into the folders where they began. In the example of the previous paragraph, Mac OS 9 puts the Mouse control panel *back* into the Control Panels folder.

Finally, if you click the Create New Set button, you're asked to name a new Extensions Manager set—"My Settings 2," for example—that reflects the new reality of your System Folder items' locations.

You might also occasionally get a message that says, "There are extensions in this set that are not installed in your computer." In this case, somebody didn't just move extensions or control panels between their folders and (Disabled) folders—somebody took them completely *out* of the System Folder. Click Cancel to open Extensions Manager and get on with your life, or click OK to save a SimpleText document onto your desktop that, when opened, lists the missing icons.

### Managing sets

Using the pop-up menu above the list, you can create—and choose from among—different canned sets of extensions and control panels. One might contain the full set you use every day. Another might contain only the extensions necessary to run Photoshop (so that you maximize the free memory on your machine) or to operate your CD-ROM burner (so that you minimize the potential of your extensions' influence on the CDs that you create). A third—a standard one on everyone's copy of Extensions Manager—is the "Mac OS 9.0 All" set, which includes only the original Apple extensions and nothing else.

To create a new set, click Duplicate Set. Type a name for your new set; click OK. Now you can turn extensions and control panels on or off; the new set will remember the status of these various checkboxes. At any time, you can reinstate some other set by choosing its name from the Selected Set pop-up menu (and then restarting).

## File Exchange

This very technical control panel helps the Mac cope with a very technical problem: opening documents the Mac doesn't recognize, including those that were created on Windows PCs. To be specific, it does three things:

- Lets your Mac read PC-(DOS or Windows) floppy disks, Zip disks, and other removable disks, along with Apple II and Apple III floppies. (Without File Exchange, your Mac simply reports that these kinds of disks are "unreadable.")

- Intervenes when you double-click a document icon whose parent program—the one used to make it—isn't actually on your Mac. (A downloaded Internet graphic is a common example.) File Exchange offers a list of programs that *can* open it. See page 109 for details on this useful intrusion.

- Lets you establish relationships between certain kinds of PC files and the programs on your Mac that can open them. For example, when you double-click a Windows file whose name ends in the suffix *.aif,* File Exchange is set up to recognize it as a sound file (AIFF)—and to open (and play) it using the QuickTime Player program on your Mac. The scrolling list (on the PC Exchange panel of this control panel) lists several dozen of these relationships, and you can create your own by clicking the Add button.

File Exchange offers several additional features, all of which are fairly obscure, such as the "Map PC extensions to Mac OS file types on PC disks" checkbox. If they intrigue you, choose Help→Show Balloons, and then point the cursor at them; a pop-up cartoon balloon appears to describe each item as you point at it.

## File Sharing

This program is useful only if your Mac is connected to an office network. It lets you specify whether or not other people on the network are allowed to see your files—and *which* people on the network. For complete instructions on setting up such a network—and in using this control panel—see Chapter 16.

## File Synchronization

If you're running Mac OS 9 on a desktop computer, such as an iMac, you probably don't have this control panel. Mac OS 9 ordinarily installs it only on laptops. But you can install it onto *any* Mac using the Custom installation option described on page 428.

You may find installing it worthwhile, because File Synchronization is a clever and nearly effortless backup program. It ensures that the contents of two particular folders remain identical and up-to-date. For laptop owners, File Synchronization can copy your important work *onto* the laptop before a trip, and move it *back* to your desktop computer when you return. For desktop computer owners, File Synchronization can safely and efficiently back up your important folders onto another disk—such as a Zip disk, SuperDisk, or iDisk. (iDisk is described in Chapter 14).

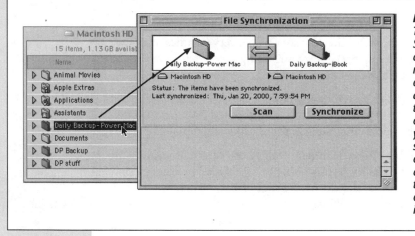

*Figure 12-4:*
*To set up the File Synchronization program, drag the folder from your main Mac onto the left side of the synchronization pair, as shown at left. Then drag the backup folder (or corresponding folder from your laptop) onto the right side. (If you prefer choosing the folders in a dialog box to dragging their icons, double-click one of the folder buttons instead.)*

Start by setting up the source and backup folders, as shown in Figure 12-4. (To keep your head straight, create folders that have the same names on both sides.) And if you'd like more than one folder backed up in this way, choose File→New Pair, and repeat the procedure.

When you open the File Synchronization control panel and then click Synchronize, the Mac automatically compares the contents of the two folders you designated, and copies the *most recent* files both ways until both folders contain the identical material. For example, if you created a new document on your laptop, File Synchronization copies it into its mirror folder on the desktop Mac. If you updated a document on the Mac, it replaces the older version on the backup disk.

---

*Caution:* If, since the last time you synchronized the folders, a particular document was edited *both* on the desktop Mac and on the laptop, File Synchronization gives you no warning. Instead, it simply gives you the most recently edited document in *both* folders. Even if you had done seven hours of work on the laptop copy, but *more recently* changed only a single punctuation mark in the desktop copy, the desktop version wipes out the laptop draft.

---

# General Controls

Apple might as well have named this one Miscellaneous, because its settings and options have nothing particular in common. Nevertheless, some can be useful:

- **Show Desktop when in background.** Ordinarily, when you launch, say, your word processor, you can still see pieces of the Finder (such as the Trash icon) behind the word processor's window. For beginners, this arrangement can be disconcerting; with one errant mouse click outside of the word processor window, the Finder, and all of its windows, spring to the front. The word processor window disappears, having been sent to the background; many a novice has shrieked in horror, assuming that the word processing document is gone forever.

  When you turn off this checkbox, the Finder windows and icons become invisible when you're using any other program. This arrangement prevents the kind of accidental clicks that might send a beginner tumbling into a different program.

  On the other hand, it also deprives the Mac user of a handy feature—the ability to jump into another program by clicking any visible portion of its window. Whenever "Show desktop" is turned off, the only way to switch from one open program to another is to use the Application menu or its keystroke (page 101).

- **Show Launcher at system startup.** Turning on this option puts an alias of the Launcher (see page 43) into your System Folder→Startup Items folder. As a result, the Launcher window appears automatically every time you turn on the computer.

- **Shut Down Warning** (called **Check Disk** in Mac OS 9.1 and later). You're supposed to turn off the computer by using the Special→Shut Down command, or by pressing the Power button on your keyboard (and then clicking the Shut Down button). If the Mac turns off in any other way—because of a system crash, power outage, or accidental unplugging, for example—it doesn't have a chance to do its usual end-of-session house cleaning. The next time it's turned on, therefore, the Mac scolds you with an error message that says, "Your computer did not shut down properly." The Mac then runs its Disk First Aid program to insure that no damage occurred to your hard drive as a result of the crash.

  By turning off this checkbox, you tell the Mac not to show that message. But you also prevent the Mac from performing that important disk-repair routine, which often nips nascent problems in the bud. In other words, leave the Shut Down Warning checkbox turned on.

- **Folder Protection.** In previous versions of the Mac OS, these two checkboxes provided handy protection against the destructive acts of very young or very mischievous people. These options prevented icons from being dragged into or out of the System Folder or Applications folder.

  Apple decided, however, that the Multiple Users feature of Mac OS 9 (see Chapter 17) provides enough protection. As a result, Apple removed this feature from the General Controls box—but didn't even bother to remove the checkboxes! There they sat, dimmed and unavailable, until they disappeared in Mac OS 9.1's redesigned, Multiple Users-compatible General Controls panel.

• **Insertion Point Blinking.** This control governs the blinking rate of the *insertion point* (the cursor that shows where typing will begin when you're word processing). The option to change its speed is, no doubt, primarily a nostalgic gesture: this was one of the few settings you could change on the very first 1984 Macintosh.

• **Menu Blinking.** When you click a menu command, it blinks several times before executing the command. That's one second of your life wasted waiting for the computer, several times per hour. If you believe that life is too short, click Off.

• **Documents.** The three choices here represent Apple's attempt to prevent you from losing documents by inadvertently saving them into some random folder. Instead, the first time you save any document, the Save dialog box (see Chapter 8) appears, proposing one of three locations as the location for the file you're about to save. "Folder that is set by the application" refers to the home folder of whenever document you first double-clicked to launch this program. "Last folder used in the application" refers to whatever folder you've most recently opened while using the program you're currently in.

For novices and experts alike, the third option, "Documents folder," can be a perfect solution to the lost-documents syndrome; Figure 12-5 has the details. This feature also makes it very easy to back up your work, because all of your documents are contained in a single folder.

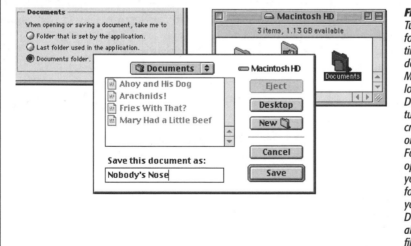

**Figure 12-5:**
*Turn on the Documents folder option (left). The next time you save a new document (middle), the Mac proposes a special location for it—the Documents folder. As it turns out, the Mac has just created this special folder on your hard drive (right). For now on, whenever you open or save a document, you won't have to navigate folders to find a location—you'll always be shown the Documents folder, so you'll always know where your files are.*

# Internet

In the dark and time-consuming days of the early 1990s, the worst aspect of using the Internet was having to *set up* your Internet programs: your email program, Web browser, FTP client, and so on. Each required you to input several pounds of information about you, your Internet connection, and so on.

This control panel neatly solves the problem. It provides a central location where you can record all of this information *once*. After you've done so, you don't need to type these settings into your Internet programs; most of them can retrieve the information they need from the Internet control panel. (If America Online is your road to the Internet, ignore this control panel entirely.)

The Internet control panel has five tabs: Personal, E-mail, Web, News, and Advanced. Each screen contains blanks where you can record the kind of information required by your email, Web, newsgroup, and other Internet software.

For most purposes, you don't need to fill in all of these fields; but filling in a few choice ones can save you a lot of time down the road:

- **Personal.** Fill in your name, email address, and *signature* (what you want to appear at the end of each email you send—just your name, for example, or perhaps a witty quote from some book or movie).

- **E-mail.** Fill in all four blanks; if you're not sure what to type, contact your Internet access company (or its Web page) for help. By far the most important setting here, however, is the Default E-mail Application pop-up menu. Use this pop-up menu to indicate which email program you use. From now on, whenever you click a "Click here to send email" link on a Web page, your favorite email program opens automatically.

- **Web.** Almost all of the settings on this panel are useful and important. Fill in the Home Page (the Web page you want to open when you click the Home button in your browser) and the Search Page (the Web page you want to open when you click the Search button in your Web browser; try *http://www.yahoo.com* or *http://www.google.com*). Next, click Select to specify a Downloads folder—files you download from the Internet will be stored here. (Many people create a Downloads folder on the desktop for this purpose, or choose the Desktop itself. Either method eliminates the frustration of not being able to find something that you downloaded.)

  The most important setting is the last one: Default Web Browser. Use it to indicate which browser—Internet Explorer or Netscape Communicator, for example—you prefer. This is the browser that will open automatically whenever you double-click an Internet location file (see Chapter 14) or a Sherlock Internet-search result (see Chapter 15), for example.

- **News.** If you're a fan of Internet newsgroups (electronic bulletin boards), you can use this panel to specify your server, name, password, and preferred newsreader program.

• **Advanced.** The Advanced tab is ordinarily hidden—it's a little secret reserved for Internet jocks who know what they're doing. To make it appear, choose Edit→User Mode, click Advanced, and then click OK. The Advanced tab that now materializes offers seven panels of its own. They let you specify your preferred FTP servers, the Mac programs you want to handle various kinds of Internet file transfers, the fonts you prefer for email, firewall information (for people who work in a corporation), and so on. Look over the options here; if you know what they are, you're already qualified to use them.

(The other advanced option in Edit→User Mode is called Administration. It's exactly like Advanced, except that it requires a password before any of the Internet control panel's settings can be changed. It's designed to keep mischievous little hands out of your carefully constructed network settings when your Mac is in a lab situation.)

---

**FREQUENTLY ASKED QUESTION**

## The Ignored Internet Control Panel

*Hey! I spent 20 minutes setting up my Internet control panel, but my Internet programs are ignoring my settings. What gives?*

After you've established your Internet control panel settings, some Internet programs recognize them immediately. Outlook Express and Netscape Communicator, for example, suck in their settings from the Internet control panel instantaneously. (This behavior can actually be confusing. When you choose Edit→Preferences in Netscape, for example, the "home page location" field is dimmed and unavailable—because Netscape is extracting this information from your

settings in the Internet control panel. You're not allowed to type in anything here.)

But in other programs, including Internet Explorer, Eudora, and Claris Emailer, you must use the preference commands to *tell* the program to adopt the Internet control panel settings.

In some programs, furthermore, the option to adopt the Internet control panel settings is called "Use Internet Config." That's a reference to the free program (Internet Config) from which the Internet control panel is descended.

---

**Tip:** Not everybody uses the same set of Internet information all the time. For example, your laptop might require one set of preferences when you're home, and another when you're on the road. That's why the Internet control panel lets you create, and name independently, different *sets* of information. To name the one you've just set up, choose File→Rename Set. To create a new set of preferences, click Duplicate Set, give your new set a name, and then visit each of the tabs to change the details that need changing.

Then, when you travel (or otherwise need to change the settings), use the Active Set pop-up menu.

## Keyboard

This peculiar little control panel has three uses. Two are practical and convenient, and one is useful to only a tiny minority of Mac fans. Here they are, in order of appearance:

### Keyboard layout

As you can read in Chapter 13, the Mac is the world's most impressive polyglot: it can handle many different languages on the screen at the same time. But the symbols you use when you're typing Swedish aren't the same as when you're typing English. Apple solved this problem by creating different *keyboard layouts,* one for each language. Each keyboard layout rearranges the letters that appear when you press the keys. For example, when you use the Swedish layout and press the semicolon key, you don't get a semicolon (;)—you get an ö. (Apple even includes a Dvorak layout—a scientific rearrangement of the standard layout that puts the most common letters directly under your fingertips on the home row. Fans of the Dvorak layout claim greater accuracy, better speed, and less fatigue.)

Use the list in the Keyboard control panel to indicate which keyboard layout you want to use. (To see what your new keyboard arrangement looks like, choose  →Key Caps.) If you check off more than one keyboard layout, a tiny flag icon appears in the upper-right corner of your screen—a keyboard *menu* that lets you switch from one layout to another just by choosing its name.

---

*Tip:* You can rotate through the different keyboard layouts in the script you've selected by pressing ⌘-Space bar. If this keystroke already does something in one of the programs you use, open the Keyboard control panel, click Options, and click the "Use Command+Option+Space" checkbox to substitute this less-common keystroke.

---

The Keyboard control panel also includes a Script pop-up menu; yours probably lists only a single command, Roman. For more on script systems, see page 235.

### Keyboard behavior

You're probably too young to remember the antique once known as a *typewriter.* On some electric versions of this machine, you could hold down the letter X key to type a series of XXXXXXXs—ideal for crossing something out in a contract, for example.

On the Mac, *every* key behaves this way. Hold down any key long enough, and it starts spitting out repetitions, making it easy to type, for example, "No WAAAAAAAY!" or "You go, girrrrrrrrrl!" The two sliders in the Keyboard control panel govern this behavior. On the right: a slider that determines how long you must hold down the key before it starts repeating (to prevent triggering repetitions accidentally, in other words). On the left: a slider that governs how fast each key spits out letters once the spitting has begun.

### Function Keys

At this writing, the Function Keys button appears only if you have an iMac, recent PowerBook, or iBook. That's too bad, because it offers a very useful feature: the ability to assign functions to your otherwise mostly function-less function keys (the F-keys on the top row of your keyboard). For step-by-step instructions in making these keys open your favorite programs and documents, see page 105.

---

## Keychain Access

This control panel represents one of the biggest new features in Mac OS 9: the ability to define a single password that then unlocks than dozens of other ones that you used to have to remember. For details, see Chapter 16.

## Launcher

The Launcher "control panel" is bizarre: when you open it, no control panel opens up. Instead, you get the Launcher window, showing the icons of your favorite programs, documents, disks, folders, and so on. Chapter 2 contains a full description.

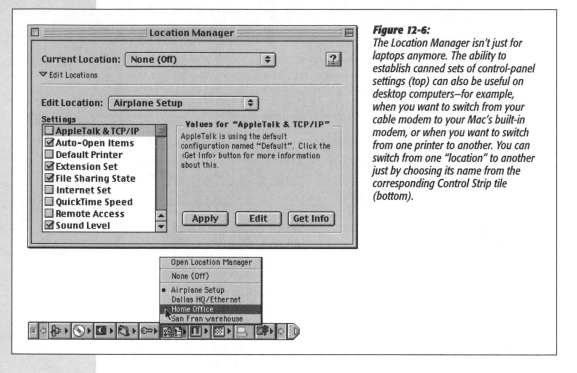

**Figure 12-6:**
*The Location Manager isn't just for laptops anymore. The ability to establish canned sets of control-panel settings (top) can also be useful on desktop computers–for example, when you want to switch from your cable modem to your Mac's built-in modem, or when you want to switch from one printer to another. You can switch from one "location" to another just by choosing its name from the corresponding Control Strip tile (bottom).*

## Location Manager

If you travel with a Mac laptop, you know the drill: at the office, you enjoy your high-speed Internet connection by Ethernet. You keep your Mac's speaker volume low, so you won't disturb the people in the surrounding cubicles. You print on the high-speed laser printer down the hall. But when you return home every night, you have to reconfigure your laptop. You set it to use the modem for Internet connections, you turn up the volume so you can hear it, and you open the Chooser to select your family's color inkjet printer. The next morning, you go to work and start all over again.

If you're willing to endure some grueling setup, the complex but powerful Location Manager can eliminate that treadmill of repetitive configuration. As Figure 12-6 shows, you just specify which control panels you want changed for each location you visit with your laptop. Thereafter, you can switch all of the control panels simultaneously to predefined settings—just by choosing your current location's name from a pop-up menu on your Control Strip.

### Creating a new Location

Turn off the phone and cancel your appointments for the next 25 minutes; setting up Location Manager isn't always simple.

To create a *Location*, which is nothing more than a set of memorized settings, get every control panel exactly the way you like it *first*—and then open Location Manager, which will take a snapshot of the current settings.

To make it do so, choose File→New Location. Type a name for the location you're defining –"Home Office," for example. When you click OK, the list of Location Manager-controllable control panels appears, as shown at left in Figure 12-6. Here's what they do:

- **AppleTalk & TCP/IP.** The AppleTalk and TCP/IP control panels define how your Mac is connected—to an office network and to the Internet, respectively. (For more on the AppleTalk control panel, see Chapter 16; for more on TCP/IP, see Chapter 14.)

  The AppleTalk & TCP/IP option in Location Manager can be extremely useful. If you have an iBook, for example, you might create two "locations"—one that sets TCP/IP to connect to the Internet using your wireless AirPort card, and another (for use in hotel rooms) that makes it use the built-in modem.

  But here's the peculiar thing about Location Manager: it can't memorize your AppleTalk and TCP/IP control panel setups if those settings are called *Default* in their respective control panels. Open your AppleTalk control panel, choose File→Configurations, and check it out for yourself. If Default is the highlighted list item, click Duplicate, type a more distinctive name, click OK, and then click Make Active. Repeat this process with the TCP/IP control panel.

  Now, at last, you can open the Location Manager control panel to turn on the AppleTalk & TCP/IP checkbox—and then click Apply. Location Manager has now memorized your current network and Internet settings, and associated them with the Home Office.

- **Auto-Open Items.** As described on page 183, any icon you put into your System Folder→Startup Items folder opens automatically when you turn the computer on. But although you might like Excel to auto-open when you're at work, you might want Tomb Raider to auto-open when you're at home. When you click this checkbox, the standard Open File dialog box appears, as described in Chapter 8; navigate to the first item you'd like to open automatically when you're in the Home Office, highlight it, and then click Add Item. (You can choose programs, documents, even folders and disks in this way.) Continue navigating to, selecting, and adding items until you're satisfied with the arsenal of startup items—and finally, click Apply.

Whatever items you've chosen open immediately when you switch Locations; you don't have to restart the machine.

- **Default Printer.** If you turn on this checkbox, the currently selected printer is associated with the location you're defining. (The *selected* printer is the one highlighted in the Chooser, or the one indicated by a black outline on your desktop— see Chapter 19.)

- **Extension Set.** Earlier in this chapter, you read about Extensions Manager, the program that lets you define groups of extensions and control panels that you want turned on. You might want a stripped-down set when you're using a laptop on the plane (for battery savings), but the whole enchilada when you're at your office and plugged into an outlet; Location Manager can accommodate you. Just turn on this checkbox; whatever *set* of extensions you're using at that moment will be turned on again whenever you use this Location.

- **File Sharing State.** See Chapter 16 for details on file sharing; click this checkbox if you want this Location to memorize the current on/off status of your File Sharing feature.

- **Internet Set.** This checkbox refers to the currently selected *set* of settings in the Internet control panel, which is described earlier in this chapter. Each group of Internet control panel settings can store the information for a different Internet account, email address, and so on; in other words, Location Manager gives you an easy way to switch between accounts (such as Earthlink at home and the account your company provides at work) without having to fiddle around with your control panels.

- **QuickTime Speed.** As you can read in Chapter 20, the QuickTime feature of Mac OS 9 lets you watch TV and movie clips that reach your computer from the Internet. They look good, however, only if the QuickTime software knows what kind of Internet connection you have; movies that come to you via traditional modem are much smaller and jerkier than movies that arrive by cable modem, for example. When you check this checkbox, Location Manager memorizes the current setting in the Connection Speed panel of the QuickTime Settings control panel.

- **Remote Access.** Meet the number one use of the Location Manager control panel: the ability to switch Internet access phone numbers as you move your laptop from city to city. Specifying the local Internet phone number is, after all, is the primary purpose of the Remote Access control panel; if you travel regularly, you can use Location Manager to build a long list of city locations, each of which "knows" the local phone number for your Internet access company.

As described under "AppleTalk & TCP/IP," however, the Location Manager refuses to memorize the current settings in the Remote Access and Modem control panels if they're set to *Default.* Open  →Control Panels→Remote Access, and then choose File→Configurations; if Default is selected, click Duplicate, type a more distinctive name, and then click Make Active. Repeat the process with the

Modem control panel. Only now can Location Manager memorize the currently selected Internet phone number.

- **Sound Level.** When you click this checkbox, Location Manager memorizes the current volume setting for your Mac, which it records on a scale from 0 to 7.

- **Time Zone.** This option memorizes your current time zone, as it's selected in the Date & Time control panel. Now, every time you travel coast to coast, for example, you won't have to reset your Mac's clock to reflect the new local time—instead, you'll just choose, say, "LA Office" from the Location Manager tile on the Control Strip. Your clock will be instantly adjusted.

---

*Tip:* Don't miss the options in the Edit→Preferences command. In the dialog box that appears, you can set up Location Manager to offer the list of Locations you've defined *as* the Mac is starting up–every time, or only when you're holding down, say, the Control key. This way, you won't forget to make the switch when you arrive at your new real-world location.

The Preferences box also offers the option to ask you about each setting independently–first the sound level, then the time zone, and so on–in case you want only some of the changes to kick in.

---

## Memory

See Chapter 7 for complete instructions on using this important control panel, which governs how your Mac uses memory.

## Modem

For such a tiny program, the Modem control panel causes a lot of grief for people trying in vain to get on to the Internet. You're supposed to choose, from its single pop-up menu, the precise modem model your Mac uses. If you choose the wrong model, you'll find yourself on a permanent truck stop of the information superhighway. (Fortunately, most modern Mac models have a *built-in* modem—known as the Apple Internal 56K Modem or PowerBook G3 Internal Modem, for example—and the Modem control panel comes already set to the correct option.)

The items in this pop-up menu correspond to the *modem script* files in your System Folder→Extensions→Modem Scripts folder. If your modem model doesn't show up here, it's your job to nag the manufacturer of the modem until they provide one. (The modem company's Web page should be your first stop on this quest—if you can even get online.) Drop the script onto your System Folder icon, click OK, and then open the Modem control panel again. At last, your modem's name shows in up in the pop-up menu, where you can choose it to get on with your online life.

## Monitors

The options in this useful program depend on your Mac model. Most Macs, however, offer at least two of these big buttons at the top of the window:

---

## Monitor

This panel lets you make two settings: Color Depth and Resolution. Both settings are discussed on page 75; for now, it's enough to know that the Color Depth affect how many colors your screen can display at once, and Resolution lets you magnify or reduce the screen image.

---

*Tip:* You can adjust the color depth and resolution of your monitor without having to use the Monitors control panel. In most cases, using the Control Strip is quicker and easier (see page 68).

---

## Color

If your ColorSync software is installed correctly (see Chapter 19), this icon appears. When clicked, it summons a list of *ColorSync profiles*—files that identify the color-display characteristics of your monitor. ColorSync information is primarily useful to people who use a scanner and a color printer, but you do no harm by clicking the name of the monitor you're using in this list.

---

**POWER USERS' CLINIC**

### Many Monitors, One Mac

From the dawn of the color-monitor era, Macs have had a terrific feature that Windows computers lacked for 10 years: the ability to exploit multiple monitors all plugged into the Mac at the same time. You can choose to have every monitor display the same thing—useful in a classroom—or to have one monitor act as an extension of the next. For example, you might have your Photoshop image window on your big monitor, but keep all the Photoshop controls and tool palettes on a smaller screen. Your cursor passes from one screen to another as it crosses the boundary.

To bring about this delicious arrangement, you need a Power Mac with more than one video card installed, or a PowerBook G3 (bronze keyboard). (You can rig certain other PowerBook, iBook, or iMac models with a second monitor, but these setups generally limit you to seeing the same picture on both screens—an arrangement called *video mirroring.)*

When you open the Monitors program on those Power Macs and PowerBook G3s, you see a different Monitors control-panel window on each screen. Using this control panel, you can change the color and resolution settings independently for each screen.

If your Mac can show different images on each screen, you get another icon at the top of your main screen, called Arrange. The Arrange window shows a miniature version of each

monitor. By dragging them around each other, you can specify how you want the second monitor's image "attached" to the first. Most people position the second monitor immediately to the right of the first, but you're also free to position it on the left, above, below, or even directly on top of the first monitor's icon (which produces a video-mirroring setup). For the least likelihood of going insane, consider placing the actual monitor into the corresponding position in the real world—to the right of your first monitor, for example.

For deep-down multiple-monitor fanatics, the fun doesn't stop there. See the microscopic menu bar on the first-monitor icon? You can drag that tiny strip onto a different monitor icon, if you like, to tell Monitors where you'd like the *actual* menu bar to appear. You can even control which monitor gets the startup slide show (the Mac OS 9 logo, the parade of extensions, and so on): turn on the "Identify the startup screen" checkbox. Now the tiny smiling-Mac icon appears on the startup monitor icon; you can drag this tiny smiling Mac to a different monitor icon, thus changing the stage for the startup slide show.

Finally, once you've got a multiple-monitor setup running, your Control Strip changes. The Resolution and Color Depth tiles (see page 74) each show two sets of options, so that you can control each monitor independently.

---

***Tip:*** The way your monitor displays colors can vary widely, depending on the lighting, the temperature, its age, and its mood. On some rainy Saturday afternoon, therefore, you might enjoy *calibrating* (adjusting) your monitor. To do so, open the Monitors control panel, click Color, and then click Calibrate. The Monitor Calibration Assistant appears; by answering the question that appears on each screen, using the visual aids the program presents, you can fine-tune the color display of your monitor until it's extremely accurate. At the end of the process, you'll be asked to name and save the new ColorSync profile you've created. If you care about color fidelity, repeat this entire procedure every couple of months.

### Geometry

This button appears only if you're using certain monitors, such as the iMac's built-in monitor. Click this button to summon a new panel that offers fantastic control over the way the screen image appears on the glass of your monitor. You can make it larger, smaller, higher, lower, wider, shorter, puffier in the middle, and so on, just by adjusting the corresponding controls.

## Mouse

It may surprise you that the cursor doesn't move five inches when you move the mouse five inches on the desk. Instead, the cursor moves farther when you move the mouse faster. How *much* farther depends on how you set the first slider in this control panel (see Figure 12-7). The Fast setting is nice if you have an enormous monitor, because it means that you don't need an equally large mouse pad to get from one corner to another. The Very Slow setting, on the other hand, can be frustrating, because it forces you to pick up and put down the mouse a lot as you scoot across the screen; it offers no acceleration at all. Experimentation is the key.

The Double-Click Speed setting specifies how much time you have to complete a double-click. If you click too slowly—beyond the time you've allotted yourself with this slider—the Mac "hears" two *single* clicks instead.

***Figure 12-7:***
*On a PowerBook or iBook, the Mouse control panel offers additional options. Mouse Tracks adds a special effect to your arrow cursor as it moves across the screen—a trailing parade of duplicate cursors. (In the day of low-cost, slow-to-respond laptop screens, this option could help you find a lost cursor; on modern Mac laptops, it's just distracting.) The Thick I-Beam option fattens up the vertical cursor when you're editing text.*

## Multiple Users

One of Mac OS 9's most heavily hyped features is its ability to permit different people in the same family, school, or office to use the same Mac. In OS 9, you can make it so that each user sees only the appropriate set of folders, programs, and documents, and benefits from a personalized set of settings for each program. This control panel is where you set up these "accounts" for each person. You'll find details in Chapter 17.

## QuickTime Settings

Most of the controls in this control panel do nothing at all. They're remnants of an age when Apple had high expectations for its QuickTime technology—expectations that never materialized. (Nobody enters passwords to unlock movies in the Media Keys section of this control panel, for example.)

There are, however, two settings worth changing in this control panel. First, by choosing Registration from the pop-up menu, you can type in a password you've purchased for $30 from the Apple Web site that turns QuickTime into QuickTime Pro—a much more flexible movie kit described in Chapter 20.

Second, by choosing AutoPlay from the pop-up menu, you can turn off the option called Enable CD-ROM Auto Play. In Apple's master plan, this feature would have let you insert specially created CD-ROM game discs that would begin running instantly (without your having to double-click). As it turns out, however, only a single programmer took advantage of this opportunity: the sociopath who wrote the Auto Start virus, one of the few Mac viruses. Fortunately, by turning this checkbox off, you ensure that your Mac will never catch that virus.

The other option on the screen, Enable Audio CD AutoPlay, is perfectly harmless—and, in fact, is handy. When turned on, this option plays music CDs automatically when you insert them into the machine. (See Chapter 13 for more on playing music CDs on your Mac.)

## Remote Access

This control panel connects you to the Internet over a telephone line (as opposed to, say, a cable modem or DSL modem). This control panel stores the phone number, password, and other aspects of your Internet account. (It was called the PPP control panel in some earlier versions of the Mac OS.) For more on this control panel and its useful hidden options, see page 256.

## Software Update

Few operating-system ideas are simpler or better than this one: whenever Apple improves or fixes one of the 2,000 software pieces that make up Mac OS 9, the Software Update program can notify you, download the update, and install it into your System Folder automatically. Figure 12-8 shows the procedure.

Software Update doesn't run rampant through your system software, however; it's quietly respectful. For example, in the beginning, you must manually click the Update Now button when you want the program to dial the Internet for updates. Furthermore, unless you turn off the "Ask me" checkbox, Software Update doesn't actually download the new software without asking your permission first.

For maximum effortlessness, turn on the checkbox called "Update software automatically." Then click Set Schedule to specify how often the program is allowed to hunt for new and improved software pieces. Even then, Software Update doesn't actually dial the Internet on its own at these times; instead, it goes about its business the next time *you* connect to the Internet for any reason.

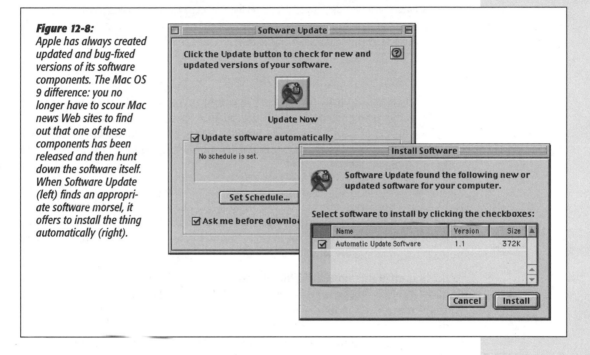

**Figure 12-8:**
*Apple has always created updated and bug-fixed versions of its software components. The Mac OS 9 difference: you no longer have to scour Mac news Web sites to find out that one of these components has been released and then hunt down the software itself. When Software Update (left) finds an appropriate software morsel, it offers to install the thing automatically (right).*

# Sound

It's possible to go your whole life without visiting this little program, but you'll miss out on a lot of Macintosh fun. Using the four control categories listed at the left side of the window (or, in Mac OS 9.1 and later, in tabs across the top), you can configure the sound system of your Mac in the following ways:

### Alert Sounds (Alerts tab)

"Alert Sound" means *error beep*—the sound you hear when the Mac wants your attention, or when you click someplace you shouldn't. (Want to hear yours? Choose File→Page Setup and then click anywhere outside of the dialog box.)

The big news in Mac OS 9 is the new set of choices in the list of alert sounds—the first new sounds Apple has provided in a decade. A few of the old favorites are still here, including Indigo, Simple Beep, and the famous Sosumi (named, the legend goes, when Apple Records threatened to sue Apple Computer for adding sound-recording features to the Mac). But the newcomers, including Glass, Pong2003, and Temple, add even more variety and wit to the collection. (If you've connected a microphone to your Mac, you can record new error sounds of your own. See Chapter 20 for details.)

---

**Tip:** See the volume slider on the Alert Sounds panel? Some Mac users are confused by the fact that even when they drag this slider all the way to the left, the sound from games and music CDs still plays at full volume.

The actual *master* volume slider for your Mac is on the Output panel of this control panel. (You can also use the Control Strip for this purpose.) The slider on the Alert Sounds panel is *just* for error beeps; Apple was kind enough to let you adjust the volume of these error beeps independently.

---

### Input

As Chapter 20 makes clear, any Macintosh can record sound. The question is: What would you like it to record? After all, several sources of sound are available to the Mac, including the built-in mike (iMac and PowerBook models), the CD-ROM drive (when you play music discs), an external microphone plugged into the microphone jack, and so on.

To specify what you want recorded, click Input, and then choose from the list on the right. (The Built-in choice, in this case, means, "All jacks on the outside of this computer." Depending on your model, this may refer to the Sound Input jack, the Microphone jack, the RCA audio input on AV models, and so on. Use the Input Source pop-up menu to specify which source you want to record from.)

At the bottom of this panel lurks the "Play sound through output device" checkbox. In English, it means, "Let me hear this sound while I'm recording it." When you're recording from a microphone, you usually *don't* want this box turned on—you'd get feedback from your Mac's speaker. But when you're recording from a CD, you *do* want this box turned on. Otherwise, you wouldn't be able to hear what you're recording.

### Output

"Output" means speakers. For 99 percent of the Mac-using community, this panel offers nothing useful except the master volume slider. The "Choose the device" wording seems to imply that you can choose which speakers you want to use for playback. But Built-in is generally the only choice, even if you have external speakers. (The Mac uses your external speakers automatically when they're plugged in.)

---

**Tip:** If you have a Mac with stereo speakers attached—you're in for a sonic treat. Using the Appearance control panel (see Chapter 3), turn on the Platinum sound effects. As you drag items around your screen, you'll hear sounds coming from the appropriate places in the stereo "field." Menus work the same way—when you pull down the  menu, the sound comes from the left speaker; when you open the Application menu, the sound comes from the right. You've got to give Apple credit: somebody was actually paid to come up with this idea.

---

### Speaker Setup (Speakers)

Some Macs, like Power Books and iMacs, have built-in stereo speakers; other Macs attain stereo-dom with the addition of external speakers. (Such special computer speakers are inexpensive—under $50.) If your Mac is thus equipped, you'll get a kick out of the Speaker Setup panel. By clicking Start Test and then dragging the sliders underneath the pictures of left and right speakers, you can adjust the relative balance between them (see Figure 12-9). That's useful if, for example, your desk is triangular, and you've been forced to put the left speaker farther away from your head than the right one.

**Figure 12-9:**
*The Speaker Setup screen lets you adjust the relative balance between your two stereo speakers. If your Mac has a headphone jack (this means you, iMac owners), something magical happens when you plug in head-phones: a picture of them appears instantly beneath the speakers in this window. Click the headphone picture, and then Start Test to perform balance adjustment between the two sides of your headphones.*

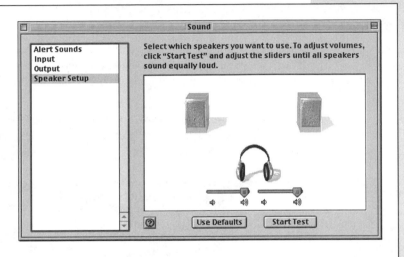

## Speech

Despite the *hundreds* of dollars Apple must have spent developing the Mac's speech capabilities, most people don't use it for anything serious. Sure, a few ultra-nerds record their answering-machine greeting using the Mac's voice. But for most people, the novelty of this feature wears off quickly.

If you're game to play around with it, however, using the Speech control panel is easy enough. When the Options pop-up menu is set to Voice, you can use the Voice pop-up menu to choose one of the Mac's 18 male, female, and alien voices.

The other choice in the Options pop-up menu can be marginally useful: Talking Alerts. When the "Speak the alert text" option is checked, the Mac reads, out loud, any error message that appears on the screen. This feature comes in handy on those occasional days when the Mac is busy doing something time-consuming—compiling a QuickTime movie, installing new software, downloading something big—and you go over to the couch to read a magazine while waiting. Instead of reading long into the night, unaware that the Mac has finished the job, you'll now be alerted by the sound of the Mac talking in its bizarre accent. When you get up to look at the screen, you'll realize that the Mac was trying to tell you something.

For much more on Apple's speech features, see Chapter 21.

## Startup Disk

As noted in the previous chapter, your Mac can't start up without a System Folder. However, the Mac generally doesn't care *where* it finds the System Folder; it doesn't necessarily have to be on the built-in hard drive. You can start the Mac up instead from a CD-ROM, Zip disk, external hard drive, and so on.

Advanced Mac users often capitalize on this feature by keeping a different version of the system software on each disk. For example, they might have Mac OS 9 on the hard drive, for example, but keep a slimmed-down copy of Mac OS 8.6 on a Zip disk when they need to run software that's incompatible with Mac OS 9.

That's all fine with the Mac. It just wants to know: "The next time I start up, *which disk* am I supposed to start up from?" This control panel lets you answer that question. It shows the icons of any System Folder–equipped disks currently inserted into the Mac. Just click the one you want, and then restart the machine.

*Note:* Not every kind of disk can start up your machine, even if its icon shows up in the Startup Disk control panel. Many external FireWire drives can't start up the Mac; neither can a DVD-RAM disc. A RAM disk can't start up any modern Mac model (but can start up most pre-G3 models).

---

**FREQUENTLY ASKED QUESTION**

### Network Disk: the Mystery Startup Icon

*I've only got one startup disk: the hard drive built into my iMac. So how come my Startup Disk control panel shows another hard drive called Network Disk?*

Certain Macs, such as iMacs, iBooks, and recent Power Macs, were designed to be *net-bootable*. That means that, in corporate or school situations, a bunch of these Macs can use, as their startup disk, the hard drive of a single, central *server* machine (usually running a special networking operating system called Mac OS X Server).

When your iMac starts up from a startup disk elsewhere on

the network in this way, you wait a lot longer for the startup process to finish. But for whoever has to run the network, the payoffs are considerable: now there's only *one* System Folder to configure, troubleshoot, maintain, and so on. As long as the server's System Folder is running well, every Mac connected to it runs well.

That's why a special icon called Network Disk appears in your Startup Disk control panel: it's there for the day when your Mac is connected to a central server disk, and you're instructed to start up from it, instead of from your own hard drive.

---

## TCP/IP

This control panel is the heart of your Mac's Internet connections. The strings of numbers and codes displayed here tell your Mac how to connect to the Net, whether by phone line or a higher-speed connection (such as cable modem or DSL). Better still, you can use the File→Configurations command to create *several* TCP/IP connection settings—a huge time-saver for anyone who must occasionally switch from, say, America Online to a regular ISP account, or from dial-up modem to cable modem. You can read more on this arrangement on page 256.

## Trackpad

This control panel is exclusively for laptops. Its Tracking Speed and Double-Click Speed controls correspond to those in the Mouse control panel, described earlier in this chapter.

Much more interesting are the "Use Trackpad for:" controls. Under normal circumstances, you touch your laptop's trackpad exclusively to *move* the cursor. For clicking and dragging, you're supposed to use the clicking button beneath the trackpad.

Many people find, however, that it's more direct to tap and drag directly on the trackpad—using the same finger that's been moving the cursor—instead of trying to hit the clicker button with the thumb. That's the purpose of these three boxes:

- **Clicking.** When this box is turned on, you can tap the trackpad surface to register a "mouse click" at the location of the cursor. Double-tap to double-click.

- **Dragging.** Turn on this option if you want to be able to move icons, highlight text, or pull down menus using the trackpad. Start by tapping twice on the trackpad—but *immediately* after the second tap, begin dragging your finger. (If you don't start moving promptly, the laptop assumes that you were double-clicking, which could wind up opening some icon you didn't intend to open.) You can stroke the trackpad repeatedly to continue your movement, as long as your finger never leaves the trackpad surface for more than about one second. When you finally stop touching the pad, you "let go," and the drag is considered complete. (Fortunately, all of this is much easier to do than to describe.)

- **Drag lock.** If the dragging maneuver described above makes you too nervous that you're going to "drop" what you're dragging if you stop moving your finger, consider this option instead. When it's on, you can take your sweet time about continuing the movement. In between strokes of the trackpad, you can take your finger off the laptop for as long as you like. You can take a phone call, a shower, or a vacation; the Mac still thinks that you're in the middle of a drag. Only when you tap *again* does the laptop consider the drag a done deal.

## USB Printer Sharing

New in Mac OS 9.1, this control panel lets every Mac on the network use the same USB printer (such as a color inkjet). Getting all this working may require a bit of fiddling on big networks (see the Mac Help topic "USB Printer Sharing"); but if the technology gods are smiling, all you have to do is click the Start button, click the My Printers tab, and turn on the Share checkbox for the printer to be shared.

Thereafter, you can use that shared printer from another Mac on the network like this: First, install the printer's driver software. Second, open USB Printer Sharing, click the Network Printers tab, and turn on the printer's checkbox. Finally, select the shared printer in the Chooser, just as you would any printer.

## Web Sharing

See page 245 for details on this control panel.

# The Extensions: What They're For

In your System Folder→Extensions folder, over 150 pieces of software wriggle, squirm, and compete: your extensions. Each adds one feature or another to your Mac. Many of them also use up memory, make the Mac take longer to start up, and can increase the likelihood of crashes, freezes, and glitches (see Appendix C).

In the Mac OS X, Apple has eliminated extensions, for these very reasons. In the meantime, you can improve your Mac's health and speed by turning off the extensions (and, therefore, features) you don't need. You turn them off using Extensions Manager, described earlier in this chapter.

One more point about extensions: Apple's programmers are fond of splitting them up into several extensions per feature. Mac OS 9's password-protection feature requires five extensions; your Mac's ATI video card requires six; the collection of Quick-Time movie-playing extensions, seven. In the following discussion, your extension parade is presented, therefore, feature by feature.

## Extensions for Software Features

Most of your extensions are designed to offer one software feature or another. They include:

- **Basic Mac features.** Many of the basic Mac features you've read about in other chapters of this book rely upon software helpers in the Extensions folder. Such features include the Control Strip *(Control Strip Extension)*, tear-off Application menu *(Application Switcher)*, Control-key contextual menus *(Contextual Menu Extension, SOMobjects for Mac OS)*, the Location Manager *(Location Manager Extension, Location Manager Modules)*, Software Update control panel *(Software Update Engine, Software Update Scheduler)*, automatic clock-setting by Internet *(Time Synchronizer)*, online help *(HTMLRenderingLib)*, and, if you have a Zip drive, the software that lets your Mac read Zip disks *(Iomega Driver)*.

- **Your Web browser.** A few of the software chunks in your Extensions folder are helper programs for your Web browser. For example, Microsoft Internet Explorer installs translators like *ActiveX Controls, Indeo Video,* and *Intel Raw Video.* (The latter are for playing Windows-format movies you encounter on the Web.) *Macromedia* and *MacromediaRuntimeLib* let your Web browser interpret certain kinds of animations online. And the *MRJ Libraries* (Macintosh Runtime for Java) represent the Mac's interpretation of the famous Java language, which lets certain Web pages perform sophisticated, application-like tasks. Chances are good that your favorite bank or investment Web site requires Java.

• **Your Microsoft programs.** If you use Microsoft Office 98, the world's largest software company has endowed your Extensions folder with *Microsoft Hyperlink Library, Microsoft OLE Automation, Microsoft OLE Library, Microsoft RPC Runtime Library, Microsoft Structured Storage, MS Font Embed Library (PPC), MS Library Folder,* and *Microsoft Component Library.*

• **Movies.** QuickTime is the software that lets your Mac show movies, whether played from your hard drive, from a CD, from the Internet, or from a camcorder (if your Mac, like the iMac DV, has movie-making circuitry). The components that make all of this work include *QuickTime Extensions, QuickTime, QuickTime MPEG Extension, QuickTime Musical Instruments,* and *QuickTime PowerPlug.* A few are more specialized: QuickTime VR lets your Mac display panoramic "virtual-reality" photos, as described in Chapter 20. You need the *QuickTime FireWire DV Support* and *QuickTime FireWire DV Enabler* extensions only if your Mac has a FireWire jack for connecting to your digital camcorder.

• **Security.** Mac OS 9 is the most secure, password-protectable operating system in the Mac's history. The Multiple Users feature described in Chapter 17 requires the extensions called *Multi-User Startup* and *Voice Verification.* Both that feature and the password-protection feature described in Chapter 2 require the *Security Cert Module, Security Library, Security Manager, Security Policy Module,* and *Security Storage Module* extensions.

• **AppleScript.** The extensions called *AppleScript, Folder Actions,* and *AppleScriptLib* make possible AppleScript, the software robot described in Chapter 10.

• **Your fonts.** The font extensions in your System Folder include *Type 1 Scaler* (helps your Mac display special font categories, including Unicode and vertical-typing languages) and the *Type Libraries* folder, which provides typographical information to your Microsoft Office programs, if any.

• **Your applications.** Some of your extensions are designed to help the Mac run programs—a function that occasionally comes in handy. The *Shared Library Manager* and *Shared Library Manager PPC* extensions let your Mac use shared libraries, which are described on page 188. The *CarbonLib* extension is a forward-looking bit of code that will let your Mac OS 9 machine run programs written for Mac OS X. Finally, the *Text Encoding Converter* extension helps prevent you from seeing U's instead of apostrophes in your email. (That's the simplified explanation. The technical one is that this extension helps the Mac translate between various text systems, such as ASCII and Unicode.)

- **Speech.** As described in Chapter 21, your Mac can talk. The *MacinTalk 3* extension, *MacinTalk Pro, Speech Manager,* and *Voices* folder make it possible.

- **Sherlock.** The Sherlock searching program gets Chapter 15 to itself. Among its components are *Find By Content* (searches for the words inside your files), *FBC Indexing Scheduler* (FBC stands for Find By Content—lets your Mac index your hard drive at a time you specify), *Find,* plus the Internet-searching files *LDAP Client Library* and *LDAPPlugin.*

- **The Internet.** The *Internet Access* extension lets you go online. The two *StuffIt Engine* files, in conjunction with the StuffIt Expander program (in your Internet folder), help you decompress and decode files you download from the Internet.

---

**Tip:** The rarely discussed *Internet Config Extension* adds a useful feature to every program you use: any time you see a Web or email address written in one of your programs, you can highlight and then ⌘-click it to launch your Web browser or email program. You're taken directly to the address you clicked.

---

- **Extensions Manager.** Ironically, the Extensions Manager *control panel* requires an extension—the one called *EM Extension.* Because Apple has preceded its name with an invisible space, this item appears first in the alphabetical list of extensions—and when you turn the Mac on, it therefore loads into memory first. That's why you can press the Space bar at startup to summon Extensions Manager: this extension has already loaded, preparing the Mac to watch for your Space bar-press.

- **Apple Guide.** Apple Guide is one of the Mac's built-in Help features, as described in Appendix A. The various text and graphics that appear in these help screens are stored in Guide files: *Apple Guide, Location Manager Guide, Macintosh Guide, SimpleText Guide,* and so on.

- **Your CD-ROM drive.** The *Apple CD/DVD Driver* extension is the critical component here; without it, your Mac's CD drive is nonfunctional. Additional files— *Audio CD Access, Foreign File Access, High Sierra File Access, UDF Volume Access, Apple Photo Access,* and *ISO 9660 Access*—are plug-in files that let your Mac read various specialized kinds of CDs, including music CDs, Kodak photo CDs, DVDs, and hybrid Mac/Windows discs.

- **Printing software.** Your Extensions folder also contains the software the Mac needs to print. These components include *Desktop Printer Spooler, Desktop PrintMonitor, PrintingLib,* and *PrintMonitor.* (You can turn the first two off, if you like, as described in Chapter 19.) The *Printer Descriptions* folder contains individual files for dozens of individual printer models, each of which describes to the Mac that printer's specific features. You'd be well advised to throw away the Printer Description files for printers you don't use. Finally, you'll find the *Printer Share* extension, which lets you share an old Apple StyleWriter with other Macs on the network—slowly. See Chapter 19 for much more on printing and these options.

- **Network Browser.** The extensions called *SLPPlugin, NSL UI Library, URL Access,* and *NBP Plugin DNSPlugin* are associated with the Network Browser, described in Chapter 5. Each lets your Network Browser "see" a different kind of computer on the Internet.

## Extensions for Hardware Features

Fortunately, the software for such fundamental Mac elements as the mouse, keyboard, and basic monitor functions are invisible to you; they're embedded into the system software itself. Most other hardware attachments, however, require special software:

- **Your video card.** In its efforts to make the Mac an excellent computer for playing video games, Apple and ATI, its video-card partner, have created numerous pieces of software that control your video circuitry. They include *ATI 3D Accelerator, ATI Resource Manager, ATI Video Accelerator, ATI Video Accelerator Update, Apple IX3D Graphics Accelerator, Apple IX3D RAVE Engine,* and *Apple IX3D Video Memory Manager.*

- **Your printer.** Over the years, Apple has marketed dozens of printer models, all of which have now been discontinued. For the benefit of Mac customers who still use these old printers, however, Apple still clutters your Extensions folder with the necessary printer software: *Apple Color SW Pro CMM, Color SW 1500, ImageWriter, CSW 6000 Series, LaserWriter 300/LS,* and so on. (SW stands for StyleWriter.) If you have one of the popular Epson or Hewlett-Packard inkjet printers, you'll see files here in your Extensions folder with the word Epson or HP in their names. Throw away or turn off all of them except the one that corresponds to the printers you actually use. (The one called LaserWriter 8 can control most laser printers, however, even if they aren't made by Apple.)

- **Your network.** A sprawling array of extensions is dedicated to a single purpose: letting your Mac connect to other computers in your office over network wiring. These include *Network Setup Extension, Apple Enet* (for Ethernet networks), and *Open Transport.* Some of the files are specifically for use in sharing files with other Mac users (*File Sharing Library, File Sharing Extension*), and still others are for making your Mac available for sharing over the Internet (*Web Sharing Extension, ShareWay IP Personal Bgnd*). For more on networking, see Chapter 16.

- **ColorSync.** Apple has put a lot of effort into its color-fidelity software, as you can read in Chapter 19. In addition to the ColorSync control panel described earlier, the ColorSync software suite includes such extensions as *ColorSync Extension, Color Picker, Default Calibrator,* and *Heidelberg CMM* (color-matching module). All of this helps keep colors consistent from scan to finished color printout.

- **Video games.** Many of your extensions are dedicated to providing special graphics features for computer games. They fall into three categories: sprocket libraries (*NetSprocketLib, InputSprocket Extension, DrawSprocketLib*), QuickDraw 3D (*Apple QD3D HW Driver, Apple QD3D HW Plug-In, QD3DCustomElements, QuickDraw 3D, QuickDraw 3D IR, QuickDraw 3D RAVE, QuickDraw 3D Viewer*), and OpenGL software (*OpenGLEngine, OpenGLLibrary, OpenGLMemory, OpenGLRenderer, OpenGLRendererATI,* and *OpenGLUtility*).

Sprocket libraries are primarily designed to let the Mac use external game-playing equipment, such as joysticks. QuickDraw 3D is a built-in software suite that makes it easier for programmers to create three-dimensional characters in their computer games. OpenGL, which stands for Open Graphics Library, is a set of standard programming tools, originally designed by Silicon Graphics and now available on many different kinds of computers, that helps game programmers create special effects like fog, shadows, three-dimensional scenes, and so on. If you don't play computer games, you can turn all of these extensions off.

• **Your speakers.** *Sound Manager, SoundSprocket Filter,* and *SoundSprocketLib* are all designed to help your Mac process sound, especially from games.

• **Your modem.** Even your humble modem requires software. The Modem Scripts folder contains drivers for every conceivable modem brand; as noted earlier in this book, feel free to open this folder and throw away the files corresponding to all modems but your own. *OpenTpt Modem, OpenTpt Remote Access,* and *OpenTpt Serial Arbitrator* are other extensions that help your Mac manage its modem and modem port.

# CHAPTER 13

# Apple Leftovers, Apple Extras

The System Folder—described exhaustively in the preceding chapters—is the heart, brains, and most abdominal organs of Mac OS 9, but it's not the only component. The hard drive of even a brand-new Mac OS 9 Macintosh comes with several additional folders—Apple Extras, Assistants, Applications, and so on—filled with software both useful and frivolous. And if even that's not enough software for you, the *custom installation* option of the Mac OS 9 installer, described in Appendix B, offers several hundred megabytes more.

This chapter guides you through these extras, add-ons, and accessories. It's not likely that you'll use very many of them—but here and there, among all the chaff, you might find a surprisingly useful nugget.

## The Apple Extras Folder

The folder name "Apple Extras" is Apple's cute way of saying, "Stuff we had no good place to install." It contains an utterly random assortment of utility programs. By all means, throw away the ones you don't intend to use.

### Apple LaserWriter Software

The only useful item in this folder is the Desktop Printer Utility. As you can read in Chapter 19, it lets you adjust various settings on your laser printer. (If you don't have a laser printer, toss it.)

### AppleScript

This folder is the home of AppleScript, the Macintosh automation software described in Chapter 10. It contains Script Editor, the program you use to write, inspect, and edit AppleScripts, as well as two folders filled with useful, ready-made AppleScripts. Here's a quick summary of the scripts Apple includes with Mac OS 9:

### Automated Tasks

Inside this folder is a document called About Automated Tasks that, for a document written by Apple, is fairly easily understood. It describes each of this folder's *AppleScripts*—tiny double-clickable programs that perform tiny, one-shot functions—in detail. There you'll discover that four of these scripts are useful only to people on a network who frequently turn File Sharing on and off, and so on.

One of these scripts, however, is fantastically useful, and belongs in the  menu of every Macintosh: *Add Alias to Apple Menu.* If you've read the discussion on page 79, you know how useful it can be to have your favorite icons in the  menu—but how annoying it is to install them there. You must make an alias of the icon, take the word *alias* off the icon's name, open three folders, and so on.

But all that changes if you add this AppleScript to your  menu. From now on, just highlight any icon, and then choose Add Alias to Apple Menu from the  menu— instantly, the highlighted icon appears in your  menu. (If you can't find the Automated Tasks folder, click the Missing CD-ROM link at *www.missingmanual.com* to download a copy.)

### More Automated Tasks

Why are these three additional scripts segregated into their own folder? Must be office politics.

In any case, the one called *Alert When Folder Changes* is another tool for people on networks—it checks a particular shared folder every 15 minutes. If anyone puts any new files into that folder, a message appears to alert you. The one called *Synchronize Folders* is a more confusing version of the File Synchronization program described in the previous chapter.

The remaining script, *Hide/Show Folder Sizes*, is easy to overlook, but can save a lot of time in certain situations. When you double-click it, the "Calculate Folder sizes" option, described on page 26, is turned on for all open windows. Being able to switch this option on or off so easily is helpful when you're comparing the contents of two disks, when trying to find out whether or not you've prepared the right amount of material for a CD-ROM you're about to burn, and so on.

## ColorSync Extras

If you've become handy with AppleScript (see Chapter 10), and you work in the graphic design or printing industry, you may well find it worthwhile to get to know the 21 AppleScripts included in this folder. As the accompanying Sample AppleScripts ReadMe document makes clear, these arc AppleScript examples that illustrate how you might be able to automate the processing and ColorSync profiling of graphics files in your publishing system. Very few of these scripts are meant to be used as is; you're supposed to modify them so that they make sense for your own particular equipment, learning volumes about AppleScript in the process.

## FireWire

As described in Chapter 18, FireWire is the high-speed jack on the side or back of most current Mac models. This folder contains only a text file explaining as much.

## Font Extras

The FontSync control panel, the primary document of this folder, is a noble Apple attempt to solve an old problem for desktop publishers. You finish designing some beautiful newsletter, you take it to the local printing shop for printing on a high-quality press, and you have to throw out the entire batch—because the fonts didn't come out right. The printing shop didn't have exactly the same fonts you had when you prepared the document. Or, worse, it *did* have the same font—but from a different font company, with the same name but slightly different type characteristics.

FontSync could give you early warning for such disasters. When you double-click the Create FontSync Profile program, several minutes elapse—and then the Mac generates a FontSync Profile document. This file contains staggering amounts of information about the design, spacing, and curlicues of every font installed in your system. When you hand that profile over to your print shop, they can drop it onto the accompanying program, called Match FontSync Profile; Mac OS 9 will tell them precisely what fonts are different on their Macs and yours.

The wishful-thinking aspect of this technology is, of course, that it assumes a lot: that your print shop uses Mac OS 9, that the print shop knows how to use FontSync, and that you remember to create the profile and submit it.

## Iomega

This software contains the Tools program that lets you erase, format, or lock Zip and Jaz disks.

## Mac OS Runtime for Java

There's nothing useful in this folder—just Read Me documents. The actual Mac Java software is in your Extensions folder, as described on page 217.

## Map Control Panel

This handy little program lets you tell, at a glance, what time it is in any other country in the world. As shown in Figure 13-1, a click anywhere on the map shows you the current time at that spot, along with its longitude and latitude. Drag your cursor over the edges of the picture to scroll the map. You can also type in the name of the major city and then click Find to locate it (or the closest alphabetic match in the Map database).

---

*Tip:* Repeatedly Option-click the Find button, or press Option-Return, to visit each of the cities in the Map program's database in turn.

And if you're *really* bored, type *Mid* and press Return.

---

To get the most use out of the Map, tell it where *you* are. To do so, click on the Map, or search for a major city in your time zone; when the cursor is blinking in the correct spot, click Set. Now you can perform useful time and distance comparisons with *other* cities, as shown in Figure 13-1. (The current time in the other city appears at the bottom of the window; the number of hours' *difference* is displayed in the Time Zone boxes—the + symbol means that the distant city's clocks are set *ahead* of yours.)

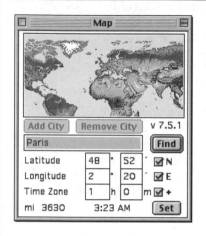

**Figure 13-1:**
*After you've set your home city (by locating it on the map and then clicking Set), you can click any other Map location to view your distance from it, as shown in the lower-left corner. Click that "mi" readout repeatedly to view your distance from the other city in kilometers or degrees.*

Until 1998, the Map was a staple of the Mac's Control Panels folder. It was finally exiled to the Apple Extras folder because of one simple failing: it doesn't observe Daylight Saving Time, which occasionally throws off its time calculations. The Date & Time control panel has far surpassed it in the time-keeping regard, but nothing can match the Map's charm and usefulness in providing distance readouts—and a sense of your world.

*Tip:* You can enlarge the Map picture, although blotchily, by pressing Shift just after double-clicking the Map control panel icon (for 200% size), Option *while* double-clicking, (400%), or Shift and Option just after double-clicking (800%).

## Monitors Extras Folder

The Digital Color Meter program in this folder is yet another Apple tool that helps designers and publishers maintain consistent colors in the rough translation between screen and printout. When this program is running, point the cursor to anything you see on your screen—in the design you're working on, on a Web page, and so on. As you point, the color meter shows you what percent of the color at the cursor tip is composed of red, green, and blue. (You can click any of the other buttons to view the color as expressed in various other technical ways.)

If you have an Apple ColorSync or AppleVision monitor, an additional feature awaits. If you press ⌘-F, the program computes the corresponding Pantone shade (a printing-industry standard color-matching system), so that you can figure out how to reproduce a particular monitor-displayed color when printed.

## Note Pad

Steve Jobs may have brought Apple back from the dead when he returned to run the company in 1997, but he's one arbitrary fellow. Among the changes he made upon his return: taking the Note Pad, a favorite  menu item since 1984, out of the  menu.

The banishment to the Apple Extras folder is a shame, because the Note Pad is a handy little storage center for phone numbers, to do lists, Web addresses, brainstorms, and other bits of text you run across in your day-to-day activity. Here's what you can do with the Note Pad:

- Resize or scroll the display—each page holds a maximum of 32 KB of text (several real-world pages' worth).

- Drag-and-drop text (see page 138, within the Note Pad page, to and from the desktop, or to and from other drag-and-drop programs.

- Create additional pages (choose File→New Note).

- Change the typeface (choose Edit→Preferences).

- Search for text (choose Edit→Find).

- Jump to a specific page (click the page number at the bottom).

- Maintain multiple Note Pad files, as described on page 181.

Actually, the Stickies program in the  menu does everything the Note Pad does, and more—for example, it lets you see all of the "pages" simultaneously. But for nostalgia fans and neat freaks, there's something about the tiny, real-world feeling of the Note Pad that screams out, "Move me back into the  menu!"

---

*Tip:* Have you ever wished you could edit or add to a "Read Me" file, but couldn't because the Read Me was, of course, a *read-only* SimpleText file? (See "The Uneditable SimpleText File" on page 231.) The solution: Open Note Pad and drag the Read Me *icon* into the Note Pad window. Now you have normal, editable text in your Note Pad.

---

## Register with Apple

This tiny program does nothing more than open your Web browser to the Apple Registration Web page, where you can put yourself on Apple's junk-mail list. (Registering in this way is optional—you don't have to register to get technical and warranty support from Apple, for example.)

## On the Desktop

After you install Mac OS 9, or when you buy a computer that comes with Mac OS 9 on it, a few alias icons litter the right side of your screen. As you can tell from the following descriptions, there's no real reason to leave them on your desktop—even if you find them useful, the  menu makes a better, and more often available, location for them. Here's what they do:

## Browse the Internet

Double-click this icon to launch your Web browser; that's all this program does.

---

**Tip:** Mac OS 9, of course, comes with *two* Web browsers—Netscape Communicator and Internet Explorer. Which one opens when you double-click the Browse the Internet icon?

The sneaky answer: whichever one you designated in the →Control Panels→Internet control panel. Details on page 201. (If you don't make a choice in the Internet control panel, you get Microsoft Internet Explorer.)

---

## Mail

Like the preceding item, this one does nothing more than launch an Internet program—in this case, your e-mail program. (As described in the previous tip, your email program is Microsoft Outlook Express unless you specify a different one using the Internet control panel.)

## QuickTime Player

You can read about the QuickTime Player program, which plays movies and sounds, in Chapter 20.

## Register with Apple

This alias launches the Register with Apple program, which is described in the previous section.

# The Applications Folder

Apple gives you a few starter programs in this folder; as you download and buy more programs of your own, you may find this folder a good place to store them. Not only does it have a handsome custom icon that distinguishes it from mere mortal folders, but it appears near the top of the alphabet when you view your hard drive window as a list.

## AppleCD Audio Player

By a happy coincidence, the equipment your Mac uses to play CD-ROM discs is exactly the same equipment found in a stereo-system music CD player. All you need is a little bit of software—this program—to serve as the "front panel," and suddenly your Mac is the world's best CD player.

Put a music CD into your Mac, launch this program, and the music begins. You can change the color scheme to your liking, using the Options menu. Adjust the volume using the right-side slider, and then switch into whatever program you're using for work—the CD player program retreats into the background, but the music continues so that you can listen as you work.

*Tip:* If you regularly listen to music as you work, you can bypass AppleCD Audio Player entirely. Choose ☀→Control Panels→QuickTime Settings, choose AutoPlay from the pop-up menu, and make sure that Enable Audio CD AutoPlay is turned on. Now music CDs play as soon as they're inserted into the Mac—no special action on your part is required.

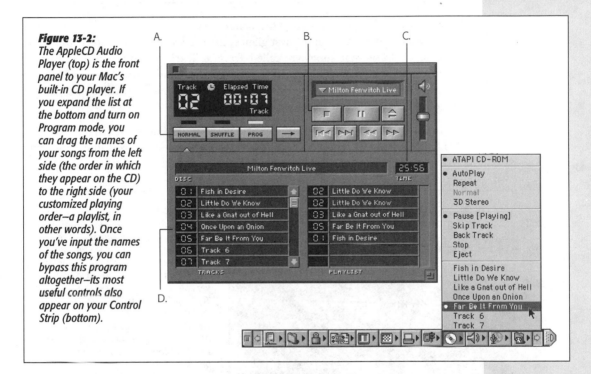

**Figure 13-2:**
*The AppleCD Audio Player (top) is the front panel to your Mac's built-in CD player. If you expand the list at the bottom and turn on Program mode, you can drag the names of your songs from the left side (the order in which they appear on the CD) to the right side (your customized playing order—a playlist, in other words). Once you've input the names of the songs, you can bypass this program altogether—its most useful controls also appear on your Control Strip (bottom).*

The controls in this program correspond to the labels in Figure 13-2.

A. **Normal, Shuffle, Prog, [Arrow].** The first three buttons here determine how the CD songs are played. "Normal" means in sequence, "Shuffle" means in a random order, and the Prog (Program) button means that you can rearrange the songs manually, as shown in Figure 13-2.

The arrow button is the Repeat button. Click it to switch between Repeat mode (the CD plays over and over again, as represented by the loop that appears on this button) and Standard mode (the CD plays to the end and then stops, as represented by the straight arrow that appears on the button).

**B. Primary transport controls.** The top row of buttons here mean Stop, Play/Pause, and Eject; the bottom buttons mean Previous Track, Next Track, Rewind, and Fast Forward. Above all this, where it says Audio CD, is a pop-up menu of the tracks on the CD, so that you can jump immediately to a particular song.

**C. Time display.** This readout shows the total lengths of the songs on the CD (or, if you're building a playlist, the total lengths of the songs you've selected).

---

***Tip:*** Speaking of time: click the tiny clock at the upper-left corner of the window. You're offered a pop-up menu that controls what the large time display shows—the elapsed time or remaining time, either for the current track or the entire CD.

---

**D. Track list.** To make this part of the window appear, click the tiny triangle just below the Normal button. At first glance, the track list doesn't appear to be terrifically helpful—the songs are called Track 1, Track 2, and so on. Fortunately, you can click the name of a track and type in its name. (You can also click the words "Audio CD" above the list and type in the name of the disc.) As you go, press Return or Tab to move down to the next blank.

The information you type here is stored in your System Folder→Preferences folder, in a file called CD Remote Programs. As a result, whenever you insert this particular CD again, the Mac will remember its track names and title.

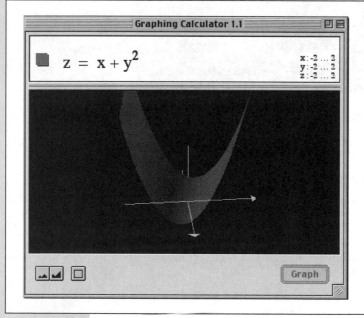

**Figure 13-3:**
*Showing off is easy with the Graphing calculator. Graphical equations like z=x+y2 or y=7z+x3 produce the most impressive results. For more examples of the kinds equations the Mac OS 9 version can solve, choose Help→ Types of Graphs. There you'll find out that version 2.2, for sale at www.PacificT.com, can graph dozens of more complex equations, including spherical coordinates and contour plots.*

*Tip:* You're not condemned to typing the names of every track on every CD you own. The free program NetCD Player (available at *www.missingmanual.com*) automatically downloads the lists of tracks for each of your CDs from one of the Internet's gigantic CD databases. The CD and track names show up in AppleCD Audio Player automatically.

## Graphing Calculator

If you work in math or the sciences, you may get actual use out of this dazzling display of computer horsepower—otherwise, you can use it just to dazzle people. You type an equation into the top window (one that begins with $y=$ or $z=$) and press Return; the Graphing Calculator solves the equation as a graphic in two or three dimensions (see Figure 13-3).

Use the color swatch pop-up menu to specify a color for your graph; drag the horizontal divider bar up or down to adjust the size of the graph area; drag the graph (not the background) to rotate it in a different direction; zoom in or zoom out by clicking the mountain buttons at the lower-left corner; and adjust the resolution (quality) of the graph by clicking the icon to the right of the mountains and dragging the slider. For truly mind-blowing demos of the commercial 2.0 version (for which this 1.1 version is a glorified advertisement), choose Demo→Version 2.

In the meantime, once you've got a graph or animation of which you're particularly proud, you can capture it. You can drag the graph background directly to the desktop, for example, to produce a picture clipping; you can choose Edit→Copy Graph; or you can even save the animation as a QuickTime movie (see Chapter 20) by choosing File→Save as Movie.

## Network Browser

For a complete discussion of this program, which also appears in your  menu, see page 90.

## QuickTime

This folder contains several components of the QuickTime movie, picture, and sound-playing software described in more detail in Chapter 20. These items include:

- **PictureViewer.** The world hasn't given nearly enough attention and glory to this humble, versatile, powerful picture viewer. All those graphics that you download from the Internet, every photo attachment someone sends you by email— PictureViewer opens them all, every standard graphics file type, in a fraction of a second. In fact, PictureViewer does so much faster than, say, the $800 Photoshop program. You can't *edit* pictures with this program, but for just looking at them, nothing's better. (PictureViewer's Image menu contains commands that let you enlarge or reduce the image, rotate it, and so on.)

  Consider putting this icon, or an alias of it, right on your desktop; then, whenever a graphic arrives on your Mac, you can look at it by dragging its icon on top of the PictureViewer icon.

- **QuickTime Player.** This program plays digital movies, as described in Chapter 20.

- **QuickTime Plugin.** This software lets your Web browser view *streaming* QuickTime movies—those that are transmitted to your Mac over the Internet. (In fact, this file is just a backup—duplicate copies of this plug-in are already installed in the two browsers that come with Mac OS 9.)

- **QuickTime Updater.** Like the Software Update control panel described in Chapter 12, this little program connects to the Internet to see if Apple has released a newer version of the QuickTime software. If so, QuickTime Updater offers to download and install it for you. (You can perform the same function from within the QuickTime Player program, if you like. Just choose Help→Check for QuickTime Updates.)

## Security

This folder contains the Apple File Security program, which is at the heart of the icon password-protection scheme described on page 49. You can drag an icon that you'd like to password-protect onto the Apple File Security icon—or, conversely, you can *un*protect a previously encrypted icon by dragging it onto Apple File Security. (Of course, you can also unprotect an encrypted icon by double-clicking it and entering the correct password—but doing so also *opens* the file you double-clicked. Dragging it onto the Apple File Security icon is the only way to decrypt a file without opening it.)

This folder also contains the Apple Verifier program. It detects the presence and authenticity of *digital signatures*—codes that are embedded into certain files to prove that they haven't been tampered with in transit over the Internet. If you receive a file from a company that uses digital signatures, drag it onto Apple Verifier's icon. If your Keychain (see Chapter 16) recognizes the digital signature, you can open the file. If not, you can either teach your keychain that this particular signature is legitimate—or worry that the file is bogus, and leave it unopened on your hard drive.

## SimpleSound

SimpleSound is a small and useful sound-recording program; if your Mac has a microphone, consider moving this one into your  menu. Instructions on using SimpleSound are in Chapter 20; for now, note that SimpleSound's most useful feature is its ability to record extremely long sounds. It's not limited to 10-second snippets, like the Sound control panel.

## SimpleText

SimpleText is a stripped-down word processor. Apple created it years ago to answer this question: "If we want new Mac owners—who haven't yet bought a word processor—to read our Read Me files, how will they read 'em?" When you double-click a Read Me file, in other words, it launches this program.

SimpleText's greatest limitation is that it can't display a document containing more than 32 K of text (a handful of pages long). It doesn't have any paragraph formatting features (like single-spaced vs. double-spaced)—in fact, the only formatting you can do is to change the fonts, sizes, and styles of the text in a document you're writing. You can't paste in graphics, either.

---

*Tip:* Mac experts may suggest workarounds for the "no graphics in SimpleText" rules, but these methods are more trouble than they're worth. Instead, prepare your SimpleText-based Read Me file with the much more powerful Tex-Edit, a shareware program available from *www.missingmanual.com.* It lets you paste or drag graphics directly into your text document; when you save the resulting file as a SimpleText–Read Only document, your work is done.

---

All of this is a long way of saying that while SimpleText isn't great at *creating* documents, it's terrific at showing them. SimpleText can play sounds or QuickTime movies, open almost any kind of graphics file, or show any kind of text-only file. It can also, by the way, read to you out loud—use the commands in the Sound menu. (Details on using the Mac's speech capabilities are in Chapter 21.)

---

*Tip:* Because a Read Me file comes with almost every new program, the average Mac hard drive eventually gets littered with copies of SimpleText. There's nothing inherently wrong with having 36 copies of it occupying various corners of your hard drive (unless you, like some Mac fans, believe that SimpleText copies spontaneously reproduce while the computer is turned off). But if the thought bothers you, use your Sherlock program to search for *SimpleText*—and throw away all but one copy.

---

# The Assistants Folder

An Assistant, in Apple-ese, is an interview program. (In Microsoft-ese, it would be called a Wizard.) It presents a series of screens, posing one question at a time; after answering each question, you're supposed to click the right-arrow (or Next) button.

---

At the end of the interview, the Assistant program incorporates your answers into some finished product—such as configuring numerous control panels all at once.

### Internet Setup Assistant

When you buy an iMac or iBook or first install Mac OS 9, you can't miss this one: it walks you through the process of creating an Internet account. Type in your name, address, and credit-card number, and you're in business. (Behind the scenes, the Internet Setup Assistant fills in the necessary blanks in three control panels: Remote Access, TCP/IP, and Modem; details are at the end of Chapter 14.)

### Mac OS Setup Assistant

This program pokes up its obtrusive little head the first time you turn on *any* modern Macintosh. As you click your way through its various question screens, you're asked about your time zone, geographic location, and printer connection. Several of the questions pertain to your network setup—you're asked to give your computer a name and password, for example (you can't skip this question, even if you have no intention of connecting your Mac to a network). Behind the scenes, the Setup Assistant makes the corresponding changes to your File Sharing, AppleTalk, and Date & Time control panels.

---

*Tip:* There's nothing wrong with just choosing File→Quit as soon as the Setup Assistant appears. The Mac works perfectly well without your slogging through this interview—the only crucial setting to make manually, in that case, is the time and time zone in the Date & Time control panel.

---

## The Internet Folder

In this folder, you'll find two folders of substance: Internet Applications and Internet Utilities. You'll also find aliases to many of the contents inside.

The big-ticket items, of course, are the three Internet programs in Internet Applications: Internet Explorer (Web browser), Netscape Communicator (Web browser), and Outlook Express (email program). The remaining folder, Microsoft Internet Self-Repair, contains the auto-installing items that allow Microsoft's programs to run the first time you double-click them, without even having to officially install them first. (Microsoft's self-install scheme also means that if you turn off or move one of its extensions, your Microsoft programs still run.)

The Internet Utilities folder, meanwhile, contains the Mail and Browse the Internet programs (for which aliases appear on your desktop, as described in the previous section), a folder of Internet Assistants, and the Aladdin Folder. (The Aladdin Folder contains StuffIt Expander, which translates compressed Internet downloads into usable files, and DropStuff, which converts usable files into compressed Internet uploads. For example, DropStuff can compress an entire folder into a single file icon, which you can then email to somebody—that is, if your email program doesn't do this automatically.)

***Tip:*** One of your first acts as a Mac OS 9 owner should be to open the Aladdin→StuffIt Expander folder, and drag the StuffIt Expander icon onto your desktop. Almost everything you download from the Internet, either from a Web page or as an email attachment, needs to be decoded and decompressed before you can use it; you can do that by dragging the download onto the StuffIt Expander icon.

## The Utilities Folder

This folder contains three disk-management programs that most people use once in a blue moon, if ever: Disk Copy, Disk First Aid, and Drive Setup.

### Disk Copy

This program creates *disk images*—electronic versions of disks or folders that you can send electronically to somebody else. The world's largest disk-image fan is Apple itself; the company often releases new software as a disk image. When you download a disk image and double-click its icon, Disk Copy re-creates the original disk icon on your screen (although most people never realize that Disk Copy was involved). Figure 13-4 shows the routine.

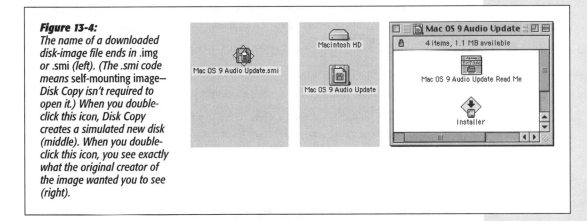

***Figure 13-4:***
*The name of a downloaded disk-image file ends in .img or .smi (left). (The .smi code means self-mounting image—Disk Copy isn't required to open it.) When you double-click this icon, Disk Copy creates a simulated new disk (middle). When you double-click this icon, you see exactly what the original creator of the image wanted you to see (right).*

You can also use Disk Copy to create disk images of your own—just drag a folder or disk icon into the Disk Copy window.

### Disk First Aid

Most people have encountered this disk-repair program without even being aware of it. Disk First Aid is the software that runs automatically, behind the scenes, whenever you start the Mac up after a system crash.

If you double-click the program's icon in the Utilities Folder, you're shown the icons of your hard drive and any other disks in your Mac at the moment. You're now supposed to click the icon of a disk and then click either Verify (to get a report on the disk's health) or Repair (which fixes whatever problems the program finds). In other words, Disk First Aid attempts to perform the same healing effects on a sick hard drive as, say, a commercial program like Norton Utilities. It does a great job at fixing many kinds of small disk problems; when you're troubleshooting, this free program should always be your first resort.

If Disk First Aid reports that it's unable to fix the problem, *then* it's time to invest in Norton Utilities or its rival, TechTool Pro.

---

***Tip:*** If Disk First Aid finds nothing wrong with a disk, it reports: "The volume appears to be OK." Don't be alarmed at the wishy-washy, not-very-confident wording of that message—that's the strongest vote of confidence Disk First Aid can give. Even a brand-new, perfectly healthy hard drive only *appears* to be OK to Disk First Aid.

---

## Drive Setup

Drive Setup is Apple's hard-drive erasing and partitioning program. If you make the proper sacrifices to the software gods, your hard drive will never be so damaged that it requires total erasure. As Appendix B should make clear, you can solve the vast majority of Mac problems by *replacing* the ailing software, not wiping it out.

Still, if you're determined to erase a disk completely—when you plan to sell your Mac, for example—Drive Setup is your tool. Click the name of the drive you want to erase, and then click Initialize.

---

***Caution:*** Technically, the Initialize button only marks the hard drive as *available* for storing new files—it doesn't actually scrub the disk to remove all traces of your old files. In other words, if you're selling your Mac, your buyer could theotically use a program like Norton Utilities to resurrect some of the files you erased.

If you're concerned about security, choose Functions→Initialization Options before clicking Initialize; turn on the two checkboxes there, and then click OK. Erasing the hard drive will now take much longer, but you can be confident that every last scrap of information has been obliterated.

---

# Custom Installation Options

As though all of the supplementary and utility software on your hard drive weren't enough, the Mac OS CD comes with enormous gobs of software that doesn't get automatically deposited on your Mac. You must specifically request this stuff by performing a *custom installation,* as described in Appendix B. If you go through with it, here's what you can request:

## English Speech Recognition

Don't get excited—Mac OS 9 by itself doesn't take dictation. By "speech recognition," Apple means executing commands—opening programs, printing, quitting, shutting down, running AppleScripts, and so on—not typing out words. For details on this speech-recognition feature, which is called PlainTalk, see Chapter 21.

## Language Kits

If you've scanned Chapters 11 and 12, you might have been struck by the quantity of system-software components dedicated to displaying non-English alphabets on the screen. So many control panels—Date & Time, Text, Numbers, Keyboard, and so on—are designed to accommodate this feature.

If you work in only one language, this flexibility may seem like no big deal. You probably bought your Mac with a *localized* operating system—that is, a version of Mac OS 9 that already runs in your own language.

But if you need to *switch* between your Mac's native language and other languages, on an occasional basis—when writing documents in both languages, when viewing Web pages, and so on—then Apple's WorldScript software is just what you need. Each WorldScript kit includes fonts, keyboard layouts, and software that helps the Mac word process from right to left across the screen, or top to bottom, as necessary. (Such a kit doesn't affect your actual OS language—the menus, dialog boxes, and so on.)

Before Mac OS 9, Apple sold these language kits for $79 apiece. Fortunately, *all* of these kits are included in Mac OS 9 at no extra charge.

---

**POWER USERS' CLINIC**

### Partitioning a Hard Drive with Drive Setup

It took years for Apple to get around to offering *partitioning* software in the standard operating system, but the current Drive Setup offers exactly that feature. Using its Custom Setup command, you can erase a hard drive in such a way that you subdivide its surface. Each chunk is represented on your screen by two (or more) different hard-drive icons.

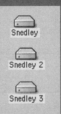

Actually, these days, there's not much reason to partition a drive; a partitioned hard drive is more difficult to resurrect after a serious crash, requires more navigation when you want to open a particular file, and offers no speed or safety benefits. Still, some people prefer to keep one category of files, or a different operating system, on each of several partitions.

To partition your drive—which involves *erasing it completely*—launch Drive Setup. Click the name of the hard drive, and then click Initialize. In the dialog box, click Custom Setup. From the Partitioning Scheme pop-up menu, choose the number of partitions you want. Now drag the horizontal lines in the Volumes map to specify the relative sizes of the partitions you want to create. When you're finished, click OK, and then click Initialize in the two final dialog boxes.

---

## Installing a WorldScript Kit

To install a new language kit, run the Mac OS 9 installer on your Mac OS 9 CD. On successive screens, click Continue, Select, Add/Remove, and Language Kits. From the None Selected pop-up menu, choose Customized Installation.

Now you're offered a list of language kits, including Arabic, Gujarati, Punjabi, Hebrew, Japanese, Korean, Chinese simplified, and Chinese traditional. Some of the other options listed here aren't immediately clear—each contains the necessary fonts and alphabets for *several* languages:

- **Central European.** With this kit, you can type in Polish, Hungarian, Czech, and Slovak.

- **Cyrillic.** For Russian, Bulgarian, and Ukrainian.

- **Devanagari.** For typing in Hindi, Marathi, Nepali, Sanskrit, and others.

Click the checkboxes for the language kits you want to install. Click OK, Start, Continue, and—when the installation is complete—Restart.

---

**Note:** You can also install Persian—it's in the Language Kits CD Extras folder on your Mac OS 9 CD—but it's incompatible with the Arabic kit. Install only one or the other.

---

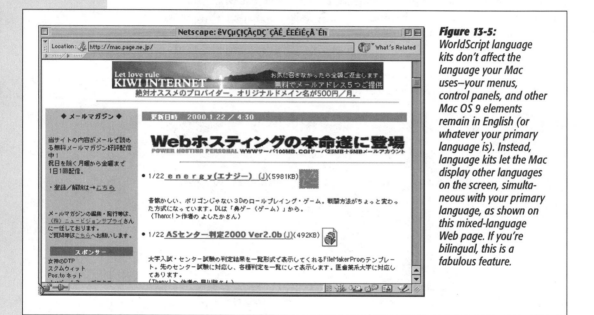

***Figure 13-5:***
*WorldScript language kits don't affect the language your Mac uses—your menus, control panels, and other Mac OS 9 elements remain in English (or whatever your primary language is). Instead, language kits let the Mac display other languages on the screen, simultaneous with your primary language, as shown on this mixed-language Web page. If you're bilingual, this is a fabulous feature.*

## Using a Language Kit

When the installation is complete, a new menu appears at the upper-right corner of your screen, resembling the flag of the currently selected language kit. Using this menu, you can choose the newly installed language kit. (Technically, you use this menu to specify a new *keyboard layout,* as described on page 203, but doing so simultaneously switches to the appropriate language kit.)

---

**Tip:** If you're using Chinese, Japanese, or Korean, choose Help→Mac Help and search for *languages.* There you'll find instructions on using Mac OS 9's special ideogram-entry palette.

---

Unfortunately, having a globally aware operating system doesn't necessarily mean that you have globally aware *programs.* In fact, relatively few programs sold in America can handle non-English language kits. Mac OS 9 comes with three: SimpleText, Netscape Communicator, and Internet Explorer. (The latter pair let you visit foreign-language Web pages, as shown in Figure 13-5.) The NisusWriter word processor *(www.nisus.com)*, ClockWork networkable calendar *(www.centsoft.com)*, and Statview math program *(www.sas.com)* are some examples of commercial programs that are WorldScript-savvy.

## Network Assistant Client

Apple sells a program called Apple Network Administrator that lets corporate networking pros control your Mac from over the network—but only if you've installed this special "receiving-end" software at that person's request.

---

**WORKAROUND WORKSHOP**

## Fixing Language-Kit Problems

As you can imagine, the challenges involved in making a computer work smoothly in 30 different languages are considerable. Glitches, therefore, are inevitable.

You can turn off all language kits by restarting the Mac; as it's starting up again, press Option and the Space bar. Do so when, for example, the language kits are causing problems in some of your non-WorldScript compatible programs.

If the names of your folders—and Sherlock results—show up as gibberish, it's because the Mac is still trying to use the Geneva typeface to display characters that don't exist in the English alphabet. Choose  →Control Panels→Appearance, click Fonts, and choose a font for folders belonging to the script system you installed—Osaka, for example, if you installed Japanese.

Finally, if you're getting gibberish in your menus and dialog boxes, drag the icon of the troublesome program onto the icon of the Language Register program. (It's on your hard drive in the Utilities folder.) You'll be offered the chance to specify what language the menus and dialog boxes *should* be showing in that program.

---

*Figure 13-6:*
*Using the Easy Access control panel, you can turn each of three special keyboard modes on or off. One lets you move the mouse by pressing keys; one filters out accidental keypresses; and one lets you trigger multiple-key combinations by pressing one at a time.*

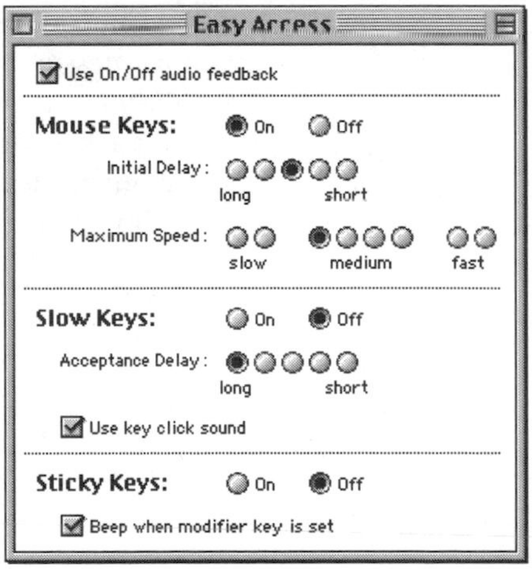

# Easy Access and CloseView

Apple offers two control panels that may be of particular interest to people who have trouble with their eyes or hands. Using the Easy Keys program, you can point, click, and drag without using the mouse—a feature that's also handy when the mouse is broken or missing. And using a control panel called CloseView, you can magnify the screen image, which is useful if you're visually impaired.

To install these programs, open the CD Extras→Universal Access folder on your Mac OS 9 CD. Drag the Easy Access and CloseView control panels onto your System Folder, click OK, and then restart the Mac. (Alternatively, run the Mac OS 9 installer on your Mac OS 9 CD. On successive screens, click Continue, Select, Add/Remove, and Mac OS 9. From the Recommended Installation pop-up menu, choose Customized Installation; on the next screen, turn off everything except Universal Access. Click OK, and proceed with the installation.)

When the Mac restarts, you'll be able to perform the following stunts:

### *Control the cursor without the mouse*

The Easy Access control panel offers three features designed to help people who can't use the mouse or who want more precision when working in graphics programs (see Figure 13-7):

- **Mouse Keys.** Using this feature, you can click, drag, and otherwise manipulate the cursor by pressing the keys on your numeric keypad.

  To turn on this mode, click On in the Easy Access control panel—or just press ⌘-Shift-Clear; a scientific-sounding ascending arpeggio chirp tells you that you've turned the feature on. To turn this mode off, press the Clear key to alone; you'll hear a descending arpeggio. (The Clear key is in the upper-left corner of your numeric keypad.)

  When Mouse Keys is turned on, the 5 key acts as the clicker—press it once to "click the mouse," twice to double-click, and so on. Move the cursor around the screen by pressing the eight keys that surround the 5 key. (For example, hold down the 9 key to move the cursor diagonally up and to the right.) If you hold one of these keys down continuously, the cursor, after a pause, begins to move smoothly in that direction—according to the settings you've made for Initial Delay and Maximum Speed into the Easy Access control panel.

---

**Tip:** Press the 0 key to lock down the mouse button, and the period key to unlock it.

---

- **Slow Keys.** This typing mode is designed for people who may sometimes press keys by mistake. You can turn it on and off either by clicking the On or Off buttons in the Easy Access control panel, or by holding the Return key down for 10 seconds or more. (A pair of beeps lets you know that you've turned Slow Keys on or off.)

At this point, the Mac ignores any keystrokes unless you press a key for, say, a full second or a second and a half, depending on the Acceptance Delay setting you've made in the Easy Access control panel.

- **Sticky Keys.** This feature is designed to help people who have difficulty triggering complex keystrokes, such as ⌘-Option-P; it lets you "press" such a combination by striking the keys one at a time instead of simultaneously. To turn this mode on or off, press the Shift key five times in a row. (Another ascending or descending series of notes lets you know you've been successful in turning the feature on or off.)

Once this feature is turned on, a tiny symbol appears at the very upper-right corner of your screen; it tells you what's going on, as shown at left in Figure 13-7.

---

**Figure 13-7:**
*When you press a modifier key (such as Shift, Option, Control, or ⌘), an arrow appears in the Sticky Keys special marker (middle), telling you that Sticky Keys is waiting for a letter or number key to complete the keystroke. If you press the modifier key twice, you lock that key down; now, as you type letter keys, the Mac acts as though you're holding down the modifier key continuously (right).*

| 10:18 AM | 📭 Finder |
| 10:18 AM | 📭 Finder |
| 10:18 AM | 📭 Finder |

---

### Enlarging the screen image

If you have trouble seeing the screen, by far the best solution is to reduce your monitor's *resolution,* thus magnifying the image, using the Monitors control panel (see page 207). If you have a 17-inch or larger monitor set to, say, 640 x 480, the result is a crisp, high-contrast, extremely magnified picture.

---

**Figure 13-8:**
*If you wish, CloseView can invert the screen, black-for-white (an effect that works better when you set your monitor to grayscale instead of color). It can also enlarge the screen picture—an effect that's difficult to depict in an illustration, because the resulting image is many times the size of this book.*

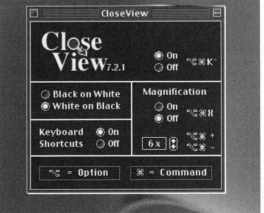

---

If even that magnification doesn't suffice, however, you may get some assistance from the CloseView control panel. Its purpose is to enlarge the area surrounding your cursor from 2 to 16 times—and, if you like, also to invert the colors of the screen so that white is black, blue is yellow, and so on, as shown in Figure 13-8.

To make it work, turn CloseView on by clicking On in the CloseView control panel—or by pressing ⌘-Option-K. A rectangle appears, a few inches square, that follows your cursor around the screen. It indicates the amount of screen area you'll see if you now turn on the Magnification feature (or press ⌘-Option-X). When you do so, the Mac will fill your screen with a gigantically enlarged screen picture that scrolls as you move the mouse.

You can increase or decrease the magnification by pressing ⌘-Option-plus or –minus (or by clicking up or down arrow buttons in the CloseView control panel).

# Part Four:
# Mac OS 9 Online

4

# Web Sharing, iTools, and Other Internet Integration

*I*nternet Copilot was an advertising slogan Apple dreamed up to emphasize the new Internet features of its operating system. While no Web browser is built directly into the OS (as it is in, say, Windows 98), Mac OS 9 does have several surprising built-in Internet features. Some are quirky, others are important time savers—but all of them are hidden to the uninitiated.

These features include *iTools:* a set of powerful features hosted by Apple's Web page. The various iTools let you send email greeting cards, sign up for a free email account, build a free Web page, back up your documents, and so on. (Without resorting to special tricks, iTools are available only to people running Mac OS 9.)

This chapter covers both ends of the Mac OS 9 Internet strategy: the features on your Mac, and the features on Apple's end of the Internet. (Of course, Mac OS 9's biggest new feature of all, Sherlock 2, is also an Internet feature, but it gets Chapter 15 to itself.)

## Mac OS 9 Internet Featurettes

Mac OS 9's scattershot collection of Internet features fall into three categories: Internet location files, Web sharing, and the Network Browser's ability to view FTP sites.

### Internet Location Files

One of the least convenient aspects of using the Internet, whether email, Web, or the software-library sites known as FTP, is having to remember the often cumbersome addresses for these Internet locations. The Mac offers a clever way to manage and memorize these addresses: storing them as *Internet location files*. Figure 14-1 shows the procedure for creating one of these special clipping files.

The idea is simple: when you double-click an Internet location file, your Web browser opens automatically to that page, or your email program launches and generates a new, blank, pre-addressed outgoing message, or your FTP program opens to the specified site, and so on. In other words, an Internet location file is like a system-wide Bookmarks feature. You might consider gathering together the location files for Web sites you frequently visit, put them into a folder, and put that folder into your  menu. Do the same with addresses to which you frequently send email. Thereafter, you save a step every time you want to jump to a particular Web page or send email to a particular person—just choose the appropriate name from the  menu.

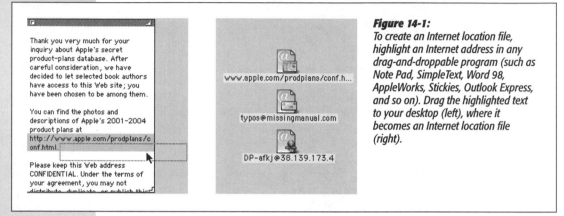

Thank you very much for your inquiry about Apple's secret product-plans database. After careful consideration, we have decided to let selected book authors have access to this Web site; you have been chosen to be among them.

You can find the photos and descriptions of Apple's 2001-2004 product plans at http://www.apple.com/prodplans/conf.html.

Please keep this Web address CONFIDENTIAL. Under the terms of your agreement, you may not distribute, duplicate, or publish this.

www.apple.com/prodplans/conf.h...

typos@missingmanual.com

DP-afkj@38.139.173.4

**Figure 14-1:**
*To create an Internet location file, highlight an Internet address in any drag-and-droppable program (such as Note Pad, SimpleText, Word 98, AppleWorks, Stickies, Outlook Express, and so on). Drag the highlighted text to your desktop (left), where it becomes an Internet location file (right).*

**Tip:** Rename your Internet location files. Doing so doesn't affect their original programming—they still take you to the same Web pages or email addresses—but lets you substitute plain English names ("Bob Smith" instead of *bsmith@earthlink.net,* for example).

Although Web and email addresses are by far the most popular uses of the Internet location file feature, they're not the only ones. You can actually create *seven* different kinds of Internet location files; each displays a distinctive icon and, when double-clicked, launches a particular program. Here's the rundown:

- **Web addresses (such as *www.apple.com*).** Connects to the Internet and shows the Web page in your default Web browser—the one you selected on the Web tab of the Internet control panel.

- **Email addresses (such as *john@apple.com*).** Creates a pre-addressed outgoing email, using the email program you've selected in the Internet control panel's Mail tab.

- **Newsgroup addresses (such as *news:news.apple.com*).** Shows you the specified *newsgroup* (Internet bulletin board) in your favorite newsreader program, which once again you've selected in the Internet control panel (on the News tab).

- **FTP sites (such as *ftp://ftp.apple.com*).** Shows you the software files sitting on a particular Internet hard drive (FTP site), using your favorite FTP-access software. (Fetch, Anarchie, the Network Browser, and even your Web browser can show you the contents of FTP sites.)

Specifying which FTP program you want to use requires several steps. First, open the Internet control panel. Choose Edit→User Mode; click Advanced; click OK; click the Advanced tab; click Helper Apps; and, in the list, click *ftp*. Now click Change. Finally, navigate to, and double-click, the FTP program you want the Mac to use when you double-click an FTP Internet location file.

- **AppleShare servers (such as *afp://at/Engineering:IL5 3rd Floor)*.** Connects you to a particular hard drive on your office network.

- **AppleTalk zones (such as *at://IL5 2nd Floor)*.** Connects you to a particular *zone* of your office network, from which you can then select a particular server.

- **Web pages stored on your Mac (such as *file:///Macintosh HD/Website Stuff/ home.html)*.** When you double-click one of these Internet location files, the particular HTML (Web-page) document opens in your chosen Web browser. The slashes in the address show the file's *path name*—that is, the example above is a file on the hard drive Macintosh HD, in a folder called Website Stuff; the document is called *home.html*. (Note the three slashes at the beginning of the address. They specify a file on your hard drive, rather than a Web-page address.)

*Tip:* As far as your Mac is concerned, an Internet location file and a Favorite (or bookmark), as defined by Internet Explorer, are the same thing. As Figure 14-2 illustrates, you can create one from the other just by dragging.

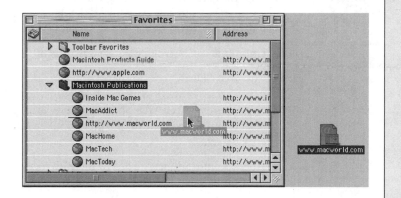

**Figure 14-2:**
*In Internet Explorer, choose Favorites→Edit Favorites. Now, impressively enough, you can drag Internet location files from the desktop directly into your bookmarks list. Oddly enough, this trick even works with email location files: if you add one to your Favorites menu, then choosing it (from within Internet Explorer) launches your email program and pre-addresses an outgoing message.*

## Web Sharing

Using the Web Sharing control panel, you can turn your Mac into a tiny Web site (or *server)* on the Internet. (This process assumes that you've already created some Web pages—using a program like PageMill, GoLive, Home Page, or BBEdit.) After you provide your friends and co-workers with your Mac's particular Web site address, they can view your Web pages, graphics, and documents in their own Web browsers.

Suddenly your Web site is on the Internet—but you haven't had to pay a penny to a Web-hosting company.

You still may want to, however, when you realize the limitations of this feature. It only works when your Mac is actually online, connected to the Internet. Worse, you can't realistically use this feature if you connect to the Internet by modem; as it turns out, your Mac's Web address *changes* every time you dial, making it impractical to provide its address to your friends and co-workers. (Unless you just want to fool around with this feature, that is; for experimentation's sake, you could always connect by modem, then call up a buddy to advertise your temporary address). In other words, the Web Sharing feature is designed for people who are connected to the Internet full-time— by cable modem, DSL connection, or office network, for example.

Finally, the Web Sharing feature can't handle much traffic. In fact, Apple didn't design it for posting Web pages to the Internet at large; instead, it had in mind *intranets,* small in-office connections. For example, a business might create its own private Web site that's available only to people in the company.

---

***Tip:*** Personal Web Sharing is an extremely easy and efficient way to share your Mac files with Windows PCs, either those on your office network or those on the Internet. No special software or translation is required, and posting your files on the Web page avoids all the usual complexities of sending files by email.

---

Here's how you turn your Mac into a low-budget Web site:

1. **Put the HTML documents, graphics, and files you want to publish into the Web Pages folder on your hard drive.**

   Mac OS 9 creates this Web Pages folder exactly for this purpose. You don't *have* to use this folder to contain your mini-Web site; but doing so will save you a step, as you'll see in a moment.

2. **Choose ⌘→Control Panels→Web Sharing.**

   The Web Sharing control panel appears, as shown in Figure 14-3. If your Web pages aren't in the Web Pages folder on your hard drive (see step 1), take this opportunity to tell Web Sharing where your pages *are.* To do so, click the *top* Select button. Navigate to, and highlight, the folder that contains your Web pages; click Select.

   Now you must designate one of the Web pages in that folder as the home page— the first one that appears when someone connects.

3. **Click the *lower* Select button. Navigate to, and double-click, the home page in your Web Pages folder.**

   If you don't specify a home page, your visitors won't see a Web page at all when they connect to your Mac—they'll see a simple list of the files and folders in your Web Pages folder. This arrangement, called Personal NetFinder, can be useful if the purpose of your Web site is simply to make documents available in a central place.

**4. Click Start.**

You've just made the contents of your Web Pages folder available to *anyone* who can connect to your Mac. If you prefer to limit who has access, however, click the "Use File Sharing to control user access" button. Now you can use the File Sharing control panel to specify exactly who can access your private Web site. (You'll find a complete description of the File Sharing control panel in Chapter 16.)

**5. Choose Edit→Copy My Address. Paste your new Web address into an email to your friends and co-workers.**

In general, your Mac's Web address is based on its very unmemorable *IP address,* which is a string of numbers separated by periods. Tell your friends to bookmark it so they won't have to remember this number.

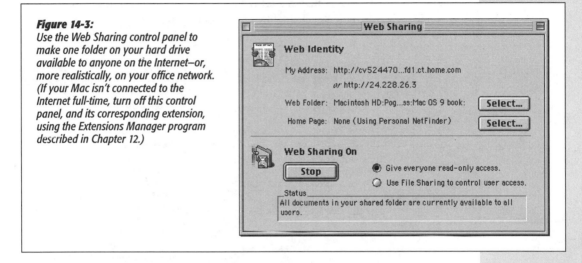

**Figure 14-3:**
*Use the Web Sharing control panel to make one folder on your hard drive available to anyone on the Internet—or, more realistically, on your office network. (If your Mac isn't connected to the Internet full-time, turn off this control panel, and its corresponding extension, using the Extensions Manager program described in Chapter 12.)*

You've done it: you've put your folder-based Web page on the Internet for all to see—that is, all who know your secret Web address. (You can find out who's been visiting you, and when, by using the Log feature in the Web Sharing control panel.) If you are one of the lucky ones whose Mac is connected to the Internet around-the-clock, you'll be amazed at how quick and satisfying this little-known feature turns out to be.

---

***Tip:*** If your Web Sharing visitors complain that they're getting "not enough resources" error messages when they try to open files on your mini-Web site, your Mac isn't giving Web Sharing enough memory. Choose **⌘**→Control Panels→Web Sharing. Choose Edit→Preferences, and use the lower-left pop-up menu to increase the Memory Allocation number. (Increasing Web Sharing's memory allotment the usual way, by using the Get Info command as described in Chapter 7, doesn't work to solve this problem.)

---

## FTPing with the Network Browser

*FTP* (file transfer protocol) sites are software libraries on the Internet. If you've heard of FTP at all, it was probably under one of two circumstances—either you've downloaded software from an Internet FTP site, or you've created and maintained your own Web site. (Popular shareware programs like Fetch and Anarchie Pro let Web designers view a list of all the text and graphics documents, sitting there on some Internet-connected computer somewhere, that make up their Web pages. When they want to update one of those pages, they add it to this list; to delete a Web page, they remove it from this list.)

In Mac OS 9, for the first time, you can access FTP sites using the Network Browser in your  menu. Because Mac OS 9's Keychain feature (see Chapter 16) eliminates your having to type in your name and password each time you connect to an FTP site, the Network Browser actually makes a fairly handy FTP program. (On the other hand, Anarchie works with the Keychain, too, saving you the same step.)

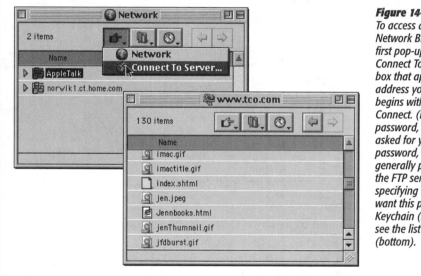

**Figure 14-4:**
*To access an FTP site, open the Network Browser (top). From the first pop-up menu, choose Connect To Server. In the dialog box that appears, type the FTP address you've been given (it begins with ftp://), and then click Connect. (Enter your Keychain password, if asked.) You'll be asked for your name and password, which are also generally provided by the host of the FTP server. Finally—after specifying whether or not you want this password added to your Keychain (see Chapter 16)—you see the list of files on the FTP site (bottom).*

Figure 14-4 shows the step-by-step procedure for opening the list of software on an FTP server. Once you're looking at the list, you can add items to it by dragging them from your desktop into the list; copy them to your Mac by dragging them out of the list onto your desktop; or open them by double-clicking (Network Browser copies them to your own Mac first). (To rename or re-organize the files on the FTP site, you still need a more powerful program—like Fetch.)

## iTools @ Apple.com

In January 2000, Apple CEO Steve Jobs explained to the Macworld Expo crowds that he and his team had had a mighty brainstorm based on the fact that Apple controls *both ends* of the connection between a Mac OS 9 computer and the Apple Web site. As a result, he went on, Apple ought to be able to come up with some pretty clever new Internet-based features as a reward to loyal Mac fans. And sure enough, later that same day, the Apple Web site appeared with its completely new look (see Figure 14-5).

Click the iTools tab to view the Mac OS 9–only features. Here's what you'll find:

**Figure 14-5:**
*The current Apple Web site features special tabs across the top; some of them are available to anyone. For example, the iReview feature lets readers rate popular Web sites, giving first-time Internet fans a useful list of good places to go. The iCards feature lets you send attractively designed electronic greeting cards by email to anyone on the Internet. The four special features on the iTools tab, however, work only if you're running Mac OS 9: Email, KidSafe, iDisk, and HomePage.*

## Email

Apple offers a free email account to any Mac OS 9 user. Of course, anyone who's able to *get* to the Apple Web site probably already *has* an email account, provided by EarthLink, America Online, or whoever is providing the Internet service. Furthermore, the Apple Web site feature offers no way to read or write email—this particular iTool offers you only an email *address* (account). You're still expected to use Outlook Express, Eudora, Claris Emailer, or another email program to get and send your Mac.com email.

---

**Note:** If America Online is your Internet company, you can't use the iTools email feature. AOL, alas, uses a nonstandard email format that's incompatible with standard Internet email—and with services like iTools email.

---

So why bother? The iTools advantage is, very simply, the clean and simple address: *YourName@mac.com.* Furthermore, because iTools is a Macintosh-only service, untrafficked by 200 million Windows users, the odds are good that you'll be able to claim the name you want. Praise be: no longer must you be known as *dpogue28514@ earthlink.net.*

---

***Tip:*** If Outlook Express or Entourage is your email program, you need to take an extra step when creating a Mac.com account. Choose Tools→Accounts; click the Mail tab (Entourage only); double-click the Mac.com account. In *that* window, click the Account Settings tab; enter your mac.com email address in the "E-mail address" field. In the "POP server" box, enter *mail.mac.com;* in the "SMTP server" box, enter *smtp.mac.com.*

Finally, click where it says "Click here for advanced sending options." In the resulting fold-out panel, turn on "SMTP server requires authentication"; close the fold-out panel, then click OK. Now your Mac.com looks and acts as though it were a bona fide ISP, and that your Mac.com address were a "real" one.

---

The Apple Web site gives you two additional features that help you process your email. First, it offers a Forward function that can route any incoming Mac.com email to another address of your choice. Second, you can set up your Mac.com email account to send automatic "I'm out-of-town" replies to anyone who emails you. In this case, you still get your email—or if you really *are* out-of-town, it piles up until you you return—but each incoming message gets the response you've created.

Of course, most email programs, including Outlook Express, Claris Emailer, and Eudora, already offer these forwarding and auto-reply features—but for the beginner, the Apple Web site version is easier to set up.

## Getting Ready for iTools

The most complicated part of using the Apple iTools services is setting them up. To do so, you need a Mac running Mac OS 9 that already has an Internet account (America Online is OK).

Go to *Apple.com.* Click the iTools tab at the top of the window. Click the big Start button. You'll be guided through the process of downloading the iTools Installer. Eventually, you'll see its icon appear on your desktop. It looks like a red toolbox; if your Web browser window is covering up your desktop, choose Hide Netscape Communicator, or Hide Internet Explorer, from your Application menu.

Now double-click the iTools Installer and follow the instructions on screen. Switch back to your browser when the installation is over; you'll be asked to type in your name, address, phone number, and so on. Click Continue, and then Accept. Now you're supposed to make up a member name (such as *alincoln* or *skibunny*) and password. You're also asked to make up a question and answer (such as, "First-grade teacher's name?" and "Smithers") If you ever forget your password, the iTools software will help you—but only if it knows that you're you when you answer this question correctly.

The next Web page asks whether you want to configure your email program to get and send email for your new Mac.com email account. An account summary screen now appears (make sure to print it or save it), and then, finally, the system offers to send an email message to your friends letting them know about your new email address (which is *whatever-name-you-chose@mac.com).*

From now on, when you visit the Apple Web page and click the iTools tab, you'll see buttons for the four primary iTools services, as described in this section: KidSafe, Email, iDisk, and HomePage.

## KidSafe

If you're a parent who's concerned about your kid stumbling onto questionable Web sites, you can buy and install *filtering* software, which doesn't let your child see any Web pages containing certain forbidden words. But filtering software sometimes blocks innocent sites (such as chicken-breast recipes), yet misses smut sites with innocent addresses (such as *www.whitehouse.com,* which is *not* the White House).

The alternative is to take the opposite tack: install software that specifies which Web sites your kid *can* visit. That's how Apple's KidSafe works. A panel of teachers and librarians helps Apple select and approve Web sites—55,000 at the outset, and then 10,000 more per month, says Apple.

The drawback here is, of course, that your own home page—or mine—probably isn't on the list. Fortunately, when you, the master account holder, are on the KidSafe page, you can click the Edit Settings button to add new addresses that you'd like to the list of approved sites. (You'll also need to click that Edit Settings button if you want your kid to be able to play games, access FTP software sites, or chat.)

Using KidSafe requires that you download another special installer. When the Mac "comes to," KidSafe protection is automatically turned on for everybody *except* you, the owner of the Mac. In other words, KidSafe has no effect unless you turn on the Multiple Users feature of Mac OS 9, which is described in Chapter 17.

## iDisk

For many people, the crown jewel of the Apple Mac OS 9 Internet services is iDisk. It creates a 20 MB phantom hard drive icon on your desktop. Anything you drag into the folders on this gets copied—apparently onto this miniature Zip disk on your desktop, but actually to Apple's secure servers on the Internet.

In other words, iDisk is a free backup disk. It's the clever solution for people whose Macs don't have floppy drives or Zip drives—and even a good idea for those who do, because this backup disk is off-site. If a fire or thief destroys your office *and* your backup disks, your iDisk is still safe. Furthermore, you can pull the iDisk onto *any* Mac OS 9 computer's screen—at your office, at your home, at your friend's house— so you don't have to carry around a physical disk to transport important files. The sole, and considerable, drawback to the iDisk system is its speed. Connecting to it over a standard modem is a procedure measured in minutes, not seconds.

### Using iDisk

To pull the iDisk onto your screen, follow the instructions in Figure 14-6 (or see the following Tip). At this point, using iDisk is exactly like using a very, very slow—but very, very safe—floppy disk or Zip disk. You can drag files or folders from your hard drive into one of the folders that appear on the iDisk. (You can't create your own folders on the iDisk. You must put your files and folders into one of the folders *already on the iDisk,* such as Documents or Pictures. If you try to drag an icon directly into the iDisk window, or onto the iDisk icon, for example, you'll be told you don't have enough "access privileges.") Because you're actually sending things over the Internet, this process is slow; feel free to switch into some other program to continue working while the copying takes place.

Thereafter, you can retrieve or open whatever you copied to the iDisk. Open one of the folders on it; you can now open, rename, throw away, or copy (to your hard drive) whatever you find inside. Unfortunately, you can't leave your iDisk on the screen all day; you're only allowed to keep it on your screen for an hour at a time. (Warnings that you're soon to be disconnected appear ten minutes and then two minutes before the actual disconnection.)

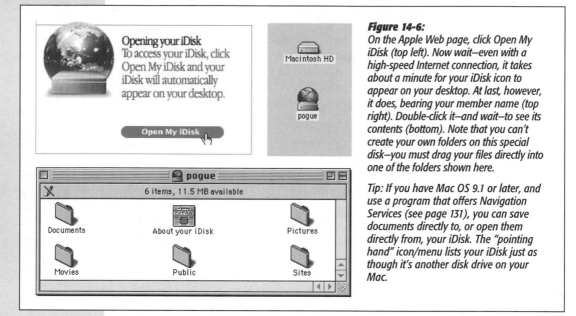

**Opening your iDisk**
To access your iDisk, click Open My iDisk and your iDisk will automatically appear on your desktop.

Open My iDisk

**Figure 14-6:**
*On the Apple Web page, click Open My iDisk (top left). Now wait—even with a high-speed Internet connection, it takes about a minute for your iDisk icon to appear on your desktop. At last, however, it does, bearing your member name (top right). Double-click it—and wait—to see its contents (bottom). Note that you can't create your own folders on this special disk—you must drag your files directly into one of the folders shown here.*

*Tip: If you have Mac OS 9.1 or later, and use a program that offers Navigation Services (see page 131), you can save documents directly to, or open them directly from, your iDisk. The "pointing hand" icon/menu lists your iDisk just as though it's another disk drive on your Mac.*

**Tip:** Once you've got your iDisk icon on the screen, make an alias of it. From now on, whenever you want your iDisk, just double-click this alias icon. You don't have to launch your browser, go to Apple.com, click iTools, or any of that jazz; when you double-click the alias, you connect to the Internet (if you're not already on), type your password, wait a minute—and the iDisk icon appears.

### The Public folder

In general, whatever you put onto your iDisk is private; nobody (except people who know your name and password) can see what you've stored there. There's one exception, however: the Public folder on every iDisk. Anything you put into this folder can be seen by any other iTools member—all they need is your member name. They *don't* need to know your password to open the Public folder.

The Public folder is a great mechanism. It's terrific for storing family photos, for example, where anyone who's interested can look at them. It's also great when you're working on some collaborative project (where security isn't an issue); you can post the latest drafts of your work in the Public folder for your co-workers to review.

*Tip:* To view someone *else's* Public folder, visit the Apple Web site. Click iTools; click iDisk; and type the member name of the person whose Public folder you want to look at into the Name: blank. Click Open Public Folder. After a minute or so, a new iDisk icon appears on your desktop, bearing that member's name. Double-click it to view the contents of that person's Public folder; you can copy these files to your hard drive, or double-click them to open them directly.

## HomePage

Creating a Web page isn't difficult; using a program like PageMill (which once came with every iMac), Home Page, or even Word 98, you can design the text and graphics for a simple Web page in an afternoon. It's much more difficult, however, to figure out how to *post* that Web page—to hang it on the Internet where the world can see it. To do that, you need special software, several passwords and codes, and a lot of help from whoever is hosting your Web page (such as your Internet access company).

The iTools HomePage feature eliminates all that hassle. All you have to do is drag your Web-page documents and graphics into the Sites folder on your iDisk (which is described in the previous section). Your Web page is instantly available for viewing by the 200 million people on the Internet.

### Creating a Web page using your own tools

If you already know how to design Web pages, great; put the HTML documents and graphics you've created into the Sites folder of your iDisk.

Then tell your friends its Web address. Suppose the Web page you designed is called Index.html, and that your iTools member name is SkiBunny. In that case, your custom-designed Web address is *http://homepage.mac.com/skibunny/index.html.*

*Note:* Unlike pages created by the HomePage tools described here, Web pages you design using your own software *don't* show up when using the administrative tools on the Apple iTools Web site. Nonetheless, they're full-fledged, working Web pages the instant you put them into your iDisk's Sites folder.

### Creating a simple Web page using HomePage

If you have no experience designing Web pages, you can use iTools itself to create gorgeous, if simple, Web pages. Sign into the Apple Web site's iTools screen; click HomePage. Click Start on the welcome screen. You're offered several standard Web page templates:

• **Photo Album.** Your Web page will look like a beautifully designed page full of slides, each showing a miniature version of one of the pictures you've selected. Your Web-page visitors can click one of the slides to view the picture at full size.

If this is the kind of Web page you want, prepare by saving your graphics, photos, or scans as *JPEG files* (use File→Save As in your graphics, scanning, or digital-camera software). (Unfortunately, iTools doesn't work with GIF files or the emerging PNG graphics format.) Create an iDisk, as described in the previous section; open your iDisk, and copy these graphics into the Pictures folder.

*Tip:* When editing the text of your photo-album page, be sure to add the words, "Click a slide to view the full-sized photo," so that your Web page visitors will *know* that that option is available.

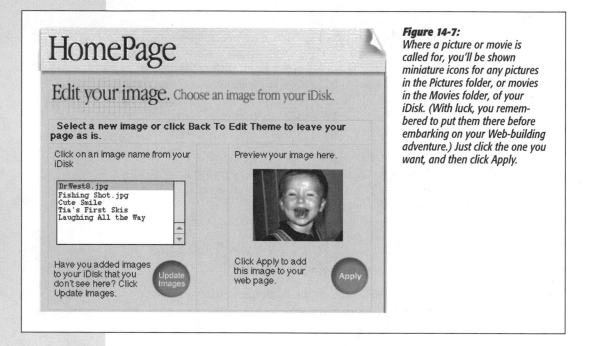

**Figure 14-7:**
*Where a picture or movie is called for, you'll be shown miniature icons for any pictures in the Pictures folder, or movies in the Movies folder, of your iDisk. (With luck, you remembered to put them there before embarking on your Web-building adventure.) Just click the one you want, and then click Apply.*

- **iMovie Theater.** If you've ever tried to put digital movies on a Web page, you'll fall over in a dead faint to find out how easy it is using iTools.

  Prepare for this project by saving your QuickTime movies in a Web-friendly format—that is, with a small window size and a low frames-per-second rate. If you're using iMovie (the movie-editing software that comes with the iMac DV line of Macs), do this by choosing File→Export Movie, and then choosing "Web Movie (small)."

  Making your movies small in this way isn't just thoughtful for your Web site visitors, who must wait for the movie to download before it plays; it also acknowledges that your iDisk is only 20 MB in size, and bigger movies might not fit.

  Put the resulting movies in the Movies folder of your iDisk.

- **Invites.** Use this option for Web-based invitations to parties and other events.

- **Baby Announcements.** You'll be offered a choice of Boy or Girl announcement, and given the chance to insert a digital photo.

- **Resume.** This template may owe its existence to the high-turnover job market in Silicon Valley, where Apple is based; in any case, it lets you post your résumé online for all headhunters to see.

On the next screen, click the miniature image of the design you want. Finally, you arrive at a full-size mock up of the finished Web page, filled with little Edit buttons that let you change the chunks of dummy text. (For example, the Edit buttons let you change what the baby-announcement template lists for height, weight, and date of birth; on the invitation Web page, click the Edit buttons to specify the time, place, and driving directions for your party; and so on.) Click Preview to see how the Web page will look.

---

**UP TO SPEED**

## Using iTools on Older System Software

Apple says that its iTools are available only to Macs running Mac OS 9. In fact, however, many of them are also available to Macs running, say, Mac OS 8.5 or even System 7.6—if you're willing to take some sneaky extra steps.

At this writing, instructions for running iTools on pre-Mac OS 9 machines are posted at *www.acts.org/itoolstrick.* In

essence, using iTools boils down to installing an extension called AppleShare 3.8.3 and then taking a number of tweaky steps.

Even then, you won't have access to KidSafe or iCards (the greeting-card feature). But you'll gain the mac.com e-mail address and access to the iDisk (including its Sites folder for posting your Web page).

---

*Tip:* If you would like to omit one of the proposed pieces of information—if you don't have any particular "additional message" to add to the baby announcement, for example—edit it anyway, if only to delete the dummy text that appears there. Otherwise, your baby announcement will appear in final form with the words "Your message here"!

---

When you finally click the Publish button at the top of the screen, three things happen. First, new Web-page (HTML) documents appear in the Sites folder of your iDisk; if you know how to use a Web-page creation program like PageMill, you can make changes to your Web page just by editing these documents. Second, the URL (Web address) for your Web page appears on your screen, which you can copy and then email to anyone who'd be interested. (Unfortunately, it's not particularly catchy: it's along the lines of *http://homepage.mac.com/YourMemberName/baby.html*).

And finally, your Web page is now available for anyone on the Internet to see. Corporations and professional Web designers may sniff at the simplicity of the result—but it takes *them* a lot longer than ten minutes, and more than $0, to do their thing.

---

*Tip:* You can create as many Web pages as you want (within the space constraints of your iDisk). When you return to the HomePage screen, a list of your existing Web pages appears (complete with Edit Page and Delete Page buttons). So does the Add A Page button, which you can click to start the process of building another Web page.

## How the Mac Meets Internet

If you used the Internet Setup Assistant to sign up for your Internet account, you never even saw the various control panels involved—the Setup Assistant made all the appropriate settings automatically, behind the scenes. It set up three control panels: TCP/IP, Remote Access, and Modem—all parts of Apple's Open Transport networking software suite.

The **TCP/IP control panel's** "Connect via" pop-up menu specifies how you're connecting to the Internet—using, for example, PPP (by modem); Ethernet (by cable modem, DSL, or corporate network); or AirPort (by wireless card). Your ISP or network geek is supposed to tell you how to fill in the remaining settings (IP Address, the Configure pop-up menu, Name Server Address, and so on).

The Mac stores your TCP/IP setup in the System Folder→ Preferences folder, in a file called TCP/IP Preferences. It's worth backing up this file; whenever you upgrade machines or perform a clean system install, you'll save 10 minutes of fiddling by dragging the TCP/IP Preferences into the corresponding place in the new System Folder. Your Internet connection will be ready to go.

In the **Remote Access control panel,** you specify your account name, password, and phone number for your ISP, if the Internet Setup Assistant didn't already do so. The Save Password box, shown here, lets you avoid having to type your password every time you dial. (If you don't connect by dial-up modem, you don't need this control panel at all.)

If you click Options, you're offered three tabs: Redialing, Connection, and Protocol. Several of these options are extremely useful. For example, the Connection options include

"Launch Status application when connecting," which automatically opens the Remote Access Status program (page 93) every time you're on the Net. As a result, you can easily monitor your connection speed and disconnect when ready—a very useful feature. The Protocol options inlcude "Connect automatically when starting TCP/IP applications," which makes your Mac dial automatically when your email program or Web browser tries to go online.

The settings you make in Remote Access are stored in your System Folder→Preferences→Remote Access folder; this, too, is a folder worth backing up (see page 436).

The third piece of the Open Transport Internet collection is the **Modem control panel,** which you use to specify what kind of modem you have. (Most modern Macs have a built-in "Apple Internal 56K" model.)

All three of these control panels offer a File→Configurations command. It produces a list of memorized connection settings, so you can easily switch. In the TCP/IP control panel, for example, you might create one configuration for America Online, and another for an EarthLink account; or one for modem connections, and another for your cable modem.

A laptop example: After choosing File→Configurations in the Remote Access control panel, click your main setup name, click Duplicate, and then type the name of a new city. Click Make Active; you return to the main screen, where you can type the phone number for the new city. After you've created several such configurations, you can switch phone numbers using the Remote Access tile of the Control Strip (page 76), or using Location Manager (page 204).

# CHAPTER 15

# Finding Files and Web Sites with Sherlock 2

S herlock 2 is the most famous of Mac OS 9's new features. It's the one feature newspaper reporters wrote about when Mac OS 9 debuted, and it's the Mac OS 9-only feature with the widest appeal.

Sherlock 2 is Mac OS 9's Find command. Like its Mac OS 8.5 predecessor, called simply Sherlock, version 2 can quickly find three kinds of things:

- **Icons.** Like the Find command of previous Mac OS versions, Sherlock can look for a particular file or folder based on its description—by its name, size, date stamp, and so on.

- **Words.** Sherlock can also look for the words *inside* your files. That's a powerful feature if you remember having typed or read something, but can't remember the file's name.

- **Web sites.** Most intriguingly of all, Sherlock can look for words that appear on Web pages, exactly like such search engines as Yahoo.com or AltaVista.com. But there's a difference: each of those Web-based search engines "knows about" only a tiny subset—maybe 30 percent—of the world's Web pages. You'd need to search several times with different search engines to ensure that you've actually searched most of the Internet.

But Sherlock can harness the power of several Internet search engines simultaneously—all right from your desktop, without even having to open your Web browser. Sherlock 2 can even compare prices on shopping Web sites and track bids on auction Web sites.

This chapter covers these three searching systems in sequence.

# Finding Icons

Most people, most of the time, use Sherlock to search for files by name. Here's how the process works:

## Preparing to Search

To open Sherlock in readiness for searching for icons, choose Sherlock from the  menu. Or, if you're already in the Finder, choose File→Find (or press ⌘-F).

The window that appears may take you by surprise. It's enormous, filled with unlabeled icons and blanks, and apparently made of stainless steel (see Figure 15-1). For your purposes, you can ignore the row of icons at the top of the screen; except for the leftmost one, these icons are exclusively for searching the Internet.

The list in the middle of the window is important, however: it lets you specify *where* you want Sherlock to do its searching. Every disk attached to your Mac at the moment—your hard drive, a Zip disk, a CD-ROM, a networked disk you've mounted, and so on—shows up here with its own checkbox. Most of the time, you just want to search your primary hard drive; ensure that a checkmark appears next to its name, and then proceed.

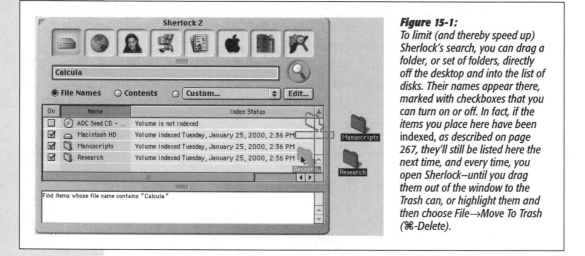

**Figure 15-1:**
*To limit (and thereby speed up) Sherlock's search, you can drag a folder, or set of folders, directly off the desktop and into the list of disks. Their names appear there, marked with checkboxes that you can turn on or off. In fact, if the items you place here have been indexed, as described on page 267, they'll still be listed here the next time, and every time, you open Sherlock—until you drag them out of the window to the Trash can, or highlight them and then choose File→Move To Trash (⌘-Delete).*

---

**Tip:** This window acts like a Finder list view: you can drag the dividers between the column names to make the columns wider or narrower, and you can click the name of a column to sort the list by that criterion. (For details on what the Index Status column represents, see "Finding Words" later in this chapter.)

---

It's worth noting, however, that you can greatly speed up the searching by telling Sherlock which specific *folders* you want it to search. Figure 15-1 shows how to do that.

To find a file whose name you know, just type a few letters of its name into the blank. (Capitals don't matter, and neither does the position of the letters you type—if you type *John,* Sherlock will find files with names Johnson, Peterjohn, and DiJohnson.) Finally, click the magnifying-glass icon (or press Return).

---

***Tip:*** Although Sherlock isn't a program that opens quickly, it at least has the decency to memorize whatever you type while it's opening. That quirk lets keyboard fans type all of the following in rapid succession, without ever having to use the mouse: ⌘-F (to launch the program), *Sweden* (or whatever the name of the file or folder you seek), and Return.

---

While the searching is going on, the magnifying-glass icon changes to become a stop sign. To interrupt the search in progress, you can click the stop sign, press ⌘-period, or press the Esc key.

---

**WORKAROUND WORKSHOP**

## Making Sherlock Think Less Different

The brushed-metal look of Sherlock may look nifty and futuristic. Unfortunately, it also deprives Mac fans of several standard window controls of the sort described in Chapter 1. For example, there are no title-bar stripes that let you know when this window is in the foreground. There's no collapse box in the upper right, for use in "windowshading" the window. Nor is there a zoom box in the upper-right corner, which would make the window jump to full size. There aren't even traditional puffy window edges by which you could drag this window to move it, although moving

this window isn't hard—you can drag *anywhere* on the brushed metal.

If you miss some of the standard window features that Apple took out of Sherlock, help is at hand. The program called Sherlock II Window Fixer neatly restores the missing window features to Sherlock's stainless-steel incarnation. The title bar, collapse box, and zoom box go back where they belong. (You can download this program from *www.missingmanual.com.)*

---

## The Search Results

A couple of seconds after you've clicked the magnifying glass icon, the Sherlock screen changes. In place of the disk list, you now see a list of files whose names contain what you typed in the blank. (Figure 15-2 shows this list.)

You can manipulate this list much the way you'd approach a list of files in a standard Finder list-view window. You can highlight something in the list by typing the first couple letters of its name, move up or down the list by pressing the arrow keys, and so on. You can jump from place to place in the Sherlock window—from the list of found items to the "folder map" below them, and back to the blank at the top of the window—by pressing the Tab key. You can also highlight multiple icons simultaneously, exactly as you would in a Finder list view: highlight all of them by choosing Edit→Select All, highlight individual items by Shift-clicking them, drag diagonally to enclose a cluster of found items, and so on.

At this point, you can proceed in many different ways:

---

### Find out where something is

If you click *once* on any item in the results list, the bottom half of the window becomes a folder map that shows you where that item is. For example, in Figure 15-2, the notation in the bottom half of the window (read from bottom to top) means: "The Calculator icon you found is in the Apple Menu Items folder, which is in the System Folder, which is on the hard drive called Macintosh HD."

If you want to get your hands on the actual icon, you don't have to do all of that window-opening and folder-burrowing. Instead, you can just choose File→Open Enclosing Folder. Sherlock instantly retreats to the background, as the Finder highlights the actual icon in question, sitting there in its window wherever it happens to be on your hard drive.

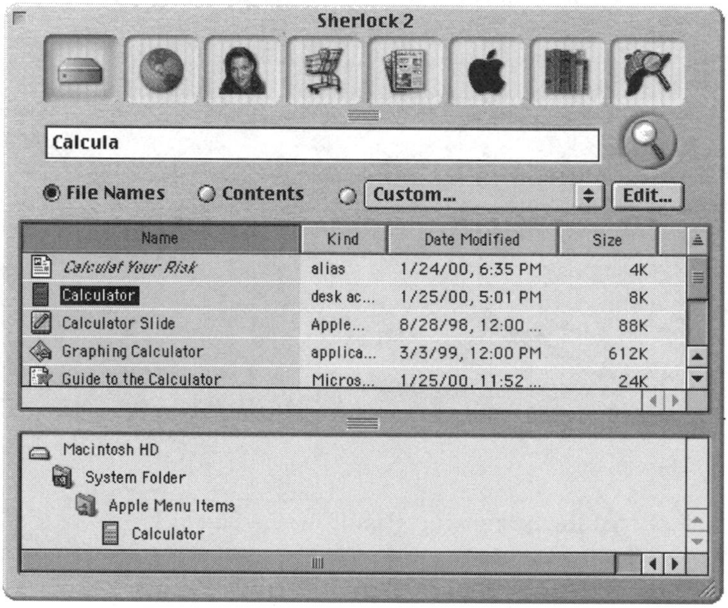

**Figure 15-2:**
*In the top half of the window: the file Sherlock found. In the bottom half: the path, or map, that shows you exactly where the highlighted found icon is filed. You can drag the horizontal divider between the halves of this window upward or downward to adjust the relative sizes of the panes. (You can also drag the lower-right corner of the window to make it bigger or smaller.)*

### Open the file (or open one of the folders it's in)

If one of the found files is the one you were looking for, double-click it to open it. This, in fact, is what most people do most of the time when using Sherlock. In many cases, you'll never even know or care *where* the file was—you just want to get into it.

**Tip:** If you press Option while double-clicking one of the files that Sherlock finds, Sherlock itself closes. When you're finished working on whatever you double-clicked, you won't have to manually quit the Sherlock program.

It's less useful, but still worth noting, that you can also double-click to open any of the folders that appear in "folder map" in the bottom half of the window. For example, in Figure 15-2, you could double-click the System Folder icon to open it, or the Apple Menu Items folder to open *it*, and so on.

### Move or delete the file

You can drag an item directly out of Sherlock's found-files list and into a different folder, window, or disk, or onto the desktop. (The icon doesn't disappear from the found-files list, but the folder map at the bottom of the window updates itself to reflect the icon's new location.)

### Print, trash, or Get Info

After highlighting an icon (or icons) in the list of found files, you can use any of the commands in the File menu: Print Item, Move to Trash, Get Info, Label, and so on.

### Adjust the list

By clicking the column headings, you can sort the list of found files in various ways: by name, size, date, and so on. (You can reverse the order by clicking the tiny pyramid button above the vertical scroll bar.) You can also make the window bigger (by dragging the lower-right corner handle) or adjust the relative widths of the columns (by dragging the column-name dividers). All of this works exactly as it does in a Finder list-view window.

### Make an alias

You can make an alias for one of the found items exactly the way you'd do in a Finder window: drag it out of the window while pressing ⌘-Option. The alias appears wherever you release the mouse (on the desktop, for example).

### Search for similar files

By Control-clicking one of the files in the list that Sherlock produces, you're offered a contextual-menu command called Find Similar Files. If you choose it, Sherlock does its best to round up other files on your hard drive that resemble the one you Control-clicked. (It tries to find files that contain similar words, have a similar name, have the same type and creator codes, and so on.) In general, Sherlock's fuzzy logic in performing this kind of search may be a bit fuzzier than you'd like—it can pull up some genuinely bizarre documents. But every now and then, the program will surprise you with its accuracy.

### Summarize File to Clipboard

This command, too, appears when you Control-click one of Sherlock's found files— if the file you click is a plain text file. (In fact, this command appears *only* when you click a text file. AppleWorks and Word files, for example, don't count, unless you'd saved such documents as text-only files.)When you choose Summarize File to Clipboard, Sherlock analyzes the text in that file, and produces—on the Clipboard— a very short version of the same document. It doesn't do any rewriting to produce its capsule version—now *that* would be an impressive feature. Instead it selects a few whole sentences from the original document that seem to represent it.

To view the summary, switch to the Finder, where you'll find the Clipboard window open and waiting with the summary displayed. (Alternatively, switch into a word processor and then choose Edit→Paste.)

Here again, the Summarize feature is half useful and half gimmick. At the very least, you can use it to provide a sneak peak at one of the files that Sherlock has rounded up, so that you'll know whether or not it found the file you're looking for.

### Index selection

When you Control-click a file in the found-file list, you get the option to add the found file to Sherlock's *index* of all the documents on your hard drive. (You can read about indexing later in this section.)

### Save the search setup

By choosing File→Save Search Criteria (or by pressing ⌘-S), you can immortalize the search you've just set up. You might use this feature if you perform the same search each day—if, for example, you like to scan the Internet each morning for newly posted articles on Rosie O'Donnell, or round up all the documents you created yesterday for backing up.

The Save File dialog box appears, so that you can name (and choose a location for) the Save Find File document you're about to create. This file describes the search you've set up—what text was in the box at the top of the window; what kind of search it was (File Names, Contents, Custom, or one of the Internet searches described later in this chapter); and so on. (It *does* remember which disks or folders you had selected for searching, even though *all* disk and folder checkboxes seem to be checked when the Sherlock window first appears.)

The next time you want to repeat that search, just double-click the Save Find File document you created. Sherlock launches automatically, instantly fills in the saved search criteria, and begins searching.

### Do another search

To start over with another search, choose Find→Find File (or press ⌘-F). The list of found files disappears, and the original Sherlock screen (showing your list of disks) reappears. (You can also start over with a different kind of search, such as the text-contents or Internet searches described in the rest of this chapter, using one of the other commands in the Find menu.)

---

**Tip:** You can conduct multiple searches simultaneously, and you can leave the found-files results windows of previous searches hanging around on your screen. The key to both techniques is the File→New Window command; each time you use it, you get another Sherlock search screen that can contain, and conduct, an independent search.

---

### Adjust your search

Instead of starting over with a blank Sherlock screen, you can also return to your original search screen—an extremely useful feature if, for example, you made a typo in the file name you were searching for. To return to the original screen, you might click around in hopes of finding a Back button, but you won't find one.

Instead, the secret is to click the hard-drive icon at the upper-left corner of the Sherlock window. You return instantly to your previous search setup.

## Searching by Date, Size, and More

Searching for a file by typing in a few letters of its name is by far the most frequently used Sherlock function. But in certain circumstances, you may not remember the name you gave a file, or you want to narrow the search by confining it to, say, only Microsoft Word files. Using the More Search Options dialog box—which opens when you click the Edit button at the right side of the window—you can limit your search to files that were created before or after a certain date, that are larger or smaller than a certain size, that were created by a specific program, and so forth. Figure 15-3 shows exactly how detailed this kind of search can be.

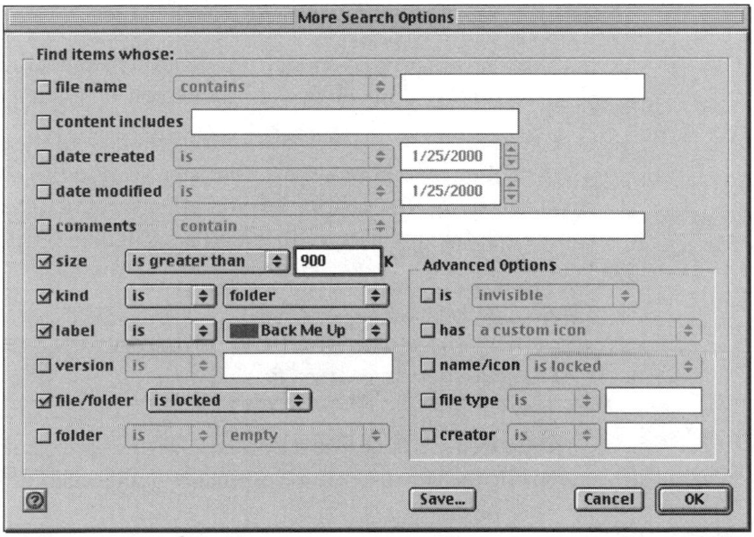

**Figure 15-3:**
*By clicking the Edit button on the Sherlock screen, you open this massive dialog box. Turn on the checkboxes of as many criteria as you'd like; each additional checkbox further narrows the search. This example would find locked folders larger than 900 K to which you've applied the label "Back Me Up."*

The checkboxes refer to the following details about your files:

• **File name.** When you turn on this checkbox, the pop-up menu becomes available—and you suddenly realize how *this* file-name search differs from the one on the main Sherlock screen. This time, Sherlock won't just find files whose names *contain* the letters you type—it can find files whose names *begin* with those letters, *end* with those letters, *don't* contain those letters, and so on.

- **Content includes.** This box lets you search for words within files, as described in the next section.

- **Date created, date modified.** These options, along with the options in the corresponding pop-up menus, let you search for files according to when you first created them or when you last saved them. Some of the fuzzy-logic commands on these pop-up menus are particularly useful: options like "is within 1 month of" are exactly what you need when you only vaguely remember when you last worked with the file.

- **Comments.** This blank lets you specify text that you'd like to search in the comments field of your files' Get Info boxes, as described on page 22.

- **Size.** Using this control, and its "is less than"/"is greater than" pop-up menu, you can restrict your search to files of a certain size. (Remember that there are 1,024 K per megabyte; this field requires a number in K, or kilobytes.)

- **Kind.** These two pop-up menus let you search for everything that is, or isn't, a certain kind of file—an alias, folder, extension, stationery file, and so on. Being able to round up all your *applications* (programs) by using this option is especially useful if you want to create an application-launching window, like one of the pop-up windows described in Chapter 1.

- **Label.** You can read about icon labels on page 40; this checkbox and pop-up menu let you round up all icons to which you've applied a particular label.

- **Version.** If you inspect the Get Info window of the programs on your hard drive, you'll discover that almost every application has a version number. So do many extensions, shared libraries, and other system-software files. This option lets you search for applications that have a particular version number.

---

***Note:*** Most documents lack built-in version numbers, so don't turn this checkbox on except when looking for applications and system files. If you specify a version number when searching for documents, Sherlock will come up empty-handed every time.

---

- **File/folder is locked/is unlocked.** Use this option to find all files that you've locked using the File→Get Info command—and the folders they're in, which are locked as a result.

- **Folder is/is not empty/shared/mounted.** This checkbox is useful when you want to round up all folders of a certain type. For example, it feels good, every now and then, to find all empty folders on your hard drive and throw them away.

  *Shared folders* are those you've made available to other people on the network using the File Sharing feature (see Chapter 16). *Mounted folders* are those on other Macs on the network that you've brought onto your screen using that same File Sharing feature.

- **Is invisible/visible.** Your hard drive is teeming with invisible files, such as the enormous "swap file" that stores the contents of your Mac's virtual memory (see Chapter 7). Using this command, you can take a look at them. (It's not wise to move or throw away invisible files, however; Apple made them invisible expressly so you wouldn't tamper with them.)

- **Has a custom icon/no custom icon.** A *custom icon* is a replacement graphic that you've pasted onto one of your icons, as described on page 32.

- **Name/icon is locked/is not locked.** This puzzling option lets you find two kinds of icons. First, it turns up icons whose *names* are locked by Mac OS 9 itself (such as the System Folder sub-folders, such as Control Panels and Fonts, that display special folder icons).

  Second, it finds folders you've locked using the File→Get Info→Sharing command. (When you use the command, the dialog box that appears offers a checkbox called "Can't move, rename, or delete this item (locked)"—that is, it prevents you or other people on the network from messing with this particular folder.)

- **File type, creator.** The *type and creator codes* associate every file on your hard drive with the programs that can open it; see page 107 for details. Technical as this option may sound, it's actually among the most useful in this entire box—by searching for a creator code, for example, you can tell Sherlock to find all documents that belong to a particular program (such as all AppleWorks files).

### How to specify all this information in half a second

Some of the information in this More Search Options window is easy to specify—such as the Kind of file you're looking for. Other bits of information, particularly the file and creator codes, are normally hidden from view. If you want to round up all documents created by, say, BeeKeeper Pro, how are you supposed to know what type codes to type?

By *showing* Sherlock. You can drag any icon directly from your desktop or any Finder window right on top of the More Search Options window; Sherlock responds by filling in *all* of the blanks described above with the information that describes the file you dragged: its size, kind, label, type code, and so on, turning the More Search Options window into the world's largest Get Info window. This doesn't mean that you must now search for documents matching all of these criteria; just turn on the checkboxes of the criteria you *do* want to match when searching.

### Saving searches

After spending an hour or two inside the More Search Options dialog box setting up elaborate search criteria, you may be relieved to learn that you can save a snapshot of this search setup. When you need to search for this kind of file again, you'll be able to restore this setup using a single pop-up menu. Figure 15-4 shows the steps. (Behind the scenes, the Mac stores your saved criteria as individual documents in the System Folder→Internet Search Sites→Files folder.)

By the way: saving a More Search Options setup in this way isn't the same as using the

File→Save Search Criteria command on the main Sherlock screen, as described earlier in this chapter. This Save button produces a saved search that (a) shows up in the Custom pop-up menu and (b) affects only the search criteria in the More Search Options dialog box. The Save Search Criteria option, on the other hand, memorizes the Custom setup you've selected *and* the list of disks you want to search. It also creates a stand-alone file that, when double-clicked, launches Sherlock and begins searching.

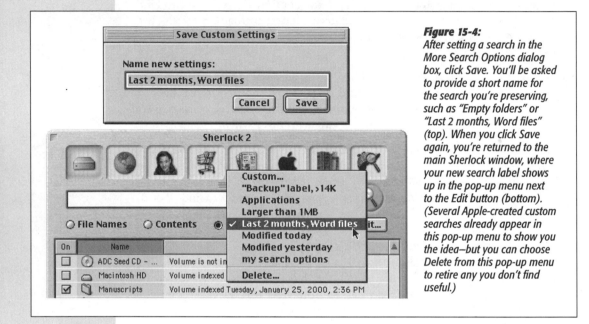

**Figure 15-4:**
*After setting a search in the More Search Options dialog box, click Save. You'll be asked to provide a short name for the search you're preserving, such as "Empty folders" or "Last 2 months, Word files" (top). When you click Save again, you're returned to the main Sherlock window, where your new search label shows up in the pop-up menu next to the Edit button (bottom). (Several Apple-created custom searches already appear in this pop-up menu to show you the idea—but you can choose Delete from this pop-up menu to retire any you don't find useful.)*

**Tip:** When you're saving a Custom search that finds files by their dates (when you created or modified them), be careful how you set up the search. For example, if you set up the dialog box to find files created "within 1 day of 11/1/2000," Sherlock will always find files created around November 1, 2000. But if your search is set up to find files created "today" or "yesterday," Sherlock will always find files created the day, or the day before, it's performing the search, even if that's years from now.

### Actually performing the search

After you've specified your complex search options, click OK. You return to the main Sherlock window, where the Custom button now appears selected. More important, the bottom of the window shows, in plain English, what you're looking for: "Find items whose name contains 'fish', date created is within 2 months of 7/4/2000, file/folder is locked," for example.

*Tip:* By typing into the text box at the top of the Sherlock window, you can specify letters to look for in your file names *in addition* to whatever criteria you've selected using the Custom menu. For example, suppose you've used the Custom pop-up menu to choose Applications (one of the pre-installed examples). By typing *Apple* into the text box above it, you can limit your search to applications whose name contains *Apple.*

At last you're ready to perform the search—by pressing Return or clicking the magnifying-glass button.

# Finding Text in Your Files

Sooner or later, it happens to everyone: a file's name doesn't match what's inside it. Maybe a marauding toddler pressed the keys while playing KidPix, inadvertently renaming your doctoral thesis "xggrjpO#$5%////." Maybe, in a Saturday afternoon organizing binge, your spouse helpfully changed the name of your "ATM Instructions" document to "Cash Machine Info," little realizing that it was a help file for Adobe Type Manager. Or maybe you just can't remember what you called something.

For this purpose, Sherlock offers a powerful Contents button that lets you search for words *inside* your files, regardless of their names. It performs this kind of search with amazing speed, and has saved thousands of Mac fans hours of frustrated searching by hand.

## The Indexing Catch

Left unaided, however, the Mac would take almost as long as *you* would to search your files for a particular phrase. To eliminate that agonizing delay, Apple programmed Sherlock to do something ingenious: like a kid cramming for an exam, Sherlock reads, takes notes on, and memorizes the contents of all of your files. Doing all of this reading—called *indexing* –may take several hours, depending on how much stuff is on your hard drive.

After having indexed your hard drive, however, Sherlock can produce search results in seconds.

### The first index—and scheduling

When you first get your Mac, the hard drive has never been indexed. When you open the Sherlock window for the first time, the Index Status column in the list of hard drives tells you as much.

The first time you index your hard drive, Sherlock requires an hour or two, during which you can continue working, but your Mac will feel drugged. That's why Apple encourages you to be absent while the indexing goes on—instead, you should set up a *schedule* for Sherlock, so that the indexing takes place in the middle of the night.

After the first indexing is over, Sherlock needs only a few minutes per day to update its miniature card catalog of your hard drive, to bone up on any new documents you've written. You can schedule this action, too.

**Tip:** This indexing concept explains the names of numerous files in your System Folder–the extensions called Find By Content and FBC Indexing Schedule, for example. It also explains the huge, multi-megabyte *invisible* file on your hard drive–the actual index itself–called TheFindByContentIndex (apparently named by a programmer with a broken Space bar). To see this file, use the "is invisible" option in the More Search Options dialog box described in the previous section.

### Scheduling unattended indexing

To set up your indexing schedule, open Sherlock. Choose Find→Index Volumes. As shown in Figure 15-5, you can click the checkbox for the hard drive you want to schedule, and then click the Schedule button. Now you can specify on which days of the week, and at what times, you want the indexing to take place.

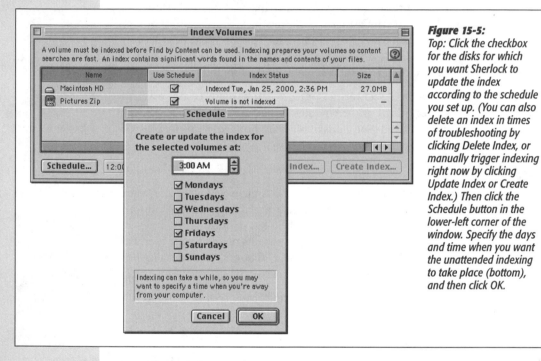

**Figure 15-5:**
*Top: Click the checkbox for the disks for which you want Sherlock to update the index according to the schedule you set up. (You can also delete an index in times of troubleshooting by clicking Delete Index, or manually trigger indexing right now by clicking Update Index or Create Index.) Then click the Schedule button in the lower-left corner of the window. Specify the days and time when you want the unattended indexing to take place (bottom), and then click OK.*

**Tip:** You don't necessarily have to leave your Mac on all night long if you've scheduled an after-hours indexing. First, remember that you can use the Energy Saver control panel to shut down the computer automatically at a certain time–say, an hour after the scheduled indexing time.

Second, if you live by a regular schedule, you can set Sherlock up to begin its indexing at the end of your workday. Then try to shut the Mac down–you'll be told that the indexing is underway, and you'll be offered the option to have the Mac shut itself down automatically when the indexing is complete.

### What gets indexed

Sherlock is smart enough to ignore files on your hard drive that don't actually contain *words,* such as applications, pictures, movies, system files, and (unfortunately) data-bases. What it does index includes word processing files, text files, clipping files, HTML (Web-page) documents, Acrobat (.pdf) files (created in Acrobat versions before 4.0), and sometimes email, depending on the program you use. (Sherlock can find text in Outlook Express messages, for example, but not Claris Emailer 2 messages.)

Sherlock can't index CDs or other hard drives on the network.

### How to control the indexing

Unless you intervene, Sherlock indexes much more than it needs to. As a result, your invisible index file takes up an unnecessary amount of hard-drive space, and the indexing takes much longer than it should. Here's how to control the process:

First, open Sherlock. Choose Edit→Preferences. Click Languages, and turn off the checkboxes of every language except the ones you use in your documents. (Chances are, the factory-installed set of languages to be indexed—Afrikaans, Catalan, Norwegian, and so on—is more inclusive than you actually need.) If you plan to work while the indexing goes on, you can also adjust the Responsiveness slider in this dialog box. ("More responsive" means that the Mac won't act quite so distracted as you work in other programs, but the indexing will take longer.)

Second, consider using icon labels (see page 40) to flag folders that you do, or don't, want indexed. You can then tell Sherlock to bypass them (or bypass all others). To do so, open Sherlock, choose Edit→Preferences; turn on the "Don't index items with this label" or "Only index items with this label" button, and use the pop-up menu to specify which label. For example, if you apply a label called Search Me to the three folders that actually contain your work, and then tell Sherlock to index only folders with that label, Sherlock's indexing and searching go like lightning.

Third, suppose you rarely use the find-by-content feature, having decided that you would rather not dedicate 25 or 50 MB of your hard drive to the invisible index file. But then, one day, you need to find a particular document in a folder that contains 75 files. You can index only that single folder—or even a single document—by Control-clicking its icon and then choosing Index Selection from the contextual menu. The Mac begins indexing that folder instantly. When you then want to use the Find By Content feature, drag the indexed folder into the list of disks, as shown in Figure 15-1.

Finally, you can make the indexing much faster—ten times faster or more, especially on large hard drives—by giving the indexing program more memory. To do that, open your System Folder→Extensions→Find folder. Highlight the icon called Find by Content Indexing, and then choose File→Get Info→Memory. Set the Preferred Size number to a much higher number—as much memory as you can afford, such as 7,000 K. The Mac's resulting indexing speed boost will be dramatic.

## How to Search for Text

After you've indexed your hard drive, you can begin to enjoy the payoff—searching for words inside your files. If Sherlock is open, you can either click the Contents button or press ⌘-G to prepare for a content search; if Sherlock isn't open, and you're in the Finder, you can summon Sherlock's contents-search screen by pressing ⌘-F, ⌘-G in rapid succession.

Now type the word or phrase you seek. Click the magnifying-glass icon (or press Return). Sherlock quickly produces a list of results, ranked by *relevance,* as shown in Figure 15-6.

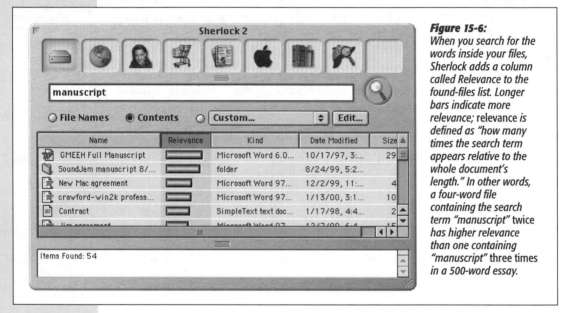

**Figure 15-6:**
*When you search for the words inside your files, Sherlock adds a column called Relevance to the found-files list. Longer bars indicate more relevance; relevance is defined as "how many times the search term appears relative to the whole document's length." In other words, a four-word file containing the search term "manuscript" twice has higher relevance than one containing "manuscript" three times in a 500-word essay.*

After the list appears, you can open, print, move, make an alias of, or otherwise handle the resulting files exactly as described in "The Search Results," earlier in this chapter.

## When Sherlock Fails

If you find yourself frustrated by Sherlock's ability to find words inside your files, it helps to understand the way it searches. For example:

- Sherlock indexes only the first 2,000 different words in each file. That's why Sherlock might miss your book manuscript if the search term occurs late in the document.

- Sherlock tries to find files containing *any* of the words you type into the search blank. If you search for *Steve Jobs,* you'll turn up every document that contains the word Steve, *and* every document that contains the word jobs. You can't tell Sherlock to a search for a specific pair of words that occur together (as you can, using quotation marks, when using Internet search pages).

- Sherlock sometimes even tries to find files containing *pieces* of what you searched for. If you search for *Steven,* Sherlock's roundup includes files containing just the word Steve. That phenomenon partly explains why Sherlock sometimes finds files that don't seem to contain the search term at all.

## Searching the Internet

Any old computer can search for the files on its own hard drive. Sherlock's special twist, however, is that you can use exactly the same program to search for information on the World Wide Web (if your Mac has an Internet account).

If Sherlock is open, you put it into search-the-Internet mode by clicking one of the icons at the top of the window, or by choosing Find→Search Internet. If Sherlock *isn't* open, but you're in the Finder, you can open Sherlock directly to Internet mode by choosing File→Search Internet (or by pressing ⌘-H).

The large icons at the top of the Sherlock window represent different kinds of Web sites that Sherlock can search (see Figure 15-6). When you click one, the screen changes to show a list of checkboxes, each corresponding to a particular Web page that you can search.

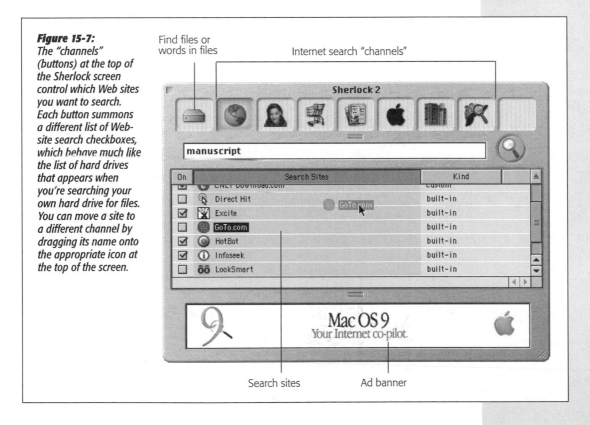

*Figure 15-7:*
*The "channels" (buttons) at the top of the Sherlock screen control which Web sites you want to search. Each button summons a different list of Web-site search checkboxes, which behave much like the list of hard drives that appears when you're searching your own hard drive for files. You can move a site to a different channel by dragging its name onto the appropriate icon at the top of the screen.*

Find files or words in files

Internet search "channels"

Search sites

Ad banner

Here's what these *channel buttons* (as Apple calls them) represent. (To identify one of these icons by name, point to it without clicking; a pop-up label appears.)

- **Internet.** When you click this channel button, you see a list of checkboxes. Each represents a popular *search engine*—a Web page, like Yahoo.com or AltaVista.com, that searches part of the Internet. The benefits of having them listed in Sherlock are that, first, you can search more than one simultaneously; and second, you can perform this kind of search without actually having to launch your Web browser.

- **People.** This tantalizing option lets you type in somebody's name; Sherlock then consults any of three different "White Pages" Web sites in an attempt to track down that person's email address and telephone number.

  Unfortunately, the technology gods don't smile on this feature. It only rarely produces an entry for the person you're seeking. When you do get results, you're usually shown only an email address (which is often out of date); a phone number shows up even less often.

- **Shopping.** Now we're talking. The checkboxes on this screen represent shopping and auction Web sites, such as Amazon, eBay, and Barnes & Noble. When you search these sites, you type in the name of a product; Sherlock shows you a list of matching items from those Web sites, sorted by price and including shipping-delay information.

  Unless you don't buy anything on the Internet beyond books and CDs, the included plug-ins for this screen may not seem very useful. But as you add new plug-ins, as described later this chapter, the Shopping channel could emerge as a powerful comparison-shopping feature.

- **News.** These checkboxes let you search various Internet-based news, sports, and financial-news services.

- **Apple.** Using the checkboxes, you can search the Apple Macintosh Products Guide, a database of 14,000 programs for the Mac (to find out if, for example, there's an interior-design program for the Mac); the Apple Tech Info Library, a huge collection of answers, troubleshooting tips, and feature explanations for every Mac model ever made; and Apple.com (the rest of the Apple site, including press releases, programming tools, news blurbs, and so on).

- **Reference.** The three checkboxes on this screen may look sparse, but they represent a delicious Mac feature: what amounts to a built-in dictionary, thesaurus, and encyclopedia. Type the term you're looking for, click the appropriate checkboxes, and let Sherlock retrieve the definition, encyclopedia entry, or list of synonyms from the corresponding Web sites.

- **My Channel.** When you click this Sherlock Holmes-cap icon, you get an empty space where the checkboxes usually appear. This is *your* channel—actually, the first of many that you can create—which is an empty screen to be filled with your own personal selection of checkboxes. To add a checkbox to this screen, switch to one of the *other* screens (by clicking a different top-row icon) and then drag a checkbox directly onto the Holmes-cap icon.

More on creating your own channels, and managing plug-ins, in the next section.

- **KidSafe.** This channel icon shows up only if you've installed KidSafe, the child-protection software described on page 250. This channel shows you only the names of Web pages that are on the approved list of 55,000 or more KidSafe pages. (Apple intends to expand this list month by month.)

## Performing a Search

Searching the Web pages listed in one of the channel screens works just like searching your own Mac disks for particular files. Begin by switching to the appropriate channel, either by clicking one of the icons or by using the Channels menu. Turn on the checkboxes of the Web sites you want to search, type the text you wish to find, and then click the magnifying-glass icon (or press Return).

---

*Tip:* You can save a canned search setup when using the Internet search features, exactly as you can with other kinds of searches (see page 265). When you double-click the saved search file, Sherlock launches, connects to the Internet, and performs the predetermined search automatically.

---

If you're not already online, Sherlock now tells the Mac to dial the Internet, sends your search request to the selected Web pages and, after a moment, shows you the results of its search. Instead of seeing a list of files, however, this time, Sherlock shows you a list of Web pages containing the text you typed. Figure 15-8 shows the idea.

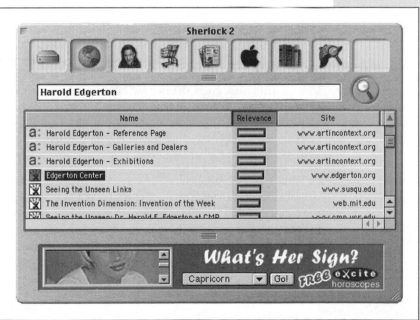

**Figure 15-8:**
*When you search the Internet, you get a list of Web sites that contain the text you seek. As with find-by-content searches, many of these results are sorted by relevance. When you're searching the Web, the Sherlock window sprouts a new element: the advertising banner at the bottom of the screen—a concession to the various Web-search pages, such as Excite and Lycos, whose Web-page ads are invisible to people using Sherlock.*

***Tip:*** Sherlock shows you only the first 20 or 30 "hits" from each Web site you searched. This limit is built into the Sherlock plug-in you're using. If you're technically savvy, however, you can tweak this number. You'll find instructions in Apple's technical note at *http://til.info.apple.com/techinfo.nsf/artnum/n58163.*

Here's what you can do with one of these results:

- **Read the first paragraph.** Click one of the Web pages listed in the search results; as shown in Figure 15-8, Sherlock shows you, just above the advertising panel, the first paragraph or so of text that appears on that Web page. This blurb is a very useful preview, one that can save you the effort of opening that Web page only to find that it's not what you were looking for.

- **Go to the Web page.** Double-click one of the listings to launch your Web browser and actually visit the corresponding page. (The Web browser that opens when you double-click is determined by the  →Control Panels→Internet control panel's Web tab.) If you double-click a name you found using one of the People channels, your email program opens, and a new outgoing message appears— pre-addressed.

***Tip:*** If your Web browser is already open, you can drag one of the Sherlock results directly into its window to switch to the corresponding new page.

- **Create an Internet location file.** If you think you might like to visit one of these Web sites later, you can drag it out of the list and onto your desktop, where it becomes an Internet location file (see page 244). You can also drag it directly into the Internet Explorer Favorites list, where it becomes a bookmark for that browser.

- **Repeat the search.** Click the same channel button again to restore your original search setup—to correct a typo, for example. Or click a different channel button to search a different kind of Web page—or even your hard drive.

## When Sherlock Fails on the Internet

If you find the Web pages that Sherlock locates inconsistent in quality, you're not alone. Remember that, first of all, it's not Sherlock doing the searching—it's the Web-search pages whose checkboxes you've selected. To understand what's going on with Sherlock, you must understand what's going on with Internet search pages.

For example: Web pages sometimes turn up in Sherlock that don't, in fact, appear to contain any of the words you searched for. When this happens, it's probably because the creator of that Web page buried your search words invisibly on the page—in its HTML *keyword list,* for example, exactly in hopes of being found by search engines like yours. That technique may seem dishonest, but it's very popular on the Internet— especially if you're searching for commonly sought terms.

Each Web-search page has different conventions, too, concerning punctuation marks in your search phrase. For example, search engines like Yahoo rely on quotation marks "like this" to indicate words that must be found together; otherwise, it turns up all Web pages containing *either* word, not necessarily together. Other Web sites accept punctuation like + and -, the words *and* and *or,* the excluding term *not,* and so on. There's no way to find out exactly how to punctuate your search request for a particular Web-search page except to visit that Web page and read its Help screen.

## Of Channels and Plug-ins

To get the most out of Sherlock, consider capitalizing on its expansion feature. By downloading additional (free) plug-ins, you can take Sherlock's Internet searching abilities far beyond Lycos and Amazon.com. By understanding how Mac OS 9 organizes these files in the System Folder, you can create and manage your own channels, stocked with your own plug-ins.

---

***Tip:*** By studying a little bit of HTML (Web-page coding), you can actually create plug-ins of your own. If you know how to write HTML code, visit Apple's "how to make Sherlock plug-ins" page at *http://developer.apple.com/macos/sherlock.html.*

---

### Getting more plug-ins

You can find additional Sherlock plug-ins all over the Internet. For example:

• **Sherlock Resource Site.** Here you'll find about 85 plug-ins ready to go, including those for Yahoo, Time Daily (Time magazine), Onelist (a list of email-based discussion groups), MacCentral (Macintosh news and opinion), MP3.com (music files to download), Internet Movie Database, Adobe, Deal Mac (a roundup of Mac-product discount offers), U.S. Government, eToys, and so on. And if you're *really* bored, the Terminix plug-in searches the Terminix Pest Library. *www.macineurope.com/sherlocksite*

• **Apple-Donuts.** Over 300 plug-ins are here, neatly organized by category (commerce, companies, entertainment, Internet search sites, and so on). Among the useful: MacZone and Price Watch USA (to check prices for Mac goods), Computer Jargon, PalmCentral (for PalmPilot software), Macworld, MacAddict, and MacWeek magazines, and so on. You can even download all 300 in a single pass. *www.apple-donuts.com/sherlocksearch/index.html*

• **Sherlock international plug-ins.** These plug-ins are specifically geared toward searching international-information databases: the U.S. State Department, Central Europe Online, Kennedy School of Government, and so on, plus French and Spanish versions of the Lycos search engine. *www.xenophone.com/sherlock*

### Installing plug-ins

When properly decompressed, a plug-in's name generally ends in the letters *.src* (for "Sherlock resource"). You can install a new plug-in by dragging it to one of these three locations:

• Directly onto one of the channel buttons. Sherlock installs the plug-in onto that channel "page."

---

- Straight into the list of plug-in/sites on any channel page.

- Onto the System Folder icon; when the message appears that says, "Put this into the Internet Search Sites folder?"—click OK. The next time you open Sherlock, you'll see the new plug-in listed on the appropriate channel screen.

    Usually, it shows up on the My Channel page. That's because the vast majority of Sherlock plug-ins were written for the original Sherlock program—the one that came with Mac OS 8.5—which didn't *have* channels. (Plug-ins designed specifically for the People, Shopping, News, or Reference channels of Mac OS 9 are less common.) As a result, Sherlock doesn't know what to do with these plug-ins except to file them on your My Channel screen.

To move a site plug-in to a different channel, drag its checkbox onto one of the channel icons at the top of the Sherlock screen. And to remove one of these new checkbox items from your Sherlock screen, drag its icon directly out of Sherlock—onto the desktop, for example, or into the Trash.

---

*Tip:* To become a Sherlock master, try deleting, adding, or moving plug-in files around the manual way. Open your System Folder→Internet Search Sites folder. Inside, you'll find a folder corresponding to each of your channels; inside each of these folders is the set of plug-ins that appears on that page. By dragging these icons around, you can assign them to different channels.

---

### Managing channels

To create a new channel, choose Channels→New Channel. In the resulting dialog box (see Figure 15-9), type a name for the channel, a description, if you like, and then choose an icon from the scrolling list at the right side of the dialog box.

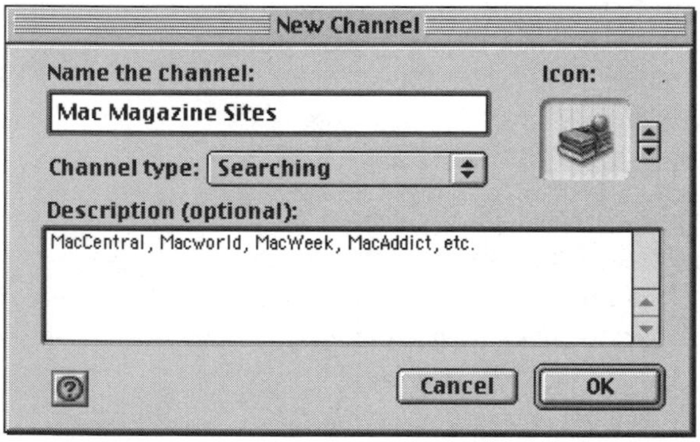

**Figure 15-9:**
*Use this dialog box to set up a new channel, or to edit an old one (but not Apple's canned channels). You can choose an icon for the channel either by using the scrolling arrows at right, or by dragging any PICT-format file (to avoid squishing, it should be about the size and shape of the channel button) off the desktop and directly onto the icon box shown here. (You can also drag a PICT file directly onto a channel icon in the main Sherlock window—but again, you can't change Apple's channel icons.)*

You can return to this channel-customizing dialog box at any time—just click one of your custom channels and then choose Channel→Edit Channel. (You can't, alas, edit any of the channels that come built into Sherlock. Despite the availability of several other people-heads in the list of available icons, your People channel is stuck with the twenty-something brunette forever.)

You can also rearrange your channel icons—just drag them into any blank slots in the channel palette. Doing so is easiest, of course, if there *are* some blank slots; you can make blank ones show up by dragging the "grip strip" handle—centered just below the channel icons—downward.

---

**FREQUENTLY ASKED QUESTION**

## It's Not Nice to Fool Mother Apple

*I keep trying to delete the People channel, which doesn't really work anyway. But it keeps coming back!*

You're welcome to play around in the System Folder→Internet Search Sites folder. Inside, each folder represents one of your channels, and each plug-in inside these folders represents the checkbox on the corresponding channel page. You can rename a channel by renaming its folder,

delete the channel by deleting its folder, reassign a checkbox by dragging it to a different channel folder, and so on.

You'll soon discover, however, that Apple doesn't want you disturbing its original channel lineup—People, Shopping, and so on. If you drag one of these folders out of the Internet Search Sites folder, Sherlock will re-create it automatically.

---

# Part Five:
# Plugging into Mac OS 9

5

# Networking in Mac OS 9

E very Mac ever made is network-ready. Buy a few cables and adapters, and you can wire all the Macs in your office together. Once that's done, you can copy files from one machine to another just as you'd drag files between folders on your own Mac. You can send little messages to each other's screens. Everyone on the network can consult the same database or calendar. You can play games over the network. You can share a single laser printer, cable modem, or fax modem among all the Macs in the office. And in Mac OS 9, you can even connect to this network from wherever you are in the world, using the Internet as the world's longest extension cord back to your office.

Best of all, all the software you need to create such a network is built right into Mac OS 9.

As you read this chapter, remember the difficulty Apple faces: It must design a networking system simple enough for the laptop owner who just wants to copy things to her desktop Mac when she gets home from a trip—and yet secure and flexible enough for the network designer at a large corporation. The Mac OS 9 networking software contains many different layers of password protection and security, which you can apply independently to every folder on your hard drive. Fortunately, you can ignore all of this if the network is just you, your two Macs, and a printer.

## Wiring the Network

These days, every Mac and laser printer has an Ethernet jack on the back panel (see Figure 16-1). If you connect all of the Macs and Ethernet printers in your small office to a central *Ethernet hub*—a compact $25 box with jacks for five or ten computers and printers—you've got yourself a very fast, very reliable network. (Most people wind up trying to hide the Ethernet hub in the closet, and running the wiring either along the edges of the room or inside the walls.) You can buy Ethernet cables, plus the Ethernet hub, in any computer store or, less expensively, from an Internet-based mail-order house. (Hubs aren't Mac-specific.)

*Tip:* If you want to connect only two Macs—say, your laptop and your desktop machine—you don't need an Ethernet hub at all. Instead, you just need an Ethernet *crossover cable*—about $8 from a computer store or online mail-order supplier. Run it directly between the Ethernet jacks of the two computers.

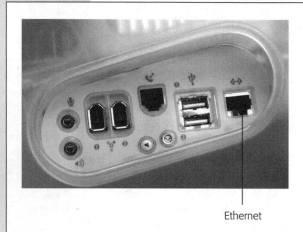

**Figure 16-1:**
*Every Mac sold today has an Ethernet jack. It looks like an overweight telephone jack. It connects to an Ethernet hub via Ethernet cable (also known as RJ-45), which looks like an overweight telephone wire. Some very old Macs, such as the Power Mac 6100, have built-in Ethernet circuitry, but may require an adapter to accommodate the actual Ethernet cable.*

Ethernet

Ethernet is the best networking system for most offices; it's fast, easy, and cheap. You may also encounter one of these two other kinds of networks, however—one for very old Macs, and the other for very new:

• **LocalTalk.** If you have very old Macs that don't have Ethernet jacks, you can plug *PhoneNet-style* connectors into your printer ports. You can then connect one PhoneNet connector to the next using ordinary telephone wire, in a continuous chain. (You can buy PhoneNet connectors—about $10 apiece—on the Internet. They're hard to find in computer stores these days.)

• **AirPort.** The latest Mac models let you install a $99 metal card, about the size of a Visa card, that lets them connect to your network without any wires at all—as long as they're within about 150 feet of a *base station,* which must in turn be physically connected to your network. (If you think about it, the AirPort system is a lot like a cordless phone; the Mac is the movable handset.)

The base station can either be the $300 AirPort Base Station—which looks like a small silver flying saucer—or another AirPort-equipped Mac that you've configured, using the AirPort Setup Assistant, to serve as a *software-based* base station. You can plug the flying-saucer base station into an Ethernet hub, thus permitting 10 or 20 AirPort-equipped Macs to join an existing Ethernet network without wiring.

After having wired your network, all that remains is for you to tell each computer which method you've used to connect it. Open the  →Control Panels→AppleTalk control panel; from the pop-up menu, choose the appropriate connection: Ethernet, Printer port (for LocalTalk), or AirPort. If the Mac informs you that AppleTalk is *inactive*, make it active before proceeding.

At this point, your network is ready. Your Mac should "see" any Ethernet printers that are turned on, in readiness to print (see Chapter 19). You can now play network games or use a network calendar. And you can now turn on *file sharing*, one of the most useful and most sophisticated features of the Mac OS.

# File Sharing in Mac OS 9

In file sharing, you can summon the icon for a folder or disk attached to any other computer on the network, as long as the owner of that computer has given you permission to do so. That folder or disk shows up on your screen underneath your own hard drive, as shown in Figure 16-2. At this point, you can drag files in or out, exactly as though the other Mac's folder or disk is a gigantic Zip disk you've inserted into your own machine.

**Figure 16-2:**
*The whole point of file sharing: to bring icons for the hard drives or folders from other Macs, such as the Jenn's iMac HD icon, onto your own screen. By dragging icons back and forth, you can transfer your work from your main Mac to your laptop; give copies of your documents to other people; create a "drop box" that collects submissions from various authors for, a publication; and so on.*

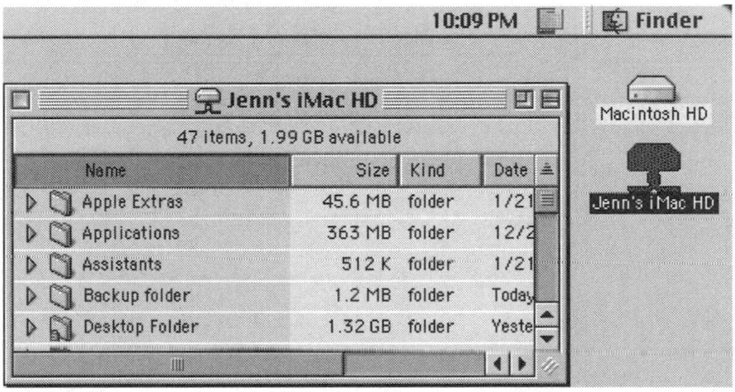

## Network 1: Fast, Easy, and Password-Free

Because security is an important issue in corporations, the Mac's file-sharing feature comes with a dizzying array of password-related features. For each folder you make available to the network, you can specify exactly which co-workers have access—and how *much* access.

But if you work alone, or with partners from whom you have nothing to hide, you may consider all of these layers of security so much red tape. The following instructions guide you through setting up a streamlined file-sharing network that doesn't require any passwords. Later in this chapter, you can read the more involved instructions for creating a full-blown, secure network.

Both sets of guidelines assume, of course, that you've already wired the network together, as described at the beginning of this chapter.

### Setting up Each Mac

Choose  →Control Panels→File Sharing. The File Sharing control panel opens (see Figure 16-3). In the Owner Name field (blank), type your name (or company name); leave the password field empty; and in the Computer Name field , type a name for the computer (such as *Front Desk iMac*). If you took the time to answer the questions of the Macintosh Setup Assistant—the program that runs itself the first time you turn on a new Mac—you may find that these fields are already filled in. Delete the password, in that case.

Click the Start button in the center of the dialog box. (While the feature "warms up," which can take up to a minute, the button says Cancel; when file sharing is finally on, the button says Stop.) Close the window.

Repeat this process on each Mac in your office—but enter the *same* Owner Name on each machine. That's all the setup needed—you're ready to use your network.

---

**Note to File Sharing veterans:** You don't have to share any disks or folders using the File→Get Info→Sharing command. If every Mac has the same Owner Name, you, the Owner, can automatically access every disk on every shared machine–without having to explicitly share them.

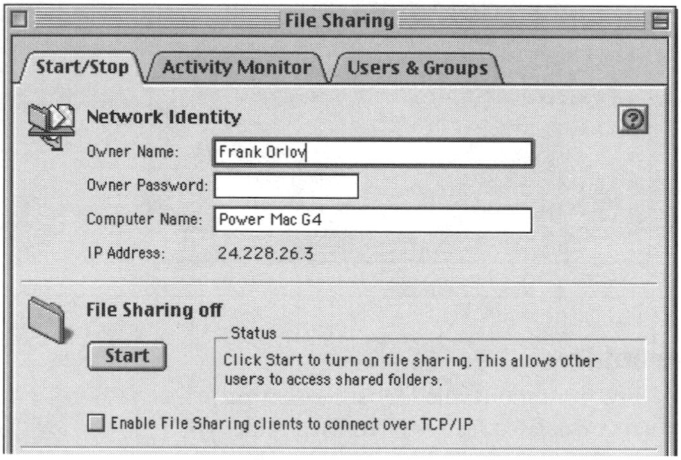

**Figure 16-3:**
*This is the setup for a security-free, high-convenience file-sharing arrangement. You'll be able to access any Mac on the network without having to type in anything– no name, no password. If you work alone with a couple of Macs, or with co-workers you trust, this is by far the most efficient arrangement.*

### Accessing the other Mac

Suppose you're seated at your Power Mac G4, but you need a file that's on the iMac DV down the hall. To bring its hard drive's icon onto your screen, follow these steps:

1. **Open the Network Browser.**

   To do so, choose  →Network Browser. (You can read more about this program in Chapter 5.)

2. **Double-click AppleTalk to see the list of Macs on your network.**

As shown in Figure 16-4, the names of the other Macs on the network appear in the list. (If they don't, then something's wrong with your network wiring, or you haven't prepared those Macs as described in "Setting up Each Mac.")

3. **Double-click the name of the Mac you want to access.**

Now the "Connect as:" box appears, where you're supposed to input your name and password (Figure 16-4, center). The Owner Name already appears in the Name field, as you specified it in the File Sharing field of every Mac. The Password field is empty.

Because you left the password empty, you can just click Connect, or press the Return or Enter key, to get rid of this dialog box.

---

***Tip:*** This "Connect as:" dialog box appears every time you try to connect to another Mac. To dismiss it, all you have to do is press Enter or Return. Still, if you wish, you can even eliminate the appearance of this dialog box itself, further streamlining the process of connecting to another Mac. Doing so requires your clicking the Add to Keychain checkbox here, and reading the discussion of the Keychain later in this chapter.

---

***Figure 16-4:***
*The sequence of connecting to another disk on the network: Open the Network Browser (top); double-click AppleTalk; double-click the name of the Mac you want. Specify your password—or, if you didn't require one, leave the password field blank. Click Connect (middle). Finally, double-click the name of the shared folder or disk you actually want to open (bottom). At any stage, you can drag an icon from the Network Browser window to your desktop to make an alias, saving you some navigation the next time you want to connect.*

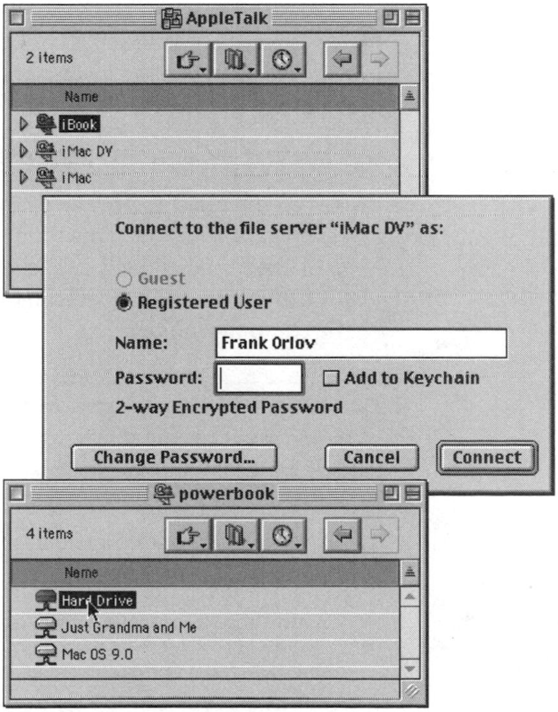

**4. Click Connect (or press Return or Enter).**

Now a list of disks connected to that Mac appears (Figure 16-4, bottom).

**5. Double-click the name of the disk you want to open.**

At last, the hard drive you've connected to appears on the right side of your screen. It usually appears just below your built-in hard drive icon. You can open this icon to open, copy, move, rename, or delete the files on it, exactly as though the files were on your own computer.

*Tip:* Make an alias of the hard-drive icon that you've just pulled onto your screen. The next time you want to connect to it, just double-click its icon—you'll skip steps 1, 2, 3, and 5 of the connection process described in this section.

## Network 2: Complex, Secure, and Specific

If security is an issue where you work, the Mac can accommodate you. Using a wide range of built-in tools, you can specify exactly which folders on your hard drive are accessible to which coworkers—and exactly what powers each person has over each folder. Although setting up such a configuration involves a lot of steps, it isn't especially difficult.

### Phase 1: Create accounts

In this first step, you'll tell your Mac about each person who may soon be visiting over the network wires.

**1. Choose  →Control Panels→File Sharing.**

If your own name, favorite password, and computer name don't show up here (see Figure 16-3), take the time to type them in. (You may find that these fields have already been filled in by the Macintosh Setup Assistant, which queried you for this information when you first installed Mac OS 9 or bought and turned on the computer.)

*Tip:* One of Mac OS 9's most intriguing new features is its ability to let you connect to a Mac over the Internet. To permit this kind of connection to your computer, turn on the "Enable File Sharing clients to connect over TCP/IP" checkbox. (See page 293 to find out the procedure for connecting.)

**2. Click the Users & Groups tab.**

As shown in Figure 16-5, this window shows a list of everybody who may conceivably access your own hard drive.

The Guest icon appears here automatically. It represents a special, password-less account that you can use for non-confidential folders to save your network comrades a few steps. (This advice will make more sense when you read Phase 3, later in this discussion.)

3. **Click New User. Type a name and password for the first co-worker.**

You can invite each co-worker to come over to stand beside you as you do this, to make up a favorite name and password.

On the other hand, you may prefer to use the "Allow user to change password" checkbox (see Figure 16-5, bottom). It lets you make up a temporary password for each co-worker when you're first creating the network—something easy, like each person's last name. Later, when you explain to your partners how they're supposed to use the network, you can advise them to change their password—to make up one of their own—at the first opportunity. (Instructions for doing so appear below, in Phase 3.)

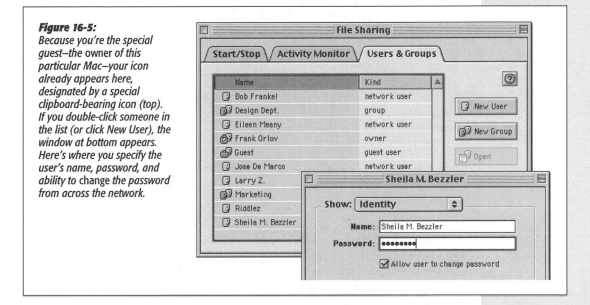

**Figure 16-5:**
*Because you're the special guest—the owner of this particular Mac—your icon already appears here, designated by a special clipboard-bearing icon (top). If you double-click someone in the list (or click New User), the window at bottom appears. Here's where you specify the user's name, password, and ability to change the password from across the network.*

**Tip:** By choosing Sharing from the Show pop-up menu, you can also turn off the "Allow user to connect" checkbox. This option is a master switch for a user's access to your Mac. The moment the memo arrives saying that Sheila has been embezzling funds, you don't have to fiddle around with each disk and folder you've shared, trying to find out which ones Sheila has been given access to. Instead, you can quickly shut down *all* of her access to your computer by turning off this checkbox.

4. **Close the window, and repeat step 3 for each co-worker on your network.**

You can also click New Group to create a *group* of people—Marketing, for example. As shown in Figure 16-6, you can then drag the names of the various individuals *on top of* these Group icons to copy them there. (You can also drag a clump of selected individuals simultaneously into a group—select them by ⌘-clicking their names, or Shift-click to select a consecutive chunk of names, before dragging onto a Group icon.) One person can belong to many different groups.

Later, when you're specifying how much access various people have to various folders, you can permit an entire group of people access to a particular folder in one fell swoop. (This, too, will become clearer in Phase 3.)

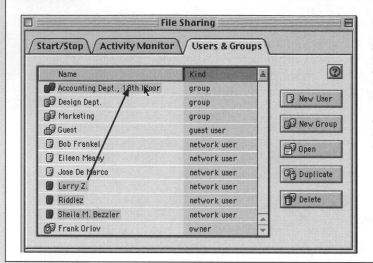

**Figure 16-6:**
*You can add a person's name to a group in one of two ways: either by dragging that name onto a Group icon, or by dragging a Group icon onto the name. To remove someone from a group, double-click the Group icon. The list of members appears; drag someone's name to the Trash, or highlight the name and press the Delete key.*

As your list grows, you can sort it either by Name or by Kind (group, network user, and so on) by clicking the column headings, exactly as in a Finder list-view window. You can also click the pyramid button just above the scroll bar to reverse the sorting order (another familiar Mac OS technique).

---

**Tip:** To see a list of people in a particular group, double-click the Group icon. Conversely, to see which groups an individual belongs to, double-click that person's icon; from the Show pop-up menu, choose Sharing. You'll see a scrolling list of groups to which this person belongs.

And one more Group tip: You can drag Group icons onto another Group icon, thus creating a larger group made up of all the individuals who compose those smaller groups.

---

Phase 1 is complete when you've typed in the names and passwords of everyone on your network who might want to access the files on your Mac. Close the File Sharing control panel.

### Phase 2: Sharing disks and folders

Now that you've identified *who* can visit your Mac, you must specify *what* they can visit. In other words, you probably don't want everyone freely rooting around through the stuff on your hard drive, reading whatever personal correspondence you have there. Instead, you'll probably want to designate specific disks or folders for sharing over the network; using the built-in file-sharing feature of Mac OS 9, you can make up to ten folders on your hard drive available (not counting folders *inside* folders). (If you need more flexibility—if you want to make more folders available, or you want to permit more than 10 simultaneous connections, or you need more speed, buy a server-software suite like AppleShare IP or Mac OS X Server.)

---

**Note:** You can't share a floppy disk. You can't share an individual file, either; it must be inside a folder or on a disk that you've shared.

---

Here's how you identify such a folder.

1. **Highlight a folder on your hard drive. Choose File→Get Info→Sharing.**

   The dialog box shown in Figure 16-7 appears.

**Figure 16-7:**
This window lets you establish who's allowed to see or use the contents of a particular folder or disk. Using the Privilege pop-up menus (lower right), you can specify how much access the Owner, a selected user or group, and everyone else has. As elsewhere in the Mac OS, the circled question-mark icon brings up a help screen, although its helpfulness may not be immediately apparent.

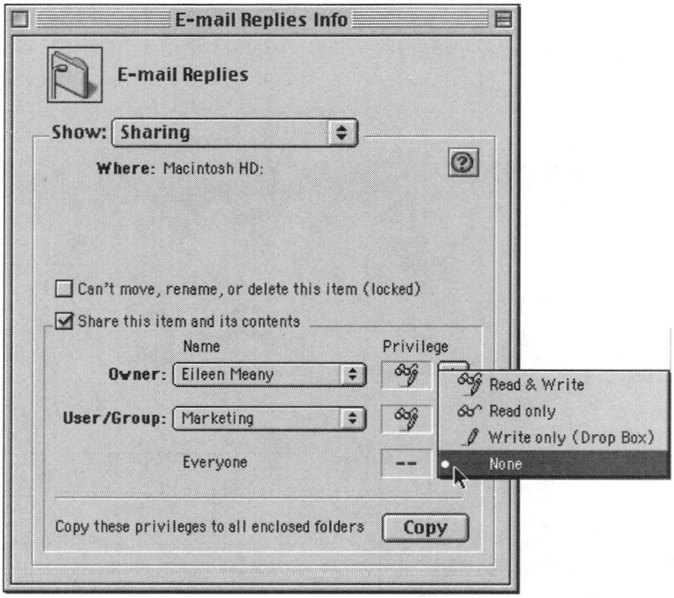

2. **Turn on "Share this item and its contents."**

   If you like, using the Owner pop-up menu, you can also designate somebody else as the *co-owner* of this folder—a concept that requires some explanation.

   This folder is on *your* hard drive; you, obviously, have complete control over it. In file-sharing lingo, you are the *owner* of it. Only the owner is allowed to specify *access privileges* to this folder, as you will in the next step—that is, to change who can access this folder, and what they can do with it.

   But in some work situations, you might want somebody *else* on the network to have control over these access privileges. For example, you may be the graphic designer who has to lay out the Arts section of the magazine, but you want the editor of that section to have control over this Articles folder, too.

---

If you decide to designate somebody else as the co-owner of this folder, use the appropriate Privilege pop-up menu (see Figure 16-7) to specify how much access the owner has to this folder. (You can read about the various degrees of access in step 5.)

3. **Turn on "Can't move, rename, or delete this item (locked)," if you like.**

A folder you've protected in this way resists your co-workers' attempts to trash, move, or rename the *folder*. They have full access over its *contents*, however (unless you protect the contents in step 5). (*You* can't move or delete a folder you've locked this way, either.)

4. **Using the User/Group pop-up menu, indicate who can access this folder.**

You can choose only one name. That's great if you want to share this folder with only one other co-worker; if you want to share it with more than one person, however, you must create a Group, as described in Phase 1. Then choose that group's name from this pop-up menu.

---

**POWER USERS' CLINIC**

## The Enclosed-Folder Conundrum

When you turn on File Sharing for a folder or disk, you also share all of the folders inside of it. If you highlight one of these inner folders and then choose File→Get Info→Sharing, you'll see a checkbox called "Use enclosing folder's privileges"—and it's turned on. The controls that let you specify who has access to this folder, meanwhile, are dimmed. After all, you've already specified who has access to this folder—when you set up the *outer* folder's access privileges.

In certain circumstances, however, you may want one of the inner folders to be protected differently from those outside it. In that case, turn off the "Use enclosing folder's privileges" checkbox; now you can use the various privileges pop-up menus in the bottom half of the window, as shown in Figure 16-7.

Because you now know that every interior folder automatically inherits the sharing settings of the outer folder, then you may wonder why there's a "Copy these privileges to all enclosed folders" button (see Figure 16-7). You use it only in one circumstance—when you *change* the access privileges for the outer folder. Click Copy to update the folders inside it to match.

---

5. **Using the Privilege pop-up menu, specify what the specified co-worker or group can *do* with this folder.**

If you choose **None**, then you're a network tease—your co-workers may be able to see the folder, but its name will be dimmed and unavailable. Choose **Write only (Drop Box)** if you want your network buddies to be able to see the folder, but not open it; all they can do is deposit files into it. The **Read only** option lets visitors open the folder, open the files inside, or copy the files inside to their own hard drives—but they can't put anything new into the folder, nor save changes to files they find there.

Finally, choose **Read & Write** if you'd like your networked colleagues to have full access to the folder. They can do anything they want with the files inside, including trashing them.

6. **Specify how much access, if any, you want *everyone else* on the network to have.**

In step 4, you gave specific folder access to a specific person or group. Using the Everyone/Privilege pop-up menu at the bottom of the dialog box, you can specify how much access everyone *else* gets, including people who sign on as Guests.

You can't give "Everyone" *more* access to the folder than you gave the User/Group people—only the same degree of freedom, or less. For example, you can't give Read & Write access to Everyone to a folder, but give the Marketing group (using the User/Group pop-up menu) only drop-box access.

7. **Close the window. Repeat steps 1 through 6 for up to nine other folders.**

### Phase 3: Connecting to shared disks and folders

The previous section describes the steps involved in preparing your Mac for invasion by other people on the network. This section details how to be one of *them*—that is, how to connect to other Macs that have been set up for file sharing.

1. **Choose 🍎→Network Browser.**

The Network Browser window appears, listing all Macs on the network that contain shared disks or files. (If you, like many Mac old-timers, prefer to use the Chooser instead of the Network Browser, choose 🍎→Chooser; click the AppleShare icon—or type the letter A; and then continue with the instructions as written here. See the sidebar "The Secret Chooser Advantage" for more details.)

If you like, you can drag the icon of the Mac to which you're connecting onto the desktop (or highlight its icon and then choose File→Make Alias; finally, click OK. When you want to access this networked Mac in the future, you can skip steps 1 and 2 by just double-clicking this special *network location* alias on your desktop.

---

*Tip:* You can also access folders and disks on your network directly from within the Open File dialog box described in Chapter 8—*if* the program you're using offers *Navigation Services* (the newer Open File box design also described in Chapter 8). To do so, click the Shortcuts button (see Figure 8-4); from the pop-up menu and choose Network. Then proceed with the instructions as written here.

---

2. **Double-click the name of the Mac that contains what you want.**

The dialog box shown in the middle of Figure 16-4 appears.

3. **Specify whether you're a Guest or a Registered User.**

You can click the appropriate button or press the keystrokes ⌘-G or ⌘-R, respectively. Although Guests access is more convenient because it doesn't require a password, remember that the shared folder you want might not be fully accessible to guests, as described in step 6 of the preceding instructions.

If you're a registered user, your name already appears here—at least Mac OS 9's guess as to your registered name. (It's whatever you've typed into the top field in the File Sharing control panel, which may not necessarily match your account name on the Mac you're invading.)

4. **Type your password.**

This is the password that was set up for you in step 3 of Phase 1, several pages back. Capitalization counts.

If you plan to access this particular folder or disk often, you might also decide to add this password to your Keychain, a feature described at the end of this chapter.

At this point, you can change your password, if the owner of the shared Mac has permitted doing so. Click Change Password. A small dialog box appears, in which you can specify both the old password (to prove that you're legitimate) and the new one before clicking OK.

5. **Click Connect (or press Return).**

Now you see the list of shared disks or folders on the Mac you're visiting. (If you plan to use the file-sharing feature regularly, master the Favorites and Recent Items pop-up menus in the Network Browser, as shown in Figure 16-8.)

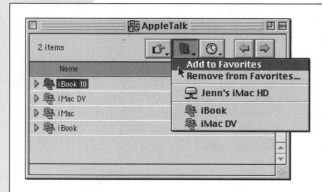

***Figure 16-8:***
*You can, if you wish, highlight one of the disks or folders in this list and then choose Add to Favorites, as shown here. (Alternatively, drag the shared disk or folder icon directly onto the Favorites menu icon.) The next time you want to connect to that particular shared item, you can choose its name from the Favorites pop-up folder/icon, which eliminates a step in the usual connection sequence. (You can also choose the name of the shared item from the Recent Items pop-up menu/icon, which looks like a clock.)*

6. **Double-click the name of the folder or disk you want to open.**

Its icon now appears at the right side of your desktop, as shown in Figure 16-2. You're now free to manipulate its contents as described in the next section.

As noted earlier, you'd be wise to make an alias of the folder or disk you've just brought your desktop. The *next* time you want to connect, just double-click the alias icon—you get to skip steps 1, 2, and 6 of the procedure above.

### Connecting over the Internet

One of Mac OS 9's most interesting new features is its ability to let you connect to your File Sharing network over the Internet. If, in Phase 1 of the setup in the previous chapter, you turned on "Enable File Sharing clients to connect over TCP/IP," you're ready to roll.

This feature is practical only if the shared Mac has a *permanent* Internet connection—a cable modem, DSL line, or other high-speed, Ethernet-based connection to the Net. That's because, when you want to connect from another location, you need to know the shared Mac's *IP address*—its unique Internet computer number. Unfortunately, Macs that connect to the Internet by dialing with a modem (instead of a permanent high-speed connection) get assigned a different IP address with *each connection*, making it much less convenient for you to connect from afar.

To connect over the Internet, follow the steps on the next page.

---

**POWER USERS' CLINIC**

## The Secret Chooser Advantage

As noted in this chapter, you don't have to use the Network Browser to access other Macs on your network. Old-time Mac fans have grown accustomed to using the Chooser for the same purpose.

In general, the Network Browser makes more sense. It offers better integration with the Keychain, described later in this chapter; has a much more attractive interface; offers "flippy triangles" that help you get a better picture of the overall network; and has pop-up menus that offer quick access to favorite disks and networked disks to which you've recently connected.

The Chooser offers two features that didn't make it into the Network Browser, however. In step 6 of the connection steps described in this section, you're shown a list of shared disks and folders on the Mac you're invading. You can select and open more than one simultaneously—a Chooser exclusive.

Furthermore, each item in the list bears a checkbox; as the dialog box tells you, "Checked items will be opened at system startup time." In other words, you can specify that you want these items brought onto your screen automatically every time you turn on your computer.

If you check one of these boxes, you're offered two additional options. Save My Name Only means that, just after you turn your Mac on, you'll be asked to type your password for the automatically summoned shared items. If you use Save My Name and Password in the Keychain option instead, you won't even have to do that; the Keychain, described at the end of this chapter, will memorize your password. The items you've checked will appear automatically without any more effort on your part.

---

1. **Open the Network Browser. From the Shortcuts menu, choose Connect to Server.**

   Figure 16-9 shows this step.

2. **Type in the IP address of the Mac to which you want to connect, and then click Connect (or press Enter).**

   If you don't know the shared Mac's IP address, pick up the phone and call somebody in the office there. That person can find out the shared Mac's IP address in any of several ways; the most convenient is to choose ▲→File Sharing, where the IP Address is prominently displayed, just beneath the name and password fields.

   If your Mac isn't already online, its modem now dials and, after a while, connects to the shared Mac.

3. **Continue with step 3 of the previous instructions.**

   You may find that this kind of connection is slower than an Ethernet hookup in the same building; but when you're in Hong Kong and need a document from your Mac in Minneapolis, you may not care.

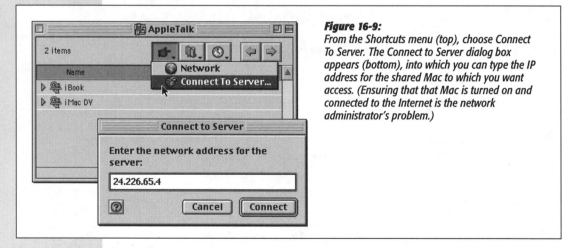

*Figure 16-9:*
*From the Shortcuts menu (top), choose Connect To Server. The Connect to Server dialog box appears (bottom), into which you can type the IP address for the shared Mac to which you want access. (Ensuring that that Mac is turned on and connected to the Internet is the network administrator's problem.)*

## What You Can Do Once You're Connected

After you've brought the icon of the shared folder or disk onto your screen, whether using the simple, password-free scenario or the more complex setup, what you can do next depends on how much access you were given in Phase 2.

Whether or not you can put icons into it, open it, take files out of it, and so on depends on how its owner set it up. Fortunately, special folder icons tell you at a glance how much access you've been given, as shown in Figure 16-10. These special icons correspond to the various options described in Phase 2 of the preceding section. For example, if somebody highlighted a folder, chose File→Get Info→Sharing, and gave you Write Only privileges, the folder now appears on your screen—as viewed over the network—with the drop-box icon shown in Figure 16-10.

Most people use the file-sharing feature to copy files between one Mac and another. You can also *open* a document that's on a shared disk.

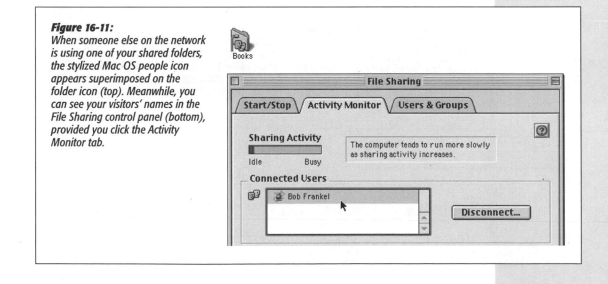

**Figure 16-10:**
*Special folder icons let you know what privileges you've been given (top). For example, you can deposit files into the Drop Box folder, but can't open it. (If you try to open it, you get the message shown at bottom.) You can't open the Salary Assignments folder at all. You can use the contents of the Important Stuff folder normally, but you can't move or rename the folder itself. But you have full control over the Advertising folder, exactly as though it were on your own Mac.*

Administrative Gunk

4 items, 1.13 GB available

Drop Box    Salary Assignments    Important Stuff    Advertising

The folder "Drop Box" could not be opened, because you do not have enough access privileges.

OK

Be careful, however—double-clicking, say, a Microsoft Word document on a shared disk works fine if Microsoft Word is actually on your machine. But if it isn't, your Mac will try to open the copy of Microsoft Word on the shared disk, elsewhere on the network—a painfully slow procedure. You'll become all too familiar with the double-headed arrow at the upper-left corner of your screen that appears when the Mac is frantically trying to copy information across the network wires.

**Figure 16-11:**
*When someone else on the network is using one of your shared folders, the stylized Mac OS people icon appears superimposed on the folder icon (top). Meanwhile, you can see your visitors' names in the File Sharing control panel (bottom), provided you click the Activity Monitor tab.*

Books

File Sharing

Start/Stop \ Activity Monitor \ Users & Groups

Sharing Activity

Idle          Busy

The computer tends to run more slowly as sharing activity increases.

Connected Users

Bob Frankel

Disconnect...

### When you want to disconnect

When you're finished using a shared disk or folder, do your network comrades a favor by getting rid of it. To do so, drag its icon to the Trash, or highlight its icon and then choose File→Put Away; once it's gone, you no longer risk slowing the network down by remaining connected. (You can also disconnect from a shared folder or disk when you shut down your Mac or, if it's a laptop, put it to sleep.)

### When you want to disconnect others

When other people on the network are accessing *your* Mac, several visual clues let you know. For example, the folder being visited displays a special icon, as shown in Figure 16-11. Furthermore, the File Sharing control panel offers several special treats.

Choose  →Control Panels→File Sharing; when the control panel opens, click Activity Monitor. Here you'll see a list of everybody on the network who's currently connected to your Mac. To boot somebody, just click a name in the Connecting Users list, and then click Disconnect. You can also disconnect people by turning off File Sharing or by shutting down your Mac.

---

*Tip:* You can also use the File Sharing/Activity Monitor panel to send little messages to people who are connected to your Mac. Figure 16-12 has the details.

---

Using any of these methods, the Mac asks you how much notice you want to give your co-workers that they're about to be disconnected—10 minutes to finish up what they're doing, for example. (If you're feeling rushed or rude, type a 0—doing so disconnects that person instantly, without warning.) Then click OK. (When you disconnect people by closing your laptop lid, having a system crash, or unplugging the network wires, your co-workers get no notice at all. A message appears on their screens that says, "The server has unexpectedly shut down.")

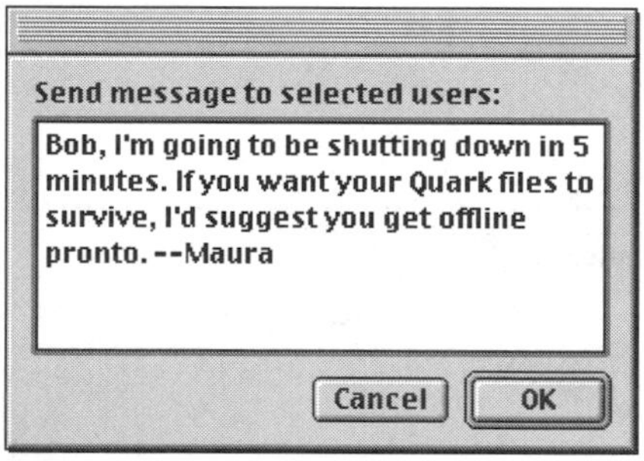

---

**Send message to selected users:**

Bob, I'm going to be shutting down in 5 minutes. If you want your Quark files to survive, I'd suggest you get offline pronto. --Maura

Cancel    OK

*Figure 16-12:*
*To send a message to someone who's connected to your Mac—to warn then that you're about to disconnect, for example, or to request that they get you a beverage—Option-double-click a name in the Connected Users list of the File Sharing control panel. A box appears, in which you can type your message.*

---

# Apple Remote Access (ARA)

As noted in Chapter 13, Mac OS 9 includes several hunks of software that used to be sold separately—for example, the WorldScript language kits. An even more useful example, for many, is Apple Remote Access, a software kit that lets you dial in to your Mac from anywhere in the world.

## When to Use Which Remote-Connection Technology

If you've read this entire book so far, you might reasonably be confused at this point. This is, after all, the *third* Mac OS 9 technology that purports to let you connect to your Mac from a distant location. You might be wondering which of these three technologies to use in which situation. Here's a quick summary:

- **File Sharing over the Internet.** As described in the previous discussions, the folders you share using the file-sharing feature can be made available to anyone on the Internet. You can use all the security features and access-privilege features of standard file sharing. If your co-workers know the IP address of your Mac, they can access its contents from anywhere in the world via the Internet. They must have a Macintosh to do so, however.

  If you travel, this is by far the most economical and convenient method of hooking up remotely. You have to pay only for a local call from your laptop to the nearest Internet access number, whether you're in LA, New York, or Paris, and your home Mac doesn't have to have its own private phone line (unlike ARA, described below). Unfortunately, this method *does* require that your home Mac have a full-time Internet connection.

- **Web Sharing.** As described in Chapter 12, this control panel lets you "publish" a folder on your hard drive that anyone on the Internet—or certain people you specify—can access. (Once again, this feature requires that your Mac have a full-time Internet connection.) Although this feature was designed to let you display Web pages, the optional Personal NetFinder feature (also described in Chapter 12) shows your visitors a tidy list of every file and folder in the shared folder. If, in the Web Sharing control panel, you turn on the button called "Use File Sharing to control user access," you can even control *which* people can access your folder, and how much access, exactly like the file-sharing feature described in this chapter.

  So how is Web Sharing different from standard file sharing over the Internet? There are two key differences. First, you can share only *one folder* using Web Sharing (using File Sharing, you can share up to ten). Second, and more important, people who visit your Web Sharing folder do so using a standard Web browser. As a result, anyone on the Internet, *including Windows users,* can access the material in your Web Sharing folder. (Without buying utility software, Windows users can't otherwise access your Mac at all.)

- **Apple Remote Access (ARA).** This feature, too, relies on the various controls and security features of standard Mac file sharing. Here again, you can specify exactly who has permission to connect to your Mac, and how much control they have over each shared folder.

  The big difference here: the Internet isn't involved. Whereas standard file sharing and Web Sharing require the shared Mac to have a high-speed, permanent Internet connection, ARA is ideal for connecting to Macs equipped only with a modem. When someone dials in, your Mac actually answers the phone, confirms the identity of the Mac calling in, and provides access to the corresponding folders.

ARA, in other words, is perfect for the laptop-carrying Mac fan who occasionally needs to dial home to check the calendar, grab a file, make a backup, and so on—provided the Mac back at home is connected to its own phone line, as described next.

## Setting up Apple Remote Access

To make ARA work, you must provide the home-base Mac—the one you'll be calling—with a phone line of its own. Otherwise, when your laptop calls from the hotel room, some family member or answering machine might pick up the phone, ruining your chances of connecting. (For about $99, you can also buy an electronic switch box that detects which kind of call is coming in—voice or computer—and routes the call accordingly.)

Then prepare the home-base Mac as follows:

1. **Choose &#63743;→Control panels→Remote Access.**

   The Remote Access control panel appears. (See the end of Chapter 14 for details on this program.)

2. **From the Remote Access menu, choose Answering.**

   The dialog box shown in Figure 16-13 appears.

3. **Turn on "Answer calls."**

   As shown in Figure 16-13, you can control the incoming calls in various other ways.

4. **Click OK. Choose &#63743;→Control Panels→File Sharing. Click the Users & Groups tab.**

   The list of people to whom you've given access to your Mac appears. Create accounts for anyone who might be dialing in by clicking New User. (Details on this process are in Phase 1, earlier in this chapter.)

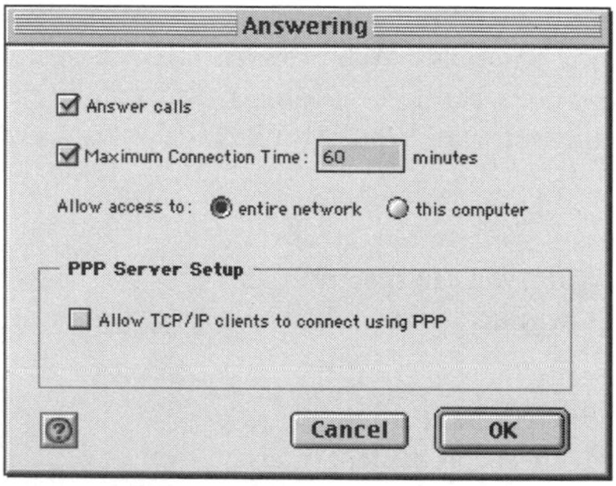

---

**Figure 16-13:**
*To permit people to dial into your computer, turn on "Answer calls." If you're worried about tying up the phone line, you can also limit the incoming calls using the Maximum Connection Time option. If your home-base Mac is part of a network, use the third control to specify whether incoming callers can "see" only your Mac, or the entire network. Finally, using the PPP Server Setup controls, you can permit people to use your own Mac's Internet services when connected to it from the road.*

5. Double-click the name of someone who might be dialing in. From the Show pop-up menu, choose Remote Access. Turn on "Allow user to dial in to this computer."

If you like, you can also turn on "Callback at #" and specify a callback number. This option makes your Mac immediately hang up on anyone who calls in (after identifying the calling Mac), and then dial the number you provide in this box. (The calling Mac must also be set up to answer calls.) You can use this option as a security measure—in other words, if you're being visited by some hacker in Germany who's masquerading as one of your telecommuting co-workers, he'll be deprived of a connection. The Mac will call the telecommuting co-worker at home.

6. Close all the windows.

That's all there is to it; your Mac is ready for invasion by laptops and other Macs outside the office.

## Preparing to Dial

Now suppose that you're the laptop-carrying traveler. Suppose, furthermore, that you want to use the calling-card number your company has provided, and that you're in a hotel room somewhere that requires you to dial 9 for an outside line.

1. Choose  →Control Panels→DialAssist.

The DialAssist control panel opens, as shown in Figure 16-14.

2. Configure DialAssist, as shown in Figure 16-14.

Using this control panel, you can let your Mac handle the dirty work of dialing complicated phone numbers.

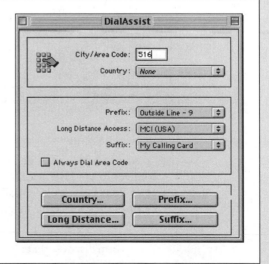

**Figure 16-14:**
In the City/Area Code box, type the area code for your current location. Change the Country if appropriate. If you need to dial 8 or 9 for an outside line, use the Prefix pop-up menu; to dial an 800 number for your calling card, use the second pop-up menu; to specify your actual calling card number, use the Suffix pop-up menu. (You can add more choices to these pop-up menus by clicking the corresponding buttons at the bottom of the window. Click Suffix and then Add, for example, to input your calling card number.)

3. **Close DialAssist. Choose ⬤→Control Panels→Remote Access.**

   The Remote Access control panel appears, as described at the end of Chapter 14.

4. **Choose File→Configurations. Click Duplicate, type a name for this configuration (such as *Dial into office*), and click OK. Click Make Active.**

   You've just saved this soon-to-be complex setup under its own name, so that you can easily reuse it later.

5. **Choose Edit→User Mode. Click Advanced, and then click OK.**

   You just made a checkbox appear called Use DialAssist.

6. **Turn on Use DialAssist. Use the Number, Area Code, and Country fields to specify the phone number for your Mac at home.**

   The Preview shows you exactly what your laptop is about to dial.

7. **Click Options. From the "Use protocol" pop-up menu, choose ARAP. Click OK. Close the window; click Save.**

At last, you're ready to connect.

## Making the Connection

Having suffered through the configuration described in the previous steps, it's time to make the call. The Mac at home is configured, attached to its own phone line, and awaiting your call.

You can place the actual call in one of two ways, as illustrated in Figure 16-15.

**Figure 16-15:**
*To place the call, choose your configuration name from the Remote Access tile of the Control Strip. Alternatively, you can open the Remote Access control panel (or the ⬤→Remote Access Status program) and click Connect. When you're finished with your connection, choose Disconnect from the Control Strip tile, or click Disconnect in the control panel or Remote Access Status window.*

Now your laptop dials and connects; the process feels much like it does when you connect to the Internet. Once you're connected, however, you won't be launching your Web browser or email program—instead, choose ⬤→Network Browser. Double-click the AppleTalk icon, and continue exactly as described in Phase 3 earlier in this chapter.

You'll soon discover that connecting by modem is agonizingly slow; remember that even "56K" modems only *receive* data at 53K (and only rarely). They still *transmit* at 28.8K, which is therefore the maximum speed of your Remote Access connection.

# The Keychain: Forgettable Passwords

The information explosion of the computer age may translate into bargains, power, and efficiency, but it carries with it a colossal annoyance: the proliferation of *passwords* we have to memorize. Web sites, shared folders on the network, files encrypted with Mac OS 9's password-protection feature, FTP sites on which we maintain our Web pages—every single one requires another password to remember. Worse, we're not allowed to use the same password over and over again, because each Web page, file server, FTP site, or protected file requires a different *form* of password—"five to seven digits, which must include both letters and numbers"; "six characters or more, beginning with a letter"; and so on.

In Mac OS 9, Apple has done the world a mighty favor by inventing the *Keychain*. The concept is brilliant: when you sit down to work on your Mac, you type in *one password*—one master code that tells the computer: "It's really me. I'm at my computer now." The Mac responds by *automatically* filling in every password blank you encounter. You can safely forget all of your passwords except the master one.

If you're not concerned about security—that is, if you work at home, and you're the only one who uses your Mac—great. Enter the Keychain master password one time, and then forget the feature entirely—except to marvel now and then that you don't seem to have to enter a lot of passwords anymore.

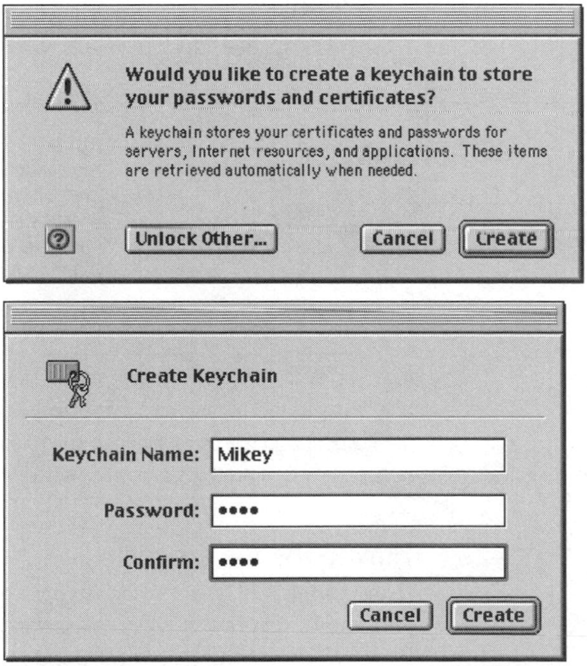

**Figure 16-16:**
*If you click Create when first asked to create a Keychain (top), the Create Keychain box appears (bottom). This is where you name your Keychain and make up the master password–the only one you'll have to remember. If your password is fewer than six characters long–or empty–a warning appears, scolding you for making up a password that some hacker with a lot of time on his hands could figure out. If you work at home by yourself, you work with people you trust, or the stuff you're protecting isn't particularly private, just click Yes and ignore the message.*

If you're concerned about the security of your Mac when you're not at your desk, however, you can "lock the Keychain" when you leave the machine. Now, should the evil hacker stroll by your desk, he'll find that every FTP site, shared network folder, and protected file once again requires its own individual password.

## Creating your Keychain

To create your Keychain, choose  →Control Panels→Keychain Access. The dialog box shown in Figure 16-16 appears. (The same window appears the first time you turn on the Add to Keychain checkbox anywhere it appears—when you encrypt a file, access a shared disk or folder on the network, or type the password for an FTP site, for example.) In any case, click Create (or press Return). As shown in Figure 16-16, you're now asked to name your Keychain and assign its master password.

## Locking and Unlocking the Keychain

When your Keychain is unlocked, you can open your password-protected files, visit your password-protected FTP sites, and connect to password-protected shared disks and folders on the network—without ever having to enter a password. Remember: if you work alone, leave your Keychain permanently unlocked. If you work in an office where someone else might sit down at your Mac while you're getting a candy bar, lock the Keychain when you wander away. (To *unlock* the Keychain when you return, you must enter your master password. Locking it requires no password.)

To unlock or lock your Keychain, you can use the Keychain Access control panel described above. On the other hand, you might find it more convenient to use the Control Strip, as shown in Figure 16-17.

**Figure 16-17:**
*You can lock or unlock your Keychain using its Control Strip icon, which looks like a padlock when locked, a key when open. Or use a shareware program like Keychain Unlocker (available at, for example,* www.missingmanual.com*) to open your Keychain automatically when the Mac starts up.*

*Tip:* By choosing File→New Keychain, you can use the Keychain Access control panel to create more than one Keychain, each with its own master password. On one hand, this might defeat the simplicity goal of the Keychain. On the other hand, it's conceivable that you might want to encrypt all of your business documents with one master password, and all of your personal stuff with another, for example.

## How to Use the Keychain

Unfortunately, when it comes to password proliferation, we're not out of the woods yet. The Keychain can't store passwords in programs that haven't been rewritten to be *Keychain-aware*. Notable among programs that ignore the Keychain are the two popular Web browsers, Netscape Communicator and Internet Explorer (including version 5). In other words, the Keychain can't store passwords for secure Web pages, such as those for your bank and online-brokerage accounts. (On the other hand, Internet Explorer has its own built-in password-memorizing feature. It's not as convenient as the master Keychain password, but it's better than nothing.)

The Keychain *does* store your passwords for password-protected files, file sharing (as described in this chapter), and FTP sites. Here's how you might use the Keychain in each of those situations:

### Protecting a file

You can read about Mac OS 9's password-protection feature in Chapter 2. Just highlight any file icon, and then choose File→Encrypt. A dialog box appears, in which you're supposed to enter the password for this file. As shown in Figure 16-18 (top), the Add to Keychain checkbox means that you can immediately forget whatever password you type here.

**Figure 16-18:**
*When you encrypt a file, turn on the Add to Keychain button before clicking Encrypt (top). The Mac stores the password you assigned to this protected file, so that you can forget it. The Add to Keychain checkbox also appears when you connect to an FTP (file transfer protocol) Internet site using the Network Browser program built into Mac OS 9 – or Anarchie, the popular shareware program.*

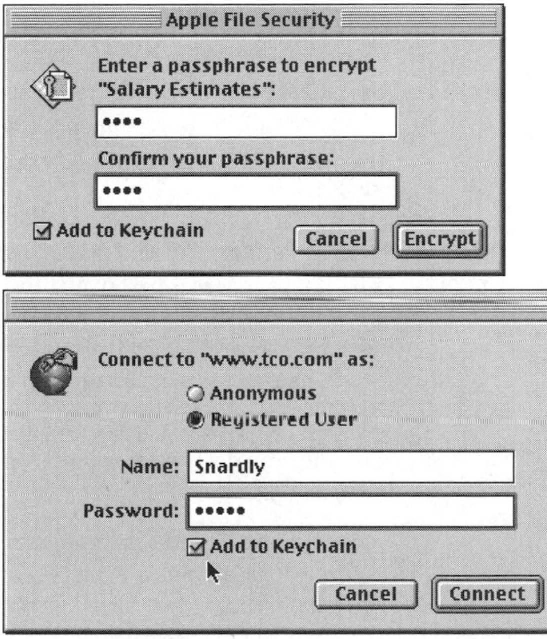

From now on, when you double-click that file, you won't be asked for any password. It will open automatically, with only a slight delay as the Mac consults your Keychain to retrieve the password, which it uses to decrypt the file. (This automatic opening feature assumes, of course, that your Keychain is unlocked. If not, you'll be asked to unlock it—and if you decline, you'll have to remember the password you gave this specific encrypted file.)

### Accessing an FTP site

If you frequently download software from a corporate hard drive somewhere, or if you maintain a Web site, you may already be familiar with an *FTP server*. This is just like a Web site, except that it exists solely for storing files. Many FTP sites, including your Web page's FTP site, require a password.

At this writing, two FTP programs can work with the Keychain. One is the Network Browser, described in Chapter 5. When you choose the Connect to Server command from its Shortcuts pop-up menu/icon (see Figure 16-9), you can type in the address of the FTP site you want to visit. When you click Connect, you're asked for your name and password—here again, the Add to Keychain checkbox appears (see Figure 16-19, bottom). Click it before clicking Connect to avoid having to enter this password the *next* time you connect.

The other FTP program that's Keychain-aware is the popular shareware program Anarchie, which is available from *www.missingmanual.com,* among other places. Here again, the Add to Keychain checkbox appears automatically whenever you try to connect to an FTP site. Click it to avoid having to remember your password for this site in the future.

### Accessing shared files and folders on the network

Finally, if your Mac is part of an office network, of the sort described in the first part of this chapter, the Keychain pays off every time you connect to another disk on the network. It saves you the trouble of typing in your password each time—indeed, you don't even *see* the name-and-password dialog box.

The Keychain's behavior is peculiar in this instance, however. It doesn't really save you time until the *third time* you connect to a particular shared disk or folder. Here's the drill:

- **First connection.** As instructed in "Phase 3," earlier in this chapter, you generally connect to a shared Mac by choosing &#63743;→Network Browser. Double-click AppleTalk, and then the name of the Mac you want. As shown in Figure 16-9, you must now type your password—for the last time. Click Add to Keychain before clicking Connect.

  The list of shared folders and disks appears; double-click the one you want to open. (If you don't yet have a Keychain, you're asked to create one now.)

- **Second connection.** Open the Network Browser. Double-click AppleTalk. Double-click the name of the Mac to which you want to connect.

  Now, however, the Mac displays the message shown in Figure 16-19. The bottom option means: "Don't ask me for a password the next time I connect to this shared item *using the Network Browser*." In other words, the Mac wants you to approve Keychain power over *each method* you might use to open the password-memorized item. This message will appear again when you connect to this shared item using the Chooser, for example; again when you double-click its alias (a shortcut described earlier in this chapter); and so on.

The first checkbox avoids all of that red tape. It means, "Don't ever ask me for the password, no matter how I connect to this shared item."

If you turn on either checkbox, a confirmation box appears; click Yes, and then click Allow.

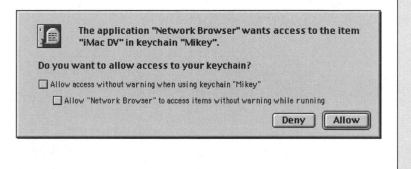

**Figure 16-19:**
*The second time you connect to a Keychain-added network folder, this message appears. It seeks final confirmation that you want to Keychain to automatically fill in your password the next time you connect to the shared item. For the easiest existence, turn on the top checkbox, click Yes, and then click Allow.*

The application "Network Browser" wants access to the item "iMac DV" in keychain "Mikey".

**Do you want to allow access to your keychain?**

☐ Allow access without warning when using keychain "Mikey"

☐ Allow "Network Browser" to access items without warning while running

[ Deny ]  [ Allow ]

• **Subsequent connections.** The next time you connect to that particular shared folder or disk, you connect instantly—without being asked for a password. As long as your Keychain is unlocked, you can bring that other Mac's hard drive onto your screen with very little effort. Provided you've selected the top checkbox in Figure 16-19, you can just double-click the shared item's alias or choose its name from the ☰→Recent Servers command, for example.

## Managing Your Keychain

Keychains are represented by separate files in your System Folder→Preferences→ Keychains folder.

### Deleting a Keychain

You can delete a Keychain if you like, but first make sure that:

• You remember all the individual passwords that this Keychain has memorized. For example, suppose you encrypted a file on your desktop, but didn't pay much attention to the password you gave it, assuming that your Keychain would do the memorizing. If you delete the Keychain file, you can open the encrypted file only by typing the exact password you gave it. If you don't remember, the file remains closed forever.

• You lock the Keychain first. You can't discard an open Keychain.

If you've considered both of these points, then you can safely drag a Keychain file out of your System Folder→Preferences→Keychain folder and into the Trash.

### Renaming a Keychain

To rename a keychain, open the System Folder→Preferences→Keychain folder. There you'll find the icons representing any Keychains you've created; you can rename them just as you'd rename any icon.

### Copying a Keychain

Knowing about this Keychain file is useful for another reason, too—you can copy it into the corresponding location on another computer, such as your laptop. It carries with it all the information concerning your FTP, network, and file passwords.

### Viewing your Keychain setup

At any time, you can see a list of the passwords the Keychain has memorized—and even what those passwords are. To do so, choose &#63743;→Control Panels→Keychain Access. The control panel opens, bearing a list of all the passwords it has memorized, as shown in Figure 16-20.

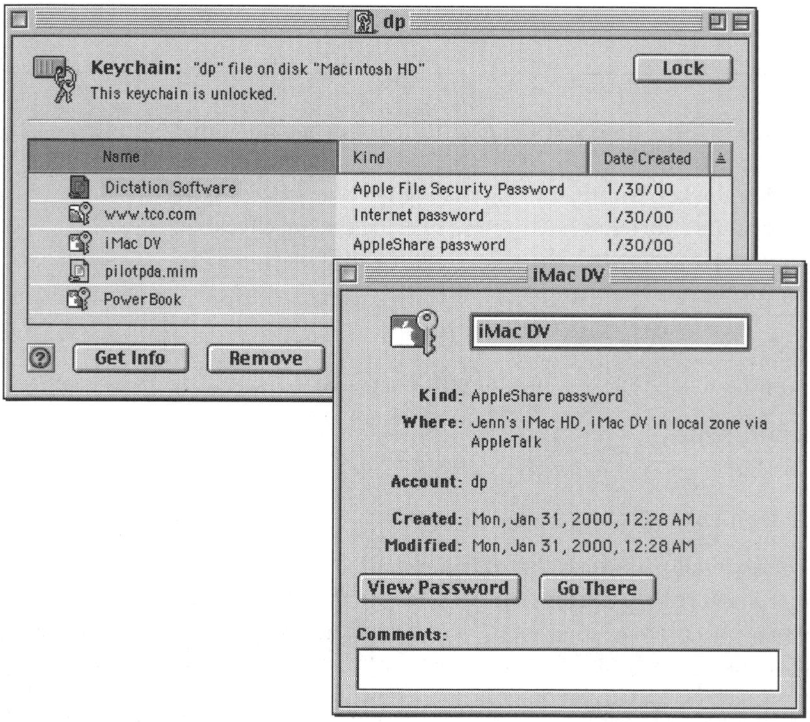

**Figure 16-20:**
*The Keychain Access control panel shows you a list of every password your Keychain has memorized (top). Double-click one to view its Get Info screen (bottom), where (if you prove that you're you by re-entering your master password) you can view the corresponding memorized password.*

# One Mac,
# Many Users

For years, teachers, parents, and computer-lab instructors have struggled to answer a difficult question: How do you rig one Mac so that several different people can use it throughout the day, without interfering with one another's files and settings? And how do you protect a Mac from getting fouled up by mischievous (or bumbling) students and employees?

Some schools, labs, families, and businesses just muddled through as best they could. Others tried installing balky and sometimes destabilizing software like Apple's old At Ease program. It wasn't until the release of Mac OS 9 that a solid, reliable, built-in solution to this traditional problem emerged: the Multiple Users control panel.

## Introducing Multiple Users

This new program lets you create an *account* for each student, family member, or employee. When you turn on the Mac, it doesn't start up as usual; instead, it asks you to *log in,* as shown in Figure 17-1. It may even ask for a password, which you can either type or speak; if your Mac has a microphone, Mac OS 9 can actually recognize your "voice print" for security purposes.

When you identify yourself, you arrive at the Mac desktop in your own customized world: *your* desktop picture fills the screen, the Web browser lists *your* bookmarks, the  menu lists *your* favorite documents, and so on. On the desktop is a folder bearing your name, and all of your files are stored there.

Furthermore, you may find yourself with restricted access to some parts of the Mac—you may not be allowed to print, use certain CD-ROMs, launch certain programs, and so on. In other words, the Multiple Users feature has two components: first, a convenience element that hides everyone else's junk; and second, a security element that protects both the Mac's system software and other people's work.

In designing Multiple Users to be as flexible and secure as possible, Apple created a very complex set of screens and options; that's why this is a long chapter. But as with the networking software described in the previous chapter, setting up a multiple-user Macintosh doesn't require any particular technical skill; it's just time-consuming.

**Figure 17-1:**
*When you enable the Multiple Users feature—the successor to the old At Ease kid-proofing software—you don't turn on the Mac so much as sign in to it. A new command appears in the Special menu called Log Out, too, which also returns you to this sign-in screen. Double-click your own name, and type or speak your password, to get past this box and into your own stuff.*

## Four Degrees of Freedom

The master control center for the Multiple Users feature is the Multiple Users control panel (choose  →Control Panels→Multiple Users). Among other controls, it harbors the master on/off switch, as shown in Figure 17-2.

In the next part of this chapter, you can read about how to use this control panel to create and configure accounts for each of your underlings. For now, however, it's important to understand the four different kinds of accounts the control panel lets you create. Each kind offers a different degree of security—and therefore, a different degree of freedom over the Mac itself. If you can understand this idea, most of the Multiple Users concept should be easy to grasp.

As the administrator of the Mac, you must describe each member of your crew as one of these four kinds of people: Normal, Limited, or Panels. (The fourth account type is Owner, and only one person has it: you.)

**Figure 17-2:**
*The Multiple Users control panel features the master on/off switch for this feature (at the bottom of the window). Turning Multiple Users on means that, whenever you turn on the Mac or use the Special→Log Out command, the sign-in screen shown in Figure 17-1 appears. Turning Multiple Users off means that the Mac behaves as it always has.*

## The Owner

If you've specified your name in the File Sharing control panel, as described in the previous chapter, your account in the Multiple Users control panel already exists. (It also already exists if you tolerated the questions of the Mac OS Setup Assistant on the day you first turned on the computer or installed Mac OS 9.)

If you're the owner, life doesn't change much once you've turned on Multiple Users. Every feature described in this book works exactly as it did before. In other words, Multiple Users doesn't protect the Mac from *you*. In fact, you have several powers that nobody else who uses this Mac can have: only you can install new programs, configure printers, and turn the Multiple Users feature off.

---

*Tip:* Even if you don't share your Mac with anyone and don't create any other accounts, you might still be tempted to use Multiple Users because of its ability to password-protect the entire computer. Open the Multiple Users control panel, click the On button at the bottom of the window, double-click your own name, and type a password. From now on, your Mac is protected against unauthorized visitors fiddling with the computer when you're away from your desk.

---

## "Normal" users

If responsible adults use your Mac—in the office, for example, or some other no-kids environment—you'll probably want to create Normal accounts for them. When someone you've designated as a Normal user signs in to use your Mac, it's *almost* as though there's no Multiple Users feature at all. That person can use all the programs and features of the Mac with just a couple of exceptions:

- Certain important control panels appear, but don't open. If you try to open the AppleTalk, Memory, Modem, Remote Access, TCP/IP, or Multiple Users control panel, for example, you get a message like the one shown in Figure 17-3.

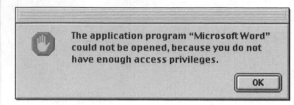

The application program "Microsoft Word" could not be opened, because you do not have enough access privileges.

OK

**Figure 17-3:**
*If you use the Multiple Users feature, those in your office, home, or school will quickly become accustomed to seeing this message. It appears whenever you double-click something that the owner of this Mac has declared off-limits to you, or whenever you try to use a control panel (or some other feature) that's off-limits to Limited account holders.*

- The folders that contain the personal files of other account holders are invisible to you. You see only your own stuff.

## "Limited" users

This kind of account restricts much more of the Mac. When you, the owner, create this kind of account, you get to choose from a list of programs on this Mac, specifying exactly which ones the Limited account holder can use. If you're setting up this Mac for classroom use, for example, you might want to put AppleWorks onto the "approved" list, but declare games and Kid Pix off-limits. If, while you're trying to teach, inattentive students try to distract themselves by launching a game, they'll get another message of the kind shown in Figure 17-3.

Limited account holders can't save documents into any folder except their own, which makes it both easier for them to find their documents again later and more difficult for them to scatter unidentifiable documents across your hard drive.

You can limit this kind of account in other ways, too—for example, a Limited user generally can't open any control panels, Zip disks, or other removable disks. You can prevent printing, using  menu items, or accessing the network. You can even create a list of approved CD-ROMs and DVDs; if the Limited user tries to insert a disk that isn't on the list, the Mac ejects it automatically.

## "Panels" users

This kind of account is designed for young children or others who could do without the complexity of the regular Mac interface. It offers exactly the same kinds of freedoms and restrictions as the Limited type described above, with one giant difference: when a Panels user logs on, he doesn't see the standard Macintosh desktop at all. Instead, he encounters the Panels screen shown in Figure 17-4. No disk or Trash icons appear—in fact, the hard drive icon itself is missing. Only programs that you, the owner, have approved even show up here, providing maximum protection against any accidental messing up of your Mac.

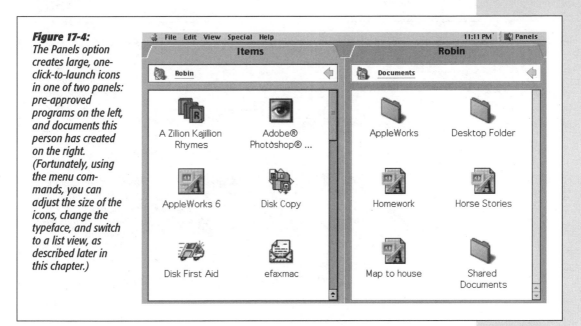

**Figure 17-4:**
The Panels option creates large, one-click-to-launch icons in one of two panels: pre-approved programs on the left, and documents this person has created on the right. (Fortunately, using the menu commands, you can adjust the size of the icons, change the typeface, and switch to a list view, as described later in this chapter.)

## Setting up Accounts

To get going with the Multiple Users feature, start by opening  →Control Panels→File Sharing. Confirm that your own name and (if you like) password appear here—these will be the settings for *your* account, the owner account.

Now choose  →Control Panels→Multiple Users. As shown in Figure 17-2, the Multiple Users window appears. Click On at the bottom of the window, and then click New User to set up the first account (other than your own owner's account). The window shown in Figure 17-5 appears, where you can type a person's name and, if security is an issue, a password. If you're looking into Multiple Users more for convenience than for security, you can leave the password blank.

---

**Tip:** Behind the scenes, creating a new account also creates a Keychain for that person, as described at the end of the previous chapter. Whenever she signs into the Mac, Mac OS 9 opens the corresponding Keychain automatically, so that she won't have to type in passwords for her protected files, network connections, and so on. (If she deliberately changes her Keychain password in the Keychain Access control panel, of course, she loses this convenience—she'll have to type the new password every time she signs on.)

---

At this point, you could close the window. You'd return to the Multiple Users list, having created a new, Normal-level account that now shows up in the list of users. You could then click New User again to set up the next account, and so on, until you had created 40 accounts (the maximum).

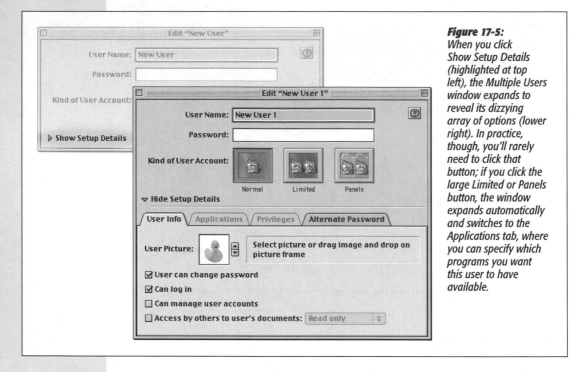

**Figure 17-5:**
*When you click Show Setup Details (highlighted at top left), the Multiple Users window expands to reveal its dizzying array of options (lower right). In practice, though, you'll rarely need to click that button; if you click the large Limited or Panels button, the window expands automatically and switches to the Applications tab, where you can specify which programs you want this user to have available.*

Most of the juicy Multiple Users options, however, appear only if you expand the window (see Figure 17-5). The raft of additional options is split among four separate tabbed windows called User Info, Applications, Privileges, and Alternate Password. Here's what they do:

## The User Info Tab

You can use the options on this pane regardless of the kind of account you're creating (Normal, Limited, or Panels). (The other three tabs apply only to Limited and Panels people—after all, the other restrictions don't apply to Normal people.)

- **User Picture.** As shown in Figure 17-1, each account holder on your Mac is represented, on the sign-in screen, by a small picture. If you click the tiny arrow buttons (next to the duck in Figure 17-5), you can scroll through the 40 charming, if cutesy, images of fruits, baby animals, iMacs, and flowers included by Apple for your selection pleasure.

  It's much more fun, however, to drag a picture of your own, as represented by a graphics file you've created, onto the little User Picture box, where it now appears as one of the selections. (You can also *paste* a graphic onto the User Picture.)

*Tip:* If you drag or paste a very large graphic, Multiple Users may give you an out-of-memory message. If you're handy with Photoshop, AppleWorks, GraphicConverter, or another graphics program, reduce the image to 64 pixels square before pasting or dragging it into the Multiple Users control panel.

- **User can change password.** When this option is turned on, the account holder can change his own password when signing on. (A Change Password button appears there, as shown in Figure 17-1.) This feature makes it convenient for you to set up accounts when your underlings aren't around, assigning each a temporary password. Later, when they arrive at the computer, each person can change the temporary password to a more difficult-to-guess, permanent one.

- **Can log in.** Turning off this checkbox, naturally, means that this account holder can't sign in at all. Her name won't even appear in the list of users.

  You're entitled to wonder: "Why provide this option? If I didn't want this person accessing the Mac, I wouldn't have given her an account." Actually, though, you might indeed enjoy this option for *temporary* suspension of an account. When that Mac user returns from vacation, suspension, or sabbatical, you can turn this checkbox back on again. All of her documents and settings are instantly reinstated—which they might not have been if, for example, you had *deleted* the account.

*Tip:* Many a Mac OS 9 parent has created two accounts for her child in the Multiple Users control panel: one that includes free access to every program, including games, and another that omits games (for use during homework time). Turning off the "Can log in" option for the games account is a means of cyber-grounding the kid, too.

- **Can manage user accounts.** Under most circumstances, nobody except you, the owner, can even open the Multiple Users control panel, let alone create or delete accounts. Thanks to this checkbox, however, you can bless a Normal account holder with the ability to open the Multiple Users control panel. You might use this feature if, for example, you want to give a teaching assistant the flexibility to create a new account when you're not there (such as if another student joins the class). Even then, however, a Normal account holder can't make any changes to the owner account. (This checkbox isn't available if you're creating a Limited or Panels account.)

- **Access by others to user's documents.** This option was designed to answer an intriguing question: If each account holder sees only his own files—and everyone else's files are invisible—how then can people collaborate on a document?

  As noted at the beginning of this chapter, one hallmark of the Multiple Users feature is its creation of a special folder on the desktop named for the account holder. If your account name is Bob, the desktop folder is called Bob, for example; it contains every document you create. (Figure 17-10 illustrates this folder.) Except as noted later in this chapter, this folder is invisible to everyone else who uses the Mac.

If you turn on the "access by others" checkbox, however, other people *can* see Bob's documents folder (by opening a folder called Other Users).

*Tip:* Technically, both the user-named folder on the desktop and the Shared Documents folder are *aliases* (see Chapter 2), not real folders. If you'd like to find the actual corresponding folders—for backup purposes, for example—you'll find them in the Users folder on your hard drive, inside individual folders named for each account.

After turning on this option, use the pop-up menu next to it to choose *Write only* (other users can't open Bob's folder, but can deposit files into it), *Read-only* (others can open the folder and look at the files inside, but can't make changes and can't put in anything new), or *Read & Write* (others can do whatever they want to Bob's folder). You can find the discussions of these options in the preceding chapter—they correspond to the various degrees of folder protection you can use when setting up a network.

## The Applications Tab

When you create a Limited or Panels account, you can specify exactly which programs each person can launch. If you're a parent, for example, you can set up an account that permits your child to launch educational games, but not your copy of Quicken or FileMaker Pro. (Then again, depending on the child, you might want to reverse that logic.)

When you click the Limited or Panels button for the first time, or when you click the Applications tab, the Mac creates a massive list of every program on the hard drive, including duplicates, AppleScripts (see Chapter 2), and strange background programs you've probably never even heard of. By turning on these checkboxes, you can specify exactly which programs this account holder can open. (If you're creating a Normal account, this tab isn't available; a Normal account holder can open *any* program on the hard drive.)

*Tip:* The list of programs includes applications on any Zip disks, SuperDisks, CD-ROMs, and other disks in your Mac at the moment. As a result, the Applications list may show duplicates and programs that aren't usually available. That's why it's a good idea to eject such disks before setting up accounts.

You can manage this enormous Applications list by using some of the buttons and pop-up menus that surround it:

- **Add Other.** Using the Privileges tab, described in the next section, you can choose whether or not each of your underlings can open control panels. But what if you want someone to be able to open one *specific* control panel, or a handful? (Control panels don't generally show up in the scrolling list of applications.) In that case, you can click Add Other. An Open File dialog box appears, which you can use to add control panels, document templates, and other nonstandard program-like files to the Applications list.

- **Select All, Select None.** Suppose the Applications list reveals that you have 384 programs on your hard drive—and there are only *two* that you want off-limits for your kids. Obviously, if you had to turn on 382 checkboxes, you'd be sitting there until next October.

  Fortunately, you can click Select All to turn on *all* the checkboxes—and then manually turn off the few that you *don't* want included. The Select None button works the opposite way—it turns off all checkboxes, so that you can begin turning checkboxes on again from scratch.

- **Show:.** Using this pop-up menu, you can dramatically shorten the list, making the application-selection process much easier. Choose **all but AppleScripts,** for example, to hide all of the AppleScripts that make this list twice as long—now you see only genuine programs. (Choose **all applications** again to make them return to the list.) Finally, to review your approved list in progress, choose **selected items only.** The Mac hides all programs whose checkboxes you *haven't* turned on.

After you've finished creating this person's account, the Mac makes it easy for that person to see her list of approved programs. When the Limited account holder named Sheila signs in, she'll see a folder on the desktop called Sheila's Items, containing aliases for the list of programs you just selected. If she has a Panels account instead, the programs you've selected will show up on her Items panel, as shown in Figure 17-4. (All of this will become clearer in "Signing In," later in this chapter.)

## The Privileges Tab

This panel of restrictions, too, is available when you're setting up a Limited or Panels account. (You can't open this pane when you create a Normal account, because Normal users automatically have all of the options here turned on.)

- **Allow access to: CD/DVD-ROMs.** In some situations—schools, for example—you might not want to permit your charges to use CD-ROMs or DVD-ROMs. If that's the case, turn off the CD/DVD-ROMs checkbox.

  If it's fine with you that your wards can use CDs (including music CDs), turn on this checkbox and then click Any.

  On the other hand, you might want to permit access to *some* CD-ROMs—just not, say, the Sports Illustrated Swimsuit CD. In that case, turn on "List for restricted users." You can now create a master list of approved CD-ROMs for your Limited account holders. (All of this is irrelevant to Panels users, who can't access any discs at all.) Unfortunately, you can't create a separate list for each user—you can create only one master CD-ROM list for everyone who uses this Mac.

  To create the list, finish setting up this account using the options described in the following sections. Then close the window. You return to the Multiple Users window shown in Figure 17-2. Click Options, click CD/DVD-ROM Access, insert the first disc you'd like to approve, wait until its name shows up in the "Inserted" pop-up menu, and then click Add to List (see Figure 17-6). Now its name appears in the "List for restricted users."

When you're finished approving a disc and its contents, switch to the Finder, where the disc's icon appears on the desktop; drag its icon to the Trash. Insert the next disc, and repeat the process. Finally, click Save.

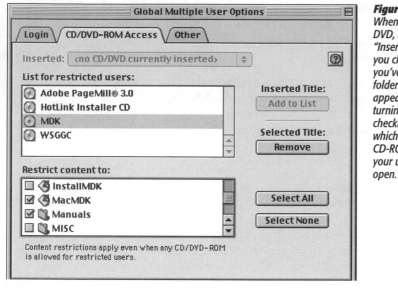

*Figure 17-6:*
*When you insert a CD or DVD, its name appears in the "Inserted" pop-up menu until you click Add to List. Once you've done so, the actual files, folders and programs on the disc appear in the lower list. By turning on and off these checkboxes, you can specify which individual items on each CD-ROM or DVD-ROM you want your underlings to be able to open.*

If a Limited person tries to insert a CD that isn't on the list, the Mac ejects the disc automatically. If he inserts an approved disc, but tries to open an *unapproved* icon on it, he gets the "not enough privileges" message like the one in Figure 17-3.

- **Other removable media.** This item refers to Zip, Super-, floppy, and other cartridge-style disks. When you turn on this checkbox, this account holder can use such disks; if not, the disks automatically pop out when inserted.

- **Shared Folder.** When you turned on the Multiple Users feature of your Mac, you also created a Shared Documents folder. You (the owner) and all Normal account holders can see it and use the files inside.

Limited and Panels people see this folder only if you want them to, however (by turning on this checkbox). If you're creating a Limited account for, say, Harold, and you turn off the Shared Folder option, then when he logs in and opens the Harold folder on the desktop, he won't even see the Shared Documents folder that everybody else sees. (Figure 17-10 should make this clearer.)

- **Chooser and Network Browser.** Turn on this option only if you want to permit access to other disks on the network, as described in the previous chapter. (Access to the Chooser also means that this account holder can switch printers— if you've permitted it, as described on the next page.)

- **Control Panels.** Turn this checkbox on if you'd like the Control Panels command to return to the  menu, where it normally appears. Even then, your dependents can open only certain control panels—the ones that let you change the Mac's look and behavior, not the ones that let you configure your network, for example. (Apple's rationale: Why should *each user* be able to specify different network settings? This Mac's network settings are the same no matter who's using it.)

- **Other Apple Menu Items.** When you turn this checkbox off, the  menu gets a lot shorter. Your underling will find only six of the standard items in the  menu: the Chooser, Favorites, Network Browser, Recent Applications, Recent Documents, and Recent Servers. All of the other goodies are absent, including the Calculator, Scrapbook, and so on.

- **User Can Print.** If you turn this box on, then this account holder can make printouts. If more than one printer is available, you can even use the pop-up menu to specify *which* printer is available. (If you leave the All Printers setting in this pop-up menu, your account holders can switch to a different printer using the Chooser, as described in Chapter 19.)

---

***Complicated note:*** If you specify that this account holder can print only on a particular printer, he can still select a different printer using the →Chooser program, just as described in Chapter 19. But the printing process won't begin until he types in the *owner's* password–yours. In other words, in a classroom situation, the student must to call you over to his desk to approve of the printout on the non-authorized printer.

---

## Speaking Your Password: the Alternate Password Tab

One of Mac OS 9's most heavily hyped offerings is its voice-password feature. If your Mac is equipped with a microphone, then your wards don't have to type their passwords when they sign into the machine—instead, they can speak them. This pane of the Multiple Users control panel is where you set up this feature.

**Figure 17-7:**
*If you can't operate the Voice Verification pop-up menu, that's normal—it's the only choice. (Apple evidently hopes that someday, the Multiple Users feature will offer such more exotic authentication procedures as eyeball scanners and thumbprint analyzers. Only then will this pop-up menu be useful.)*

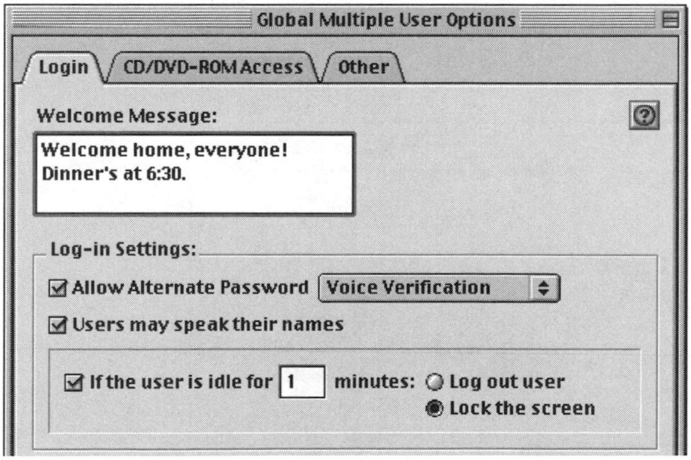

However, the tab that lets you access this pane appears dimmed and unavailable until you throw the master switch for permitting voice passwords. Here's the whole process for turning on that master switch and then recording voice passwords:

1. **Sign in as the owner, if you haven't already. Open the Multiple Users control panel.**

   The window shown in Figure 17-2 appears.

2. **Click Options.**

   Now the Login options screen appears, as shown in Figure 17-7.

3. **Turn on Allow Alternate Password.**

   If you can't turn this checkbox on, it's because your Mac doesn't have a microphone.

4. **Click Save. Double-click the name of the first person you want to be able to sign in by speaking her password.**

   The Edit screen appears, as shown in Figure 17-5. Make sure that you've created an actual typed password (in the Password blank) for this customer; doing so ensures that she'll have a backup means of getting into the Mac if the speech-recognition password doesn't work for some reason—such as when she gets a cold.

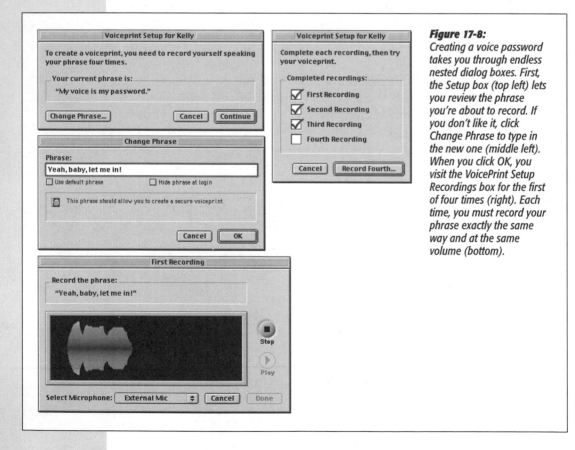

**Figure 17-8:**
*Creating a voice password takes you through endless nested dialog boxes. First, the Setup box (top left) lets you review the phrase you're about to record. If you don't like it, click Change Phrase to type in the new one (middle left). When you click OK, you visit the VoicePrint Setup Recordings box for the first of four times (right). Each time, you must record your phrase exactly the same way and at the same volume (bottom).*

5. **Click the Alternate Password tab. Turn on the "This user will use the alternate password" checkbox.**

   At this point, you must bring the actual human being in question over to the Mac. Recording her actual voice isn't something that you, the owner, can do for her.

6. **Click Create VoicePrint.**

   If your Mac doesn't have a microphone connected, a message will tell you so.

   Now the Voiceprint Setup dialog box appears, as shown in Figure 17-8. This is your opportunity to choose a voice password (if you don't care for Apple's suggestion, that is).

7. **Click Change Phrase.**

   Now the Change Phrase window opens, where your underling can specify what pass phrase she wants to use for voice-print purposes (Figure 17-8, middle left). Obviously, it can't be the same as the normal typed password—every time the account holder signs in, she'll be saying the password out loud, so that everyone else can hear it! Instead, she should select a five-to-seven syllable pass *phrase,* along the lines of Apple's suggestion, "My voice is my password." It can be anything, though—"Open Sesame, little Mac!" or "It's Harriet! Open up!", for example. It doesn't even have to be English. The Mac is just going to learn the spoken sounds.

8. **Type the pass phrase.**

   Actually, what you type here is just a reminder of what the account holder should say when signing in. The Mac isn't actually going to compare what she says with what's typed here.

   If you click "Use default phrase," her selected pass phrase disappears, now replaced with the original suggestion, "My voice is my password." If you click "Hide phrase at login," meanwhile, the Mac won't reveal what the pass phrase is supposed to be at sign-in time, as it ordinarily would.

   In either case, when you type your phrase, the message in the bottom part of the window lets you know whether or not it's the right length for a secure voiceprint.

9. **Click OK. Now click Continue (or press Return).**

   Now the Voiceprint Setup window appears (Figure 17-8, right). Your underling will now have to record the chosen pass phrase four times—exactly the same each time.

10. **Click Record First (or press Return).**

    The First Recording box appears. Use the pop-up menu at the bottom to specify what microphone you'll be using, if your Mac offers a choice.

11. **Click Record. After about one second, speak the pass phrase. Wait one more second, and then click Stop. Finally, click Done.**

    You can see this colorful process in action in Figure 17-8 (bottom). When you click Done, you return to the Voiceprint Setup window, where a check mark now appears in the First Recording box.

12. **Click Record Second (then repeat step 11), Record Third (repeat step 11), and Record Fourth (repeat step 11).**

    You return to the Voiceprint Setup box.

13. **Click Try It (or press Return). Speak your pass phrase one last time to see if it works.**

    If so, you hear a drum roll sound, and a message tells you that the voice password is now ready to use.

This process certainly isn't quite as streamlined as other Mac processes, but maybe that's the price you pay for this high-tech, Star Trek-esque feature. For instructions on actually using the voice-password feature, see "Signing In," later in this chapter.

---

***Caution:*** If you change your name or password as it appears in the File Sharing control panel, you'll confuse the voice-password feature—it will no longer recognize your pass phrase when you try to sign in. (You'll have to type your traditional password to access the Mac.) If all you changed was your password, you can fix the problem just by opening the Multiple Users control panel once. But if you also changed your owner name, you'll have to create a new voiceprint from scratch.

---

# Setting Up the Global Options

For most of the setup options described so far in this chapter, you can create different settings for *each* person who uses this Mac. The Multiple Users control panel offers one final set of options, however, that applies to everyone. To view these choices, sign in as the owner, if you haven't already, and open the Multiple Users control panel (Figure 17-2). Click Options.

Now the dialog box shown in Figure 17-7 appears, once again offering three different tabs filled with options.

## The Login Tab

These settings control what happens when your underlings try to sign in, as described in "Signing In," later in this chapter:

- **Welcome Message.** By changing the text in this box, you control what message appears in the dialog box shown in Figure 17-1.

---

***Tip:*** You can use the welcome message as a sort of low-tech bulletin board—instead of saying, "Welcome, freedom-restricted citizens!," you can use it to say, for example, "School closes at 1 PM today!"

---

- **Allow Alternate Password.** Turn on this checkbox to permit the voice-recognition password system described in the previous section.

- **Users may speak their names.** Generally, when confronted with the list of account holders pictured in Figure 17-1, each account holder will click his own name to select it. On a microphone-equipped Mac, however, each person can *speak* his own name to select it—a savings of two-tenths of a second. (This is not the same thing as the voice *password,* which he'll have to speak next.)

---

***Tip:*** This feature requires that you've installed the PlainTalk speech-recognition software described in Chapter 21.

---

- **If the user is idle for __ minutes:.** As you can read at the end of this chapter, the usual procedure for finishing up a work session is for each person to choose Special→Log Out. The sign-in screen then appears, ready for the next victim.

  But sometimes people forget. These options are provided as a security measure: If you turn on this checkbox and then select "Log out user," then the Mac will display the sign-in screen automatically (Figure 17-1) after the number of unattended minutes you specify. If you choose "Lock the screen," then after the specified number of minutes, the Mac shows a message that says: "This machine has been idle for too long. Kelly, you must verify your identity to continue." If Kelly (or whoever is currently signed in) clicks OK and specifies the correct password, the work session resumes; otherwise, the Mac remains unusable until somebody clicks Logout.

---

***Tip:*** The automatic logout or screen-lock feature doesn't work if you left the Password field empty when setting up the account in question.

---

## The CD/DVD-ROM Access Tab

Use the controls on this pane to specify which CD-ROMs and DVD-ROMs you want your Limited and Panels Users to have, as described in "The Privileges Tab," earlier in this chapter.

## The Other Tab

This final collection of random options offers a few additional security precautions.

- **Allow a Guest User Account.** When you turn on this option, you create a new account holder, called Guest, that doesn't require a password. This account is perfect for assigning to visitors, new students, and so on. You can give this account any level of freedom, exactly as you would with a standard account. Most of the time, however, you'll probably want to give this account fairly limited access to the Mac because of its password-free status. In other words, consider switching it to Limited or Panels mode—not Normal, which is the factory setting.

- **Notify when new applications have been installed.** Limited and Panels people can't install new programs onto this Mac. But you can, and so can Normal Users. The trouble is, you've presumably spent a lot of time specifying which programs your Limited and Panels users are allowed to use. How should the Mac handle newly installed programs? Should it make them available to the limited accounts, or unavailable?

The Mac doesn't make a decision for you. Instead, if you turn on this checkbox, the next time you, the owner, sign out or shut down, you'll get a message warning you that new programs have arrived. You'll then be offered a tidy list of accounts; for each of the newly installed programs, you can then click the checkboxes of the people you want to let have access.

- **When logging in:.** Usually, the Multiple Users feature presents a list of account holders when the Mac is first turned on, as shown in Figure 17-1. That's the "Users choose their names from the list" option in action.

  If you're especially worried about security, however, you might not even want that list to appear. If you turn on "Users type their names," each person who signs in must type *both* his name (into a blank that appears) *and* his password—a very inconvenient, but secure, arrangement.

- **User account will be from:.** You can safely ignore this option unless you are the administrator of a network that runs Mac OS X Server. If you are that person, then you already know about the Macintosh Manager server software that lets you maintain a list of user accounts on one central computer. If you're using such an arrangement, choose the "Macintosh Manager account" option; otherwise, leave "Multiple User accounts" selected.

## Editing, Duplicating, and Deleting Accounts

To edit one of your accounts—to change any of the settings described so far—sign in as the owner, open the Multiple Users control panel, and double-click the name of the account you want to edit. The four tabs, seething with options, are once again at your disposal.

To save time when you have to create many accounts, by the way, don't miss the Duplicate button. It creates a copy of a highlighted account name, with all of its settings intact. You can then edit this copy, if necessary, to introduce whatever minor changes you want.

To delete an account, click it and then click Delete. After you confirm your decision, the Mac offers you the chance to delete the *account,* but leave behind the User *folder* containing all of that person's settings and documents. (If you decide to preserve that folder—which is in the Users folder on your hard drive—then later, you can reinstate that person by creating a new account in the Multiple Users control panel with *exactly* the same name. At that time, you'll be offered the opportunity to have this "new" account inherit all the old settings and documents of the previously deleted one.)

# Signing In

Without a doubt, the Multiple Users feature requires a massive amount of setup. Fortunately, the payoff eventually arrives. Here's what it's like using a Mac with the Multiple Users feature turned on. (For the purposes of this discussion, "you" are no longer the owner—you're one of the students, employees, or family members for whom an account has been set up.)

## Identifying Yourself

When you first turn on the Mac—or when the person who last used this computer chooses Special→Log Out—you get the welcome screen shown in Figure 17-1. At this point, you can proceed in any of several ways:

### Shutdown

Click this button if you're done for the day, or if sudden panic about the complexity of Multiple Users makes you want to run away. The computer turns off.

### Change Password

Click this button to summon the Change Password window, where you can create a new password for yourself (after typing the old one first to prove that you're you). If you also turn on the "Reset alternate password" option, you'll then proceed to *another* dialog box, where you can change and re-record your voice pass phrase.

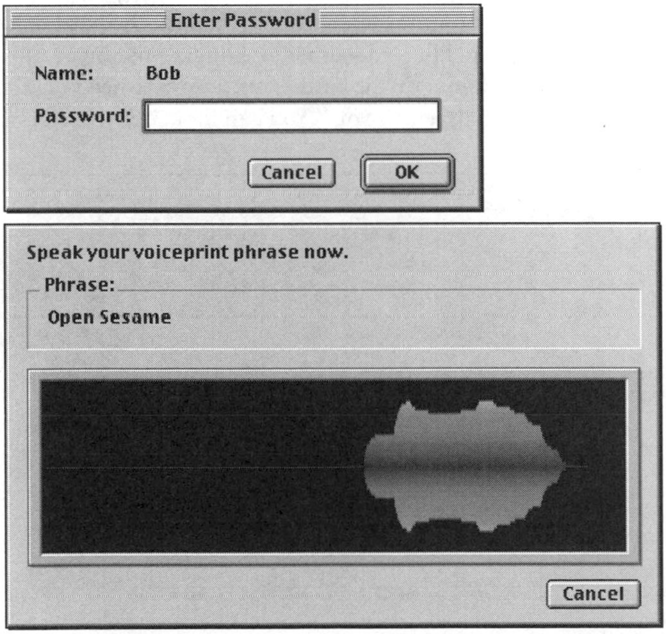

**Figure 17-9:**
*If your account was set up with a password, you now encounter either the Password box (left) or the voiceprint Phrase box. You can try as many times as you want to type the password in; with each incorrect guess, the entire dialog box shudders violently from side to side, as though shaking its head "No." On the other hand, you can try to speak your voice password only one time. If it doesn't work—and it often doesn't, because it's a very sensitive mechanism—then you're shown the typed-password box as plan B.*

If the Change Password button is dimmed, it's because the owner of this Mac decided not to give you password-changing freedom. (The checkbox that governs this feature is on the User Info tab shown in Figure 17-5.)

### Log in

To sign in, double-click your account name in the list. Or, if you prefer using the keyboard, highlight your name by typing the first couple of letters of it, and then press Return or Enter to "click" the Log-in button.

The Password box now appears, where you can either type your password or, if the voice feature has been set up, speak your pass phrase (see Figure 17-9).

## Opening Icons (Normal and Limited Accounts)

Once you're in, what you see depends on what kind of account was set up for you.

If you have the Normal account, of course, the Mac's screen and the desktop look just as they always do. As noted at the beginning of this chapter, only a few control panels, and the Documents folders of your fellow account holders, are off-limits.

If you're a Limited user, the Mac desktop looks as it always does. But if you try to double-click something for which you haven't been given access, you get the "not enough privileges" message shown in Figure 17-3.

If you have a Limited account, you'll also find, just underneath the hard drive icon, two folders bearing your name. The first, called Shawn's Items (for example), contains the aliases of your approved applications. You're not allowed to open any other programs that you may find on the hard drive, even if you try to do so by double-clicking a document belonging to one of those programs. And when you open any folder on the hard drive, a tiny slashed pencil icon appears in the left side of the title bar, telling you: "You can look, but you can't touch."

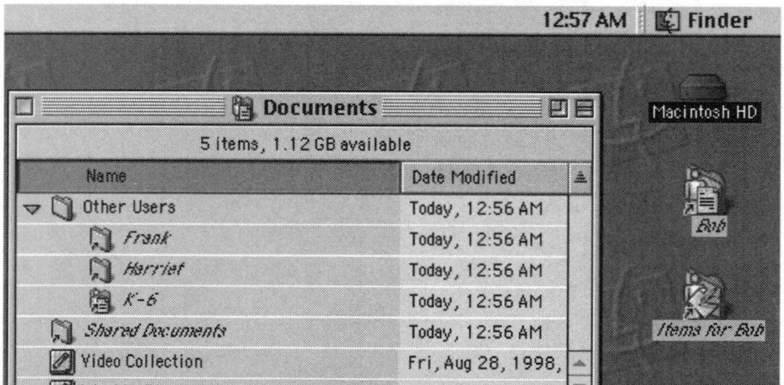

**Figure 17-10:**
*Bob has just signed in. He double-clicks his Bob folder on the desktop. Inside, if the owner of this Mac has so directed, he can see the global Shared Documents folder. The Other Users folder is populated by individual folders for the other account holders, where Bob can take a look at their documents.*

The other folder is named after your account: Shawn, for example. This is the *only* folder into which you're allowed to save new documents. Inside this folder you may find two existing folders (see Figure 17-10):

• **Shared Documents.** Shared Documents are public files for everyone's enjoyment, visible to every account (unless the owner has declared them off-limits for some account holders).

• **Other Users.** This folder contains individual folders for each *other* account holder (called Bob, Frank, Harriet, and so on); if the Mac's owner has so designated, you can open these inner folders to see the documents your fellow Mac-sharers have created. (You may not be able to change or delete these documents, however, depending on how much protection the owner has given them.)

---

*Tip:* If you are the owner or a Normal account holder, you can rebuild the desktop file (a troubleshooting technique described in Appendix C) without even having to restart the computer. Instead, just press the ⌘ and Option keys just after entering your password. The "Rebuild the desktop?" message will appear shortly.

---

## Opening Icons (Panels Accounts)

If the owner of this Mac thinks that either you or the computer need some extra help, you may find yourself signing in and finding, in place of the standard Mac desktop, the strange world shown in Figure 17-11. (Educators and parents who once used Apple's discontinued At Ease software will feel a distinct sense of déja vu.)

On the left: the Items window that shows the list of programs you've been authorized to use. On the right: the contents of your Documents folder, where every new file you create appears.

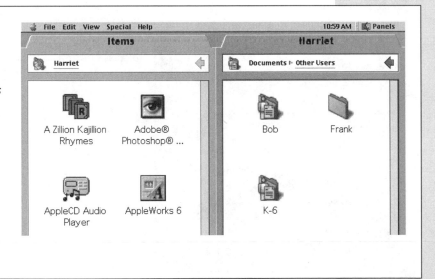

**Figure 17-11:**
*Every now and then, when you click a folder icon in the Panels world, it doesn't open into a new panel. Instead, it fills the existing panel. The left-arrow (Back) button darkens, and the name of the window changes (such as this one, where it says Documents→ Other Users) to suggest that you're now looking at a window within a folder—not that you would understand this notation if you're five years old.*

### Idiosyncrasies of Panels

For a system that's supposed to be idiot-proof, the Panels world is fairly confusing. It works like this:

- Click an icon *once* to open it. When you open an application, both of the Panels panels collapse to the bottom edge of your screen, so that you can call them back again when you need them. (If they get covered up, you can also bring them back by choosing Panels from the Application menu.)

- If you click a folder icon, you sometimes get a *third* vertical panel that shows its contents. To make this additional panel go away, click its tab.

- However, you can't ever make the two original panels go away—if you click their tabs, they just collapse to the bottom of the screen, much like the pop-up windows described in Chapter 1. If you click only one of these tabs, the remaining panel expands to fill the entire screen.

- When you click some folders, such as Other Users, you don't get a third panel—instead, your Documents window disappears, now replaced by the contents of the Other Users folder. For more on this peculiar situation, see Figure 17-11.

- The File menu offers Get Info, Rename, Find, Delete, and Copy commands. Trouble is, how are you supposed to select an icon before performing one of these functions—when a single click *opens* each icon?

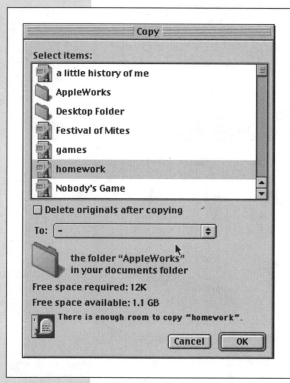

**Figure 17-12:**
*Using the Copy command from within the Panels interface is awkward—you must specify where you want the copy to appear first, by choosing Other from the pop-up menu beneath the list. (When you do so, yet another dialog box appears, in which you're supposed to choose the destination folder for the copying. You must choose a folder that's* within your own named *folder.) Finally, you return to this dialog box, where you click Copy to perform the copying operation.*

As it turns out, each of those commands summons a special dialog box like the one shown in Figure 17-12—containing a list of every folder and document in your Documents folder. You're supposed to indicate, by clicking an item in this list, which one you want to manipulate.

### Customizing your Panels

When you choose Edit→Preferences, you're offered the dialog box shown in Figure 17-13. These options work like this:

- **Turn Sound On.** This checkbox makes the Mac play a crisp clicking sound when you click an icon.

- **Apply Label colors to icons.** Ordinarily, the jumbo icons of the Panels interface don't reflect the label colors that the Mac's owner may have applied to them. (You, the Panels person, can't apply labels.) All icons appear exactly as though they did the day they were born—with no label shading. Turn on this option if you'd like the icons to reflect the label colors the owner, or any Normal users, have applied. (See page 40 for more on labels.)

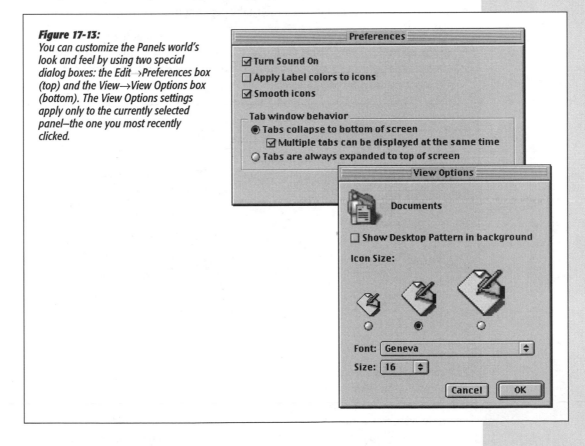

**Figure 17-13:**
*You can customize the Panels world's look and feel by using two special dialog boxes: the Edit→Preferences box (top) and the View→View Options box (bottom). The View Options settings apply only to the currently selected panel—the one you most recently clicked.*

- **Smooth Icons.** In the process of enlarging the icons on the Panels, the Mac simply magnifies each dot that composes one of these icons. The result: jagged edges. This option smoothes the jagged edges on the large-size icons.

- **Tabs collapse to bottom of screen.** When you click the tabs at the top of one of your panels, the panel collapses, becoming a tab hugging the bottom of the screen. This option is responsible for that behavior.

If you also turn on the "Multiple tabs can be displayed at the same time" option, sure enough, multiple tabs can be displayed at the same time (as you open more than one folder, for example; Figure 17-14 shows this arrangement). The alternative—turning off the "multiple tabs" box—means that only one panel at the time fills the entire screen. All other panels become tabs at the bottom edge of the monitor, exactly like the pop-up windows described in Chapter 1.

- **Tabs are always expanded to top of screen.** If you find the collapsing-to-the-bottom-of-the-screen business disconcerting, use this option instead. It creates a series of overlapping, full-screen panels, each with its own tab always visible at the top of the screen, ready for clicking (see Figure 17-14). The effect is that of a stack of file folders in a drawer, their tabs peeking up.

The only downside of this arrangement is that when you actually launch a program, all trace of the Panels disappears. You don't see the tabs hugging the bottom of the screen, as you usually do. To return to the Panels, you must either quit the program or choose Panels from the Application menu.

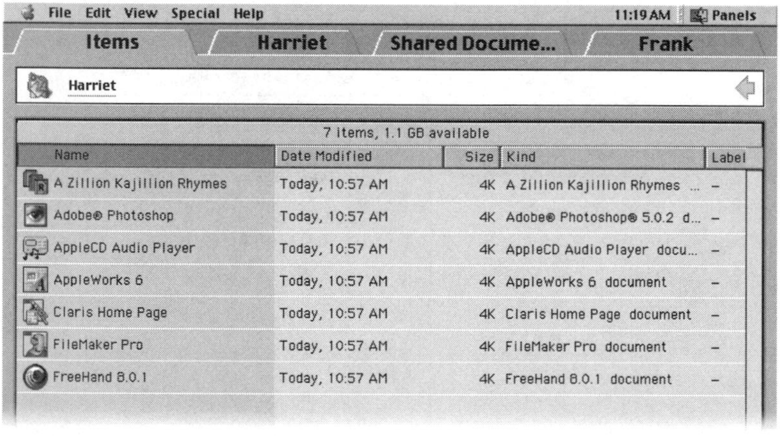

**Figure 17-14:**
*With enough fiddling, you can make Panels look a lot more sophisticated. Here's what a list view looks like when the "Tabs are always expanded" option is turned on. You can't close a panel just by clicking its tab when you're using this setup—you must click the tab and then choose File→Close.*

### List views and icon sizes

Fortunately, you're not condemned to looking at these gigantic icons with their gigantic names. You can use the View menu to control how your panels look. For example, you can choose View→as List (for one particular panel) to create a list view, as shown in Figure 17-14. You can sort one of your panels, either by icon or by list, using the View→Sort command.

*Tip:* As in the actual Finder, you can click the column headings in a list view to sort the list by that criterion: Date Modified, Size, and so on.

Finally, you can choose View Options to choose a different size for your icons and a different typeface for their names. As in the real Finder, in fact, the options that appear in the View Options dialog box depend on whether a panel is in icon view or list view. As shown in Figure 17-13, the icon view offers the "Show Desktop Pattern in background" option, which makes your icons float on the background of whatever pattern or photo this Mac's owner has established using the Appearance control panel. The list view offers the "Use relative date" and "Calculate folder sizes" options described on page 24.

## Setting Preferences

Regardless of which kind of account you have, the genius of the Multiple Users feature is that it lets you customize your own world. Changes you make to the look and feel of your Mac using the control panels (if, in fact, you can open the control panels) affect only your environment. You can change the mouse speed, desktop picture, bookmarks list in your Web browser, favorite font in AppleWorks, and so on; the Mac remembers who you are and how you like things.

## Logging Out

When you're finished using the Mac, regardless of your account level, choose Special→Logout (or press the ⌘-Q key combination—a Mac OS 9 Finder debut). A confirmation message appears; if you click No, you return to whatever you were doing. If you click Yes, or press Return, you return to the screen shown in Figure 17-1, and the entire Multiple Users sign-in cycle begins again.

# Technical Underpinnings

Behind the scenes, the Multiple Users feature works very cleverly. If you, the owner, learn to master its folder system, then you can perform various kinds of administration without even having to open the Multiple Users control panel.

Every scrap of information that creates the Multiple Users configuration on your Mac resides in two folders: the Users folder on your hard drive, and the System Folder→Preferences→Multi-Users folder.

## The Users Folder

After you've turned on Multiple Users, you'll discover a new Users folder sitting on your hard drive. Inside is a folder for each account you've created. And inside that is a microcosm of your own System Folder, as described in Chapter 11. Here, in other words, are duplicates of your Apple Menu Items, Favorites, Internet Search Sites, Launcher Items, Preferences, and Startup Items folders, for example. And yet the contents of each affect only its particular account.

**Note:** The Multiple Users feature, in effect, duplicates much of the System Folder for each account holder; but remember that the System Folder is one of the largest on your hard drive. Creating many accounts—especially Normal accounts—can therefore occupy quite a bit of disk space.

Once you understand this relationship between these System Folder-clone folders and the accounts you create, it becomes very easy to customize many different accounts simultaneously, without even opening the Multiple Users control panel. Figure 17-15 offers an example.

**Tip:** The Desktop folder (inside each account holder's folder) contains the icons that appear on each person's desktop when he signs in. If you want to place a Read Me First file on each student's screen where he can't miss it, for example, drop it into this folder.

In fact, the *positions* of the icons in the Desktop folder window correspond to the icon positions on the account holder's desktop. If you make the Desktop-folder window as large as possible, choose View→as Icons, and drag icons around inside this window, you can determine exactly where they'll show up when the account holder signs in.

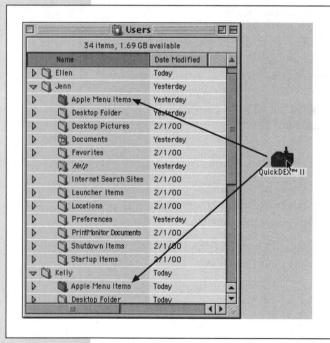

**Figure 17-15:**
*Here's how you might go about adding a particular  menu item to two of your account holders at once. After opening the Users folder on your hard drive, open each user's folder, and then ⌘-Option-drag the  desired icon into each Apple Menu Items folders. (⌘-Option-dragging makes an alias.) Using the same trick, you could customize the Startup Items, Shutdown Items, or Favorites of several account holders simultaneously.*

The Documents folder inside each of these user-named folders, moreover, contains the actual files each person has created. Now that you know where they are, making backups is easy. In fact, you might find it more efficient to back up this entire Users folder; that way, you'll sleep easy, knowing that you've backed up not only the documents but also the account configurations it took you so long to create.

## The Multi-Users Folder

The other folder you, the owner, might find interesting is deep inside the System Folder. It's the System Folder→Preferences→Multi-User Items folder.

Here's where you'll find additional configuration data for each of your account holders. The Groups folder is especially important: inside, within folders named for your accounts, are aliases for the applications you've approved for each person. If you discover that four of your students have been playing Tomb Raider during history class, you can rapidly deprive them of this privilege in the future—open each of these account-named folders, and discard the Tomb Raider alias inside.

If you spend some time exploring this folder, you'll find several other items worth backing up or tracking. For example, the Pictures folder contains the custom graphics you've used as icons for each account holder on the sign-in screen; the CD-ROM Prefs icon stores the names of CD-ROMs and DVD-ROMs for which you've given approval; and so on.

## Breaking Through Security

Unlike some other Mac security products, casual hackers can't easily bypass the Multiple Users feature. If they press the Shift key during startup, which turns off all of your extensions (see Appendix C), they'll still be asked for the owner's password when the Mac starts up. Even if someone tries to start the Mac up with a Mac OS 9 CD-ROM, virtue will still triumph: a "Please enter owner's password" message will appear.

Young evildoers may even try to press the Space bar while the Mac is starting up, in hopes of opening Extensions Manager (see page 195), with the intention of turning *off* the Multiple Users control panel. No such luck—you *can't* turn off the Multiple Users control panel using Extensions Manager. (If even the attempt is bothering you, the owner, take the EM Extension file out of your System Folder→Extensions folder. Now pressing the Space bar during startup does nothing.)

---

*Caution:* There is one way to get past Multiple Users security: Insert a system-software CD-ROM that can start up your Mac. By pressing the C key during startup, someone could start up the Mac from this CD, open the System Folder→Preferences folder, and throw away the Multiple Users preferences file. The trespasser would then have full access to the Mac. (Remember this when you forget your password, too.)

---

## When Things Go Wrong

Most programs work gracefully with the Multiple Users feature. That is, most programs that store their preference settings in the System Folder→Preferences folder work gracefully. A few programs, however, use oddball schemes for storing their settings. Here are a few examples of trouble that Limited and Panels account holders may encounter:

- **America Online.** When you try to launch AOL 3, it quits abruptly; when you launch AOL 4, you get an error message that says the "Main Database couldn't be opened." The fix: while signed in as the owner of the Mac, drag the entire America Online application folder into the System Folder→Application Support folder.

---

- **Microsoft programs.** The first time you open a freshly installed copy of Word 98, Internet Explorer, or another Microsoft program, it launches a program called Microsoft First Run. This little program's job is to copy all of the necessary Microsoft support files into your System Folder.

  But Limited and Panels people aren't allowed to change the System Folder, so an error message results. You can solve this and many related problems by running such programs once, yourself (as the owner), before turning on the Multiple Users feature.

- **Genuinely incompatible programs.** There are, unfortunately, a very few programs that don't run at all in Limited or Panels accounts; until the software companies fix their software, you have no choice but to give your account holders Normal access in such cases.

  But those aren't the only glitches you may encounter using Multiple Users. You should also be aware of these troubleshooting spots:

- **Programs that call other programs.** Every now and then, one of your Limited or Panels customers may receive an error message when double-clicking some application—because it requires *another* application. The classic example is the Mac Help program (in the Finder, choose Help→Mac Help): many of the help topics feature buttons that say, for example, "Click here to change your desktop appearance." But if you haven't added Appearance to the list of approved programs, clicking that Help link will produce nothing but an error message. Similarly, clicking an email or Web link in, say, a Net-savvy word processor (like word or AppleWorks) will produce an error message if you haven't given the account holder access to a Web browser or email program.

  Another example: If you try to use the Location Manager (described in Chapter 12) to change your network settings, another error message may appear—because Limited and Panels account holders are never allowed to change network settings.

- **Startup Items problems.** Limited and Panels account holders aren't allowed to change what's in their Startup Items folders (see page 183). Error messages result, therefore, when they use programs that offer to install aliases of themselves in the Startup Items folder. These include the General Controls control panel (when you turn on the "Show Launcher at system startup" checkbox) and the Stickies program (when it offers to start up automatically whenever you turn on the computer). If this bug is biting you, get the owner to install the necessary Startup Items aliases manually, as described earlier in "The Users Folder."

- **The Case of the Missing Sherlock Channels.** When you first run Sherlock after turning on Multiple Users (see Chapter 15), you don't see the usual assortment of "channel" icons at the top of the window. In fact, you see only three of them. To solve the problem, click the My Channel (hat) icon, click OK to dismiss the error message, and wait while Sherlock connects to the Internet and reinstalls the missing channels. (Even Apple's *bugs* are creative.)

- **Epson printers.** To make Epson printers work when using Multiple Users, you, the owner, must take two precautions. First, allow access to All Printers when you're configuring a Limited or Panels account, as described earlier in this chapter.

  Second, help your underling redirect the Epson *spool folders* to a location where he's allowed to save new files—that is, in his own folder on the desktop. To do that, launch a program that can print. Choose File→Print; in the Print dialog box, click the Tools button, then Configuration. Store the Temporary Spool and Temporary High Speed Copies folders in the desktop folder that bears the account holder's name.

- **The endless-loop log out.** If you choose Special→Log Out while unsaved documents are still open, the Mac offers you its usual "Save changes?" dialog box. If you click the Cancel button, Multiple Users instantly tries again to shut down your account, and displays the same dialog box again. This cycle will repeat endlessly—or until you click Save or Don't Save instead.

---

**UP TO SPEED**

## Simple Finder

Before there was Multiple Users, there was Simple Finder. It's a special mode designed to streamline the Finder's menus and remove commands that could get novices and kids into trouble, and it's still available in Mac OS 9.

If you choose Edit→Preferences, you'll see an option called Simple Finder. When you turn it on and close the dialog box, you'll find yourself in a stripped-down Finder world. Look at your menus—they're practically empty. The File menu, which usually offers 17 commands, now offers only 6; such commands as Get Info, Label, Make Alias, Add to Favorites, and Encrypt are absent. All keyboard shortcuts (except ⌘-? for Help) are disabled, too; forget about summoning Sherlock by pressing ⌘-F. You can't create pop-up windows, change view options, or clean up the icons in a window. You can't erase a disk or even restart the Mac—you can only shut it down.

The most important thing to know about Simple Finder, however, is how to *turn it off.* Mac gurus get emailed questions like this about once a week: "How come I can't find the Get Info command?" (Answer: Choose Edit→Preferences once again and turn off the Simple Finder checkbox.)

In other words, Simple Finder may be well intentioned. But in the world of Mac OS 9's Multiple Users, Simple Finder has lost much of its purpose in life. Today, its most common effect on Mac users is to confuse them.

# Disks, Cables, and Other Insertions

Technically speaking, the way the Mac interacts with disks and cables isn't a Mac OS 9 topic. After all, whether you have Mac OS 8 or Mac OS 9, you insert a CD or USB cable the same way.

Still, behind the scenes, your attachments and disks do interact with the system software. These methods of bringing outside-world information into your Mac are an important aspect of using *any* Mac—and are therefore worth exploring in this chapter.

## How the Mac Does Disks

Apple shocked the world when, in 1998, it introduced the iMac without a floppy-disk drive—and proceeded to eliminate the floppy drive from all subsequent Mac models in the following years. Apple argues that the floppy disk is dead—it's too small to serve as a backup disk, and, in this day of the Internet, it's a redundant method of exchanging files with other computers.

### Disks Today

But the floppy disk didn't disappear entirely. Millions of older Macs still have floppy drives, and many modern-Mac owners buy add-on floppy drives. In fact, you can insert all kinds of disks into a Mac these days. Here are the most popular examples:

### *Zip disks*

When you buy a new Power Mac from the Apple Web site, you can specify that you'd like a Zip drive built into the front panel for another $100. If, instead, you're willing to plug an external box into your Mac, you can get an external Zip drive for any Mac model. Either way, you wind up with an inexpensive system for backing up and transferring files: each $10 or $20 Zip disk holds 100 or 250 megabytes (depending on the model you buy)—that's 70 to 178 times as much as a floppy.

Modern Macs require a *USB* Zip drive; it plugs into one of the USB jacks on your Mac. On older Macs, you plug the Zip drive into your SCSI jack. (More on USB, SCSI, and other such terms later in this chapter.)

---

*Tip:* You move files on and off Zip disks just as you would any Mac disk. You also rename, copy, and share Zip disks like any other Mac disks.

To erase or lock a Zip disk, however, you must use the Iomega Tools program. A version of this software comes in your Apple Extras→Iomega folder, but the Iomega Web site (*www.iomega.com*) already offers a free, even newer version.

---

### SuperDisks

A SuperDisk drive—another gadget you can plug into your Mac's USB connector—poses a fascinating alternative to the Zip drive. Its disks look exactly like floppies, but hold 20 times more. The real advantage of a SuperDisk drive, though, is that it *also* accepts standard floppy disks. The only downsides: (1) SuperDisk drives are slow, and (2) it's up to you to figure out how to tell a SuperDisk disk apart from a floppy disk.

### Floppy drives

Despite Apple's conviction that the era of floppy disks is over, millions of floppies continue to populate the earth. In Chapter 16, you can find out how to connect Macs by network wires; Chapter 14 covers the world's best file-transfer system: the Internet. But if, despite those file-transfer systems, you still crave the hands-on, in-your-pocket solidity of the good old floppy disk, about $80 buys an external floppy-disk drive for your floppy-less Mac. (This device, too, connects to your USB jack.)

### CD-ROMs

You wouldn't get far in today's computer world without a CD-ROM drive. All commercial software comes on CD—not to mention the music CDs that the Mac can play so expertly (see page 226). You may also encounter DVD-ROMs (which look like normal CDs but hold several times more data).

### Recordable CDs

CD-ROM stands for "compact disc, *read-only* memory"—in other words, you can't put your own files on them. Read-only means you can't write (save files) onto them.

Yet some of the most popular Mac drives these days are various kinds of *CD burners*—drives that can record onto specially designed CDs; in fact, CD burners are standard or optional equipment in all current Mac models. All of these discs look like normal CDs, but they (and the drives that accommodate them) may fall into any of these categories:

- **CD-R.** You can fill such a disc with your own files—once. The disk can't be changed thereafter.

- **CD-RW.** The initials stand for *rewritable;* you can record such discs over and over again. Of course, both the recorders that do this and the blank discs are more expensive than the one-shot kind.

- **DVD-RAM** is just like a CD-rewritable, but holds five times more, thanks to the DVD format. Apple offers a built-in DVD-RAM drive in the Power Macs it sells on the Apple Web site.

## How All Disks Are Alike

Yes, you can insert all kinds of different disks into a Mac. But as far as the Mac is concerned, they're all just disks. (Actually, the Mac thinks of them as *volumes*—that's how your Apple System Profiler describes them, for example.) They all have the following aspects in common:

### They need driver software

A Mac can't communicate with *any* add-on gadget—printer, CD-ROM, mouse, keyboard, whatever—without special software that tells the computer how to communicate with that add-on. Inside your System Folder→Extensions folder, you'll find dozens of specialized icons, each designed to *drive* one kind of appliance or another. The floppy-drive software is invisible, because it's built into the System file. But it's easy to spot the CD-ROM driver (called *Apple CD/DVD Driver),* the Zip-disk driver (called *Iomega Driver),* and so on.

CD-ROM and Zip drives are very common, so Apple does you the favor of including the necessary driver software in the standard Mac OS 9 System Folder. But if you add a SuperDisk drive, external floppy drive, or any form of rewritable CD drive, you must install the included driver software yourself.

### They appear as icons on the desktop

Another standard element of Mac disk behavior: When you insert a disk, its icon shows up at the right side of the screen. (It shows up, that is, *if* the proper driver software is in the System Folder.) If you've used only Windows computers, this behavior may throw you at first; you don't have to go hunting for the inserted disk's icon in some My Computer icon, as you do on a PC. To see what's on a disk you've inserted, double-click its icon.

To get a disk out of your Mac, use one of these two methods:

- **Drag its icon onto the Trash can.** For years, this technique has confused and frightened first-time computer users; doesn't the *Trash* mean *delete?* Well, yes, but only when you drag document or folder icons there—not disk icons. Dragging disk icons onto the Trash makes the Mac spit them out.

- **Highlight the disk icon, and then choose Special→Eject Disk (⌘-E) or File→Put Away (⌘-Y).** Either way, the disk now pops out. (Alternatively, you can Control-click the disk's icon and then choose, from the pop-up menu, Eject Disk.)

### They sometimes need repair

Any disk that you can erase, including hard drives, can go bad. When this happens, you may get an error message that reports the disk as being "damaged" or "unusable." (If you get the –39 error message, then a particular *file* on the disk has gone bad, and must be replaced.)

## The Eject Button That Doesn't

*When I push the button on my CD-ROM drawer, how come it doesn't open?*

Once you've inserted a CD (or Zip disk), the Mac won't let go unless you eject it the official way–by dragging its icon to the trash, using the Special→Eject Disk command, or pressing the Eject key on the new Apple keyboard. Pushing the button on the CD-ROM door (on Mac models that *have* a door) opens the drawer–when it's empty. But if it's got a

disk in it, you can push that button 'till doomsday; the Mac will simply ignore you.

That behavior especially confuses people who are used to using Windows; on a Windows PC, pushing the CD button does indeed eject the disc. But on the Mac, pushing the CD or Zip-drive Eject button ejects an inserted disk only in one circumstance: when the disk drive's driver software isn't installed, and the disk's icon never did show up on the screen.

The most common causes of disk corruption are freezes, crashes, and other instances of shutting off the Mac improperly (that is, in any way other than using the Shut Down command or Shut Down button). Fortunately, you can often correct the problem using the Disk First Aid program described on page 233.

*Tip:* If at first you don't succeed, run Disk First Aid again. Sometimes running the program's Repair function several times in a row can correct a hard-drive problem that's too stubborn for a single pass.

And, if after several times you don't succeed, try running Norton Utilities or TechTool Pro (which are commercial, more powerful versions of Disk First Aid).

## Startup Disks

When you turn the Mac on, it frantically hunts for a *startup disk*—that is, a disk containing a System Folder. If you've ever seen the dispiriting blinking-question-mark icon on a Mac's screen, you know what happens when the Mac *can't* find a startup disk. It blinks like that forever, or until you find and insert a startup disk.

### Creating a startup disk

By installing the Mac OS onto a disk—be it a Zip disk, hard drive, or rewritable CD-ROM—you can create a startup disk. Not all disks are capable of starting up the Mac, however; a few that can't include RAM disks (except on some discontinued Mac models), some external FireWire disks, and DVD-RAM discs formatted with a program *other* than Apple's own Drive Setup program. Even with a System Folder installed, these kinds of disks can't start up the Mac.

### Selecting a startup disk

It's perfectly possible to have more than one startup disk attached to your Mac simultaneously. That's the setup, for example, whenever you've inserted the Mac OS 9 CD into your Mac—now you've got both it and your hard drive. Each contains a System Folder, and each is a startup disk. Some veteran Mac fans deliberately create other startup disks—on Zip disks, on other hard drives, or on burnable CDs, for example—so that they'll easily be able to start the Mac up from a backup startup disk, or a pure and virginal System Folder, or a different version of the OS.

So how does the Mac know *which* disk to use as its startup disk? After all, only one System Folder can be operational at a time. The Mac has a control panel dedicated to answering just this question: the Startup Disk control panel (see Figure 18-1, and also page 214). Use it to specify which disk you want the Mac to start up from the next time it starts up.

---

***Tip:*** If you're in a hurry to start the machine up from a different disk, just click the disk icon you want and then restart the Mac. You don't have to close the control panel window first.

---

**Figure 18-1:**
*In the Startup Disk control panel, the currently selected disk—the one that will be "in force" the next time the machine starts up—is always highlighted. If you click in the white area, so that no disk is selected, be prepared for a very long startup cycle, as the Mac searches its various network, SCSI, and other connections for a working startup disk.*

*In Mac OS 9.1 and later, the control panel looks slightly different. It offers "flippy triangles" that offer a selection of System Folders on each of your drives—a nod toward making it easier for people who like to switch back and forth between Mac OS 9 and Mac OS X.*

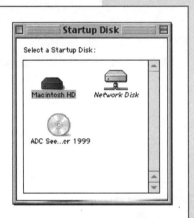

## Erasing, Formatting, and Initializing

To erase a disk, just highlight its icon on the desktop and then choose Special→Erase Disk. You won't be able to do so, though, if:

- The disk is a CD-ROM or DVD, which means it can't be erased.

- You've got File Sharing turned on (see Chapter 16).

- You're trying to erase the startup disk. You can't wipe out the disk that contains the currently running System Folder any more than you can paint the floor directly beneath your feet. You can only erase a disk that's *not* the one you started up from. (To erase your built-in hard drive, for example, you must start up from, for example, the Mac OS 9 CD-ROM.)

---

But Mac OS 9 includes another, more flexible way to erase a disk: a program called Drive Setup. (It's in your Applications→Utilities folder.) As described on page 235, you can use this program to erase or subdivide *(partition)* a hard drive. You can also use it to lock a hard drive or cartridge so that it behaves like a CD-ROM: people can look at what's on it, but they can't store anything new on it.

---

**FREQUENTLY ASKED QUESTION**

## Network Disk: the Mystery Startup Icon

*I've only got one startup disk: the hard drive built into my iMac. So how come my Startup Disk control panel shows another hard drive called Network Disk?*

Certain Macs, such as iMacs, iBooks, Power Mac G4s, and others, were designed to be *net-bootable.* That means that, in corporate or school situations, a bunch of these Macs can use, as their startup disk, the hard drive of a single, central *server* machine (usually running a special networking operating system called Mac OS X Server).

When your iMac starts up from a startup disk elsewhere on the network in this way, you wait a lot longer for the startup process to finish. But for whoever has to run the network, the payoffs are considerable: now there's only *one* System Folder to configure, troubleshoot, maintain, and so on. As long as the server's System Folder is running well, every Mac connected to it runs well.

That's why a special icon called Network Disk appears in your Startup Disk control panel: it's there for the day when your Mac is connected to a central server disk, and you're instructed to start up from it, instead of from your own hard drive.

---

**DVD-RAM note:** If your Mac has a DVD-RAM (erasable DVD) drive, you can use the Special→Erase Disk to wipe out a DVD-RAM disc. But if you want the disc to be a *startup* disk, you must use Drive Setup instead, and you must use one of the two *HFS* formatting options, as described in the next section.

---

### Understanding Mac OS Extended formatting

Whether you use the Special→Erase Disk command or the Drive Setup program to erase a disk, you'll be confronted with one option that confuses many beginning (and even intermediate) Mac users: a choice between two formatting options called *Mac OS Standard (HFS)* and *Mac OS Extended (HFS Plus).*

The history of these options is long and technical, but it boils down to this: Until Mac OS 8.1, the Mac chopped up every hard drive surface into thousands of individual "parking places" for data called *blocks.* The size of each block depended on the size of the hard drive, but 16K, 32K, or 64K blocks were typical on 200MB and larger hard drives. Trouble was, the least amount of space a single file on your hard drive can consume is *one block.* Even if a document has just a paragraph in it—2K worth of text, for example—it was still required to occupy a full block of hard drive space. The remaining 30K of space in its block were simply wasted. Multiply that space waste by the hundreds or thousands of tiny files generated by your Web browser and email programs, and you can see how this old Mac OS Standard scheme wasted hundreds of megabytes per hard drive.

That's why all modern hard drives come with the *Mac OS Extended* formatting, in which the block sizes are much tinier—along the lines of 4K each. As a result, small files waste much less space, and each hard drive—particularly if it's a big one—offers hundreds more megabytes' worth of space (see Figure 18-2).

**Figure 18-2:**
*The fine print in a Get Info window shows how much disk space is wasted by an alias icon on a Mac OS-Extended-formatted hard drive (left) and a Mac OS Standard-formatted one (right). The actual file is only 740 bytes, less than one kilobyte (K); about 127K is wasted on the hard drive at right, where every block is 128K.*

So why didn't the vastly superior, faster, more economical Mac OS Extended (HFS Plus) scheme immediately rule the earth? Because Macs running Mac OS 8 or earlier don't understand the new formatting scheme. If you try to hook up an HFS Plus formatted disk—an external hard drive, for example—to a Mac with an older System Folder, the disk appears completely blank. All you get is a single text file called, believe it or not, "Where_have_all_my_files_gone?" (If you open the document, it'll explain that your files are perfectly safe—but that you need to insert this disk into a Mac OS 8.1-or-later Mac to view them.)

---

**GEM IN THE ROUGH**

## Startup Keys for Startup Disks

The leaflet that accompanies Mac OS 9 lets you know that you don't actually need to open the Startup Disk control panel just to start up the Mac from a CD-ROM. If you insert, say, the Mac OS 9 CD into the Mac, just restart the computer—and as it comes to life again, hold down the letter C key. The Mac then uses the CD-ROM as its startup disk.

But that's by no means the only startup disk-related key you can hold down during startup. If you press ⌘-Option-Shift-Delete just after turning on the Mac, you make the machine *ignore* its built-in hard drive. You force the Mac to start up from the next startup disk it finds, such as an external hard drive.

In fact, if you add a number key (1 through 6) to that keystroke, you tell the Mac *which* startup disk to use, as they're listed in your Startup Disk control panel. Of course, if you're a person who actually has six external startup disks, you don't need a book to tell you that—you've probably written a book or two of your own!

---

*Tip:* To see which formatting scheme your hard drive uses—Mac OS Standard or Mac OS Extended—highlight its icon. Choose File→Get Info. You'll see the formatting scheme listed at the top of the window (see Figure 18-2).

In other words, the bottom line is this: format any disk that's bigger than 300 MB or so using the Mac OS Extended option, which makes each disk hold many more files—*unless* you plan to use the disk on a Mac that's running system software older than Mac OS 8.1. (On disks smaller than 300MB, including Zip disks, the older, HFS [Mac OS Standard] formatting is actually more space-efficient.)

# Macintosh Cable Crash Course

Understanding the various connectors on the back panel of a Mac entails distinguishing between B.I. (before iMac) or A.I. (after iMac) models. When creating the iMac, Apple did away with several kinds of jacks that had been on every previous Mac. The switch caused temporary pain for millions of Mac fans whose scanners, printers, Zip drives, and other add-ons suddenly required adapters or replacements. But in theory, at least, the benefits of the newer connector types pay off in convenience and savings.

## Older Macs (before iMac)

Older Macs had these jacks on the back panel:

### Modem port

This round, eight-pin connector accepts the *serial cable* from such add-ons as modems, digital cameras, digitizing (drawing) tablets, MIDI (music synthesizer) interfaces, inkjet printers, and the PalmPilot synchronizing cradle.

As jacks go, the modem port isn't bad; for example, you're not compelled to shut the Mac down every time you want to connect or disconnect something. The one infuriating limitation of the modem port is that there's only *one* of it. Short of buying a $200 modem-port expander card to install into your Mac, you can't plug both your MIDI interface and your digital camera (for example) into the Mac at the same time.

### Printer port

This connector looks identical to the modem port. And when you turn off the networking feature called AppleTalk (using the AppleTalk Inactive button in the  →Chooser, for example), it also behaves exactly like the modem port. When AppleTalk is turned off, the printer port accepts exactly the same kind of serial cables as the modem port.

Trouble is, many Mac users need AppleTalk turned *on*. It must be turned on if, for example, you intend to connect your Mac to a LocalTalk network (described in Chapter 16) or if you use a laser printer.

Some older-Mac owners are lucky enough to connect to the network or printer via an Ethernet jack. In that situation, you can use the AppleTalk control panel (described in Chapter 12) to switch the networking features to your Ethernet jack; the printer port, in that situation, becomes just another modem port. Now you *can* connect both your MIDI interface and your digital camera simultaneously—but still only two devices. If you add a PalmPilot to the mix, you're back into the old plugging-and-unplugging game.

### ADB (keyboard/mouse) jack

Older Macs' keyboards and mice plug into this peculiar jack (whose initials stand for Apple Desktop Bus). It, too, is small and round, and looks almost exactly like the modem and printer ports. But for the most part, it accepts only one kind of appliance: Keyboards, mice, and specially designed joysticks.

The ADB connector was adequate for its era, but has several distinct disadvantages: namely, that you're not supposed to plug or unplug anything from the Mac's ADB connector while the computer is turned on. Doing so risks damaging the keyboard/mouse, the Mac's main circuit board, or both, occasionally requiring massively expensive repairs. If you're lucky, you can re-plug a loose ADB mouse or keyboard without causing such horrific damage—but even then, you'll find that your replugged mouse now operates frustratingly slowly, requiring furious repeated scrapes across the mouse pad just to move the cursor to the top of the screen. To restore normal speed, you must restart the computer anyway.

### SCSI port

The widest connector on the back of pre-iMac Mac models is called the SCSI connector (pronounced *scuzzy*). It accommodates such add-ons as scanners, hard drives, and removable-disk systems like Zip and Jaz.

But for user-friendliness, SCSI is a disaster. You can't plug or unplug something while the computer (or the add-on) is turned on. You have to flip switches to give each SCSI appliance its own unique *address*. If you connect more than one SCSI gadget to your Mac, you must *terminate* (place a special transistor plug on) the last device in the chain. This chain is limited to six gadgets, which can begin to misbehave if the total cabling between (and inside) them is longer than 18 feet. Then again, SCSI gadgets can misbehave just whenever they feel like it: often, something as seemingly irrelevant as the sequence of devices can affect whether or not your scanner works or your Mac turns on. The cables are fat, expensive, and sometimes flaky.

## Today's Macs

Modern Mac models lack modem, printer, ADB, and SCSI jacks; Apple finally got fed up with their limitations and dangers. In their place, you get two new kinds of connectors: USB and (on most models) FireWire. These connections offer freedom of plugging: you can connect or disconnect USB and FireWire devices whether the Mac is turned on or not. There's no such thing as ID numbers, termination, or six-gadget limitations with USB and FireWire, either; these devices are as plug-and-play as plug-and-play gets.

USB and FireWire are not perfect yet, however; some knowledge is still required.

## USB connectors

Every modern Mac model comes with one or two of these *Universal Serial Bus* jacks. ("Bus" is geek-speak for *circuit.*) This jack replaces the modem, printer, ADB, and (to some degree) SCSI connectors of older Macs; USB can accommodate your mouse, keyboard, PalmPilot, MIDI interface, digital camera, inkjet printer, Zip drive, scanner, and so on. (Figure 18-3 shows this kind of jack.)

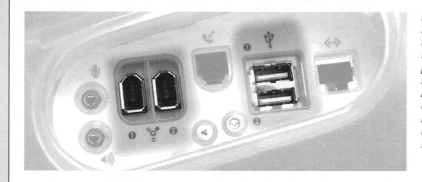

**Figure 18-3:**
*Highlighted at right: the two USB ports on a typical iMac. Note the peculiar three-pronged icon that represents it. At left: a pair of FireWire connectors. The icon looks like a cross between a Y and a "Danger: Radiation" logo.*

Obviously, you can't plug *all* of those gadgets into your Mac simultaneously; your keyboard itself occupies one USB connector. To the delight of electronics companies everywhere, you must buy a USB *hub,* a multiplier that grants you four or eight more USB jacks, if you want to connect additional USB add-ons. You can plug hub into hub, furthermore, until you've got a seething tangle of 127 USB devices all connected to the same Mac.

Before falling in love with USB, however, you should know these three USB facts:

- **USB gadgets still need software.** USB devices aren't really plug-and-play; they're actually install-the-software, then-plug-and-play. When you plug in a new gadget—a USB scanner, for example—the Mac is smart enough to display a message that says, in effect, "I sense that you've plugged something new into me, but I don't have the software I need to operate it." It's up to you to insert the CD that came with your new gadget and install the software. (The exception: Some keyboards and mice work fine without installing software, thanks to a set of standard drivers Apple has built in to Mac OS 9.)

- **USB still needs power.** On paper, USB looked like an especially attractive technology because it can actually send electricity down its cable. Imagine it: Your new scanner, Zip drive, or printer wouldn't require a power cord! It's the end of desk-clutter cabling mess!

    In real life, however, things aren't so simple. True, the Mac does send a *trickle* of juice down the USB cable—but only enough to power, say, your keyboard and mouse. More complex equipment, such as scanners and Zip drives, still require their own power cords.

The trickle of juice, moreover, dissipates quickly. When you need more USB slots, you can buy two different kind of hubs: *Powered* hubs, which have power cords of their own; and *nonpowered* ones, which get their electricity from the USB cable itself. To the dismay of thousands of Mac fans when USB first debuted, many USB add-ons don't work when plugged into a nonpowered hub.

---

*Tip:* The distinction between powered and nonpowered hubs becomes especially important if you plan to connect keyboard into keyboard, or hub into hub. When chaining together multiple USB hubs, don't plug a nonpowered one into another nonpowered one (if you expect everything to work); if you must use nonpowered hubs, alternate them with powered ones.

Desktop Macs' keyboards are themselves USB hubs; that is, you can find a free USB slot open at each end of it. Most people plug the mouse into one end, leaving the other USB connector available for, say, a printer. But the keyboard is a nonpowered hub! Therefore, you can't plug a power-hungry USB gadget into it—such as another keyboard.

---

- **USB is still getting there.** Even if you follow all the rules of powered hubs and nonpowered, USB is still an evolving technology. As many iMac fans can tell you, keeping both a USB printer and USB scanner connected at once can lead to freezes and crashes. Apple has updated its USB software several times, and so have the companies that make those printers and scanners; you'll do yourself a big favor by keeping on top of the new software releases.

  When it comes to Mac OS 9's USB software, keeping up to date is easy—just use the Software Update control panel, as described in Chapter 12, to make sure your Mac always has the latest version. Keeping track of your printer and scanner software is more difficult, but periodically looking up your equipment at *www.versiontracker.com* is an excellent way to stay informed.

### FireWire connectors

As noted above, Apple eliminated the troublesome SCSI connector from the standard Mac (although for $50, the Apple Store at *www.apple.com* will install a SCSI jack into any Power Mac you buy there). The USB technology is great for "slow" devices like printers and scanners, but doesn't transfer data fast enough for such speed-intensive gadgets as hard drives and video equipment.

That's why most of today's Mac models also include one or two *FireWire* connectors, into which you can plug specially designed hard drives, digital cameras (see Figure 18-3), and digital camcorders. (If you use an iMac DV, you may have already discovered the joy of editing your own footage by plugging a digital camcorder into this jack.) You can plug one FireWire doodad into the next, for a total of 40 devices—without ever having to think about ID numbers, termination, or even turning the Mac off in between hookups.

At this writing, there are few FireWire gadgets other than hard drives, cameras, and camcorders. Still, the advice provided in the USB discussion earlier still applies. Keep your driver software updated; and remember that the FireWire wire itself supplies some power—enough for one hard drive, say—but adding on additional gadgets may require power adapters.

---

***Tip:*** FireWire is Apple's friendlier name for IEEE-1394, which is what other electronics companies call this particular kind of connector. That's a handy fact when you're shopping for, say, a DV camcorder. It may not come with a "FireWire" connector—but if it has an "IEEE-1394" connector, you're in business.

---

### The Ethernet jack

All modern Macs also include an Ethernet connector, which looks like an overweight telephone jack. Into this jack you plug, of course, your Ethernet cables when you create a network (as described in Chapter 16).

But the Ethernet jack is also where your pre-USB printer winds up. That is, if you have, say, an old StyleWriter printer, the modern Mac offers no printer port into which to plug it. But for $80 or so, you can buy an AsantéTalk adapter (www.asante.com) or iPrint adapter (www.farallon.com) that lets you plug your old printer into your modern Mac's Ethernet socket. As a bonus, that printer is now available for use by any Mac on your Ethernet network.

# CHAPTER 19

# Printing, Fonts, and ColorSync

When Apple advertises the 50 new features of Mac OS 9, it could very well be talking just about the many new printing options, which, for the most part, appeal primarily to printing shops. After all, the printing industry is a Mac stronghold, so Apple's engineers spend a good amount of their energy making sure that every conceivable printing and font-management feature is built into the Mac.

Another elaborate set of software components is dedicated to the Mac OS's *desktop printing* feature, which is primarily useful to people who work on a network that offers several connected printers.

A final batch of features is aimed at people who scan, edit, and then print color photographs. As anyone who's tried to do such a thing knows, what's burnt umber to your scanner is rarely the same shade as burnt umber to your inkjet printer. Apple's ambitious ColorSync software is designed to be the negotiator between your scanner or camera, monitor, and printer, so that colors remain consistent throughout the process.

This chapter tackles all of these features: printing, managing multiple printers, fonts, and ColorSync.

## Mac Meets Printer

Grand Central Station for Macintosh printers is the Chooser program (choose  →Chooser). As you can see from Figure 19-1, it displays an icon for several discontinued Apple printers. (Apple no longer makes printers.) These icons represent the software—the *drivers*—that the Mac needs to communicate with each of the corresponding printers.

When you buy a modern printer from, say, Epson, Canon, or Hewlett-Packard, its icon doesn't show up in the Chooser until you run the installer program on the CD that accompanies the printer. For example, if you install the software for an Epson Stylus 740 inkjet printer, the Chooser now displays an icon called SC740 (which is the Epson programmers' cryptic way of saying "Stylus Color 740").

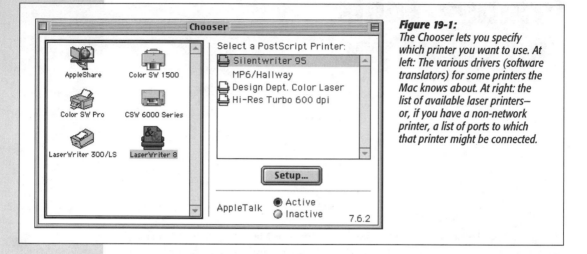

**Figure 19-1:**
*The Chooser lets you specify which printer you want to use. At left: The various drivers (software translators) for some printers the Mac knows about. At right: the list of available laser printers— or, if you have a non-network printer, a list of ports to which that printer might be connected.*

---

**Tip:** Each icon in the Chooser is represented by a piece of software in your System Folder→Extensions folder. Feel free to discard the icons of printers you don't imagine you'll be using. If you think it's unlikely that you'll be printing on, say, an ImageWriter printer (which was discontinued in 1996), by all means throw away its icon. (Keep the LaserWriter 8 icon on hand, however; it's the driver software for almost any brand of laser printer.)

---

Before making any printouts at all, in other words, you must first install the software for your new printer—and then you must open the Chooser and click the corresponding icon. On the right side of the screen, you may have to make another click:

- If you click the icon for a networkable office laser printer (such as the LaserWriter 8 icon), and you are, in fact, connected to a network, the names of all operational office printers appear on the right side of the window. (If your corporate network is so big that it has multiple *zones,* first click the appropriate zone at the lower-left of the Chooser window.) Click the name of the printer you'd like to use.

- If you click the icon for a non-networkable printer, such as an inkjet printer from Epson, Canon, or Hewlett-Packard, the right side of the screen offers a list of Mac connectors to which that printer might be attached. If you have a modern Mac, the inkjet printer is probably connected to your USB socket, and you have no further choices to make. If you have an older Mac, you must specify whether the printer is connected to the modem or printer port.

***Note:*** If you intend to connect your inkjet printer to the printer port, the controls at the bottom of the window should say *AppleTalk Inactive*. AppleTalk should be active *only* when you want to connect a networkable laser printer to your printer port.

- If you click the LaserWriter 8 icon, you can, if you like, also click the Setup button on the right side of the screen. Now you're offered an enormous list of laser printers (exclusively discontinued Apple models, unless you've bought a new laser printer and run its installer). By double-clicking the one you actually own, you can inform your Mac of that printer's special capabilities—the largest paper it can handle, double-sided printing features, additional paper trays, and so on. (If your printer doesn't show up in this list, click Generic.)

In any case, your primary mission, upon installing a new printer, is to select its name in the Chooser and then close the window. (You can also use the Desktop Printing Utility program, described later in this chapter, to set up a new printer.) Now you're ready to make printouts, as described in "Making the Printout," also later in this chapter.

---

**FREQUENTLY ASKED QUESTION**

## The Forgetful Chooser

*Every time I open the Chooser, I have to click my printer icon again. Why can't it remember what I chose the last time?*

Actually, it can, and it does. If you try printing another document, you'll discover that the Mac uses the same printer again—proof that the Chooser does indeed remember your choice.

What's probably confusing you is the fact that when you open the Chooser again later, the printer *icon* is no longer selected. That's standard behavior. As it turns out, the Chooser is the command center for more than just printers. Sometimes you use it to configure your fax modem; other times you use it to connect to your network, as described in Chapter 16.

Each time you open it, in other words, the Mac doesn't know what settings you intend to change—printer, fax modem, or network—so it highlights *nothing*. Behind the scenes, however, the Mac is still perfectly aware of your preferred printer.

(On the other hand, if, each time you print, you get a *message* that instructs you to choose a printer in the Chooser, then the Mac really *is* forgetting your printer choice. It's likely that your Mac's built-in 5-year lithium battery, whose purpose is to maintain such settings when the computer is turned off, has died. An Apple dealer can replace it for you for about $25.)

---

## Desktop Printer Icons

If you work alone, with one printer attached to one Mac, you can afford to skip this section.

But some people have more than one printer. You might have a laser printer attached to your Ethernet port, for example, and a color inkjet attached to your USB port. You may also have a choice of printers if you work in a networked office—maybe an old black-and-white Apple LaserWriter, plus an expensive color laser printer for printing mockups of brochure designs. Either way, you need a way to specify, on a printout-to-printout basis, which printer you want to use.

Of course, you can always open the  →Chooser whenever you want to switch print-ers, and then click the corresponding icon. If you switch infrequently, this method works perfectly well.

---

**Note:** If your printer isn't an Apple model, using the Chooser may be the *only* way you can switch printers; not every printer comes with software that's compatible with the Desktop Printing feature described below.

---

If you switch more often, however, you may wish for a more convenient method of switching printers. That's why Apple created its Desktop Printing feature: as shown in Figure 19-2, you can set up your desktop with an icon representing each printer. You also wind up with a Printing menu that unlocks several additional printing options.

Even Mac users with only a single printer sometimes encounter this feature. They wind up with a big bold desktop icon representing that one printer, and have no idea what it's for or how it got there. Now you know.

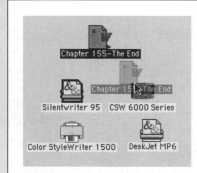

**Figure 19-2:**
*You can direct each printout to a particular printer just by dragging its icon onto the corresponding desktop printer icon. When you print using the File→Print command, the printer with the big bold icon (top left) is the one that does the job.*

---

**FREQUENTLY ASKED QUESTION**

## The Xed-Out Desktop Printer Icon

*I've got a big bold printer icon on my desktop, like the ones you describe. But it has a huge X through it. What's it for?*

The Desktop Printing software described in this section re-quires two extensions in your System Folder→Extensions folder, called Desktop Printing Extension and Desktop Printer Spooler. If you turn these extensions off, you cut out the sys-tem software's communication with the printer icons on your desktop—the Mac responds by displaying the X. It means, "This desktop printer icon isn't working at the moment, but when you turn your extensions back on, all will be well."

You'll encounter this syndrome not just when you move or turn off the desktop printing extensions, but also whenever

you press the Shift key while the Mac is starting up. Doing so turns off all extensions, *including* the two Desktop Print-ing ones.

*OK, you're probably going to say that this is a related ques-tion—but how can I get rid of those desktop icons entirely?*

This is a related question. As you may have discovered, you can't ditch desktop printer icons by dragging them to the Trash; the Mac recreates at least one of them automatically. You must first turn off the two desktop printing extensions (using Extensions Manager, described in Chapter 12) and then restart the computer. Only then can you throw out your desktop icons, which now appear with Xes on them.

## Creating Desktop Printer Icons

If you found a printer icon already on your desktop after installing Mac OS 9, it's probably because you patiently answered questions posed by the Mac OS Setup Assistant that runs just after installation of Mac OS 9. (One of those questions asks what kind of printer is connected to your Mac.) You may also wind up with an automatic desktop printer icon after upgrading to Mac OS 9 from an earlier OS version, in which you had already selected a printer.

Creating another desktop printer icon is as easy as choosing ⌘→Chooser and clicking another printer icon. Each time you do so and then close the Chooser, another printer icon appears on your desktop. (The exceptions, as noted earlier, are the icons for non-Apple printers that still aren't compatible with the desktop-printer feature.)

Once you've got a few printer icons, they don't necessarily have to remain *desktop* printer icons. You can move these icons anywhere you like—for example, into a folder, into the ⌘ menu, or someplace else where they create less clutter. You can rename them, too—click the name once, and then type the replacement name, exactly as you would rename any Mac icon.

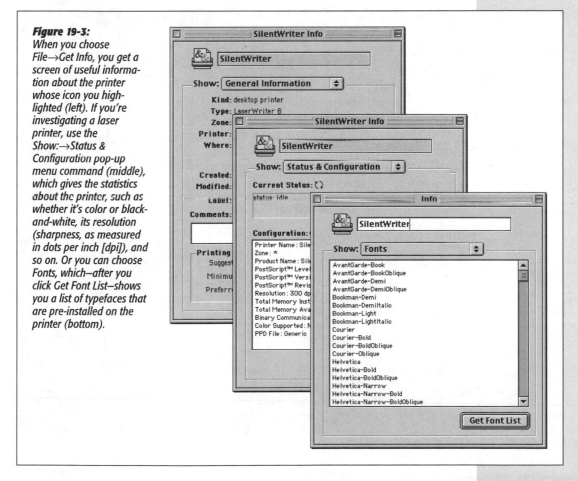

*Figure 19-3:*
*When you choose File→Get Info, you get a screen of useful information about the printer whose icon you highlighted (left). If you're investigating a laser printer, use the Show:→Status & Configuration pop-up menu command (middle), which gives the statistics about the printer, such as whether it's color or black-and-white, its resolution (sharpness, as measured in dots per inch [dpi]), and so on. Or you can choose Fonts, which—after you click Get Font List—shows you a list of typefaces that are pre-installed on the printer (bottom).*

If you ever forget a printer's original name, highlight its icon and then choose File→Get Info. As shown in Figure 19-3, printer icons have Get Info windows all their own; the first one, General Information, identifies the printer's original information.

## Using Desktop Printer Icons

Despite their innocent appearance, desktop printer icons are teeming with sophisticated features for managing your printouts.

### Choosing your favorite

If multiple printers are indeed connected to your Mac, the first thing Desktop Printing lets you do is indicate which you'd like to use for your next printout. To do so, click once on its icon. When you do so, a new menu appears on your menu bar called Printing. The commands it offers depend on what kind of printer icon you've clicked—for example, if you clicked an inkjet printer, the Printing menu lets you specify how the printer is connected to your Mac; if you clicked a laser printer, you get a Setup command that duplicates the functions of the Setup button in the Chooser; and so on.

---

**POWER USERS' CLINIC**

## Desktop Printer Utility

In your Apple Extras→Utilities→Apple LaserWriter Software folder is a forgotten little program called Desktop Printer Utility. As shown here, it offers a method of creating special mutant breeds of desktop printer icons.

The first kind, Printer (AppleTalk), creates a standard laser-printer desktop printer icon, exactly as though you had clicked Laser-Writer 8 in the Chooser. The next item, Printer (LPR), is for office networks that rely on TCP/IP (the protocol used by the Internet); it creates a printer icon for a printer elsewhere on your TCP/IP network. (If you're a network administrator who set this up, you'll know what this is about.)

A Printer (no printer connection) icon doesn't print anything; it's just a holding tank, like a desktop printer that's been put on permanent hold. When you're using your laptop at 39,000 feet, you can freely use your Print command. The laptop will do the dirty work of converting your documents into printout files, which this icon houses. Later, when you return to the ground—or someplace where there's an actual printer—you can drag the pent-up printout icons from this "printer's" window onto one of your other desktop printer icons to get the hard copy.

Finally, the Translator (PostScript) desktop printer type is a converter. When you use this kind of "printer," the Mac converts your printed file into a PostScript file, as described later in this chapter.

After selecting the kind of special printer icon you want, you face another dialog box in which you must specify additional settings—for the TCP/IP printer, for example, you must enter the printer's network address. Finally, click Create, and then save the new icon with the location—and the name—you want it to have.

**New Desktop Printer**

With  LaserWriter 8  ⬍

Create Desktop...

Printer (AppleTalk)
Printer (LPR)
Printer (no printer connection)
Translator (PostScript)

Converts file to PostScript™ format. The file will be placed in a folder that you specify.

Cancel    OK

---

But regardless of the kind of printer icon you clicked, the Printing command always contains a Set Default Printer command. That command, or its ⌘-L keyboard shortcut, establishes the highlighted printer as the *default printer*—the Chosen One. A thick black border appears around its desktop icon, letting you know that your next printout will go to that printer.

Actually, though, there are three faster ways to choose a new favorite printer:

- Control-click the desktop printer icon; choose Set as Default from the pop-up menu.

- If your Control Strip is open, as described in Chapter 4, choose a printer's name from the Desktop Printing tile. A dot appears in the pop-up menu beside the name of the currently selected printer.

- Just drag a document icon (one that you want to print) onto a desktop printer icon, which automatically becomes the new default printer.

### Managing printouts

The real fun of desktop printer icons only begins when you've actually tried printing something. (To print something, see "Making the Printout," later in this chapter; it boils down to opening a document and then choosing File→Print.)

Once you've done so, an amazing thing happens: your chosen desktop printer icon suddenly behaves like a folder that contains the printouts-in-waiting. Double-click one of these icons to see something like Figure 19-4: the printouts that will soon be sliding out of your printer appear in a tidy list.

**Figure 19-4:**
*Waiting printouts show up in a desktop-printer window. You can manipulate this window exactly as you would any Finder list view: for example, you can sort the list by clicking the column headings Name, Pages, and so on; make the columns wider or narrower by dragging the column-heading dividers horizontally; or reverse the sorting order by clicking the triangle button above the scroll bar.*

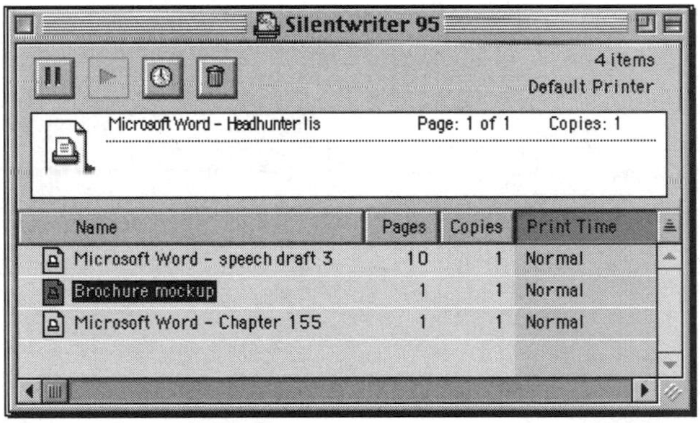

There's no end to the control you now have over these waiting printouts, which Apple collectively calls the *print queue:*

- **Rearrange them.** By dragging the names of your printouts up and down in the list, you can specify which ones get printed first—namely, the ones at the top of the list. (This works only when you're viewing the list sorted in Print Time order, as shown in Figure 19-4.)

- **Delete them.** By clicking an icon, or Shift-clicking several, and then clicking the tiny trash icon at the top of the window, you remove items from the list of waiting printouts. If you prefer, you can also drag icons directly into the real Trash in the corner of your screen. There they become separate printout icons, which you can truly delete—by emptying the Trash—or rescue by dragging back onto a desktop printer icon.

- **Duplicate them.** After highlighting the name of a waiting printout, you can choose File→Duplicate to make a copy of it in the same window. Now you'll get two printouts of the same thing.

- **Add to them.** You can drag document icons—Word or AppleWorks documents, for example—directly onto a desktop printer icon (or into its open window). Doing so prints the document and establishes that printer icon as the new default printer, as noted above.

- **Change your mind.** By highlighting a printout and then clicking the Pause button (the leftmost of the four VCR-style icons above the list), you put that printout on hold. It won't print out until you highlight it again and click the Play button (the second icon at the top of the window).

- **Schedule them.** Click one of the printouts and then click the tiny clock icon above the list. As shown in Figure 19-5, you can reschedule this printout for a time when the printer isn't so busy, as a favor to those co-workers with more urgent print jobs.

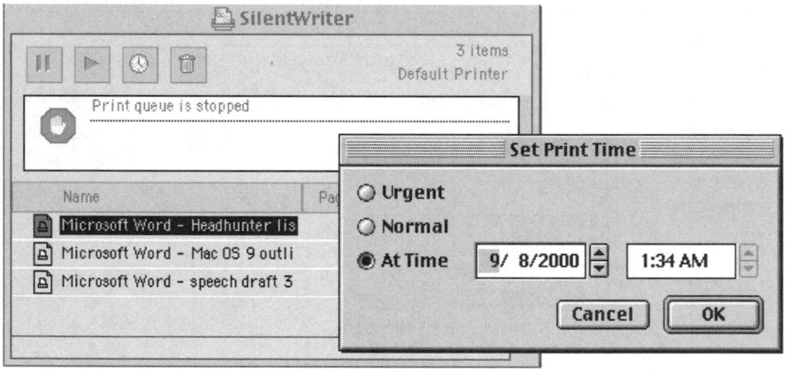

**Figure 19-5:**
Choose Urgent to force your printout to the top of the list, so that it will be printed first. Or click At Time to schedule your printout for some later time—so that your 75-page thesis prints out in the middle of the night to avoid tying up the printer, for example.

- **Halt them all.** You can stop all printouts for a specific printer (whose window is open) by choosing Printing→Stop Print Queue. (Choose Printing→Start Print Queue to re-enable printing on this printer.)

---

**Tip:** If menus aren't your thing, hold down Shift and Option to make the Pause button turn into a tiny stop-sign icon button, which you can click to stop the print queue. Hold down the same two keys to make the Play button take on the shape of a printer icon, which means Start Print Queue.

---

- **Switch them to another printer.** If this is the day your 75 co-workers are all printing out their résumés, you can drag your printout-in-waiting onto the icon (or into the window) of another desktop printer, thus forcing your work to print out on a different printer. (This works only if you're dragging it to the icon of the same *kind* of printer—from one laser printer icon to another, for example.)

# Printing Without Desktop Icons

Suppose you've got one Mac and one printer, and you'd really rather not get into the complexity of the desktop-printer icons described in the previous section. And yet, having scanned the preceding pages, you're feeling left out—why shouldn't you, too, be able to rearrange printouts, put printouts on hold, and perform other kinds of printout manipulation?

Actually, you can. If you regularly use *background printing,* described in the next section, you get most of the same benefits as the desktop-printing feature, even though you use only a single printer.

---

***Tip:*** You won't encounter PrintMonitor, the program described in the following section, or any of its features when the desktop printing feature described in the previous section is turned *on.* To turn Desktop Printing off, choose &#63743;→Control Panels→Extensions Manager, turn off the icons called Desktop Printing Extension and Desktop Printer Spooler, and then restart the Mac.

---

## Meet PrintMonitor

When you print a document, the Mac does two things. First, it launches a printing-management program called PrintMonitor. Many people aren't even aware that this program has been launched, but if you check your Application menu about 10 seconds after printing something, you'll see PrintMonitor in the list of open programs.

---

**Figure 19-6:**
*You can rearrange the sequence of printouts waiting to happen by dragging their names up or down in the Waiting area of the PrintMonitor window. If you click Set Print Time, you can put a printout on hold or reschedule it for a less busy printing time.*

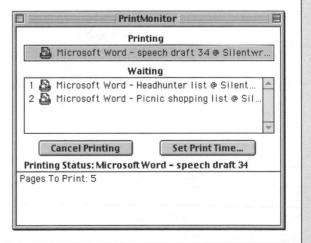

---

Second, the Mac creates a *spool file*—a printout-in-waiting, exactly like the ones described in the previous discussion. Most of the time, however, you never see these spool files. They're buried in the System Folder→PrintMonitor Documents folder—and even then, only for a moment. Once the Mac prints these documents, they disappear from the PrintMonitor Documents folder forever.

## Controlling PrintMonitor Printouts

To gain some control over the printout process, choose PrintMonitor from your Application menu. As shown in Figure 19-6, this funny little program pops to the foreground, showing a list of the documents waiting to be printed.

Before you know it, your Mac will actually print these documents, and you'll have lost whatever control you hoped to gain. But if you act quickly, you can manipulate the printouts like this:

- **Rearrange them.** Drag printouts up or down the list to make them print sooner or later than other documents.

- **Cancel them.** Click a waiting printout's name and then click Remove From List if you change your mind about printing it.

- **Reschedule them.** Click a waiting printout and then click Set Print Time. You'll be offered the chance to specify a later date for printing this document. You can also click Postpone Indefinitely, which puts the printout on hold until you highlight the printout again, click Set Print Time again, and indicate a printing time.

- **Collect printouts for later.** Even when there's nothing listed in the PrintMonitor window, you may enjoy this trick: While the PrintMonitor window is open, choose File→Stop Printing. Now, whenever you use the Print command, the Mac will convert your document into a printout-to-be, but won't actually attempt to send it to a printer.

    As described in "Using Desktop Printer Icons," earlier in this chapter, that can be a great feature when you're on the plane with your laptop, for example; when you touch down and connect to the printer, you can choose File→Resume Printing. All of your saved printouts will tumble out in short order.

---

***Tip:*** PrintMonitor normally appears only when you're actually printing something. You might wonder, therefore, how you can get to its menus—in order to choose Stop Printing, for example—without having to make a printout of something.

Fortunately, PrintMonitor is a genuine program with a genuine double-clickable icon. To find it, open your System Folder→Extensions folder. You can double-click the PrintMonitor icon just as you would any application.

---

## PrintMonitor Preferences

While PrintMonitor is open, you can also choose File→Preferences. A dialog box appears, offering these choices:

- **Show the PrintMonitor window.** Actually, the No/Yes options here have no effect; PrintMonitor *always* launches in the background when you make the printout, regardless of the setting you make here.

- **When a printing error needs to be reported.** If the printer is out of paper or ink, for example, how urgently do you want PrintMonitor to try to get your attention? You can have it display a message, make your Application menu blink, or just display a tiny black diamond beside the PrintMonitor name in the Application menu. (You won't even see that diamond until you actually open the Application menu.)

- **When a manual feed job starts.** Suppose that your printer has a "manual feed" option (which takes one sheet at a time from a special tray or slot), and that you've selected that option when making your printout. How do you want PrintMonitor to say, "It's time to put in the next sheet"? Once again, you can specify how much flashing or message-showing PrintMonitor should show you.

# Making the Printout

This chapter so far has covered the elaborate printout-manipulation features built into Mac OS 9. You're not compelled to use any of these fancy options; many Mac users don't. Almost everyone, however, sooner or later makes a basic printout. You can print your documents either from within the programs you used to create them—or directly from the Finder.

## Printing from Within Your Programs

The experience of printing depends on the printer you're using—laser printer, color inkjet, or whatever. In every case, however, all the printing options hide in two commands: Page Setup, which you need to adjust only occasionally, and Print. You'll find these two commands in the File menus of almost every Macintosh program in existence—Word, Excel, AppleWorks, Photoshop, your email program, your Web browser, and on and on.

### Page Setup

Most people use this command only when they want to print a document rotated sideways on the page, so that it prints "the long way." But even some of the less-used options here are sometimes useful (see Figure 19-7). The Scale or Scaling control, for example, lets you reduce or enlarge your document, which can be handy if the program you're using doesn't offer such a control.

The remaining choices vary; the Page Setup options for an Epson inkjet, for example, differ dramatically from those for a laser printer. Only your printer's user manual can tell you exactly what these choices do. Because most laser printers offer the standard LaserWriter 8 options, here's a rundown of some of the most useful. (They're listed here by the corresponding command in the pop-up menu at the upper-left corner of the dialog box.)

• **Page Attributes.** Use the Paper pop-up menu to specify what size paper you're printing on—US Letter, US Legal, or one of the standard European paper sizes (A4 and B5). Don't be confused by the "small" variants listed here (such as US Letter Small); these paper *dimensions* are identical to the non-small versions. The only difference is the margin: if you turn on the Small option, the laser printer chops off any part of the printout closer than half an inch to the edge of the page. (The non-small page sizes can get to within a quarter of an inch.)

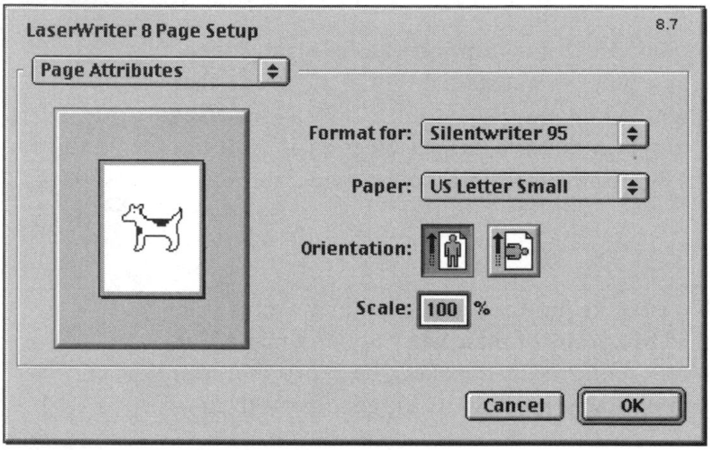

**Figure 19-7:**
*The options included in this dialog box depend on the printer model you're using. Sometimes, as when printing on a laser printer, the pop-up menu at upper-left lets you switch among different screens full of choices. The effect of each printing option is illustrated by the little animal in the dialog box, which is known as the Dogcow. (The rumor that the Dogcow is related to the animal on the cover of this book is pure speculation.)*

*Tip:* Clearly, "US Letter Small," with its fatter non-printable margin, is usually less useful than "US Letter." Who wants to risk having printouts chopped off at the margins? Yet your Mac insists on using the Small option, no matter how many times you change this pop-up menu.

There is a secret, however, to changing the setting once and for all: Option-click the OK button. You'll be asked if you're sure you want your new Page Setup options preserved; click Save.

(Note: You must perform this ritual once for each program that offers its own Page Setup options, as described in the next paragraph—and again, once, for all *other* programs.)

• **Microsoft Word.** To see a window full of printing options unique to the program you're actually using—Word is just one example—choose its name from the pop-up menu. (If you don't see your program's name listed in this pop-up menu, then this program offers no special options of its own.)

• **PostScript Options.** The vast majority of these checkboxes are novelty items or leftover workarounds from the days when most Mac users printed from MacWrite and MacPaint. Most of the time, you should turn them all off.

For example, **Flip Horizontal** prints out a mirror image of your document—useful if you intend to create iron-on logos, read the printout in a mirror or reflected off of your car windshield, and so on. **Invert Image** creates a black-on-white, negative image, suitable for Halloween posters and using up your printer cartridge quickly.

- **Unlimited Downloadable Fonts** can be useful when you're printing on a laser printer with limited memory—especially if it's a document containing lots of different fonts. Then, instead of overwhelming the printer's memory by trying to transmit too many fonts, the Mac instructs the printer to "forget" one set of fonts before receiving the next. All of this makes the printout take much longer to appear; furthermore, this process can wreak havoc (or, more precisely, wreak Courier) with the fonts embedded in EPS graphics.

### The Print command

Although you can grow to a ripe old age without ever seeing the Page Setup dialog box, you can't miss the Print dialog box. It appears, whether you like it or not, whenever you choose File→Print in one of your programs.

Once again, the exact options you encounter depend on the printer you're using (or more specifically, they depend on the driver you've selected in the Chooser). You're always offered a few standard options, however, including these:

- **Copies.** Type the number of copies you want printed.

- **Pages.** You don't have to print an entire document—you can print, say, only pages 2 through 15.

***Tip:*** You don't have to type numbers into both the "From:" and "To:" boxes. If you leave the first box blank, the Mac assumes that you mean "from Page 1." If you leave the second box blank, the Mac understands you to mean "to the end." To print only the first three pages, in other words, leave the first box blank, and type 3 into the second box. (These page numbers refer to the physical pages you're printing, not to any fancy numbering you've set up in your word processor. As far as the Print dialog box is concerned, the first printed page is Page 1, even if you've told your word processor to label it page 455.)

If you have a color inkjet printer, you can also specify what print quality you want, what kind of paper you're printing on, and so on.

If you're using a laser printer, you get dozens of additional options. They're divided into separate screens, accessible using the unnamed pop-up menu just below the "Printer:" pop-up menu. Many of these options are extremely technical, designed for use by graphic designers and print shops; fortunately, you can choose Help→Show Balloons and then, by pointing to each option, read a description of its function.

In the meantime, a few of the options can occasionally be useful. For example:

- **General.** Specify the number of copies, range of pages you want printed, and whether or not you intend to print one page at a time (Manual Feed).

- **Microsoft Word.** Whatever program you're using—Word, AppleWorks, or anything else—may offer its own special printing options on this screen.

- **Background Printing.** You can read about background printing in the upcoming sidebar called "Background Printing Basics." The beauty of using a laser printer, however, is that you can turn background printing on or off independently for *each* printout, using these controls. (You can also specify when you want this document printed.)

- **Color Matching.** Use these controls to specify how you want the colors in your document, if any, translated on their way to the printer. For example, you can print a color document in black-and-white even on a color printer, if that's what you want. (Unfortunately, Apple's programmers have yet to devise a way to make a color printout on a *black-and-white* printer.)

If you choose ColorSync Color Matching (described later in this chapter) or PostScript Color Matching, you can also use the Intent pop-up menu. These options are designed to address a characteristic problem of color printers: they can't actually reproduce every color in the rainbow. That could be a problem if you're printing a photograph of, for example, a rainbow.

You can choose from among the various visual/psychological compromises here. For photos, Perceptual Matching is usually best; for graphs and charts, Saturation Matching may be more successful. If you use the "Auto selection" option, the Mac automatically uses Saturation matching for graph-like drawings (object-oriented artwork), but Perceptual for photos (bitmapped artwork).

When you choose one of the color matching choices from the Print Color pop-up menu, you can also specify a printer profile; this, too, is described later in this chapter under "ColorSync."

- **Cover Page.** If you turn on this option (by clicking **Before Document** or **After Document**), the Mac will tack an extra page onto your printout. It bears the name of your file, your name, and the time. The **Paper Source** pop-up menu lets you specify which of your printer's paper trays you want to use for the cover page—so that you can stock that tray with scrap paper, for example.

- **Font Settings.** If you plan to save your file as a PostScript file, as described in "Save as File," below, **Annotate Font Keys** embeds textual comments to your PostScript file that describe the fonts you used—which can be useful in times of troubleshooting. The other settings here affect what happens when you use a typeface in your document that isn't one of the fonts built into your printer. For example, the **Preferred Format** option applies only when your Mac has both TrueType and PostScript versions of a particular font installed.

- **Job Logging.** Using these controls, you can specify what you want to happen when the laser printer reports a PostScript error (when your document is too complex for the printer's memory, for example)—whether you want a short message to appear on the screen, or a more detailed and technical message to print out.

You can also ask your Mac to keep a record of the printouts it makes. (Specify where you want the file kept by clicking the Change button.) You can choose from

Generate Job Copy, which keeps a duplicate of the actual printout in the journal, or Generate Job Log, which just makes a journal of what was printed when.

- **Layout.** As shown in Figure 19-8, these options can be very useful. For example, you can save paper and toner cartridges by printing several miniature "pages" on a single sheet of paper.

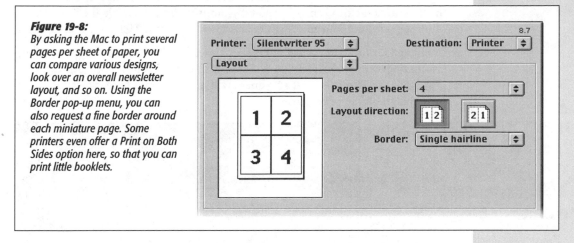

**Figure 19-8:**
*By asking the Mac to print several pages per sheet of paper, you can compare various designs, look over an overall newsletter layout, and so on. Using the Border pop-up menu, you can also request a fine border around each miniature page. Some printers even offer a Print on Both Sides option here, so that you can print little booklets.*

- **Save as File.** Using the Destination→File pop-up menu command at the top of this dialog box, you can turn your printout into a file on your hard drive rather than sending it to the printer. You can then send the resulting file—a *PostScript file*—directly to a print shop. This file contains a complete, self-contained computer-language description of your printout that the print shop can use to print your document without requiring the program you used to create it—or even the document itself.

The options on the Save as File screen let you describe the file you'll be creating. Use the **Format** pop-up menu, for example, to specify whether you want a standard PostScript file, as described above, or an *EPS* (Encapsulated PostScript) graphic that you can insert into a page-layout program. (In general, choose EPS Mac Enhanced Preview, which is in color, from the pop-up menu here; the Standard Preview is in black and white, and the No Preview doesn't let you see the image at all when placing it into your page-layout program.)

---

**Tip:** If you have the software called Acrobat Distiller, the Format pop-up menu offers another choice: Acrobat PDF. This choice lets you create an Adobe Acrobat document—a file that any Mac or Windows user can view, read, and print using the free Acrobat Reader program included with every Mac and PC. (You must buy Adobe Acrobat 4 to gain this option—or get it with the purchase of a program like Adobe PageMaker or InDesign.)

---

The **PostScript Level** command specifies what kind of laser printers you intend your file to be printed on (keeping in mind that Level 1 printers—very old ones—offer fewer advanced graphics features, such as color handling and patterns).

Use the **Font Inclusion** pop-up menu to answer the question: "What happens if I used fonts in my document that aren't built into the printer that will be printing this PostScript file?" If you choose None, you'll get the Courier typeface in place of your special fonts. If you click All, you won't have that problem—but the resulting PostScript file will be gargantuan, taking up lots of disk space; it will incorporate every character of every font in your document. Choosing All But Standard 13 instead helps the problem a little bit, by omitting from your file the standard 13 fonts that are built into almost every laser printer (Times, Helvetica, and so on).

- **Imaging Options.** This panel of choices appears only if you're using one of the discontinued Apple printers that offered printout-enhancement features called FinePrint and PhotoGrade. Experiment with these options to see what gives your text and graphics the best printouts.

### Background Printing Basics

In the beginning, there was no such thing as background printing. The Mac simply locked you out whenever it was printing. You couldn't do anything with the Mac except stare at the "now printing" message.

With the invention of background printing, your options are more interesting. Background printing lets you keep using your Mac while the printing takes place. It hands the printing tasks off to a special program—PrintMonitor or Desktop PrintMonitor—that feeds the printout, a little bit at a time, to your printer, in the tiny pauses between your keystrokes and mouse clicks. As a result, the printout takes longer—but you can keep working in the meantime.

You can turn background printing on or off fairly easily—once you find the control, whose location depends on the printer in question. If you're using a laser printer, for example, you turn background printing on or off independently for each printout. Just choose Background Printing in the dialog box that appears when you choose File→Print, as described in this chapter. (Unless you intervene, background printing is always on.) Similarly, if you're using an Epson inkjet, click the fourth of the five icons in the Print dialog box—the one whose icon is a clock superimposed on a printout—to turn background printing on or off.

For most Apple non-laser printers, you can't turn background printing on or off one printout at a time—only for the entire printer. To do so, choose ♦→Chooser, click the icon for the printer, and then click the Background Printing On or Off button that appears on the right side of the Chooser window.

## Printing from the Finder

You don't necessarily have to print a document while it's open in front of you. You can, if you wish, print it directly from the Finder, using one of these three methods:

- Highlight the document icon, and then choose File→Print.

- Control-click the document icon; choose Print from the contextual menu that appears.

- If you're using the desktop-printer icons described at the beginning of this chapter, drag the document icon onto one of these printer icons.

Now the Mac launches the program that created it—Word or AppleWorks, for example—and the Print dialog box appears, so that you can specify how many copies you want and how many of the pages you want printed. When you click Print, your printer springs into action, and then the program quits automatically (if it hadn't already been open).

---

**Tip:** If you're using a laser printer, and you print a PostScript, EPS, JPEG, or PICT graphics document, the Mac doesn't have to launch the parent program. Instead, the Mac sends the file directly to the printer, saving you a little bit of time and itself a little bit of memory.

---

You can also highlight several icons and print them simultaneously, even if you used different programs to create them. (If they're in different windows, consider dragging their icons onto the desktop, so that you can highlight them all simultaneously. Then, after the printing is over, choose File→Put Away, which makes the icons jump back into their original folders.)

---

**Tip:** The Finder's File menu also contains commands for printing Finder windows—Page Setup and Print Window (or, if no window is open, Print Desktop). You may find the Print Window command useful when you want a quick table of contents for, for example, a Zip disk. It's also very useful when you're trying to find out whether or not a printer is working—just open any window and then choose Print Window. You save the time and effort of finding some test document to print.

---

# Fonts

Over the years, Macintosh fonts have improved considerably. No longer do you have to pray to the printer gods that your beautiful flyer won't come out with jagged-looking typeface because you chose the wrong font *type,* one that doesn't have smooth edges. (Jagged-printing *bitmapped fonts* were standard on original Macs, but have now, mercifully, almost completely disappeared from the Earth.)

## TrueType Fonts

If you stick to the fonts that came with your Mac (and the additional ones installed by AppleWorks, Microsoft programs, and so on), your font life is fairly uneventful. Whether you know it or not, every font in your System Folder→Fonts folder is what's known as a *TrueType* font. TrueType fonts are easy to use and easy to understand; no matter what point size you select for these fonts, they look smooth and professional, both on the screen and when you print. Figure 19-9 reveals the simplicity and common sense in the design of TrueType fonts.

## PostScript Fonts

If you're a graphic designer, however, you may well have inherited or purchased fonts that come in another format: *PostScript* fonts. These fonts have several advantages: first, in the professional publishing world, they're everywhere; the PostScript fonts listed in the Adobe catalog, for example, number in the thousands. Second, if you send your finished work to a print shop, PostScript fonts will be met with a friendlier reception, because TrueType fonts can choke some older typesetting equipment.

But PostScript fonts have some considerable disadvantages, too. For example, each comes in two pieces—one that provides the information necessary to display the typeface on the screen, and a set of additional files required by your printer. (Figure 19-9 illustrates this clutter in your Fonts folder.) If you print a document for which some of these printer files are missing, you'll get the wrong font in your printout, even if the document looks fine on the screen.

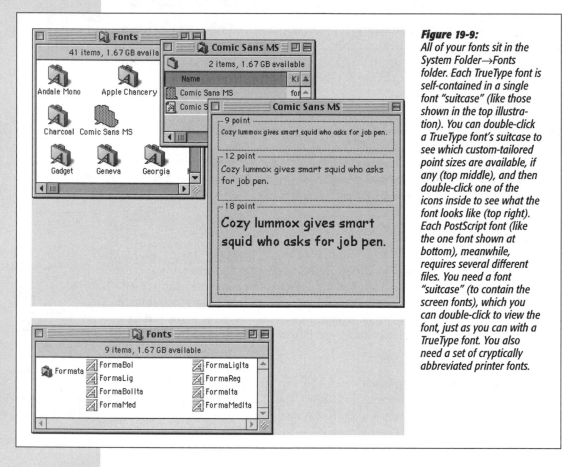

**Figure 19-9:**
*All of your fonts sit in the System Folder→Fonts folder. Each TrueType font is self-contained in a single font "suitcase" (like those shown in the top illustration). You can double-click a TrueType font's suitcase to see which custom-tailored point sizes are available, if any (top middle), and then double-click one of the icons inside to see what the font looks like (top right). Each PostScript font (like the one font shown at bottom), meanwhile, requires several different files. You need a font "suitcase" (to contain the screen fonts), which you can double-click to view the font, just as you can with a TrueType font. You also need a set of cryptically abbreviated printer fonts.*

But your document probably *won't* look fine on the screen unless your Mac has Adobe Type Manager (ATM), a special control panel. Without it, PostScript fonts that you use in your documents at nonstandard sizes (anything other than, for example, 9, 10, 12, 14, 18, or 24 points) appear jagged on the screen.

Fortunately, ATM is easy to get—and it's free: just install the free Acrobat Reader program. Acrobat Reader is on your Mac OS 9 CD, or you can download the latest version from *www.adobe.com*. (Acrobat Reader is designed to let you read the PDF, or Adobe Acrobat, files, which are becoming increasingly popular on the Internet—especially as user manuals for downloaded software.)

## Managing Your Fonts

As shown in Figure 19-9, every font that appears in the Font menus of your various programs is represented in your System Folder→Fonts folder by an icon—or several.

### Installing fonts

Mac OS 9 comes with 18 great-looking TrueType fonts: Apple Chancery, Capitals, Charcoal, Chicago, Courier, Gadget, Geneva, Helvetica, Hoefler Text, Monaco, New York, Palatino, Sand, Skia, Symbol, Techno, Textile, and Times. (When you install Microsoft Internet Explorer, you inherit another handful, including Andale, Arial, Impact, Trebuchet, Verdana, and the symbol fonts Webdings and Wingdings.) But the world is filled with additional fonts. You may find them on the CD-ROMs that come with Mac magazines, on Mac software Web sites, or in the catalogs of commercial typeface companies.

To install a new font, drag its suitcase (if it's TrueType) or its suitcase *and* accompanying printer files (if it's PostScript) either into the Fonts folder or directly onto the System Folder icon. (In the latter case, the Mac offers to install them into the Fonts folder automatically. You'll be notified that the newly installed fonts won't appear in your Font menus until the *next* time you launch your various programs.)

### Removing fonts

When you've had enough of a font, you can remove it from your Mac. To do so, quit all running programs. Then open the System Folder, open the Fonts folder, and drag the offending font suitcase into any other folder (or the Trash). Now when you launch your programs, that font will be absent from the Font menus.

### More about font suitcases

It's Mac OS 9's least publicized new feature: your Fonts folder can contain up to 512 font suitcases—quadruple the limit in previous OS versions—each of which can contain either TrueType fonts or the screen half of PostScript fonts.

If you, owner of more fonts than Felix J. Adobe himself, feel hemmed in by this limitation, you're not out of luck. As it turns out, you can combine font suitcases by dragging one on top of another. By doing so, you can not only organize your fonts (in font suitcases called, for example, Campbell Project or Old-Fashioned), but neatly thwart the 512-suitcase limit—because a single font suitcase can contain dozens of different fonts. (You can also, of course, buy a program like Suitcase *[www.extensis.com]* or MasterJuggler Pro *[www.alsoft.com],* which not only dodge the suitcase limit, but also let you load or unload canned sets of fonts on the fly, as you need them.)

# ColorSync

As you may have read elsewhere in this book—or discovered through painful experience—computers aren't great with color. Every appliance that expresses color—such as your scanner, monitor, and printer—can "see" a different subset of the universe of color. Worse, each piece of equipment "describes" each color differently; if you've ever printed a scanned photograph on your color inkjet printer and wondered why the flesh tones, sky shades, or fruit colors didn't match the original photo, you've seen this syndrome in action. (Apple's ColorSync Web site, *www.apple.com/colorsync*, points out that "off" colors are an even bigger deal in the commercial world. A customer might return a product after discovering, for example, that the actual product color doesn't match the photo on a company's Web site.)

---

**GEM IN THE ROUGH**

## The Secret Screen-Capture Keystrokes

If you're reading a chapter about printing, you may someday be interested in creating *screenshots*—printable illustrations of the Mac screen. Screenshots are a staple of articles, tutorials, and books about the Mac (including this one).

The Mac offers an enormous number of different ways to create screenshots of what you see on the screen. All of them involve pressing the ⌘ and Shift keys. Here's the rundown:

Press ⌘-Shift-3 to create a picture file on your hard drive, in the PICT graphics format, that depicts the entire screen image. A satisfying camera-shutter sound tells you that you were successful. (The file is called Picture 1. Each time you press ⌘-Shift-3, you get another file, called Picture 2, Picture 3, and so on.) You can open this file into SimpleText, Photoshop, AppleWorks, or another graphics program, in readiness for editing or printing.

Press ⌘-Shift-4 to turn your cursor into a tiny + symbol. Now drag diagonally across the screen to capture only a rectangular chunk of it. When you release the mouse, you hear the camera-click sound, and a Picture 1 file appears on your hard drive.

Add Caps Lock to the ⌘-Shift-4 keystroke to turn your cursor into a bullseye symbol. Now you can capture *only* one window or dialog box—after you click inside it. This trick saves you the trouble of cropping out unnecessary background details in your graphics program.

Add Control to either of those keystrokes if you want the resulting image to be copied onto your Clipboard, ready for pasting into (for example) Photoshop or AppleWorks, instead of creating a PICT file on your hard drive.

You can even capture a menu using these keystrokes if you first open the menu by clicking its name. (You can't capture a menu if you've dragged down it with the mouse button pressed.)

Of course, if you're really serious about capturing screenshots, opt instead for a more powerful add-on program like Snapz Pro *(www.ambrosiasw.com)*, which can capture virtually anything on the screen and save it into your choice of graphics format.

---

Apple's ColorSync software, newly enhanced in Mac OS 9, represents a giant stride toward solving the problem. It relies on individual *profiles* for each scanner, monitor, printer, digital camera, copier, proofer, and so on—tiny files that tell the Mac how each device handles color, and which colors it can express. These profiles become part of your color documents themselves, so that every color device they en-

---

counter knows where the document came from and what it's supposed to look like. The ColorSync software then tries to supervise the color processing process, shifting colors so that they remain as consistent as possible through the scanning, editing, and printing process.

## Getting ColorSync Profiles

ColorSync profiles for most Apple color printers, scanners, and monitors come built into Mac OS 9. When you buy equipment or software from Kodak, Agfa, Heidelberg, Pantone, Scitex, Imation, Barco, and Tektronix, you may get additional profiles. If your equipment didn't come with a ColorSync profile, visit Profile Central *(www.chromix.com)*, where hundreds of model-specific profiles are available for downloading. (Put new profiles into the System Folder→Preferences→ColorSync Profiles folder.)

*Tip:* Even if your particular color appliance doesn't have a ColorSync module, you should still use the ColorSync profiles you *do* have for the other elements of your system. Every little bit helps.

## Choosing Your System's Profiles

You specify which equipment you're using by opening two control panels: Monitors and ColorSync.

### Specifying your monitor's profile

Choose &#63743;→Control Panels→Monitors. Click the Color button. Click the name of your monitor in the scrolling list. If you don't see it, download the list of all Apple monitor profiles from *www.apple.com/colorsync/software*. Or create your own profile by clicking Calibrate, as described on page 209.

**Figure 19-10:**
*Tell the Macintosh what scanner and printer you intend to use. Don't bother trying to select the Display profile here; you can't adjust it. This pop-up menu merely reflects whatever choice you made in the Monitors control panel.*

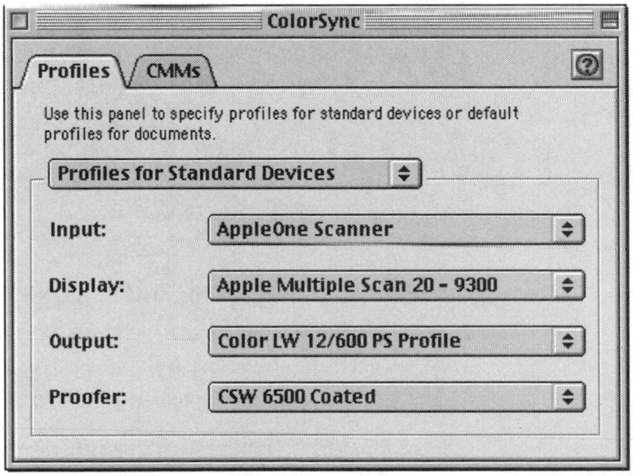

### Specifying your other profiles

To indicate the scanner and printer you plan to use, choose &#xF8FF;→Control Panels→ ColorSync. As you can see in Figure 19-10, you're supposed to identify the appropriate Input profile (for your scanner or camera), Output profile (for your printer), and Proofer profile (if you use a less expensive printer for checking over the work).

### Saving all of this for quick switching

Fortunately, you're not condemned to using the same scanner and printer forever. Nor are you forced to switch the ColorSync control panel settings every time you switch printers or scanners.

Instead, you can save a "snapshot" of the current ColorSync control panel settings into a configuration called a ColorSync Workflow. To do so, choose File→ColorSync Workflows. A special dialog box appears, in which you can create, delete, name, or duplicate your Workflow configurations. Then, to switch from (for example) your Agfa Scanner/Kodak Printer configuration to your Kodak Camera/Proofer configuration, just click the appropriate name in this list and then click Make Active. (Using the Export and Import commands, you can also save a Workflow setup as a stand-alone file, suitable for transferring to other Macs so that they can duplicate your setup without your having to redo the work. And using AppleScripts, as described at the end of this chapter, you can automate Workflow switching.)

---

**POWER USERS' CLINIC**

## AppleScript and ColorSync 3

Using AppleScript, described in Chapter 10, you can harness ColorSync in elaborate ways. Just by dragging document icons onto AppleScript icons, for example, you can embed ColorSync profiles, modify the already incorporated profiles, remove profiles, review the profile information embedded in a graphic, and much more. Better yet, you don't even have to know AppleScript to perform these functions—you can use the built-in AppleScripts that come with Mac OS 9.

To find them, open the Apple Extras→ColorSync Extras→AppleScript Files folder. The centerpiece of this collection of 20 ready-made AppleScripts is the Sample Scripts ReadMe, which tells you how to use them. As this document makes clear, however, Apple's real hope is that these example scripts will give you a leg up on creating your own AppleScripts. One day, Apple hopes, you, the print shop operator, will be able to automate your entire color processing routine using AppleScript and ColorSync as the centerpiece of your operation.

---

## Teaching Photoshop to Use ColorSync

Just specifying what equipment you have isn't enough to make ColorSync work for you. Now you must tell your applications to embed ColorSync data into your documents, so that the Mac's color-correcting features will respect their color characteristics.

Each program (page layout, graphic editing, and so on) may handle ColorSync differently; some may not offer ColorSync features at all. Photoshop, for example, doesn't have ColorSync features built in—but you can add them in the form of *plug-ins*.

Because Photoshop is a core tool for most people who'd be interested in ColorSync, here's the procedure for embedding ColorSync data into your Photoshop work:

Start by downloading the ColorSync plug-ins for Photoshop from *www.apple.com/ colorsync/software*. Put these three files into the Photoshop→Plug-Ins→Acquire/ Export folder. Thereafter, you can ColorSync-ize an open Photoshop image by choosing Filter→Color Match→ColorSync Filter. A dialog box appears, in which you're supposed to specify the profiles for the original scanner or camera ("Source Profile") and the printer you intend to use ("Output Profile"). When you click OK, Photoshop embeds all of this information directly into the file; you're automatically on track for consistent color.

---

***Tip:*** You can also use the File→Export→TIFF with ColorSync Profile command to *export* a Photoshop image with ColorSync profiles embedded in it—a great way to transfer Photoshop's familiarity with ColorSync to any program that can accept images.

---

# Sound and Digital Movies

For years, as other computer companies whipped themselves into a frenzy attempting to market one "multimedia computer" or another, Mac fans just smiled. Macs have been capable of displaying sound and graphics—no add-on sound, graphics, or video boards required—from day one, years before the word multimedia was even coined.

The Mac's superiority at handling sound and video continues in Mac OS 9. In particular, QuickTime, the software that lets you play digital movies on your screen and watch live "streaming" broadcasts from the Internet, is more powerful than ever. This chapter covers both creative pursuits: Creating and using sound, and playing and editing movies.

## Recording Sound

The Mac includes two different sound-recording programs. First, there's the Sound control panel, which is exclusively for recording *error beeps*—the very short sound that plays whenever you click somewhere you shouldn't, or when the Mac otherwise needs your attention. Second, there's SimpleSound, which can preserve much longer recording sessions—many hours long, in fact.

### Preparing to Record

To record sound, your Mac needs a microphone. If you have an iMac or PowerBook, you're in luck: you have a microphone built into the monitor—the tiny hole in the plastic. If you have a Power Mac, you probably got the special Apple PlainTalk microphone in the package; it's designed to be perched on the front top edge of your monitor. If you have an iBook, you'll need a USB microphone adapter, such as the iMic *(www.griffintech.com),* which can accommodate any standard Radio Shack-type microphone.

Then, before you try to record sound, you need to tell the Mac which of its sound sources—its CD-ROM drive, your microphone, or whatever—it's supposed to record. Do so by opening the Sound control panel, clicking Input, and choosing External Mic or Built-In Mic from the input source pop-up menu, as appropriate.

*Tip:* If, after clicking the Record button in SimpleSound or another sound-recording program, you wind up with five seconds of nothing, it's because the Mac is trying to record from the wrong sound source. Return to the Sound control panel→Input screen and confirm the Input Source.

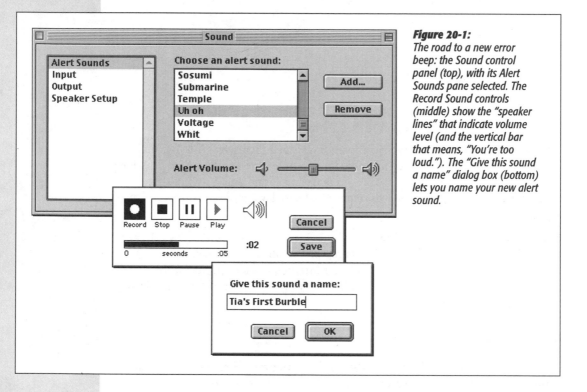

**Figure 20-1:**
*The road to a new error beep: the Sound control panel (top), with its Alert Sounds pane selected. The Record Sound controls (middle) show the "speaker lines" that indicate volume level (and the vertical bar that means, "You're too loud."). The "Give this sound a name" dialog box (bottom) lets you name your new alert sound.*

Once you've set up the Mac this way, you're ready to go.

## Recording a New Error Beep

Mac OS 9 comes with an especially generous assortment of error beeps: the spooky Submarine, the glassy Temple, and so on. But no error beep is as delightful as one that you've made yourself—of your two-year-old saying, "Nope!" for example, or your own voice saying, "Drat!"

.If that's what you want to use your microphone for, proceed like this:

1. Choose  →Control Panels→Sound.

   The Sound control panel opens, as shown in Figure 20-1. (You can also use SimpleSound, described in the next section, to create new alert sounds. Just follow the steps here, starting from step 2.)

2. Click Alert Sound, and then click Add.

   You get a special panel of recording buttons, as shown in the middle of Figure 20-1. Get ready to record your sound—when it comes to recording an error beep, you want to avoid dead space at the beginning and end of the sound at all costs. (You'll quickly discover why if you record a sound that winds up being ten full seconds long—and then the next day, the Mac tries to beep five times.)

3. Click Record, make the sound, and then click Stop as soon thereafter as possible.

   If you see animated speaker lines coming out of the tiny speaker icon, great—that's your VU (sound level) meter. It tells you that the Mac is hearing you. If you don't see these speaker lines, however, then the sound isn't getting through. The problem is most likely that your Sound control panel isn't set to record the appropriate sound source, as described at the beginning of this chapter.

   If it's impossible to get a clean sound, free of dead space—because you're recording babies or animals who refuse to perform on cue, for example—you're not out of luck. You can always edit out the dead space, as described later in this chapter.

   At this point, you can click the Play button to see what you've got. If it isn't quite what you had hoped, repeat step 3; your first take is automatically obliterated.

   When you've got something worth keeping, go on:

4. Click Save.

   Now the "Give the sound a name" box appears, as shown at the bottom of Figure 20-1.

5. Type a name for your new sound, and then click OK.

   Your newly recorded sound appears in the list of alert sounds. Click it to hear it again; if you leave it highlighted when you close the control panel, it becomes the new error beep for every mistake you make on your Mac.

*Tip:* You can remove an error beep from the list, too—click its name and then click Remove. The Mac won't let you remove Simple Beep, however; the poor thing has to have *some* means of getting your attention.

## Recording Longer Sounds with SimpleSound

Recording the occasional error sound is fine if you just want to dabble, but you're not exactly exploiting the 16-bit, 44.1-kHz, CD-quality sound circuitry built into your Macintosh. To record sounds that last longer than the feeble 10 seconds of an alert beep, you need to unleash the raw, seething power of SimpleSound.

If you've used previous versions of the Mac OS, you're probably already flicking your mental mouse up to the ✿ menu, where SimpleSound has lived for years. You won't find it there. In Mac OS 9, Apple inexplicably moved this cornerstone of the Mac's sonic empire into the Applications folder on your hard drive. (If you intend to do much sound recording, by all means restore it to the ✿ menu, as directed on page 79.)

To use this little recording utility, first see "Preparing to Record" at the beginning of this chapter. Now open SimpleSound, which at first looks like nothing more than a list of your error beeps (see Figure 20-2).

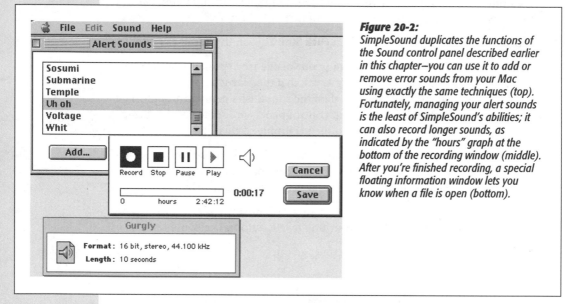

**Figure 20-2:**
*SimpleSound duplicates the functions of the Sound control panel described earlier in this chapter—you can use it to add or remove error sounds from your Mac using exactly the same techniques (top). Fortunately, managing your alert sounds is the least of SimpleSound's abilities; it can also record longer sounds, as indicated by the "hours" graph at the bottom of the recording window (middle). After you're finished recording, a special floating information window lets you know when a file is open (bottom).*

## Specifying the sound quality

To make a new sound file, start by choosing a recording quality from the Sound menu. The four options here represent different trade-offs: the choices near the top of the menu offer higher fidelity, but produce larger files on your hard drive. (The numbers provided below indicate the technical specifications of quality: for example, 16-bit sounds are more authentic than 8-bit ones, and 44 kHz is twice as good as 22 kHz.) Furthermore, while you're recording, SimpleSound must hold the sound in progress in your Mac's memory—so higher-quality recording settings also affect the maximum length of the sound you record.

Here's a breakdown of your options:

- **CD Quality.** This is the Mac's best quality. If you're an audiophile, you'll smile knowing that this option gives you 16-bit sampling, in stereo, with a 44.1 kHz sampling rate—in other words, exactly the same fidelity as a commercial audio CD.

  The file you create with a recording like this, however, takes up quite a bit of space: over 10 MB per minute of recorded sound. (You won't want to email one of *these* babies to a friend—unless it's very short or your friend has a cable modem.) Furthermore, on a Mac with 128 MB of RAM, the longest sound file you can record is about two and a half hours—certainly nothing to sneeze at, but a far cry from the hours possible at lower sound quality settings.

- **Music Quality.** Choose this command when absolute CD-level clarity isn't required, but you still want a terrific recording. In technical terms, this kind of recording gives you eight-bit samples, in mono, recorded at 22 kHz.

  As your reward for giving up some quality, you create much more compact sound files: each minute takes up only about 1.2 MB of disk space. Plus, the Mac with 128 MB of RAM can record over 21 hours of sound at this quality in a single pass. You could create your own books-on-tape with this kind of recording—like *Roots*.

- **Speech Quality.** You'll hear the difference when you try to listen to one of these sounds; they sound decidedly tinny. (And no wonder—you're getting a monophonic sound at 22 kHz that's compressed using what's called MACE three-to-one compression, which discards additional sound quality.) On the other hand, the files are fairly small on the hard drive—about 550 K for one minute—and a Mac with 128 MB of RAM can record 63 continuous hours at this quality.

- **Phone Quality.** As the name suggests, this kind of sound is quite muffled—it's about what you'd expect from a cheap answering machine or a bad phone connection. Technically speaking, it's the same scheme as Speech Quality, except that the MACE compression is applied twice as severely (6:1). Don't attempt to record music with this option—only voices—and only voices that are crisp and clear to begin with. The payoff is that these files are tiny on the hard drive—about 224 K for one minute—and the Mac can record 128 continuous hours in a single sound file. (Who needs the Watergate tapes?)

### Recording the sound

Now you're ready to record. Choose File→New. As shown in the middle of Figure 20-2, the usual Record/Stop/Pause/Play controls appear. Once again, you click Record to begin the recording, you watch the sound waves coming out of the speaker icon to make sure that the Mac is hearing you, and you click Stop as soon as possible after you're finished, so as not to record "dead air."

When you click Save, the standard Save File dialog box appears. This isn't the same procedure you get when recording a new error beep, in which the Mac automatically installs the newly recorded sound into your System file (see Figure 20-3). The System file can't accommodate these long sounds of different quality levels, so the Mac is asking you to save your new recording onto your hard drive as an independent, stand-alone file.

### Playing back SimpleSound files

After you've saved your SimpleSound file, you'll see a new icon on your desktop; you'll also see a small SimpleSound window that represents it (see Figure 20-2, bottom). When this floating window is open, you can play the sound by choosing

Sound→Play (or pressing ⌘-P). Once the sound is under way, you can interrupt it by choosing Sound→Stop (or pressing ⌘-period).

---

**Tip:** SimpleSound is perfectly content to play multiple sound files simultaneously. Open all the files you'll want to play; each is represented on your screen by a floating information window. Click the first one you want to play, and then start it playing (press ⌘-P). Switch to the next file's information window, and start *it* playing (⌘-P); and so on.

Using this technique, you can perform dialog skits with yourself, sing harmonies with yourself, and otherwise operate the world's cheapest multi-track studio.

---

### About SimpleSound files on the desktop

Unfortunately, the files SimpleSound saves aren't what are known as "System 7" sounds, which play when double-clicked. Instead, when you double-click one of these icons, SimpleSound itself opens. To hear the recording, you must choose Sound→Play.

The fact that SimpleSound doesn't create System 7 sound files may seem to be a great limitation; after all, only standard System 7 sounds in the System Folder→Startup Items folder play automatically at startup, or perform the other tricks described in the next section. Fortunately, you can edit and convert these sound files into more accessible formats; just read on.

## What to Do With Recorded Sounds

You can have a lot of fun with recorded sounds—if you know where to find them, where to put them, and how to edit them.

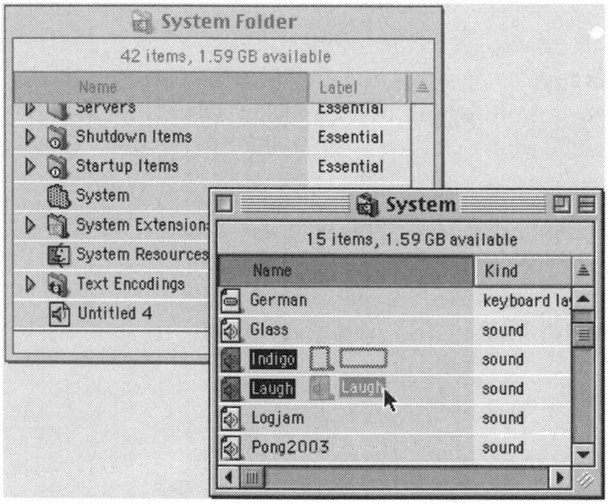

**Figure 20-3:**
*Open your System Folder, and then double-click the System suitcase file. Inside, nestled among your foreign-language keyboard-layout files, you'll find icons representing your various error beeps. You can remove one from your System file by dragging it out of this window and, for example, to the desktop; to copy it instead, press Option as you drag. You can also add new error-beep sounds by dragging sound files into this window.*

### Files in the System File

All of your error beeps, including the ones you've recorded yourself, are stored in the System file itself. To see and manipulate them, follow the instructions shown in Figure 20-3.

### Fun with System 7 sounds

Sounds that have the "System 7" file format, like the error beeps in your System file, play when double-clicked. (To cancel playback before it's finished, press ⌘-period.) That double-click-to-play feature makes them ideal for special kinds of treatment:

• **Play them at startup.** This is by far one of the most popular uses of sound files: put one into your System Folder→Startup Items folder. When you next turn on the computer, the Mac plays this sound automatically.

  Some people use this feature to leave a vocal note for themselves or for someone else who uses the computer—"Great work last night! There's a little something for you in the fridge." Others populate the Startup Items folder with sounds just for fun—"Kirk to Enterprise!"—or, more pragmatically, to let them know when the lengthy startup process has finished. (The sound in the Startup Items folder doesn't play until all of the extension loading and startup checking is complete.)

• **Play them at shutdown.** Same idea, different time: If you put a System 7 sound into the System Folder→Shutdown Items folder, the Mac plays the file whenever it's just about to shut down. Popular sound files for this purpose include funny clips from TV and movies ("She's dead, Jim!").

• **Use them as clock chimes.** As noted in Chapter 12, the Date & Time control panel can, if you wish, make your Mac chime on the hour, half-hour, or even quarter-hour. You can choose any sound you like to represent the chime sound—provided that the sound is (a) a System 7 file and (b) installed in your System file.

• **Transfer them to other people.** Because System 7 sounds play when double-clicked—unlike any other sound format—they're great for emailing to other Mac users, posting on Web sites, transferring over the network, and so on. Many a Bart Simpson sound clip proliferates via the Internet in exactly this way.

### Converting and editing sounds

You're not stuck with whatever recording you got; if there's excess silence at one end of the clip, or a few too many "uh"s and "um"s in the middle, you can edit them out. Meanwhile, you can convert any sound, including the files you've recorded with SimpleSound, into System 7 format, so that you can use the sounds for some of the purposes described above.

To pull this off, however, you need a sound-editing program. The Internet's shareware libraries are filled with sound-editing programs, but the most useful, economical, and powerful include these:

• **SoundApp.** This program is the ultimate file-conversion tool. It can open almost any kind of sound file and convert it to almost any other kind—including System

7 sound format. This program doesn't let you *edit* the sound—just convert it—but it's free. You can get it at *www.missingmanual.com,* among other places.

- **SndSampler.** This extremely powerful, yet friendly, program lets you open *and edit* virtually any sound file (see Figure 20-4). This program, too, is available at *www.missingmanual.com.*

- **QuickTime Player Pro.** You can read about QuickTime Player in the next section: it's already on your hard drive. Unfortunately, the version included with Mac OS 9 does little more than *play* sounds and QuickTime movies. But if you pay $30 for QuickTime Player *Pro,* you can both edit sound files and convert them into different sound formats. (See the sidebar on the next page.)

Unfortunately, you can't edit sound files *visually,* as you can using SndSampler—that is, QuickTime Player Pro doesn't show the actual sound waves. You do your editing simply by noting the position of the pointer that moves as the sound plays. Still, if you also intend to edit your QuickTime movies using this program, the $30 fee may be a good investment.

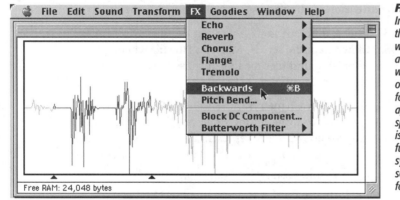

*Figure 20-4:*
*In SndSampler, you can see the entire sound file in one window; you can drag across a section of sound waves to highlight the piece of the sound, in preparation for deleting, copying, or applying one of the many special effects. The program is shareware; it's fully functional, but the honor system suggests that you send the programmer $20 for his efforts.*

## QuickTime Movies

A QuickTime movie is a digital movie—a file on your hard drive, on a CD-ROM, or on the Internet, that flashes many individual *frames* (photos) per second before your eyes, while also playing a synchronized sound track.

Because they require a great deal of computer horsepower and disk space, these movies have taken over a decade to become commonplace. Today, however, they're becoming increasingly popular—partly because they're now available on Windows PCs too, partly because computers have become very powerful, and partly because the iMac DV has made it very easy to make your *own* QuickTime movies (as described in *iMovie: The Missing Manual).* QuickTime movies now show up on Web pages, as email attachments, on CDs that people burn at home, and so on.

Still, watching a QuickTime movie isn't anything like watching a real movie—or even like watching TV. Even filling a "movie screen" three inches square with smoothly playing video requires an enormous amount of computer effort—behind the scenes, the Mac is pumping 15 or 30 color pictures *per second* off the hard drive and onto the screen. If the "movie screen" were any larger than a few inches square, many Macs wouldn't be able to pull off this stunt at all.

## QuickTime Player

Dozens of modern Mac programs can open QuickTime movies, play them back, and sometimes even incorporate them into your documents: Word, FileMaker, AppleWorks, PowerPoint, Internet Explorer, Netscape Communicator, America Online, and so on.

But the cornerstone of Mac OS 9's movie-playback software is QuickTime Player, the small program that comes in your Applications→QuickTime folder. This version, QuickTime Player 4.0 or 4.1, bears little resemblance to the Movie Player program that came with previous versions of the system software (see Figure 20-5). Still, it does what it's designed to do: show pictures, play movies, and play sounds.

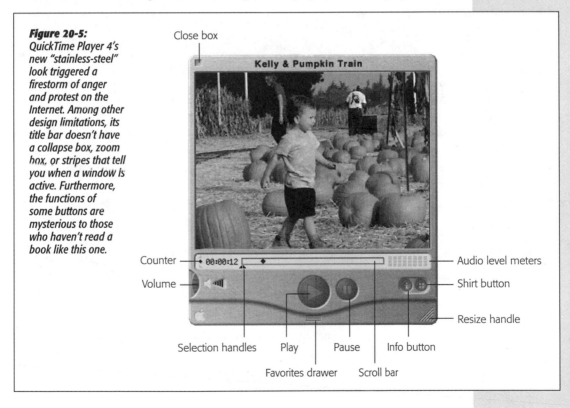

***Figure 20-5:***
*QuickTime Player 4's new "stainless-steel" look triggered a firestorm of anger and protest on the Internet. Among other design limitations, its title bar doesn't have a collapse box, zoom box, or stripes that tell you when a window is active. Furthermore, the functions of some buttons are mysterious to those who haven't read a book like this one.*

Close box

Kelly & Pumpkin Train

Counter — 00:00:12

Audio level meters

Volume — Shirt button

Resize handle

Selection handles  Play  Pause  Info button

Favorites drawer  Scroll bar

**Tip:** Like Picture Viewer, another program in the QuickTime folder, QuickTime Player can also open many graphics files—such as JPEG, GIF, TIFF, PICT, and even native Photoshop documents. You can either drag these graphics files onto the QuickTime Player icon, or—from within QuickTime Player—choose File→Open Movie. Find the graphics file you want to open, and then double-click it.

---

**FREQUENTLY ASKED QUESTION**

## QuickTime Player vs. QuickTime Player Pro

*Every time I launch QuickTime Player, I get this stupid ad about upgrading to QuickTime 4 Pro. How can I get rid of it?*

By clicking the Later button—every time you launch the program.

The permanent solution is more expensive. When you install Mac OS 9, you get a free program called QuickTime Player. It has one function, which it performs very well: to *play* QuickTime movies, both those on your Mac and those you receive over the Internet.

QuickTime Player does not, however, let you *edit* QuickTime movies—you can't cut out a scene you don't like, insert a title, and so on. There's not even a Save As or Export command—after all, if you can't make changes to the movies you're viewing, there's little call for a Save command.

For $30, however, Apple will sell you a password that turns your copy of QuickTime Player into something called QuickTime Player Pro. (To obtain this password, call 888-295-0648, or visit *www.apple.com/QuickTime.*) To record your password, choose  →Control Panels→QuickTime Settings; choose Registration from the pop-up menu, and

click Enter Registration. Your password gets stored in the System Folder→Preferences folder, in a file called QuickTime Settings; remember that fact when you upgrade your System Folder or your Mac. (You don't need a new password for QuickTime 4 if you bought one for QuickTime 3—the same serial number works.)

Once you've done so, you gain several immediate benefits—not the least of which is the permanent disappearance of the "upgrade now" advertisement. Now QuickTime Player is QuickTime Player Pro, and is capable of editing your movies, as described later in this chapter. It can also import many more sound and graphics formats, and—via the File→Export command—convert sounds, movies, and graphics into other formats.

Still, you should remain vigilant; new versions of QuickTime Player are always on the way. Since Mac OS 9 debuted, new versions of QuickTime, 4.1 and even 5, have already arrived. Check Apple's Web site for updates—or let your Software Update control panel do the work.

---

### Playing movies with QuickTime Player

You can open a movie file either by dragging it onto the QuickTime Player icon or by launching QuickTime Player and then choosing File→Open. As shown in Figure 20-5, a number of controls help you govern the movie's playback:

- **Close box.** Click to get rid of this movie window, exactly as you would any Mac window.

- **Audio level meters.** This little graph dances to indicate the relative strength of various frequencies in the sound track, like the VU meters on a stereo. If you don't see any dancing going on, then you've opened a movie that doesn't have a sound track.

- **Shirt button.** Click this peculiar button to open up a special panel of additional options, as described below.

- **Resize handle.** Drag diagonally to make the window bigger or smaller.

---

**Tip:** When you drag the resize handle, QuickTime Player strives to maintain the same *aspect ratio* (relative dimensions) of the original movie, so that you don't accidentally squish it while resizing the window. If you *want* to squish it, however—perhaps for the special effect of seeing your loved ones as they would with different sets of horizontal and vertical genes—press the Shift key as you drag.

---

If you hold the Option key while dragging, meanwhile, you'll discover that the movie frame grows or shrinks in sudden jumping factors of two—twice as big, four times as big, and so on. On slower Macs, keeping a movie at an even multiple of its original size in this way ensures smoother playback.

- **Info button.** Click here to view the copyright information, if any, for this movie. (Click the same button again to hide the copyright information.)

- **Scroll bar.** Drag the diamond to jump to a different spot in the movie.

---

**Tip:** You can also press the right and left arrow keys to step through the movie one frame at a time. If you press Option-right and -left arrow, you jump to the beginning or end of the movie. In the Pro version, Option-arrow also jumps to the beginning or ending of the selected stretch of movie, if any.

---

- **Pause button.** Actually, it's the Stop button. (Clicking it a second time, in other words, doesn't make playback resume, as clicking a true Pause button would.)

- **Favorites drawer.** Drag these ridges downward to open up the Favorites panel, as described later in this chapter.

- **Play button.** Click once to start, and again to stop. You can also press the Space bar, Return key, or ⌘-right arrow for this purpose. (Or avoid the buttons altogether and double-click the movie itself to start or stop playback.)

---

**Tip:** You can make any movie play automatically when opened, so that you don't have to click the Play button. To do so, choose Edit→Preferences→General, and turn on "Play movie from beginning when opened."

---

- **Selection handles.** These tiny black triangles appear only in the $30 Pro version; you use them to select, or highlight, stretches of footage.

- **Volume.** If you like, you can make the soundtrack louder or softer by dragging this thumbwheel up or down with your mouse. You may find it easier, however, to drag *horizontally* across the small speaker design to its right, which accomplishes the same thing. (So does pressing the up or down arrow key.)

---

• **Counter.** In hours: minutes: seconds, this display shows how far your diamond cursor has moved into the movie.

If you have QuickTime Pro, and you've highlighted a stretch of movie by dragging the tiny triangles underneath the scrollbar, you can make this counter show the start and end times of the selection. To do so, click the tiny gray triangle above and to the left, or below and to the left, of the number display.

### "Advanced" controls

When you click the shirt-button button described earlier, a sleek black "drawer" slides out of the bottom of the window, containing various additional navigation and sound controls, as shown in Figure 20-6. Here's what they do:

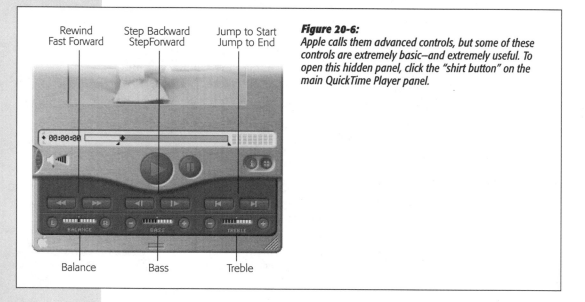

Rewind
Fast Forward

Step Backward
StepForward

Jump to Start
Jump to End

Balance

Bass

Treble

**Figure 20-6:**
*Apple calls them advanced controls, but some of these controls are extremely basic—and extremely useful. To open this hidden panel, click the "shirt button" on the main QuickTime Player panel.*

• **Rewind, Fast Forward.** When you click one of these buttons and keep the mouse button pressed, you speed through your movie, backward and forward, respectively, complete with sound. This is a terrific way to navigate your movie quickly, regardless of whether you're using QuickTime Player or QuickTime Player Pro.

• **Step Backward, Step Forward.** These two buttons make the movie advance by a single frame backward or forward, respectively. (Pressing the left and right arrow keys does the same thing.)

• **Jump to Start, Jump to End.** These buttons do exactly what they say: scroll to the beginning or end of your movie. In the Pro version, they can also jump to the beginning and ending of the selected portion of the movie, if any. All of this, in other words, is exactly the same as pressing the Option-left arrow or -right arrow keystrokes.

- **Balance.** This control works only if you have stereo speakers on your Mac. You can adjust the relative sound balance between them by clicking the L or R buttons repeatedly—or by simply dragging inside the Balance graph with the mouse.

- **Bass, Treble.** Exactly as on a stereo, you can use these controls to adjust the relative low frequencies and high frequencies of your soundtrack. (Click the – and + buttons repeatedly, or drag horizontally in the slider area.) Without external speakers attached to your Mac—and sometimes even *with* external speakers—you might not hear much difference.

### Fancy playback tricks

Nobody knows for sure what Apple was thinking when it created some of these additional features—exactly how often do you want your movie to play backward?—but here they are. Some of these features are available only in the unlocked Pro version of the QuickTime Player, as indicated below.

- **Change the screen size.** Using the Movie menu commands, such as Double Size and Fill Screen, you can enlarge or reduce the actual "movie screen" window. Making the window larger also makes the movie coarser, because QuickTime Player simply doubles the size of every dot that was present in the original. Still, when you want to show a movie to a group of people more than a few feet back from the screen, these larger sizes are perfectly effective.

- **Play more than one movie.** You can open several movies at once and then run them simultaneously. (Of course, the more movies you try to play at once, the jerkier the playback gets.)

  As a sanity preserver, QuickTime Player plays only one soundtrack—that of the movie you most currently clicked. If you really want to hear the cacophony all of the soundtracks being played simultaneously, choose Edit→Preferences→ General, and turn off "Only front movie plays sound." (The related checkbox here, "Play sound in background," controls what happens when you switch out of QuickTime Player into another program.)

---

**Tip:** If you have Player Pro, you can use the Movie→Play All Movies command to begin playback of all open movies at the same instant.

---

- **Play the movie backward.** You can play the movie *backward*—but not always smoothly—by pressing ⌘-left arrow, or by Shift-double-clicking the movie itself. (You must keep the Shift button pressed to make the backward playback continue.) There's no better way to listen for secret subliminal messages.

- **Loop the movie (Pro only).** When you choose Movie→Loop and then click Play, the movie plays endlessly from beginning to end, repeating until you make it stop.

- **Play a selection (Pro only).** When you choose Movie→Loop Back and Forth and then click Play, the movie plays to the end—and then plays *backward*, from end to beginning. It repeats this cycle until you make it stop.

---

• **Play every frame (Pro only).** If you try to play a very large movie that incorporates a high frame rate (many frames per second) on a slow Mac, QuickTime Player skips individual frames of the movie. In other words, it sacrifices smooth motion in order to maintain synchronization with the soundtrack.

But if you choose Movie→Play All Frames and then play the movie, QuickTime Player says, "OK, forget the soundtrack—I'll show you every single frame of the movie, even if it isn't at full speed." You get no sound at all, but you do get to see each frame of the movie.

## QuickTime TV (Internet Streaming)

QuickTime TV got a few raised eyebrows when Steve Jobs announced it in 1998, but few Mac fans have even noticed it since. That's too bad—it's a clever and well-implemented feature that basically lets you watch TV, or listen to the radio, as you work on your Mac—at no charge.

### Streaming video from your browser

With ever-increasing frequency, modern Web sites advertise *streaming video* events, such as Steve Jobs keynote speeches and the occasional live rock-group performance. You'll find a note on a Web page that says, for example: "Watch the live presidential debate by clicking here on October 15, 2000, at 9:00 p.m. EST."

If you do so, you'll find yourself transported once again into QuickTime Player, which connects to the appropriate Internet "station" and plays the video in its window. (You can also choose File→Open URL from within QuickTime Player to type in the Web address.)

---

**FREQUENTLY ASKED QUESTION**

## Why QuickTime TV Looks so Bad

*I was curious to try this streaming video business, but it looks absolutely terrible on the screen. The video picture changes only about once every few seconds, the audio drops out sometimes, and the picture quality is terrible. What am I doing wrong?*

You're trying to do streaming video when the Internet is still in its infancy. Audio and video require huge amounts of data, and today's phone lines simply aren't fast enough to transmit all of this information to your computer. (In fact, streaming video often looks bad even if you have a high-speed cable modem or DSL connection.) As a result, you get only snippets of it, as you discovered; QuickTime Player

does its best to create some rude imitation of actual TV, but it's not the next best thing to being there.

Until technology improves, there's only one small step you can take to make sure you're getting the best possible playback. In QuickTime Player, choose Edit→Preferences→Connection Speed. In the resulting dialog box, click the button corresponding to the kind of Internet connection you have. (If you have a cable modem, choose "112K Dual ISDN.") Some streaming video broadcasts are actually transmitted over several different "channels," geared for different connection speeds; specifying your connection speed here ensures that you'll get the best possible stream.

---

*Note:* You don't have much control when watching a live broadcast. You generally can't rewind, and you certainly can't fast forward. You may be able to pause the broadcast, but when you un-pause, you wind up at the current broadcast moment–not where you had stopped.

### Streaming video in QuickTime Player

Fortunately, if you're eager to experience the early-technology thrill of watching live Internet video, you don't have to wait until you stumble onto a broadcast advertised on a Web page. Thanks to Apple's QuickTime TV initiative, a number of TV and radio broadcasts are going on at this very moment—24 hours a day. A list of them is built right into QuickTime Player.

To access these "channels," drag downward on the ridges at the bottom center of the QuickTime Player window. (Alternately, choose Favorites→Open Favorites Drawer.) A "drawer" slides downward, revealing the list of installed channels, as shown in Figure 20-7. (The QuickTime player window must be high enough on your screen for the drawer to have room to emerge.)

**Figure 20-7:**
*The Favorites "drawer" contains icons for various Web sites that offer streaming audio and video. Click one to have a look or listen–but be prepared to wait. You can also add your favorite QuickTime movies to the drawer; if they begin with a fade-in, they look like black squares here (lower right).*

When you click one of these channel buttons, your Mac connects to the Internet and, after a while, begins to play the corresponding channel in all its flickering glory. As you'll soon discover, some of these channels are more useful than others. They fall into these categories:

- **Live TV.** You might expect that this format would be the standard for QuickTime TV—it's certainly the most exciting. Unfortunately, few channels use this approach—at this writing, only the BBC News and Bloomberg actually show you a live TV broadcast, 24 hours a day.

- **Live radio.** These channels let you listen to the radio while you work. They include the ESPN, WGBH radio, and NPR channels. (You don't get any video with these channels.)

- **Canned videos.** Most of the channels work like this: when you click the channel icon, you summon a "billboard" that offers several buttons, each of which plays one short video clip. The VH-1, HBO, Rolling Stone, Weather Channel, Disney, and Warner Records channels take this sometimes self-promotional approach. (So do the CNN and Fox News channels, but at least these videos are updated almost every day.)

- **Web-site buttons.** Some channels provide little more than links to the corresponding Web sites, which then open in your Web browser. The Nickelodeon channel and parts of others take this approach, for example.

*Tip:* Since Mac OS 9 debuted, Apple has already created additional QuickTime TV channels. You'll find a list of these new channels at *www.apple.com/quicktime/qtv.*

While you're there, don't miss the links at the bottom of the page, which direct you to over 100 more radio stations, rock videos, and other Internet QuickTime sources that aren't actually QuickTime TV channels. But they're live, streaming audio and video sources that can *become* QuickTime TV channels—that is, icons in your Favorites drawer—as soon as you choose the Favorites→Add Favorite command.

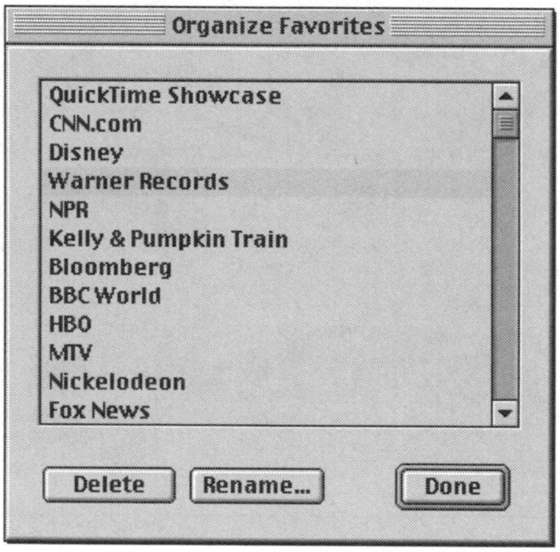

**Figure 20-8:**
*To delete one of your "favorites," click its name and then click Delete. (No confirmation box appears.) You can rename one by clicking its name and then clicking Rename. Click Done to return to the QuickTime Player window, where your changes are now in effect.*

**Organize Favorites**

QuickTime Showcase
CNN.com
Disney
Warner Records
NPR
Kelly & Pumpkin Train
Bloomberg
BBC World
HBO
MTV
Nickelodeon
Fox News

Delete   Rename...   Done

### Manipulating your Favorites

Technically, the channel icons below the QuickTime Player window are known as Favorites. You can manipulate them by choosing Favorites→Organize Favorites; a window listing your channels opens. As you can see in Figure 20-8, this list is your key to deleting or renaming the QuickTime TV channels.

You can also reorganize the locations of the Favorites icons just by dragging them around. Unfortunately, you can't drag one on top of another one in hopes of switching their locations—you wind up wiping one of them out. You must drag these icons only onto empty slots if you hope to preserve the full collection. (Pull the drawer down farther if you can't see any open slots.)

### Adding your own Favorites

Although few people have use for this feature, it's possible to add the icons of your own QuickTime movies to the Favorites drawer—not QuickTime TV channels, but actual movies on your hard drive. To do so, you can use any of these three methods:

- Drag the icon of a QuickTime movie, picture file, or sound file directly off of your desktop and into the QuickTime Player window—onto an empty slot in the Favorites drawer.

- Open a movie, picture, or sound, and then choose Favorites→Add Favorite.

- Open a movie or picture, and then drag its image out of the QuickTime Player movie screen and onto a Favorites drawer slot.

No matter which method you use, an icon for that movie, sound, or picture now appears on the Favorites drawer.

---

**FREQUENTLY ASKED QUESTION**

## All the Lonely Black Squares

*When I add one of my own movies to the Favorites drawer, how come it shows up as a black square? Makes it kinda hard to tell my movies apart, especially since there are no text labels.*

When QuickTime Player creates the icon for a movie in your Favorites drawer, it uses the *first frame* of that movie as the icon. But because so many QuickTime movies fade in from darkness at the beginning, you wind up with a lot of plain black squares.

If you have QuickTime Player Pro, you can control which frame of the movie serves as its icon. Scroll to a frame that will remind you of the movie, and then choose Movie→Set

Poster Frame. If you now add the movie to your Favorites drawer, you'll see that your favorite frame has become its icon. (You can now use the Movie→Go To Poster Frame command, meantime, to jump directly to that frame after you've been playing the movie.)

Using this trick isn't ideal, however. First, if you've already added this movie to your Favorites, you must first delete it from the drawer using the Favorites→Organize Favorites command. Second, whenever you open this QuickTime movie in the future, QuickTime Player jumps directly to the poster-frame frame instead of playing it from the beginning. You must rewind to the beginning manually (by pressing Option-left arrow, for example).

---

## Editing in QuickTime Player Pro

If you've spent the $30 to upgrade your free copy of QuickTime Player to the Pro version, you've unlocked a number of useful features. For example:

- Your Movie menu contains additional playback options, such as those described in "Fancy playback tricks" on page 383.

- When you find a QuickTime movie on a Web page, you can save it to your hard drive. (Click on the movie; hold down the mouse button until a pop-up menu appears; choose Save Movie to Disk, or the equivalent in your browser.)

- Using the commands in the Edit menu, you can view, turn on and off, add, or delete the individual *tracks* in a particular movie. (Most movies have nothing but a video track and a soundtrack. But a few specialized movies may also contain a text track, an animation track, alternate soundtracks, and so on.)

- The File→Present Movie command is extremely useful. It's the best possible way to view a QuickTime movie on your screen, in fact. When you use this command, QuickTime Player blacks out the screen, automatically makes your monitor zoom in to a lower resolution (see page 75) so that the movie fills more of the screen, and devotes all the Mac's processing power to playing the movie smoothly. (To interrupt the movie, press ⌘-period.)

---

**Tip:** The dialog box that appears when you choose File→Present Movie gives you a few other options, such as Full Screen. These movie-enlarging features are terrific when you want to show a group of people a movie, but remember that an enlarged QuickTime movie is also a jerkier and grainier one.

---

By far the most powerful feature you gain in the Pro version, however, is its ability to *edit* QuickTime movies. You can rearrange scenes, eliminate others, and save the result as a new movie with its own name. (Even QuickTime Player Pro doesn't let you *create* QuickTime movies; for that, you need a digital camcorder, a FireWire-equipped Mac, and editing software (such as iMovie, Final Cut Pro, Premiere, or EditDV). QuickTime Player Pro simply lets you edit existing movies.)

### Selecting footage

Before you can cut, copy, or paste footage, QuickTime Player needs to provide a way for you to specify *what* footage you want to manipulate. Its solution: the two tiny black triangles that begin at the left end of the scroll bar, as shown in Figure 20-9. These are the "in" and "out" points; by dragging these triangles, you're supposed to enclose the scene you want to cut or copy.

**Figure 20-9:**
To select a particular scene, drag the tiny black triangles apart until they enclose the material you want. As you drag, QuickTime Player updates the movie picture to show you where you are. The material you select is represented by a gray strip of the scroll bar.

---

*Tip:* You can gain more precise control over the selection procedure shown in Figure 20-9 by clicking one of the black triangles and then pressing the right or left arrow key. Doing so expands or contracts the selected chunk of footage by one frame at a time.

You may also prefer to select a piece of footage by Shift-clicking the Play button. As long as you hold down the Shift key, you continue to select footage; when you release the Shift key, you stop the playback, and the selected passage appears in gray on the scroll bar.

---

Once you've highlighted a passage of footage, you can proceed as follows:

- Jump to the beginning or end of the selected footage by pressing Option-right arrow or -left arrow key.

- Deselect the footage by dragging the two triangles together again.

- Play only the selected passage by choosing Movie→Play Selection Only. (The other Movie menu commands, such as Loop, apply only to the selection at this point.)

- Drag the movie picture out of the Player window and onto the desktop, where it becomes a *movie clipping* that you can double-click to view.

- Cut, copy, or clear the highlighted material using the commands in the Edit menu.

---

*Tip:* If you paste some text you've copied directly into QuickTime Player Pro, you get a two-second title (such as an opening credit) at the current frame, professionally displayed as white type against a black background. QuickTime Player automatically uses the font, size, and style of the text that was in the text clipping. You can paste a graphic image, too; once again, you get a two-second "slide" of that still image.

If you find it easier, you can also drag a text or picture *clipping file* directly from the desktop into the QuickTime Player window; once again, you get a two-second insert. (For details on text clippings, see page 138.) To make the text or picture appear longer than two seconds, drag or paste it several times in a row.

---

### Pasting footage

After cutting or copying footage, you can move it elsewhere in the movie. Specify where you want the pasted material to go by first clicking or dragging in the horizontal scroll bar, so that the black diamond marks the spot; then choose Edit→Paste. The selection triangles (and their accompanying gray scroll-bar section) appear to show you where the new footage has appeared. (That makes it easy for you to promptly choose Edit→Cut, for example, if you change your mind.)

By pressing secret keys, moreover, you gain two clever variations of the Paste command. They work like this:

- If you highlight some footage before pasting, and then press Shift, you'll find that the Edit→Paste command has changed to become Edit→Replace; whatever footage is on your clipboard now *replaces* the selected stretch of movie.

- If you highlight some footage, and then press Option, the Paste command changes to read Trim. It's like the Crop command in a graphics program (or the Crop

---

command in iMovie)—it eliminates the outer parts of the movie, the pieces that *aren't* selected. All that remains is the part you first selected.

> **Tip:** You can edit sounds exactly as you edit movies, using precisely the same commands and shortcuts. Use the File→Open command in QuickTime Player Pro to locate a sound file you want to open; it opens exactly like a QuickTime movie, except with only a scroll bar—no picture.

### Saving the finished movie

After you've finished working on your sound or movie, you can send it back out into the world in any of several ways. If you choose Edit→Save As, for example, you can specify a new name for your edited masterpiece. You must also choose one of these two options:

- **Save normally.** The term "normally" is a red herring—in fact, you'll almost never want to use this option, which produces a very tiny QuickTime file that contains no footage at all. Instead, it's something like an alias of the movie you edited—the "Save normally," edited file works only as long as the original, unedited movie remains on your hard drive. If you try to email the newly saved file, your unhappy recipient won't see anything at all.

- **Make movie self-contained.** This option produces a new QuickTime movie—the one you've just finished editing. Although it consumes more disk space, it has none of the drawbacks of the "save normally" file described above.

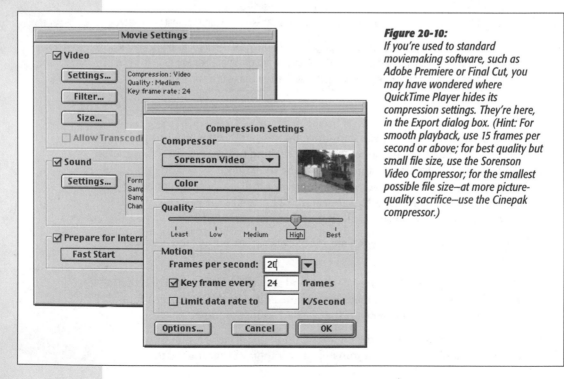

**Figure 20-10:**
*If you're used to standard moviemaking software, such as Adobe Premiere or Final Cut, you may have wondered where QuickTime Player hides its compression settings. They're here, in the Export dialog box. (Hint: For smooth playback, use 15 frames per second or above; for best quality but small file size, use the Sorenson Video Compressor; for the smallest possible file size—at more picture-quality sacrifice—use the Cinepak compressor.)*

## Exporting the finished work

Instead of using the File→Save As command, you can also use the File→Export command. The resulting dialog box offers two pop-up menus that can be very useful in tailoring your finished work for specific purposes:

- **Export:.** Using this pop-up menu, you can convert your movie to AVI (Windows movie) format, DV Stream (for use with digital-video editing programs like iMovie, Final Cut, and EditDV), Image Sequence (which produces a very large collection of individual still frames), and so on. This pop-up menu also lets you convert a sound you've been working on to (for example) AIFF, System 7, or Wave (Windows) formats.

- **Use:.** This pop-up menu lets you establish your preferences for the export format you've just specified above. For example, if you're exporting your movie as individual still frames, you can use this pop-up menu to specify the format for those individual still frames—BMP (Windows format), JPEG, and so on. If you're exporting your work as a QuickTime movie, you can specify how much QuickTime Player should compress it. (Compression makes a file much smaller, but decreases the video quality.) For example, if you intend to let people watch this movie over the Internet, you should use one of the Streaming options, which makes the movie extremely small and extremely cruddy-looking. If you plan to burn your movie onto a CD-ROM, use one of the "CD-ROM" options at the bottom of the pop-up menu.

---

**GEM IN THE ROUGH**

## QuickTime Virtual Reality

If they live to be 100, most Mac users will probably never encounter a *Quick-Time VR* movie. Yet this kind of "panorama movie" technology is built into every Mac, and the extension that enables it loads in your Mac every time you turn it on.

The trick is *finding* a QuickTime VR movie; your best bet is, as usual, the Web. (The best starting point is Apple's own QuickTime VR page, *www.apple.com/quicktime/qtvr.*)

When you open a QuickTime VR movie, you might think at first that you've simply opened a still photo; there's no QuickTime-style scroll bar, for example. The trick is do *drag* your cursor around inside the photo. Doing so rotates the "camera," permitting you to look around you in all directions.

Then try pressing the Shift key, to zoom in (move forward) as much as you like. If you go to far, the image gets too grainy. Press the Control key to zoom out (move backward).

Using the free tools on the Apple Web site, you can even make your *own* QuickTime VR panorama movies—provided you've got a camera, tripod, and a good deal of patience.

---

### *Changing the compression; applying special effects*

One of QuickTime Player's most powerful features is hidden in the Export dialog box, in a place where you might never find it. If none of the canned compression settings appeals to you, you can click the Options button in this dialog box. In the Settings dialog box that appears (see Figure 20-10), QuickTime Player Pro offers a staggering degree of control over the movie you're exporting.

When exporting a movie, for example, here's where you can specify what *compression format* you want to use, how many frames per second you want, and (by clicking Size) what dimensions you want the finished movie to have. As a bonus, you even get a Filter button that offers 14 special video effects. They let you blur or sharpen your movie, adjust the brightness or contrast, fiddle with the color balance, and so on.

Similarly, when you're exporting a sound file, the Options button lets you specify what sound quality you want, what compression method, and so on—all various ways of manipulating the trade-off between file size and sound quality.

---

***Tip:*** Once you're finished editing a QuickTime movie, rename it *startup movie* and put it into your System Folder. It plays automatically every time the computer starts up—alas, without its soundtrack.

---

# CHAPTER 21

# Speech Recognition and Synthesized Speech

Although it comes as a surprise to many Mac users, the Mac is quite talented when it comes to speech—especially if you're running Mac OS 9. Its abilities fall into two categories: reading text aloud, using a synthesized voice; and taking commands from your voice. This chapter shows you how to capitalize on both of these features.

---

**FREQUENTLY ASKED QUESTION**

## Speech Recognition vs. Dictation Software

*Can I dictate to my Mac so that it types out everything I say?*

Not without add-on software. If you really want dictation software, you need a Mac program like IBM ViaVoice (*www.ibm.com*) or Voice Power Pro (*www.voicepower-pro.com*).

By itself, Mac OS 9 still doesn't take dictation. But if your

Mac has a microphone, you can speak *commands* very effectively, instructing the Mac to open and close windows and programs, click the navigation buttons in your Web browser, and so on. That's what the Mac OS 9 feature called PlainTalk Speech Recognition actually does—and that's the feature described in this chapter.

---

## PlainTalk Speech Recognition

The Apple marketing machine may have been working too hard when it called this feature "speech recognition"—as noted in the sidebar, the Mac OS feature called PlainTalk doesn't take dictation. Instead, PlainTalk is what's known as a *command-and-control* program. It lets you open programs, trigger AppleScripts, and click menu items by speaking their names.

---

Few people use PlainTalk speech recognition, probably because it isn't installed as a part of the standard Mac OS 9 package, or perhaps because, until Mac OS 9, it didn't do very much. But if your Mac has a microphone, as described at the beginning of the previous chapter, PlainTalk is worth at least a 15-minute test drive; it may become a part of your work routine forever.

## Installing PlainTalk Speech Recognition

To install the speech recognition software, follow these steps:

1. **Insert your Mac OS 9 CD. Double-click the Mac OS Install icon. When the welcome screen appears, click Continue.**

   Now you're asked to specify what hard drive you want to receive the installation. Almost always, the Destination Disk is your regular built-in hard drive.

2. **Click Select.**

   A small dialog box appears, letting you know that you already have Mac OS 9 installed.

3. **Click Add/Remove; on the next screen, scroll down to turn on the checkbox called English Speech Recognition. Click Start, and then click Continue.**

   When the installation is complete, you'll be asked to restart the computer; do so.

## Your First Conversation with the Mac

When the Mac restarts, you'll see a few new windows on the screen (Figure 21-1). They include the Feedback window, the Speakable Commands list, and the Speech page of the Mac's online help.

### The Feedback window

This is the window showing the cartoon of a young woman. The word *Esc* just below her head indicates the "listen" key—the key you're supposed to hold down when you want the Mac to respond to your voice. (You wouldn't want the Mac listening all the time—especially when you said, for example, "Hey, it's cold in here. *Close the window.*" Therefore, the Mac comes ready to listen to you only when you're pressing that key.)

You can specify a different key, if you wish, or eliminate the requirement to press a key altogether, as described in the next section.

When you start talking, you'll also see the Mac's interpretation of what you said written out here.

---

**Tip:** The Feedback window doesn't need to occupy as much space as it does. By clicking its Zoom box, you can collapse it down to just the cartoon head, saving a lot of horizontal space. You can also click its collapse box to shrink it vertically.

If you like having the visual feedback, though, you might simply prefer a less space-consuming "character" to appear here. The secret is to open the Speech control panel, choose Options→Feedback, and choose Character→Lights. The Lights "character" has no face at all, and makes the Feedback window very small.

---

## The Speakable Commands window

Here's the most important single fact to understand about PlainTalk speech recognition: the only commands it understands are listed either in the Speakable Commands window, which you can't edit, or in the ⬛→Speakable Items submenu, which you *can* edit. (More on making up your own commands in a moment.)

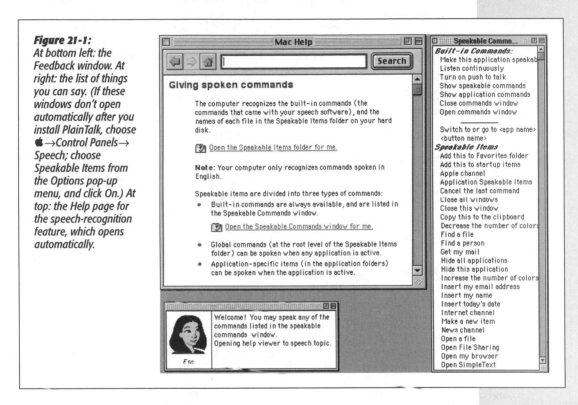

**Figure 21-1:**
*At bottom left: the Feedback window. At right: the list of things you can say. (If these windows don't open automatically after you install PlainTalk, choose ⬛→Control Panels→Speech; choose Speakable Items from the Options pop-up menu, and click On.) At top: the Help page for the speech-recognition feature, which opens automatically.*

Especially when you start using PlainTalk, the Speakable Commands window is handy: it offers a complete list of every *built-in* command (that is, those not represented by icons in the Speakable Items folder, described in this chapter). As you can see, some of them are extremely useful, and represent shortcuts that would take several steps if you had to perform them manually. Here are a few examples:

- **Switch to AppleWorks.** Here's one of the best uses of the speech-recognition program: you can launch, or switch to, one of your programs, just by using this command. (AppleWorks is just one example.)

---

**Tip:** The Mac can open two kinds of programs using this command: those listed in your ⬛→Recent Applications submenu, and those in your Speakable Items folder, as described below.

---

- **Add this to startup items.** Puts an alias of the highlighted icon into your System Folder→Startup Items folder, as described on page 183.

- **Close all windows.** Closes every desktop window instantly.

- **Take a window picture.** Turns your cursor into a small + symbol, so that you can drag across a rectangular area of your screen. When you release the mouse, the Mac creates a graphics file on your hard drive called Picture 1. As described in Chapter 19, this trick is useful when, for example, you want to illustrate a computer book.

- **Insert my email address.** Works in whatever program you're using. (The Mac gets your email address from the information you provided in the Internet control panel.)

- **Quit all applications.** Saves you the trouble of switching into each program and choosing File→Quit.

- **Show me what to say.** Opens the Speakable Commands window.

- **What day is it?** Tells you the date.

- **Tell me a joke.** Begins a pathetic/funny knock-knock joke. You've got to play along, providing the "who's there?" and "so-and-so *who?*" answers.

The commands listed in this window aren't the only ones you can speak, of course. You'll find out how to create new commands of your own later in this section.

### Speaking to the Mac

When you decide you're ready to try talking to your computer, position the microphone. If it's the gray PlainTalk microphone that comes with Power Macs, perch it on the top of your monitor, with the Apple logo facing you. (Apple recommends that you place it between one and three feet from your mouth.) If it's a headset microphone, make sure it's plugged in. If your Mac has a built-in microphone, such as the iMac or PowerBook, you can use PlainTalk, but its recognition may not be as accurate.

In any case, finish up by opening the  →Control Panels→Speech control panel; choose Options→Listening, and use the Microphone pop-up menu to specify which microphone you'll be using (if you have a choice).

Now you're ready to begin. While pressing the Esc key (if that's still the one identified in the Feedback window), begin speaking. Just speak normally and clearly; don't exaggerate or shout. Try one of the commands in the Speakable Commands list, for example—perhaps "What time is it?" If the Mac doesn't understand you, try a couple of more times, and try slowing down. (And if the Feedback window doesn't show animated sound waves, indicating that the Mac is hearing you, something's wrong with your microphone setup. Open the  →Control Panels→Sound control panel again, and confirm that the Input source—your microphone—is selected correctly.)

## Customizing Speech Recognition

You can tailor the speech-recognition feature in two ways—by adjusting the way it looks and operates, and by adding new commands to its vocabulary.

### Changing when the Mac listens

Early experimentation quickly showed Apple's speech engineers that having the micro-phone "open," listening full-time, was an invitation for disaster. Everyday phone con-versations, office chatter, and throat-clearings completely bewildered the software, trig-gering random commands or puzzled expressions from the little cartoon character.

Therefore, you must explicitly *tell* the Mac when you're addressing it. When you first install the speech-recognition feature, the Mac expects you to get its attention by press-ing a key when you speak, such as the Esc key at the upper-left corner of your keyboard.

---

*Tip:* You can change the key you hold down when you want the Mac to listen. To do so, choose  →Control Panels→Speech; choose Options→Listening. Click in the Key(s) field, and then press the keyboard key you'd prefer to use. Your choices are Esc, tilde (~), Delete, F5 through F15, or the keys on your numeric keypad—with or without one or more of the Shift, Control, or Option keys.

---

If you'd rather not have to press some key whenever you want the computer's atten-tion, click the other option in this box, "Key(s) toggle listening on and off" (see Figure 21-2). Now you must get the computer's attention by speaking its name—which you type into the Name box—before each command. For example, you might say, "Computer, open AppleWorks," or "Hal, what day is it?" (The "push to talk" key, in this case, serves as a master on/off switch for the Mac's listening mode.)

---

*Note:* This method of getting the computer's attention is generally less reliable than the push-a-key-to-talk system. *Especially* if you name the computer Hal; although that's hilarious in theory, multisyllable names work better in practice.

---

Using the "Name is" pop-up menu, meanwhile, you can specify how big your win-dow of opportunity is:

- **Before every command.** When this option is selected, nothing you say is inter-preted as a command unless you say the computer's name first, as in, "*Macintosh, switch to Microsoft Word.*"

- **15 seconds after last command, 30 seconds after last command.** Apple offers these options for those occasions when you want to issue several commands in a row, and would feel foolish saying, "Computer, close all windows. Computer, empty the trash. Computer, switch to AppleWorks." When you turn on this op-tion, you can say the computer's name just once; all commands that you issue in the next 15 or 30 seconds "belong to" that first salutation.

---

*Tip:* If you're not using the push-to-talk method, you can still turn speech recognition off temporarily by saying, "Turn on push to talk." (Now the Mac listens to you only when you're pressing the designated key. Your Feedback cartoon character, meanwhile, makes it clear that the Mac isn't really paying attention to you—by sleeping, reading the paper, daydreaming, and so on.) When you want to return to listening-all-the-time mode, say, "Listen continuously."

---

Finally, note that the Speech control panel also lets you turn off PlainTalk recognition completely. From the Options pop-up menu, choose Speakable Items, and then click Off (see Figure 21-2). (Turning off PlainTalk doesn't affect other speech features of the Mac, including voice passwords and the text-to-speech feature described at the end of this chapter.)

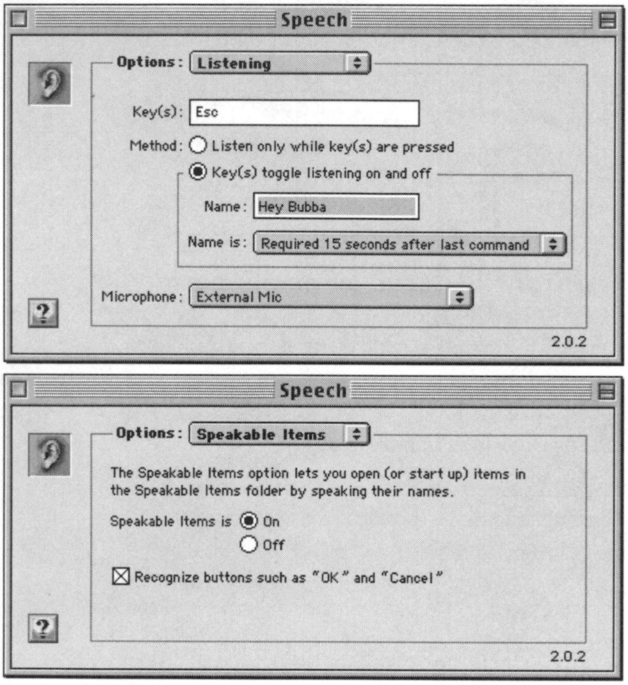

**Figure 21-2:**
*Top: If you turn on "Key(s) toggle listening on and off," then you don't have to press a key to make the Mac listen. (Instead, pressing the designated key turns the speech-recognition feature on or off completely.) In the Name field, type the name you want the Mac to listen for as it monitors the sound from your mike. Bottom: Turn off listening altogether using this On/Off control.*

### Changing the Feedback character

Another set of options in the Speech control panel governs the little cartoon character in the Feedback window. Choose Options→Feedback to see these choices.

- **Character.** You have a choice of nine different cartoon characters, each with basic animations, and most with an obvious lineage to popular TV. There's Connie (Chung), Sally (Jessy Raphael), Raymond (Dustin Hoffman in *Rain Man*), Phil (Hartman)—and Vincent (van Gogh), the severed ear—for example. (See Figure 21-3 for some illustrations.)

- **Speak text feedback.** Sometimes the Feedback window shows you a message of its own—when you use the "Empty the Trash" command, for example, text in the Feedback window may inform you that a locked item prevents the emptying. The Mac generally reads this text aloud to you; turn this checkbox off if you'd rather have the Mac be silent. (You can specify which of the Mac's 18 voices you want your character to use, too, by choosing Options→Voice in the Speech control panel. There's nothing to stop you from associating a male voice with a female Feedback character, and so on.)

- **Recognized.** The Mac generally makes a sound whenever it recognizes something you've said. Use this pop-up menu to control which of your built-in beeps you want it to use—or choose None.

**Figure 21-3:**
*Some say Apple's programmers have been heavily influenced by "Saturday Night Live" and other pop TV shows. How can you look at Pat, for example, without seeing the androgynous character from the SNL skit?*

### Improving the PlainTalk vocabulary

As you'll soon discover, PlainTalk has an extremely limited vocabulary—in fact, in addition to the canned set of Speakable Commands, it understands *only* the names of the icons in your System Folder→Apple Menu Items→Speakable Items folder. When it comes to offering you an enhanced vocabulary, the software really can't do anything more than double-click an icon—such as a document, program, folder, or alias—for you.

---

***Tip:*** Actually, PlainTalk can do *one* other thing for you—it can click button names like OK, Yes, No, Quit, and Cancel. To turn on this feature, choose  →Control Panels→Speech. In the Speech control panel, choose Options→Speakable Items. Turn on the checkbox called "Recognized buttons" (see Figure 21-2).

---

At first, you might imagine that this limitation means that PlainTalk can do little more than open programs or documents—"Open AppleWorks," "Open Internet Explorer," and so on. And indeed, that's one of PlainTalk's primary functions. By putting an alias of the favorite document or program into the Speakable Items folder, you've just taught PlainTalk to recognize its name, and to open it for you when you so command. (You can name these icons anything you want; you can also rename the starter set that Apple provides.)

---

***Tip:*** PlainTalk can do the dirty work of putting favorite icons' aliases into the Speakable Items folder for you. Just highlight an icon in a desktop window and then say, "Make this speakable."

---

Although PlainTalk commands can't do much more than double-click icons, AppleScript icons are among them—a fact that dramatically expands PlainTalk's repertoire. (See Chapter 10 for instructions on using AppleScript.) If you choose  →Speakable Items, you'll discover that most of the built-in speakable-item icons are, in fact, AppleScript icons (which look like little scrolls). As it turns out, all of the other ones—displaying a little ear—are based on AppleScripts, too. The point is that you can make PlainTalk do almost anything you want, especially in the Finder, simply by creating AppleScripts and putting them into the Speakable Items folder.

---

*Tip:* With a little bit of add-on software, PlainTalk can pull down menus for you, and type out predefined sentences or paragraphs of canned text. You could say, for example, "sign this" to have PlainTalk type out *Yours very sincerely, Jacob C. McGillicuddy, DDS.*

To make all this possible, you need a free PlainTalk add-on called ListenDo. It's available for download from *www.macspeech.com.*

---

### Application-specific commands

Most of the pre-installed PlainTalk commands work in any program. You can say, for example, "Find a file" to launch Sherlock from within any program.

In Mac OS 9, however, you can create commands that work only in a specific program. As proof, look in your Speakable Items folder—there you'll find a folder called Application Speakable Items. And inside *that* folder are individual folders for each of the programs you might use—Internet Explorer, Outlook Express, the Finder, and so on. These commands work only when you're using those particular programs. (If you can't, or don't like to, use your hands when Web surfing, for example, you might enjoy the pre-defined browser commands like Go Back, Go Forward, Page Down, and so on.)

If you get good at AppleScript, you can create your own application-command folders in the Speakable Items→Application Speakable Items folder. Follow these steps:

1. **Launch the program for which you want to create special commands.**

   Make sure PlainTalk is on and listening.

2. **Say, "Make this application speakable."**

   The Mac creates a folder for the program in the Speakable Items folder.

3. **Drag the AppleScripts you've created into the newly created Speakable Items→ application folder.**

Of course, not every program is equally suitable to being voice-controlled—since PlainTalk is based on AppleScript, only programs that are AppleScriptable (see Chapter 10) thrive with this treatment.

---

*Tip:* If you give an application-specific icon the exact same name as one of the global commands, the Mac executes the application-specific one—if that program is running.

---

### PlainTalk tips, tricks, and troubleshooting

When you're creating new commands, keep this advice in mind:

- The Mac understands longer icon names better than shorter ones. "Save the file" works better than "Save."

- If the name of an icon includes an acronym (such as *FTP)*, put spaces between the letters (F T P), if you'll be pronouncing them as individual letters.

- PlainTalk ignores any digits and punctuation in the Speakable Items icons' names. To open the Date & Time control panel, for example, you can say either "Open Date and Time" or, if you're in a hurry, "Open Date Time."

- You can precede the name of something in your Speakable Items folder with the word "Open." PlainTalk doesn't care—"open Excel" and "Excel" do the same thing.

- PlainTalk treats "this " and "these" identically (as in, "Add this to startup items").

If you can't seem to make the speech recognition feature work, consider this checklist:

- If your Feedback cartoon character doesn't emit sound-wave lines when you're speaking, something's wrong with your microphone arrangement. Revisit the Speech control panel, and make sure you've selected the correct microphone. Also make sure you've plugged the microphone into the correct jack on the back or side of the computer.

- Make sure you're pressing the correct key (if you're using the push-to-talk method), or speaking the name of the computer before each command (if not).

- Make sure you're saying the name of the working command, as listed either in the Speakable Commands window (which appears when you say "What can I say?") or the  →Speakable Items list.

- Be aware of what program you're in. Remember that application-specific commands don't work when you're not in those programs.

## PlainTalk Text-to-Speech

So far in this chapter, you've read about the Mac's listening ability. But the conversation doesn't have to be one-way. It's even easier to make the Mac talk.

In fact, the Mac can read almost anything on your screen, using your choice of 18 synthesizer voices. You hear it—the Mac speaks with a twangy, charmingly Norwegian accent—coming out of your speaker, reading whatever is on the screen in SimpleText, AppleWorks, America Online, Microsoft Word, FileMaker Pro, and several other programs.

Unlike the speech recognition feature, this talent doesn't require you to install anything special; the software is part of the standard Mac OS 9 installation. In fact, you may remember having been startled by the Mac's voice the very first time a dialog box appeared on the screen in Mac OS 9—this version of the operating system comes set to read these dialog boxes aloud, in order to get your attention.

**Note:** If your Mac won't talk, it's probably because you or somebody else turned off the necessary extensions and control panels in your System Folder. You need the Speech control panel, plus the extensions called Speech Manager, MacinTalk 2, and MacinTalk Pro. See Chapter 12 for more on extensions and control panels.

## Setting Up the Mac's Voice

To configure the way the Mac talks, choose ⌘→Control Panels→Speech. In the Speech dialog box, choose Options→Voice. As you can see in Figure 21-4, you can control which of the Mac's 18 voices you want your computer to use, as well as how fast it should speak.

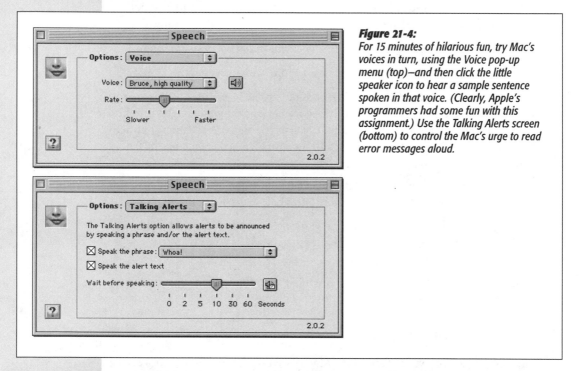

**Figure 21-4:**
*For 15 minutes of hilarious fun, try Mac's voices in turn, using the Voice pop-up menu (top)—and then click the little speaker icon to hear a sample sentence spoken in that voice. (Clearly, Apple's programmers had some fun with this assignment.) Use the Talking Alerts screen (bottom) to control the Mac's urge to read error messages aloud.*

---

**FREQUENTLY ASKED QUESTION**

## High-Quality Voices

*Why do Agnes, Bruce, and Victoria appear in my Speech control panel with alternate, "high quality" versions?*

These are the so-called MacinTalk Pro voices. As a little experimentation will show you, they sound much better and more natural than their non-high-quality versions. The trade-off is that they take up much more memory (1.5 MB) when you're using the speech features of your Mac—which was a much bigger drawback in 1990 than it is today, where the least expensive Mac comes with 64 MB of memory.

*Tip:* As with the other aspects of Mac OS speech, this one is filled with whimsical touches. Four of the voices, as it turns out, *sing* rather than speaking. (They're Good News, which sings to the tune of "Pomp and Circumstance," otherwise known as the Graduation March; Bad News, which sings to the tune of the Chopin Prelude in C minor, better known as the Funeral March; Cellos, which sings to the tune of Grieg's "Peer Gynt" suite; and Pipe Organ, which sings to the tune of the Alfred Hitchcock TV-show theme.)

In other words, these voices sing whatever words you type to those melodies. (To hear the melody in its entirety, don't use any punctuation.)

## Where to Use Text-to-Speech

Not every program on the Mac can speak. And not every program that *can* speak includes an obvious way to produce the voices. Here are a few tips to get you started.

### Error messages

You don't have to do much to hear this example of the Mac's speech feature—as already noted, it happens automatically whenever a Mac OS 9 error message appears on the screen. You can control the specifics of this behavior in the Speech control panel—choose Options→Talking Alerts to see the controls shown in Figure 21-4. There you'll find options like these:

- **Speak the phrase.** Use this pop-up menu to specify what utterance the Mac speaks before the actual error message—for example, "*Shoot!* The Trash could not be emptied" or "*It's not my fault!* The document could not be printed." (Yes, "It's not my fault!" is actually one of the choices here.) If you don't want any such preamble, turn off the checkbox.

  For added hilarity, choose "Next in the list" or "Random from the list" from this pop-up menu, so that you never hear the same expletive twice. Better yet, choose Edit Phrase List to open a dialog box where you can make up your own phrases of frustration. (Apple Computer, Inc. is not liable for any trouble you may get into with people in neighboring cubicles.)

- **Speak the alert text.** If you turn off this checkbox, the Mac won't read the actual error message at all. (That is, if you turn on "Speak the phrase" but leave this checkbox off, the Mac will shout, for example, "Oh dear!" to get your attention, but will leave it up to you to read the actual message on the screen.)

- **Wait before speaking.** The entire purpose of the Talking Alerts feature is ostensibly to get your attention if you've wandered away, mentally or physically, from your Mac, when there's some urgent problem that, if left undetected, could get you into trouble. (A 500-page printout brought to its knees by a paper jam comes to mind.)

  In other words, if you're still sitting in front of your Mac, you may not need the Mac to speak to get your attention; you'll simply read the message on the screen. That's why you can set this slider to make the Mac wait, after the error message appears, for up to a minute before trying to flag you with its voice. (Click the small icon above the word "Seconds" to get a feeling for how long the Mac will delay before speaking.)

## SimpleText

SimpleText is by far the most direct route to hearing your Mac speak. It includes a Sound menu with a Speak All command (when no text is selected) or a Speak Selection command (when you've highlighted some text). There's nothing more to it—choose Sound→Voices to specify the voice you want to listen to, and then choose Sound→Speak to hear your text read back to you.

## AppleWorks 5

Most people miss out on AppleWorks' ability to speak, because the feature is buried. You must add a special button to one of your button bars in order to initiate it. Follow these steps:

1. **By clicking the downward-pointing arrow button at the left end of a button bar, choose Edit Button Bars.**

   The Edit Button Bars dialog box appears.

2. **Click one of the button bars, click Modify, and then choose Word Processing from the Button Category pop-up menu.**

   A special set of icons appears.

3. **Click the tiny "talking Mac" icon, and then click Add.**

   This icon looks like a tiny Mac Plus with a speech balloon coming out of its mouth.

4. **Click OK.**

   The icon you clicked now appears at the right end of the button bar. Click it to hear your Mac speak any highlighted piece of text, using whatever voice you've most recently selected in the Speech control panel.

## AppleWorks 6

1. **Choose Edit→Preferences→Button Bar.**

   The Customize Button Bars dialog box appears.

2. **Scroll down to the Word Processing triangle; click it. Scroll down even more, until you see the Speak Text button. Drag it out of the dialog box and onto the button bar. Click Done.**

   The icon you clicked now appears on the button bar whenever a word-processing document (or box) is open. Click it to hear your Mac speak any highlighted piece of text, once again using the voice you've selected in the Speech control panel.

## Microsoft Word 98

As in AppleWorks, you must manually set up your copy of Word to speak. To do so, insert the Microsoft Office CD-ROM. Open the Value Pack folder; double-click the Value Pack Installer. In the Value Pack Installer checkbox screen, click Word Speak, and then click Install.

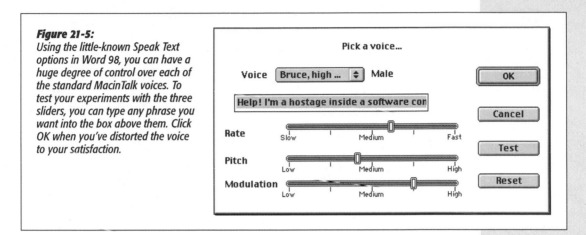

When the installation is over, your copy of Word has two new commands in the Tools menu: Pick Voice and Speak Selection. As you can see in Figure 21-5, Word offers far more control over the standard MacinTalk voices than any other program—you can actually change the pitch and modulation (sing-songiness) for each voice.

Moreover, when you finally use the Speak Selection command, you don't just hear your text read aloud—you get a visual sound-wave display, too. Don't say Microsoft never did anything for you.

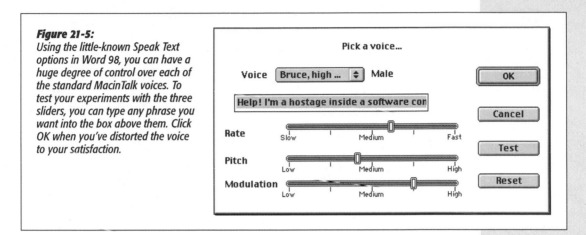

**Figure 21-5:**
*Using the little-known Speak Text options in Word 98, you can have a huge degree of control over each of the standard MacinTalk voices. To test your experiments with the three sliders, you can type any phrase you want into the box above them. Click OK when you've distorted the voice to your satisfaction.*

Pick a voice...

Voice [ Bruce, high ... ] Male        [ OK ]

[ Help! I'm a hostage inside a software cor ]        [ Cancel ]

Rate    Slow      Medium      Fast        [ Test ]

Pitch   Low       Medium      High        [ Reset ]

Modulation   Low   Medium   High

### FileMaker Pro

You can use the Speak script command to build speech features into a FileMaker database. You can read about this script command in FileMaker's built-in help; it's worth noting, however, that you can have it speak either a canned phrase or the contents of a database field. You can also specify which voice you want to use.

---

**Tip:** Regardless of which program you use for speech, you can use four special codes to govern inflection. Add a comma for a large pause in the speaking, a single quote (') for a shorter pause, and the peculiar clause *[[emph +]]* or *[[emph –]]* to give more or less stress to the following syllable. (There's a space before the + or – symbol in that phrase.)

Finally, you can control how fast the Mac talks by inserting a double-bracketed comment like this one into your text: *[[rate 160]] I'm in no hurry!* The number in double brackets can be between 160 and 210; the speed control is subtle, but effective.

---

6

# Part Six:
# Appendixes

# Mac OS 9, Menu by Menu

M ac OS 9 includes Balloon Help (described at the end of this appendix), which serves admirably in identifying the primary menu functions in Mac OS 9.

But you didn't buy this book because you wanted to use online help. Here's a plain-English rundown of the Mac OS 9 menu commands (those that aren't described in other chapters of this book).

## Apple (🍎) Menu

For complete documentation of these commands and programs, see Chapter 5.

## File Menu

Most of these commands operate on a *selection*—that is, you're supposed to highlight an icon, or several icons, before using the menu.

### New Folder

Creates a new folder, called *untitled folder,* inside the open window (or, if no window is open, on the desktop). Keyboard equivalent: ⌘-N (for *New folder*).

### Open

Opens a highlighted document, program, folder, or disk, exactly as though you had double-clicked its icon. Keyboard equivalent: ⌘-O.

## Print

Sends the highlighted document to your printer, after first opening the necessary application (such as your word processor) and offering you the Print dialog box, where you can specify how many copies you want. For more on this "print from the desktop" feature, see the end of Chapter 19. Keyboard equivalent: ⌘-P.

## Move To Trash

Puts the highlighted file icon (or icons) into the Trash. The Mac is now ready to delete it forever (when you choose Special→Empty Trash). (This command doesn't operate on disk icons—only files and folders.)

Actually, what's more useful than this command is its keyboard equivalent, ⌘-Delete. Using the keyboard shortcut saves you a long and awkward mouse drag across your monitor. Note that, to prevent accidental trashings, the Mac permits you to throw away icons only from the active (frontmost) window. If you double-click a folder icon on the desktop, for example, the Move To Trash command doesn't work—because that folder's window has now been moved in front of the icon itself. Only if you then click the desktop (or press ⌘-up arrow), thus making it active, can you use the Move To Trash command or its keyboard shortcut. Keyboard equivalent: ⌘-Delete.

## Close Window

Closes the active (frontmost) window, exactly as though you had clicked the Close box in its upper-left corner. Keyboard equivalent: ⌘-W (for *Window*).

## Get Info

Opens the Get Info window for the highlighted icon. If you've highlighted multiple icons, you get multiple Get Info windows. Keyboard equivalent: ⌘-I (for *Info*).

The Get Info window itself looks different, and the File→Get Info submenu offers different options, depending on the kind of icon you selected. The File→Get Info submenu may offer one, two, or three commands. (Instead of using one of these submenu commands, you can also choose File→Get Info and then choose from the pop-up menu in the Get Info window itself, as shown in Figure A-1.) These commands may include:

- **General Information.** Available for every kind of icon. Here's where you can view (and edit) the name of the icon, see statistics about its size, creation date, most recent change date, label, and so on. If you've highlighted a disk, this info window shows you its capacity and how full it is; if you highlighted the Trash, you see how many items are in it; and so on.

  Here, too, you can type in random comments for your own reference, as shown in Figure A-1. And by pasting over the icon picture in the upper-left corner of the window, you can replace the picture itself used for this icon—a technique described on page 32.

- **Sharing.** Available for folders, disks, and programs (not documents). This window lets you specify who, on your office network, can open and root through this particular folder or disk—or, if the icon represents an application, who can send AppleScript commands to it over the network. See Chapter 16 for complete details on setting up folder or disk network privileges, and Chapter 10 for details on sending AppleScript commands.

- **Memory.** Available for applications only. Lets you view and adjust a program's memory appetite, as described in Chapter 7.

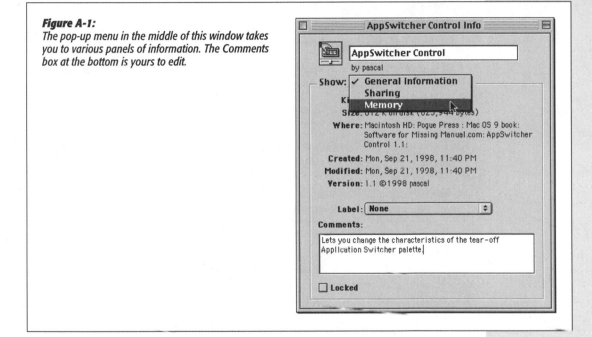

**Figure A-1:**
*The pop-up menu in the middle of this window takes you to various panels of information. The Comments box at the bottom is yours to edit.*

## Label

As noted on page 40, the submenus of this command let you apply a text and color label to various icons for the purposes of categorizing them. (If "Essential," "Hot," and "In Progress" aren't exactly what you want as the labels for your icons, choose Edit→Preferences to edit them.)

## Duplicate

Makes a copy of the highlighted icon, exactly as though you had Option-dragged it into a different window. The Mac adds the word "copy" to the end of the file's name to distinguish it from the original.

## Make Alias

An alias is a duplicate of a file's *icon*—not the file itself—which you can double-click to open the original, in effect permitting you to have one file in more than one place on your hard drive. (More on aliases on page 37.) This command creates an alias of a highlighted icon, exactly as though you had ⌘-Option-dragged it.

## Add To Favorites

Creates, in the System Folder→Favorites folder, an alias of whatever icon you've highlighted. That icon's name instantly appears, as a result, in the  →Favorites submenu. For details on this feature, see page 87.)

## Put Away

This command has three functions:

- If you've dragged an icon out of a window and onto the desktop, this command puts the icon back into the folder it came from.

- This command takes a highlighted icon out of the Trash and puts it back into whatever folder it last occupied.

- This command ejects a disk or CD whose icon you've highlighted.

---

*Tip:* One of the most useful aspects of Put Away is its ability to fling multiple highlighted icons back to their respective starting points—even if that means filing different icons into different windows on different disks. For example, you might decide to print four documents, all of which are in different folders. Drag each one to the desktop; highlight all four; choose File→Print. When the printing is over, choose File→Put Away; the Mac moves them back into their original folders, none the worse for the wear.

---

## Encrypt

New to Mac OS 9, this command brings up the Apple File Security window, into which you're supposed to type a password (twice) for the file icon you've highlighted. (You can password-protect only files, not folders or disks.)

If you then click Encrypt, the Mac encodes the file, password-protecting it, using an ultra-secure coding method that even Apple can't break. (You'll also be offered the chance to add this password to your Keychain, as described in Chapter 16.) More on file encryption in Chapter 2.

## Find

This command summons Sherlock 2, the file- and Internet-searching program described in Chapter 15. When the program opens, it's ready to search for the names of files on your hard drive.

## Search the Internet

This command, too, summons the Sherlock 2 program described in Chapter 15—but this time, it opens configured to search the Internet for a phrase you type.

## Show Original

This command is available only if you've highlighted an *alias* (see page 37). It highlights the original icon, the one from which you made the alias, wherever it may be on your hard drive, in whichever window happens to contain it.

## Page Setup

Brings up the Page Setup command described in Chapter 19, so that you can specify (for example) what kind of paper you've put into your printer.

## Print Desktop/Print Window

Prints a copy of the current Finder window; on the printout, you'll see whatever icons you can see in the window on the screen. If no window is open, this command says Print Desktop, and prints a copy of the entire desktop, even if doing so requires several sheets of paper.

As noted in Chapter 19, this command represents a quick, handy way to test your printer without having to launch a program and type up a fake document just so you'll have something to print.

# Edit Menu

When you work in, say, your word processor, you use the Edit menu quite a bit—its Cut, Copy, and Paste commands are very useful. In the Finder, however, these commands rarely come in handy. The Preferences command in this menu, on the other hand, is useful indeed.

## Undo

This command is rarely available; it can't undo moving an icon, creating a folder, emptying the Trash, and so on. In fact, it can undo only one fairly obscure action: typing or pasting while editing an icon's name. (See page 31 for more on the process of renaming icons.)

## Cut, Copy, Paste, Clear

Like Undo, these commands do very little in the Finder. (See Chapter 6 to find out how these commands are useful in other programs.) You can't copy and paste files themselves from one window to another, as you can in, for example, Microsoft Windows.

These commands *are* operational when you're editing file names, which is sometimes useful—for example, if you're renaming a long list of icons *Case History 12, Case History 13,* and so on, you could save yourself a lot of typing by pasting "Case History" and then manually typing the numbers.

You can also use these commands when replacing a file's icon (by using the Get Info window as described on page 32).

***Tip:*** After highlighting a group of icons, you can use Edit→Copy, switch to a word processor, and then choose Edit→Paste to produce a neat list of all the icons' names.

The Clear command is similar to Cut—it removes a selected chunk of text or graphics—but doesn't put the removed material on the invisible Clipboard, as Cut would. In other words, you can't then paste what you've removed.

## Select All

Highlights all of the icons in the open window (or, if no window is open, on the desktop).

If you're editing an icon's name, and your cursor is blinking in the renaming rectangle, this command highlights the entire file name instead.

## Show Clipboard

Opens a window that reveals whatever material you've most recently cut or copied. (You can achieve the same effect, by the way, by double-clicking the Clipboard icon in the System Folder.)

## Preferences

Opens the Finder Preferences dialog box, as shown in Figure A-2. This dialog box offers three tabs that govern the way the Finder works:

- **General.** Lets you turn on or off Simple Finder (see the end of Chapter 17) and the spring-loaded folders feature. Also lets you choose between two underlying invisible grid spacings for icons you've neatened using the View→Clean Up and View→Arrange commands (see page 18).

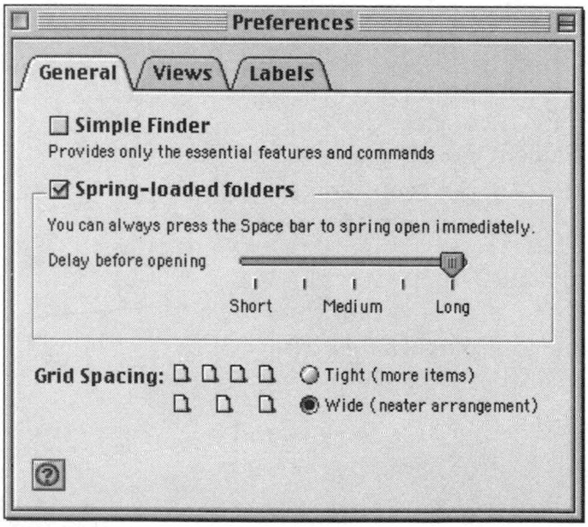

***Figure A-2:***
*The Edit→Preferences command summons this dialog box. Use the three tabs to adjust several miscellaneous Finder-related settings; the General tab, for example, governs the Simple Finder command, the grid spacing (used for icons when you apply the View→Clean Up command), and so on.*

- **Views.** Lets you define what you want to be the *standard* characteristics for list, icon, and button views. For example, you can specify which columns of information (size, date, and so on) you want to see in list views; what icon size you want to see in icon views; and so on. (Use the pop-up menu to specify which view you want to edit.) For details on these options, see Chapter 1.

  Any new folders you create automatically inherit the settings you've just made. But what about older folders that don't display your preferred characteristics? If you open such a window, choose View→View Options, and then click Set to Standard Views, you'll apply your "standard" settings to that window.

- **Labels.** Lets you define the text and colors you want as your seven available labels (see Chapter 2). (To change the color, click the color swatch next to a label name. The Color Picker dialog box appears, offering several different methods of specifying a new color.)

# View Menu

The commands in the View menu apply *only* to the active Finder window: the one that's open and in front of all the others.

## as Icons, as Buttons, as List

These commands let you view the files in a window as *icons* (which you move by dragging freely), as *buttons* (large, "pillowed" buttons that open with a single click), or as a *list* (a neat list view that's automatically sorted). Chapter 1 contains complete descriptions of these three views and their relative advantages.

## as Window, as Pop-up Window

Most desktop windows are viewed "as Window"—as a standard window. If you choose "as Pop-up Window," however, the window collapses to the bottom edge of your screen, where it becomes a tab. This handy organizational helper is described in detail in Chapter 1.

## Clean Up, Arrange/Sort List

These commands, too, are described in Chapter 1; they're both useful for tidying a window filled with randomly spaced icons. "Clean Up" is unavailable in list views; the second command says Arrange when the open window is in an icon view, and Sort List when the open window is a list view.

## Reset Column Positions

After you've fiddled with the sequence and widths of the columns in a list-view window (see Chapter 1), you can use this command to restore those columns to their original, factory-installed widths and column order.

## View Options

Opens the View Options dialog box, which is described in Chapter 1. Its offerings depend on which view the open window was in (list, button, or icon), but the point is the same: to let you adjust icon sizes, column selection, automatic grid positioning, and so on, for the current window.

# Special Menu

The Special menu, the only Finder menu that's not a verb, would have been better named "Arbitrary"; its commands have little in common, except that they don't belong in any of the other menus.

## Empty Trash

Deletes the icons you've dragged onto the Trash can icon, as described on page 46. Available only if there's something actually *in* the Trash.

---

***Tip:*** Using the Empty Trash command generally produces an "Are you sure?" dialog box message. If you're *always* sure, you can instruct the Mac not to display this confirmation message, as described on page 48.

You can tell by a glance at the Special menu whether or not the confirmation message will appear: If you see the ellipsis (…) after the Empty Trash command, the confirmation message will appear; if no ellipsis appears, the Mac will empty the Trash without requesting confirmation.

---

## Eject

Available only if you've first highlighted a disk icon that is, in fact, removable. (If you've turned on File Sharing, as described in Chapter 16, your removable disks probably aren't removable.) This command makes the Mac spit the disk out.

## Erase Disk

Available only if you've highlighted an erasable disk icon. (You can't erase the disk you started up from, a CD-ROM or DVD-ROM, or any disk larger than 2 MB while File Sharing is turned on.) You're then shown the dialog box in Figure A-3, where you can specify a new name (and other options) for the disk you're about to erase.

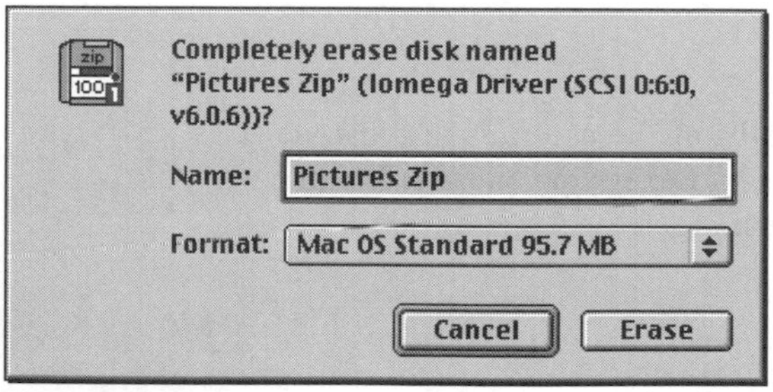

***Figure A-3:***
*Using the pop-up menu, you can specify how you want this disk erased. For example, if you're erasing a floppy disk, you can specify whether you want it formatted for Mac or Windows (DOS). See Chapter 18 for more on formatting and erasing disks.*

## Sleep

Puts your Mac into Sleep mode, darkening the screen and putting the computer into a low-power, dormant state. Press a key, or click the mouse, to wake it up again. (More on Sleep mode on page 72.)

## Restart

Turns the Mac off, then on again. You'll most often use this command after a program has crashed (to rule out the possibility that it left your Mac in an unstable condition), after installing new software, or after using Extensions Manager to turn some extensions or control panels on or off.

## Shut Down

Turns the Mac off, quitting all running programs (and asking you to save any unsaved work) in the process.

---

*Tip:* You can change your mind about shutting down the Mac if you launch a new program before the machine has completely shut down. For example, suppose you choose Special→Shut Down. The Mac disconnects from the Internet (five seconds), quits three programs (five seconds), and ejects a disk or two. During that time, you can open a new program by choosing its name from the  menu, by pressing an Fkey, and so on—thus forcing the Mac to abandon its shutdown in progress.

---

*Figure A-4:*
*When you choose Help→Help Center, you're shown a master list of the broad help categories available on your Mac. Each topic in the Help Center (top left) corresponds to a folder in your System Folder→Help folder (lower right). Click a blue underlined link to begin your exploration of the help topics.*

# Help Menu

Over the years, Apple has attempted several different forms of online help screens. No one Help format is available in every Mac program; and even the oldest of these systems still lurks in Mac OS 9. Still, one of these commands or another may occasionally be useful.

## Help Center

Mac OS 9's primary help mechanism is a Web-browser-like program that reads help files in your System Folder→Help folder. Each new component of the Mac system software you install may come with its own suite of help screens. Figure A-4 should make this relationship clearer.

As always, using an online, electronic help system is often an exercise in frustration; the Mac's help browser gives you no sense of context that indicates where you are in the greater pile of help screens. Searches produce only 10 results per screen, no matter how tall you make the window. Furthermore, the help screens themselves may leave something to be desired. (The topic "Inserting a DVD-Video disc," for example, offers these instructions: "If you don't know how to insert a disc in your drive, see the documentation that came with the drive.")

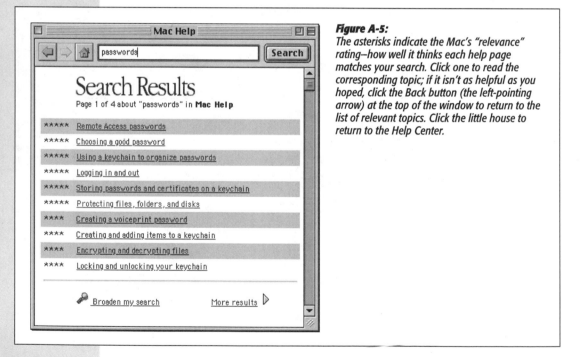

**Figure A-5:**
*The asterisks indicate the Mac's "relevance" rating—how well it thinks each help page matches your search. Click one to read the corresponding topic; if it isn't as helpful as you hoped, click the Back button (the left-pointing arrow) at the top of the window to return to the list of relevant topics. Click the little house to return to the Help Center.*

You're expected to find the topic you want in one of these two ways:

- **Use the Search blank.** Type the phrase you want, such as *printing* or *switching* *applications,* into the blank at the top of the window, and then click Search (or press Return).

The Mac responds by showing you a list of help-screen topics that may pertain to what you're seeking (see Figure A-5).

• **Drill down.** That is, keep clicking blue underlined links until you find the topic you want. You might start at the Help Center screen shown in Figure A-4, for example, and then click Mac Help. The next screen shows you a list of general Mac help topics; you might click Security to find out how to password-protect a file. The next screen shows you individual security-related topics; you could click, for example, "Protecting files, folders, and disks," which takes you at last to some actual instructions.

As with the Search method, you can backtrack by clicking the Back button at the top of the "browser" window.

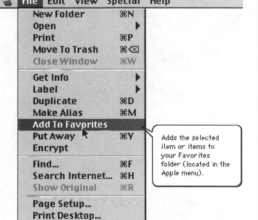

**Figure A-6:**
*Balloon Help may not get much respect, but it's an extremely effective means of learning about a new program. It offers many "Oh, so that's* what it's for!" *moments.*

**Tip:** Not only is the Help browser *like* a Web browser, it *is* a Web browser. The help documents in your System Folder→Help folder are, in fact, standard Web pages written in HTML (Web-page) language.

You can harness this useful fact in two ways: First, you can add your own comments to the help screens just by opening the corresponding help files in a Web-page-editing program like Claris Home Page, BBEdit, or Adobe PageMill. Second, you can open one of these help files in your *real* Web browser, such as Internet Explorer or Netscape Communicator. Doing so offers some features not available in the built-in Help browser: the ability to copy sections of help text for pasting into another program, for example, or the ability to bookmark a particular Help-screen page.

Both of these tricks involve your figuring out *which* help-screen file to open, which isn't always easy; the files in your Help folder have names like *baRtoc.htm* and *baVers.htm*. Trial and error is the only way to go.

## Show Balloons

In many programs, including the Finder itself, a secondary help feature is available: Balloon Help. When you choose Help→Balloon Help, a cartoon balloon springs out of your cursor as you point to various icons and menu commands. The message in the balloon explains the function of the menu, command, icon, window, checkbox, or button you're pointing to (see Figure A-6).

This help feature doesn't get much respect in the Mac community, but that's unfortunate; a huge number of secrets, tips, and pointers lurk in its little messages. A surprising number of programs supply balloons when you turn on Balloon Help, including Microsoft Office programs, iMovie, AppleWorks, Appearance, the Chooser, Sherlock 2, SimpleSound, AppleCD Audio Player, Network Browser, Stickies, the Note Pad, Palm Desktop, the Help Center described above, and so on. (A few programs lack balloon help, such as Photoshop, FileMaker Pro, and even some of Apple's own programs, such as Apple System Profiler and the Calculator. In these programs,

---

**FREQUENTLY ASKED QUESTION**

### The Forgotten Help: Apple Guide

*I found something else in the Help menu. What's SimpleText Guide?*

The Guide system is yet another Mac help-file system that lurks in the Help menus of such programs as Quicken, SimpleText, Drive Setup, AppleCD Audio Player, Apple Video Player, Apple IR File Exchange, File Synchronization, iMovie, Location Manager, and so on.

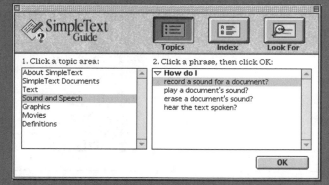

When you choose it, you're asked to click a broad help topic at the left side of the window, and then a specific topic on the right side. But now a strange and wonderful thing happens: a floating window appears (usually near the bottom of your screen) that gives you a single instruction, the first step in accomplishing the task you selected. It might tell you to choose a certain menu command, for example; with each step, a fat, ghostly, red marker draws a bright red circle around whatever menu command or button you're sup-

posed to click. When you click the Next button, the next instruction appears.

It would be hard to imagine a more effective help system than this one, which feels as though a personal coach is guiding you, step by patient step, through a particular task. Unfortunately, for a software company, designing an Apple Guide help file is almost as complex a task as writing the software to begin with; few software companies actually write Guide files for their programs. That software-company reluctance is what inspired Apple to switch to its newer, Web-browser-like help feature; after all, Web pages are *extremely* easy for software companies to write, involving almost no programming at all.

Few programs, in other words, offer all three kinds of Mac help systems, but it would be nice if they did: Balloon Help to tell you what it is, Mac Help to tell you how it works, and Apple Guide to tell you how to use it.

---

the Show Balloons command is indeed available—but the balloons that appear don't identify anything beyond built-in Mac basics, such as "This is a window.")

The next time you're stuck in one of your programs, or confused about the function of some menu command or icon, try turning on Balloon Help; you may be surprised by its effectiveness.

## Mac Help

This command, available only in the Finder, takes you directly to the list of Mac help topics—which is only one of the broad help categories listed on the Help Center screen shown in Figure A-4.

# Installing Mac OS 9

I f your Mac came with Mac OS 9 already installed, great; you won't have to go through the educational but time-consuming process of updating your operating system. (You may still want to consider reading about the *clean install,* described at the end of this chapter, because it's a sensational troubleshooting technique.)

If your Mac is running some earlier version of the Mac OS, however, and you've obtained a copy of the Mac OS 9 CD-ROM, almost all of this chapter pertains to you. It covers all three kinds of installation:

- **The standard installation,** in which your existing System Folder is simply updated to Mac OS 9, in the process preserving your preferences files, font collection, ☗ menu configuration, and so on;

- **The custom installation,** in which you install only the Mac OS 9 components you want; and

- **The clean installation,** in which the Mac OS 9 installer gives you a virginal, clean, complete Mac OS 9 System Folder, setting aside and retiring your existing, older System Folder.

---

***Tip:*** Technically, Mac OS 9 costs $99; you can buy it at the computer store, from the Apple Web site (*www.apple.com*), or from any Mac mail-order joint (such as *macwarehouse.com, macmall.com,* or *maczone.com*). But Apple will give you a $20 rebate if you have Mac OS 8.5 or Mac OS 8.6. And if you have an iBook, Power Mac G4, or any other Mac model that was released after Mac OS 9, you can buy Mac OS 9 for $20. For details on these offers (which involve mailing in a considerable amount of paperwork), call 800-335-9258, or visit *www.apple.com/macos/uptodate*.

---

# Before You Install

Mac OS 9 requires a Mac with a PowerPC processor, which includes every Mac sold since late 1994. PowerPC-equipped Macs include every Power Macintosh, iMac, and iBook model, along with any Performa, PowerBook, or LC model with a four-digit model number. (You can't install Mac OS 9 on a Mac model that you've enhanced with a PowerPC upgrade card.)

Mac OS 9 also requires a Mac that has 32 MB of RAM *and* virtual memory (see page 117) turned up to at least 40 MB. For faster, smoother operation, however, Apple recommends 64 MB of memory or more. You need 100 to 250 MB of empty disk space when you install Mac OS 9, too, depending on how many of its components you plan to install.

If you're upgrading from Mac OS 8.1 or earlier, consult the Before You Install document on the Mac OS 9 CD. It contains special steps for Macs with ultrawide SCSI cards, DOS compatibility cards, and Macs in the 5000 and 6000 model lines. It also warns you about hard drives that you've formatted using non-Apple hard drive software (such as HDToolkit); you'll probably have to contact the manufacturer about getting an update before you can install Mac OS 9.

# The Standard Installation

If you're upgrading to Mac OS 9 from an earlier Mac OS version, Apple assumes that you've already got a lot of customized stuff in your existing System Folder: fonts you've added, extensions and control panels deposited by your application installers, the preference files that store serial numbers for your software,  menu items you've installed, and so on. The idea behind the standard Mac OS 9 installation is to *preserve* all of that customized stuff. Mac OS 9 installer treads carefully around it, updating or adding only the components it cares about—the ones needed to give you a genuine Mac OS 9 System Folder.

Most people, most of the time, perform this kind of upgrade. There *is* another way to install Mac OS 9—the clean install, described later in this appendix—but the standard installation is the one you get if you don't take any special steps.

Most Mac OS 9 upgrades go very smoothly. Still, when things do go wrong, the standard installation is generally at fault. That's because some of your older extensions, control panels, and other System Folder components—the very items the Mac OS installer takes care not to disturb—may be incompatible with Mac OS 9. When you start up the machine after the installation, therefore, your first experience with the new operating system may be freezes or other glitches.

The bottom line: If things go well, the standard installation can save you a lot of time and hassle. It simply upgrades your existing System Folder, maintaining your customizations. If things don't go well, and your Mac is crashy after the upgrade, you can always perform a clean install afterward. Consider jumping directly to a clean install only if:

- You're having glitches and freezes already, while running your older system software. Installing Mac OS 9 over such a system would simply exacerbate the problems.

- You're a utility junkie. You've loaded down your System Folder with add-on extensions and control panels, such as Kaleidoscope and other shareware goodies from the Web. If so, you're probably better off performing a clean install—unless you first revisit the Web sites in question to make sure you've got the latest, Mac OS 9-compatible versions of your System Folder clutter.

Here, then, are the steps for performing a standard installation.

*Tip:* If you're installing Mac OS 9 onto a laptop, plug it in before you begin, so that it won't go to sleep or run out of battery power in the middle of the process. Check your Energy Saver control panel, too, to make sure that the computer isn't set to sleep after only a few minutes of inactivity.

1. **Insert the Mac OS 9 CD-ROM. Choose Special→Restart; immediately hold down the letter C key until you see the light-colored desktop pattern that's filled with pictures of CDs.**

   That special background tells you that you've started up the Mac from the CD-ROM. (Technically, you can install Mac OS 9 without starting up from the CD-ROM, but this approach is more likely to go smoothly. It rules out the possibility that one of your own extensions or control panels might interfere with the installation process.)

   On the screen now, you should see the Mac OS 9 CD window. It contains Before You Install, a Utilities folder, and the Mac OS Install icon.

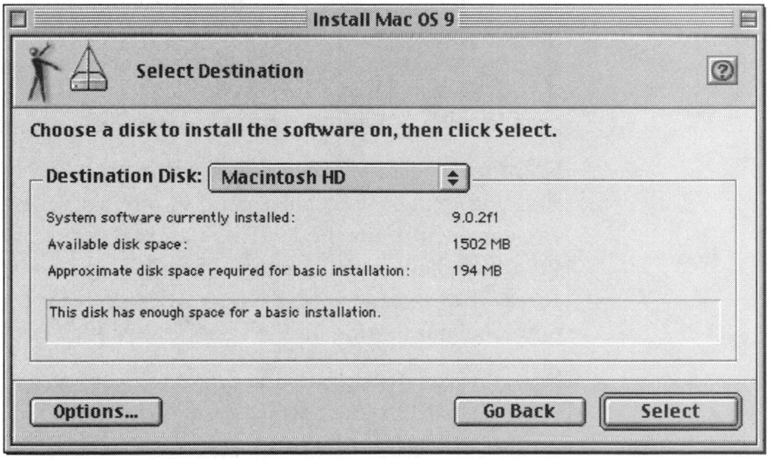

*Figure B-1:*
*The Select Destination screen that lets you specify which disk you want to receive Mac OS 9. It's possible to cram Mac OS 9 onto a Zip disk, but only if you use a customized installation, as described in the next section, and request only a few of Mac OS 9's features—and then use the Memory control panel's "Select Disk" pop-up menu to specify a different disk for virtual-memory storage.*

2. **Double-click Mac OS install.**

A welcome screen appears. There's nothing particularly interesting on it except for the circled question mark in the upper-right corner, which you can click for some help screens.

3. **Click Continue (or press Return).**

Now the Select Destination screen appears, as shown in Figure B-1. This is where you're supposed to specify which disk you want Mac OS 9 installed on. Most people accept the proposed choice, which is the built-in hard drive. It's possible, however, to install Mac OS 9 onto a different drive, such as an external hard drive, a Jaz cartridge (if you have version 6.0.2 or later of its driver software), and so on.

4. **From the Destination Disk pop-up menu, specify the disk on which you want Mac OS 9 installed. Then click Select (or press Return).**

Now you're shown the Before You Install document; it's the same one that appears in the Mac OS 9 CD window.

5. **Click Continue (or press Return). Click Continue on the next screen, too, to bypass the software license agreement. Click Agree on the pop-up warning.**

At last you arrive at the Install Software screen. At this point, you could click Options to turn off one of two special features: **Update Apple Hard Disk Drivers** makes sure that your hard drive (if it's an Apple hard drive) has the latest hard drive software installed—an excellent idea. The **Create Installation Report** checkbox produces a folder on your hard drive called Installer Logs; inside are text files that identify every software component the Mac OS 9 installer added, deleted, or replaced.

This screen also contains the Customize button. More on this topic in "The Custom Installation," later in this appendix.

6. **Click Start.**

If you're warned that other applications are running, click Continue. (The Mac can't install new system software if any other programs are running.)

Now the installation process begins in earnest. A status box lets you know what's going on—first the installer checks your hard drive and automatically repairs any damage it finds there. (This step makes the transition to Mac OS 9 much smoother than, say, the one to Mac OS 8, whose installer didn't perform this check. The upgrade to Mac OS 8 caused grief for thousands of people who had tiny problems lurking on their hard drives.)

Next, the installer updates the driver software on your hard drive (unless it's not an Apple hard drive, in which case you're responsible for obtaining Mac OS 9-compatible driver software).

Finally, the actual software installation begins. You can click Cancel at any time; you'll be asked whether you want to abort the entire installation, just skip the installation of the component currently being installed (such as ColorSync or speech recognition), or start the installation over again.

The entire installation process takes about 10 minutes. When the installation is complete, you'll be asked to restart the Mac.

**7. Click Restart.**

That's it—you've just installed Mac OS 9.

When the Mac starts up again, the Mac OS Setup Assistant runs automatically; it's an inconsequential startup program designed primarily for people whose Macs are connected to office networks. On successive screens, you're asked to specify the current time zone, the current time and date, your name and password (for networking purposes), what kind of printer you plan to connect, and so on.

**Figure B-2:**
*If you click Customize, you're offered these primary 10 chunks of software (top). If you choose Customized Installation from one of the pop-up menus at the right side of that window, you're shown the individual software pieces that make up the larger module (bottom). A checkmark means you're going to get the entire collection; a – means that you're going to get some of the items within each collection; and an empty checkbox means you're not going to get any of the items in that collection. Click the little **i** button for a terse explanation of its contents.*

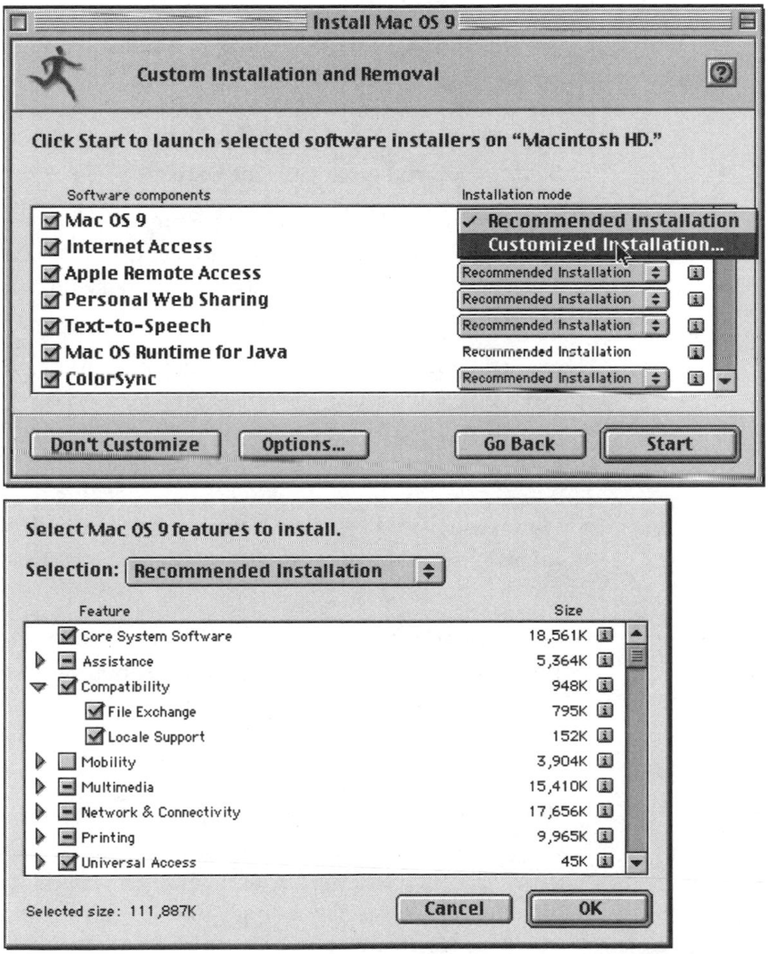

*Tip:* You can skip the Mac OS Setup Assistant; just choose File→Quit at any time, and then confirm that you do indeed want to abandon the process. If you're not on office network, the only meaningful setting the Setup Assistant makes for you is the time and date, which you can do much more quickly yourself (by choosing  →Control Panels→Date & Time).

On the final screen, you can click Quit (to begin using your Mac) or Continue (if you'd like to set up an Internet account). If you choose to continue, you're shown the Internet Setup Assistant, which walks you through the process of setting up an Internet account with EarthLink.

Then, at last, you're ready to begin using your Mac and enjoying the features described in this book.

# The Custom Installation

In step 5 of the preceding instructions, you come face-to-face with a button called Customize. It brings up the screen shown in Figure B-2, where you can specify which components of the Mac OS you want installed. Unless you're an absolute terrified novice who'd just as soon not have to confront unnecessary options, turning off the components you don't need can save you installation time and a lot of disk space. This option lets you order your software meal *à la carte* instead of as a fixed package.

To the right of each item is a pop-up menu. (You must turn on the checkbox to undim the pop-up menu.) It lets you further break down this customized installation into the individual chunks of software that make up each of the modules listed here, as shown in Figure B-2.

Here are the individual modules you can turn off or on—and the sub-options that appear when you choose Customized Installation from the pop-up menu:

## Mac OS 9

This item gives you the basic System Folder, lacking only the nine other major modules items listed on this screen. If you choose Customized Installation from the pop-up menu to its right, you discover that Mac OS 9 is composed of these elements (see Figure B-2, bottom):

- **Core System Software.** Here it is: Mac OS 9 in its tiniest, most stripped-down form— a mere 18-MB chunk that's just barely enough software to let your Mac turn on. This option is useful when you want to create, for example, an "emergency" Zip disk or even RAM disk, so you'll have something to start up your Mac when all else fails (and you've lost your Mac OS 9 CD, which is an ideal startup disk).

  This miniature System Folder is rather shocking to use: it starts up your Mac almost instantaneously, seems to double your Mac's speed, and uses very little RAM. Of course, it's lacking just about every useful feature of the standard Mac— in fact, it gives you only a single font (Geneva), which makes your menus look extremely peculiar.

*Tip:* Don't miss the Selection pop-up menu above the list of checkboxes (you can see it in the bottom dialog box of Figure B-2). It lets you turn all of the checkboxes on or off with a single click.

- **Assistance.** This item means "help files," including two of the help systems (Apple Guide and Mac OS Help) described in Appendix A, the Mac OS Setup Assistant program described above, and SimpleText.

- **Compatibility.** Grants you File Exchange (a control panel described in Chapter 12) and Locale Support. Locale Support creates a folder in your System Folder called Language & Region Support, containing 13 resource files for various languages. The Mac relies on the information in these files when it offers you various international choices in its control panels, such as Date & Time, Numbers, and so on.

- **Mobility.** These programs for laptops include Apple IR File Exchange (lets PowerBooks connect with each other through the air, via infrared communication), a battery-draining application (designed to eliminate the "memory effect" of very old PowerBook batteries), the Trackpad control panel, and the drivers for various PowerBook and iBook modems and monitors.

- **Multimedia.** In this category are the drivers for various Apple sound and video products, including its CD/DVD drive, game drivers like OpenGL and Game Sprockets, QuickTime, and the useful AppleCD Audio Player (see Chapter 5).

- **Network & Connectivity.** Most of these items are for setting up an office network, as described in Chapter 16: AppleShare, Ethernet drivers, File Sharing, the Network Browser, Open Transport (see Chapter 14), and so on. Buried in this option, however, are several of the big-ticket Mac OS 9 features—the Multiple Users control panel, the password-encryption feature, and so on.

- **Printing.** This batch includes all the software described in Chapter 15—various drivers for discontinued Apple printer models, the Desktop Printing software, and so on.

- **Universal Access.** You can read about these two control panels—CloseView and Easy Access—in Chapter 13.

- **Utility.** This broad category includes some of the most useful Mac OS 9 components: AppleScript (Chapter 10), the application switcher (Chapter 6), the Control Strip (Chapter 4), Disk Copy (Chapter 13), Disk First Aid (Chapter 13), Drive Setup, FontSync (Chapter 12), the Graphing Calculator (Chapter 13), Note Pad (Chapter 13), SimpleSound (Chapter 20), and so on.

- **Video.** Here are the drivers for various Apple monitors, plus the DigitalColor Meter program described in Chapter 13.

- **International.** This software gets your Mac ready for the international language features described in Chapter 13.

- **Apple Menu Items.** Here are the Calculator, Chooser, Key Caps, Sherlock, and other  menu items that aren't part of the bundles of software described so far.

• **Control Panels.** This category includes all of the control panels described in Chapter 12—except the ones included in software chunks described so far.

---

***Tip:*** Nestled among these control panel options is File Synchronization, which is generally installed only on laptops. If you have a desktop Mac, you can use a custom installation to turn it on here.

---

• **Fonts.** Using these checkboxes, you can turn on or off each of the 19 TrueType fonts that come with the Mac (see Chapter 19).

---

**GEM IN THE ROUGH**

## The Universal System Folder

When you install the Mac OS 9 component by itself, the installer gives you a System Folder that can start up your Mac model. Unbeknownst to most Mac fans, however, not every Mac OS 9 System Folder is alike. The installer can create several subtly different versions of Mac OS 9—one for an iMac, another for Power Mac G4 models, another for the old beige Power Mac G3 models, and so on.

In other words, the Mac OS 9 you installed onto a Zip disk connected to your iMac may not actually be able to start up a Power Mac G3 in the next office.

The solution: create a *Universal* System Folder. This extra-large version of Mac OS 9, once installed on a portable disk large enough to contain it, can power up any Mac OS 9-compatible machine.

To create it, run the Mac OS 9 installer, exactly as described in steps 1 through 5 at the beginning of this appendix. Once again, you'll wind up facing a Customize button. Click it, make sure the Mac OS 9 checkbox has a checkmark, and then—from the Installation Mode pop-up menu—choose Customized Installation. Finally, from the Selection pop-up menu above the checkboxes, choose Universal Installation.

Unless you further customize the installation by turning off some of the checkboxes described below, you'll get a System Folder that occupies 140 MB—but that can start up any PowerPC Mac with enough RAM for Mac OS 9.

---

## Internet Access

A better name for this item would have been "Internet programs," because this is the component that gives you two Web browsers (Internet Explorer and Netscape Communicator), an email program (Outlook Express), and so on. If you use the pop-up menu to specify Customized Installation, you may save yourself a lot of disk space; the individual components you can turn on or off include:

• **Apple Internet Access.** This checkbox refers to the Internet Access extension, which you need to go online.

• **Internet Utilities.** This item grants you StuffIt Expander, the useful utility program that can decompress software you download from the Internet via email or Web pages, and DropStuff, which lets you *create* compressed files for sending. (Most email programs perform this compression automatically, however.)

*Tip:* Newer versions of both StuffIt Expander and DropStuff are already available, at no charge, from *www.aladdinsys.com.*

- **Microsoft.** Turn on this checkbox to acquire Internet Explorer and Outlook Express, Microsoft's Web browser and email program.

- **Netscape Communicator.** An alternative, faster Web browser with fewer browsing features—but a built-in Web-page editor.

## Apple Remote Access

This bundle includes the Apple Remote Access Personal Server software, which lets you dial into your Mac from the road (see Chapter 16).

## Personal Web Sharing

As described in Chapter 14, Web Sharing lets you make one folder on your hard drive available to the entire Internet. This package includes the necessary control panel, Control Strip module, extension, and instruction manual (in Web-page format; you'll find it in a folder called Web Pages on your hard drive).

## Text-To-Speech

If you want your Mac to be able to read your text back to you out loud, in a nasal voice, this is the option you want (see Chapter 21).

## Mac OS Runtime for Java

You can read about Java on page 217; it's a fancy programming language required by some Web pages (such as banking and game sites).

## ColorSync

As described in Chapter 19, ColorSync is a collection of software components that help ensure color consistency throughout the scanning, viewing, editing, and printing process. This bundle gives you that software, including the Photoshop plug-ins described in Chapter 19 and the profiles for many Apple color products.

## English Speech Recognition

Here's the software you need for the Mac to understand your spoken commands, as described in Chapter 21. It's not ordinarily installed; a customized installation is the only way to get it.

## Language Kits

You can read about these kits in Chapter 13; they let you word process or surf the Web in any of dozens of different languages—Hebrew, Japanese, Korean, Chinese, and so on—complete with foreign-language fonts and alphabet systems.

## Network Assistant Client

Network administrators can buy a program called Apple Network Administrator that lets them install software onto an entire network's worth of Macs—remotely, from one central computer. Administrators can also maintain the software, trouble-shoot problems, and even see what's on your screen. But to do that, your Mac must have this special software installed.

---

***Tip:*** You can also *remove* selected components from an existing copy of Mac OS 9. Suppose, for example, that in reading the preceding pages, you become alarmed at how much junk gets installed during a standard installation. By following the steps for performing a customized installation, and then choosing Customized Removal from one of the pop-up menus (shown at top in Figure B-2), you can turn on the checkboxes of software components you want removed, thus saving a lot of disk space.

Finally, open the more detailed list of components shown at bottom in Figure B-2. Click the ones you want deleted, and then click Remove. When the process is over, you'll be asked to restart your Mac, just as though you had installed something.

---

### POWER USERS' CLINIC

## Labeling the Mac OS 9 Components

Regardless of the kind of Mac OS 9 installation you per-form, one syndrome will befall you in the coming months: over time, you and your applications will deposit more files into the System Folder. As you install programs, your Exten-sions and Preferences folders will collect more accompany-ing modules; as you explore the Internet, you'll stumble across more shareware that sounds like fun. And then one day, your Mac will start acting up. You'll stare hopelessly at your System Folder, filled as it is with over 2,000 icons, and have no idea where to begin your troubleshooting.

If you plan ahead, you can avoid this situation. Immediately after installing Mac OS 9, use the icon-labeling trick described on page 40. The routine goes like this: open your System Folder. Choose Edit→Select All. Then press ⌘-Option-right arrow, which expands every flippy triangle so that you can see every icon in every folder.

Now choose Edit→Select All again, and then choose File→Label→Essential (or any label you prefer). (You may even want to choose Edit→Preferences→Labels and type in a very specific label, such as "Clean install 8/2000.") You've just tinted every icon in every System Folder folder orange (or whatever color that label represents). Finally, press ⌘-left arrow to collapse all the folders again, and close the System Folder.

When the day of troubleshooting arrives, you'll be able to narrow down your list of culprits instantly. You'll open your System Folder and look for items that *aren't* orange. These are the icons that didn't come from Apple, and are there-fore the ones most likely to be causing your problems. (Be alert, however: System components that Mac OS 9's Soft-ware Updates control panel have automatically downloaded and installed won't be orange, either.)

## The Clean Installation

A standard Mac OS 9 installation packs in Mac OS 9 around your fonts, control panels, ⌘ menu items, startup items, and so on. If all goes well, when your Mac restarts after the installation, you'll be running the new operating system with all of your familiar modifications intact.

But if anything goes wrong, and your Mac behaves oddly—whether at the time of installation or later—you may want to consider a *clean installation*. In this special mode, the Mac OS 9 installer gives you a new System Folder—a fresh, perfect, smoothly operating System Folder that doesn't contain any of the junk you've added to your Mac over the months. Nothing else on your hard drive is disturbed—your programs and documents are just fine—but the System Folder itself is surgically replaced.

When you do a clean installation of Mac OS 9, the installer retires your existing System Folder and renames it *Previous System Folder* to avoid confusion. Figure B-3 shows the effect.

**Figure B-3:**
Your new, fresh Mac OS 9 System Folder is easily identifiable–it's the one now called System Folder, and it's also the one bearing the traditional Mac OS logo, as shown here at right.

Previous System Folder

System Folder

It's impossible to overstate the power and usefulness of the clean install. Unless your Mac has actual hardware problems, whatever glitch you've been experiencing, in any program—crashes, freezes, cosmetic anomalies, or whatever—goes away after a clean install. That's why this technique is so adored by Mac phone staff, trouble-shooters, and consultants the world over.

What makes a clean install inconvenient, however, is that when it's over, you have to hand-install every component that made the old System Folder *your* System Folder—all of those preference files, fonts, ⌘ menu items, and so on that you and your programs had added over the months. This section gives you guidance both on performing a clean install and on performing this follow-up procedure.

## Performing a Clean Installation

To give yourself a fresh, new System Folder, follow these steps:

1. **Insert your Mac OS 9 CD-ROM. Double-click the Mac OS Install icon.**

   The Welcome screen appears.

2. **Click Continue; from the pop-up menu, choose a destination disk for the installation.**

   In general, this is your built-in hard drive.

   Now you've arrived at the critical step:

3. **Click the Options button in the lower-left corner of the window.**

   As shown in Figure B-4, you're now offered the chance to specify a clean installation.

4. Turn on the "Perform Clean Installation" checkbox and then click OK. Click Select, and then continue with step 5 on page 426.

When the installation is complete, you'll see two System Folders—as shown in Figure B-3—one of which is named Previous System Folder. That's your old one. You should notice that the Mac starts up faster, windows and programs open faster, and the entire machine feels smoother and more responsive.

**Figure B-4:**
Click Options (background) to summon the "Perform Clean Installation" dialog box, which briefly explains what's about to happen. Turn on the checkbox and then click OK.

## Reinstalling Fonts, Preferences, and Other Components

If you have a current version of the commercial program called Conflict Catcher (*www.casadyg.com*), bringing over your fonts, preference files, control panels, menu items, and other personal items from the Previous System Folder into the new one is easy. The Clean Install Merge command in Conflict Catcher automatically prepares for you a list of each item in the *old* System Folder that isn't in the new one. You just click the checkboxes of the ones you want copied into the new System Folder, and call it a day.

If you don't have Conflict Catcher, you can perform the same steps manually, although you'll spend more time doing it. Here's how to go about it:

1. Open the Previous System Folder and the new one in tall, skinny windows, side-by-side, as shown in Figure B-5.

   For each window, choose View→as List.

2. In each of the two windows, click the flippy triangle next to the Apple Menu Items folder, so that you can see its contents.

   The idea is that you want to compare the contents, to find elements in the left-side (Previous System Folder) window that *aren't* in the new System Folder. When you find such an icon in the Apple Menu Items folder, do this:

3. While pressing Option, drag each unique icon in the left-side Apple Menu Items window into the corresponding folder in the right-side window (the new System Folder).

Option-dragging creates a copy of the original. You're copying, rather than moving, these items in order to leave your previous System Folder intact, just in case you need to go back to it.

Incidentally: an item in your ★ menu can't cause instability on your Mac. You're perfectly safe copying these items into the new System Folder.

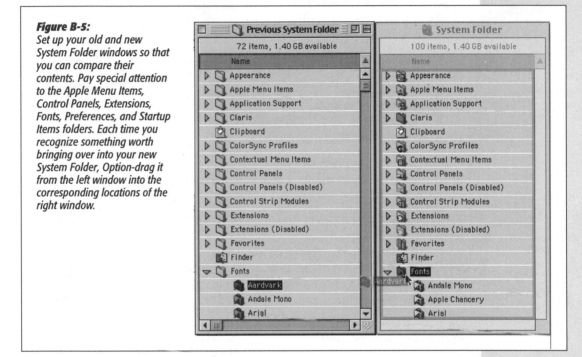

**Figure B-5:**
*Set up your old and new System Folder windows so that you can compare their contents. Pay special attention to the Apple Menu Items, Control Panels, Extensions, Fonts, Preferences, and Startup Items folders. Each time you recognize something worth bringing over into your new System Folder, Option-drag it from the left window into the corresponding locations of the right window.*

4. Repeat the compare-and-copy procedure with the Control Panels, Extensions, Startup Items, and Fonts folders.

Be judicious, however. The last thing you want is to re-introduce problem components into your new System Folder. If possible, install fresh versions of these control panels, extensions, and fonts—updated versions, if you can find them—instead of copying them from the old System Folder.

If you find something in the Previous System Folder window that you can't identify—that is, you're not sure whether you need it or not—consider living without it as you get used to your new System Folder. Part of the joy of the clean install is leaving behind hundreds of arbitrary files installed unnecessarily by your various applications.

**5. Repeat the compare-and-copy procedure with your Preferences folder.**

Corrupted preference files are a common cause of problems on the Mac. You should grow especially suspicious when you begin having problems in one specific program, as described in Appendix C.

Therefore, consider dragging preference files from your old System Folder into your new one *only* if they contain key information, such as the password or serial number necessary to run a particular program. (Unfortunately, some programs rely on *invisible* serial-number files; you'll have to reinstall such programs from scratch.) You should also copy over the files that contain your Internet connection information (phone numbers, passwords, and so on)—namely, the TCP/IP Preferences, Modem Preferences, and Remote Access folder.

---

*Tip:* The Mac won't let you replace the Remote Access folder in your new System Folder; it will claim that the existing Remote Access folder is "in use." The solution: *throw away* the new Remote Access folder before Option-dragging the old one.

---

**6. Close all windows, and then restart the Mac.**

With luck, you'll be exactly where you want to be: running a clean, fresh, fast new System Folder that nonetheless contains your most treasured fonts, control panels, and so on.

At this point, it's a good idea to live with *both* System Folders on your hard drive for a couple of weeks. (Contrary to the Apple advice of the 1980s, these days, it's perfectly safe to have multiple System Folders on your hard drive. The Mac "blesses"—activates—only one System Folder at a time, as indicated by the Mac OS logo on the folder.) After some time has elapsed, and you're comfortable that your new System Folder works the way you like, you can throw away the one called Previous System Folder.

---

*Tip:* If the installation didn't go well, you can always return to your earlier System Folder, even if it was an earlier version of the Mac OS. To do so, open your new System Folder. Move the Finder out of the window—to the desktop, for example. Doing so cripples the new System Folder; you'll see the Mac OS logo disappear from its folder, and the colorful special folder designs inside it all turn plain.

Now just open and close the Previous System Folder to make the Mac OS logo reappear on *it.* You've just "blessed" the older System Folder; when you restart, it will be in control. (You can leave its "Previous" name, or rename it; the name of the System Folder makes no difference.)

---

# Mac OS 9 Compatibility Problems

A major system-software upgrade always invites a few headaches, and Mac OS 9 is a prominent example. Dozens of programs—especially utility programs—require minor upgrades to be compatible with Mac OS 9. Not every item in this list, by the way, is *completely* broken in Mac OS 9; some have only minor incompatibilities. Here's a partial list of the programs that have compatibility issues, along with the software companies' Web sites and the *lowest* version number that works completely in Mac OS 9:

### Mac OS 9 Compatibility Problems

| Product | Web site | Requires version |
| --- | --- | --- |
| Acrobat Reader | adobe.com | 4.0 |
| Adobe Type Reunion | adobe.com | 4.5.2 |
| AppleWorks 5 | apple.com | 5.0.4 |
| ATM | adobe.com | 4.5.2 |
| Avara | Ambrosiasw.com | 1.0.1 |
| Barrack | Ambrosiasw.com | 1.0.4 |
| Conflict Catcher | casadyg.com | 8.0.6 |
| Cythera | Ambrosiasw.com | 1.0.4 |
| Excel 98 | microsoft.com | (unnumbered updater available) |
| Final Cut Pro | apple.com | 1.2.1 |
| Final Draft | finaldraft.com | 5.0.2d |
| Fourth Dimension | acius.com | 6.5.3 |
| InstallerMaker | aladdinsys.com | 6.5 |
| Kensington trackballs | kensington.com | 5.31 |
| MenuFonts | dublclick.com | (no fix yet) |
| Norton Anti-Virus | symantec.com | 6.0 |
| Norton Utilities | symantec.com | 5.0 |
| PaperPort | visioneer.com | (unnumbered updater available) |
| Premiere | adobe.com | 5.1c |
| RAM Doubler 8 | connectix.com | 9 |
| Retrospect | dantz.com | 4.2 |
| SpaceSaver | aladdinsys.com | (no fix yet) |
| Speed Doubler | connectix.com | (no fix planned) |
| StatView | statview.com | (fixed by the Mac OS 9.0.2 update) |
| StuffIt Deluxe | aladdinsys.com | 5.5 |
| StuffIt Expander | aladdinsys.com | 5.5 |
| StyleWriter 4000 | apple.com | (no fix yet) |
| Toast | adaptec.com | 4.1 |
| VirtualPC | connectix.com | 2.1.2 |

You can find much more exhaustive Mac OS 9 compatibility lists at any of these Web sites:

- **MacFixit.** Point your browser to *www.macfixit.com/reports/macos9-2.shtml# updated* for a long list of updates and software patches, with links.

- **Macintouch.** The Mac OS 9 compatibility report is at *www.macintouch.com/ m90_compatibility.html.*

- **VersionTracker.** This outstanding resource tracks current versions of *everything* Mac-related. It has a special Mac OS 9 page at *www.versiontracker.com/systems/ system9.shtml.*

## All About Mac OS 9.0.4

In April 2000, Apple released an update called Mac OS 9.0.4. You can get it in one of three ways:

- Open your Software Update control panel, as described on page 210, and click the Update Now button. If your Internet connection and karma are both good, you'll be offered the chance to download and install the new software.

- Second, you can download the updater directly from *http://asu.info.apple.com.* (Search for *9.0.4.)*

- Buy a CD-ROM containing the updater by sending $19.95 to *Apple Order Center, Attn: 9.0.4 CD Upgrade, Box 2270, Buffalo, NY 14240-2270.*

So what do you get for your trouble? Bug fixes. Your Apple DVD Player software, for example, is less likely to exhibit "sound drift," in which the soundtrack gradually gets more and more out of sync with the picture. The Mac now recognizes more FireWire gadgets (camcorders and hard drives, for example), makes networking more reliable, solves some laptop battery problems, and improves the stability of audio, video, and graphics software. (Mac OS 9.0.4 otherwise offers no new features.)

Installer beware, however; like any updater these days, this one brings with it further incompatibilities. For example, Action Utilities and Palm Desktop require free updaters to remain compatible with 9.0.4. If you're on the fence about performing this installation, consult the Mac OS 9.0.4 reports at *www.macfixit.com* and *www. macintouch.com*—fully armed, however, with the acknowledgment that most people don't send their reports to such Web sites if everything went *well* with the upgrade.

## All About Mac OS 9.1—and Later

Mac OS 9.0.4 isn't the end of the line for Mac OS 9. In addition to more bug fixes, the Mac OS 9.1 updater gives you two new control panels, updated General Controls and Sound control panels, and a Window menu in the Finder that lists (and lets you manipulate) your open desktop windows. See page 6 for details.

As this book went to press, yet another system-software version was in testing, tentatively numbered Mac OS 9.2. The book in your hands is fully 9.2-ready; the Mac OS 9.2 software update offers no new features except bug fixes and—this is the big one—better service as the "Classic" mode in Mac OS X.

# Troubleshooting Cue Card

I n an operating system with over 2,000 parts, the occasional technical hiccup is to be expected. If you choose Help→Mac Help to open the Mac's Web browser-like help system, and then click the "Preventing and solving problems" link, you'll be shown a few helpful topics pertaining to hardware problems (such as USB difficulties), error messages, and so on. Your particular Mac model probably came with a small booklet that outlines troubleshooting steps unique to that model, too.

The purpose of this appendix is to help you troubleshoot problems with the system software itself. Try the numbered troubleshooting steps listed here in sequence until the problem goes away.

## Freezes, Crashes, and Strange Glitches

The first question: Is your Mac freezing or crashing in just one particular program? Or is it randomly freezing and crashing regardless of the program?

### Problems in One Particular Program

This kind of problem is fairly easy to solve, since it's limited to one particular application.

1. **Give the program more memory.**

   You'll find step-by-step instructions on page 115.

2. **Throw way the Preferences file for that program.**

   To do so, quit the troublesome program. Open the System Folder→Preferences folder; find and throw away the preferences file for the application in question.

The next time you run the program, it will build itself a brand new preference file that, if you're lucky, lacks whatever corruption was causing your problems.

3. **Contact the manufacturer to see if there's a newer version.**

It's possible that you have one of the programs that doesn't work well with Mac OS 9, as described at the end of Appendix B.

4. **Reinstall the program.**

If possible, first throw away all traces of it, including its Preferences file(s).

## Problems in No Particular Program

If your crashes and glitches don't seem to be limited to one program, your task is more time-consuming.

1. **Unplug all of your USB and SCSI gadgets, and then restart the Mac.**

(You can leave your USB keyboard and mouse plugged in, of course.) If the problem goes away, then you probably have a USB or SCSI cabling problem, as described in Chapter 18.

2. **Turn off all of your extensions.**

To do so, restart the Mac while pressing the Shift key until you see the words "Extensions off" on the screen.

If you're able to launch your favorite programs while all of the extensions are turned off, and the Mac doesn't seem to be crashing anymore, then you're half-way home: you've determined that an extension conflict is indeed the problem. (Conflicting or outdated extensions are by far the most common cause of random glitches, crashes, and other troubles.) Move on to step 3.

If the problem persists, however, skip to step 5.

3. **Turn on only Apple's extensions.**

Restart the Mac while pressing the Space bar. After a moment, Extensions Manager should appear (see Chapter 12), listing all of your extensions and control panels. Note the name of the current set, as identified by the Selected Set pop-up menu at the top of the screen, so that you can return to it when the troubleshooting exercise is over.

Now, from the pop-up menu, choose Mac OS 9.0 Base, and then click Continue. Try out your Mac now. If the problem is gone, then one of your *own* extensions or control panels—not the ones that came from Apple—is responsible for the problem; move on to step 4. If the problem persists, then you need to perform a *clean system install,* as described in Appendix B.

4. **Perform a conflict test.**

In other words, use trial and error to figure out which specific extension or control panel is causing the problem. This step is fairly easy if you have a program like Conflict Catcher, which automates the procedure. (You can download a free seven-day working version of this program at *www.casadyg.com.*)

You can also do the test manually, however. Doing so involves opening Extensions Manager (see Chapter 12), turning off half of your extensions and control panels, restarting the Mac, testing to see if the problem is resolved, and repeating this procedure until you've narrowed the problem down to one particular extension or control panel. (Hint: It's usually the one you most recently installed.)

You can find a more detailed description of this process in Mac OS 9's Help→Mac Help command. (Search for *extensions conflicts.*)

5. **Try "zapping the PRAM."**

This procedure involves restarting the Mac. While it's rebooting, press the improbable keystroke ⌘-Option-P-R. (You may have to invite a friend over to help you hold down all of these keys.) The screen goes dark, and the startup process begins again, with a second chime. Keep the keys down until the third or fourth chime, and then let go.

You've just reset the parameter RAM, or PRAM ("PEE-ram"), which is an electronic storage area for your Mac's control panel settings: time, date, networking method, mouse speed, and so on. You'll have to reset these settings manually, but now and then, this procedure can shake an unruly computer back to its senses.

6. **Perform a clean system install, as described in Appendix B.**

Doing so goes beyond replacing troublesome extensions and control panels—it also lets you escape corrupted fonts, preferences, resource files, and so on.

7. **Run the Disk First Aid program (see Chapter 13) to check for hard drive problems.**

---

**UP TO SPEED**

## Two Keystrokes Worth Learning

When a program has crashed, press ⌘-Option-Esc. You'll be offered a button called Force Quit that, when clicked, lets you escape the frozen program. This trick works about 25 percent of the time; the other times, it just further locks up your Mac, which you must then restart. When it works, the force-quit procedure lets you jettison the frozen program, switch into your other open programs to save the open documents there, and then restart the Mac anyway, which is probably unstable this point.

So, what if your Mac does completely freeze? In that case, you need the more dramatic ⌘-Control-power key sequence, which makes the Mac restart even if it's frozen solid. And if even that keystroke doesn't work (because your USB chain is locked up, for example), press the actual reset *button,* or insert a straightened paper clip into the reset *hole,* on the side or back of your Mac. (It's marked by a left-pointing triangle.)

---

# Other Common Problems

Not every problem you encounter is related to running applications. Sometimes trouble strikes before you even get that far. For example:

## The Blinking Question Mark at Startup

When a small flashing question-mark icon appears in the middle of the screen, your Mac can't find a working System Folder. Fortunately, you have your Mac OS 9 CD-ROM, which you can now insert; the Mac will use *its* System Folder instead, which will at least get you into your machine.

From there, you should investigate why your regularly scheduled System Folder isn't working. For example, the Finder and System icons must both be inside it, and yet not filed away into some inner folder. You'll know you've got the problem fixed when the Mac OS logo appears on the System Folder icon itself.

If you can't figure out what's wrong, perform the universal problem-solver: the clean install, as described in Appendix B.

## Endless Wait at Startup

Recent Mac models may experience another startup peculiarity: after you turn the machine on, it sits there for two or three minutes, apparently brain-dead, before suddenly starting up normally.

The problem is that your Startup Disk control panel has forgotten which hard drive is your startup drive, perhaps because you zapped your PRAM. (The Mac is actually spending that time searching the network for a *net-boot* hard drive, described in Chapter 5 under "Startup Disk.") The solution is easy: choose  →Control Panels→Startup Disk; click your hard drive's icon; and restart the machine.

## Freezes During Startup

If the Mac locks up during the startup process, it shouldn't take you long to trouble-shoot:

1. If your Mac is an older model that has equipment plugged into the SCSI connector, unplug the Mac to cut the power—and then unplug everything from the SCSI jack.

   If the problem goes away, then you've got a SCSI cabling problem, as described in Chapter 18.

   If that doesn't solve the problem, your Mac has an extension conflict.

2. Restart the computer by pressing ⌘-Control-power key. Then, as it's restarting, press the Shift key until you see the words "Extensions off" on the screen.

   As described earlier in this appendix, your Mac now starts up fine—but without any of the extensions and control panels that make life worth living. Perform a conflict test, as described above, to ferret out the problem. Or, if you don't have the time, perform a clean install, as described in Appendix B.

## Double-Clicking a Document Doesn't Work

If you double-click, say, a Word 98 document, but Microsoft Word doesn't open in response, your desktop database files have become confused (see page 51 for an introduction to the desktop database). Another symptom of the same problem: your documents appear without their magnificent, full-color icons, and instead appear with boring, blank sheet-of-paper icons.

In either case, the solution is to *rebuild the desktop file*. Do so by restarting the Mac (or logging out, if you're using Multiple Users). As the machine starts up again, or as you sign in again, press ⌘ and Option until a message asks if you're sure you want to rebuild the desktop file. Click OK. (If you continue to press those two keys, you'll eventually be invited to rebuild the desktop files on any other disks attached to your Mac.)

---

**FREQUENTLY ASKED QUESTION**

### Numbered Error Messages

*I got a message that says, "Error Type 11." What does that mean?*

There's no translation table somewhere that says, for example, "Type 11: You crashed because you tried to print a table formatted in Helvetica, which is a bug in Word 98." Numbered error messages, such as "Error type 11," are meaningful only to programmers, and even then they're extremely vague (the messages, not the programmers). If you're really interested, you can visit *http://til.info.apple.com/*

*techinfo.nsf/artnum/N1749* to read a list of these extremely technical error descriptions.

Numbered error messages simply mean that something went wrong—usually because of an extension conflict or an outdated program—and that you'll have to restart the Mac. (The exception is the –119 error message, which does indeed have a specific meaning: Your program is incompatible with Mac OS 9, and needs an update.)

---

# Where to Get Troubleshooting Help

## Help Online

These Internet sites contain nothing but troubleshooting discussions, tools, and help:

- MacFixIt *(www.macfixit.com)*.

- Macintosh Crash/Freeze Tips *(www.zplace.com/crashtips)*.

- Mac newsgroups (such as *comp.sys.mac*). A newsgroup is an Internet bulletin board, which you can access using a program like Outlook Express (which is included with Mac OS 9) or by visiting, in your Web browser, *www.deja.com/usenet*. If you're polite and concise, you can post questions to the multitudes here and get more replies to them than you'll know what to do with.

- No Wonder *(www.nowonder.com)*. This sensational Web site provides personal, free technical help for your questions, written and sent to you by actual human beings.

---

- **The Apple Tech Exchange bulletin board** *(http://support.info.apple.com/te/te.taf)*. Tech Exchange is Apple's own bulletin board, where you can post questions that live Apple technicians read and answer. Actually, you're more likely to benefit from this resource by reading the answers that have already been posted; chances are good that somebody else has had your problem.

- **Other Apple support resources** *(apple.com/support)*. Apple's help Web site also includes downloadable manuals, software updates, frequently asked questions, and many other resources. (Click long enough, for example, and you'll find the Mac OS 9 troubleshooting page, which is at *www.info.apple.com/support/pages.taf?product=macos9.)*

The mother of all troubleshooting resources, however, is Apple's own Tech Information Library. This is the collection of over 50,000 individual technical articles, organized in a searchable database, that the Apple technicians themselves consult when you call for help.

If you like, you can visit this library using your Web browser; the address is *http://til.info.apple.com.* You just type in what you're looking for, such as *iMac DV and crashing,* and your Web browser shows you a list of matching articles.

You'll save a step, however, if you use the Sherlock 2 program that's built right into your  menu. As described in Chapter 15, if you click the black Apple logo at the top of its screen, you're offered checkboxes that search any of three Apple databases—one of which is the Tech Info Library. In other words, you can search the Tech Info Library directly from your desktop, without having to launch your browser first. (You can then double-click one of the resulting listings to read the topic in your Web browser.)

## Help by Telephone

Finally, consider contacting whoever sold you the component that's making your life miserable: the printer company, scanner company, software company, and so on.

If it's a Mac OS 9 problem, you can call Apple at (800) 500-7078. For the first 90 days following your purchase of Mac OS 9 (which, as far as Apple knows, is the date of your first call, or the day you registered by double-clicking the Register with Apple icon on your desktop), the technicians will answer your questions for free.

After that, unless you've paid for AppleCare for your Mac (a three-year extended warranty program), Apple will charge you to answer your questions—unless the problem turns out to be Apple's fault, in which case they won't charge you.

# A

## Colophon

The animal on the cover of *Mac OS 9: The Missing Manual* is a dog. It may be a distant relative of the Dogcow, the genetically dubious animal that appears in every Macintosh Page Setup dialog box.

Due to a wrist ailment you really don't want to hear about, the author wrote the chapters of this book by voice, using Dragon Naturally Speaking on a Windows PC. The Microsoft Word files were then transferred as quickly as possible to a Power Mac G3, where they were spell-checked, illustrated, and transmitted to the book's editors. Ambrosia Software's Snapz Pro was used to capture illustrations; Adobe Photoshop and Macromedia Freehand were called in as required for touching them up.

The book was designed and laid out in Adobe PageMaker 6.5 on a Power Mac 8500 and Power Mac G3. The fonts used include Formata (as the sans-serif family) and Minion (as the serif body face). To provide the  and ⌘ symbols, a custom font was created using Macromedia Fontographer. The index was created using EZ Index, a Mac-only shareware indexing program available at *www.northcoast.com/~jvholder*. The book was then generated as an Adobe Acrobat PDF file for proofreading and transmission to the printing plant.